WOMEN IN POLITICS:

OUTSIDERS OR INSIDERS?

A Collection of Readings

Second Edition

Lois Lovelace Duke, Editor
Clemson University

PRENTICE HALL, Upper Saddle River, New Jersey 07458

BFN 7966 - 0/2

...ary of Congress Cataloging-in-Publication Data

...en in politics : outsiders or insiders : a collection of readings /
...is Lovelace Duke, editor.-2nd ed.
    p.   cm.
...ncludes bibliographical references.
...SBN 0-13-185240-X (pbk. : alk. paper)
... Women in politics -United States. 2. Feminism -United States.
... Duke, Lois Lovelace.
...1236.5.U6W663 1996
...0'.082-dc20
                                                            95-34262
                                                            CIP

...rial/production supervision: Rojean Wagner
...isition editor: Mike Bickerstaff
...tant editor: Jennie Katsaros
...r in Chief: Nancy Roberts
...uyer: Bob Anderson
Cover photo: Jeffrey Markowitz/Sygma

© 1996, 1993 by Prentice-Hall, Inc.
Simon & Schuster/A Viacom Company
Upper Saddle River, New Jersey 07458

Printed in the United States of America
10 9 8 7 6 5 4 3 2 1

ISBN 0-13-185240-X

PRENTICE-HALL INTERNATIONAL (UK) LIMITED, *London*
PRENTICE-HALL OF AUSTRALIA PTY. LIMITED, *Sydney*
PRENTICE-HALL CANADA INC., *Toronto*
PRENTICE-HALL HISPANOAMERICANA, S.A., *Mexico*
PRENTICE-HALL OF INDIA PRIVATE LIMITED, *New Delhi*
PRENTICE-HALL OF JAPAN, INC., *Tokyo*
SIMON & SCHUSTER ASIA PTE. LTD., *Singapore*
EDITORA PRENTICE-HALL DO BRASIL, LTDA., *Rio de Janeiro*

CONTENTS

PREFACE

It is always gratifying to have a professional work well received by one's peers. Thus, the second edition of this volume has been altered somewhat, while attempts have been made to maintain and update many of the pieces in the original edition. The basic thrust of the book is essentially unchanged. That is, this book is designed to provide a supplemental reader on the topic of women and politics to accompany texts for American government courses to aid in integrating the study of women in the political system, as well as for use in women and politics courses and even as a supplement for graduate-level courses. This reader provides relevant research on women and politics across a spectrum of topics and perspectives; thus the book can provide only a "snapshot." Each author has added a "Further Readings" section at the conclusion of his or her article to help in explaining more fully where the essays fit into the overall picture of other research.

We begin with a feminist theoretical framework, examine some gender differences in political attitudes and voting, and explore how women have fared in competing for public office. Next we look at the various branches of government and see how women are (and in some cases are not) participating in the functions of government. Then we explore public perceptions of Hillary Rodham Clinton and gender cultural reflections in the mass media and about the mass media and end with discussing how female activists put into practice some of the more theoretical components to change public policy and create feminist public discourse.

ORGANIZATIONAL FRAMEWORK

The book is organized into nine chapters, which are arranged into four parts. Part I includes an analysis of "Women, Equality, and Feminist Theory." Part II explores the topic of "Women and Politics," including how women and men have changed in their opinions about women's roles in politics, gender differences in voting to include the nature of the gender gap in the 1992 presidential election, the concept of occupational stratification and how this affects political attitudes, and women and elections. Part III, "Gender and Government," examines women and their role as policy makers in political institutions. This topic includes women as chief executives; females in the U.S. Congress and projections for their future role; females within the judicial system; women's rights struggles and the U.S. Supreme Court's responses; and women, media, and public opinion. Part IV looks at "Women and National Policy" in such public policy areas as family and medical leave, sex at risk in insurance classifications, and affirmative action. We conclude with a chapter on activism and tactics that includes an article on coffee drinking and the importance of free speech. The following is a brief summary of the chapters included in the book:

CHAPTER 1   THE STUDY OF WOMEN: THE NEW FRAMEWORK

Feminist Theory and the Politics of Empowerment   *Iva Ellen Deutchman*

This study critically evaluates feminist theories about power. The concept of power has long fascinated not only political analysts but political activists as well. Among many reasons to support an increase in the number of women officials, one overriding reason has been based on the belief that women feel differently about power and use power differently than men. Men, it is argued, see power as *power over*, an ability to influence or dominate, whereas women see power as *power to*, or empowerment. Thus, power for women can be seen as less confrontational and more cooperative than power for men. Deutchman critically examines the claim that women and men are different in both their concept of power and their use of power.

The Riddle of Consciousness: Racism and Identity in Feminist Theory   *Nancie E. Caraway*

Utilizing the political and epistemological contributions of contemporary Black feminist theory, Nancie E. Caraway points up the intersections of gender, race, and class as determinants of oppression. She argues that the texts of Black feminists teach us that feminist theory and politics should address this "multiple jeopardy." She cautions that feminists need to be wary of the damaging consequences of conceptions like identity and self, which have set up White norms. In her discussion of identity politics, Caraway questions many of the assumptions of mainstream White feminism. She proposes instead multicultural goals in which the themes of racism and identity come together in a configuration that can address the theoretical issues about the female subject. She argues that a critical identity politics cautions us not to become too comfortable too long in one spot with one identity lest we forget and stifle the ways in which we change, contradict, and grow in history.

CHAPTER 2   GENDER DIFFERENCES IN POLITICAL ATTITUDES AND VOTING

Changing Views about Gender Equality in Politics: Gradual Change and Lingering Doubts   *Linda L. M. Bennett/Stephen E. Bennett*

This article looks at how women and men have changed in their opinions about women's roles in politics. Creating a Political Gender Roles Index from data in the National Opinion Research Center's (NORC) General Social Surveys between 1974 and 1993, the Bennetts find that while there are few gender differences about the role of women in politics, there are differences in the rate of change toward favoring more modern roles. The authors warn against assuming that there will be a natural progression in opinion favoring more modern roles, particularly among young, even well-educated, men.

The Generations of Feminism   *Elizabeth Adell Cook*

Previous research has found that younger women are more likely to hold feminist attitudes than are older women. There is also some evidence, however, that young women in the 1980s are less supportive of feminism than were older women. This suggests there may be some generational influences at work. Cohort analysis of the 1972 to 1992 American National Election Studies indicates that women who came of age during the period of social activism of the 1960s and the growth of the women's movement in the 1970s exhibit higher levels of politicized feminist consciousness than do women of earlier generations; that women who came of age during the more conservative late 1970s and early 1980s exhibit lower levels of feminist consciousness than do women of the "Sixties" and "Women's Liberation" cohorts. Specifically, a comparison of the "Complacent/Reagan" cohort with the Women's Liberation cohort on feminist issues included in the 1992 study revealed the two cohorts were quite similar in the attention they paid to women's issues, their views on the seriousness of the problem of sexual harassment, and their anger about the way women are treated in society. However, the Complacent cohort was less likely to favor government funding of abortion for poor women and to express pride in the accomplishments of women. The greatest difference between the two generations is on the issue of government-sponsored child care; women of the Complacent cohort are much more likely to believe that the government should provide child care assistance to low and middle income working parents.

More than Pink and Blue: Gender, Occupational Stratification, and Political Attitudes   *Gertrude A. Steuernagel/Thomas A. Yantek/Irene J. Barnett*

Women's lives are changing, and these changes are not without implications for political life in the United States. One of the most significant changes in women's lives during the twentieth century has been in their roles as workers. A number of researchers have established the importance of understanding the relationship between employment and women's political behavior. Since it has been established that workforce participation is linked to women's political behavior, there is a need to focus on the realities of women's employment and the details of the kind of workplace environment in which women find themselves. This study is concerned with the effects of occupational segregation on women's political attitudes. The authors use data from the 1992 University of Michigan National Election Study as well as statistics on occupational segregation and integration from the U.S. Department of Labor. The conclusions suggest a need to go beyond the sex of respondents in order to comprehend the significance of gender and its relationship to political attitudes. As a result of sex-role socialization, life-cycle demands, and discrimination, women tend to cluster in what the authors refer to as *female-segregated jobs*. They conclude that the experiences women have in these jobs affect their political attitudes.

Gender and Ideological Polarization among Southern Grassroots Party Activists
Anne E. Kelley/William E. Hulbary/Lewis Bowman

The authors use the traditionally politically conservative South and data from the 1991–1992 Southern Grassroots Party Activist Study to reexamine and update the link between gender, party, and political ideology. Specifically, they focus on these questions: (1) How do the political ideology and issue attitudes of southern party activists divide along party and gender lines? Is there a "gender gap?" (2) Are party and gender differences in ideology and issues linked with other relevant factors such as age, race, ethnicity, socioeconomic status, and regional differences? Their data show that partisanship explains a large portion of the variation in political ideology among southern party activists. Regardless of any other consideration, Democrats were consistently more liberal and Republicans consistently more conservative. Gender accounted for considerable variation in political liberalism among Democrats but was less useful in explaining political conservatism among Republicans. Both Democratic and Republican women activists in rapidly growing Rim South states were more liberal or less conservative than their counterparts in other southern states. The authors found that the political conservatism of the Deep South did not diminish party and gender differences; instead, it magnified the conservative orientation of women and men in both parties. Occupational status, education, and family income also helped explain ideological and issue differences among southern party activists.

Whither the Gender Gap? Converging and Conflicting Attitudes among Women

Cal Clark/Janet Clark

Janet Clark and Cal Clark maintain that, by the mid-1990s, some scholars seemed to be turning to the clash between feminists and "traditional" women over such "culture wars" issues as abortion, indicating the splintering of women into contending groups. This article examines the nature of the gender gap and the divisions of opinion among women at the time of the 1992 presidential election to see whether women's "political interests" are in fact fragmenting. The first section of the article discusses the evolution and current nature of the gender gap on nine sets of issues; the second portion of the essay analyzes the extent of the gender gap within different socioeconomic groups; and the third focuses on what groups of women are most likely to support and oppose representative issues in each set. The authors find little evidence that women's social and political interests were cohesive in the 1980s and have recently become much more fragmented. Rather, the gender gap in the 1980s represented the overlapping concerns of somewhat disparate groups of women; and despite the growing salience of the "culture wars" issues, there was little change in this situation as of 1992.

CHAPTER 3   WOMEN AND ELECTIONS: THE UPHILL STRUGGLE

On the Eve of Transition: Women in Southern Legislatures, 1946–1968

Joanne V. Hawks/Carolyn Ellis Staton

Many scholars considered the post–World War II era a quiescent time for White middle-class American women. After a period of wartime involvement, many women supposedly retreated into a more traditional lifestyle. Yet, between 1946 and 1968, almost 100 women entered legislatures in the South, a particularly traditional region. Data indicate that they were predominantly women who were already involved in the public sphere in one or more ways. Even though many were serious legislators, the press emphasized their domesticity and femininity instead of their legislative achievements.

Second Best? Women Mayors and Council Members: A New Test of the Desirability Thesis   *Susan A. MacManus/Charles S. Bullock III*

The authors examine the reasons for a marked increase in the number of women elected to mayoral and city council positions in U.S. municipalities over the past decade. They ask: (1) Are women most often winning in jurisdictions where the mayoral and council positions are less powerful and prestigious or less desirable? (2) Are women winning offices in the 1990s because these positions are "second-best"? The authors use data from a 1991 "Form of Government" survey conducted by the International City/County Management Association (ICMA). The desirability hypothesis suggests that women will most frequently serve as mayors or council members when the post is least attractive. Findings show women more frequently serve on councils than as mayors; women mayors are more likely to be found among the ranks of those for whom the post is part-time; women mayors more often serve in mayor-council arrangements and when the mayor is elected directly by the voters; and, in general, the overall explanatory power of the desirability thesis is rather weak. Formal structural measures of office desirability do not account for very much of the variation in the gender makeup of U.S. mayoral and city council posts.

CHAPTER 4   LEGISLATURES, WOMEN, AND POLICY MAKING

Women in Congress   *Marcia Lynn Whicker/Malcolm Jewell/Lois Lovelace Duke*

In recent years, women have made some inroads in obtaining elected political office. Those inroads, however, have not included gains in female representation in Congress. During the more than seventy years since women secured the right to participate politically with the passage of the Nineteenth Amendment, female representation in Congress has increased from a minuscule 2 percent of total membership in 1922 to only 5.2 percent in 1988. At that rate of increase, women will not achieve equality in representation until the year 2582. By the 104th Congress, the percentage of women grew to 10.4 percent, a sizable increase, but still much below the 50 percent proportion that representation by gender would entail. Womeicantly fewer terms, and are more likely to decline to seek reelection. The gap between democratic rhetoric and representational reality for women is great, despite a significant narrowing in the experiential backgrounds of men and women who are elected to Congress. Even though the number of women serving in the U.S. Congress roughly doubled with the 1992 election, many obstacles remain for women seeking congressional office.

Why Are More Women State Legislators?   *Wilma Rule*

This research analyzes why women's recruitment in the fifty state assemblies and senates increased 100 percent in the decade from 1974 to 1984 but has slipped over the past decade. Specifically, the author asks the following: (1) What were the reasons for women's steady advance from 1974 to 1984? (2) What has changed in 1994? (3) What are the factors that were more favorable in the 1980s than in the 1970s? (4) How does 1994 compare with 1984? Analysis reveals that women's recruitment to state legislatures has almost tripled in the past twenty years. For the 1970s there was a building on the gains in the Republican-moralistic states most favorable to women in the 1960s. In the 1980s no political party or political culture was dominant in the states where women legislators had the most dramatic increases. States that led in the 1970s and 1980s continued to advance, with most of their state senates at least doubling the number of women members by the 1994 elections. Also, in 1994, the South broke out of its mold as the "solid Democratic South" for the first time in some 100 years. The author also finds that, at the same time, the Republican Party dominance was modified as a favorable factor for women's recruitment.

Contemporary Women State Legislators: A Diverse Group with Diverse Agendas
Lynne E. Ford/Kathleen Dolan

The authors explore the puzzle of female representation in state legislatures. To study this issue of whether there has been a new-style female legislator over time, the authors analyzed demographic, political, and legislative data on all women serving in the legislatures of fifteen states in 1972, 1982, and 1992. The authors also used a mail survey of the 1,373 women serving as U.S. state legislators in all fifty states during the 1992 legislative session. Their examination of women state legislators both over time and during the contemporary period reveals a diverse group of women in the political arena, both in experience and in interests these women bring to politics. As a group, women state legislators serving in the 1990s exhibit greater educational, occupational, political, and legislative diversity than the women who served in the past. Conclusions indicate that, if the launching role that state legislative experience has provided for men holds true for women, this diversity and greater numbers of women serving in elective office at the state level should ultimately mean larger and more diverse pools of future female candidates at the national level.

CHAPTER 5   THE EXECUTIVE BRANCH: WOMEN AND LEADERSHIP

The Maleness of the American Presidency   *Marcia Lynn Whicker/Todd W. Areson*

The authors explore why the U.S. presidency has historically been a bastion of maleness despite comments during the early Clinton administration that First Lady Hillary Rodham Clinton would be a "copresident." The authors identify factors that account for the unlevel presidential "playing field" that women candidates face; the presidential system of direct, popular election; the paucity of women who have gained experience in the three presidential "launching roles" of the vice presidency, the U.S. senate, and governorships; the difficulty women face in securing campaign funding for national and subnational races; and long-standing public images of a conflict for women—but not for men—between familial and political roles.

Women as Governors: State Executive Leadership with a Feminist Face?   *Sara J. Weir*

Focusing on the growing importance of the governorship in U.S. politics, Sara Weir explores a new area of scholarly inquiry—women as governors. She shows how the ten women elected to the governorship since 1974 have worked against gender stereotypes to serve in an office that demands knowledge of budgeting and fiscal policy and administrative leadership—abilities most often associated with males by voters. Although the numbers are too small to generalize, the author speculates about changing patterns in the candidacy and election of women state chief executives and the ways in which some female governors empower women and support women's issues. Positive developments include the success of two female gubernatorial candidates in defeating incumbent governors since 1990, and the high number of women serving as lieutenant governors in 1995—increasing the numbers of women in the "pool" of qualified gubernatorial candidates for the future. Still, the number of women running for and winning in gubernatorial contests is very small. At this time only one woman is serving as a state governor, and all nine women who were major political party candidates in the November 1994 elections were defeated. According to the author, the success of women as state chief executives is mixed at best. She concludes by speculating about the governorship as an avenue to the presidential ticket, looking especially at the Republican Party's interest in New Jersey governor, Christine Todd Whitman.

CHAPTER 6   THE COURTS: WOMEN AND DECISIONS

Women's Rights and Legal Wrongs: The U.S. Supreme Court and Sex Discrimination
Karen O'Connor

The author traces the intertwined quest for expanded rights for women and the U.S. Supreme Court's responses to those actions. She begins with an overview of the colonial period, moves to the Civil War years, addresses the suffrage movement litigation, reviews the press for state laws and for the Supreme Court to address the issue of gender, and explores the legal status of women at the workplace as well as more contemporary attempts to expand women's rights. She finds that fewer and fewer constitutional cases involving sex discrimination are coming before the Supreme Court each year—perhaps because women's rights groups are using their time and money to fend off challenges to a series of decisions adverse to abortion rights. Also, the author maintains that most of the "easy" constitutional cases have been decided, and there is fairly uniform application of the intermediate standard of review in the lower courts. Thus, most gender cases that the Supreme Court now chooses to hear involve employment discrimination and the scope of bona fide occupational qualifications permissible under Title VII. The author concludes that the consensus evidenced by the Court and the addition of two Democratic appointees by conservative Republicans leaves women's rights activists far more optimistic than they were just a short time ago.

Women within the Judicial System: Changing Roles   *Elaine Martin*

Women judges are unlike other women in politics in the way they attain public office and the way they are free to behave once they attain such office. The author examines three aspects of change for women within the judicial system: (1) the increase in the numbers of women judges; (2) the growing evidence in judicial research that women judges are more supportive of women's rights than are male judges; and (3) the possibility that female judges' support of women's rights is related to a feeling of obligation to represent other women. The author finds that even though the relative numbers of female judges lag far behind the relative numbers of female state legislators, their numbers are rapidly increasing. Two factors have improved women's chances of becoming judges: (1) All presidents since Carter have followed his precedent in seeking to appoint women, and (2) more women have become lawyers. Results from studies done in the 1970s and early 1980s suggested that men's and women's similar legal training and socialization as lawyers minimized any potential gender differences in judicial behavior. However, more recent studies indicate that, as women's numbers move beyond the token stage and as younger females educated after the women's movement become judges, differences based on gender emerge more clearly. This study used hypothetical cases to create a situation where large numbers of male and female judges would be deciding the same case. Results indicate that both gender and feminist ideology are important in predicting how judges may decide women's rights cases. The author finds that, within ideological types, women are more likely than men to vote in a pro-female manner. Based on questions answered in a sample of female judges, the author concludes that some female judges have a strong sense that part of their job is to "act for" the interests of other women.

CHAPTER 7   WOMEN, MEDIA, AND PUBLIC OPINION

Women and Sex Stereotypes: Cultural Reflections in the Mass Media   *Lois Lovelace Duke*

The editor explores some of the research that has been done concerning the manner in which the mass media have portrayed American political women in the news. Comparisons are drawn between the news about women and men in the American political environment. The editor considers influences on the news-making process, considers how specific agendas are passed through the media, looks at some of the myths and stereotypes about women that are portrayed in the media, and describes the white male domination of the news organization. She concludes that clearly the role of women in all facets of American political life is changing; these changes have been and are being reported by the mass media. However, the question then becomes, What is the content of this media coverage? What has been the role of the media in assessing the "reality" of some of these changes? Do women in politics not deserve a great deal more coverage than the media give them? She concludes that additional studies appear warranted as the number of female candidates increases in American politics. Studies especially are needed that would systematically compare the coverage about women who run for elective office with that of male candidates.

Gender Differences in State Legislators' Perceptions of Media Coverage of Public Affairs   *Glen Sussman/Nicholas P. Lovrich Jr.*

This article examines gender differences in attitudes among state legislators about media coverage of state legislatures generally and support for gavel-to-gavel continuous televised coverage of legislative affairs in particular. The study is based on data collected from a sizable sample of female and male legislators in the fifty states. The authors find that, in the area of media perceptions and legislative process reform to provide for greater access for broadcast journalists, there continues to be a gender difference. Female legislators tend to be less satisfied with the performance of the broadcast media than do male legislators; they are also more inclined to presume that the average citizen is interested in greater access to the work of the legislature than are their male counterparts. Particularly for urban-based Democratic female state legislators, perhaps the most pro-feminist agenda state-level political elite, the concept of broad access to unedited, live coverage of legislative debate and formal decisional processes represents an important goal of legislative work. The authors find that for male solons, the pragmatic issues of managerial and professional competence reign supreme; for female legislators a definite geopolitical social agenda construction of the issue seems to have been a common inclination.

Public Opinion of Hillary Rodham Clinton as First Lady

Barbara C. Burrell/Linda J. Penaloza

The authors contend that Hillary Rodham Clinton has transformed the role of First Lady—that she represents a new era and a new generation of the professional woman who is also smart. This article traces the historical perspective of public opinion polls on the popularity of the First Lady back to Pat Nixon in 1969; the authors focus more specifically on public response to Hillary Rodham Clinton as captured through public opinion measured in national surveys. These national polls have explored such areas as overall impressions, Hillary Clinton's role as First Lady, perceptions about her involvement in public policy, how much influence she has had on the president, her role as head of President Clinton's Task Force on Health Care Reform, perceptions of her personal character and qualities, and the Whitewater incident. The authors found a good deal of variation in people's evaluations of Hillary Rodham Clinton and her actions. Substantial numbers have felt warm toward her, and a significant minority have not. The authors conclude that rather than the First Lady being an albatross around President Clinton's neck, she developed a positive image among the public in the early stages of the Clinton administration. Findings also show that, while 80 to 90 percent of the people polled have come to say they would support a woman as president, not all of the questions asked in the polls about the role of the First Lady show a general acceptance of a more political role for that position or a ready transition from that job to being chief executive.

CHAPTER 8   PUBLIC POLICY: THE FEMINIST PERSPECTIVE

The Handmaid's Tale and *The Birth Dearth*: Prophecy, Prescription, and Public Policy
Diane D. Blair

This essay deals with the politics of reproduction. It compares and analyzes Margaret Atwood's novel *The Handmaid's Tale* (1986) and Ben Wattenberg's book *The Birth Dearth* (1987). Blair argues that Atwood, writing from a feminist perspective, posits a dystopia in which women have been reduced to the function of breeders. By contrast, Wattenberg, writing from what Blair describes as a "nationalistic perspective," deplores the current American "birth dearth," attributes it primarily to "working women," and proposes a variety of pro-natalist remedies. Blair maintains that among the significant implications of these two books, especially when they are read in tandem, are the following: that pro-natalism, justified by the United States' relatively low fertility rate, has climbed high on many conservative agendas; that this movement seriously jeopardizes many of the gains achieved by feminists in recent years; and that the contemporary pro-natalist drive has long and powerful historical precedents.

The Family and Medical Leave Act: A Policy for Families   *Joan Hulse Thompson*

The author traces the history and origin of the Family and Medical Leave Act (FMLA). This legislation was passed in 1990 and again in 1992, but President Bush vetoed the bill both times and the Congress was unable to override either veto. Both chambers passed the bill again in 1993, and President Clinton signed it, making it effective on August 5, 1993. The author describes the influence of the Congressional Caucus for Women's Issues (CCWI) in developing this legislation, building a bipartisan coalition across committee jurisdictions, and coordinating the efforts of outside advocacy groups. The author concludes that the caucus symbolizes what has been called the "second stage" of the women's movement because it is a partnership of congresswomen and congressmen. On a more grim note, however, after the 1994 election the very survival of the caucus appeared to be in doubt when the Republican Conference voted to eliminate provisions in the House rules that permit representatives to use office staff funds to support legislative service organizations.

Sex at Risk in Insurance Classifications? The Supreme Court as Shaper of Public Policy
Ruth Bamberger

Although numerous laws have been passed prohibiting sex discrimination in a variety of public policy areas, the insurance industry has retained the practice of discriminating by sex in determining prices of its products. The industry argues its position on cost-efficiency and actuarial grounds. Women's rights and civil rights groups have criticized such discrimination on grounds of fairness and prevailing social policy. Although they have pursued their cause through multiple channels of government, the Supreme Court is perceived to be a primary agent of policy change. The Court has signaled that sex may be at risk as an insurance classification, but its role as shaper of public policy on this issue has been incremental at best.

Affirmative Action as a Woman's Issue   *Roberta Ann Johnson*

This reading offers a generic definition of affirmative action and then does three things. First, it raises the development of the federal affirmative action policy from the issuing of executive orders by Presidents Roosevelt, Kennedy, and Johnson to its full implementation in the Department of Labor. Second, the paper summarizes and evaluates all the affirmative action cases decided by the Supreme Court, starting with the *Bakke* decision. Finally, using Census Bureau and Department of Labor statistics and secondary sources, the study considers the ways in which affirmative action increases opportunities for women. Throughout the paper, the author recognizes affirmative action for its redistributive thrust.

CHAPTER 9   WOMEN ACTIVISTS: ATTITUDES, TACTICS

Anarchist Feminism and Student Power: Is This Any Way to Run a Women's Studies Program?   *Kathleen P. Iannello*

This study analyzes systems of power within the framework of organizations. The author argues that it is from the notion of power as a type of energy or "empowerment" that a feminist framework for organizations emerges. Two feminist organizations were selected for in-depth study—the feminist peace group and the women's health collective. From the study of these two anarchist feminist groups, a modified consensual structure is identified. The most important defining element is the outward, not downward, delegation of routine decisions to the few and the reserving of critical decisions for the entire membership. Other important elements of the model include: (1) the recognition of ability or expertise rather than rank or position; (2) the notion of empowerment as a basis of consensual "process"; and (3) clarity of goals that are arrived at through this consensual process. The author uses a case study of the governing body of one women's studies program, the Women's Studies Program Advisory Council (WSPAC) at a small liberal arts college, to illustrate the challenges and benefits of organizing consensually in an academic environment. The implications for women in this modified consensual structure include experiences in an environment of trust and support as opposed to the more traditional hierarchical organizations in which only those at the top (all too often male figures) make critical policy with varying degrees of input from lower levels.

Grounds for Criticism: Coffee, Passion, and the Politics of Feminist Discourse
Elizabeth A. Kelly

This essay explores the relationship between coffee and political discourse, paying particular attention to the role of coffeehouses as alternative public spheres. It also examines the often-complex relationships between coffee, coffeehouse cultures, and gender, along with how these relationships have shifted historically. The author concludes with a look at the countercultural institutions that have emerged in the last two decades that draw on the traditions of free speech and cultural and political criticism that were integral to the coffeehouse cultures of centuries past. She describes the GI coffeehouse movement during the Vietnam Conflict and the feminist community organizing and cultural work since the late 1960s, which has often centered around coffeehouses, sometimes in tandem with feminist bookstores and other forms of cultural expression. Finally, the author describes two feminist coffeehouses and the political struggles attached to building alternative social and cultural institutions that prioritize the concerns or needs of women.

ACKNOWLEDGMENTS

This book is specifically dedicated to the women and men who have contributed to, supported, and been loyal to this project from its inception more than five years ago. I would also like to thank the members of the Women's Caucus for Political Science for their encouragement and advice—even though you are too numerous to name here, you know who you are, and I value and appreciate you. A special word of thanks goes to the Clemson University students who have suffered through my Gender and Politics courses over the past several years. This volume has been enhanced by your suggestions. I would be remiss if I did not thank the three reviewers commissioned by Prentice Hall to study the original essays in the first edition: Ellen Riggle, University of Kentucky; M. Margaret Conway, University of Florida; and Maureen Moakley, University of Rhode Island. Your suggestions and recommendations are invaluable. (A special word of thanks to the reviewer who referred to the first edition as a "wonderful pedagogical tool for the instructor.")

Many thanks also go to Angela Newell and Kim Gibby at Clemson University for their excellent secretarial support in this endeavor. Finally, I would like to thank Mike Bickerstaff, senior editor, and Jennie Katsaros, assistant editor, and the staff at Prentice Hall.

Lois Lovelace Duke

 **Chapter 1**

The Study of Women: The New Framework

Until the 1960s, most of the research about movements for women's rights centered on women's suffrage in the nineteenth and early twentieth centuries. Since the 1960s, however, an enormous number of studies on women and politics have been added to the scholarly literature. Even a superficial review of the wealth of books, journal articles, and other publications analyzing the relationship between gender and politics reveals that the field of research in this area has grown substantially.

Over the past twenty-five years, scholars who wished to research the influence of women's political behavior in the American political process experienced numerous "growing pains." These included limited financial support for research on the topic, initial efforts to study a field that had established norms identified and defined from a male perspective and male-shaped understanding of the political world, and a tendency to view gender-related research as a "special-interest" focus, "outside" the normal theoretical framework. For all these reasons, many studies on women and politics turned out to be simply descriptive narratives drawn from traditional concepts, as opposed to empirically driven research studies.

The early pioneers of scholarly research on gender and politics, however, may currently reflect on a significant legacy of contributions. These include the present solid body of literature analyzing gender socialization, women's political behavior (at both the individual and the group level), and women's role (to include officeholding) in the political sector. As we enter the next century, however, it appears that the early scholars analyzing the issue of women in American politics have passed along to the next generation of researchers on this topic a clear challenge: to ascertain why it is that women are still represented in such small numbers in both elective and appointive political offices. Clearly there is a need to use the previously researched information to provide a new agenda in which findings on the role and performance of females in the public sector can be more conclusive. Why are more women not serving as elected and appointed officials in politics? Why are more issues of concern to women not being addressed in our public policies? Why are women still being discriminated against and still suffering sexual harassment? What are the political implications for women in the mid-1990s as one looks at the congressional legislative agenda? Will the advances made during the women's rights movement of the 1960s be sustained?

The next research agenda to explore further this issue of women and politics should address these questions. It would seem that only when women are able to mobilize support for continued advancement in the equal rights arena will the women's movement remain viable. We begin this book by considering the issue of equality for women from the perspective of feminist theory. We will then move to an examination of gender differences in political attitudes and voting and examine how women have competed for public office. We will look at women in U.S. government and address gender cultural reflections in the mass media. We will then continue with an analysis of women and national policy. We will conclude with a look at female activism within an organization and the implications for political discourse among women centered around coffeehouses. Along the way we hope to provide some insight into the questions raised herein. First, however, let us consider several issues of concern to women from a theoretical feminist framework. For our purposes here, we define *feminist framework* as an overall analysis of the nature and causes of female inequality and an accompanying alternative or proposal for ending women's discrimination.

In our first reading, Iva Ellen Deutchman critically evaluates feminist theories about power. The concept of power has long fascinated not only political analysts but political activists as well. Among the many reasons to support an increase in the number of women officials, one overriding reason has been based on the belief that women feel differently about power and use power differently from men. Men, it is argued, see power as *power over*, an ability to influence or dominate, whereas women see power as *power to*, or empowerment. Thus, power for women is seen as less confrontational and more cooperative than power for men. Deutchman critically examines the claim that women and men are different in their concept of power and their use of power. Since power is intertwined with the ultimate political fallout, the real implication for public policy then becomes who wins and who loses?

Nancie E. Caraway uses the political and epistemological contributions of contemporary Black feminist theory to point up the intersections of gender, race, and class as determinants of oppression. She argues that the texts of Black feminists teach us that feminist theory and politics should address this "multiple jeopardy." She cautions that feminists need to be wary of the damaging consequences of conceptions like *identity* and *self* that have set up white norms. In her discussion of identity politics, Caraway questions many of the assumptions of mainstream white feminism. She proposes instead multicultural goals in which the themes of racism and identity come together in a configuration that can address the theoretical issues about the female subject. She argues that a critical identity politics cautions us not to become too comfortable too long in one spot with one identity, lest we forget and stifle the ways in which we change, contradict, and grow in history. We begin with these two essays.

Feminist Theory and the Politics of Empowerment

Iva Ellen Deutchman

INTRODUCTION

Power is often seen as one of the most important concepts for political analysis. Indeed, many political scientists would define *politics* as concerned primarily with the allocation and distribution of power.[1] It is perhaps surprising, then, that there is so much disagreement about how to define, let alone measure, power.

Most contemporary scholars define *power* as a relationship rather than a property or quality. In other words, power is not something an actor has or possesses. Rather, it is an ability to influence another actor or actors. Someone can exercise power in a proactive manner, meaning that he or she engages in a behavior designed to influence another actor or actors. Alternatively, someone can choose *not* to act when he or she might be expected to do so; that, too, is an exercise of power.

Consider, for example, that you are an unseen witness to an important conversation. If you make your presence known and stop the conversation, that would be an exercise of power. But if you remain hidden and learn information you aren't supposed to know, that, too, would be an exercise of power.

The concept of power has long fascinated not only political analysts but political activists as well. Since the rise of the modern feminist movement in the late 1960s, many female political activists have argued that we need more women in

Iva Ellen Deutchman is an associate professor of political science at Hobart and William Smith Colleges.

I would like to thank Professors Peter Beckman, Ilene Nicholas, Lee Quinby, and William Waller, as well as my former honors students Susan Fletcher and John Monahan, for their careful attention to an earlier version of this paper.

politics. Among the many reasons to support an increase in the number of women officials, one overriding reason has been based on the belief that women feel differently about power and use power differently from men. Men, it is argued, see power much as I have described it here. Women, by contrast, see power as less confrontational and more cooperative. From this it follows that we will have a more humane government with better policies if we elect more women to political office.

Before we come to such conclusions, however, it is wise to examine critically the claim that women and men are very different in their concept of power and their use of power. It is to this task that I now turn my attention.

While offering important critiques of more traditional theories, some feminist theories about power are themselves deeply problematic in their understanding of power. The particular difficulties in these theories include a tendency toward essentialism (seeing men and women as inherently different in their natures), an ahistorical understanding of some nonfeminist theories of power, and some unresolved contradictions in implementing a feminist approach to power. What is needed is a feminist approach to power that is nonessentialist, structural, and historical.

POWER AS GENDER-RELATED

Although there are a variety of approaches to the treatment of power within feminist scholarship, feminist analysis insists that to talk about power is to discuss gender; in other words, power relations are themselves gendered. Holding perhaps the most extreme position, Jean Lipman-Blumen considers gender roles as "the model for power relationships between generations, socio-economic classes, religious, racial and ethnic groups, as well as between imperial powers and their colonies, and between less developed and post-industrial societies."[2] Gender as model implies that the dominance–submission roles that men and women play are the basis for power relations of all kinds.

Other feminist theorists hold that it is difficult and perhaps impossible to sever gender from power. As Joan Scott reminds us, "gender is a primary way of signifying relationships of power. It might be better to say, gender is a primary field within which or by means of which power is articulated."[3] Because men and women do not have the same access to resources that are associated with power and because they are socialized to use power differently, "gender becomes implicated in the conception and construction of power itself."[4] That is, women do not have (much) power because their gender has denied them access to resources (such as inheritance) that often yield power. Lynda Sagrestano, a major researcher of gender-based power differences, flatly states that "men have more power and resources in modern American society and tend to be more effective than women in using power."[5]

Power as gender-related goes beyond discussions that consider authority and wealth as primary attributes. Many feminist theorist hold that conditions of oppression often reveal real strength in the oppressed, challenging traditional notions that women are perpetual victims. Jean Lipman-Blumen and Elizabeth Janeway,[6] among others, speak of the reciprocal relationship between influencer and influencee. As Elizabeth Janeway says, "The two members of the power relationship—we can call them the powerful and the weak, or the governors and governed, rulers and ruled, leaders and followers—do not interact at the ultimate level of total dominance and utter subordination.[7] Linda Gordon, in her brilliant social history of family violence, argues the need to recognize women victims' "bravery, resilience, and ingenuity, often with very limited resources, in trying to protect and nurture themselves and their children."[8] To argue that gender relations are power relations, as much feminist theory does, is not to argue that women are perpetual victims.

Feminist theory argues not only that power is gendered but also that women both define power and use power differently than men do. Feminist theorists such as Janet Flammang[9] and Nancy Hartsock[10] argue that women define power as empowerment or *power to* or *power for*, while men see power as domination or *power over*. Certainly, as Jeffrey Isaac states, "[E]mpiricist power theorists have confined themselves to one particular locution, 'power over,' corresponding to their belief that a proper social science is a science of behavioral regularities."[11] These empiricist theorists have clearly monopolized the power debate,[12] and hence their definitions of power have predominated. Power as gender-related thus forces us to reconsider our everyday relationships as models of power.

For a better understanding of the power debates, it is useful to know that traditional social science has often made a distinction between what is called empirical and normative theory. *Empirical theory* refers to theory about what is or what exists—in other words, "is"-based theory. *Normative theory* refers to "shoulds" or "oughts"—what *should* exist in a prescriptive sense. While this duality is extreme in that it is arguably impossible to separate what is from what should be, many theorists have seen themselves as representative of one position and sometimes hostile to the other. This is certainly true regarding conflicting theories of power, both feminist and nonfeminist.

The concept of empowerment or "power to" suggests a broadness that "power over" lacks. "Power over" only captures the ability to act or compel actions, whereas "power to" is more inclusive, comprising both the ability to act and the ability to refrain from action. However, the power to refrain from action, when exercised, is never quantifiable.[13] Hence, empirical theorists cannot fully capture the feminist concept of "power to" or empowerment.

EMPOWERMENT AS A FEMINIST CONCEPT

Some feminist theorists have argued that empowerment is a particularly feminist concept which stands in striking opposition to masculinist ideologies of power. Such theorists argue that empirical differences in women's and men's power behaviors are apparent. Lipman-Blumen asserts that "men and women engage in the gender power relationship with notably distinct styles."[14] Janet Flammang asserts that whereas "[f]eminists recognize that women have been denied power . . . women do not want power if what that means is business as usual, 'getting yours at someone's expense,' a zero-sum game where one person's gain is another's loss."[15] Feminist theory thus calls for women's empowerment without calling for men's subordination. As Flammang notes, "The best way to put an end to the theory and practice of masculinist 'power over' is to bring into being the theory and practice of feminist 'power to.'"[16]

Nancy Hartsock emphasizes the benefits to community that empowerment brings when she says that "women's stress on power not as domination but as capacity, on power as a capacity of the community as a whole, suggests that women's experience of connection and relation have consequences for understandings of power and may hold resources for a more liberating understanding."[17] Sarah Lucia Hoagland suggests:

> "Power-over" is a matter of dominance, of forcing others, of bending them to our will through a variety of overt and covert methods. It is the power of control, and our attention is riveted on those who blatantly exercise it, because it is backed by coercion, threats, and instances of destruction.
> "Power-from-within," on the other hand, is a matter of centering and remaining steady in our environment as we choose how we direct our energy . . . . "Power-from-within" is the power of ability, choice and engagement. It is creative and hence it is an affecting and transforming power, but not an imposing power.[18]

Hilary Lips displays again the despair some women feel at conforming to androcentric power structures:

> Many people who are trying to restructure the relationships between women and men in the direction of greater equality find the issue of power problematic. While trying to break free of sexual stereotypes, they are torn between the desire to increase their power and the distaste they feel for the idea of imposing their will on others. Those involved in the women's movement, for instance, often question the ethics of building up power that can be exerted over others, sometimes fear and mistrust powerful individuals within their own ranks, and are wary of becoming part of powerful institutions.[19]

Flammang and other feminist scholars envision power as essentially social and cooperative. Rather than argue that one person's gain necessitates another's loss, these feminist critics of power argue that everyone can win. Jane Jaquette reminds us, however, that as long as the male model of power is the only one accorded any legitimacy, women's cooperative vision of power is easily and effectively discounted.[20]

RESULTS OF EMPOWERMENT

Feminist theory thus argues that power is gendered, that a particularly feminist alternative to traditional definitions of power has emerged, and that this concept of empowerment is not only a theory but also a way of describing and analyzing women's actual power behavior. Women, it is argued, not only should use power differently from men; in fact they do.

Because power is so intimately connected to political participation, the argument follows that women's increased political participation opens up the possibility that both politics and policy would change substantially in the future. The way in which one sees power—as empowerment (a shared or cooperative effort) or domination (a zero-sum game with clear winners and losers)—is a critical determinant of one's political behavior. For example, it is often argued that women delegate or share authority whereas men prefer a hierarchical model of power with one (white) male in control.

The feminist vision of power, as a cooperative non-zero-sum relationship called empowerment, is heralded as better than the masculinist view it opposes. By "better than," feminist theorists mean more humane, less destructive, more fully human. For many feminist theorists, women's cooperative vision of power will have a salving, if not saving, political effect. Joan Griscom calls this a major mistake made by some feminist theorists in their analysis of power: "There is a tendency to consider *power over* 'bad' and *power for* 'good.' The former is seen as domination and lack of connection, the latter with relationality."[21] To understand this better it is helpful to examine in more detail the male model of "power over" which these feminist theorists reject.

"POWER TO" VERSUS "POWER OVER"

Feminist theory defines itself in opposition to what it labels male-based theories of power, which range from antifeminist to nonfeminist. The initial impulse of post-1968 feminist theory was in opposition to overtly misogynist (or antiwoman) theories. The vigorous debate about power that has occurred over the last twenty years has not addressed feminist concerns. Part of the reason is simply historical: Feminist theory has had its transformative impact in the social sciences after the early debates about power that took place in the 1960s.

The zero-sum, masculinist model of power that feminist theory opposes sees power as a causal relationship of domination: One agent causes another agent to perform some act he or she would not otherwise perform.[22] This understanding of power is clearly in the empiricist tradition to which Jeffrey Isaac earlier referred, and it is a conception of power that predominated for many years. This definition was later challenged by Peter Bachrach and Morton Baratz, who claimed that it excluded nondecisions.[23] In other words, by focusing only on observable activity, theorists like Robert Dahl ignored the mobilization of bias,[24] which prevents some interests from being heard. Hence, they discount or overlook examples of power that can prevent issues from becoming issues. This understanding of power, as suggested earlier, is not sensitive to the idea of "power to," or the ability to refrain from acting.

Steven Lukes extends the argument of Bachrach and Baratz even further.[25] He suggests that power can and does involve the shaping of preferences so that an issue might not reach the policy agenda because one agent's preferences have already been thoroughly shaped by another's. No conflict between these parties may be observed because the power was exercised long before the analyst could observe it.

I would argue that this debate about power is more nonfeminist than antifeminist. The "genderedness" of power, which feminist theorists take as their starting point, is clearly missing. The male critics of Dahl and others, who are clearly sensitive to the way in which the political system shapes and manipulates preferences, do not see gender as a critical aspect of power relations.

Even recent articles on power, which have the benefits of fifteen years or more of feminist theory, still do not foreground gender in their understanding of power. For example, Jeffrey Isaac argues that power must be understood in terms of actors' "enduring, socially structured relationships,"[26] a claim to which many feminist theorists would subscribe. He defines social power as deriving from "enduring structural relationships in society and exercised by individuals and groups based on their location in a given structure,"[27] but only acknowledges in a footnote that this view is being argued by some contemporary feminist theorists of patriarchy. Gender is thus a footnote or an incidental rather than a place from which to begin the analysis of power. Thus, feminist theory counterposes itself against a theory of power that does not see gender as critical.

PROBLEMS WITH THE FEMINIST TREATMENT OF POWER

Feminist theorists have leveled important charges against traditional theorists in their exposition of the gendered nature of power. Before adopting separate power models for men and women, however, let us examine some aspects of feminist theory that do not enable us to generalize and thus can be considered weak at this point in time.

Feminist theory associates empowerment ("power to" or "power-from-within") with feminism. In other words, it posits that empowerment is a particularly *feminist* alternative to the zero-sum model of power. Many nonfeminist thinkers, however, have also promoted this model. Certainly E. E. Schattschneider, Bachrach and Baratz, and Michel Foucault, among others, are sensitive to the nonhierarchical, empowerment model.[28] As Sara Evans recounts, the early social movements of the 1960s embraced this notion of power.[29] Clearly, however, neither Schattschneider, Bachrach and Baratz, nor the New Left leaders of the 1960s were *feminists*. (In fact, as Evans among others argues, the opposite is the case concerning the New Left.) When feminists argue that empowerment is particularly feminist, they need to be aware that the concept itself has a prefeminist history and has in fact been attractive to activists (like those of the New Left) whose commitment to feminism is indeed questionable.

There is also an increasing tendency to associate empowerment, or power to, not merely with feminism as a political movement but with women as a gender group. As Cynthia L. Miller and A. Gaye Cummins suggest, embedded in many modern feminist theories of power "is the assumption that power is a gendered concept (e.g., dominating as a male form of power and empowering as a female form of power)."[30] Joan Griscom also complains about "the tendency to identify power-over as masculine and power-for as feminine."[31]

Therefore, in reading scholars like Janet Flammang or Jane Jaquette, it is difficult to understand what they see as distinctly feminist about empowerment. If they mean that the women's movement embraces this theory, although it is not the first to do so, they need to be clearer in telling us that. If they mean to associate empowerment exclusively with feminism, they are making a historical error. If they mean to suggest that empowerment is female and power over is male, they are going out on a dangerous limb, as there is no empirical proof that the sexes neatly divide on the use of power.

There are further problems with these feminist theories of power. To claim, as some feminist theorists do, that women define and use power differently than men do is to make an essentialist argument—that is, an argument that posits that men and women are somehow inherently different from one another. Sandra Morgen and Ann Bookman suggest:

> Essentialist theory has once again taken root today and has found receptive audiences among many feminists. Unlike traditional or nineteenth-century feminist theories, current perspectives rarely explicitly endorse a biological essentialism. "Difference" is often conceived in more psychosocial terms, with the link to biology implicit, and sometimes denied. Nevertheless, essential male and female natures are posited.[32]

Linda Alcoff concurs, noting the tendency within many radical and cultural feminist theories "toward setting up an ahistorical and esssentialist conception of female nature."[33] She goes on to suggest an "essentialist definition of woman makes her identity independent of her external situation."[34] Gender differences are thus seen to be fixed, permanent, innate because they are ultimately connected to, if not rooted in, biology.[35] On the basis of her reading of Nancy Hartsock, Sondra Farganis suggests that "a 'feminist theory of power' would no longer speak of 'power as dominance or domination,' but would build on the particularities of a feminist standpoint that comes out of feminine contributions to human subsistence and to mothering."[36]

Thus, the argument that men see power as domination while women see power as cooperation has an essentialist component, making it both politically and philosophically problematic. Politically, it is a partial resurrection of the nineteenth-century doctrine of separate spheres,[37] a doctrine with both antifeminist and feminst potential. The separate spheres doctrine argues that women are of a higher moral caliber than men. Because of their better natures, women would purify public life. Alternatively, because of their more delicate natures, women should retreat to the relative "safety" of the home. Some strands of modern-day feminist theory have thus, in effect, breathed life into this possibly dangerous doctrine. As Alcoff remarks, "Belief in women's innate peacefulness and ability to nurture has been common among feminists since the nineteenth century and has enjoyed a resurgence in the last decade, most notably among feminist peace activists."[38]

Philosophically, essentialism underlies the claims of both many radical and cultural feminists and their historical and contemporary antifeminist opponents. It is critical that feminist theorists appreciate the antifeminist potential of essentialist arguments because of our inability to control the direction of the debate. In other words, in arguing for women's unique and missing voice, an antifeminist, rather than feminist, position may be the result. Ruth Milkman says that "feminist scholars must be aware of the real danger that arguments about 'difference' or 'women's culture' will be put to uses other than those for which they were originally developed."[39] Milkman suggests that, given the political posture of the patriarchal state, the likelihood is great that essentialist arguments made by feminists will lead to antifeminist policies.

If women and men are truly "different," the policy implications can cut both ways. This can be seen in a variety of contemporary debates about issues like maternity leave, which pits many feminists against one another. Some argue, for example, that women should receive both lengthy and paid maternity leaves because having a child is obviously a sex-based ability. However, it is easy for employers to turn this reasoning around on women and use it as an excuse not to hire them. Therefore, other feminists believe the right strategy is to minimize biological differences. In the maternity leave example, such feminists would treat pregnancy as a temporary "disability," akin to a man being out of work for six weeks to recover from a football injury.[40]

Historical, political, and philosophical problems mandate moving beyond essentialism. Such a move, however, does not mean denying the reality of gender differences. Rather, we need a theory that acknowledges the complex relationship between gender and social structure. Mary Poovey suggests an antiessentialist, feminist position in her argument:

> We must recognize that what [most] women now share is a positional similarity that masquerades as a natural likeness and that has historically underwritten oppression, *and* we must be willing to give up the illusory similarity of nature that reinforces binary logic even though such a move threatens to jeopardize what is "special" about women. My argument is that the structural similarity that pretends to reflect nature masks the operation of other kinds of difference (class and race, for example) precisely by constructing a "nature" that seems desirable, because it gives women what seems to be (but is not) a naturally constructive and politically subversive role.[41]

Similarly, Joan Scott reminds us:

> An insistence on differences undercuts the tendency to absolutist, and in the case of sexual difference, essentialist categories. It does not deny the existence of gender difference, but it does suggest that its meanings are always relative to particular constructions in specified contexts. In contrast, absolutist categorizations of difference end up always reinforcing normative rules.[42]

Feminist theory about power needs to reject essentialist implications, grounding itself, as Scott and Poovey argue, in the specific and real-life conditions of our existence.

EMPIRICAL DIFFERENCES IN GENDER-BASED POWER BEHAVIOR

Feminist theorists who deny essentialist claims believe we must confront gender differences in designing political theories about power. It is first necessary to discover whether or not gender-based behavioral differences exist and to uncover their causes and assess their importance. To agree that significant gender-based behavioral differences exist in general does not necessarily mean there are gender-based differences in power behavior or, in fact, that power behavior is politically relevant. The empirical questions, in the case of gender-based differences and gender-based power differences, are as difficult as the normative questions.

Many of us would like to believe that women and men have different power behaviors, and that women's methods of exercising power would be less violent, less hierarchical, less destructive than men's. Virginia Sapiro suggests:

> There is also reason to believe that women and men may have different orientations toward political processes (as opposed to policy issues); they may, for example, deal with conflict in different ways. . . . They seem to react to human association differently. . . .[43]

However, she aptly cautions that "when we find differences such as these in social psychological or developmental literature, however, it is necessary to establish empirically their relationship to politics and political process.[44]

Most of the research on gender-based differences in power behavior comes from social psychologists.[45] These scholars have primarily investigated power drive (need for power) and power style (the way in which one customarily exercises or blocks influence attempts). Although the corpus of this research suggests a similarity in male and female orientations toward power, the relationship between access to power resources, one's position in the power structure, and actual use of power is more complex than gender-only accounts of power behavior might suggest. It is therefore a high-risk strategy to assert the existence of gender-based differences in power behavior in the face of evidence, which, though inconclusive, tends to suggest the absence of such differences.

EMPOWERMENT AND THE EXERCISE OF POWER

The empowerment model, though arguably more comprehensive than the "power over" locution, faces several substantial problems. In particular, I am concerned that the coming into being of empowerment involves several contradictions that are either ignored or finessed by the model's supporters. Janet Flammang has noted that her position on empowerment "is naive wishful thinking in a world of scarce resources and tight budgets."[46] Frederick Frey has argued that a power vacuum, or a situation where no one exercises power, cannot exist indefinitely.[47] Sooner or later someone will "take charge." An ideal of power devoid of domination (or at least hierarchical leadership) may thus be impossible to attain.

As Frey suggests, power is not given up voluntarily; rather it is taken. If men have more access to structural power and the resources that translate into power than do women, and if men benefit from their power superiority, we should not expect them suddenly to cede power to women. Groups with access to political and economic power rarely undergo a consciousness-raising experience culminating in their renunciation of privilege. Thus, feminists who wish to replace "power over" with "power to" may never be in a position to enforce such a choice.

Moreover, in order to enforce such a choice, feminists would be in the contradictory position of using "power over" in order to make the world safe for "power to." Were feminists able to exercise that kind of power—that is, the power necessary to redefine power—it is quite likely they would lack the consciousness to thus redefine it. Another way of saying this is to suggest that "power to" is not distinctly feminist; rather, it is distinctly "outsider." When outsider status no longer applies, the ideology supporting it is transformed to conform with the new (insider) status.

Flammang asserts that women do not want power if it means obtaining power at someone else's (presumably men's) expense. This surely implies that either there is no serious opposition to women's empowerment or that women will graciously concede defeat in the face of opposition rather than use "power over." Clearly, the cooperative vision of power will have enough serious and dedicated opponents that it would not be instituted cooperatively. As the zero-sum model suggests, feminists would thus need to defeat their "power over" opponents or be defeated themselves.

It is difficult to know whether Flammang thinks that most feminists should wish to be on the winning or the losing side. Assuming, however, that most feminists would prefer to win, a second problem arises. Once they have used "power over" in order to win, it is not clear in what form the feminist consciousness of empowerment would survive. Ends and means are connected in such a way that to use any means to achieve desirable ends may clearly compromise the ends themselves. Feminists who use "power over" in order to achieve "power to" may, in the final analysis, no longer have a feminist consciousness. But if they do not use "power over" they are going to be political losers, in no position even to articulate alternative political frameworks. It is this contraction that is particularly ignored in the relevant literature. How long an outsider consciousness remains uncorrupted by praxis is a perennial question in political analysis and a crucial one, which needs to be considered in arguing for an alternative conception of power.

The tendency toward essentialism, which I argued earlier undergirds the women and empowerment debate, further complicates the question of how empowerment could come into being. If women's nature is responsible for their conception of power as shared and cooperative (as male nature, presumably, results in seeing power as domination and hierarchy), then women would be unable to adopt a zero-sum model of power because it would not be in their nature to do so. If, however, Frey is correct that power must be taken, as the zero-sum model suggests, then women would never be able to seize power.

If we reject essentialism and argue that women could adopt a zero-sum orientation toward power in order to replace it later with "power to," we still confront the argument that the feminist vision of power as cooperative and non-zero-sum could only work in a situation where everyone shared a conception of a common (and probably self-evident) public good. In such a world, power might well consist of cooperative, non-zero-sum relationships based on mutual support

in realizing desired goals. Obviously, that is not the existing state of political affairs, where issues are won and lost. Clearly, the current choice is not whether we
will have "power over" or "power to": It is, rather, who wins and who loses.

Some feminist theorists may dismiss my critique of empowerment because
they perceive it to be male-centered. Hilary Lips expresses this uneasiness very well:

> Feminist groups constitute a good example of what happens when power is viewed
> with suspicion. Initially, many such groups actively avoided having formal leaders in
> order to avoid the negative effects of power. After a time, however, a more sophisti-
> cated approach gained ground, and it was recognized that a lack of structural leader-
> ship can sometimes pave the way for unchecked tyranny by informal "leaders." . . .
> However, some feminists still voice skepticism about those in power, even when the
> powerful are also of feminist persuasion.[48]

Lips suggests, however, that "it is questionable whether the transforming power
can be attained without, in some sense, power over others."[49]

In arguing that the empowerment model poses substantial problems, theo-
retically and in its potential for realization, I am not suggesting that women do not
have a substantial claim to exercise power, politically or otherwise. Quite the opposite. It is dangerous to base women's claims to political power on the argument
that they would use power differently from (read: better than) men. Men's claim to
power is not, after all, based on their ability to use power in particularly beneficial
ways. Perhaps all such claims to power should be so argued, but that is another
issue. What I am saying is that the empowerment model is as deeply problematic,
albeit in different ways, as the androcentric "power over" model it opposes. Moreover, it is not necessary to argue that women use power differently from men in
order to make the case for women's increased political power.

SUMMARY

Feminist theory thus suffers from a lack of clarity as to what is distinctively feminist about empowerment. More important, it exhibits a tendency toward essentialism in its insistence that women think about and use power differently than
men do. That women think about or use power differently than men has not been
sustained by the empirical social psychological studies that have attempted to
quantify power behavior. Finally, feminist thinking about power runs into a series
of contradictions when confronting the implementation of "power to" in a zero-
sum world of "power over."

If we are to evaluate subsequent feminist theories of power, at least three criteria must be considered. A feminist theory of power that is both normative and
empirical and that does not lend itself to antifeminist uses must be historical,
structural, and nonessentialist.

It must confront and account for the (limited) empirical evidence that argues
for a convergence in men's and women's power behavior. It must delineate what
is specifically feminist about empowerment in light of that model's appeal to non-

feminist thinkers. It must address the questions of how nonhierarchical, nonmasculinist behaviors will or can come to replace the zero-sum politics of winners and losers. The questions that should shape such a feminist discourse about power cannot be answered here. Until we begin to be more responsive to these questions, however, we cannot hope to replace "power over" with "power to."

NOTES

1. A citation of the relevant literature on power would be enormous. Many scholars have argued for the centrality of power in political analysis, beginning as far back as Plato.

2. J. Lipman-Blumen, *Gender Roles and Power* (Englewood Cliffs, NJ: Prentice-Hall, 1984), p. 5.

3. J. Scott, "Gender: A Useful Category of Historical Analysis," *American Historical Review*, 91 (1986), p. 1069.

4. Ibid.

5. L. M. Sagrestano, "The Use of Power and Influence in a Gendered World," *Psychology of Women Quarterly*, 16 (1992), p. 445.

6. E. Janeway, "Women and the Uses of Power," in H. Eisenstein and A. Jardine (Eds.), *The Future of Difference* (New Brunswick, NJ: Rutgers University Press, 1980), pp. 327–344.

7. Ibid., p. 328.

8. L. Gordon, *Heroes of Their Own Lives* (New York: Viking, 1988), p. 251.

9. J. A. Flammang, "Feminist Theory: The Question of Power," in S. G. McNall (Ed.), *Current Perspectives in Social Theory*, vol. 4 (Greenwich, CT: JAI Press, 1983), pp. 37–83.

10. N. Hartsock, *Money, Sex and Power: Toward a Feminist Historical Materialism* (Boston: Northeastern University Press, 1983).

11. J. Isaac, "Beyond the Three Faces of Power: A Realist Critique," *Polity*, 10 (1987), pp. 20–21.

12. Ibid.

13. P. Bachrach and M. Baratz, "The Two Faces of Power," *American Political Science Review*, 56 (1962), pp. 947–952.

14. Lipman-Blumen, *Gender Roles and Power*, p. 21.

15. Flammang, "Feminist Theory," p. 71.

16. Ibid., p. 74.

17. Hartsock, *Money, Sex and Power*, p. 253.

18. S. Hoagland, "Lesbian Ethics: Some Thoughts on Power in Our Interactions," *Lesbian Ethics*, 2 (1986), p. 7.

19. H. M. Lips, *Women, Men and the Psychology of Power* (Englewood Cliffs, NJ: Prentice-Hall, 1981), p. 10.

20. J. Jaquette, "Power as Ideology: A Feminist Analysis," in J. H. Steihm (Ed.), *Women's Views of the Political World of Men* (Dobbs Ferry, NY: Transnational, 1984), pp. 9–29.

21. J. L. Griscom, "Women and Power: Definition, Dualism and Difference," *Psychology of Women Quarterly*, 16 (1992), p. 406.

22. R. Dahl, "The Concept of Power," *Behavioral Science*, 2 (1957), pp. 201–215.

23. P. Bachrach and M. Baratz, "Decisions and Non-Decisions: An Analytic Framework," *American Political Science Review*, 57 (1963), pp. 632–642, and "The Two Faces of Power," *American Political Science Review*, 56 (1962), pp. 947–952.

24. E. E. Schattschneider, *The Semi-Sovereign People* (Hinesdale, IL: Dryden Press, 1960).

25. S. Lukes, *Power: A Radical View* (London: Macmillan, 1974).

26. Isaac, "Beyond the Three Faces of Power," p. 21.

27. Ibid., p. 28.

28. M. Foucault, *Power/Knowledge: Selected Interviews and Other Writings, 1972–1977* (New York: Pantheon, 1980).

29. S. Evans, *Personal Politics: The Roots of Women's Liberation in the Civil Rights Movement and the New Left* (New York: Random House, 1980).

30. C. L. Miller and A. G. Cummins, "An Examination of Women's Perspectives on Power," *Psychology of Women Quarterly* 16 (1992), p. 417.

31. Griscom, "Women and Power," p. 406.

32. S. Morgen and A. Bookman, "Rethinking Women and Politics: An Introductory Essay," in A. Bookman and S. Morgen (Eds.), *Women and the Politics of Empowerment* (Philadelphia: Temple University Press, 1988), p. 21.

33. L. Alcoff, "Cultural Feminism versus Post-structuralism: The Identity Crisis in Feminist Theory," *Signs*, 13 (1988), p. 411.

34. Ibid., p. 433.

35. Ibid.

36. S. Farganis, *The Social Reconstruction of the Feminine Character* (Totowa, NJ: Rowman and Littlefield, 1986), p. 160.

37. C. Degler, *At Odds: Women and the Family in America from the Revolution to the Present* (New York: Oxford University Press, 1980).

38. Alcoff, "Cultural Feminism versus Post-structuralism," p. 413.

39. R. Milkman, "Women's History and the Sears Case," *Feminist Studies*, 12 (1986), pp. 394–395.

40. See Zillah Eisenstein, *The Female Body and the Law* (Berkeley: University of California Press, 1988), for a good discussion of these issues.

41. M. Poovey, "Feminism and Deconstruction," *Feminist Studies*, 14 (1988), p. 63.

42. J. Scott, "Deconstructing Equality-versus-Difference: Or, the Uses of Post-structuralist Theory for Feminism," *Feminist Studies*, 14 (1988), p. 47.

43. V. Sapiro, "Reflections on Reflections: Personal Ruminations," *Women and Politics*, 7 (1987), p. 25.

44. Ibid.

45. A review of the relevant literature would make a good-sized book. A recent volume of *Psychology of Women Quarterly*, 16 (1992) is devoted to the topic of "Women and Power" and is a good resource for empirical studies on gender and power.

46. Flammang, "Feminist Theory," p. 71.

47. F. W. Frey, "The Motivation to Power," paper presented at the American Political Science Association, 1984.

48. Lips, *Women, Men and the Psychology of Power*, p. 13.

49. Ibid.

FURTHER READING

Alcoff, L. "Cultural Feminism versus Post-structuralism: The Identity Crisis in Feminist Theory." *Signs*, 13 (Spring 1988), pp. 405–436.

Bachrach, P., and Baratz, M. "The Two Faces of Power." *American Political Science Review*, 56 (December 1962), pp. 947–952.

Bachrach, P., and Baratz, M. "Decisions and Nondecisions: An Analytic Framework." *American Political Science Review*, 57 (September 1963), pp. 632–642.

Dahl, R. "The Concept of Power." *Behavioral Science*, 2 (July 1957), pp. 201–215.

Degler, C. *At Odds: Women and the Family in America from the Revolution to the Present*. New York: Oxford University Press, 1980.

Eisenstein, Z. *The Radical Future of Liberal Feminism*. New York: Longman, 1981.

Evans, S. *Personal Politics: The Roots of Women's Liberation in the Civil Rights Movement and the New Left*. New York: Random House, 1980.

Farganis, S. *The Social Reconstruction of the Feminine Character*. Totowa, NJ: Rowman and Littlefield, 1986.

Flammang, J. A. "Feminist Theory: The Question of Power." In S. G. McNall (Ed.), *Current Perspectives in Social Theory* (vol. 4, pp. 37–83). Greenwich, CT: JAI Press, 1983.

Foucault, M. *Power/Knowledge: Selected Interviews and Other Writings, 1972–1977*. New York: Pantheon, 1980.

Frey, F. W. "The Motivation to Power." Paper presented at the American Political Science Association, 1984.

Gordon, L. *Heroes of Their Own Lives*. New York: Viking, 1988.

Hartsock, N. *Money, Sex and Power: Toward a Feminist Historical Materialism*. Boston: Northeastern University Press, 1983.

Hoagland, S. "Lesbian Ethics: Some Thoughts on Power in our Interactions." *Lesbian Ethics*, 2 (1986), pp. 5–32.

Isaac, J. "Beyond the Three Faces of Power: A Realist Critique." *Polity*, 10 (Fall 1987), pp. 4–31.

Janeway, E. "Women and the Uses of Power." In H. Eisenstein and A. Jardine (Eds.), *The Future of Difference* (pp. 327–344). New Brunswick, NJ: Rutgers University Press, 1980.

Jaquette, J. "Power as Ideology: A Feminist Analysis." In J. H. Steihm (Ed.), *Women's Views of the Political World of Men* (pp. 9–29). Dobbs Ferry, NY: Transnational, 1984.

Lipman-Blumen, J. *Gender Roles and Power*. Englewood Cliffs, NJ: Prentice-Hall, 1984.

Lips, H. M. *Women, Men and the Psychology of Power*. Englewood Cliffs, NJ: Prentice-Hall, 1981.

Lukes, S. *Power: A Radical View*. London: Macmillan, 1974.

Milkman, R. "Women's History and the Sears Case." *Feminist Studies*, 12 (Summer 1986), pp. 375–400.

Morgen, S., and Bookman, A. "Rethinking Women and Politics: An Introductory Essay." In A. Bookman and S. Morgen (Eds.), *Women and the Politics of Empowerment* (pp. 3–32). Philadelphia: Temple University Press, 1988.

Poovey, M. "Feminism and Deconstruction." *Feminist Studies*, 14 (Spring 1988), pp. 51–66.

Sapiro, V. "Reflections on Reflections: Personal Ruminations." *Women and Politics*, 7 (Winter 1987), pp. 21–27.

Schattschneider, E. E. *The Semisovereign People*. Hinesdale, IL: Dryden Press, 1960.

Scott, J. "Gender: A Useful Category of Historical Analysis." *American Historical Review*, 91 (December 1986), pp. 1053–1075.

Scott, J. "Deconstructing Equality-versus-Difference: Or, the Uses of Post-structuralist Theory for Feminism." *Feminist Studies*, 14 (Spring 1988), pp. 33–50.

The Riddle of Consciousness: Racism and Identity in Feminist Theory

Nancie E. Caraway

INTRODUCTION

Feminist scholarship offers both an intellectual and a political stimulus to undergraduate students in political science. It may fruitfully be called syncretic because it "brings together" so many threads about knowledge, political action, and power—and the implications of scholarship in general. Formally, it is akin to African-American studies, gay studies, and other moments in ethnic studies (Chicana, Latina, Asian, Arab, Native American) because it crosses disciplines and introduces students to historical, theoretical, empirical, and interpretive modes of inquiry. And, importantly, these academic initiatives recognize their ties to grassroots constituencies and movements for social justice. Being explicitly tied to social movements belies the claims of "neutrality" and "objectivity" professed by much social science conventional wisdom.

The increasing encounter of feminist scholarship with traditional concerns of political science (such as the Constitution, the judiciary, and electoral politics) has been challenging and revitalizing. It has displaced naturalized taboos (as in, "It's not natural for women/Blacks to participate in the nation's civic life") and exposed as riddles what were considered universal truths (as in, "We all know that politics is about state and national security, not sexual double standards, parenting, or housework"). It has resulted in the inclusion of courses in feminist theory in most political science departments at U.S. universities. This inclusion, however, carries with it the important caveat that one can't "just add women and stir."

Nancie E. Caraway is a political theorist and feminist scholar. She lives, writes, and teaches in Hawaii and in Washington, D.C.

The feminist imperative expands knowledge because it requires that we rethink old categories and accepted truths that have excluded women and women's experiences. What this means is that the concept of gender (the socially constructed "masculine" and "feminine" meanings attached to our biological plumbing) is now considered along with political authority, freedom, democracy, justice, race, and class as one of the important markers of political experience. The challenge requires as well new explanatory theories of "how things came to be this way" and new agendas for stimulating critical consciousness and accountability for oppression—whether oppression is practiced by the state, men, corporations, whites, *or* women.

The history of feminism itself is crucially a history of theory. Feminist scholarship has worked to demystify theory's abstractions by insisting, not only that the personal is political, but that the very meanings of the political and what counts as political experience are open to radical reinterpretation. This rethinking of traditional categories such as democracy, citizenship, and consciousness has enabled feminist theorists to ask subversive questions of the "canons" of political science: Which actions and experiences are considered political? How has the liberal public–private split rendered invisible women's contributions to culture? Who benefits from a social and political structure that subjugates women? What processes of identity and consciousness "produce" female and male political actors? And, importantly, how have traditional concepts of citizenship excluded women of all races?

So, although traditional concerns of political science remain legitimate, the perspectives from which they are examined are radicalized by feminist theory. Feminist political theorists have also turned to their own practices. They are attempting to examine the interlocking oppressions based on sex, gender, race, class, sexual preference, national origin and ethnicity—and to devise strategies for overcoming those oppressions. Feminist theory describes (never unproblematically) the world from the perspectives of women by asking what kinds of political power and actions contribute to a more egalitarian society. This probing critique of traditional theories of citizenship and democracy has highlighted women's alternative political practices and the masculinist thought that has relegated women to inferior positions in the public world.

An analysis of grass-roots activism of diverse women in the United States and other parts of the world historically has redefined the way "politics" is often thought of in our culture—as the actions of male elected officials. By making the activities of previously invisible women central, feminist scholars are helping to write both them and a new conception of democracy into the history of social change.

One of the most compelling turns in contemporary feminist theory is the emphasis on racism within feminism and the ways in which "women's oppression" has reflected the concerns of middle-class white women. This affords many new voices and feminisms the opportunity to negotiate community. Feminist women of color have insisted on articulating their own identities and experiences. In response, white feminists are working to contribute to this expanded understanding of "women" by interrogating their own racism, privilege, and the need for historical accountability for American apartheid and white supremacy. This is a painful but potentially liberating process, which views racism and sexism not solely as "problems" but as textured ways of defining reality and living our lives. White feminists have learned that they too are "racialized."

The emphasis in feminist theory on identity politics, ethical commitments to creating coalitions of diverse women, and reflections on critical consciousness itself sets a new agenda for students of politics. These new configurations inhabit a challenging world of social theory to which I hope to introduce female and male political science students. A gentle warning to readers: Theoretical language provokes and often frustrates newcomers. But try to work with it. Think of theory's often technical terminology as an occasion for high-spirited translation (of the type required when we strain to "understand" the riffs of a Dylan concert)—and intellectual growth.

Multicultural feminist theory (the name for the dynamics I've been discussing) has its own mode of communicating—like rap, blues, jazz, or African-American gospel testifying. The language of theory, however, does pose problems: It's dense, and it may ask that we read against the grain, follow the flow a bit while it teases us into a new coded way of thought. Much of these sentiments derive from something called *postmodernism* or *poststructuralism*—an intellectual attitude that offers skeptical insights, some of which are helpful to thoughtful feminists, some obfuscatory. This essay tries to sort out the criteria. Think of your frustration with theory-talk not as a declaration of verbal warfare, but as a meeting place of thought and spirit, a process of riddle solving.

As you travel the sometimes demanding terrain of this essay, remember the goal of creating a more robust "woman-friendly polity."[1] Toward this end, I employ two symbolic images of identity and consciousness in this essay as an entrée to these issues in current feminist theory: Toni Morrison's narrative in her novel of slavery, *Beloved*, and the autobiographical essay "Identity: Skin Blood Heart" by the white feminist Minnie Bruce Pratt.

KNOWING AND BEING: RACISM AND QUESTIONS OF FEMINIST THEORY

> Here, she said, in this place we flesh; flesh that weeps, laughs; flesh that dances on bare feet in grass. Love it. Love it hard. Yonder they do not love your flesh. They despise it. They don't love your eyes; they'd just as soon pick em out. No more do they love the skin on your back. Yonder they flay it. And O my people they do not love your hands. Those they only use, tie, bind, chop off and leave empty. Love your hands! Love them. Raise them up and kiss them. Touch others with them, pat them together, stroke them on your face 'cause they don't love that either. *You* got to love it, *you*![2]

With this extraordinary declaration from her novel of enslavement,[3] Toni Morrison's "unchurched preacher" Baby Suggs articulates the passion of collective self-affirmation to her congregation of ex-slaves. Morrison's narrative speaks to the symbolic project that has defined the African-American quest for agency and free space in the world the "whitethings" created.

This white world condemned by Morrison's text is a world in which African-Americans have had their stories, identities, and very being defined by hegemonic white culture. I, as a white feminist, inhabit a similarly hegemonic terrain, that of the community of feminist scholars and activists whose legacy, too often, has been one of "whitethings" defining feminist life and aspirations for women of color. Fortunately, for our ethical health and our political direction, new stories, theories, and strategies voiced by feminist women of color are retooling feminist thought in penetrating and passionate modes to transform a deracinated "whitething" feminism. In this article, I want to chart some contours of this new multicultural direction, situate them within certain themes of identity politics, and provide a pedagogy about accountability for overcoming racism and developing critical consciousness, themes that come to us from Minnie Bruce Pratt.

As a political theorist, not a literary critic, I began to engage the coda of subjectivity and identity not through a technical philosophical discourse, but from the sheer emotional pull of Morrison's exhortation about the flesh of Black slaves—that is, the *identity* project of African-Americans. The graphic physicality of Baby Suggs's statement concretizes for us that theory is truly never removed from the power-laden context of specific historical lives. When intellectuals consider utterances such as "deconstruction of the subject"—a provocative but often tediously hollow postmodernist challenge to certainties that we can truly "know" our "selves"—we need only return our thoughts to Morrison's prayerful *subjects* in the sun-dappled forest clearing to remember what social analysis is "about." This focus alerts us to the contributions of Black feminist theory to "our" (all women's) sense of the female subject. What can we learn about a revitalized polity and a newly committed series of feminisms if we look for the theoretical issues entangled within the arc narrated by Morrison?

Morrison's statement "*You* got to love it. *You!*" rejects the stigmas of otherness and difference inculcated by white supremacist culture, and validates, albeit tenuously, subjectivity and identity. This statement thus intersects in important ways with current epistemological debates—debates over "how we know what we know"—in feminist theory.[4] In particular, it demonstrates the creative challenges of Black feminism to feminist theory and politics.[5]

I have used Morrison's words to call attention to white racism within feminism and to validate feminist efforts at ending racist oppression as the central goal of feminist politics today. Let me note that the militant voices and courage of African-American women were first to insist on the important task of decentering "whiteness" as the norm in feminist politics. In many historical moments, they have served as the conscience of feminist practice, the spirit that drives the movement back to the essential commitment feminist scholars ought to have toward enhancing the lives of marginalized women.

Contemporary Black feminist theory arises from the same spirit of affirmation and specificity reflected in Morrison's exhortation to the nineteenth-century

Black community. The analysis that I will develop here characterizes such a project as "identity politics." But how do we reconcile this concern with agency and identity, given the red flags postmodernism sends up? The cultural power of our symbolic systems to seduce, delude, and encourage conceits about "self" and "authenticity" bear the footprints of metaphysics and take us away from the social and historical moorings in which such needs are produced. I want to think of identity politics as a contextual, not essentialist, process evolving out of political commitments and struggles for justice in multicultural feminist coalitions.[6] Identity is in the etched details of mediated lives and struggle. The reflective and reflexive political biography of the white feminist Minnie Bruce Pratt, to which I will return, is a luminous example of such a justice-seeking identity. Pratt's story is a chronicle of the fits and starts of seeking to know "how" one "is," a crucible of how a white feminist in a racist movement can be politicized through identity politics into a deeply personal interrogation of her own historical and racial roots.

What I hope to suggest in this essay is that questions about the self, about knowing and being, are not mutually exclusive. I am arguing that we must be able to articulate *some experiential foundation,* some notion of self, before we may act in the world. Rather than polarize antagonisms between feminists who "think" and feminists who "act," we need to see reflection and resistance as equally valid requirements of political and civic experience. Questions about and strategies for experiencing "identity" are crucial in this process. The perspectives derived from identity politics seek to emphasize the deep context, the "situated knowledges" (to use Donna Haraway's term), of our connected lives. Such a foundation is powerfully rendered in Morrison's preacher Baby Suggs's commentary: "In this place we flesh . . . *You* got to love it, *you!*" As Black feminist Cheryl Townsend Gilkes has pointed out, questions of identity have both historical and spiritual resonance for Black women *and* men. Black women's life experiences are grounded in a context that derives personal identity collectively, from a larger racially oppressed community "bound together by common interest, kinship, and tradition."[7] In charting the heroic and courageous activism of Black women in their struggle for dignity and equality ("uplift of the entire race") throughout American history, contemporary Black feminist historians *assume* the necessity of political agency, subjectivity, and identity as the very condition for social change.[8]

As a corollary to this understanding of the self as an entity that *is,* but is always in process, under seige, evolving as persons and events touch and change, African-American women insist that for feminist discourse and politics to be relevant to their daily concerns, they must acknowledge the intersections of gender, race, and class as determinants of oppression, and not view gender as the *primary* form of oppression. This revolutionary paradigm shift is transforming feminism; we all are emerging from a new feminist "text" freshly educated about redefining the boundaries and connections of otherness. One need only observe the spectrum of contemporary feminist communities and activities to see the impact of such thinking. The writings of Black feminists are teaching us, in this regard, that feminist theory and politics should address the "multiple jeopardy" and "multiple consciousness" of Black women, in Deborah King's formulation.[9]

IDENTITY POLITICS: POSITIONAL RESISTANCE TO WHITE RACISM

As articulated by the Black feminist Combahee River Collective in a 1977 manifesto, "Our politics evolve from a healthy love for ourselves, our sisters, and our community. . . ." Their first commitment was to the cultural center they shared as women within the Black community.

> Even our Black women's style of talking, testifying in Black language about what we have experienced, has a resonance that is both cultural and political. We have spent a great deal of energy delving into the cultural and experiential nature of our oppression out of necessity because none of these matters have ever been looked at before. No one before has ever examined the multilayered texture of Black women's lives.[10]

The collective determined to align with progressive Black men in solidarity to resist racist oppression—struggling with them against sexism—and to frame their own oppression within the overlapping networks of family and community ties. More recently, Deborah King has spelled out these webbed commitments of Black feminists to the "special circumstances of our lives in the United States: the commonalities that we share with all women, as well as the bonds that connect us to the men of our race." King acknowledges the "distinctive context for Black womanhood," which she insists be defined and interpreted by Black women themselves: "While drawing on a rich tradition of struggle as blacks and as women, we continually establish and reestablish our own priorities."[11]

These statements argue for a politics of identity that is embodied in experiences and cultural spaces whose meanings are determined by those who live their daily lives in the tissue of interwoven contradictions. Alliances, priorities, and interpretations of self are relational and not responses to any set of given objective needs. Identity politics here finds affinity with a conceptualization of Donna Haraway in her explication of a feminist "objectivity" grounded in "partial local knowledges": "Feminism is about the sciences of the multiple subject with (at least) double vision. Feminism is about a critical vision consequent upon a critical positioning in unhomogeneous gendered social space."[12]

The operative phrase here is "critical positioning." For homophobes and chauvinists along with racists may well lay claim to a particular locus of cultural groundings and alliances that teach intolerance and racial and sexual revanchism. One might envision a mythologizing of David Duke as a southern populist, white male grass-roots expression of Arcadian-inspired public will, or even "white male, ex-Klansman and neo-Nazi"—that is to say, Duke's "identity." But it is not enough to issue a cultural-demographic schemata of one's identity-defining characteristics. In order to meet the politicized and justice-seeking criteria of identity politics, a fully articulated resistance and a critical positioning to oppression must be present. The multiple "subject" or shifting self that often comes to life in "nonfeminist" settings—as the women of the Combahee River Collective recognized—provides a more democratized terrain for feminist civic potential.

One colloquial way of stating this principle is to say that, as feminists, we need to "start where people are at," not insisting that feminist identity be based on shedding familial, regional, or religious local skins. How is it then that Black feminism's embodiment of identity politics demonstrates a *critical* and thus valorized stance?

One would be on dangerous ground in projecting a romanticized image of "the oppressed" as beyond criticism. We diminish our critical edge if we dismiss postmodernist admonitions about the human potential for culpability in projecting illusions, of adopting institutionalized discourses of truth, reason, and certainty as foundations for political life. At the same time, however, we can look to the political *knowledge* that comes from the oppositional worldview Black feminist bell hooks locates in living "on the edge" of white society.[13]

Such a critical and protean version of identity politics advances a space for political action and collective transformation. All feminists need to see value in the experience of those "on the edge" because such a vantage point embodies a negative moment, inherently attuned to flesh-and-blood deprivation and pain as central to political attention. As one feminist theorist has conceptualized such a stance, the knowledge gained by living "on the other side of the tracks" is justified by the critical positioning of those persons on the margins of societies.[14] The struggle against hierarchies of power is the substance that merits our allegiance to the practices and knowledge of the marginalized.

Toni Morrison in *Beloved* makes clear that "stories" and "identities" in America's apartheid have been far from reciprocal, far from the bridges of empathy and human understanding that ethical consciousness demands of human commerce. The "other" may indeed be alien and murderous. And one "identity" has not been as good as another. Morrison gives us a story about "subjects" struggling to wrest definition of what human beings are supposed to be from white masters. It is their *critical position* vis-à-vis the dominant racist society that must be endorsed, their determination to re-vision an "other" that does not annihilate, rather than their essence as "pure" petitioners.

BE THE RIGHT THING: POSITIONING WHITE FEMINIST IDENTITY AND RACIAL IMPERATIVES

This emerging portrait of identity politics tantalizes the theoretical imaginations of feminist scholars in its bonding of epistemological considerations with imperatives for historical political action. Feminist thinkers/activists may embrace knowledge about the "fluid" and unfixed construction of identity—albeit described in specific, historic local narratives. Such portraits need not be racially (or otherwise) specific; they surely fulfill the intertextual criteria of the most provocative multicultural feminist scholarship by speaking to "us all." Collectivities of multicultural, multiracial, sexually diverse feminists may find empowerment in the resources of identity politics about the shared and differentiated faces of female oppression.

Identity politics is the terrain of social outlaws.[15] It militantly asserts who "we" are and what "we" mean (this holds, especially so, for white feminists given the history of white assumptions in much feminist theory) and engages the potential for those explorations in coalition or affinity venues. It demands accountability for correcting the racism of everyday life which the expanded vision of multicultural feminism reveals to us. I want to briefly explore one of the most penetrating and transformative instances of identity politics work by a non-Black, non–person-of-color (to reverse the white solipsistic linguistic norm "non-white")— Minnie Bruce Pratt's 1984 essay "Identity: Skin Blood Heart."[16]

Pratt's text, an intensely probing mediation on her own shifting selves, is a powerful model for other white feminists to follow in order to question our own complicity in and accountability for correcting the myriad racist practices existing in the world around us—a precondition for successful coalition building. Pratt, a white, Southern-born, Christian-raised, lesbian woman, takes her reader inside an exploration of a divided consciousness, demonstrating the postmodernist feminist thesis that the "wholeness" of the self involves an inescapably protean encounter with others. The manner in which Pratt frames her experiential/political project of struggling to derive an "identity" from which the various layers of her life "fit," empowering her to act, foregrounds questions of otherness and accountability. Pratt uses her feminism, a politics of everyday life, as a springboard from which to investigate self-consciously those many "edges" on which she stands: ". . . I will try to be at the edge between my fear and outside, on the edge at my skin, listening, asking what new thing will I hear, will I see, will I let myself feel, beyond the fear."[17] Pratt is able to let her multiple experiences of otherness float in an uneasy alliance, allowing them to open her eyes to other scenarios of domination and oppression. Her own outsider status as a lesbian alerts her to the marginalization of others with whom she attempts to ally, without collapsing them all into one "grand polemics of oppression."[18]

Central to Pratt's articulation of her search for self and identity are two important metaprocesses that are important tools for white feminists' antiracist efforts. She has the ability to problematize, to evaluate reflectively, every encounter with another and to take nothing for granted in interracial relationships. These displacements provide a valuable corrective to status quo attitudes. Pratt encourages white women to scrutinize the historical and ideological layers attendant to encounters with "others"—paying particular attention to the concealments and exclusions, the buried "holes in the text,"[19] that submerge and mystify the violations of race, class, and gender.

Pratt is frustrated and doubtful of overcoming the chasm of racism. But Pratt keeps on keeping on. These painful incidents become challenges to overcome, not paralyzing dead ends in Pratt's story; they stand as markers of the quotidian signs of racism. As Pratt assays the cost to those whom her own protection and privilege as a southern white woman have disadvantaged, she is able to "free" herself from the poisonous racism by acknowledging her own family's participation in its system. She is empowered to locate the harm, to identify the victims that the vision of the society of her white childhood excluded. By seeking the absences, she may now "gain truth" when she expands her constricted eye, "an eye that has only let in what I have been taught to see."[20]

Revelation and psychological unpeeling continue when Pratt's professor husband takes her and their children to a new town, a Southern "market town." Geography and history again stimulate her questioning of the town whose center, tellingly, is not a courthouse, but a market house. With complacent, middle-class white friends at dinner in a private club overlooking the town's central circle, she queries them about the marketplace. They chat about the fruits and vegetables, the auctioned tobacco that were sold at the market. "But not slaves," they said. It is left to the Black waiter—a silent figure who boldly breaks through "the anonymity of his red jacket"—to assume the role of educator, disrupting white historical amnesia to tell them of the men, women, and children who were sold at the market near where they now dine.

> What he told me was plain enough: This town was a place where some people had been used as livestock, chattel, slaves, cattle, capital, by other people; and this use had been justified by the physical fact of a different skin color and by the cultural fact of different ways of living. The white men and their families who had considered Black people to be animals with no right to their own children or to a home of their own still did not admit that they had done any wrong, nor that there had been any wrong, in *their* town. What he told me was plain enough: Be warned: they have not changed.[21]

The narrative of Pratt's identity journey is a useful feminist teaching precisely because her project does not become a study in narcissism, a withdrawing from political reality. Her newfound knowledge of racist history through a probing of her own personal history serves as a spur toward further inquiry and action. Her ability to approach the world and structures of domination as interlocked, as "overlapping circles," elicits knowledge of other traditions of struggle whose experiences she might draw upon. And importantly in the framework of coalition politics, Pratt perceives scenarios of persons in whose service she might present herself as an ally in their struggles.

> I knew nothing of these or other histories of struggle for equality and justice and one's own identity in the town I was living in: not a particularly big town, not liberal at all, not famous for anything: an almost rural eastern North Carolina town, in a region that you, perhaps, are used to thinking of as backward. Yet it was a place with so many resistances, so much creative challenge to the powers of the world: which is true of every county, town, or city in this country, each with its own buried history of struggle, of how people try to maintain their dignity within the restrictions placed around them, and how they struggle to break those restrictions.[22]

The potency of Pratt's story at this point in her account of the accumulated identities that she wrestles to incorporate has to do with her own connection to Southern racism. When she sought to find out what had been or was being done "in her name," the knowledge was shattering. "I had set out to make a new home with other women, only to find that the very ground I was building on was the grave of the people my kin had killed, and that my foundation, my birth culture, was mortared with blood."[23] The cracking and heaving and buckling Pratt experienced in what she describes as "the process of freeing myself" afforded no relief, no sanctimony. "This breaking through," she admits, "did not feel like liberation but like destruction." Her expanded sense of political accountability; her endeavors to locate a new "home," a chosen political community of women committed to justice; and her confession of loss are the flashpoints of Pratt's journey toward political conscience. This voice does not mute the pain and alienation such a process entails. Feel the drama in her telling:

> I think this is what happens, to a more or less extreme degree, every time we expand our limited being: it is upheaval, not catastrophe: more like a snake shedding its skin than like death: the old constriction is sloughed off with difficulty, but there is an expansion: not a change in basic shape or color, but an expansion, some growth, and some reward for struggle and curiosity. . . .
>
> As I try to strip away the layers of deceit that I have been taught, it is hard not to be afraid that these are like wrappings of a shroud and that what I will ultimately come to in myself is a disintegrating, rotting *nothing*: that the values that I have at my core, from my culture, will only be those of negativity, exclusion, fear, death. And my feeling is based in the reality that the group identity of my culture has been defined, often, not by positive qualities, but by negative characteristics: by the absence of: "no dogs, Negroes, or Jews"; we have gotten our jobs, bought our houses, borne and educated our children by the negatives: no niggers, no kikes, no wops, no dagos, no spics, no A-rabs, no gooks, no queers [emphasis in original.][24]

Pratt's essay resonates in so many ways with wisdom and warnings vital to struggling antiracist feminists. The integrity with which she describes her story encourages our own probings. Her identity project can stand as a document of feminist politicization precisely because Pratt resists those self-destructive urges that are anathema to enacting social change: the reactionary extreme of abandoning her own complexly vexing Southern culture, the paralyzing guilt and fear that come with the knowledge of the enormity and barbarity of white privilege. Throughout this powerful essay, Pratt reveals herself determined to understand the volatile psychic hold of home, childhood, and patriarchal "protection" of white women in her class. There is no denouement in Pratt's search for "identity," only continued working-through. Hers, and ours, entails a long-term commitment, a meditation on consciousness that is grounded in daily actions that allow us to connect with or bypass the "others" with whom we seek community. This seeking is the riddle of consciousness to be grappled with through political struggle.

Pratt also shows her readers the psychic dangers of denial and its opposite, absorption into the other: the desire to cover her "naked, negative [self] with something from the positive traditions of identity which have served in part to help folks survive our people."[25] Finally Pratt can come to an awareness and acceptance of her own *whiteness*—while resisting the culture of white supremacy, on the one hand, and, on the other, avoiding the condescending trap of "cultural impersonation," of attempting to "become Black." We come to see such gestures for what they are—sentimental balms of political quietism.

In the language of postmodern thought, Pratt's essay provides a "genealogy," a deep sifting through of the ideological and historical practices that render the tangle of "self." She asks how the contradictions that regulate her life came to be—in discourse, in history, in region, in family. Pratt offers a response to the issues of racism within feminism that takes us to the other side of paralyzing white guilt. In the "knowing and being" philosophical frame of feminist thought, Pratt's example ties reflection with the crucial next step of political engagement and activism for justice. She offers us the gift of openness to begin again each day that struggle to turn our received "identities" upside down.

CONCLUSION

The concept of identity politics I have attempted to sketch questions many of the troubling assumptions of mainstream white feminism. It brings to life the need for white feminists not only to endorse a call for *inclusion* and *diversity* within feminist organizations, but to go "beyond the inclusion of persons and texts," as Sandra Harding has recently argued, and ask "what should *we* be doing in order to be desirable allies from *their* perspectives?"[26] Identity politics with a postmodern tilt, then, facilitates such a commitment by rejecting the possibility of a common "woman's experience" that can be objectively derived. This reading follows Minnie Bruce Pratt's example in cautioning against the tendency to substitute a critical consciousness, or therapy, or other premises that assume we have an unchanging "essence." We are encouraged to focus instead on strategic discourse, by asking under which conditions we may work together democratically, and on political action toward common goals.

Feminists interested in multicultural goals may employ these ideas with the model of political action in strategic coalitions of diverse women. The themes of racism and identity come together in a configuration that can address the theoretical issues about the female subject so vital to current feminist thought. I hope my epigrammatic beginning, with Toni Morrison's searing accomplishment in *Beloved* of textually imparting the criminal genealogy of Black flesh in America, reminds us all just what is at stake in questions of identity and racial memory.

We ought not forget how the construction of a "self" that sees its own reflection in those "semiotic technologies"[27] created by the culture that creates us can still feel injustice and endure pain. At the same time, a critical identity politics cautions us not to become too comfortable too long in *that spot* with *that identity*, lest we forget and stifle the ways in which we change, contradict, and grow in history. The achievement of identity itself must be viewed as one moment of political struggle, a struggle that precludes our standing, innocent, on the other side of our cultural mediations.

Identity politics calls for practices of deep contextualization, with accounts of persons that are always explicitly described, colored, gendered, situated—that, to borrow from Louis Althusser, resist simplification in the last instance. And, more importantly, it gives us grounds for politics and coalitions in the renegade terrain of that "real" world of shared struggle in feminist community.

NOTES

1. Kathleen B. Jones, "Citizens in a Woman-Friendly Polity," *Signs*, 15 (4) (Summer 1990), pp. 781–812.

2. Toni Morrison, *Beloved* (New York: Knopf, 1987), pp. 88–89.

3. Although most critics have characterized Morrison's novel as a novel "of slavery," I wish to adopt the term *enslavement*. Black feminist and longtime civil rights activist Ruby Sales has made a strong case for rejecting the word *slavery* in favor of *enslavement*. In her analysis, the former term suggests a passivity and renders the process of enslavement benign. Using the word *slavery* diminishes the moral and political responsibility demanded of the one who enslaves. If there's enslavement, there's an enslaver and an enslaved person. The term *enslaved*, according to Sales, doesn't mean a person is passive; it implies coercive force was used against that person. Further, importantly, the term implies that the enslaved person is resisting. See Ruby Sales, "In Our Own Words: An Interview with Ruby Sales," *Woman's Review of Books*, 7 (5) (February 1990), p 24.

4. The problematic has been identified in these debates as one of "subject-centered discourse" and is occasioned by currents in what is intellectually framed as "postmodernist skepticism" of the founding categories of Western Enlightenment thought—truth, objectivity, the coherent self, agency, identity—all constructs from which feminism itself derived. For lucid discussions of these issues and feminism's encounter with postmodernism, consult Kathy Ferguson, "Interpretation and Genealogy in Feminism," paper presented at the Western Political Science Association, San Francisco, March 1988; Kathy Ferguson, "Subject-Centeredness in Feminist Discourse," in Kathleen B. Jones and Anna G. Jonasdottir (Eds.), *The Political Interests of Gender* (London: Sage Publications, 1985), pp. 66–78. Linda J. Nicholson (Ed.), *Feminism/Postmodernism* (New York and London: Routledge, 1990); Jane Flax, "Postmodernism and Gender Relations in Feminist Theory," *Signs*, 12 (4) (Summer 1987), pp. 621–643; Linda Alcoff, "Cultural Feminism versus Post-Structuralism: The Identity Crisis in Feminist Theory," *Signs*, 13 (3) (Spring 1988), pp 406–436; Leslie Wahl Rabine, "A Feminist Politics of Non-Identity," *Feminist Studies*, 14 (2) (Spring 1988), pp. 11–31; the entire volume on "Feminism and Epistemology: Approaches to Research in Women and Politics," in *Women & Politics*, 7 (3) (Fall 1987); Donna Haraway, "A Manifesto for Cyborgs: Science, Technology, and Socialist Feminism in the 1980s," in Nicholson, *Feminism/Postmodernism*, pp. 190–233; Donna Haraway, "Situated Knowledges: The Science Question in Feminism and the Privilege of Partial Perspective," *Feminist Studies*, 14 (3) (Fall 1988), pp. 575–599.

5. See bell hooks, *Feminist Theory: From Margin to Center* (Boston: South End Press, 1984); bell hooks, *Ain't I a Woman* (Boston: South End Press, 1989); bell hooks, *Yearning: Race, Gender, and Cultural Politics* (Boston: South End Press, 1990); Audre Lorde, *Sister Outsider* (Trumansburg, NY: Crossing Press, 1984).

6. I am persuaded by Judith Butler's reading of the identity problematic in postmodern thinking that the deconstruction of identity need not lead to the deconstruction of politics. Through the dynamic of political confrontation and coalition politics, we understand who we are and what we mean in our explication of feminist common differences. Butler argues the case "that there need not be a 'doer behind the deed,' but that the 'doer' is variably constructed in and through the deed." Butler does not, but I will, tip my voluntarist hat to Marx for the originary seeds of the insight about the self-defining character of political struggle. Judith Butler, *Gender Trouble: Feminism and the Subversion of Identity* (New York: Routledge, 1990), pp. 148, 142.

7. Cheryl Townsend Gilkes, "Dual Heroisms and Double Burdens: Interpreting Afro-American Women's Experience and History," *Feminist Studies*, 14 (3) (Fall 1989), pp. 573–590, esp. p. 573.

8. In reviewing Paula Giddings's excellent history of Black feminist activism, *When and Where I Enter: The Impact of Black Women on Race and Sex in America* (New York: William Morrow, 1984), Chery Townsend Gilkes states clearly that self-definition has historically been a major theme in Black feminist thought. Gilkes, "Dual Heroisms," p. 589, n. 4

9. Deborah H. King, "Multiple Jeopardy, Multiple Consciousness: The Context of a Black Feminist Ideology," *Signs* 14, (3) (Autumn 1988), pp. 42–72.

10. "A Black Feminist Statement: The Combahee River Collective," in Gloria T. Hull, Patricia Bell Scott, and Barbara Smith (Eds.), *But Some of Us Are Brave* (Old Westbury, NY: Feminist Press, 1982), p. 17.

11. King, "Multiple Jeopardy," pp. 42, 72.

12. Haraway, "Situated Knowledges," p. 579.

13. hooks, *Feminist Theory*, preface.

14. Linda Alcoff has developed a related conceptual framework of positionality as a basis for feminist activism that does not depend on an identity that is "essentialized"—that is, on an identity that is idealized as "transcendent" and "pure," without fault. Positionality, as she defines it, is a contextual strategy of achieving one's subjectivity. Positionality views woman's identity "relative to a constantly shifting context, to a situation that includes a network of elements involving others, the objective economic conditions, cultural and political institutions and ideologies, and so on. . . . The position of woman is relative and not innate, and yet neither is it 'undecidable.' " Alcoff, "Cultural Feminism," pp. 433–434.

15. See Shane Phelan's highly original study of the political and theoretical dimensions of lesbian identity politics, *Identity Politics: Lesbian Feminism and the Limits of Community* (Philadelphia: Temple University Press, 1989).

16. Minnie Bruce Pratt, "Identity: Skin Blood Heart," in Elly Bulkin, Minnie Bruce Pratt, and Barbara Smith, (Eds.), *Yours in Struggle: Three Feminist Perspectives on Anti-Semitism and Racism* (Ithaca, NY: Firebrand Books, 1984).

17. Ibid., p. 18.

18. I don't wish to replicate here the emphasis on the subjectivity question in Pratt's project taken up by Chandra Talpade Mohanty and Biddy Martin in their essay, "Feminist Politics: What's Home Got to Do with It?," in Teresa de Lauretis (Ed.), *Feminist Studies/Critical Studies* (Bloomington: Indiana University Press, 1986), p. 206. My approach in considering Pratt is to understand the powerful symbol of political transformation she represents vis-à-vis white racism and multicultural feminist politics. But I do want to acknowledge Mohanty and Martin's skepticism about the potential of identity politics to be incorporated into feminist work for social change. The translation of discourses of self-revelation into strategic grassroots work is not axiomatic; we need to insist that the achievement of critical consciousness is a political, not solely a psychological, achievement. In this sense, a heightened consciousness leads to and requires moving from the local to the global, moving from psychic transformation to concrete acts in the material world to subvert systematic forms of oppression.

19. This is the phrase Friedrich Nietzsche employs in his critique of representation. Friedrich Nietzsche, *The Dawn of Day*, section 523, in Oscar Levy (Ed.), *The Complete Works of Friedrich Nietzsche*, Vol. 9 (New York: Gordon, 1974).

20. Pratt, "Identity: Skin Blood Heart," p. 17.

21. Ibid., p. 21.

22. Ibid., p. 29.

23. Ibid., p. 35.

24. Ibid., p. 39.

25. Ibid., p. 40.

26. Sandra Harding, "The Permanent Revolution," *Women's Review of Books*, 7 (5) (February 1990), p. 17.

27. Eloise Buker offers an incisive path through the dense thicket of semiotic discourse. She argues that feminists need not be "put off" by its technical jargon nor should they fall into a depoliticized passivity in the face of its abstractions. "In Fact," Buker argues, "we may well find [postmodernism's skepticism of Enlightenment notions of truth] liberating because we do not have to pretend that we have found THE universal laws, or even patterns that characterize all persons for all times. We can figure out what we think best in our own limited worlds. We will not defer our decisions until we know for sure what to do since we will understand that we always act in the midst of both our knowledge and our ignorance. Putting-off politics is not possible." Eloise Buker, "Rhetoric in Postmodern Feminism: Put-offs, Put-ons and Political Plays," paper presented at the annual meeting of the American Political Science Association, San Francisco, August 30–September 2, 1990, p. 7.

FURTHER READINGS

Caraway, Nancie. *Segregated Sisterhood: Racism and the Politics of American Feminism*. Knoxville: University of Tennessee Press, 1991.

Bulkin, Elly, Minnie Bruce Pratt, and Barbara Smith. *Yours in Struggle: Three Feminist Perspectives on Anti-Semitism and Racism*. New York: Long Haul Press, 1984.

DuBois, E. C., and Vicki L. Ruiz, (Eds.), *Unequal Sisters*. New York: Routledge, 1990.

Nicholson, Linda (Ed.), *Feminism/Postmodernism*. New York: Routledge, 1990.

Flax, Jane. "Postmodernism and Gender Relations in Feminist Theory." *Signs* 12 (4) (1987), pp. 621–643.

Giddings, Paula. *When and Where I Enter: The Impact of Black Women on Race and Sex in America*. New York: William Morrow, 1984.

 CHAPTER 2

GENDER DIFFERENCES IN POLITICAL ATTITUDES AND VOTING

Socialization partly explains our attitudes about politics and how politically active we later become as adults. For example, we know that women who have grown up in households in which their mothers took a relatively active role in politics are more likely themselves to vote and become active politically. Working under the assumption that political socialization can bring about ultimate political change, we first examine gender differences and similarities in political behavior and attitudes. Are younger Americans coming to greater agreement than their parents or grandparents on the issue of gender equality in the political arena? Linda L. M. Bennett and Stephen E. Bennett find that there are few gender differences in the rate of change toward favoring more modern roles. However, the authors warn against assuming that there will be a natural progression in opinion favoring more modern roles for women, particularly among young, even well-educated, men.

Previous research has found that younger women are more likely to hold feminist attitudes than are older women. There is also some evidence, however, that young women in the 1980s were less supportive of feminism than were older women, suggesting there may be some generational influences at work. Elizabeth Adell Cook explores this question using a technique called *cohort analysis*. Cohort (or generational) analysis of the 1972 to 1992 American National Election studies indicates that women who came of age during the period of social activism of the 1960s and the growth of the women's movement in the 1970s exhibit higher levels of politicized feminist consciousness than do women of earlier generations. Women who came of age during the more conservative late 1970s and early 1980s exhibit lower levels of feminist consciousness than women of the Sixties and Women's Liberation cohorts. A comparison of the Complacent/Reagan cohort with the Women's Liberation cohort on feminist issues included in the 1992 study revealed the two cohorts were quite similar in the attention they paid to women's issues.

Women's lives are changing—and these changes are not without implications for U.S. politics. One of the most significant changes for women during the twentieth century has been in their roles as workers. There has been a major social restructuring as large numbers of married women and women with preschool-aged children have become wage earners. What have women found in their work environment?

The next essay in this chapter, by Gertrude A. Steuernagel, Thomas A. Yantek and Irene Barnett, delves into some of the consequences for women and attitudes about employment. They study the issue of occupational segregation. The authors use data from the 1992 University of Michigan National Election Study as well as statistics on occupation segregation and integration from the U.S. Department of Labor. Among their findings, they conclude that occupational segregation is one of the factors in explaining why women on the whole earn less than men. Their study then examines the effect of occupational segregation on women's political attitudes. The authors argue that if we want to understand the significance of gender and its relationship to political behavior, we need to examine the relationship between the specific circumstances of employment and politics. For example, the authors point up how sex-role socialization, life-cycle demands, and discrimination result in women being clustered in what they refer to as female-segregated jobs. There are indications that the experiences these women have in these jobs affect their political attitudes.

The next essay, by Anne E. Kelley, William E. Hulbary, and Lewis Bowman, reports the importance of the link between gender, party, and political ideology in the traditionally politically conservative South. Utilizing data from the 1991–1992 Southern Grassroots Party Activist Study, they find that partisanship explains a large portion of the variation in political ideology among southern party activists. Regardless of any other consideration, Democrats were consistently more liberal and Republicans consistently more conservative. Gender accounted for considerable variation in political liberalism among Democrats but was less useful in explaining political conservatism among Republicans. Both Democrat and Republican women activists in rapidly growing Rim South states were more liberal or less conservative than their counterparts in other southern states. The authors also found (1) that male activists in each party exhibited similar regional differences and (2) that political conservatism of the Deep South did not diminish party and gender differences; instead it magnified the conservative orientation of women and men in both parties.

Are women more alike than they are different in certain aspects of political behavior? For example, some studies have shown that women tend to be more liberal on issues relating to social programs and economic security; that is, women have shown more humanitarian, social welfare–oriented attitudes. Women have also tended to be less supportive of militarist or aggressive action in foreign affairs. However, by the mid-1990s, Janet Clark and Cal Clark maintain, some scholars seemed to be turning to the clash between feminists and "traditional" women over such "culture wars" issues as abortion, indicating the splintering of women into contending groups. In the final essay in this chapter, the Clarks examine the nature of the gender gap and the divisions of opinion among women at the time of the 1992 presidential election to see whether women's "political interests" are in fact fragmenting. The authors find little evidence that women's social and political interests were cohesive in the 1980s and have recently become much more fragmented. Rather, the gender gap in the 1980s represented the overlapping concerns of somewhat disparate groups of women; and despite the growing salience of the "culture wars" issues, there was little change in this situation as of 1992. We turn now to this study.

Changing Views about Gender Equality in Politics: Gradual Change and Lingering Doubts

Linda L. M. Bennett
Stephen E. Bennett

INTRODUCTION

An important difference between women and men in the United States disappeared in the 1980s. Since ratification of the Nineteenth Amendment in 1920, women had voted in national elections in smaller proportions than men. But in the 1988 presidential election, the U.S. Census Bureau estimated that 58.3 percent of women eighteen years old and older turned out, compared to 56.4 percent of similarly aged men. Similarly, the Census Bureau reported that 62 percent of women eighteen years old and older reported voting in the 1992 election, compared to 60 percent of men eighteen years old and older.[1] The turnout gap between women and men has also disappeared in local elections.[2]

Exercising the franchise is but one way a citizen can participate in this political system, and profound gender differences remain in other modes of participation (for example, running for political office). The end of turnout differences is significant, however, because it calls into question some of the ways researchers have explained gender differences in political behavior and attitudes. Do we need to revise our thinking about the different factors that affect women and men and their involvement in politics? Are women and men becoming more alike in how they view politics? And what is happening in opinions among younger Americans? For

Linda L. M. Bennett is an associate professor and chair of the Department of Political Science at Wittenberg University. Stephen E. Bennett is a professor of political science and director of the Center for the Study of Democratic Citizenship at the University of Cincinnati.

example, are the young coming to greater agreement than their parents or grand-parents on the issue of gender equality in the political arena?

These are the questions we hope to answer in this essay. We begin with a review of explanations for gender differences in political behavior and attitudes. We will describe three basic explanations for gender differences: (1) *sex-role socialization* (how girls and boys learn "gender-appropriate" attitudes and behavior that affect how they view politics); (2) *structural* (the impact of education, occupation, income); and (3) *situational* (marital status, motherhood, homemaking). We create a way to measure what people think about political gender equality and describe those who still hold traditional conceptions of a "woman's place" in politics and society, and those who are taking on a more "modern" perspective that allows for full participation regardless of gender.

Even while some attitudes are changing, women are far from full participation in the political arena. The sex-role socialization process continues to encourage political passivity among women, although its effects are clearly weakening in areas such as voting. Socialization remains an important factor that can help us to understand the lingering differences between women and men on a host of political attitudes and behaviors.

THREE EXPLANATIONS FOR GENDER DIFFERENCES

Sex-role Socialization

In 1960 researchers defined sex-role socialization as "that portion of expectations about behavior proper for a male or female that involves political responses."[3] The authors went on to explain that the "role definitions" between women and men, and women's willingness to "leave politics to men," were the source of gender differences in attitudes during the 1950s. Socialization literature of the 1960s and early 1970s supported research from the 1950s and argued that the passive role learned by young girls was a significant reason they avoided politics later in life.[4] Studies in the 1980s asserted that girls were still learning passivity from their mothers and that this learning process accounted for their political passivity as adults.[5] Political roles are learned not only from parents, but also at school, in church, from peers, and from the media. In other words, four decades of research concluded that as a result of exposure to a number of socializing agents, many women and men grow up believing that politics is a "man's world."

The problem with sex-role socialization research is that much of it was developed from studies of children, with little evidence offered of a conclusive link between childhood experience and adult attitudes or behavior. Attempts to bridge the period between childhood and adult years depended on researchers' eliminating the influence of as many other factors as possible (some of which are discussed under structural and situational factors) and then concluding that only socialization was left as a reasonable explanation for gender differences in political thought, feelings, and actions.[6]

Structural Factors

Socioeconomic factors such as education, occupation, and income have long been known to be important in shaping a variety of attitudes. Education has been one of the strongest predictors of women's involvement and participation. In a study comparing brothers and sisters differentiated only by college attendance, the sibling with college exposure was consistently more politically interested, informed, and participatory than the one without the benefit of a college education.[7]

Along with education, women's employment status has been found by some to have an impact on political participation. In a study from the early 1970s, Kristi Andersen found a combined effect of employment and holding feminist opinions on women's willingness to participate. Working women who were supportive of an equal role in society for their sex were more participatory than their working sisters who did not back gender equality in society.[8] Still others found no differences in voting turnout between working and nonworking women and attributed gender differences to the greater political passivity of older women, who were more likely to be socialized into the notion that politics was a "man's business."[9] Tapping into the paycheck reality of work, Ellen McDonagh emphasized that work is not "liberating" if it is low-paid drudgery.[10]

Situational Factors

The number of women who become wives and/or mothers or who remain at home in the traditional role of homemaker has changed tremendously in recent years.[11] For this reason, recent research on situational factors disputes the conclusions of earlier studies. Studies from the 1950s argued that the duties of motherhood depressed women's political participation. It was assumed that women adopted the political attitudes of their husbands and looked to them for guidance when voting.[12] Lower levels of participation were most evident among less educated, low-socioeconomic-status women. The assumption was that women's absorption with the "private sphere" of the home created a major obstacle to their participation in the "public sphere" of politics.

Older, untested assumptions about women's political participation do not always hold up to empirical scrutiny. Later studies challenged the tendency of earlier studies to focus only on national elections and urged more attention to participation in state and local politics. More recent research offers more complex descriptions of the impact of motherhood and reveals an increased likelihood to participate in local politics among women with school-aged children.[13] Virginia Sapiro found that a complex joint effect of motherhood and education was linked to higher levels of community participation among women. She also argued that educational achievement is more important than marital status, homemaking, or motherhood in leading women to a general interest in politics.[14] On the other hand, Nancy Romer found that young women who were politically active while in high school *expected* to be less politically active if they took on the roles of wife and mother.[15]

In reviewing the three explanations that have been offered for gender differences in political attitudes and participation, it should be evident that it is difficult to keep each explanation distinct. Researchers have tried to separate the effects of socialization from those of socioeconomic status and role choices such as being a wife and mother, but it is less clear that most women could separate them as easily. Even those who have argued for the impact of structural and situational factors find themselves returning to the key factor of how roles are learned, or socialization. As one group of researchers note, "Socialization into the traditional feminine role in our culture produces a sense of self which is relatively more dependent on the definitions of others and a concern with homes and families, and matters related to them, over more 'distant' matters."[16] In addition, structural and situational factors have been easier to study because there are clearer indicators by which their impact can be measured. Education, occupation, marital status, number of children—these are all simple questions on any public opinion survey, whereas socialization, a slow process of learning, is more difficult to uncover with surveys. Still, it remains a compelling explanation for how women and men view politics.

Having outlined the three explanations for gender differences, it is easy to see that socialization could be related to how much women strive to achieve in education and work, as well as their choices of marriage, motherhood, and whether they stay at home as caretakers to others.[17] Are there empirical indicators that can help us to measure attitudes developed from the socialization process? We find there are such indicators, although they are far from perfect, and we turn next to how sex-role socialization shows up in attitudes about women's "proper place" in the political world. If socialization does have an impact on how interested and involved people are in politics, then we need to understand how those views are shaped. Have opinions about where women belong in the political arena changed in recent years?

MEASURING OPINIONS ABOUT GENDER ROLES IN POLITICS

The next section will present data on how much involvement in the political arena people feel is appropriate for women. Before presenting those data, we offer a brief section on where the data come from and how attitudes are being measured.

The six time periods covered in this analysis are 1974–1975, 1977–1978, 1982–1983, 1985–1986, 1988–1989, and 1991–1993. Beginning in 1974, the National Opinion Research Center (NORC) at the University of Chicago included a series of questions on its General Social Survey (GSS) asking a national sample of voting-age Americans about women's roles in business, industry, and politics. These questions have been asked on most General Social Surveys since. Three of the questions focus on gender roles and politics:

1. Do you agree or disagree with this statement? Women should take care of running their homes and leave running the country up to men.
2. If your party nominated a woman for president, would you vote for her if she were qualified for the job?
3. Tell me if you agree or disagree with this statement: Most men are better suited emotionally for politics than are most women.

For this study, these items were combined to form a "Political Gender Roles Index."[18] An index allows the combination of several narrower items into a single indicator measuring a more general concept. The Political Gender Roles Index groups responses to the three items on a scale ranging from "very modern" (disagrees that women should leave running the country up to men, would vote for a woman for president, and disagrees that men are better suited emotionally for politics) to "very traditional" (agrees the country should be run by men, would not vote for a woman, and agrees that men are more emotionally suited for politics). Those with a mix of responses were labeled "slightly modern" or "slightly traditional." The few people who said they "didn't know" what to think about any of the questions were placed in a middle "neutral" category. As you will see, there are very few people who take a neutral position on what women's political roles should be.

TRENDS IN OPINIONS ABOUT GENDER ROLES IN POLITICS

We begin with a general overview of what people think about women's appropriate roles in politics. Table 1 shows how much change there has been from 1974–1975 to 1991–1993. There has been a sharp increase in the percentage of people adopting "very modern" responses to the three items constituting the Gender Roles Index.[19] The largest increase occurs in the period from 1977–1978 to 1982–1983, though there was another sharp surge toward a modern orientation about women's roles in politics during the most recent period of 1988–1989 to 1991–1993. By the time Representative Geraldine Ferraro (D-NY) was selected by Walter Mondale as his vice presidential running mate in the 1984 presidential election, a majority of Americans were claiming to have a very modern orientation toward gender roles in politics.

The percentage of those expressing a very traditional orientation toward, gender roles was cut by almost two-thirds between 1974–1975 and 1991–1993. By 1991–1993 only one in every eight respondents to the GSS agreed with the more traditional responses to the Political Gender Roles Index. Given the prominence

Table 1   Public Opinion about Political Gender Roles for Various Years, from 1974–1975 to 1991–1993, in Percentages

	1974–1975	1977–1978	1982–1983	1985–1986	1988–1989	1991–1993
Very modern	41	42	53	51	57	64
Slightly modern	23	23	22	23	21	19
Neutral	3	3	3	2	3	3
Slightly traditional	20	20	15	16	13	8
Very traditional	13	12	8	8	6	6
(N)	(2,237)	(3,053)	(2,498)	(2,980)	(1,975)	(2,087)

Source: NORC's General Social Surveys.

achieved by women in government at all levels during the 1970s and 1980s—including city mayors, governors, members of Congress, U.S. senators, a United Nations ambassador, cabinet secretaries, and a vice presidential candidate from a major party—the persistence of traditional ideas about political gender roles is intriguing. Even so, those expressing such opinions are a dwindling group.

Do women and men differ in their views about the roles that are appropriate for women to take in the political arena? Figure 1 shows that there are more similarities than differences in what women and men think about gender roles in politics. There is a sizable gap between the percentage of women and that of men who hold very modern views compared with those who hold very traditional views. By 1991–1993 only 6 percent of women and 5 percent of men were steadfast in the belief that women should stay out of politics. The percentage of women subscribing to very modern views increased by 23 percentage points from 1974–1975 to 1991–1993. The percentage of men adopting a modern view of gender roles increased similarly (24 percent) during the same period. The rate of change in women's and men's opinions does differ. Men's expression of a more modern view of women's political roles lagged behind women's opinions until a sharp surge in the period between the 1988–1989 and 1991–1993 surveys. Between 1985–1986 and 1988–1989 the percentage of men expressing modern views remained stable, while 8 percent more women voiced very modern views. The differences in the rate of movement between sexes toward a more modern view aside, by 1991–1993 there were virtually no gender differences on the Political Gender Roles Index. If we are to understand why some people hold very modern views about political gender roles while others hold very traditional views, factors other than sex will have to be considered.

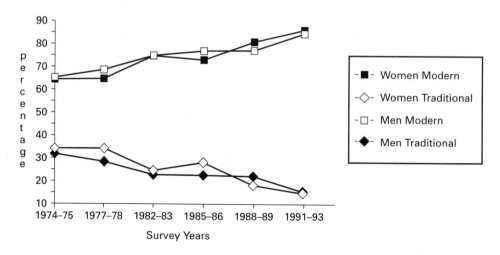

Figure 1   Political Gender Role Index Opinions by Gender and Survey Years

Source: NORC's General Social Surveys.

A MULTIVARIATE ANALYSIS OF THE SOURCES OF POLITICAL GENDER ROLE OPINIONS

A better understanding of who holds modern opinions about political gender roles and who holds traditional opinions is possible by using a statistical technique called *multiple regression*, which allows a researcher to gauge the relative impact of several factors, or variables, on a phenomenon—in this case, beliefs about women's proper roles in politics. Several variables were included in this analysis for each survey year: structural factors such as years of schooling (an imperfect but usable measure of education), family income, and occupational prestige (the social status connected with the respondent's occupation);[20] situational factors such as marital status and whether the respondent had children; socialization indicators that attempt to provide empirical links in experience between childhood and adult years, such as whether or not the respondent's mother worked when the respondent was a child, the level of education achieved by the respondent's father and mother, and measures of religious fundamentalism; and finally, additional factors said to be related to how people view politics, such as race, age, political party identification, political ideology (liberal to conservative), region of the country the respondent lived in (the southern states are noted for harboring a more traditional culture), whether the respondent reads newspapers with any regularity, and the survey year to see if the passage of time had any impact on opinions.

From 1974–1975 to 1991–1993, what factors help to explain people's opinions about the appropriate roles for women in the political arena? The answer is largely structural and socialization factors with some help from a variety of political measures such as political ideology and partisanship. Table 2 lists the significant variables in order of importance. The most important predictor of opinions about political gender roles is age. Younger people are far more likely to express modern

Table 2   Significant Factors Affecting Opinions on the Political Gender Roles Index, in Rank Order, for All Survey Years from 1974–1975 to 1991–1993

Age
Respondent's education
How often respondent attends church or synagogue
Region where respondent lives (South/not South)
Political ideology
Religious fundamentalism
Respondent's family income
Partisanship
Did respondent's mother work?
Gender
Does respondent read newspaper?
Occupational prestige
   Adjusted R^2 = .21

Source: NORC's General Social Surveys.

views than are older people. In fact, younger women are slightly more likely than younger men to express modern views even when education, the second most important predictor in Table 2, is taken into consideration. Rounding out the top three predictors is the year of the survey, reaffirming what Table 1 shows in percentages—that opinions have changed remarkably within a relatively short period of time. Considering the thirteen indicators that were found to be important in predicting opinions about women's roles in politics, the structural factors of education, family income, and occupational prestige, along with socialization factors tapping religious fundamentalism (including church or synagogue attendance) and whether the respondent's mother worked outside the home, constitute more than half of the significant predictors in the model. This is allowing that the region variable probably taps an important dimension of socialization into a more traditional culture. Even as the South is changing, the region's cultural conservatism continues to have an impact on its residents. Gender enters as an important predictor because of the differing patterns of change in opinions discussed in relation to Figure 1. Note that not a single situational factor is included as an important predictor. Although it would be risky to say that situational factors should be ignored in studies of gender and politics (as we will see in Table 3), they are clearly less important than previous literature would suggest.

Analyzing all the survey years together, as Table 2 does, can tell us about significant factors affecting opinions during that entire period, but it can hide changes that occur between the survey years included. Because the survey year does enter as a significant predictor of gender roles in politics, the passage of time is having an impact on the development of more modern orientations.

Gender does enter the overall regression model as a significant predictor, even though Figure 1 shows that by 1991–1993 women and men shared the same opinions about women's roles in politics, at least as measured by our index. A closer look, using the same analysis technique as in Table 2, makes it possible to see if different forces work to shape women's and men's opinions on the Political Gender Roles Index. Table 3 lists in order of importance the factors that shape these opinions for both women and men. Although a number of the same items appear for both women and men, the difference in ordering is intriguing. For women age is the most important factor, while for men it is level of education. Scanning the list for both sexes, one notes that, as in Table 2, structural and socialization factors predominate; for both women and men, however, the situational factor of marital status does squeeze in—at the end of the list for men and next to last for women.

Items measuring religious fundamentalism, including frequency of church attendance, appear in both Table 2 and Table 3. This is consistent with the expectation that religious conservatism (be it Protestant, Catholic, or Jewish) holds to more traditional roles for women in the private and public spheres of life. Although women are more frequent church attenders than men, the two items tapping this aspect of socialization enter all three regression models.

A separate percentage analysis of the most recent survey year (1991–1993; not shown here to save space) revealed an irony about the impact of education and age on the opinions of women and men. Among respondents who would be part of the

Table 3 Significant Factors Affecting Women's and Men's Opinions on the Political Gender Role Index, in Rank Order, for All Survey Years, 1974–1975 to 1991–1993

Women	Men
Respondent's age	Respondent's level of education
Year of survey	Respondent's age
Respondent's level of education	Region where respondent lives
Frequency of church attendance	Year of survey
Political ideology of respondent	Frequency of church attendance
Region where respondent lives	Respondent's family income
Did respondent's mother work?	Religious fundamentalism
Religious fundamentalism	Political ideology of respondent
Partisanship of respondent	Partisanship of respondent
Respondent's family income	Level of mother's education
Respondent's marital status	Respondent's marital status
Read newspaper regularly?	
Adjusted R^2 = .25	Adjusted R^2 = .18

Source: NORC's General Social Surveys.

"baby boom" generation (aged thirty to forty-four), receiving a college education appears to equalize opinions among women and men in favor of a more modern orientation toward women's political roles. Among the youngest respondents (aged eighteen to twenty-nine), however, a different tale is emerging. Young men, even if they have completed a college education, are less likely to express a preference for very modern roles for women than are similarly educated young women. In fact, 92 percent of college-educated women aged eighteen to twenty-nine favored "very modern" roles for women, compared with 72 percent of college-educated young men. Among college-educated men, only those aged sixty-five and older have a lower level of support for modern roles (67 percent). These gender differences are echoed for every education level among the youngest respondents. Is there a "gender gap" emerging, with younger men lagging behind young women in acceptance of very modern roles? Has the impact of education changed for younger Americans? Do the items in the Political Gender Roles Index have a different meaning to these youngest respondents than to their older survey counterparts? The number of cases in the 1991–1993 surveys is too small to make sweeping generalizations, but these are important differences to watch in the future.

How successful are the regression models in explaining opinions about political gender roles? Success is defined as the cumulative ability of significant predictors to explain changing opinions on the Political Gender Roles Index. No social science model we know of is able to explain 100 percent of any phenomenon. Our models are able to explain from 18 to 25 percent (see the R^2 figures in Tables 2 and 3) of change on the index. Although we can point to previous studies that have relied on regression models of similar modest capacity,[21] that is cold comfort.

There are two reasons for the modest explanatory power of the regression models. First, given the limits of secondary survey analysis, the models probably leave out key factors accounting for opinions about gender roles in politics because there are not indicators in the data sets tapping respondent's relationships with parents and how parents passed on their political views. Recall that one reason some researchers have favored structural and situational factors to explain gender differences has been their ease of measurement. Second, the items making up our Political Gender Role Index are too few and too imprecise to capture the entire range of opinions about political gender roles.

CONCLUSIONS

Does it make a difference for grassroots political behavior if people have traditional views of political gender roles? Yes, according to data from the 1993 GSS. There was a 10 percentage point difference in reported turnout in the 1992 presidential election among respondents, depending on whether they were "very modern" in their orientation toward women's roles (73 percent reported turning out to vote) or "very traditional" in their view of women's political roles (63 percent).

The disappearance of the turnout gap between women and men is only in part a result of increased voting among women. It is also the result of a sharp decline in turnout among men. Women remain less politically interested and less likely to follow media accounts of campaigns, even when education is taken into account.[22] Behind women's continuing tendency to be less politically interested is their greater likelihood to agree that "sometimes politics and government seem so complicated that a person like me can't really understand what's going on." According to data from the University of Michigan's Center for Political Studies' National Election Surveys, between 1972 and 1992, 73 to 80 percent of women said they did not feel competent to understand public affairs, compared with 59 to 66 percent of men. Controlling for education does not eliminate gender differences on this item. If anything, differences between men and women are more pronounced among the college-educated than among those whose formal schooling ended prior to graduation from high school.

With the passage of time allowing less educated, traditionally socialized Americans to leave the voting-age public, and increased exposure to higher education among the young, support for modern views of gender equality in politics will probably increase. Still, the process will not be automatic. Recall that younger men, even those with a college education, are most likely to lag behind similarly educated young women in favoring modern roles. The differences may not yet signal a transformation in well-educated young men's opinion, but they remind us that the momentum toward acceptance of gender equality in politics can be lost, even among the well educated, unless continual effort is made to overcome older notions of where women "belong." The sex-role socialization process endures, and its impact is still felt in the political arena.

NOTES

1. U.S. Bureau of the Census, *Voting and Registration in the Election of November 1988*, Current Population Reports, Series P-20, No. 440 (Washington, DC: U.S. Government Printing Office, 1989), pp. 4–5. U.S. Bureau of the Census, *Voting and Registration in the Election of November 1992*, Current Population Reports, Series P-20, No. 466 (Washington, DC: U.S. Government Printing Office, 1993), p. v.

2. Closure in the "turnout gap" is evident in data from the National Opinion Research Center (NORC). In 1967 NORC reported that 27 percent of women said they *never* voted, compared to 22 percent of men. Even this gap was smaller than it would have been in the 1920s and 1930s, immediately after the Nineteenth Amendment's ratification. By 1987 NORC data revealed women and men equally likely to report having voted (68 percent for both).

3. Angus Campbell, Philip Converse, Warren E. Miller, and Donald Stokes, *The American Voter* (New York: Wiley, 1960), p. 484.

4. Robert D. Hess and Judith V. Torney, *The Development of Political Attitudes in Children* (Chicago: Aldine, 1967); Fred I. Greenstein, *Children and Politics* (New Haven, CT: Yale University Press, 1969).

5. Ronald B. Rapoport, "The Sex Gap in Political Persuading: Where the 'Structuring Principle' Works," *American Journal of Political Science*, 25 (1) (February 1981), pp. 32–48; "Sex Differences in Attitude Expression: A Generational Explanation," *Public Opinion Quarterly*, 46 (1) (Spring 1982), pp. 86–96; "Like Mother, Like Daughter: Intergenerational Transmission of DK Response Rates," *Public Opinion Quarterly*, 49 (2) (Summer 1985), pp. 198–208.

6. Anthony Orum, Roberta S. Cohen, Susan Grassmuck, and Amy W. Orum, "Sex, Socialization, and Politics," *American Sociological Review*, 39 (2) (April 1974), pp. 197–209.

7. Kent L. Tedin, David W. Brady, and Arnold Vedlitz, "Sex Differences in Political Attitudes and Behavior: The Case for Situational Factors," *Journal of Politics*, 39 (2) (May 1977), pp. 448–456; Ethel Klein, *Gender Politics* (Cambridge, MA: Harvard University Press, 1984).

8. Kristi Andersen, "Working Women and Political Participation," *American Journal of Political Science*, 19 (3) (August 1975), pp. 439–454.

9. Raymond E. Wolfinger and Steven J. Rosenstone, *Who Votes?* (New Haven, CT: Yale University Press, 1980).

10. Ellen L. McDonagh, "To Work or Not to Work: The Differential Impact of Achieved and Derived Status upon the Political Participation of Women," *American Journal of Political Science*, 26 (2) (May 1982), pp. 280–297.

11. Klein, *Gender Politics*.

12. Robert E. Lane, *Political Life* (New York: Free Press, 1965); Campbell et al., *The American Voter*.

13. M. Kent Jennings, "Another Look at Politics and the Life Cycle," *American Journal of Political Science*, 23 (4) (November 1979), pp. 755–771.

14. Virginia Sapiro, *The Political Integration of Women* (Urbana: University of Illinois Press, 1983), pp. 89–90, 136–138.

15. Nancy Romer, "Is Political Activism Still a 'Masculine' Endeavor?" *Psychology of Women Quarterly*, 14 (2) (June 1990), pp. 229–243.

16. Kristi Andersen and Elizabeth Cook, "Women, Work, and Political Attitudes," *American Journal of Political Science*, 29 (3) (August 1985), pp. 606–622.

17. Cal Clark and Janet Clark, "Models of Gender and Political Participation in the United States," *Women and Politics*, 6 (1) (Spring 1986), pp. 5–25.

18. Before summing the three items, it was first determined if they belonged in a composite index. When all survey years were combined and the three items were fed into SPSS's RELIABILITY routine, the value of Cronbach's coefficient *alpha* was .70. The items have an average interitem correlation of $R = .44$. Although the Political Gender Roles Index contains some measurement error, it is a satisfactory device for tapping opinions about gender roles in politics.

19. Unfortunately, the 1994 General Social Survey data were not available when this chapter was written. However, thanks to Marilyn Potter of the Roper Center for Public Opinion Research at Storrs, Connecticut, we were able to see marginals on each item. The 1994 data indicate that the public continues to move toward a more "modern" view of gender roles in politics at the rate of approximately 2 percentage points a year.

20. The NORC codebook describes the occupational prestige rating process as one guided by the "respondents' estimation of the social standing of occupations." The respondents' ratings generally range along a nine-point scale and are useful in assigning some order to the thousands of occupational codes in U.S. Census Bureau data.

21. See esp. Sapiro, *The Political Integration of Women*.

22. M. Margaret Conway, *Political Participation in the United States* (Washington, DC: Congressional Quarterly Press, 1985); Linda L. M. Bennett and Stephen E. Bennett, "Enduring Gender Differences in Political Interest: The Impact of Socialization and Political Dispositions," *American Politics Quarterly*, 17 (1) (January 1989), pp. 105–122.

FURTHER READING

Beckwith, K. *American Women and Political Participation: The Impacts of Work, Generation, and Feminism.* New York: Greenwood Press, 1986.

Bennett, L. L. M., and S. E. Bennett. "Enduring Gender Differences in Political Interest." *American Politics Quarterly*, 17 (January 1989), pp. 105–122.

Carroll, S. J. "Gender Politics and the Socializing Impact of the Women's Movement." In R. Sigel (Ed.), *Political Learning in Adulthood*, pp. 306–339. Chicago: University of Chicago Press, 1989.

Erskine, H. "The Polls: Women's Role." *Public Opinion Quarterly*, 35 (Summer 1971), pp. 275–290.

Klein, E. *Gender Politics.* Cambridge, MA: Harvard University Press, 1984.

Mathews, D. G., and S. DeHart. *Sex, Gender, and the Politics of ERA: A State and the Nation.* New York: Oxford University Press, 1990.

Matthews, G. *The Rise of Public Woman: Woman's Power and Woman's Place in the United States, 1630–1970.* New York: Oxford University Press, 1992.

Sapiro, V. *The Political Integration of Women: Roles, Socialization, and Politics.* Urbana: University of Illinois Press, 1983.

Simon, R. J., and J. M. Landis. "Report: Attitudes about a Woman's Place and Role." *Public Opinion Quarterly*, 53 (Spring 1989), pp. 265–276.

Witt, L., K. M. Paget, and G. Matthews. *Running as a Woman: Gender and Power in American Politics.* New York: Free Press, 1993.

The Generations of Feminism

Elizabeth Adell Cook

It is often observed that young people have different political values and beliefs than older people. On many issues, such as abortion, gender equality, and the willingness to allow atheists to teach in college, young people are more liberal than their parents, and much more liberal than their grandparents. Some of these differences will endure over time, and others will diminish. These differences can occur as the result of (1) generational effects and (2) life-cycle effects.

Generational effects refer to differences in the political values and behaviors of two different generations; these are the result of the different social and political context in which each generation grew up or came of age. Thus, members of a generation bear the imprint of a particular period even as they age and times change. Think about the attitudes of Americans toward Japan. We would not expect Americans who grew up with the phrase "Remember Pearl Harbor" (and who in fact do) to feel as warmly toward Japan as Americans who learned about World War II in history class. Most likely, these younger Americans grew up thinking of the United States and Japan as allies. Therefore, we would expect them to view Japan more warmly than older Americans, and we would not expect the views of younger Americans to change as a result of growing older.

Life-cycle effects are defined as those differences in the political values and behaviors of two different generations resulting from different lifestyles and responsibilities as a function of age. When we compare the young to the middle-aged, the young are less likely to be married, to have children, to own homes, to be saving

Elizabeth Adell Cook is a visiting assistant professor of government at The American University.

for retirement, and to be concerned about elderly parents. Although a generation may marry later than preceding generations, or have fewer children, eventually all young generations will become middle-aged and assume many of the trappings of middle age. ("Just wait until you have children of your own.") When a younger generation becomes more like an older generation as it ages and its lifestyle changes, we refer to this as the life-cycle effect. The original differences observed between younger and older people were primarily the result of the differing life circumstances of the two generations. Thus, as the younger generation matures and experiences the changes in lifestyle usually associated with aging, it adopts the values and behaviors of the older generation. As generational effects occur, generations remain distinct over time. When life-cycle effects occur, the younger generation becomes more like the older generation as it ages.

A third kind of effect looks at changes affecting all generations. *Period effects* occur when the social and political context changes members of all generations. For example, intensive media coverage of drug problems during the early 1990s led Americans of all ages to express concern. In 1994, crime was listed as the most serious problem facing the country among all age groups in many polls.

GENERATIONS AND ATTITUDES ABOUT WOMEN

There have clearly been some period effects in attitudes toward the role of women. For example, the public has become more supportive of working women over time. Although we take it for granted that women who do the same work as men ought to receive the same pay (even though they may in fact not), this view has not always been universally endorsed. And not all generations have responded similarly in how they view women's role.

Most studies have reported that age is a significant predictor of support for feminist programs and organizations. Studies in the 1970s and 1980s found that younger women were more supportive of egalitarian values, had higher levels of gender consciousness, and were more supportive of gender equality than were older women.

During the second half of the 1980s, however, controversy arose concerning the possibility of generational change in support for feminism. Bolotin reported the emergence of a postfeminist generation among young women—part of a general retreat from liberalism among the young.[1] Most of the scholarly research on this question has focused on the attitudes of college students. Studies have found that college women may support feminist ideals but reject the collective efforts of the women's movement,[2] that there is support for equal rights but not for feminism,[3] and that the term *feminist* evokes negative connotations even among students who support gender equality.[4]

Others have argued, however, that college students do not reject feminism per se, but want to redirect the movement to their own needs.[5] Research has suggested that college women become progressively more supportive of feminism during their academic years as they experience sex discrimination.[6]

All these studies limit their analysis to college students. Although there is good theoretical reason to focus attention on the attitudes of college women (college education is a strong predictor of support for feminism), it is important to examine changing support for feminism among all women. Moreover, most research has not been conscious of its assumptions: Some studies assume that support for feminism among the young is related to life cycle, but others assume lasting generational differences. This study, therefore, will examine the pattern of support among different generations of women over the period from 1972 to 1992. The period covers the rise of feminism through the election of Clinton. The data come from the American National Election Studies of 1972, 1976, 1980, 1984, 1988, and 1992.[7]

POLITICIZED FEMINIST CONSCIOUSNESS

Scholars who focus on the women's movement have argued that feminist support is best understood in terms of group consciousness. One of the earliest activities of the feminist movement was consciousness raising—attempting to develop a politicized feminist consciousness among women.[8] Klein suggested that individuals who acquire a feminist consciousness must go through three steps.[9] First, women must recognize their membership in a group (women) and that they share interests with that group. Second, women must reject the societal rationale for the situation of the group; that is, they must blame society and not women for the disadvantaged status of women. Finally, women must recognize the need for group solutions to problems.

Gurin, Miller, and Gurin adopt a similar strategy, arguing that group consciousness consists of social group identification, power discontent, system blaming, and a collectivist orientation.[10] In other research, feminist consciousness has been defined as follows: Nonfeminists are defined as those women who do not believe that women should have an equal role with men in society, potential feminists are classified as those who believe in an equal role for women but do not support the women's liberation movement, and those who believe in an equal role and who support the movement are defined as having a politicized feminist consciousness.[11]

Support for the women's liberation movement was measured by a feeling thermometer items, which asked respondents in the 1972 to 1984 surveys to place the women's liberation movement (along with other social and political groups) on an imaginary scale that ranges from 0° (representing extreme coolness) to 100° (representing extreme warmth). Because individuals differ in the patterns of their responses to these items, responses were adjusted to account for individual differences.[12] In the 1988 and 1992 surveys, respondents were asked to place feminists on this thermometer. Thus, there is not continuity in the measure, and we should not make direct comparisons between the earlier surveys and the later ones.

Table 1 presents the frequency distributions of the measures across the period of this study. Feminist consciousness increases from 1972 to 1976 and again in 1980, then declines somewhat in 1984. Even though other research has shown that respondents respond less positively to the term *feminists* than to the term *women's lib-*

Table 1 Distribution of Feminist Consciousness

	1972	1976	1980	1984	1988	1992
Not feminist	61	51	41	47	36	28
Potential feminist	25	23	32	30	43	44
Feminist	14	26	27	21	21	29
(N)	(1,224)	(1,153)	(676)	(1,024)	(933)	(1,081)
PDI	−37	−25	−14	−26	−15	1

Note: Because the feeling thermometer for the women's liberation movement was used for 1972–1984 and the feeling thermometer for feminists was used for 1988 and 1992, the earlier years should not be directly compared with the later years.

eration movement, feminist consciousness increased from 1984 to 1988 (when the feeling thermometer changed) and again in 1992.[13]

Table 1 also contains the Percentage Difference Index (PDI) for each of the four studies. The PDI is a summary measure created by subtracting the percentage of women who are nonfeminists from the percentage of women with a politicized feminist consciousness. It provides us with a single number to compare across years.

POLITICIZED FEMINIST CONSCIOUSNESS AND GENERATIONS

Cohort, or generational, analysis allows us to compare women who came of age at different times across years. That is, instead of comparing samples of individuals of the same age group (which is forever in flux as individuals age into or out of the group), we can compare samples of a constant coming-of-age cohort. Cohort analysis allows us to start to sort out life-cycle (or maturation) effects from generational (or cohort) effects.

In order for cohort analysis to be meaningful, the cohorts need to be defined according to eras. That is, the boundaries of each cohort should to the greatest extent possible represent transitions in the relevant social context. Fortunately, the task of defining cohorts relevant to the women's movement has already been taken on. Sapiro (1980) defined seven coming-of-age cohorts relevant to women's history:

> The eras or transitions are marked by either events of particular importance to women or by the type of broad characterizations we often use to mark off historical periods. Thus, the ratification of the Nineteenth Amendment serves as a time marker, and the twenties, characterized by a post-suffrage flurry of recognition of women, is distinguished from the Depression era. Of particular interest is the transition from World War II, the era of Rosie the Riveter and national day care centers, to the thirteen-year period characterized by Betty Friedan as the time of the "Feminine Mystique," a "dark age" in women's history according to feminist observers. Although the entire post-1960 period saw the growth of social movements and policy-making aimed at equality, it is further divided by the birth of the Women's Liberation Movement.[14]

In addition to Sapiro's seven cohorts, an additional cohort is defined in the 1984 and later studies, the Complacent or Reagan era cohort. Table 2 shows a breakdown of these cohorts. Whereas Sapiro defined cohorts according to when respondents turned twenty-one, for this analysis, respondents are placed in cohorts according to the year they turned eighteen. Sapiro chose age twenty-one because it was for most of this century the legal age of majority, the age at which young people struck out on their own, and the average age of marriage for women. In this analysis, the younger age of eighteen is used because individuals would seem to be more impressionable at this age—and will be making the choices in very early adulthood about education, careers, and forming their own families. These decisions will affect their life circumstances even three years into their futures when they turn twenty-one.

COMING-OF-AGE COHORTS AND FEMINIST CONSCIOUSNESS

Table 3 shows politicized feminist consciousness by coming-of-age cohort. Because of changes in the definition of feminist consciousness between 1984 and 1988, we cannot directly compare the later period with the earlier one. Therefore, we can look at change in feminist consciousness from 1972 through 1984, and compare the relative position of the cohorts in 1988 and 1992.

The oldest cohort, women who came of age before women won the right to vote, exhibited very low feminist consciousness in 1972 and did not increase its level of consciousness in 1976. By 1980 there were too few members of this cohort left to analyze (only twenty in the sample; the youngest members would have been seventy-eight years old). Women who came of age during the twenties also exhibited very low levels of feminist consciousness in 1972 and, unlike women as a whole, did not increase their level of feminist consciousness in 1976. This cohort did increase its level of consciousness somewhat by 1980, but then declined in 1984. By 1988 there were too few members of this cohort in the sample to include in the analysis. Overall, the cohort exhibited stability over time, with low levels of feminist consciousness.

Table 2   Coming-of-Age Cohorts*

Presuffrage	Pre-1920
Twenties	1921–1929
Depression	1930–1939
World War II	1940–1945
Mystique	1946–1959
Sixties	1960–1966
Women's liberation	1967–1977
Complacent/Reagan	1978–1992

*The cohorts are defined according to periods in which the respondent turned eighteen.

Table 3   Coming-of-Age Cohorts and Feminist Consciousness

	1972	1976	1980	1984	1988	1992
Presuffrage						
Not	78	78	—	—	—	—
Potential	18	16	—	—	—	—
Feminist	*4*	*7*	—	—	—	—
PDI	[−74]	[−71]				
(*N*)	(124)	(83)	—	—	—	—
Twenties						
Not	73	74	63	74	—	—
Potential	22	15	25	16	—	—
Feminist	*5*	*11*	*12*	*10*	—	—
PDI	[−68]	[−63]	[−51]	[−64]		
(*N*)	(135)	(110)	(57)	(51)	—	—
Depression						
Not	67	61	54	66	50	43
Potential	20	24	27	20	33	36
Feminist	*13*	*15*	*19*	*14*	*17*	*21*
PDI	[−54]	[−46]	[−35]	[−52]	[−33]	[−22]
(*N*)	(181)	(168)	(84)	(119)	(90)	(94)
World War II						
Not	69	50	46	67	37	35
Potential	25	29	38	20	44	39
Feminist	*6*	*21*	*16*	*13*	*19*	*26*
PDI	[−63]	[−29]	[−30]	[−54]	[−18]	[−9]
(*N*)	(128)	(103)	(50)	(75)	(73)	(75)
Mystique						
Not	57	48	38	46	45	36
Potential	29	25	38	27	39	40
Feminist	*14*	*27*	*24*	*27*	*16*	*23*
PDI	[−43]	[−21]	[−14]	[−19]	[−29]	[−13]
(*N*)	(290)	(216)	(130)	(178)	(163)	(153)

(continued)

The Depression cohort followed the overall pattern of women as a whole but with lower levels of feminist consciousness. The exception to this pattern is that the increase in feminist consciousness from 1972 to 1976 was not as sharp for this co-hort as for women as a whole. Yet there was an increase for this cohort that did not occur in the older cohorts. This suggests that perhaps these women were still at a phase in the life cycle (aged fifty-one to sixty) in 1972 when they were more sus-ceptible to changes in attitudes than were the older cohorts of women.

The World War II cohort, like the older cohorts, exhibited very low levels of feminist consciousness in 1972—when these women were forty-five to fifty. The level of feminist consciousness increased in 1976 and declined in 1984.

The Mystique cohort, the mothers of the baby boom, in each year exhibit a higher level of feminist consciousness than the older cohorts. Despite the fact that this cohort bucked the demographic trends by marrying earlier and having more children than the older cohorts, in the 1972 to 1992 period it was more feminist than

Table 3 (continued)

	1972	1976	1980	1984	1988	1992
Sixties						
Not	53	38	34	38	33	23
Potential	30	23	31	36	44	46
Feminist	*17*	*39*	*35*	*26*	*24*	*32*
PDI	[−36]	[1]	[1]	[−12]	[−9]	[−9]
(N)	(207)	(179)	(108)	(141)	(115)	(120)
Women's Liberation*						
Not	45	40	34	35	23	24
Potential	23	24	33	36	48	41
Feminist	*32*	*36*	*34*	*29*	*29*	*35*
PDI	[−13]	[−4]	[0]	[−6]	[6]	[11]
(N)	(154)	(284)	(190)	(295)	(258)	(273)
Complacent†						
Not	—	—	—	40	28	20
Potential	—	—	—	36	50	51
Feminist	—	—	—	*24*	*22*	*29*
PDI				[−16]	[−6]	[9]
(N)	—	—	—	(136)	(181)	(279)

*Only part of the Women's Liberation cohort had turned eighteen in 1972. The complete cohort did not come of age until 1977.

†Only part of the complacent cohort had turned eighteen in 1980. The complete cohort did not come of age until 1992.

Note: Because the feeling thermometer for the women's liberation movement was used for 1972–1984 and the feeling thermometer for feminists was used for 1988 and 1992, the earlier years should not be directly compared to the later years.

the older cohorts. Feminist consciousness among this cohort seesawed; it increased from 1972 to 1976, declined in 1980, and increased again in 1984.

The Women's Liberation cohort displayed a higher level of feminist consciousness than the Sixties cohort in 1972. This suggests that the cohort was aptly named; these women responded more quickly to the women's movement than women who were older at its inception. However, these two cohorts exhibit similar levels of feminist consciousness from 1976 to 1984. During this period these two cohorts exhibit the highest levels of feminist consciousness. However, even for these two cohorts, the PDI is not positive during this time period. There are more women at the lowest level of consciousness than at the highest level.

By 1984 the Complacent cohort was coming of age. While the overall trend had been for each successive cohort to exhibit a higher level of feminist consciousness than older cohorts, this youngest cohort reversed the trend and in each year is slightly less feminist than the Women's Liberation cohort.

Does the lower level of feminist consciousness as measured here mean that women of the Complacent cohort are less supportive of feminist issues than women in the Women's Liberation cohort? We can compare the Complacent cohort to the Women's Liberation cohort on feminist issues that were included in the 1992 study. These include measures of attitudes toward abortion, sexual harassment, government funding of child care, the power of women and men in the family and society, pride in women's accomplishments and anger about their status, and the strategy women should pursue. Also included is a question of whether respondents think of themselves as feminists.

The Complacent Cohort and Women's Liberation cohort took very similar positions on abortion and parental consent for abortions for minors. However, the Complacent cohort was less likely to favor government funding of abortion for poor women and more likely than the older cohort, to favor a law requiring a married woman to inform her husband about an abortion. The two cohorts were quite similar in the attention they paid to women's issues, their views on the seriousness of the problem of sexual harassment, and their anger about the way women are treated in society. However, the Complacent cohort was less likely to express pride in the accomplishments of women. They were as likely to believe men have more power in society and the family, and they were more likely than the Women's Liberation cohort to express the belief that men and women ought to have equal power in society. The greatest difference between the two generations is on the issue of government-sponsored child care; women of the Complacent era are much more likely to believe that the government should provide child care assistance to low- and middle-income working parents. One might suspect that this is a life-cycle effect; those in the Complacent cohort were more likely to have young children at home in 1992 than the older cohorts. However, even after controls for children in the home are introduced, the Complacent cohort is still significantly more likely to favor government aid to child care than the Women's Liberation cohort.

SUMMARY

A number of events that occurred during the 1972 to 1992 time period shaped attitudes: the mobilization of the women's movement, the passage by Congress of the Equal Rights Amendment (ERA) and its early successes, the formation and mobilization of the anti-ERA coalition, the strong antifeminist platform of the Republicans in 1980, the Reagan presidency, and the Webster decision. Moreover, the tenor of news coverage of the movement changed markedly over the course of this period, from strongly negative to evenhanded.

In 1972 the women's movement did not have very much support. Only 13 percent of women in the study demonstrated a politicized feminist consciousness, and 61 percent did not even appear to have the potential for developing one. Although the measures are not directly comparable, 29 percent demonstrated a politicized feminist consciousness, in 1992.

The biggest increase in feminist consciousness during this period (1972–1976) occurred among women who were in their thirties and forties in 1976 (The Sixties, Mystique, and World War II cohorts). Older women showed little or no increase, and younger women (the Women's Liberation cohort) had less room to move because they had started out with higher levels of support than any other cohort.

Cohort analysis revealed that generational turnover helped to increase the level of feminist consciousness from 1972 to 1976, as more feminist younger women replaced more traditional older women. The most feminist women were those who came of age during the development of the women's movement in the 1970s. The youngest women, those who came of age in the late 1970s and 1980s, were less feminist than the Women's Liberation cohort but more feminist than women overall. There is some evidence for a postfeminist cohort here, but the level of decline in support was not precipitous. Furthermore, in 1992 these younger women were about as supportive of feminist issues as were women of the Women's Liberation cohort.

Although it is impossible to speak with certainty, there appear to have been both generational and period effects at work. Moreover, clear cohort differences persist over time, suggesting that generational effects are strong.

Whether the Complacent cohort will increase is not clear. A number of studies have reported changing attitudes among this cohort as they are exposed to sex discrimination.[15] Although sex discrimination was much more blatant in earlier eras, young women who grew up during a period of rapid role change and increasing expectations for women are unlikely to be as tolerant of discrimination as those who grew up expecting it. It is difficult to be complacent in the face of discrimination.

NOTES

1. Susan Bolotin, "Views from the Post-Feminist Generation," *New York Times Magazine*, October 1982.

2. Mirra Komarovsky, *Women in College* (New York: Basic Books, 1985).

3. M. Jacobson, "You Say Potato and I Say Potato: Attitudes toward Feminism as a Function of Its Subject-Selected Labels," *Sex Roles*, 7 (1981), pp. 349–354.

4. M. Jacobson and W. Koch, "Attributed Reasons for Support of the Feminist Movement as a Function of Attractiveness," *Sex Roles*, 4 (1978), pp. 169–174.

5. Betty Friedan, *The Second Stage* (New York: Summit Books, 1981).

6. Alan Bayer, "Sexist Students in American Colleges," *Journal of Marriage and the Family*, 37 (1975), pp. 391–397; Mirra Komarovsky, *Women in College* (New York: Basic Books, 1985); C. Renzetti, "New Wave or Second Stage? Attitudes of College Women toward Feminism," *Sex Roles*, 16 (1987), pp. 265–277.

7. The data used in this article were made available by the Interuniversity Consortium for Political and Social Research. The data for the American National Election Studies were originally collected by the Center for Political Studies. Neither the collectors of the original data nor the consortium bear any responsibility for the analyses or interpretations presented here.

8. C. Renzetti, "New Wave or Second Stage?" pp. 265–277.

9. Ethel Klein, *Gender Politics* (Cambridge, MA: Harvard University Press, 1984).

10. Patricia Gurin, Arthur Miller, and Gerald Gurin, "Stratum Identification and Consciousness," *Social Psychology Quarterly*, 43 (1980), pp. 30–47.

11. Elizabeth Adell Cook, "Measuring Feminist Consciousness." *Women and Politics*, 9 (1989), The measure used here differs slightly from that described in the article cited in note 10. pp. 71–88.

12. Support for the women's movement is based on the relative feeling thermometer for the "women's liberation movement" (1972 through 1984) and "feminists" (1988 and 1992). Because of changes in the question, the measure is not strictly comparable from the earlier period to the later. This relative feeling thermometer is calculated as follows. First, a personal mean is calculated for each respondent across four social groups: liberals, conservatives, labor, and big business. These groups were used because they are common to all six studies and respondents' mean scores on this set of items is not correlated with their ideology. (See Clyde Wilcox, Lee Sigelman and Elizabeth Cook, "Some Like It Hot: Individual Differences in Responses to Group Feeling Thermometers," *Public Opinion Quarterly*, 53 [1989], pp. 246–275 for a detailed discussion of using adjusted feeling thermometers.) This personal mean is subtracted from a respondent's rating of the women's liberation movement, and the remainder is divided by the personal mean [(score − mean)/mean]. The relative feeling thermometer thus represents percentage difference from the mean for the four groups. A score of 10 percent or more above their personal mean is defined here as support for the women's liberation movement.

13. Elizabeth Adell Cook and Clyde Wilcox, "A Rose by Any Other Name: Measuring Support for Organized Feminism Using ANES Feeling Thermometers," *Women and Politics*, 12 (1992), pp. 35–52.

14. Virginia Sapiro, "News from the Front: Intersex and Intergenerational Conflict over the Status of Women," *Western Political Quarterly*, 33 (1980), p. 263.

15. Renzetti, "New Wave or Second Stage?"; Bayer, "Sexist Students in American Colleges;" Komarovsky, *Women in College*.

FURTHER READINGS

Bayer, Alan. "Sexist Students in American Colleges." *Journal of Marriage and the Family*, 37 (1975), pp. 391–397.

Bolotin, Susan. "Views from the Post-Feminist Generation." *New York Times Magazine*. October 1982.

Conover, Pamela. "The Influence of Group Identifications on Political Perception and Evaluation." *Journal of Politics*, 46 (1984), pp. 760–785.

Costain, Anne N. "Representing Women: The Transition from Social Movement to Interest Group." *Western Political Quarterly*, 34 (1981), pp. 100–113.

———. *Inviting Women's Rebellion: A Political Process Interpretation of the Women's Movement*. John Hopkins, 1992.

Freeman, Jo. *The Politics of Women's Liberation*. David McKay, 1975.

Gurin, Patricia. "Women's Gender Consciousness." *Public Opinion Quarterly*, 49 (1986), pp. 143–163.

Jacobson, M. "You Say Potato and I Say Potato: Attitudes toward Feminism as a Function of Its Subject-Selected Labels." *Sex Roles*, 7 (1981), pp. 349–354.

Jennings, Kent, and Richard Niemi. *Generations and Politics*. Princeton, NJ: Princeton University Press, 1981.

Komarovsky, Mirra. *Women in College*. Basic Books, 1985.

Klein, Ethel. *Gender Politics*. Cambridge, MA: Harvard University Press, 1984.

Rinehart, Sue Tolleson. *Gender Consciousness and Politics*. Routledge, 1992.

Sapiro, Virginia. "News from the Front: Intersex and Intergenerational Conflict over the Status of Women." *Western Political Quarterly*, 33 (1980), pp. 260–277.

Thornton, Arland, and Deborah Freedman. "Changes in Sex Role Attitudes of Women, 1962–1977." *American Sociological Review*, 44 (1979), pp. 831–842.

More than Pink and Blue: Gender, Occupational Stratification, and Political Attitudes

Gertrude A. Steuernagel
Thomas A. Yantek
Irene J. Barnett

There have been revolutionary changes in the lives of twentieth-century American women. Foremost among these changes are those related to women's employment outside the home. This is not to imply, of course, that prior to the 1900s women were not involved in paid employment. African-American women in particular have a history of combining family and work responsibilities. What is unprecedented about the current employment situation of American women, however, are the numbers of married women and women with preschool-aged children who are employed as wage earners in a part-time or full-time capacity. A few statistics are useful in understanding the depth and scope of this major social restructuring. In 1880 women constituted 14 percent of this nation's work force. One hundred years later this figure had increased to 42 percent.[1] By 1992 it reached 45.5 percent.[2] During the same period, 1880 through 1980, the percentage of all women who were employed outside the home increased from 16 percent to 51 percent.[3] By 1992 this figure had increased to 57.8 percent.[4] Equally dramatic changes occurred in the demographic profile of working women. In 1880, by far the largest segment of working women were single. Today, a majority of married women are numbered in the ranks of working women; and women with children are a significant part of

The authors wish to acknowledge the use of data contained in the 1992 National Elections Study, published by the University of Michigan's Center for Political Studies, which bears no responsibility for its use or interpretation here.

Gertrude A. Steuernagel is a professor of political science and Thomas A. Yantek is an associate professor of political science at Kent State University. Irene J. Barnett is a doctoral student in Kent State University's Department of Political Science.

the labor force.[5] As of 1992, over half of all children under the age of six had a mother in the labor force.[6]

WOMEN AND OCCUPATIONAL SEGREGATION

An emphasis on these changes, however, obscures an important reality concerning American women's working lives. There is a significant characteristic of women's employment that has not radically changed in recent times and is not likely to be altered in the near future. Most American women work in so-called pink-collar ghettos. An employed American woman today is more likely than not to find herself in an occupationally segregated profession. She will work with other women in jobs traditionally held by women—jobs that reflect what society sees as appropriate to women's roles as wives, mothers, and caregivers and that reflect women's supposed strengths as nurturers and helpmates. As of 1992, for example, women account for 98.8 percent of all dental assistants, 97.1 percent of all child care workers in private households, 84.9 percent of all data entry keyers, 85.4 percent of all elementary school teachers, 87.6 percent of all librarians, and 94.3 percent of all registered nurses. In contrast, women account for only 8.6 percent of all dentists, 1.0 percent of all carpenters, 3 percent of all computer programmers, 40.9 percent of all college and university professors, 21.4 percent of all lawyers and judges, and 20.4 percent of all physicians.[7] Women, despite their race or ethnic group, are concentrated in low-paying and low-status jobs. Certain factors, such as changing attitudes concerning appropriate sex roles and legislation that has outlawed sex discrimination, have led to a small decline in the degree of occupational segregation by gender; but there is substantial reason to believe that it will continue to affect the lives of working women well into the next century.[8]

Some of the consequences for women of occupational segregation have been better documented than others. There is clear evidence that occupational segregation is involved in the wage gap. That is to say, it is one of the factors, possibly the most important, in explaining why women on the whole earn less than men.[9] In 1991, for example, the median annual income for men who work year-round in a full-time capacity was $29,421; the income for comparable women was $20,553.[10]

In contrast, more information is needed on the impact of occupational segregation on women's conditions in the workplace. The area of workplace health hazards is a case in point. The risks to women in traditionally female occupations, for example, are less obvious than the risks to men in fields such as construction and welding.[11]

In particular, it is important to explore the effects of occupational segregation on women's political attitudes. Although there has been considerable research into the effect of workforce involvement on women's political behavior, little has been done on the specific effects of occupational segregation. If we want to understand the political behavior of U.S. women, we need to understand the circumstances of their lives. Because there is considerable evidence that women's employment and their political behavior are related, we need to examine the relationship between the specific circumstances of that employment and their politics. Some research, for example, indicates that housewives and women employed in low-status, low-paying occupations, such as hairdresser and waitress, tend to show less support for feminism than do women in higher-status, higher-paying jobs, such as teacher and accountant.[12] This study, therefore, will address questions about the effects of occupational segregation on women's political attitudes, with special attention to the intersection of occupational segregation and gender as they affect the political attitudes of women and men.

FINDINGS

Fortunately, there are available data that permit us to examine the effects of occupational segregation on political attitudes. We utilize data from the 1992 University of Michigan/Survey Research Center (SRC) National Election Study (NES), as well as statistics on occupational segregation and integration from the U.S. Department of Labor. To give just one example of the selection process, consider the case of identifying women in female-dominated occupations at the managerial/professional (white-collar) level. Data from the Department of Labor reveal that the two professional occupations with the heaviest concentrations of women are registered nurse (94.6 percent) and teachers at the kindergarten and prekindergarten level, (98.2 percent).

In the NES those occupations are clustered together into categories 07 and 09, respectively, on Variable 3921: Respondent's Main Occupation, and contain totals of twenty-seven and forty-two women, respectively (and also seven and twenty men, respectively). Thus, those sixty-nine women comprise our subsample of women in female-segregated, professional occupations (and the twenty-seven men our subsample of males in female-segregated, professional occupations). A similar pattern of identification was used for selecting the other subsamples, which then were aggregated across the different professional classifications to produce groups of men and women in male-dominated, integrated, and female-dominated occupations.*

As an initial pass at the data, we examine in Tables 1 and 2 the differences between men and women generally in terms of their interest in and discussion of politics. Although the differences are not overwhelming, nevertheless it is clear that men express both more interest in and a greater tendency to discuss political affairs.

That they follow and talk about politics slightly less frequently than their male counterparts does not mean that women fail to perceive meaningful differences in social organization. Table 3 reveals that women are more likely than men to perceive the latter as holding the reins of power in American society (although the differences are only borderline significant in the statistical sense). Those differences in perception are reflected also in gender-differentiated *prescriptions* con-

*The SRC's method for classifying occupations does not allow for a precise identification of individual occupations. Rather than list the respondent's occupation by means of the Census Bureau's 1980 Standard Occupational Classification (SOC) code, the SRC collapses several SOC categories into a single category of similar occupations. In utilizing the more generic categorizations in the NES for selecting our subsamples, we have been careful not to do harm to the segregated nature of the occupational categories identified from the Labor Department's tables. In other words, if too many nonsegregated occupations were included in an SRC-encoded category, we chose to exclude all those respondents from our analysis, rather than contaminate the results.

Table 1   Attention to Campaign (V5102)

	Men	Women
Very much interested	52.1%	46.0%
Somewhat interested	39.2	40.4
Not very interested	8.8	13.6

Chi-square: $p = .00035$; $n = 2,246$.

Table 2   Frequency of Political Discussion (V5106)

	Men	Women
Every day	16.4%	10.8%
Three to four times per week	23.8	19.8
Once or twice per month	35.1	37.6
Less often	24.7	31.6

Chi-square: $p = .00013$; $n = 1,834$.

cerning the exercise of societal power, with men not surprisingly more willing to say that they *ought* to exercise the greater power in society (Table 4).

Similar differences—significant in the statistical sense, even if they are not overpowering in magnitude—between men and women can be found when we turn our attention to substantive issues. Rather than examine a long series of individual issues in a search for policy-relevant differences between the sexes, we have chosen to simplify the investigation by combining eight separate issue areas into a single index measuring liberalism or conservatism. Responses (measured in terms of the SRC's traditional, seven-point scale—ranging from most liberal to most conservative) to questions concerning governmental spending and services (Variable 3701 in the 1992 NES), defense spending (V3707), government-provided health insurance (V3616), a government-guaranteed standard of living (V3818), governmental assistance for blacks (V3724), government-provided child care (V3745), urban unrest (V3746), and women's role in society (V3801) constitute the index. Respondents were classified into three groups based on the sums of their responses to the eight questions. As Table 5 demonstrates, there exist mild but statistically sig-

Table 3   Perceived Power of Men, Women in American Society (V6007)

	Men	Women
Men have more power	80.4%	84.0%
Men, women about equal	16.5	13.4
Women have more power	3.1	2.1

Chi-square: $p = .05963$; $n = 2,234$.

Table 4 Desired Power for Men, Women in American Society (V6008)

	Men	Women
Men should exercise the greater power	15.0%	11.2%
Men, women should exercise equal power	83.9	86.7
Women should exercise the greater power	1.1	2.1

Chi-square: $p = .00618$; $n = 2,212$.

nificant differences between men and women on the overall liberalism–conservatism scale. As expected, women hold more liberal views than do men, and men hold more conservative views than do women, although an overwhelming majority of each group falls into the moderate category.

A nearly identical pattern can be discerned when the focus shifts from issues as such to spending on various public policies. An index measuring preferences for governmental spending was constructed in much the same manner as was used previously. For the spending index the eight areas covered are Social Security (V3811), science and technology (V3812), child care (V3813), the environment (V3815), unemployment assistance (V3816), the poor (V3817), schools (V3818), and cities (V3819). Based on their preferences, respondents were placed into one of three categories, as demonstrated in Table 6. Once again, small but statistically significant differences emerge between men, who are less likely to favor increased social spending and more likely to favor budget cuts, and women, who exhibit the opposite tendencies.

The central argument of this analysis, however, is that simple differences between men and women may miss much of the dynamic that actually drives attitude formation. Instead, we have argued earlier, social roles—particularly, in this case, the effects of sex-based segregation in the workplace—may play a part in the construction of political opinions. With that in mind, we make a second pass at the data summarized in the tables, this time controlling for occupational segregation.†

We turn first to a reexamination of the political-interest and political-discussion variables. Table 7 reveals that men in female-segregated jobs (i.e., jobs where

†In the discussion to follow, male-segregated occupations encompass jobs that are held by men at an 80 percent rate or higher; female-segregated jobs are those held by women at an 80 percent rate or higher; and integrated occupations generally fall into the 40 percent to 60 percent range.

Table 5 Eight-Issue, Liberalism–Conservatism Index

	Men	Women
Liberal	5.6%	10.6%
Moderate	87.7	86.3
Conservative	6.7	3.1

Chi-square: $p = .00005$; $n = 1,348$.

Table 6   Eight-Issue, Government-Spending Index

	Men	Women
Big spender	3.3%	5.8%
Mixed bag	89.2	90.5
Budget cutter	7.5	3.8

Chi-square: $p = .00003$; $n = 2,222$.

women make up 80 percent or more of the workforce) are much more interested in politics than are men in either integrated or male-dominated occupations (for chi-square, $p = .00368$). Interestingly, we see this same pattern—reflected in the job-segregation mirror, as it were—for women (albeit in more muted tones), with women in male-segregated occupations significantly more interested than women in traditionally female-dominated professions (although the differences are not statistically significant, with p (chi-square) $= .51184$). With respect to discussing politics, Table 8 reveals a pattern nearly identical to that characterizing political interest. That is, males in female-dominated occupations are significantly more engaged in political discussion than are men in the male-segregated occupations (p [chi-square] $= .05056$), while females in male-dominated trades are more regular discussants than are their counterparts in female-dominated jobs (although p [chi-square] $= .77498$) We might speculate that being in the minority on the job serves as an inducement to keep one's political antennae attuned to the surroundings. Occupational segregation, in other words, does appear to play a role in attitude formation.

We next turn our attention to the findings encompassed originally by Tables 3 and 4, dealing with the perceived and prescribed power of women in our society. Whereas the simple breakdown by sex revealed statistically significant differences (although not overwhelming in magnitude) in both cases, controlling for occupational segregation here demonstrates no significant distinctions.[‡] Tables 9 and 10 re-

---

[‡]p (chi-square, men, V6007) $= .16195$; p (chi-square, women, V6007 $= .51387$; p (chi-square, men, V6008) $= .76506$; p (chi-square, women, V6008) $= .92027$.

Table 7   Attention to Campaign (V5102)

	Male-Dominated Occupations		Integrated Occupations		Female-Dominated Occupations	
	Men	*Women*	*Men*	*Women*	*Men*	*Women*
Very much interested	45.0%	51.9%	58.2%	51.4%	70.4%	43.3%
Somewhat interested	45.4	37.0	36.4	36.4	27.8	46.1
Not very interested	9.7	11.1	5.5	12.1	1.9	10.6
	$n = 269$	$n = 27$	$n = 110$	$n = 107$	$n = 54$	$n = 245$

Table 8   Frequency of Political Discussion (V5106)

	Male-Dominated Occupations		Integrated Occupations		Female-Dominated Occupations	
	Men	Women	Men	Women	Men	Women
Every day	14.3%	19.2%	19.2%	7.9%	29.4%	11.5%
Three to four times per week	23.5	19.2	17.3	18.0	25.5	20.1
Once or twice per month	36.5	34.6	45.2	38.2	29.4	36.8
Less often	25.9	26.9	18.3	36.0	15.7	31.6
	$n = 230$	$n = 26$	$n = 104$	$n = 89$	$n = 51$	$n = 209$

veal that all subgroups overwhelmingly perceive men to exercise the greater power in society, while also calling in like proportions for a leavening of societal strength.

Finally, we reexamine the issue-based ideology and spending indexes, in Tables 11 and 12. Looking first at Table 11, among the men, only the most imperceptible (and, appropriately, statistically insignificant: p [chi-square] $= .19676$) differences can be detected across the occupational-segregation categories. Interestingly, to the extent that any sizable difference can be detected, it shows that men who toil as part of the minority (in female-segregated work) are noticeably more conservative than are their counterparts in male-dominated trades. Among women, on the other hand, the opposite pattern can be observed. Female workers in male-segregated occupations are discernibly more liberal than women in female-segregated positions. Overall, the breakdown for women by occupation-segregated categories is borderline significant, with p (chi-square) $= .09123$.

For the spending index, on the other hand, the significant differences are to be found among the men (p [chi-square] $= .01145$). Those in traditionally female trades are markedly more budget-conscious than are their counterparts in the male-dominated professions. Among women, however, any perceived differences are statistical artifacts (p [chi-square] $= .91781$).

Table 9   Perceived Power of Men, Women in American Society (V6007)

	Male-Dominated Occupations		Integrated Occupations		Female-Dominated Occupations	
	Men	Women	Men	Women	Men	Women
Men have more power	78.8%	88.5%	86.5%	85.8%	90.7%	89.8%
Men, women about equal	18.2	11.5	10.8	12.3	7.4	7.3
Women have more power	3.0	—	2.7	1.9	1.9	2.9
	$n = 269$	$n = 26$	$n = 111$	$n = 106$	$n = 54$	$n = 245$

Table 10   Desired Power for Men, Women in American Society (V6008)

	Male-Dominated Occupations		Integrated Occupations		Female-Dominated Occupations	
	Men	*Women*	*Men*	*Women*	*Men*	*Women*
Men should exercise the greater power	17.6%	8.0%	15.6%	6.6%	15.1%	9.0%
Men, women should exercise equal power	81.7	92.0	82.6	92.5	84.9	89.8
Women should exercise the greater power	0.8	—	1.8	0.9	—	1.2
	n = 262	*n* = 25	*n* = 109	*n* = 106	*n* = 53	*n* = 244

The contrary findings of Tables 11 and 12 present something of a puzzle. Why is the effect of occupational isolation among the opposite sex in the conservative direction for men, but in the liberal direction for women? Can it be a reflection of the more assertive or feminist nature needed by women who seek to invade traditionally male citadels of employment? Are men in heavily female occupations more likely to want to cut public spending due to their own precarious economic situations in lower-paying "women's jobs"? Definitive answers to these kinds of questions are not possible with the given data. At this point, all we can do is reiterate the theme that emerges from our analysis here: Gender segregation in the workplace does appear to play a role in the organization of various political attitudes. Although the simpler, broader distinction between men and women may be the more important influence on opinion formation, nevertheless anyone seeking to understand the differences between the sexes must dig deeper. Biology is not solely determinative; culture matters.

Table 11   Eight-Issue, Liberalism–Conservatism Index

	Male-Dominated Occupations		Integrated Occupations		Female-Dominated Occupations	
	Men	*Women*	*Men*	*Women*	*Men*	*Women*
Liberal	6.9%	21.1%	2.7%	17.5%	4.5%	6.9%
Moderate	86.8	78.9	88.0	77.8	79.5	89.6
Conservative	6.3	—	9.3	4.81	15.9	3.5
	n = 189	*n* = 19	*n* = 75	*n* = 63	*n* = 44	*n* = 144

Table 12 Eight-Issue, Government-Spending Index

	Male-Dominated Occupations		Integrated Occupations		Female-Dominated Occupations	
	Men	Women	Men	Women	Men	Women
Big spender	2.5%	3.8%	0.9%	5.5%	—	6.0%
Mixed bag	89.3	88.5	93.7	89.9	79.2	90.0
Budget cutter	8.2	7.7	5.4	4.6	20.8	4.0
	$n = 280$	$n = 26$	$n = 111$	$n = 109$	$n = 53$	$n = 250$

SUMMARY

The findings of this study are consistent with much of the current research in the field of gender and politics. Research has indicated, for example, that women and men differ on certain "humanitarian" issues.[13] The women in our study, through their liberal positions on issues and their positions on spending, did display a more consistent pattern of support for humanitarian positions than did their male counterparts.

More importantly, however, our study suggests the need to look beyond the sex of the respondents if we want to understand the significance of gender and its relationship to political behavior. Biological males and females become gendered males and females in the context of particular cultures and particular historical periods. It is useful to think of gender in terms of what it represents for individuals. Gender viewed this way becomes for an individual a set of opportunity structures that a particular culture values. In the United States today, for example, gender is involved in the kinds of work experiences people choose or find themselves directed toward. As a result of sex-role socialization, life-cycle demands, and discrimination, women tend to cluster in what we have referred to as female-segregated jobs. The figures we have looked at indicate that the experiences they have in these jobs affect their political attitudes. We can also speculate that since adult socialization appears to affect political attitudes, the longer women remain in those positions, the more their work experiences will affect their political attitudes. This is a subject for additional research. As the workplace changes, so will American political life. The hows and whys of these changes present a challenge to citizens and political scientists alike.

NOTES

1. Lynn Weiner, *From Working Girl to Working Mother: The Female Labor Force in the United States, 1820–1980* (Chapel Hill: University of North Carolina Press, 1985), p. 4.

2. Cynthia Costello and Anne J. Stone for the Women's Research and Education Institute (Eds.), *The American Woman 1994–95* (New York: Norton, 1994), p. 283.

3. Weiner, *From Working Girl*, p. 4.

4. Costello and Stone, *The American Woman 1994–95*, p. 283.

5. Weiner, *From Working Girl*, p. 7.

6. Costello and Stone, *The American Woman 1994–95*, p. 303.

7. Ibid., pp. 298, 300.

8. Andrea H. Beller, "Occupational Segregation and the Earnings Gap," in *Comparable Worth: Issue for the 80's*, vol. 1 (Washington, DC: U.S. Commission on Civil Rights, 1984), p. 23.

9. Beller, "Occupational Segregation," p. 32.

10. Costello and Stone, *The American Woman 1994–95*, p. 314.

11. *Women's Health: Report of the Public Health Service Task Force on Women's Health Issues*, vol. 2 (Washington,

DC: U.S. Department of Health and Human Services), p. 16.

12. Ethel Klein, *Gender Politics* (Cambridge, MA: Harvard University Press, 1984), p. 108.

13. See, for example, Sandra Baxter and Marjorie Lansing, *Women and Politics: The Invisible Majority* (Ann Arbor: University of Michigan Press, 1983); Cal Clark and Janet Clark, "The Gender Gap 1988: Compassion, Pacifism, and Indirect Feminism," in Lois Lovelace Duke (Ed.), *Women in Politics: Outsiders or Insiders* (Englewood Cliffs, NJ: Prentice-Hall, 1993), pp. 32–45; Nancy E. McGlen and Karen O'Connor, *Women, Politics, and American Society* (Englewood Cliffs, NJ: Prentice-Hall, 1995), pp. 71–72.

FURTHER READINGS

Anderson, Kristi, and Elizabeth Cook. "Women, Work and Political Attitudes." *American Journal of Political Science*, 29 (3) (August 1985), pp. 606–625.

Banaszak, Lee Ann, and Jane E. Leighley. "How Employment Affects Women's Gender Attitudes." *Political Geography Quarterly*, 10 (2) (April 1991), pp. 174–185.

Coyle, Angela, and Jane Skinner (Eds.). *Women and Work*. New York: New York University Press, 1988.

Davidson, Marilyn, and Cary Cooper (Eds.). *Working Women: An International Survey*. London: Wiley, 1984.

England, Paula. *Comparable Worth: Theories and Evidence*. New York: Aldine De Gruyter, 1992.

Gerschwender, James, and Rita Carroll-Seguin. "Exploding the Myth of African American Progress." *Signs: Journal of Women in Culture and Society*, 15 (2) (Winter 1990), pp. 285–299.

Gurin, Patricia. "Women's Gender and Consciousness." *Public Opinion Quarterly*, 49 (2) (Summer 1985), pp. 143–163.

Hunt, Audrey (Ed.). *Women and Paid Work*. New York: St. Martin's Press, 1988.

Hunter, Frances. *Equal Pay for Comparable Worth: The Working Woman's Issue of the Eighties*. New York: Praeger, 1986.

Jacobs, Jerry. "Long-Term Trends in Occupational Segregation by Sex." *American Journal of Sociology*, 95 (1) (July 1989), pp. 160–173.

Kelly, Rita Mae. *The Gendered Economy: Work, Careers and Success*. Newbury Park, CA: Sage Publications, 1991.

Kodras, Janet, and Irene Padavic. "Economic Restructuring and Women's Sectoral Employment in the 1970s: A Spatial Investigation across 380 U.S. Labor Market Areas." *Social Science Quarterly*, 74 (1) (March 1993), pp. 1–25.

Nelson, Barbara, and Sara M. Evans. *Wage Justice: Comparable Worth and the Paradox of Technocratic Reform*. Chicago: University of Chicago Press, 1989.

Reskin, Barbara (Ed.). *Sex Segregation in the Workplace: Trends, Explanations, Remedies*. Washington, DC: National Academy Press, 1984.

Slavin, Sarah (Ed.). "The Politics of Professionalism, Opportunity, Employment, and Gender." *Women and Politics*, 6 (3) (Fall 1986).

Welch, Susan, and John Hibbing. "Financial Conditions, Gender and Voting in American National Elections." *Journal of Politics*, 54 (1) (February 1992), pp. 197–213.

Gender and Ideological Polarization Among Southern Grassroots Party Activists

Anne E. Kelley
William E. Hulbary
Lewis Bowman

Several years ago Jeane Kirkpatrick pointed out that women had a long way to go to overcome various forms of domination in the political process of many societies. Describing the difficulties for women in political participation in the 1970s, she wrote:

> Few aspects of social life are more completely or universally male dominated than politics. . . . The advent of democracy and women's suffrage has given women a voice in important political decisions in some countries, but in the United States and elsewhere, universal suffrage has had limited impact on male dominance of power processes.[1]

Many current assessments are not so bleak. Why not? In recent years women have turned out to vote at rates equal to or greater than those for men. Although success has been slower than many expected, women increasingly have been seeking and winning public office.[2] And, once in office, women often have been more likely to give policy priorities to issues of particular concern to women.[3] Since 1980 women have begun separating themselves from men on a range of issues, on partisan attachment itself, and on support for candidates. During the 1980s many began referring to these gender differences as a "gender gap" in contemporary politics.[4] Irene Natividad, former head of the National Woman's Political Caucus,

Anne E. Kelley is an emeritus associate professor of political science in the Department of Government and International Affairs at the University of South Florida; William E. Hulbary is an associate professor of political science in the Department of Government and International Affairs at the University of South Florida; Lewis Bowman is a retired professor of political science.

described this differentiation in terms of a gender gap "[which] is permanent, . . . keeps getting bigger, and . . . is going to change the national agenda in the
future."[5]

What can be said about this phenomenon among highly partisan political activists in a transitional party setting such as the South? In most states the political
parties are required to fill precinct committee posts, the basic political party position in local party organizations, with equal numbers of men and women. Generally the political parties' county chairs are chosen by the precinct committee members from their ranks. This has enabled women in most areas to participate at the
same rate as men in grassroots party activities. This essay examines the following
questions regarding these local party activists: (1) How do political ideology and
issues differ by gender, partisanship, and social background? (2) Is there a gender
gap at the local "grassroots" level among the South's party precinct committee
members? (3) Is there evidence that increased grassroots party activism among
women made any difference in the political attitudes they carried into the political
process? (4) Do partisanship, region of residence in the South, or social background
characteristics override the impact of gender on attitudes?

HISTORICAL PERSPECTIVE

Even after the struggle for women's suffrage granted by the Nineteenth Amendment (1920), winning the privilege of voting did not lead to great changes in
women's political behavior or in women's impact on politics. Beginning in the
1930s, women's involvement was primarily at the local level, where a relatively
large number of party posts and a few elective or appointive offices were available.
However, this availability did not lead to immediate success in winning public
office.

It was not until the 1960s and 1970s that women's political influence increased
in the South as demographic change occurred. As in the rest of the country, women
entered the region's workforce, colleges, universities, and professions in record
numbers, gradually making more and more women economically independent of
men.[6] The growing economic independence and autonomy of women coupled
with the influx of nonsouthern residents in several southern states helped produce
two cultures with differing views of the role of women. A more traditional culture
continued in the rural South with its conservative views of women's roles. Con-
currently, in many growth areas of the South, a second, nontraditional culture
evolved, a culture with more liberal views of women's roles.[7]

During the same period, women's political participation patterns changed
substantially. In several southern states women voter registrants outnumbered
men. More women were elected to public offices in the South. Many of these were
born outside of the South, or were very mobile within the South; and many were
college graduates, and tended to be more active in political party or community
organizations.

Additional changes in party rules brought far greater representation of women, as well as Blacks, youth, and other groups. For women as well as other groups, party organizations were a conduit for advancement in politics.[8] More than is generally appreciated, political party organizations have provided a point of entry for women who sought political activism. As noted, by McGlen and O'Conner,

> Women's efforts to organize, as well as the political parties' responsiveness to their demands for greater representation, aided women's efforts to play a greater role in politics. Involvement through various organized efforts played a key role in propelling women into party politics. . . .[9]

Although the success of women in politics has not been as great in the South as in other regions, party organizational activity has been a major contributor to the success of women in southern politics.[10]

The nature of the party system, and indeed the nature of politics itself, changed considerably during the same period. Accounts of electoral realignment and realignment politics often overlook the importance of party organizational changes.[11] In the South the growth of two-partyism has given party activists the opportunity to participate in a party more congruent with their political attitudes and ideologies. Over a period of time this produced "party sorting" in which the grassroots party activists switched parties to find a more comfortable ideological home.[12] This movement of activists from party to party produced greater ideological congruence within each party and wider ideological differences between the parties. If this is the case, then partisanship becomes more important in explaining ideological and issue differences, while gender and other variables become less important.

GENDER, PARTY, IDEOLOGY, AND ISSUES

Partisan differences in attitudes about political ideology and issues are sizable; Democrats tend to be more liberal and Republicans, more conservative. Of course, the fit between ideology and partisanship is not perfect, but the correlation is strong and persistent. Party activism, in turn, amplifies the size of these ideological differences. The ideological split between Democrats and Republicans is larger among party activists than in the general electorate.[13]

The emergence of a "gender gap" in the 1980s included differences in party affiliation and candidate preferences. Women tended to be somewhat more Democratic and more likely to favor Democratic candidates for public office. But the gender gap extended to issue attitudes and political ideology as well.[14] Although the term *gap* may overstate the differences between men and women on issues and ideology, women increasingly tended to be somewhat more liberal than men on a variety of issues, including, among others, social welfare issues and the role of government in redistributing income; minority rights; some social issues; and issues relating to the use of force or violence in varied situations (foreign affairs, combating crime, or personal relations). Although gender differences have developed on "women's issues" (e.g., abortion, gender equality in government policy and in the workplace), these differences generally tend to be quite small. In part this is because women themselves are more divided on these issues than men; well-educated, working women tend to be more liberal while less-educated women and those not in the workforce (by choice) are more conservative. Compared to party differences (and differences associated with socioeconomic status (SES) and employment outside the home), gender differences on issues and ideology, though important, tended to be relatively small. But gender differences persisted even after compensating for party and other factors; on most issues women were somewhat more liberal than men.

IDEOLOGY AND ISSUES AMONG SOUTHERN PARTY ACTIVISTS

In view of the ongoing political involvement and success of women in the 1990s, data from the 1991–1992 Southern Grassroots Party Activist Study enable us to re-examine and update the link between gender, party, and political ideology for one region in the United States.[15] How do the political ideology and issue attitudes of southern party activists divide along party and gender lines? Are party and gender differences in ideology and issues linked with other relevant factors such as age, race and ethnicity, (SES), and regional differences across the South?

Political and Social Issues

Southern party activists in our survey responded to a wide range of issues concerning social welfare programs, social issues and the role of women, affirmative action, domestic spending and the federal budget, and foreign policy (see Table 1). As anticipated, large differences between the parties were evident on virtually every issue. Regardless of gender, Democrats were consistently more liberal than Republicans, usually by a margin of 20 to 30 percentage points. Moreover, the differences between Democratic and Republican women were at least as large as those between Democratic and Republican men.

Apart from these large interparty differences, there were some gender differences within each party. Although smaller than interparty differences, these gender differences revealed some consistent patterns. First, consider the gender differences on "social issues and the role of women." Except for prayer in the schools, these issues are of direct and immediate relevance to women (abortion, gender equality in business and government, and federal efforts to aid the socioeconomic position of women). In both parties women were consistently more liberal than men on these issues by 6 to 10 percentage points. Only prayer in the schools showed no gender differences within either party.

Among the Democrats this difference was not limited to "social issues" but extended to "social welfare" and "affirmative action" issues as well. In all three cat-

Table 1   Liberal Attitudes on Political Issues by Party and Gender

Issue Items	Democrats		Republicans	
	Men	Women	Men	Women
Social welfare				
Cut federal spending by reducing services even in health and education	71	78	23	30
Federal government should help people get medical care at low cost	90	91	51	52
Federal government see to it that all have job and good standard of living	45	48	11	13
Increase government spending to protect/improve the environment	84	84	63	64
Social issues and the role of women				
Allow prayer in public schools	28	29	10	9
Pro-choice on abortion	72	78	40	47
Women equal role with men in running business, industry, and government	86	93	80	82
Federal government should work to improve the social/economic position of women	83	93	48	58
Affirmative action				
Federal government improve the social/economic position of Blacks/other minorities	66	73	31	33
Because of past discrimination, preference to Blacks in hiring and promotion	21	23	3	3
Domestic spending/budget				
Constitutional amendment to balance the federal budget	32	30	11	15
Raise taxes rather than cut spending in state financial crisis	29	28	7	7
Foreign policy and defense				
Increase defense spending	72	70	44	34
U.S. pay more attention to problems at home, less to other parts of world	81	84	55	54
U.S. continue to cooperate with Russia	92	89	81	79

Note: Table entries indicate the percentage giving a liberal response. For each item, respondents indicated "strongly agree," "agree," "disagree," or "strongly disagree," and responses were rescored as appropriate to indicate liberal responses.

egories of issues, Democratic women were consistently more liberal than men. For example, women Democrats were more liberal in their support for federal spending on social services (health and education) and federal government efforts to ensure a job and good standard of living for all. Women Democrats were also more liberal on affirmative action for Blacks and other minorities. On other social welfare and affirmative action issues the gender gap was smaller (only about 2 percentage points), but its direction was consistent: Women were slightly more liberal than men.

Among Republicans issue differences between men and women were generally much smaller than among Democrats. Exceptions were the social issues already noted (abortion, gender equality in business and government, and federal efforts to aid the socioeconomic position of women) and support for federal spending to maintain social services such as health and education. These exceptions suggest that Republican women are slightly more liberal than men. On other issues, gender differences among Republicans were small and not consistently liberal or conservative.[16]

These issue differences, especially the larger and more consistent ones among Democrats, seem rooted in the different socioeconomic experiences of men and women. Women are more likely than men to be single parents, and to have lower-paying jobs and a lower standard of living; they are more likely, therefore, to need and support federal social service programs in these areas. More likely to have experienced economic discrimination, women also are more likely than men to support affirmative action for other victims of discrimination. This also helps to explain the disproportionate number of Democratic women party activists who are more liberal in these policy areas. They are more likely to have observed or experienced these problems than Republican women activists and male activists in both parties.

Political Ideology

To generalize our results beyond specific issues and to focus more broadly on political ideology, we constructed a single overall political issue scale (see Table 2). The scale combined all the issue items listed in Table 1 and yielded a single measure of "issue" ideology that allowed us to classify party activists as very liberal, liberal, moderate, conservative, and very conservative.[17] Party differences in ideology were considerable. Regardless of gender, Republicans were substantially more conservative than Democrats. Within the parties, modest gender differences were apparent as well. Among Republicans gender differences were rather small, but Republican women were somewhat less conservative than men. Among Democrats gender differences were larger but in the same direction; Democratic women were about 10 percentage points more liberal than men.

SELECTED CHARACTERISTICS AND IDEOLOGY

We believe both micro and macro variables offer complementary explanations for these gender differences in political ideology. Thus we expected macro variables such as political and cultural variation across the South, as well as micro variables such as the activists' individual social and political characteristics, to help explain gender variation in political ideology.

Table 2   Political Ideology: Party and Gender Differences*

Political Issue/ Ideology Scale†	Democrats Men	Women	Republicans Men	Women
Very liberal	14	21	1	1
Liberal	30	35	4	6
Moderate	48	38	40	44
Conservative	8	5	39	33
Very conservative	1	1	17	16
(N)	(3,331)	(1,881)	(2,986)	(1,674)

*Table entries are percentages of column totals (N).

†Scale scores were computed by averaging each respondent's score on the fifteen issue items. For each item a score of "1" was the most liberal response and a score of "4" the most conservative. Scale scores were then collapsed into a five-point scale so that: 1–1.8 = 1 (very liberal); 1.9–2.2 = 2 (liberal); 2.3–2.7 = 3 (moderate); 2.8–3.1 = 4 (conservative); and 3.2–4.0 = 5 (very conservative).

Regional Variations in Ideology

States in the Rim South rather than the Deep South are generally considered less permeated by the culture, values, and traditions of the Old South. This was likely especially in Rim South states experiencing the fastest rates of population growth—the "rapid-growth Rim South" states consisting of Florida, North Carolina, Texas, and Virginia. These states were the recipients of the largest influx of migrants from the North and had experienced large-scale economic development and diversification. Consequently, we expected their political views to be less conservative and more liberal, less a product of the Old South and more like the rest of the country, than other southern states.

Regardless of where they lived in the South, Democrats were distinctly more liberal than their Republican counterparts (Table 3). Additionally, comparison of rapid-growth Rim South states with other southern states reveals ideological differences between men and women Democrats consistent with our expectations. Democratic party activists were more liberal in rapidly growing Rim South states than in other southern states, and women Democrats were more liberal than men in both areas of the South. Indeed, women Democratic activists in rapid-growth Rim South states were among the most liberal groups in either party.

In contrast to the Democrats, Republicans displayed more homogeneity across the South. Women Republicans were slightly less conservative than Republican men in both regions. Women Republicans in the rapid-growth Rim South were the least conservative Republicans but only by a small margin. But in general, Republican local activists (especially male Republicans) showed little regional variation in political ideology.

In summary, regardless of region and party, women tend to be more liberal than men, with larger gender differences among Democrats than Republicans.

Table 3   Political Ideology: Gender Differences Associated with Selected Social Background Variables*

Social Background Variables	Democrats		Republicans	
	Men	*Women*	*Men*	*Women*
Region of the south				
Rim South—rapid growth[†] (FL, NC, TX, VA)	2.33	2.12	3.68	3.50
Other southern states (AL, AR, GA, LA, MS, SC, TN)	2.62	2.43	3.67	3.60
Ethnicity/race				
White	2.61	2.39	3.70	3.58
African-American	1.91	1.81	2.49	2.40§
Hispanic	2.12	2.24§	3.38	3.42§
Occupation[‡]				
Higher-status	2.43	2.08	3.75	3.55
Lower-status	2.65	2.42	3.76	3.56
Retired	2.49	2.36	3.50	3.44
Other (not in labor force)	—§	2.61	—§	3.82
Education				
High school degree	2.72	2.62	3.52	3.52
Some college	2.59	2.47	3.66	3.60
Four-year college degree	2.53	2.08	3.74	3.62
Advanced degree	2.27	1.93	3.68	3.44
Family income				
Less than $30,000	2.54	2.42	3.60	3.47
$30,000 to $59,000	2.52	2.27	3.67	3.55
$60,000 or more	2.46	2.15	3.71	3.62
Age (years)				
Less than 40	2.39	2.12	3.84	3.59
40 to 59	2.53	2.29	3.72	3.62
60 or more	2.54	2.36	3.53	3.46

*Table entries are averages for the group on the political ideology/issue scale described in Table 2. A value of "1" is the most liberal possible score, a value of "5" the most conservative, and a value of 3 the moderate or "middle-of-the-road" position on the scale.

[†]Rapid-growth states are those with 1980–1990 population growth above the national average (9.8 percent).

[‡]Higher-status jobs include professional/technical and managerial or administrative jobs. Lower-status jobs include skilled and semiskilled blue-collar, farm, forestry, clerical, and sales jobs. "Other" consists mainly of homemakers but also includes a few students and a few who are unemployed.

§Too few cases (30 or fewer) for meaningful analysis in one or both gender groups within the party. Any interpretation is speculative.

Even among Republicans gender differences are larger in the Rim South than elsewhere. The Democratic Party in rapidly growing Rim South states has strayed farthest from the traditional conservatism of the Old South. Even in slower-growing Deep South states, the Democratic activists are less conservative than one might expect. Republican activists more closely represent the traditional conservatism of the Old South, displaying little variation and substantial homogeneity from region to region.

Ethnicity, Race, and Ideology

Some tendency for women to be more liberal than men was also evident in ethnic and racial groups (Table 3). The activists were overwhelmingly white,[18] and white women in both parties were more liberal than men. Among African-Americans, women were also more liberal than men, though the gender differences were somewhat smaller than among whites. The differences among African-Americans were complicated by relatively high ideological homogeneity across party lines (similar issue positions among Democratic and Republican African-Americans). Democratic African-Americans were the most liberal racial and ethnic group in the survey. Republican African-Americans were much more liberal than white Republicans and resembled white Democrats in their ideology scores. Gender does count in explaining attitude differences among party activists in the South, but gender does not matter as much as ethnicity (or party).

Only among Hispanic-Americans did gender differences disappear.[19] Hispanic-Americans were more liberal than whites in both parties, but men and women Hispanic-Americans within each party were quite similar in ideology. Furthermore, the partisan differences among Hispanic-Americans were quite large, almost as large as those among whites. Unlike African-Americans, Hispanic-Americans displayed much less ideological homogeneity across party lines.

Socioeconomic Status (SES) and Ideology

Recent evidence suggests that better-educated women who work outside the home in higher-status occupations also tend to be more liberal (and more Democratic).[20] They are more likely to be aware of discrimination in the workplace, to have experienced socioeconomic deprivation, and to rely on government to redress their grievances. Thus we expected higher-SES women party activists to be more liberal, particularly among the Democrats in our study.

The general connection between political ideology and SES is more problematic in the general electorate.[21] Until recently, indicators of SES such as higher occupational status, education, and family income have been associated with political conservatism. But partisan activists tend to be more ideologically homogeneous than the general population, a factor that should diminish SES-based ideological differences within the parties. Furthermore, SES differences in partisanship and ideology have always been smaller in the South.[22] The rise of "working-class conservatism" during the Reagan years and the particularly strong appeal of Reaganism to working-class southerners helped weaken the connection between SES and ideology. Consequently, we expected the association between higher SES and conservatism to be weak or even reversed among southern party activists.

Occupational Status Political ideology varied little by occupational status among Republicans. Republican men in all occupational categories and Republican women in the "other" category (primarily homemakers) were slightly more conservative than other Republicans, but the differences were small. By contrast, among Democratic activists, women with occupations outside the home, especially women with higher-status occupations, were consistently more liberal than men. *Women Democrats with high-status occupations were the most liberal group defined by party, gender, and occupation.* In comparison, men with lower-status occupations and women not in the labor force (mostly homemakers) were the least liberal Democrats, though they were still more liberal than Republicans by a large margin.

Educational Level   Gender-related educational differences were fairly small among Republicans. By a small margin, Republican women with advanced college degrees were the least conservative. With that exception, Republicans at the lowest education levels, regardless of gender, tended to be slightly less conservative than better-educated Republicans. Among Democratic activists, better-educated men and women were more liberal than those with less education. Furthermore, at each education level Democratic women were more liberal than men. The "gap" in ideology was greater at higher educational levels (four-year college degree or higher). *The most educated Democratic women were more liberal than any other group, while the most educated Republican men were among the most conservative.*

Family Income Level   Within both parties the relationship between family income and political ideology exhibited was rather weak (Table 3). More affluent Democrats (both men and women) were somewhat more liberal, while more affluent Republicans were somewhat more conservative. At all family income levels male Democrats were slightly more moderate, and male Republicans slightly more conservative, than women in their party. *The most liberal group in both parties was high-income Democratic women, while the most conservative group was high-income Republican men.*

Age and Political Ideology

Those activists who were less than forty years old in our survey matured in an era of rapid expansion in social programs, civil rights, gender equality and a period when the traditional views of men's and women's roles were being redefined. Thus we expected younger activists, especially younger women activists, to show more support for the liberalism of the period in which they reached maturity.

Our data only partially supported our expectations. Democratic activists did fit the anticipated pattern (Table 3); younger Democrats, especially younger women Democrats, were more liberal than older Democrats. Among Republicans, however, the expected pattern was reversed. Younger Republican men and women were more conservative than their older counterparts. Younger male Republicans (less than forty years old) stood out as more conservative than any others, while *older* Republican women were among the least conservative Republicans.

Although contrary to our expectations, Republican age differences in ideology epitomize the lure of the Republican Party for young conservatives and are important in understanding contemporary party politics in the South. The South continues to be one of the most conservative regions of the country, and younger conservatives, whether men or women, are increasingly attracted by the social and political conservatism of the southern Republican Party. As two-party competition becomes the norm, young conservative southerners now seek activism and organizational positions in the Republican Party. In large measure this attraction, although stronger for men than for women, explains the widespread Republican gains in the South in the 1994 elections.

SUMMARY

We have addressed these questions: (1) How are gender and party associated with the distribution of political attitudes and ideologies among southern grassroots political party activists? Is there a "gender gap"? (2) Are other social background variables (region of residence in the South, race and ethnicity, occupation, education, family income, and age) associated with party and gender differences?

Our data show that partisanship explains a large portion of the variation in political ideology among southern party activists. Regardless of any other considerations, Democrats were consistently more liberal and Republicans consistently more conservative. Party realignment within party organizations is in progress because of these ideological differences, *and* the realignment process is reinforcing these differences in a complicated "party sorting" process.[23]

Gender accounted for considerable variation in political liberalism among Democrats but was less useful in explaining political conservatism among Republican organizational activists. On virtually all issues Democratic women were as liberal as or more liberal than Democratic men. On social issues directly relevant to women (gender equality in business and government, abortion, and federal affirmative action), women party activists in each party were consistently more liberal than men. On other issues, however, the Republican men and women had similar views. Republican women reinforced the party's conservative stance in a number of issue areas.

Reflecting political and cultural differences across the South, regional contrasts enhanced issue and ideological differences among the Democratic and Republican women activists. In each party women political activists in rapidly growing Rim South states were more liberal or less conservative than their counterparts in other southern states. Male activists in each party exhibited similar regional differences. The political conservatism of the Deep South did not diminish party and gender differences. Instead it magnified the conservative orientation of men and women in both parties.

Occupational status, education, and family income also helped explain ideological and issue differences among southern party activists. Democratic women of higher occupational status, higher educational attainment, and higher income were more liberal than any others in our survey. In contrast, Republicans were more homogeneous in their conservatism. More affluent Republican women and those who did not work outside the home tended to have more conservative views. But with these few exceptions, indicators of SES among Republicans generally were not related to ideological differences in any consistent fashion.

The gender differences in political attitudes seem to be a catalyst that is pushing the Democratic Party organization in liberal directions. At the grassroots party activist level in the South, as well as at other levels, the Democratic Party and women have had a symbiotic relationship in which the party was attractive to women because it supported their political views. This is especially true for younger, affluent, better-educated women with higher-status jobs. In turn, these Democratic women supported the organization. In this process Democratic women helped push the Democratic Party farther along the road to liberalism. Similarly, Republican Party conservatism was reinforced by women party activists. But ideological homogeneity was more prevalent among Republicans than Democrats, and this homogeneity muted gender differences in the Republican Party.

NOTES

1. Jeane J. Kirkpatrick, *The Presidential Elite* (New York: Russell Sage Foundation, 1976), p. 397.

2. For a summary of the current situation, and data illustrating change in women in elective office in the United States from 1975 through 1989, see "Women in Elective Office 1989," Fact Sheet of the Center for the American Woman and Politics, Eagleton Institute of Politics, Rutgers University, December 1989.

3. See the assessments of a 1988 national survey of women and men state representatives and senators about their policy priorities in Susan J. Carroll and Ella Taylor, "Gender Differences in Policy Priorities," *CAWP News & Notes*, 7 (Winter 1989), pp. 3–4.

4. Kathleen A. Frankovic, "Sex and Politics—New Alignments, Old Issues," PS: *Political Science and Politics*, 15 (Summer 1982), pp. 439–448. For more recent discussions, see also Pamela Johnston Conover, "Feminists and the Gender Gap," *Journal of Politics*, 50 (November 1988), pp. 985–1010; and Elizabeth Adell Cook and Clyde Wilcox, "Feminism and the Gender Gap—A Second Look," *Journal of Politics*, 53 (November 1991), pp. 1011–1122.

5. Cited in Paul Taylor, "The GOP Has a Woman Problem—George Bush's Gender Gap Is Showing Throughout the Party," *Washington Post National Weekly Edition*, July 4–10, 1988, p. 9.

6. This economic independence may well be associated with a growing psychological independence, a "feminist perspective" that is attractive to liberals regardless of gender. See, for example, Susan J. Carroll's "Women's Autonomy and the Gender Gap: 1980 and 1982," in Carol M. Muller, (Ed.), *The Politics of the Gender Gap: The Social Construction of Political Influence* (Newbury Park, CA: Sage Publications, 1988), pp. 236–257. See also Conover, "Feminists and the Gender Gap," pp. 985–1010; and Cook and Wilcox, "Feminism and the Gender Gap," pp. 1011–1122.

7. For an interpretation focusing on one important southern state (Florida), see Joan Carver's chapter entitled "Women in Florida," in Manning J. Dauer (Ed.), *Florida's Politics and Government* (Gainesville: University Presses of Florida, 1980), pp. 294–308. For a more general discussion of political culture, see R. Darcy, Susan Welch, and Janet Clark, *Women, Elections, and Representation* (New York: Longman, 1987), pp. 46–53.

8. For example, from 1968 to 1992 the proportion of women among the delegates and alternates to the Democratic presidential nominating convention jumped from 13 to 50 percent; among the Republicans it jumped from 16 to 43 percent. See Harold W. Stanley and Richard G. Niemi, *Vital Statistics on American Politics*, 4th ed. (Washington, DC: CQ Press, 1994), p. 149; and Paul Allen Beck and Frank J. Sorauf, *Party Politics in America*, 7th ed. (New York: HarperCollins, 1992), pp. 285–286.

9. See Nancy McGlen and Karen O'Conner, *Women's Rights: The Struggle for Equality in the Nineteenth and Twentieth Centuries* (New York: Praeger, 1983), pp. 105–106.

10. Darcy, Welch, and Clark, *Women, Elections, and Representation*, pp. 46–85.

11. See the discussion of this omission in James L. Gibson, "The Role of Party Organizations in the Mountain West: 1960–1980," in Peter F. Galderisi, Michael S. Lyons, Randy T. Simmons, and John G. Francis (Eds.), *The Politics of Realignment: Party Change in the Mountain West.*, (Boulder, CO: Westview Press, 1987), pp. 197–219.

12. For an extended examination of this phenomenon in one southern state, see Lewis Bowman, William E. Hulbary, and Anne E. Kelley, "Party Sorting at the Grassroots: Stable Partisans and Party Changers among Florida's Precinct Officials," in Robert P. Steed, Laurence W. Moreland, and Tod A. Baker (Eds.), *The*

Disappearing South? (Tuscaloosa: University of Alabama Press, 1990), p. 56.

13. John S. Jackson III, Barbara L. Brown, and David Bositis, "Herbert McClosky and Friends Revisited: 1980 Democratic and Republican Party Elites Compared to the Mass Public," *American Politics Quarterly* 10 (1982), pp. 158–180; Warren E. Miller and M. Kent Jennings, *Parties in Transition* (New York: Russell Sage Foundation, 1986), pp. 189–219.

14. The following summary is based on Frankovic, "Sex and Politics," pp. 439–448; Robert S. Erikson, Norman R. Luttbeg, and Kent L. Tedin, *American Public Opinion*, 4th ed. (New York: Macmillan, 1991), pp. 198–201; Robert Y. Shapiro and Harpreet Mahajan, "Gender Differences in Policy Preferences: A Summary of Trends from the 1960s to the 1980s," *Public Opinion Quarterly*, 50 (Spring 1986), pp. 42–61; Daniel Wirls, "Reinterpreting the Gender Gap," *Public Opinion Quarterly*, 50 (Fall 1986), pp. 316–330. See also the citations in note 6.

15. These data are from the Southern Grassroots Party Activists Project, directed by Charles D. Hadley and Lewis Bowman, and supported by National Science Foundation grant SES-9009846. The findings and conclusions are those of the authors and do not necessarily reflect the views of the National Science Foundation. For information about the project and data, see Charles D. Hadley and Lewis Bowman (Eds.), *Southern State Party Organizations and Activists*, (Westport, CT: Praeger, 1995).

16. Relatively large differences occurred on only two other issues—"Constitutional Amendment to balance the federal budget," where Republican women were more liberal than men, and "Increase defense spending," where Republican women were more conservative.

17. Correlations between the issue items and the overall issue scale ranged between .4 and .7, indicating that the items constitute a single dimension of liberalism–conservatism. A separate measure of self-identified political ideology—a question asking respondents how they perceived themselves in terms of the five ideological categories on the scale—correlated (Person's $R = .70$) very strongly with the political issue/ideology scale. This provided further evidence of the conceptual validity of the political issue scale and indicated that the scale scores corresponded closely to the respondents' own perceptions of their political ideology.

18. More than 90 percent of Democrats and more than 95 percent of Republicans were Whites.

19. In view of the relatively small number of Hispanic-Americans in our sample, conclusions concerning this group should be considered highly speculative.

20. For example, see Carroll, "Women's Autonomy;" see also Conover, "Feminists and the Gender Gap."

21. See Erikson, Luttbeg, and Tedin, *American Public Opinion*, pp. 168–177.

22. William H. Flanagan and Nancy H. Zingale, *The Political Behavior of the American Electorate* (Washington, DC: CQ Press, 1994), pp. 103–106, 115–140.

23. See Bowman, Hulbary, and Kelley, "Party Sorting at the Grassroots," pp. 56–70.

FURTHER READINGS

Bookman, Ann, and Sandra Morgan. *Women and the Politics of Empowerment*. Philadelphia: Temple University Press, 1988.

Carroll, Susan J., and Linda M. G. Zerilli. "Feminist Challenges to Political Science." In Ada W, Finifter (Ed.). *Political Science: The State of the Discipline, II*. Washington, DC: American Political Science Association, 1993.

Conover, Pamela Johnston. "Feminists and the Gender Gap." *Journal of Politics*, 50 (4) (November 1988), pp. 985–1010.

Cook, Elizabeth Adell, and Clyde Wilcox. "Feminism and the Gender Gap: A Second Look." *Journal of Politics*, 53 (4) (November 1991), pp. 1111–1122.

Costain, Anne N. "After Reagan: New Party Attitudes toward Gender." *Annals of the American Academy of Political and Social Science*, 515 (May 1991), pp. 114–125.

Darcy, R., Susan Welch, and Janet Clark. *Women, Elections, and Representation*. New York: Longman, 1987.

Klein, Ethel. *Gender Politics: From Consciousness to Mass Politics*. Cambridge, MA: Harvard University Press, 1984.

Miller, Warren E., and M. Kent Jennigs. *Parties in Transition: A Longitudinal Study of Party Elites and Party Supporters*. New York: Russell Sage Foundation, 1986.

Mueller, Carol M. (Ed.). *The Politics of the Gender Gap: The Social Construction of Political Influence*. Sage yearbooks in Women's Policy Studies, vol. 12. Newbury Park, CA: Sage Publications, 1988.

Poole, Keith T., and L. Harmon Zeigler. *Women, Public Opinion and Politics: The Changing Political Attitudes of American Women*. New York: Longman, 1985.

Shapiro, Robert Y., and Harpreet Mahajan. "Gender Differences in Policy Preferences: A Summary of Trends from the 1960s to the 1980s." *Public Opinion Quarterly*, 50 (1) (Spring 1986), pp. 42–61.

Tilly, Louise A., and Patricia Gurin (Eds.). *Women, Politics and Change*. New York: Russell Sage Foundation, 1990.

Wirls, Daniel. "Reinterpreting the Gender Gap." *Public Opinion Quarterly*, 50 (3) (Fall 1986), pp. 316–330.

Whither the Gender Gap? Converging and Conflicting Attitudes Among Women

Cal Clark
Janet Clark

The growth of the "gender gap" in partisanship and issue positions during the 1980s has generally been taken to signify the emergence of women as a distinct constituency with an identifiable set of interests. Such a perspective, for example, underlines the need to increase women's woeful underrepresentation among America's political leaders. By the mid-1990s, in contrast, attention seems to be turning to the clash between feminists and "traditional" women over such "culture wars" issues as abortion, indicating the splintering of women into contending groups. More speculatively, the growth of such divisions among women might portend the narrowing or disappearance of the gender gap. Indeed, the gender gap was much less pronounced in the 1992 presidential election than in the three conducted during the 1980s, with attitudes toward abortion playing a key role in electoral choice.[1] More broadly, of course, such a growing divergence of interests among women would probably create new problems for the representation of women that would stand in ironic counterpoint to the proclamation of the 1992 election as the "Year of the Woman."[2]

This paper, then, examines the nature of the gender gap and the divisions of opinion among women at the time of the 1992 presidential election to see whether women's "political interests" are in fact fragmenting. The first section discusses the evolution and current nature of the gender gap on nine sets of issues; the second analyzes the extent of the gender gap within different socioeconomic groups; and

Cal Clark is professor and head of political science at Auburn University. Janet Clark is professor and chair of political science at West Georgia College.

the third focuses on what groups of women are most likely to support and oppose representative issues in each set. As will be seen, there is little evidence that women's social and political interests were cohesive in the 1980s and have recently become much more fragmented. Rather, the gender gap in the 1980s represented the overlapping concerns of somewhat disparate groups of women; and, despite the growing salience of the "culture wars" issues, there was little change in this situation as of 1992.

THE GROWTH OF THE GENDER GAP

Until the 1970s, women and men had remarkably similar attitudes on most political issues and, consequently, exhibited almost the same pattern of voting and partisan attachment. There were a few notable exceptions, though, such as women's greater concern for morality issues and opposition to policies that threatened to involve the United States in violent conflict. Over the last two decades, in contrast, significant differences in political attitudes between the sexes emerged or expanded in such areas as women's social and political roles, "social compassion," support for minority rights, protection of the environment, and basic economic issues to greatly augment the previous limited attitudinal gap concerning peace and morality. This difference in issue positions, in turn, promoted a growing partisan and ideological gender gap that remained fairly stable during the 1980s in the 6 percent to 10 percent range for presidential voting and party identification.[3]

The growing divergence between the attitudes of women and men almost certainly stemmed from women's changing role in American society as denoted by the growth of the women's movement, women's increased entrance into higher education and the workplace, and the growing "feminization of poverty" that has resulted from a combination of a rising divorce rate and declining welfare expenditures.[4] Thus, as women were able to broaden their horizons and escape the confines of traditional socialization, they began to realize that their basic values applied to a broader range of issues, such as helping the less fortunate, supporting racial equality, protecting the environment, and, most especially, demanding equal rights for women. In particular, much of the gender gap appeared to be explicable by women's rising "gender consciousness" and "feminism," since most of it could be accounted for by the difference in attitudes between feminist women and men.[5]

From this perspective, the gender gap should have been exacerbated in 1992 because many of the events surrounding the election should have raised the saliency of gender consciousness and feminism in the electorate (e.g., the strident attacks on Anita Hill by Republican senators, the Republican convention's strong emphasis on "culture wars," and Hilary Rodham Clinton's providing an attractive role model for feminists). Yet, the gender gap shrank instead of expanding. Women were more likely than men to support Clinton by 5 percentage points (46 percent to 41 percent) and less likely to vote for Perot by 4 percentage points (17 percent to 21 percent) and for Bush by only 1 percentage point (37 percent to 38 percent). Still, this was significantly lower than the gender gaps in the 1980s; and, if there had been a two-way race between Bush and Clinton, the estimated gender gap would have been only 3 percent[6]—less than half of the gender gap in Bush's first presidential race against Michael Dukakis.[7]

To a significant extent, the size of the gender gap on presidential voting in 1992 was lowered by the cross-pressures many women felt concerning abortion and other social and moral issues.[8] This suggests that the growing prominence of the gender gap during the 1980s may have diverted attention from the fact that the gap between traditional women and feminists was growing as well, as denoted by the surprising lack of a gender gap on abortion and the Equal Rights Amendment.[9] This would further imply that the gender gap should be shrinking on partisanship and probably many other political issues as well.

To test the hypothesis that a growing conflict of opinion between feminists and traditional women has eroded the gender gap, we used data from the Survey Research Center's 1992 American National Election Survey to examine the nature of the gender gap in nine areas encompassing both traditional and newer foci of attitudinal division between the sexes: (1) general ideological and partisan attachments, (2) social and social welfare spending, (3) the role of the state, (4) women's issues, (5) moral and cultural issues, (6) civil rights, (7) militarism, (8) crime, and (9) the environment.

The results of these many comparisons are fairly consistent. While there are some indications that the presumed cleavage between feminists and traditionalist women may have attenuated the gender gap in 1992, the gender gap still lived in most issue areas. The image of women as more liberal than men is confirmed by the data on general partisan and ideological positions in Table 1. In terms of self-identification, women were 8 percent less likely than men to identify themselves as Republicans and as conservatives (approximately 37 percent to 45 percent each)— almost exactly equal to the gender gap on these items in the 1980s. They also were more likely to express positive feelings toward liberals and less likely to feel warmly toward conservatives or to believe that Republican policies on the economy are better than Democratic ones by almost the same margin (5 percent to 7 percent). Women were also less supporting of Republican foreign policy by 11 percentage points, suggesting that President Bush's triumph in the Gulf War may have raised women's traditional concerns about militarism. On the other hand, this pronounced gender gap on partisanship and ideology was not universal. The gap on warmth of feelings toward both Bush and Clinton was in the right direction but relatively small at 5 percentage points; and little difference existed in the perceptions of men and women about which party could better handle poverty and health issues.

The data in Tables 2 and 3, moreover, clearly demonstrate that women were significantly more liberal than men in the "bread-and-butter" issues concerning governmental support for social welfare policies. As Table 2 illustrates, women were generally more favorable than men by 5 to 15 percentage points toward increased spending in a wide variety of liberal areas (Social Security, the poor, child care, the homeless, unemployed people, welfare, public schools, food stamps, and Blacks in descending order). They also were more likely than men by margins of 5

Table 1 Gender Gap on Ideology and Partisanship

	Male	Female	Gender Gap
Self-identification			
Conservative	45%	37%	−8%†
Republican	44%	36%	−8%†
Warm feelings* toward ideological groups			
Conservatives	31%	26%	−5%†
Liberals	19%	26%	7%†
Warm feelings* toward politicians			
George Bush	40%	36%	−4%
Bill Clinton	47%	52%	5%
Republicans better than Democrats on			
Economy	24%	17%	−7%†
Poverty	13%	10%	−3%
Health	13%	11%	−2%
Foreign affairs	52%	41%	−11%†

*Defined as a score of 60 or more on a "thermometer" of 0 to 100.

†Statistically significant at .05 level.

Source: Computed from data from the 1992 National Election Study of the Survey Research Center, distributed by the Interuniversity Consortium for Political and Social Research. Reprinted with permission.

to 10 percentage points to have favorable feelings about marginal and minority groups in American society (Blacks, the poor, gays, Hispanics, Asians, and Jews).

They were particularly supportive compared to men (generally in the range of 10 to 15 percentage points) of expanding the role and powers of government, presumably because they believed that redistributive policies were necessary to help themselves and other marginal groups in society (see Table 3). They also had more favorable opinions of the federal government and were more likely to support government's assumption of responsibilities in such areas as health insurance, guaranteeing a job, and child care by slightly lower margins (5 to 10 percentage points). In contrast, they were hardly more willing than men to pay more taxes to support an expansion of government services.

One would certainly expect a considerable gender gap on women's issues. The results in Table 4 conform to this expectation on several important dimensions and also find a consensus between the sexes in support of gender equality, which may be taken as supporting the hypothesis as well. As would be expected, women had more positive feelings than men toward the women's movement (49 percent to 38 percent and feminists (31 percent to 27 percent), although these fairly low percentages even for women suggest the strong possibility of a cleavage between feminists and traditional women. There were differences between the sexes of over 10 percentage points on several issues concerning gender equality and women's activism: Women were more likely than men to say that sexual harassment was a serious problem, that women should form groups instead of acting individually, and that they felt pride in women's achievements. On three other items, though, there

Table 2   Gender Gap on Social Welfare

	Male	Female	Gender Gap
Social spending			
Increase Social Security spending	41%	55%	14%†
Increase spending for poor	48%	61%	13%†
Increase spending for homeless	68%	77%	9%†
Increase child care spending	44%	56%	12%†
Increase AIDS spending	61%	63%	2%†
Increase public school spending	62%	69%	7%†
Increase college aid	59%	61%	2%†
Increase spending on unemployed	35%	44%	9%†
Increase spending for Blacks	23%	27%	4%†
Increase spending for cities	21%	21%	0%†
Increase welfare spending	13%	21%	8%†
Increase food stamp spending	15%	21%	6%†
Warm feelings* toward marginal groups			
Poor	55%	64%	9%†
Welfare recipients	19%	23%	4%
Catholics	44%	48%	4%
Jews	43%	49%	6%†
Blacks	41%	52%	11%†
Hispanics	35%	42%	7%†
Asians	31%	38%	7%†
Immigrants	33%	33%	0%
Illegal immigrants	7%	9%	2%
Gays	10%	18%	8%†

*Defined as a score of 60 or more on a "thermometer" of 0 to 100.

†Statistically significant at .05 level.

Source: Computed from data from the 1992 National Election Study of the Survey Research Center, distributed by the Interuniversity Consortium for Political and Social Research. Reprinted with permission.

was a surprising consensus of approximately two-thirds to three-quarters of both men and women who expressed interest in women's issues, anger at the way some women were treated, and the belief that women and men should have an equal role in business and government (as opposed to staying home). While a cynic might note greater male commitment to more abstract and symbolic issues, as opposed to the more concrete issues of feminism and women's organizing to increase their power, this generally strong support for women's equality is consistent with long-term secular shifts in American public opinion toward greater support for equality in gender relationships.[10]

Perhaps the most surprising "nongender gap" in Table 4 to those not familiar with previous findings on the subject is the fact that 46 percent of both men and women professed a pro-choice opinion on the abortion issue, since this is generally

Table 3 Gender Gap on Role of Government

	Male	Female	Gender Gap
Government powers			
Government should expand	55%	70%	15%†
Government should become more powerful	29%	44%	15%†
Strong government over free market	64%	76%	12%†
Government involved in what people should do for themselves	45%	31%	−14%†
Government services			
Increase services vs. cut spending	32%	42%	10%†
Government provide health insurance	49%	54%	5%†
Government guarantee job and standard of living	26%	34%	8%†
Government provide child care	56%	65%	9%†
Willing to pay more taxes	29%	31%	2%
Warm feelings* toward government			
Federal government	18%	23%	5%†
Congress	19%	26%	7%†

*Defined as a score of 60 or more on a "thermometer" of 0 to 100.

†Statistically significant at .05 level.

Source: Computed from data from the 1992 National Election Study of the Survey Research Center, distributed by the Interuniversity Consortium for Political and Social Research. Reprinted with permission.

Table 4 Gender Gap on Women's Issues

	Male	Female	Gender Gap
Equality issues			
Women equal rights to lead business and government vs. stay at home	75%	75%	0%
Women should have more power in society and economy	34%	40%	6%†
Sexual harassment serious problem	25%	38%	13%†
Pride in women's achievements	61%	72%	11%†
Anger at women's treatment	61%	63%	2%
Activism			
Women should form groups vs. act on own	53%	64%	11%†
High interest in women's issues	77%	80%	3%
Warm feelings* towards women's groups			
Feminists	27%	31%	4%
Women's movement	38%	49%	11%
Abortion			
Pro-choice	46%	46%	0%

*Defined as a score of 60 or more on a "thermometer" of 0 to 100.

†Statistically significant at .05 level.

Source: Computed from data from the 1992 National Election Study of the Survey Research Center, distributed by the Interuniversity Consortium for Political and Social Research. Reprinted with permission.

viewed as perhaps the most central "women's issue" of the 1980s and 1990s. In actuality, though, this continues a trend dating back to the 1970s in which the opposition of women with traditional values to the Equal Rights Amendment and abortion has pulled down women's overall level of support for these issues to or even slightly below that of men.[11] Here, then, is strong and direct evidence of the split in perspectives between feminists and traditional women.

If, in fact, a growing split between feminists and traditional women on abortion and other moral issues is occurring, one would also expect that the traditional gender gap in which women were more conservative than men on moral issues may have eroded. The evidence on this hypothesis presented in Table 5 is somewhat ambiguous. On the one hand, the gender gap on several important moral and cultural issues (i.e., the belief that family values are important or very important, warm feelings toward fundamentalists, tolerance for different moral standards, and the view that changing morals are promoting social breakdown) is insignificant, suggesting that the postulated erosion may have occurred. On the other hand, there is clearly a very strong gender gap on attitudes about gays and about several basic moral questions—whether moral values should change in response to socioeconomic change and whether extramarital sex is wrong. Thus, there is some, but far from conclusive, support for the expectation that women's and men's cultural and moral values are converging in the aggregate, possibly in response to a growing dissensus among women on basic values.

Table 5   Gender Gap on Moral Issues

	Male	Female	Gender Gap
Abortion			
Pro-choice	46%	46%	0%
Traditional values			
Family values important	81%	82%	1%
Family values very important	45%	48%	3%
Should change moral beliefs with times	58%	49%	−9%†
Should have tolerance for different moral standards	61%	60%	−1%
Changing morals leading to social breakdown	69%	72%	3%
Extramarital sex wrong	81%	86%	5%†
Warm feelings* toward fundamentalists	27%	30%	3%
Attitudes about gays			
Warm feelings* toward gays	10%	18%	8%†
Support laws protecting gays	54%	66%	12%†
Gays should serve in military	48%	68%	20%†
Permit gay adoptions	26%	30%	4%

*Defined as a score of 60 or more on a "thermometer" of 0 to 100.

†Statistically significant at .05 level.

Source: Computed from data from the 1992 National Election Study of the Survey Research Center, distributed by the Interuniversity Consortium for Political and Social Research. Reprinted with permission.

Finally, Table 6 explores the gender gap in several other spheres where it has existed in the past: civil rights, militarism, crime and punishment, and the environment. In general, significant gender gaps exist in all these areas, with women taking the more liberal position, although two analytic qualifications are needed. First, for both civil rights and militarism, men and women in America differ little on general principles, but gender gaps exist concerning turning these principles into practice. For example, women were more likely than men to support government action promoting school integration and affirmative action by 5 to 10 percentage points; and they were more supportive of draft avoiders and less supportive of the Gulf War by slightly larger margins.[12] Second, while women were less favorably disposed toward harsh punishments (i.e., the death penalty and combating urban unrest by using the police as opposed to improving social conditions), they appeared more fearful of crime than men. Thus, women supported increased

Table 6   Gender Gap on Civil Rights, Militarism, Crime, and the Environment

	Male	Female	Gender Gap
Equal rights commitment			
All should have equal rights	91%	91%	0%
Too much emphasis on equal rights in U.S.	46%	45%	−1%
Government actions and laws			
Support government involvement school integration	40%	50%	10%†
Support quotas in education	28%	37%	9%†
Support affirmative action for jobs	18%	22%	4%
General feelings toward defense			
Warm feelings* toward military	63%	61%	−2%
Increase defense spending	20%	19%	−1%
U.S. should be willing to use military force in future	25%	21%	−4%
Particular events			
Draft avoiders right	47%	55%	8%†
Gulf War right thing	82%	67%	−15%†
Protection and fear of crime			
Increase spending on crime	67%	73%	6%†
Warm feelings* toward police	59%	64%	5%†
Warm feelings* toward lawyers	18%	29%	11%†
Harsh retribution			
Favor death penalty	86%	71%	−15%†
Social services vs. police to control urban unrest	55%	47%	8%†
Environmentalism			
Warm feelings* toward environmentalists	53%	59%	6%†
Increase environmental spending	59%	63%	4%

*Defined as a score of 60 or more on a "thermometer" of 0 to 100.

†Statistically significant at .05 level.

Source: Computed from data from the 1992 National Election Study of the Survey Research Center, distributed by the Interuniversity Consortium for Political and Social Research. Reprinted with permission.

crime spending by 6 percentage points more than men. In a similar vein, they were also more appreciative of police and lawyers, implying that they might feel more vulnerable and, thus, more in need of the protection offered by these two sources. This evidence of greater fear of crime, of course, makes women's more liberal attitudes on crime and punishment all the more significant.

In sum, these data provide indirect evidence for the supposition that growing polarization between feminist and traditional women may have accounted for the decrease of the gender gap in voting and candidate evaluations in 1992 when contextual factors, if anything, should have exacerbated the differences between women and men. While there was no change from the 1980s in the absence of a gender gap on abortion, this election differed considerably from previous ones in that abortion did affect voting, thereby driving the votes of feminists and traditional women farther apart.[13]

However, the data in this section also demonstrate that the "normal" gender gap continued on partisanship and many other political issues. This suggests that the gender gap in voting and partisanship was not simply the result of feminist women taking a different perspective from men and nonfeminist women. Several such factors are readily suggested by previous research on women's attitudes and interests: (1) women's greater (as opposed to men's) "compassion" for the less fortunate in society;[14] (2) women's relative "pacifism" in both international and domestic affairs; and (3) women's "self-interest" in liberal social policies, which has been generated by the feminization of poverty.[15]

If such factors are, indeed, at least partial causes of the gender gap, the growing polarization among women over abortion and other associated moral questions may not necessarily eradicate the gender gap or the common interests that many women possess. In fact, the gender gap appeared to be resurgent as the 1994 elections approached. While the gender gap for congressional voting was only 5 percent in 1992, polls in 1994 indicated that it had multiplied by two- to threefold just two years later.[16] The next two sections, hence, seek to document the presence or absence of these other possible components of the gender gap.

VARIATIONS IN THE GENDER GAP: CONSCIOUSNESS, CULTURE WARS, COUNTERSOCIALIZATION, COMPASSION, AND COST BEARING

The previous section reported the gender gap for the American population as a whole. It is quite likely, however, that the differences between the attitudes of women and men may vary widely in size among social and political subgroups. When one looks at how the gender gap varies among subgroups of Americans, it is possible to provide a more sophisticated picture of the gender gap and to explore for several factors that have been assumed to stimulate it: (1) the gender *consciousness* that is assumed to be at the root of America's *culture wars* over women's issues and traditional values; (2) the *countersocialization* that women evidently need to escape the limitations of a patriarchal culture; (3) the greater *compassion* that women supposedly exhibit; and (4) the *cost bearing* that the "feminization of poverty" has placed upon many women.

Several important studies have found that the gender gap can be essentially explained by differences in attitudes between *feminist* women and men. Thus, the divergence in political attitudes between the sexes derives from the feminist "gender consciousness" that many (but not all) women have developed.[17] This, in turn, implies that the gender gap should vanish once the possession or nonpossession of feminist ideas is controlled. Here, we use a scale of 0 to 100 to measure warmth of feelings toward feminism to estimate this dimension; scores of 60 or above are taken to indicate a profeminist perspective, and those of 0 to 40 denote antifeminism.

Countersocialization theory supplies one answer about why some women become feminists and others do not. According to this perspective, many women need to experience some type of countersocialization to overcome their normal socialization into traditional roles. Women who have such countersocialization, especially in their adult roles, therefore, are much more likely to reject traditional values and role stereotypes.[18] Here, we use education and age to indicate exposure to countersocialization influences. In particular, we compare the attitudes of citizens with a college degree to those with less than a high school degree, assuming that the former have had many more opportunities for countersocialization than the latter. We also assume that the socialization processes in America have become much more open and nontraditional after the early 1960s; thus, we compare the attitudes of citizens under age thirty-five to those over fifty-five.

Women have also been seen as having more "social compassion" for the less fortunate in society than do men.[19] Examining subgroups of Americans provides a more precise test of this hypothesis than simply recording if women in general were more liberal on social issues than men in general, as was done in the first section. In essence, the compassion hypothesis argues that women who would normally be expected to be conservatives will support aiding the disadvantaged out of compassion. For example, since poor women would normally be expected to take such a position out of self-interest, the problem arises of how to separate "compassion" from the self-interest in reducing the "cost bearing" of poverty. If it is assumed that both men and women who are economically distressed will take liberal positions on government role and spending policies, then one would expect that the gender gap should be significantly wider among more affluent than less affluent groups. In the former instance, compassion would pull women away from men's normal attitudes, while in the latter both men and women would be pulled in the same direction by self-interest. Similarly, the gender gap should be much greater among conservatives than liberals since most liberals should be progovernment, while compassion should pull women away from conservatives' antigovernment inclinations.

The compassion and cost-bearing hypotheses, then, predict that the magnitude of the gender gap should vary among groups with different socioeconomic status (SES) and political orientations. Here, SES was measured by income, with the poor (i.e., those whose family incomes were under $15,000) being compared to the rich (i.e., those with family incomes over $50,000). Of course, education pro-

vides a similar measure because income and education are fairly highly correlated—which, as will be seen, can make it hard to untangle the predictions of the
compassion and the countersocialization theories. In addition, African-Americans
are treated as a special, disadvantaged minority in American society, although the
rest of the citizenry is certainly too heterogeneous to be considered an "elite." Political orientations are indicated by self-reported ideology (conservatives versus
liberals) and partisanship (Republicans versus Democrats).

   Table 7 presents the gender gaps among these seven subgroups of Americans
for representative items in three sets of issues—women's status, moral values, and
militarism. These three, perhaps seemingly disparate, types of questions are
grouped together for two reasons. First, previous research suggests that the absence of a gender gap on abortion, perhaps the central issue on the feminist agenda,

Table 7   Comparison of Gender Gaps* in the Attitudes of Subgroups of Americans on Women's and Moral Issues

	Like Women's Movement	Pro-Choice	Gay Adoption	Family Values Very Important	Support Gulf War	Republicans Better Foreign Policy
Population	11%	0%	4%	3%	−15%	−11%
Gender consciousness						
Like feminists	4%	4%	7%	−4%	−3%	2%
Don't like fem	2%	−4%	2%	3%	−11%	−14%
Countersocialization						
Under 35	18%	1%	3%	6%	−11%	−12%
Over 55	−2%	−6%	7%	−2%	−13%	−3%
Less than high school degree	0%	−10%	6%	13%	−13%	−9%
College	22%	13%	13%	−9%	−8%	−8%
Compassion, SES						
Family income under $15,000	2%	−6%	1%	13%	−9%	−8%
Family income over $50,000	6%	12%	7%	−2%	−9%	−12%
African-American	11%	−4%	4%	7%	−20%	−16%
Compassion, political						
Liberals	11%	2%	2%	3%	−9%	−7%
Conservatives	13%	1%	6%	5%	−7%	−7%
Democrats	8%	−3%	2%	12%	−10%	−10%
Republicans	14%	4%	1%	1%	−6%	−6%

*The gender gap is computed by subtracting the percentage of men holding an attitude from the percentage of women. Thus, a pos-
itive gender gap shows that more women than men hold an attitude, while a negative one shows that it is more popular with men
than with women. For example, for the "population" of all Americans, 49 percent of the women and 38 percent of the men had warm
feelings toward the women's movement, for a gender gap of +11.

Source: Computed from data from the 1992 National Election Study of the Survey Research Center, distributed by the Interuniversity
Consortium for Political and Social Research. Reprinted with permission.

results from its being treated as a moral, rather than a feminist, issue by many traditionalist women.[20] Thus, it makes sense to directly compare abortion with indicators of more traditional values. Second, women's presumed pacifism is a "liberal" traditional value, which should provide an interesting contrast to women's conservatism on traditional moral issues. Third, all these issues essentially involve "cultural" rather than economic or "material" matters and, thus, might be expected to be affected by somewhat similar factors. In particular, women's issues, obviously, should be strongly influenced by gender consciousness and the countersocialization assumed to create it. Traditional moral values, in contrast, should tap the "culture wars" between feminists and traditional women. The patterns of opinions concerning women's presumed pacifism should be especially interesting because they involve a mix of the liberalism associated with gender consciousness and the traditional values associated with antifeminist women. Finally, there is little a priori reason to believe that any of these issues should involve the "compassion" associated with "bread-and-butter" political cleavages over "who gets what."

The data on a positive view toward the women's movement, the principal indicator of women's issues used here, conform almost perfectly to the gender consciousness and countersocialization hypotheses. The considerable gender gap of 11 percentage points in the general population almost vanishes completely when attitudes toward feminists are controlled. Moreover, the factors of countersocialization that have been posited as promoting feminism were clearly at work as well, since there were large gender gaps of approximately 20 percentage points for those having college degrees and those being under age thirty-five, in contrast to no gender gap for the less educated and the old. The interpretation that these large differences between education and age categories indicate opportunities for countersocialization is further strengthened by the lack of such a difference between the categories of family income, which would normally behave similarly to education because of the positive correlation between these two SES factors. Finally, controlling for race, ideology, and partisanship does not materially affect the gender gap on the women's movement, again suggesting the overriding importance of gender consciousness and the countersocialization that engenders it.

The two moral issues included in the table present very different profiles. One (support for gay adoptions) looks very much like a women's issue, while the other (belief that family values are very important) clearly taps a much different attitudinal dimension. The pattern of results for allowing gay couples to adopt children is somewhat similar to the one for attitudes about the women's movement, although it is harder to judge these relationships because the tendency for women to be more liberal than men on this issue in the general population is much smaller (4 percentage points). Two important differences suggest that gender consciousness is still important but operates a little differently than for normal women's issues. First, among those who are profeminist, women were significantly more supportive of gay adoptions than men, indicating that they had a less constrained and more liberal view of gender roles than even "feminist" men. Second, countersocialization occurred only through education, not through age. This suggests that support for gays is more limited than for feminists and the women's movement because the channels of countersocialization are narrower. In sum, perhaps because it involves gender-role issues of central concern to feminists, the gay adoption issue is an aspect of the culture wars for which the gender consciousness–countersocialization model clearly applies.

The same cannot be said, however, for another issue concerned with traditional values—the belief that family values are very important. Here, women were more conservative, not more liberal, than men, although the gender gap is a relatively small 3 percentage points. Moreover, women's greater conservatism exists for almost all the subgroups (women were significantly more liberal than men on this issue only among the profeminists, for whom women's feminist consciousness should be at the maximum). Thus, this issue apparently taps a basic moral dimension separating women from men, which harkens back to their greater moral conservatism in the past but still encompasses many women who have rejected traditional values. The subgroup differences are particularly marked for those with low SES (education and income). These are precisely the groups that normally would be expected to have the highest proportion of traditional women. Conversely, college women were much less supportive of family values than were college men. The gender gap on this variable is also much wider for Democrats as compared with Republicans but not for liberals as compared with conservatives, indicating that this moral conservatism is tied to general ideological orientations but not to party identification. Presumably, the wide gender gap among the Democrats reflects the identification with that party by a significant number of morally conservative women with lower SES based on pocketbook issues.

This moral conservatism, more importantly, explains why the pattern of the gender gap on supporting abortion choice is so different from the one for supporting the women's movement, although both are central items on the feminists' (and antifeminists') agenda. Public opinion on abortion differs from many other women's issues, however, in that exactly the same proportion of men and women are pro-choice (46 percent), in contrast to the gender gap that exists for many women's issues (see Tables 4 and 7); controlling for most of the factors in Table 7 does not change this situation materially.

Significant gender gaps do emerge for two SES factors (education and income); for both, the direction of the gender gap reverses itself between high and low SES categories—a rare and perhaps remarkable situation that does not occur for any of the other cultural or economic variables in our analysis. Among those with high education and income, women were considerably more likely to be pro-choice than men by 12 to 13 percentage points. Conversely, women with low education and income were less likely to be pro-choice than were comparable men by 6 to 10 percentage points. This suggests that each group responded to a different dynamic. Women with high SES evidently were pushed in a pro-choice direction by gender consciousness and countersocialization, while those with low SES assumed a pro-life position because of their traditional morality.

Finally, two items were used in Table 7 to measure women's presumed pacifism—support for the Gulf War and belief that Republicans can handle foreign affairs better than Democrats (which exhibits a very similar pattern, presumably because of the saliency of the Gulf War). The results are almost identical to those for the indicator of traditional values, except that women are more liberal on militarism than men. The gender gap on these two issues is substantial—15 percentage points for the former and 11 percentage points for the latter. Similar to the results for changing moral values, this gender gap holds quite consistently for almost all the subgroups under consideration. The one exception is for profeminists, where men who had a positive view of feminism adopted women's more pacific values. Thus, despite the culture wars pitting feminists against traditional women on such issues as abortion, women as a group evidently retain many of the same values that have differentiated them from men since measures of public opinion became available. Since some of these values are conventionally considered conservative and others liberal, however, it has been hard for them to receive representation within America's current party system.[21]

When we turn to bread-and-butter issues, a different set of factors would be expected to influence the gender gap. First, women's alleged "compassion" for the less fortunate in society should be discernible if it exists. As noted earlier, this implies that the gender gap should be especially wide among higher-SES and more conservative subpopulations because these are the groups where compassion might exist. Second, since poor men and women have an equal incentive to support liberal economic policies, the gender gap should be relatively small for low-SES and liberal groups. Third, gender consciousness will probably be much more limited in its impact here than it was for the cultural issues.

Finally, it is much harder to isolate the effects of countersocialization than for the cultural issues because the compassion and countersocialization perspectives make exactly the same prediction about highly educated people—that there will be a large gender gap among them. The extent of the gender gap among different age groups, however, provides a better method for assessing the presence of countersocialization. It is generally agreed that the vastly changed nature of American society between the 1950s and the 1970s means that younger Americans are receiving different socialization experiences from those of previous generations. If this is true, men as well as women under age thirty-five should be much more liberal than older generations; and there is little reason to suppose that the gender gap would vary greatly among generations. In contrast, countersocialization theory would argue that women have to take special advantage of opportunities for obtaining countersocialization, such as increased access to higher education and more liberal cultural norms. Thus, it would predict that the expansion of these opportunities in the 1970s and 1980s should have created a comparatively wide gender gap within the younger generation.

Table 8 presents a breakdown of the gender gap for a series of economic issues plus one noneconomic one that evidently elicits feelings of compassion—whether government should provide more services (as opposed to cutting taxes); whether or not more should be spent for the poor, child care, Social Security, and welfare; whether the Republicans are better for economic policy than the Democrats; and whether the response to urban unrest should target underlying social conditions (as

Table 8   Comparison of Gender Gaps* in the Attitudes of Subgroups of Americans on Government Services and Compassion Issues

	More Government Services	More Poor Spending	Republicans Better Economic Policy	Social Conditions Urban Unrest	More Child Care Spending	More Social Security Spending	More Welfare Spending
Population	10%	13%	−7%	8%	12%	14%	13%
Gender consciousness							
Like feminists	−1%	5%	2%	−0%	15%	10%	6%
Don't like feminists	17%	15%	−14%	13%	12%	17%	7%
Countersocialization							
Under 35	16%	12%	−5%	11%	21%	15%	12%
Over 55	0%	9%	−1%	6%	4%	9%	3%
Less than high school degree	6%	7%	1%	−2%	4%	10%	15%
College	13%	11%	−12%	11%	20%	14%	5%
Compassion, SES							
Family income under $15,000	12%	13%	2%	4%	5%	9%	13%
Family income over $50,000	7%	10%	−9%	14%	16%	11%	−1%
African-American	−2%	8%	−4%	−3%	8%	9%	8%
Compassion, political							
Liberals	6%	6%	−2%	4%	9%	6%	3%
Conservatives	12%	16%	−8%	11%	17%	24%	5%
Democrats	10%	11%	−2%	7%	9%	15%	6%
Republicans	8%	7%	−11%	11%	14%	14%	1%

*The gender gap is computed by subtracting the percentage of men holding an attitude from the percentage of women. Thus, a positive gender gap shows that more women than men hold an attitude, while a negative one shows that it is more popular with men than with women. For example, for the "population" of all Americans, 49 percent of the women and 38 percent of the men had warm feelings toward the women's movement, for a gender gap of +11.

Source: Computed from data from the 1992 National Election Study of the Survey Research Center, distributed by the Interuniversity Consortium for Political and Social Research. Reprinted with permission.

opposed to expanding police powers). In general, the data on the gender gap form a fairly similar pattern for six of the seven items (welfare spending is the exception), which is consistent with almost all the hypotheses adumbrated previously.

All seven of these economic and potential compassion issues have marked gender gaps in the range of 10 percentage points or slightly higher, with women invariably taking the more liberal position. As expected, it is clear that these gender gaps are not simply the result of gender consciousness. While profeminist men and women were equally liberal on most of these issues, gender gaps at least as large as those for the total population existed for all the variables except welfare spending among antifeminist women and men. Thus, the antifeminist women were clearly pulled in a more liberal direction, presumably by their compassion for the less fortunate or by their own self-interest. Both these factors, in fact, appear to be in operation.

As predicted by the "compassion" perspective, the gender gap on all these variables except welfare spending was much greater for conservatives than for liberals and for college-educated people than for grade school-educated ones, although the expected larger gender gaps for high-income people and Republicans exist for only about half the items. Thus, the social compassion often attributed to women evidently exists in several of the subgroups where it was predicted, thus providing much stronger support for this perspective than could be derived from the simple gender gap between all men and all women.

There is some evidence that this compassion is more the result of counter-socialization than a basic value held by most women. First, the gender gap varies greatly among subpopulations, unlike the relatively constant gaps for changing morals and militarism. Second, women with high education (an agent of counter-socialization) are considerably more likely than comparable men to be liberal on these issues, while the relationship is much more mixed for income (not necessarily an agent of socialization by itself). Similarly, much more compassion can be seen among conservatives than Republicans, probably because the latter are inhibited from taking "atypical" positions by their party loyalties. Third and probably most convincing, comparing the gender gap between generations provides results that are totally consistent with the countersocialization perspective. That is, the gender gap is substantially wider among those under age thirty-five than among those over fifty-five for all seven items. Thus, the less constrained and patriarchal atmosphere of the last several decades has evidently provided countersocialization, making the younger generation of educated women significantly more liberal than younger males.

Several indicators of poorer women's awareness of and self-interest in their "cost bearing" can be discerned as well. First, this situation would probably create a narrowing of the gender gap among low-SES groups. As expected, the gender gaps for African-Americans and for those who had not received a high school degree were significantly lower than for the general population with the exception of the low-education gender gap for welfare spending (which, as argued next, can be explained in self-interest terms too). The support for this perspective is far from complete, however, because some categories of low income conform to it and others do not. This is a telling omission because income should, a priori, be the variable most subject to this effect.

A self-interest explanation also suggests itself for the unique pattern of the gender gap among subgroups for views on welfare spending. Here, the normal pattern of large differences between the sexes in high-SES groups and small ones in low-SES groups is completely reversed. There is little difference in support for welfare between either wealthy or well-educated men and women. Rather, among those with less than a high school degree or with a family income under $15,000, women were substantially more supportive of welfare by margins of about 15 percentage points. Probably, this reflects the reality that women are the direct recipients of most of America's welfare programs.

The gender gap, therefore, is not a constant among all subgroups of Americans. Rather, it varies substantially among different groups, with quite different patterns emerging for specific issues. Women's issues, traditional values, and militarism evoke a cross-cutting set of cleavages resulting from an interaction among feminist gender consciousness, the culture wars between traditional women and feminists, and countersocialization promoting nontraditional views. In contrast, economic issues reflect a more consistent fit between the compassion of the more fortunate and the self-interest of the less fortunate, with countersocialization again seemingly playing a significant role in who becomes compassionate. To evaluate whether this complex structure of attitudes and values is pushing women apart or together, though, it would be very valuable to examine what these different groups of women believe on specific issues—which is, thus, the subject of our third section.

WOMEN'S VALUES AND POLICY POSITIONS: CLASHING OR CONVERGENT?

A fundamental question for understanding the future dynamics of the gender gap concerns whether the culture wars between traditional women and feminists are breaking women apart as a distinct interest group or whether compassion, self-interest to reduce cost bearing, and countersocialization are bringing women together. One method for assessing this is to examine how these subgroups of women differ or are similar on various sets of issues. If traditional women and feminists are fixed in solid opposition on a wide range of cultural and economic issues, the gender gap will probably decline over time. If these issues create cross-cutting cleavages and overlapping groups, however, the right leadership of the women's movement (or even the drift of domestic politics) could bring the convergence rather than the clash of women's interests, which, in turn, would probably widen the gender gap and promote the increased representation of women among America's political leadership.

Thus, we examined how different or similar the views of the various subgroups of women were for seven items representing the cultural and economic issues treated in the past section. We included attitudes about the women's movement, abortion, gay adoptions, and family values as a group of cultural issues that will probably be central in determining whether women's interests clash or converge. In addition, attitudes about increasing government services and increasing federal spending for the poor and for child care were used as indicators of bread-and-butter issues.

Table 9 shows that both cultural and economic issues evoked considerable and consistent partisan and ideological divisions among women. Liberals were more supportive than conservatives of the liberal position on each of these seven

Table 9   Comparison of Attitudes among Ideological and Partisan Subgroups of Women

	Like Women's Movement	Pro-Choice	Gay Adoption	Family Values Very Important	More Government Services	More Child Care Spending	More Poor Spending
All Women	49%	46%	30%	48%	42%	54%	61%
Liberals	63%	70%	54%	31%	53%	66%	63%
Conservatives	29%	35%	17%	57%	26%	35%	38%
Democrats	50%	51%	34%	41%	44%	58%	65%
Republicans	27%	38%	17%	56%	21%	34%	32%

Source: Computed from data from the 1992 National Election Study of the Survey Research Center, distributed by the Interuniversity Consortium for Political and Social Research. Reprinted with permission.

issues by margins of two to one or higher. Strong differences also existed between Democrats and Republicans, although they were not quite as great as for ideology. Women, then, appear to be divided into fairly consistent ideological and partisan groups.

While there may be a stable ideological and partisan division among women, there do appear to be alternative routes to their liberal and conservative positions, as indicated by the breakdowns for these attitudes by SES categories. As discussed in the last section, the patterns of how the gender gap varied among SES categories implied that high SES for women is associated with conservative attitudes on economic issues but with liberal attitudes on cultural and moral ones; the data in Table 10 confirm this. For economic issues, the rich and the well educated were generally more conservative than were women with lower SES (the high support of college-educated women for child care forms the sole exception), while African-American women were quite liberal on bread-and-butter issues. Conversely, those with high SES as defined by education and income were more liberal than other women on abortion, gay adoptions, and family values.

The nature and extent of these relationships, however, suggest that issue divisions among American women may be somewhat fluid. First, because different types of people are pushed in conservative and liberal directions by cultural issues, on the one hand, and economic issues, on the other, many women are undoubtedly cross-pressured and, thus, more open to reexamining their loyalties than might otherwise be the case. For example, the difference in opinion between women with high or low education or with high or low family income is no greater than the difference generated by the generational division between those under age thirty-five and those over fifty-five. Second, since the younger generation was more liberal on all these issues, unlike the flip-flop for SES, the interacting effects of age and SES almost certainly create ideological cross-pressures as well. Finally, African-American and poor women were much more liberal in their views of the women's movement than they were on the other three cultural issues. This suggests that many women facing financial hardships, whether personally feminists or not, appreciate the role of the women's movement in promoting more economic opportunities for them.

Table 10   Comparison of Attitudes among SES Subgroups of Women

	Like Women's Movement	Pro-Choice	Gay Adoption	Family Values Very Important	More Government Services	More Child Care Spending	More Poor Spending
All women	49%	46%	30%	48%	42%	54%	61%
Under 35	54%	50%	34%	35%	51%	71%	63%
Over 55	43%	40%	17%	61%	30%	39%	57%
Less than high school degree	53%	21%	14%	54%	52%	51%	74%
College	58%	67%	40%	41%	38%	61%	48%
Family income under $15,000	50%	36%	24%	48%	47%	58%	68%
Family income over $50,000	41%	57%	33%	46%	28%	47%	42%
African-American	67%	44%	28%	44%	63%	71%	78%

Source: Computed from data from the 1992 National Election Study of the Survey Research Center, distributed by the Interuniversity Consortium for Political and Social Research. Reprinted with permission.

The key to whether or not women will coalesce probably lies in the seeming culture war between feminists and antifeminists. In 1992 at least, the two sides were fairly evenly balanced, although the profeminists had a slight numerical lead (31.4 percent to 27.4 percent in the National Election Survey). However, the largest number of women (41.2 percent) did not appear fully committed to either side, as they gave feminists scores of between 40 and 60 on a 0 to 100-point scale; they are the ones whose views will determine the magnitude of the gender gap for the next few years. Thus, we included this middle category of "neutral" in Table 11. We also included data on two groups widely assumed to be antifeminists (homemakers and those who had positive feelings toward fundamentalists) for comparative purposes.

The division between feminists and antifeminists on the women's movement is stark; 88 percent of the former had warm feelings toward it, compared with a mere 14 percent of the latter. While the division is not quite so spectacular, a strong and consistent issue cleavage exists between the two groups on all these issues, with the feminists invariably taking the liberal and the antifeminists the conservative side on both cultural and economic issues. Thus, there would appear to be little hope of ameliorating this conflict, especially given the size (slightly over a quarter of all American women) of the two groups. A somewhat different picture emerges when one considers the plurality (42 percent) of women in the middle. On most of these issues, including the divisive one of abortion, they were slightly liberal and significantly closer to the feminists than to the antifeminists (the two ex-

Table 11 Comparison of Attitudes among Profeminist and Antifeminist Women

	Like Women's Movement	Pro-Choice	Gay Adoption	Family Values Very Important	More Government Services	More Child Care Spending	More Poor Spending
All women	49%	46%	30%	48%	42%	54%	61%
Position on feminism							
Profeminist	88%	59%	48%	45%	48%	69%	69%
Neutral	40%	49%	28%	44%	42%	57%	64%
Antifeminist	14%	32%	16%	58%	32%	43%	40%
Presumed antifeminists							
Homemaker	49%	39%	22%	57%	40%	52%	61%
Like funda-mentalists	57%	26%	16%	63%	35%	54%	60%

Source: Computed from data from the 1992 National Election Study of the Survey Research Center, distributed by the Interuniversity Consortium for Political and Social Research. Reprinted with permission.

ceptions are gay adoptions and, to a lesser extent, the women's movement). Thus, there is at least some chance that their position could become a moderately feminist commonality that would represent the large majority of women.

This possibility is enhanced when the positions of two groups of presumed opponents of feminism are taken into account. First, being a homemaker no longer seems to reinforce traditional socialization except in a couple of areas which are closely linked to include a homemaker's social status and self-respect. Yet, in 1992 they were only moderately conservative on cultural issues and, surprisingly, almost approximated the average woman in their support of bread-and-butter issues. In sum, they were not too far away from the views of the "moderates" in the culture war battles. Moreover, the beliefs of the profundamentalists were not as contrary to feminist issue positions as is normally assumed. Certainly, women with positive views of fundamentalists were, as expected, quite conservative in terms of abortion and gay adoptions. Yet many of their views were far from stereotypical as well. They were actually liberal in having a moderately positive view of the women's movement; and their positions on economic issues were quite similar to those of the homemakers.

These perhaps surprising findings about the attitudes of homemakers and profundamentalist women have two important implications. First, being a homemaker no longer seems to reinforce traditional socialization except in a couple of areas closely linked a homemaker's social status and self-respect. Second, given the comparatively low SES of many fundamentalists (e.g., 31 percent of women who liked fundamentalists had a grade school education or less, more than double the 14 percent of those who did not), their moderate stance on many issues may reflect an awareness of vulnerability, which, in turn, makes them sensitive to the potential benefits of government assistance and organizing self-help groups.

CONCLUSIONS

The gender gap, therefore, does not appear to have been created by a monolithic group of women, either feminist or otherwise, with a wide range of similar issue positions. Rather, it is the cumulative result of a set of overlapping concerns. Several such chains of overlapping agreement can be discerned. For example, women of color and women in blue- and pink-collar occupations share common interests on and support for economic policies and welfare issues. While not as overwhelmingly liberal, perhaps, feminists are quite supportive of these issues due to their gender ideology. More surprisingly, the perspectives of homemakers and even fundamentalist women differ in degree, rather than representing strong conservative opposition. Conversely, in regard to cultural issues, feminists find more agreement from younger and more highly educated women, whether feminist or not, reflecting the prevalent mechanisms of countersocialization in the United States today. Given this complex set of interests and groups among women, the splintering of women into warring camps over cultural (or any other) issues is certainly not foreordained. In fact, the surging gender gap before the 1994 elections, despite the fact that it was caused primarily by men defecting from the Democrats,[22] suggests that such coalescence may be coming to the fore in American politics.

NOTES

1. Mary E. Bendyna and Celinda C. Lake, "Gender and Voting in the 1992 Presidential Election," in Elizabeth Adell Cook, Sue Thomas, and Clyde Wilcox (Eds.), *The Year of the Woman: Myths and Realities.* (Boulder, CO: Westview, 1994), pp. 237–254; Cal Clark and Janet Clark, "The Impact of Gender on Presidential Voting in 1992: Disappearing or Realigning?" paper presented at the 1994 Annual Meeting of the American Political Science Association, New York.

2. Elizabeth Adell Cook, Sue Thomas, and Clyde Wilcox (Eds.), *The Year of the Woman: Myths and Realities* (Boulder, CO: Westview, 1994).

3. Sandra Baxter and Marjorie Lansing, *Women and Politics: The Invisible Majority* (Ann Arbor: University of Michigan Press, 1980); Janet Clark and Cal Clark, "The Gender Gap 1988: Compassion, Pacifism, and Indirect Feminism," in Lois Lovelace Duke (Ed.), *Women in Politics: Outsiders or Insiders?* (Englewood Cliffs, NJ: Prentice-Hall, 1993), pp. 32–45; Clark and Clark, "The Impact of Gender on Presidential Voting"; Henry C. Kenski, "The Gender Factor in a Changing Electorate," in Carol M. Mueller (Ed.), *The Politics of the Gender Gap: The Social Construction of Political Influence* (Beverly Hills, CA: Sage, 1988), pp. 38–60; Ethel Klein, *Gender Politics: From Consciousness to Mass Politics* (Cambridge, MA: Harvard University Press, 1984); Keith T. Poole and L. Harmon Zeigler, *Women, Public Opinion, and Politics: The Changing Political Attitudes of American Women* (New York: Longman, 1985); Emily Stoper, "The Gen-

der Gap Concealed and Revealed: 1936–1984," *Journal of Political Science* 17 (1 & 2) (Spring 1989), pp. 50–62.

4. Baxter and Lansing, *Women and Politics*; Susan J Carroll, "Women's Autonomy and the Gender Gap: 1980 and 1982," in Carol M. Mueller (Ed.), *The Politics of the Gender Gap: The Social Construction of Political Influence* (Beverly Hills, CA: Sage, 1988), pp. 236–257; R. Darcy, Susan Welch, and Janet Clark, *Women, Elections, and Representation* (Lincoln: University of Nebraska Press, 1994); Diane Fowlkes, "Developing a Theory of Countersocialization: Gender, Race, and Politics in the Lives of Women Activists," *Micropolitics* 3 (2) (1983), pp. 181–225; Carol Gilligan, *In a Different Voice: Psychological Theory and Women's Development* (Cambridge, MA: Harvard University Press, 1982); Klein, *Gender Politics*; Carol M. Mueller (Ed.), *The Politics of the Gender Gap: The Social Construction of Political Influence* (Beverly Hills, CA: Sage, 1988); Virginia Sapiro, *The Political Integration of Women: Roles, Socialization, and Politics* (Urbana: University of Illinois Press, 1983); Barbara Deckard Sinclair, *The Women's Movement: Political, Socioeconomic, and Psychological Issues*, 3rd ed. (New York: Harper and Row, 1983).

5. Carroll, "Women's Autonomy"; Pamela Johnston Conover, "Feminists and the Gender Gap," *Journal of Politics* 50 (4) (November 1988), pp. 985–1010; Pamela Johnston Conover and Virginia Sapiro, "Gender, Feminist Consciousness, and the 1992 Election," paper presented at the 1993 Annual Meeting of the American Po-

litical Science Association, Washington, DC; Klein, *Gender Politics*; Sue Tolleson Rinehart, *Gender Consciousness and Politics* (New York: Routledge, 1992).

6. Gerald Pomper, "The Presidential Election," in Gerald M. Pomper, F. Christopher Arterton, Ross K. Baker, Walter Dean Burnham, Kathleen A. Frankovic, Marjorie Randon Hershey, and Wilson Carey McWilliams (Eds.), *The Election of 1992: Reports and Interpretations* (Chatham, NJ: Chatham House, 1993), pp. 132–156.

7. Bendyna and Lake, "Gender and Voting"; Pomper, "The Presidential Election."

8. Clark and Clark, "The Impact of Gender on Presidential Voting."

9. David O. Sears and Leonie Huddie, "On the Origins of Political Disunity among Women," in Louise A. Tilly and Patricia Gurin (Eds.), *Women, Politics, and Change* (New York: Russell Sage, 1990), pp. 249–277; Robert Y. Shapiro and Harpreet Mahajan, "Gender Differences in Policy Preferences: A Summary of Trends from the 1960s to the 1980s," *Public Opinion Quarterly* 50 (1) (Spring 1986), pp. 42–61.

10. William Mayer, *The Changing American Mind: How and Why American Public Opinion Changed between 1960 and 1988* (Ann Arbor: University of Michigan Press, 1992).

11. Shapiro and Mahajan, "Gender Differences in Policy Preferences."

12. For similar findings concerning militarism, see Cal Clark and Janet Clark, "Wyoming Women's Attitudes towards the MX: The 'Old' v. 'New' Gender Gap," *Journal of Political Science* 17 (1–2) (Spring 1989), pp. 127–140.

13. Clark and Clark, in "The Impact of Gender on Presidential Voting," provide much more detailed statistical analysis demonstrating this.

14. Clark and Clark, "The Impact of Gender on Presidential Voting"; Shapiro and Mahajan, "Gender Differences in Policy Preferences."

15. Steven P. Erie and Martin Rein, "Women and the Welfare State," in Carol M. Mueller (Ed.), *The Politics of the Gender Gap: The Social Construction of Political Influence* (Beverly Hills, CA: Sage, 1988), pp. 273–291.

16. Ronald Brownstein, "Republican Surge? It's a Guy Thing," *Birmingham News*, October 29, 1994, pp. 1A, 10A.

17. Carroll, "Women's Autonomy"; Conover and Sapiro, "Gender, Feminist Consciousness, and the 1992 Election;" Klein, *Gender Politics*; Rinehart, *Gender Consciousness*.

18. Fowlkes, "Countersocialization"; Sapiro, *Political Integration of Women*.

19. Clark and Clark, "The Gender Gap 1988"; Shapiro and Mahajan, "Gender Differences in Policy Preferences."

20. Clark and Clark, "The Impact of Gender on Presidential Voting."

21. Stoper, "The Gender Gap Concealed and Revealed."

22. Brownstein, "Republican Surge?"

FURTHER READINGS

Baxter, Sandra, and Marjorie Lansing. *Women and Politics: The Invisible Majority*. Ann Arbor: University of Michigan Press, 1980.

Bendyna, Mary E., and Celinda C. Lake. "Gender and Voting in the 1992 Presidential Election." In Elizabeth Adell Cook, Sue Thomas, and Clyde Wilcox, (Eds.), *The Year of the Woman: Myths and Realities*, pp. 237–254. Boulder, CO: Westview, 1994.

Conover, Pamela Johnston. "Feminists and the Gender Gap." *Journal of Politics* 50 (4) (November 1988), pp. 985–1010.

Darcy, R., Susan Welch, and Janet Clark. *Women, Elections, and Representation*. Lincoln: University of Nebraska Press, 1994.

Gilligan, Carol. *In a Different Voice: Psychological Theory and Women's Development*. Cambridge, MA: Harvard University Press, 1982.

Klein, Ethel. *Gender Politics: From Consciousness to Mass Politics*. Cambridge, MA: Harvard University Press, 1984.

Mueller, Carol M. (Ed.). *The Politics of the Gender Gap: The Social Construction of Political Influence*. Beverly Hills, CA: Sage, 1988.

Poole, Keith T., and L. Harmon Zeigler. *Women, Public Opinion, and Politics: The Changing Political Attitudes of American Women*. New York: Longman, 1985.

Rinehart, Sue Tolleson. *Gender Consciousness and Politics*. New York: Routledge, 1992.

Sapiro, Virginia. *The Political Integration of Women: Roles, Socialization, and Politics*. Urbana: University of Illinois Press, 1983.

Shapiro, Robert Y., and Harpreet Mahajan. "Gender Differences in Policy Preferences: A Summary of Trends from the 1960s to the 1980s." *Public Opinion Quarterly* 50 (1) (Spring 1986), pp. 42–61.

Stoper, Emily. "The Gender Gap Concealed and Revealed: 1936–1984." *Journal of Political Science* 17 (1 & 2) (Spring 1989), pp. 50–62.

 CHAPTER 3

WOMEN AND ELECTIONS: THE UPHILL STRUGGLE

Many scholars considered the post–World War II era a quiescent time for white, middle-class American women. After a period of wartime involvement, women supposedly retreated into a more traditional lifestyle. Between 1946 and 1968, however, almost one hundred women entered legislatures in the South, a particularly traditional region. Data indicate that they were predominantly women who were already involved in the public sphere in one or more ways. Even though many were serious legislators, the press emphasized their domesticity and femininity instead of their legislative achievements. Joanne V. Hawks and Carolyn Ellis Staton critique this period of transition—and reflect on the political environment for these Southern women.

We then move from the late 1960s to a study using data from a 1991 "Form of Government" survey conducted by the international City/County Management Association (ICMA). Susan A. MacManus and Charles S. Bullock III examine the reasons for a marked increase in the numbers of women elected to mayoral and city council positions in U.S. municipalities over the past decade. Testing the desirability hypothesis, which suggests that women will most frequently serve as mayors or council members when the post is least attractive, their findings show (1) women more frequently serve on councils than as mayors, (2) women mayors are more likely to be found among the ranks of those for whom the post is part-time, (3) women mayors more often serve in mayor–council arrangements and when the mayor is elected directly by the voters, and (4) in general, the overall explanatory power of the desirability thesis is rather weak. The authors conclude that formal structural measures of office desirability do not account for very much of the variation in the gender makeup of U.S. mayoral and city council posts. Let us next consider these aspects of women and elections.

On the Eve of Transition: Women in Southern Legislatures, 1946–1968

Joanne V. Hawks
Carolyn Ellis Staton

This study focuses on women who served in southern legislatures in the period following World War II, beginning with the election of 1946 and culminating in 1968. During this period—especially in the earlier years—middle-class women received many signals that their proper sphere encompassed home, family, and related activities. The willingness of women to enter the legislature against society's traditional expectations of them may have been a mild form of rebellion, but it was nonetheless real. To some extent the women serving between 1946 and 1968 were transitional figures, standing between an earlier group of legislative women whose mere presence made them important and a later group of more activist women. They set the stage for the political women of the 1970s and 1980s, the activist women who benefited directly or indirectly from the women's movement.

The postwar legislators followed a group of trailblazers, women who had emerged from the suffrage movement with new rights and imperatives. These earlier women had begun moving into southern legislatures in a slow but steady stream in the decade of the 1920s.[1] Most were short-term legislators; few served more than one or two terms. For the most part, they could be characterized as southern progressives, people who wanted to use state government as a means of

Joanne V. Hawks, Director of Sarah Isom Center for Women's Studies, University of Mississippi teaches courses on the history of Southern and American women and the role of women in society. Carolyn Ellis Staton is acting vice chancellor for academic affairs and professor of law at the University of Mississippi School of Law.

Part of the research for this paper was supported by a Basic Research Grant from the National Endowment for the Humanities.

ameliorating conditions in their communities.[2] Many of them were especially concerned with the needs of women, children, and persons with mental, physical, and moral handicaps. Even though much of their proposed legislation did not pass, they brought certain needs into focus as matters of public concern. Just as importantly, they established the right and ability of women to serve competently as state legislators.

In the Great Depression and World War II years, a slightly larger group of women were elected. By 1936 all eleven of the former Confederate states had female as well as male legislators.

After a period of wartime involvement in paid employment or volunteer services, many women in the late 1940s and early 1950s supposedly retreated into a more traditional lifestyle.[3] According to many historical and sociological treatises, the post–World War II era was a quiescent time for U.S. women, especially middle-class white women. Andrew Sinclair has called the postwar attitude New Victorianism because of its emphasis on sharp distinctions between male and female roles and proper behavior by women.[4] The prescription for the times called upon women to immerse themselves in private concerns surrounding their families and homes and to surrender activity in the public realm to the returning veterans.

In light of these generally observed patterns, it is interesting to consider the movement of women into southern legislatures in the years following the war. In a region of the nation considered to be particularly traditional, where proper sex roles had been carefully defined and political participation had long been regarded as a white male preserve, women began entering southern legislatures in increasing numbers. Although the incidence varied from a low of one person in Alabama to a high of nineteen in the neighboring state of Mississippi, a total of ninety-three women were seated in the legislatures of the eleven former Confederate states between 1946 and 1968.

HOW WOMEN ENTERED THE LEGISLATURE

One means by which women entered legislatures was what has been termed "the widow's route," a method whereby a wife succeeded to a seat formerly held by her deceased husband. During this period, twenty-four women from the eleven states in this study entered via succession. Twenty-one were widows elected or appointed to complete their husbands' legislative terms. Two were wives who ran when their husbands resigned before their terms were completed. One, Maud Isaacks, was a daughter who succeeded her father. Most were elected to office, although a few were appointed. Of the entire group of successors, only Maud Isaacks of Texas served for an extended period of time.[5] Most finished the husband's unexpired term and then retired from office. A few ran for reelection, but most of those who were reelected served only one additional term before retiring or being defeated. Their positions seemed to be regarded by many voters as a gesture of courtesy. For instance, when Governor Earl Long of Louisiana appointed Mrs. E. D.

Gleason to complete her husband's term, he expressed doubt about his authority to make the appointment, but he assured his audience that she was a nice lady and had promised not to run again.[6]

Thus, approximately 25.5 percent of the total group of women serving between 1946 and 1968 were "fill-ins" for seats that were deemed to "belong" to their predecessors. But what of the remaining 74.5 percent? Who were they, and what motivated them to seek office?

Data indicated that they were predominantly women who were already involved in the public sphere in one way or another, as professional or business women, local officeholders, political party workers, or active members of women's organizations. Fifty-four had a profession or business in which they were contemporaneously engaged or which they had previously practiced. By far the largest single group—twenty women—were teachers. Nine women were attorneys. Ten were owners or co-owners of businesses. Two were farmers, two journalists, two physicians, and two government workers. The remainder held various other positions in the business world.

At least six women had held local political office before running for the legislature, most of them as city or county council members. Even more had served on local and state executive committees of their party, worked with the women's division, or helped in the campaigns of others before seeking office themselves. Of the nine Republican women elected during this period, most had been heavily involved in Republican party politics and were committed to strengthening two-party politics in their states. Several of the women were from political families.

In addition to these two groups—professional and business women and those with political activity of one kind or another—most of the other women were involved significantly in one or more women's organizations. At least two women became interested in politics as a result of their participation in Parent–Teacher Associations (PTAs). Other women were involved in Federated Women's Clubs, Business and Professional Women, the League of Women Voters, the American Association of University Women, the Farm Bureau (or related Home Demonstration groups), garden clubs, and other groups. Through these organizations they became aware of issues and gained a sense of how to accomplish things through their club work. In many cases, their legislative interests mirrored the concerns of the organized groups in which they had worked or held leadership positions. Maxine Baker of Florida (1963–1973) said, "I wanted to serve in the Legislature to try to accomplish some of the things I had been working for during my years as member and President of the Florida League of Women Voters. . . ."[7] Others, like Carolyn Frederick of South Carolina (1964–1976), a member of the American Association of University Women, had lobbied legislators in behalf of interests supported by their organizations, only to find that legislators tended to be longer on promises than on favorable action. Kathryn Stone of Virginia (1954–1966), a national vice president of the League of Women Voters, admonished women to join service and civic organizations to learn skills and to move on to the political arena from there.[8] She believed that women should not confine themselves to any one civic group but should become involved in party politics.[9]

Stone's comments were closely echoed by Grace Hamilton of Georgia:

> If you are concerned about working in the legislative branch of government, you had better get some experience in working other than in the legislature on the matters that concern you. . . . If you look at people who have been effective legislators, they usually have been effective in something that was non-political, related to issues before them. I personally think that the League of Women Voters is a good training, very good training to have, but I think sometimes you need to graduate from the League.[10]

Some of the women worked primarily with one particular organization; many were active in several and held membership in many more. At least eighteen women appeared to be heavily involved in club work. A few of these could also be grouped with one or both of the categories previously discussed. In fact, women who had several connections with the public sphere seemed to be especially likely at some point to consider public office.

LEGISLATIVE ISSUES

A survey of the issues in which the female legislators expressed interest leads to rather predictable findings. Many issues came readily to their attention as mothers and community volunteers. Education was a key interest, with many in favor of strengthening the public schools, providing child care and kindergartens, and raising teachers' pay. Other concerns included health, mental health, aid to the handicapped, problems of children and youth, care of the aged, alcohol and drug abuse, consumer and environmental protection, and election reform. Rural legislators often focused on agricultural problems while those elected from urban districts concentrated their efforts on urban problems, including the need for adequate representation in the legislature and better services in their areas.

A few of the women expressed concern for the so-called women's issues of the day. Jury service for women appeared to be the most generally supported proposal. A federal equal rights amendment was a more problematic issue. The few who were outspoken supporters of equal rights for women were balanced by a similar number who opposed the concept. Many women preferred to equivocate or to avoid the issue altogether.

Middle-class, mature women, long trained to be conciliatory persons—peacemakers—often seemed reluctant to take on highly controversial issues. In a period when civil rights, women's rights, youth protest, and antiwar and antiestablishment issues were eroding society's postwar complacency, most of the southern legislative women avoided identification with any of these divisive movements. They concentrated instead on gradual elimination of community problems and provision of government services to segments of the society who had unmet needs.

Civil Rights Issues

Of all the contemporary issues, the civil rights issue struck nearest to home. Clearly, the easiest way to deal with the problems of the day was to ignore them, and it is amazing how many of the legislators during this period managed to do just that. But for others the issues had to be confronted, and women, like their male counterparts, lined up on both sides of the civil rights question.

In Virginia, in particular, women could not avoid the issue. In the aftermath of the United States Supreme Court's decision in *Brown v. Board of Education*, Virginia almost immediately sought to forestall school integration by a number of measures, some as extreme as closing whole school systems. One is struck by the courage of the moderates and liberals during this time in Virginia politics. Most of the women legislators favored compliance with the law and opposed massive resistance. The usually ultrachivalrous male-dominated assembly proved that it had its raw side; it could behave rudely toward them when they tried to keep the Virginia schools open.[11]

Although most of the Virginia women delegates supported compliance, such was not the case everywhere. In Mississippi, for instance, just the opposite situation prevailed. The segregation establishment reigned supreme. As Jack Bass and Walter DeVries have stated,

> These were not ordinary times. The executive director of the Citizens Council . . . had begun preparing [Governor] Barnett's speeches. Citizens Council members were named to the State Sovereignty Commission, the official state segregation committee and a propaganda arm of the Citizens Council. . . . The Citizens Council claimed 80,000 members in the state. . . .[12]

The female legislators seemed to oppose attempts to integrate the schools as stridently as most of the male delegates. At least two women were part of the segregation establishment, the White Citizens Council and the State Sovereignty Commission. Occasionally, a legislator who proclaimed that she was a segregationist would, however, champion the rights of others. A notable example occurred in Mississippi when Senator Orene Farese argued vehemently against passage of a bill that would have eliminated the property tax exemption for churches that used their facilities on an integrated basis.[13]

Because of these stands, Farese felt compelled in her next senatorial campaign to proclaim staunchly her segregationist views. In her campaign literature she maintained that her purpose in opposing the removal of tax exemptions for integrated churches was to keep segregation intact and preserve tax exemptions for churches.[14] Perhaps, like many other politicians of the day, Farese maintained a certain facade of segregation that did not always conform to other ideas that she held.

By 1967, the civil rights movement had begun to have a significant impact on portions of the South, legislative resistance notwithstanding. Because of the movement and *Baker v. Carr*, the United States Supreme Court decision that mandated "one man, one vote," legislative redistricting was required. One result of redistricting was to increase voting strength in urban areas—places where there might be a large population of Blacks. It is not surprising, then, that in 1967 three Black women in the South entered their state legislatures: Barbara Jordan of Texas, Dorothy Brown of Tennessee, and Grace Hamilton of Georgia. The civil rights movement, by changing both the social climate and the laws, gave them opportunities for political office that they had previously lacked.

PRESS IMAGES

The times were changing, but the public's image of women in politics was not changing at the same pace. This was best indicated by contemporary press coverage, which emphasized femininity. The renewed emphasis on femininity may have been a result of a covert campaign to force women out of the traditionally male jobs that many had held during the war years. It may also have been an effort to glamorize the homemaker so that she, as consumer, might aid in the improving economy. Moreover, as the country recovered from the difficult war period, some people longed to return to a less confused, less complicated world.

In the postwar period, press treatment of female legislators primarily covered personal rather than political aspects of their lives. Articles on these women tended to focus on specific female roles. A prevalent form of feature article was the portrait of the lady legislator as family member, either wife, mother, homemaker, or grandmother. Orene Farese, who served along with her husband in the Mississippi legislature during the 1950s, was consistently spotlighted in her domestic roles. The following excerpt from a feature story about her is characteristic of the coverage she received:

> Mrs. Farese, though public minded, is a very domestic and home loving person. . . .
> She is a capable housekeeper and a wonderful homemaker. With the help of a full time maid she cares for their four bedroom, two bathroom home. . . . [15]

Farese discussed her cooking, sewing, and home decorating abilities.[16] The article proceeded to describe her to the readers:

> When you see this lovely senator-elect . . . she will most likely be wearing a stunning tailored dress or suit in one of her favorite colors, the blues, aqua or yellow in medium tone.[17]

The newspaper account contained virtually no mention of Farese's legislative and political interests. She was treated primarily as a housewife who went to the legislature.

A somewhat more muted example of the lady legislator as homemaker occurred with Grace Rodenbough of North Carolina. Although Rodenbough, who served in the legislature from 1953 to 1966, was a woman of considerable stature, the press on several different occasions focused on her fondness for her antebellum home.[18] Rodenbough might play a significant role in the legislature, but she was still seen as the southern aristocratic lady.

Rodenbough's fellow North Carolinian, Mary Faye Brumby, was subjected to similar treatment. When Brumby went to the legislature, she took her eleven-year-old son along. Her child care arrangements were highlighted in the press.[19] By taking her son with her to the capital rather than leaving him at home, she avoided being seen as the abandoning mother who pursued her own interests.

Although some accounts were brief in their mention of the legislators' children, comment was usually made. For instance, Iris Blitch of Georgia, who later went to Congress, was simply described as devoted to her children.[20]

The epitome of the legislator-as-wife stories involves Lillian Neblett Scott of Tennessee. Scott, always referred to as Mrs. Scott, was being routinely interviewed by a reporter from the Nashville *Banner* when her husband entered the room. The spotlight of the article immediately became *Mr.* Scott and his stories of marital harmony: "Somebody asked me how I made out with Lillian so active in politics, I just tole 'em that I still have my hot biscuits 365 days a year."[21] Scott continued his antics: "As the couple exchanged a look of deep affection and long understanding, 'I've never had to spank her.' "[22] Throughout the article, Lillian Scott is seen not as the incredibly active woman she was, but as a wife who knew her place. As is true of all of these features, there is an implicit statement that these women legislators were all right because, first and foremost, their principal roles were as wives and mothers.

Domesticity, Femininity, and Beauty

When they were viewed primarily as domestic creatures, female legislators lost their "strangeness." The same principle applied if the emphasis was on their femininity rather than their domesticity. Moreover, by their being pigeonholed as either a domestic or a feminine type, these women, working in a nontraditional forum, threatened no one. For example, articles such as the following 1954 feature in the *Jackson Daily News* made the idea of female legislators more palatable to the public:

> The universal feminine preoccupation with weddings, babies, and bringing up children reaches strongly into the Mississippi legislature. . . .
>   Far from being a sentimental interest, confined to cooing over the newlywedded or recently born, theirs is an informed concern aimed at changes in the laws. . . . [23]

The article went on to provide an apologia for these women:

> . . . it is, perhaps, to the state's advantage to number among its lawmakers those whose beliefs are conditioned by the previous primary experience of wife, mother, and frequently teacher.[24]

Since the days of Scarlett O'Hara, femininity and gracious beauty have been part of the mystique of southern womanhood. The beauty queen has been a consistent southern type, one with which southern society felt comfortable. In many instances, by emphasizing pulchritude, southern society was able to accept women on its own terms, and by doing so, could avoid accepting them as serious legislators. Ruth Williams of South Carolina was linked with "the rustle of silk and the faint scent of perfume" and managed "somehow, to cling to her femininity and still compete with men. . . ."[25]

Mary Shadow of Tennessee, like Williams, was young and single when she entered the legislature. Shadow, however, married during her legislative stint. News of the marriage was widely featured. Shadow, a college teacher, was quoted as saying that in her forthcoming marriage she wanted to cook, keep house, and raise a large family. One article was captioned "Miss Shadow Plans to Keep House, Raise Family."[26] Upon Shadow's marriage it was assumed that she would become a traditional housewife.

Because of the emphasis on femininity, there was a never-ending discussion of physical appearance. To some extent this focus suggested to the public that, after all, these female legislators were more female than legislator. Blitch was often described as "an attractive brunette"[27] with "a perfect size 12 figure."[28] Shadow was described as a "pretty, charming legislator";[29] and Betty Jane Long of Mississippi was depicted as "lovely."[30] Mississippi's Mary Lou Godbold and Orene Farese "add[ed] much to the lustre of [the legislature]. And the men [were] all in favor of the ladies."[31]

Kathryn Stone of Virginia, in particular, was the topic of much publicity about her physical appearance. The press found it noteworthy that one Virginia senator said to another upon seeing Stone presiding in the senate, " 'Have you ever seen a lovelier creature presiding from the chair of the president of the Senate?' whereupon the other senator then responded, 'I yield to the lovely creature. . . . ' "[32] On another occasion, the press claimed that "Mrs. Stone . . . is the prettiest thing to hit the General Assembly since Sarong Siren Dorothy Lamour dropped in at the Capitol one day a few years ago. Besides looks . . . she has brains."[33] Another feature described her clothing and home decor.[34] No matter how significant these women were as legislators and politicians, their colleagues and the press trivialized them in many instances by focusing on irrelevant considerations.

As if to stereotype them even further, the press played up the emotional nature of these women. Blitch is depicted as on the verge of tears when an adverse amendment was added to her original bill.[35] When Orene Farese opposed taxing churches that did not practice segregation, she was choked with tearful emotion.[36] Although the situation may have warranted tears, no comment is made in the coverage of the heated senate debate about the emotions of her male colleagues.

How Women Legislators Were Treated

During this period when there was an emphasis on the female attributes of the women politicians, several of them were singled out for what was then considered a chivalrous tribute. When only one woman served in a legislative body, she might be entitled sweetheart of the senate or house or some honorific variation. Blitch was named queen of the Georgia General Assembly,[37] Collins was elected sweetheart of the Alabama house,[38] and Berta Lee White of Mississippi was designated sweetheart of the senate.[39] In Collins's case, this meant that the house members might on occasion be addressed as "Mister Speaker, gentlemen of the House and sweetheart of the House."[40] In some instances the chivalry was rather overdone. For example, in making seat assignments at the beginning of the session, the speaker of the Georgia house announced that "the Lady of the House [Blitch] and the physically handicapped will get their first choice of seats."[41] Sometimes the chivalry became quite time-consuming. When the speaker of the Virginia house instructed Kathryn Stone, the sole female legislator, to make a communiqué to the senate, Stone was accompanied by the entire Virginia house delegation to the senate chambers. The newspaper described the event as a "chivalry safari."[42]

When the female legislators occasionally acted out of character from the role in which the public had cast them, it was definitely noted. Thus, when the women were perceived as politicians rather than as ladies, they were likened to males. For instance, the newspaper remarked that "Mrs. Blitch had to fight like a man."[43] Perhaps it was her ability to fight like a man that won Blitch the sobriquet "the wench from Clinch."[44] In Mississippi when three women were elected to the legislature in the same term, it was noted that they could fare well against strong male opposition.[45] The tenacity of Clara Collins was editorialized as "stubbornness, albeit justified."[46] It was with Martha Evans of North Carolina that the press had a field day. Practically every story about Evans mentioned that she was a redhead with a temper to match. For instance, in one article she was referred to as "a red-headed pepperpot."[47] Evans, who was held in a certain amount of esteem for her work, was excused by the press from stepping out of the traditional role of southern womanhood:

> In Raleigh she'll stand on her own small feet. . . . That's because she's always felt she is the equal of the male politician. And she's "been around," as the saying goes among office seekers.[48]

The women were newsworthy. When they conformed to the stereotyped version of southern womanhood, they were viewed as nonthreatening. When they did not conform to the standard image, the media nevertheless tried to force them into that mold. When they were not susceptible to being molded, they were excused, as was Evans, on the basis of being an "outsider." They were less novel than the women who preceded them in the earlier decades, but the public was still not quite comfortable with them and still regarded them as curiosities.

SUMMARY

Female legislators of the post–World War II era tried to live up to societal expectations of them as women while they practiced their political skills. For some, the substance of lawmaking was secondary to their role as lady legislator. For most, the legislature was not a stepping stone to greater political heights, but it was a forum for public service. By their service these women set the stage for the more activist, more ambitious, and more political women who succeeded them.

NOTES

1. Anne Firor Scott, *The Southern Lady: From Pedestal to Politics, 1830–1930* (Chicago: University of Chicago Press, 1970), pp. 186–211.

2. Dewey W. Grantham, *Southern Progressivism: The Reconciliation of Progress and Tradition* (Knoxville: University of Tennessee Press, 1983), pp. 410–422.

3. William H. Chafe, *The American Woman, Her Changing Social, Economic, and Political Roles, 1920–1970* (New York: Oxford University Press, 1972), pp. 176–178, 199–212. Chafe's bibliography includes many other treatises on the subject.

4. Andrew Sinclair, *The Emancipation of the American Woman* (New York: Harper & Row, 1965), pp. 354–367.

5. Mary Beth Rogers (Ed.), *Texas Women: A Celebration of History* (Austin: Texas Foundation for Women's Resources, 1981), p. 100.

6. Baton Rouge *State-Times*, August 5, 1959, Sec. A, p. 11.

7. Questionnaire completed by Maxine Baker, January 21, 1986, in possession of the authors.

8. Richmond *Times-Dispatch*, March 23, 1954.

9. Ibid.

10. Taped interview with Grace Hamilton, conducted by the authors, August 8, 1984, in possession of the authors.

11. See, e.g., Richmond *Times-Dispatch*, February 23, 1958.

12. Jack Bass and Walter DeVries, *The Transformation of Southern Politics: Social Change and Political Consequence since 1945* (New York: Basic Books, 1976), p. 196.

13. Unnamed, undated clipping in possession of the authors.

14. *The Southern Advocate*, July 23, 1959.

15. *Jackson Advertiser–TV News*, September 15, 1955, p. 6.

16. Ibid.

17. Ibid.

18. *The News and the Observer* (Raleigh), January 17, 1963, p. 8.

19. Unnamed clipping, February 14, 1965.

20. *Atlanta Constitution*, October 6, 1949, p. 26.

21. Nashville *Banner*, January 10, 1957, p. 8.

22. Ibid.

23. *Jackson Daily News*, January 24, 1954.

24. Ibid.

25. *The State* (Columbia), November 6, 1964, Sec. A, p. 1.

26. *The Nashville Tennessean*, November 19, 1950, Society Section, p. 1.

27. *Atlanta Constitution*, October 6, 1949, p. 27.

28. Ibid., October 24, 1954.

29. *The Nashville Tennessean*, January 7, 1948, p. 8.

30. *Jackson Daily News*, August 29, 1955, p. 2.

31. Unnamed clipping, January 12, 1958.

32. Richmond *Times-Dispatch*, March 15, 1954, p. 4.

33. Ibid., January 13, 1954, p. 16.

34. Ibid., November 11, 1953.

35. *Atlanta Constitution*, January 27, 1953, p. 1.

36. Jackson *Clarion-Ledger*, March 27, 1956, p. 1.

37. *Atlanta Constitution*, October 6, 1949, p. 26.

38. *Advertiser-Journal* (Montgomery), Alabama Sunday Magazine, August 16, 1965, p. 12.

39. Questionnaire completed by Berta Lee White, in possession of the authors.

40. *Advertiser-Journal* (Montgomery), Alabama Sunday Magazine, August 15, 1965, p. 12.

41. *Atlanta Constitution*, January 11, 1949, p. 1.

42. Richmond *News Leader*, March 9, 1954.

43. *Atlanta Constitution*, October 24, 1954.

44. Ibid., December 28, 1970.

45. *Jackson Daily News*, August 29, 1955, p. 2.

46. *Montgomery Advertiser*, August 13, 1967.

47. *Durham Morning Herald*, November 18, 1962, Sec. C, p. 9.

48. Ibid.

FURTHER READINGS

Baxter, Sandra, and Marjorie Lansing. *Women and Politics*. Rev. ed. Ann Arbor: University of Michigan Press, 1983.

Carroll, Susan J. *Women as Candidates in American Politics*. Bloomington: Indiana University Press, 1985.

Chafe, William H. *Paradox of Change: American Women in the Twentieth Century*. New York: Oxford University Press, 1991.

Diamond, Irene. *Sex Roles in the State House*. New Haven, CT: Yale University Press, 1977.

Dodson, Debra L., and Susan J. Carroll. *Reshaping the Agenda: Women in State Legislatures*. New Brunswick, NJ: Eagleton Institute of Politics, Rutgers, State University of New Jersey, 1991.

Fowlkes, Diane. *White Political Women: Paths from Privilege to Empowerment*. Knoxville: University of Tennessee Press, 1992.

Githens, Marianne, and Jewel L. Prestage (Eds). *A Portrait of Marginality: The Political Behavior of the American Woman*. New York: David McKay, 1977.

Jewel, Malcolm Edwin, and Marcia Lynn Whicker. "The Feminization of Leadership in State Legislatures." *Quarterly of American Political Science Association*, 26 (4) (December 1993), pp. 705–712.

Johnson, Louise B. *Women of the Louisiana Legislature.* Farmerville, LA: Greenbay Publishing, 1986.

Jones, Leslie Ellen. "The Relationship between Home Styles and Legislative Styles and Its Implication for Representation: A Comparison of Women and Men in a Southern State Legislature." Ph.D. diss., Georgia State University, 1990.

Kirkpatrick, Jeane J. *Political Woman.* New York: Basic Books, 1974.

Klein, Ethel. *Gender Politics.* Cambridge, MA: Harvard University Press, 1984.

Mandel, Ruth B. *In the Running: The New Woman Candidate.* Boston: Beacon Press, 1981.

Nelson, Albert J. *Emerging Influentials in State Legislatures: Women, Blacks, and Hispanics.* New York: Praeger, 1991.

Thomas, Sue. *How Women Legislate.* New York: Oxford University Press, 1994.

Second Best? Women Mayors and Council Members: A New Test of the Desirability Thesis

Susan A. MacManus
Charles S. Bullock III

Periodic national surveys by associations like the International City/County Management Association (ICMA) and the National League of Cities (NLC) have shown a marked increase in the number of women elected to mayoral and city council positions in U.S. municipalities over the past decade. While the proportion of women serving in these posts is still below their proportional makeup in the population, sharp gains by female office seekers bring up an old question: Are they most often winning in jurisdictions where the mayoral and council positions are less powerful and prestigious, or less desirable? In other words, are women winning offices in the 1990s capturing "second-best" positions?

Previous studies have concluded that "the higher the level of office and the more power the office has, the less likely a woman is to be elected, at least in most Western nations."[1] More desirable offices are those "with more 'perks,' permanence, and power."[2] In the past, support for the desirability thesis has been stronger in state and national legislative offices than at the local level. In the second edition of *Women, Elections, and Representation*, Darcy, Welch, and Clark conclude that "comparing city councils across the nation, it does not appear that there is much relationship between the desirability of council seats and the likelihood that women will be elected."[3] Highly desirable council posts are defined as those "that pay more, have longer terms, and are fewer in number."[4] However, their conclu-

Susan A. MacManus is a professor of public administration and political science in the Department of Government and International Affairs at the University of South Florida, Tampa. Charles S. Bullock III is the Richard B. Russell Professor of Political Science at the University of Georgia.

sion is based on a limited number of studies completed in the early 1980s.[5] Thus, we are interested in whether this conclusion still stands, especially when the scope of the inquiry is broadened to include mayoral positions.

THE STUDY

The data on which our study is based are from a 1991 "Form of Government" survey conducted by the International City/County Management Association. In October 1991, the ICMA mailed the survey to all U.S. municipalities with populations of 2,500 or more and to municipalities with populations under 2,500 that are recognized by ICMA as having the council–manager form of government or as providing for a professional manager. Municipalities that did not respond to the first survey received a second mailing in December 1991. Of the 7,141 municipalities surveyed, 4,967 (69.6 percent) responded.[6]

The 1991 ICMA survey generated information on the number of women holding mayoral and city council posts. For mayors, information was collected on their city's form of government. Data were also gathered on how each mayor is selected (by council or separately elected by the voters), the length of their term, the temporal nature of the job (full-time or part-time), whether they play both mayoral and council roles (served simultaneously on both), the extent of their council voting power (full voting member; only a tiebreaker; no vote at all), their veto power, and their ability to succeed themselves (limited or unlimited terms).

For council members, the ICMA collected data on their city's form of government, council salary, council size, term limits, type of council election system (at-large versus single-member district). In summary, the 1991 ICMA survey allows us to conduct a more extensive test of the desirability thesis using a considerably larger number of cities and a more expansive list of structural features perceived by some to be measures of the prestige and power of elective offices.

MAYORAL POSITIONS AND THE DESIRABILITY THESIS

What makes a strong or powerful mayor? Studies of *formal*[7] mayoral power generally measure the strength and prestige of the position in terms of selection (which is generally dictated by the form of government created by a city charter), term length, legislative powers (votes and vetoes), and the extent of administrative responsibilities (often indicated by whether mayors serve full- or part-time).[8] The strongest mayors are those who head cities with strong mayor–council forms of government, are separately elected by the voters, are unrestricted in how many terms they can serve, can vote on council matters, can veto council decisions, and have extensive full-time administrative responsibilities.

Form of Government

According to the ICMA *Municipal Year Book*, there are three *national* forms of city government (mayor–council, council–manager, and commission), and two *regional* forms of city government, found almost exclusively in New England communities (town meeting and representative town meeting). Looking first at the national forms, it is widely accepted that executive influence is greatest under the mayor–council form, most notably the strong mayor–council form. There are clear differences in mayoral power in strong- and weak-mayor council governments. One account draws this line:

> In strong mayor–council cities, the mayor has an independent constituent base, is empowered to hire and often to fire top administrative personnel (such as department heads), is empowered to veto council action, is the top administrator (with considerable legal administrative authority), and plays major roles in structuring the budget and the public agenda. . . . In weak mayor–council cities, political power is somewhat more widely diffused. The weak mayor typically does not have the veto, budget, and appointive powers of the strong mayor. Instead the council is in a position to control appointments and, in some cases, to put the budget together from the beginning. . . . In short, power is more broadly shared in the weak mayor–council system than in the strong mayor–council scheme.[9]

The ICMA data do not distinguish between the two forms of mayor–council government, in part because both are considered to give more power to mayors than either council–manager or commission forms.

Under the council–manager form, the chief executive is the city manager who generally prepares the budget, sets the council agenda, makes top-level administrative appointments, serves full-time but is not elected, and serves at the pleasure of council. The mayor under such a form generally presides over city council meetings and is generally selected from among the council members.

Formal mayoral strength is slightly greater in commission governments than in council–manager governments, although still weaker than in mayor–council governments. In commission-governed cities, with no executive–legislative separation of power, each commissioner serves as an executive by heading a broad functional area (e.g., finance, public safety) and as a legislator in collectively making policy decisions. The mayor in such a city, while primarily serving as a presiding officer over commission meetings, still has more formal power than a mayor in a council–manager city where clear delineation of executive power is with the manager.

Form of government itself, as these examples show, is often a predictor of the other formal mayoral power.[10] But from purely a form of government perspective, the desirability hypothesis is that women are less likely to serve as mayors in cities with mayor–council and commission governments than in those with council–manager governments.

Mayors On or Off Council?

Mayors are strongest in cities where there is a clear separation of power between the executive and legislative branches (most often, as we have seen, in mayor–council cities).[11] Thus, according to the desirability thesis, we would expect a higher incidence of women mayors simultaneously serving on council.

Mayoral Voting Power

Mayoral clout is strongest in situations where the officeholder can vote on all issues before the council, as opposed to having the legal authority to vote only in the event of a tie, or having no voting power whatsoever.[12] Thus, the desirability thesis would posit that women are more often mayors in cities where chief executives are more limited in their authority to vote on issues before the city council.

Mayoral Veto Power

Mayors with the power to veto council decisions are clearly stronger than those without. This strength stems from both the actual and the threatened use of the veto, each of which "can significantly enhance a mayor's ability to force council action in a desired fashion."[13] Clearly, under the desirability hypothesis, we would expect to find fewer women mayors in cities where the chief executive has some veto power.[14]

Full-Time or Part-Time?

In general, the 1991 ICMA survey shows that only 15.5 percent of all mayors serve in a full-time capacity. Those who do usually head large cities[15] with large governmental bureaucracies and big budgets. Big-city mayors are usually high-profile mayors who get extensive press attention and often use the position to launch their political careers upward to state and national offices. Thus we would expect to see fewer women mayors serving full- than part-time under the desirability hypothesis.

Direct versus Indirect Election

The norm across all U.S. cities is for mayors to be separately elected (in 77.1 percent of all jurisdictions). The next most common method is for mayors to be selected from among the council ranks (21.1 percent). A relative handful of cities use rotational or other indirect methods to select their mayors. Naturally, greater prestige and clout come from being directly elected by the municipality's voters at large, either in a citywide election or in a town meeting. Thus the desirability hypothesis is that fewer women would be directly elected.

Short or Long Terms?

A number of studies have tested the hypothesis that the longer the term, the more desirable and competitive an elective office is presumed to be; therefore, more women will be elected to positions with shorter terms. While few have found any significant relationship between term length and the proportion of women serving on city councils, no study has tested this relationship with regard to women mayors, at least to our knowledge.

Limited or Unlimited Terms?

Term limits, while extremely popular among the electorate, are not common for the nation's mayors. Some 95 percent of the cities responding to the 1991 ICMA survey report they have no limit on their mayor's term of office, although they are more prevalent among the nation's largest cities (present in 40 percent of those over 500,000 population). However, putting population size aside, one still concludes that mayoral prestige and strength are greater where there are no term limits. If the office desirability thesis is correct, we should find that women are more likely to hold mayoral positions in cities that limit the number of terms one may hold such a post.

To our knowledge, ours is the *first* explicit test of the desirability thesis as it relates to *mayoral* positions.[16] But even tests of the thesis as it relates to city council positions have been sparse.

CITY COUNCIL POSITIONS AND THE DESIRABILITY THESIS

City council positions are clearly more powerful and prestigious in certain types of settings than others. Council members have more clout in cities where mayors are weaker and where council members are elected citywide, have no term limits, receive pay for their service, and compete for fewer seats.

Form of Government

Council positions have more authority attached to them in cities with council–manager, commission, weak mayor–council, and representative town meeting forms of government. In these jurisdictions, the council, more than the mayor or manager, appoints officials, prepares the budget, supervises departments, and performs other administrative tasks, in addition to their normal policy-making function.[17] If the desirability thesis holds, women should be less successful at capturing council seats in cities operating under these forms.

Citywide versus District Constituency Base

City council positions are also more powerful when council members are elected citywide, or at-large, rather than from single-member districts. In other words, where the constituency base is larger, council members generally have more clout and the position is considered more prestigious—and desirable. In general, at-large electoral formats have been found to promote women's election, albeit only weakly.[18] Nonetheless, the desirability thesis posits that women are less successful at capturing council seats with larger constituency bases (at-large seats).

Limited or Unlimited Terms?

Just as with mayors, the argument related to our test of the desirability thesis is that unlimited terms are more likely to make running for a council seat an attractive prospect. The thinking is that unlimited terms permit an individual council member to build up prestige and clout associated with incumbency, along with greater substantive and political expertise. While relatively few cities actually restrict council terms (4.2 percent of the ICMA survey respondents), the desirability hypothesis suggests that more women will hold limited than unlimited term council seats.

Paid or Strictly a Volunteer?

The 1991 ICMA survey asked cities whether their council members served for free or received a salary. From a desirability perspective, council positions with a salary attached are preferable to those without. Normally, there is a fairly strong relationship between the size of a city and pay; the larger the jurisdiction, the more likely it is that a salary is attached to service on the council. (There is mixed evidence with regard to whether women are more likely to win office in smaller or larger jurisdictions).[19] Thus, the desirability hypothesis leads us to predict that women are more likely to hold unpaid, rather than salaried, council posts.

Big or Small Councils?

Some argue that it is easier to win where there are more council seats because competition is less intense, leading to the conclusion that the office is less prestigious.[20] Others would challenge this premise on the grounds that larger councils are typically found in larger cities. There, virtually no office is considered to be lacking in prestige, if for no other reasons than heavy media exposure and a higher success rate in using a council post as a stepping-stone to a higher one.[21] Again, putting population size aside, the desirability thesis we will test posits that women will hold fewer council seats in cities with small councils.

FINDINGS

As noted earlier, several questions in the 1991 ICMA survey allow us to explore the relationships between aspects of municipal structure and the desirability hypothesis. The desirability hypothesis suggests that women will most frequently serve as mayors or council members when the post is least attractive. By this logic, the most attractive positions will be oversubscribed by men while the least desirable will often be passed up by men, allowing women to win in a less competitive environment.

Women as Mayors

Of the 4,860 cities that completed the ICMA survey, 634 have female chief executives. The actual number of women mayors in various components of the analysis will vary slightly as a result of cases being lost due to missing data. In the full data set, 13 percent of the cities are led by women.

Table 1 shows the distribution of female chief executives by type of government. Women most frequently lead cities in which the policy direction is set by the public in town meetings. Approximately one in five town meeting communities has a woman as chief executive. Of the major forms of government, women are substantially more likely to serve as mayor in cities with a council–manager arrangement than in those with a more traditional mayor–council. As Table 1 shows, the proportion female in council–manager cities is 50 percent greater than in mayor–council communities. Since mayors are less powerful under the council–manager format, this pattern conforms to the expectations derived from the desirability hypothesis. Also in accord with the desirability hypothesis is the infrequency with which women serve as mayors in commission cities. These communities tend to have small governing bodies, with each member elected citywide and serving simultaneously in an executive and a legislative capacity. The mayor in a commission city is primus inter pares, as the other members of the commission head up departments such as public safety.

Mayors as Members of Council　　Women are significantly more likely to serve in cities in which the mayor also serves as a member of the council. Women hold one-seventh of the mayoral positions in such cities, compared with only one in nine mayorships where the mayor is not simultaneously a member of the council.

Full-Time or Part-Time?　　There is no significant difference in the rates at which women serve depending upon the time commitment associated with being chief executive. Of the 740 cities with a full-time mayor, 103 (13.9 percent) are led by a woman. Women also serve as mayor in 521 (12.9 percent) of the 4,038 cities where being chief executive is only a part-time responsibility. The lack of patterning here does not support the expectations from desirability theory that predict women are more likely to head up cities where being mayor is a part-time job.

Short or Long Terms?　　In keeping with the desirability hypothesis, women less often serve as mayors when that position carries a longer term. They constitute just 10 percent of the mayors whose terms are four years or longer, while holding

Table 1　Women Mayors by Type of Municipal Government

	Women Mayors	No. of Cities
Mayor–council	10.0%	2,193
Council–manager	15.3	2,338
Commission	10.9	92
Town meeting	20.5	205
Representative town meeting	15.6	32

Source: International City/County Management Association, 1991 Form of Government Survey. Washington, DC: ICMA, 1991.

17.3 percent of the mayorships in cities that restrict the chief executive to a single-year term (usually rotated). When the office of mayor has a one-year term, the post is generally held by a council member so that no one has the opportunity to develop the degree of influence that can attach to long-term incumbency. In 547 of the 620 cities that grant a mayor a one-year term, the council chooses the mayor; in another 29, the position rotates among council members. When the mayor is elected by the public (the hardest test), it tends to be for a four-year term. In 56 percent of these 3,715 cities that elect their mayors, the term is four years; in another 37 percent it is for two years.

Veto or No Veto Power? Also in line with the desirability hypothesis, women are significantly more likely to serve as mayor when that position lacks veto authority over council decisions. Of 1,467 cities in which the mayor can block council ordinances, 10.9 percent have female chief executives. In contrast, women fill the ranks of mayor 13.9 percent of the time in cities where the mayor cannot thwart council preferences.

Authority to Vote on Council Matters? There is mixed evidence on the relationship between the gender of the mayor and the authority for the mayor to vote in council meetings. The desirability hypothesis suggests that women will disproportionately be mayors in communities in which that officer cannot participate in council roll calls. As Table 2 shows, women are overrepresented in cities in which the mayor cannot vote along with council members. Women are even more overrepresented, however, in cities in which the mayor participates in all votes. Women are underrepresented in the 1,862 cities in which the mayor votes only to break a tie. Thus, while there is a statistically significant relationship between gender of mayor and authority to vote in council, the pattern does not support the desirability hypothesis.

Table 2   Mayoral Voting in Council by Gender

	Mayor Votes		
	All Issues	*Tiebreaker*	*Never*
Female	377	181	57
Male	2,046	1,681	372
N	2,423	1,862	429

Notes:
Chi-square = 31.7   Sign. = .0000
   Gamma = −.182 T-value = 4.55
      Tau b = −.065 T-value = 4.55
      Tau c = −.047 T-value = 4.55

Source: International City/County Management Association, 1991 Form of Government Survey. Washington, DC: ICMA, 1991.

Term Limits   There is a growing literature on the impacts of term limits. The consequences of term limits for women, it has been suggested, are positive to the extent that this reform promotes turnover in office. The difficulty of defeating incumbents has given rise to the proposition that groups that have historically been underrepresented will have improved chances of winning an election when open seats are at stake. Thus women, as well as racial and ethnic minorities and with a community's minority political party, may fare better in open-seat contests. However, research into the election of women to Congress has shown that the availability of open seats, while facilitating the election of women, does not guarantee that additional women will be chosen. At the state level, Pritchard[22] found that open seats in Florida during the 1980s were associated with the election of additional female legislators. In a study that included Florida along with both of the Carolinas, Bullock and Gaddie[23] did not observe similar patterns outside of Florida. If limiting the tenure of incumbents opens the way for additional women to compete successfully for office by creating a more level playing field, then we would expect to find women more frequently serving in cities that limit the tenure of their chief executive. Further, in keeping with the desirability hypothesis, being mayor in a community that limits the length of tenure may be less attractive than holding the same position in a city where, through astute politicking, one could aspire to become a career chief executive while awaiting the ideal time to bid for higher office.

In 14.5 percent of the 256 cities that restrict the ability of the mayor to seek re-election, the mayor is a female. While women are slightly more likely to lead cities that limit the tenure of the mayor, this is not a statistically significant pattern, as women are also the mayors in 13.0 percent of the cities that do not limit the tenure of their chief executive.

A Multivariate Test   Examination of the variables considered earlier simultaneously in a multivariate logistic regression model uncovers few statistically significant predictors. The strongest predictors of the gender of the mayor are the selection process, the time commitment for the position, and one of the dichotomous variables for charter format. From Table 3 we determine that women more often serve as mayors in cities that have a mayor–council system, where the mayor is chosen directly by the voters, and where it is a part-time job. Only the last of these elements is in line with expectations generated by the desirability hypothesis. Mayors generally have more power in mayor–council cities and when they have their own electoral connection directly with the public.

Women City Council Members

Women more frequently serve on councils than as mayors. Women constitute almost one-fifth of all council members in the U.S. cities surveyed. The 18.7 percent female makeup of city councils varies little for the two major forms of government. Women hold 17.4 percent of the seats in mayor–council cities, as compared with 20.2 percent of the seats in council–manager cities. One in six councillors in mayor–council cities is a woman, as is one in five of the councillors in city manager communities.

**Table 3   Multivariate Model of Desirability and the Incidence
of Female Mayors**

	b	se	Wald	Sign.
Full-time mayor	−.165	.067	6.14	.013
No term limits	.011	.095	.01	.906
Term limits	−.031	.068	.21	.643
Mayor–council	.285	.112	6.47	.011
Council–manager	.068	.103	.43	.513
Commission	.230	.195	1.39	.239
Mayor's voting power	−.083	.098	.72	.396
Mayor elected by voters	.121	.056	4.66	.031
Intercept	−1.855			

Chi-square = 41.85; −2 log likelihood = 3452.89.

Women serve least often in the 94 commission cities that responded. This largely abandoned format in which each council member is also responsible for a major executive function finds women holding only one-tenth of the council posts. The paucity of women serving in commission cities is in keeping with the desirability hypothesis. Given the dual responsibilities of commissioners, these jobs should be particularly desirable and fraught with gender stereotypes since many of these posts carry labels of "occupations" typically viewed as more "malelike" (e.g., commissioner for public safety, finance, public works, roads). At the other extreme, in council–manager cities in which the manager makes the day-to-day decisions, the functions of the council and mayor are diminished and women are relatively numerous in these municipalities.

Term Limits, Pay, and Constituency Base   Bivariate analyses indicate that women are more likely to serve as councillors in cities that limit tenure on the council and pay no salaries to the council members. Both of these are aspects of the job that make it less desirable. The desirability hypothesis also suggests that women will be less likely to serve where elections are at-large (a larger constituency base). With a citywide constituency, the visibility of the position and the scope of the constituency are obviously greater than for a single ward or district. Moreover, the task of being elected citywide may be more arduous than running in a single-member district. Although empirical results are mixed, some have suggested that women are less successful in raising the necessary funds and mounting the kind of campaign needed to win at large.

We find no support for these propositions. In the bivariate analysis, the relationship between the percent of council seats elected at large and the proportion female on the council is positive and significant (b = .026; se = .005). Underscoring the lack of support for the desirability thesis as applied to the districting format in use, the percentage of seats that are nominated and elected from single-member districts is significantly and negatively associated with the percentage of women on the council (b = −.030; se = .007).

Large or Small Councils?   It has been suggested that the larger the council, the less desirable a single seat on it would be. Thus, a member of a ten-person council has less potential influence than does a member of a five-person governing body. The bivariate analysis finds support for that proposition, as the proportion of women increases along with the size of the council (b = .007; se = .001).

Second-Class or Not? A Multivariate Test   When the variables considered previously are combined into a multivariate model, all of them except a dummy variable for the council–manager format are statistically significant. As Table 4 demonstrates, the incidence of councilwomen is greater when the number of council seats is larger, when a larger share of the council is elected at large, when term limits are in place, when councillors receive no pay, and when there are fewer seats for which the nomination and election are by district.[24] In terms of charter type, women are less likely to serve in cities governed by mayor–council or by commission than in cities using town meetings. Thus, the council size, councillor pay, term limits, mayor–council and commission variables are in the direction anticipated by desirability. The two measures of election districting run contrary to the expectations derived from desirability theory.

Although all of the predictors are statistically significant, and the F score is also highly significant, the model leaves much to be desired in its ability to explain variance in the gender makeup of U.S. city councils. Only 3 percent of the variance can be explained using the measures associated with desirability that are found in the model in Table 4. An inability to bite deeply into the explanation of variance in the proportion of women in municipal government elected offices is, unfortunately, the norm for efforts to examine the presence of women in public life in general. Other models using other data sets do little to explain variance even when

Table 4   Multivariate Model of Desirability and the Incidence of Councilwomen

	b	se	T
Percent at-large	.020	.006	3.276
Percent single-member districts	−.024	.008	−3.088
Council size	.008	.001	5.883
No pay for councillors	.014	.007	1.909
No term limits	.046	.012	−3.858
Commission	−.094	.020	−4.737
Mayor–council	−.029	.011	−2.530
Council–manager	−.005	.011	−.467
Intercept	.191		

$N = 4,832$; F = 17.40; adjusted $R^2 = .03$.

they, like the effort here, find statistically significant correlates. Structure simply matters less than other factors.

Conclusion

In this chapter we have tested the desirability hypothesis, which suggests that women will be more likely to serve as mayors or city council members when the posts are least attractive, desirable, or powerful. Using data generated in the early 1990s, we generally find limited support for the hypothesis among both mayors and council members.

In keeping with the desirability hypothesis, women mayors are more likely to be found among the ranks of those for whom the post is part-time. Contrary to expectations, however, women mayors more often serve in mayor–council arrangements and when the mayor is elected directly by the voters.

There is greater support for the desirability thesis as it relates to women city council members. In line with the thesis, women are more likely to serve as councillors in cities with larger councils, where service is unpaid rather than salaried, and where there are term limits. However, contradictory to the desirability thesis, they are more likely to serve where the council constituency base is larger (at-large election systems). And there is mixed support for the thesis that women are less likely to serve in cities with governmental forms giving the council more legislative input into executive administrative functions (council–manager, commission). While it turns out women are the most likely to get elected from cities with council–manager governments (expected), they are less likely to serve in mayor–council than in commission cities (unexpected).

In general, however, the overall explanatory power of the desirability thesis is rather weak. Formal, structural measures of office desirability simply do not account for very much of the variation in the gender makeup of mayoral and city council posts across the United States.

NOTES

1. R. Darcy, Susan Welch, and Janet Clark, *Women, Elections, and Representation*, 2nd ed. (Lincoln: University of Nebraska Press, 1994), p. 44.

2. Ibid.; also see Irene Diamond, *Sex Roles in the State House*, (New Haven, CT: Yale University Press, 1977).

3. Darcy, Welch, and Clark, *Women, Elections, and Representation*, p. 45.

4. Ibid., p. 44.

5. The authors cite a review study by Richard L. Engstrom, Michael McDonald, and Bir-Er Chou, "The Election of Women to Central City Councils in the United States: A Note on the Desirability and Compatibility Explanations," paper presented at the meeting of the International Society of Political Psychology, Toronto, June 1984.

6. Susan A. MacManus and Charles S. Bullock III, "Women and Racial/Ethnic Minorities in Mayoral and Council Positions," in *The Municipal Year Book 1993* (Washington, DC: ICMA, 1993), p. 70.

7. The actual clout of a mayor also depends on her or his political skills—persuasion, negotiation, and public relations. See Jeffrey L. Pressman, "Preconditions of Mayoral Leadership," *American Political Science Review*, 66 (June 1972), pp. 511–524.

8. For an excellent overview of mayoral powers, see Thomas R. Dye, *Politics in States and Communities*, 8th ed. (Englewood Cliffs, NJ: Prentice-Hall, 1994), pp. 344–347.

9. John A. Straayer, Robert D. Wrinkle, and J. L. Polinard, *State and Local Politics* (New York: St. Martin's Press, 1994), p. 291.

10. However, as Renner and DeSantis warn, "Pure classifications of mayoral types are difficult to construct since a fair number of jurisdictions do not conform easily to one model or another" (p. 65).

Tari Renner and Victor S. DeSantis, "Contemporary Patterns and Trends in Municipal Government Structures," in International City/County Management Association, *The Municipal Year Book 1993*. Washington, DC: ICMA, 1993, pp. 57–69.

11. According to the 1991 ICMA survey, 34.6 percent of mayors in mayor–council systems serve on the council compared with 82.0 percent of mayors in council–manager systems and 97.8 percent in commission systems. See ibid., p. 63.

12. Here, too, there is some relationship between mayoral voting power and form of government, which is not surprising in light of the variation in role. Mayors have the authority to vote on all issues in 73.1 percent of the council–manager governments and in 90.3 percent of the commission governments. Mayors in mayor–council cities are the most likely (59.7 percent) to be able to vote to break a tie. See ibid., p. 65.

13. Ibid.

14. Veto powers "may range from the ability to veto entire ordinances, resolutions, appropriations, or specific sections or lines of each" (ibid.). However, the ICMA survey data only indicate whether a mayor has some form of veto power or none.

15. Eighty percent of all cities with 500,000 population or more have full-time mayors. In contrast, only 50 percent of those with populations 250,000–499,999 have full-time mayors. The percentages for various size categories under 250,000 population slope downward from 37 percent (100,000–250,000) to a low of 8 percent (cities under 2,500). See ibid.

16. We did conduct an earlier analysis that found "few sizable gender-based differences in the powers wielded by mayors" when measured in terms of mayoral voting and veto powers. See Susan A. MacManus and Charles S. Bullock III, "Electing Women to Local Office," in Judith A. Garber and Robyne S. Turner (Eds.), *Gender in Urban Research* (Thousand Oaks, CA: Sage Publications, 1995), p. 159.

17. Dye, *Politics in States and Communities*, p. 338.

18. For thorough reviews of this literature, see Charles S. Bullock III and Susan A. MacManus, "Municipal Electoral Structure and the Election of Councilwomen," *Journal of Politics*, 53 (1991), pp. 75–89; MacManus and Bullock, "Women and Racial/Ethnic Minorities" Darcy et al., *Women, Elections, and Representation*.

19. One study has suggest that women win more often in smaller jurisdictions where such council posts are less prestigious and competition for them is less keen. See Albert Karnig and B. Oliver Walter, "Election of Women to City Councils," *Social Science Quarterly*, 56 (March 1976), pp. 605–613. Other studies assert the opposite, that women win more in larger, more cosmopolitan, less traditional cities. See Darcy et al., *Women, Elections, and Representation*, and MacManus and Bullock, "Women and Racial/Ethnic Minorities," for reviews of these studies.

20. This argument is well articulated in Susan Welch and Albert Karnig, "Correlates of Female Office-Holding in City Politics," *Journal of Politics*, 41 (May 1979), pp. 478–491.

21. This argument is spelled out in MacManus and Bullock, "Women and Racial/Ethnic Minorities." Also see Timothy Bledsoe, *Careers in City Politics* (Pittsburgh: University of Pittsburgh Press, 1993).

22. Anita Pritchard, "Florida: The Big Electoral Shakeup of 1982," in Susan A. MacManus (Ed.), *Reapportionment and Representation in Florida: A Historical Collection* (Tampa: Intrabay Innovation Institute and the University of South Florida, 1991), pp. 323–336.

23. Charles S. Bullock III and Ronald Keith Gaddie, "Changing from Multimember to Single-Member Districts: Partisan, Racial, and Gender Consequences," *State and Local Government Review*, 25 (Fall 1993), pp. 155–163.

24. The excluded category for electoral districting format is cities in which council members are nominated by district but compete at-large in the general election.

FURTHER READINGS

Carroll, Susan J. *Women as Candidates in American Politics*, 2nd ed. Bloomington, IN: Indiana University Press, 1994.

Cook, Elizabeth Adell, Sue Thomas, and Clyde Wilcox, eds. *The Year of the Woman: Myths & Realities*. Boulder, CO: Westview Press, 1994.

Dye, Thomas R. *Politics in States and Communities*. 8th ed. Englewood Cliffs, NJ: Prentice-Hall, 1994.

McGlen, Nancy E. and Karen O'Connor. *Women, Politics, and American Society*. Englewood Cliffs, NJ: Prentice-Hall, 1995.

National Civic Review, quarterly.

Rajoppi, Joanne. *Women in Office: Getting There and Staying There*. Westport, CT: Bergin & Garvey, 1993.

Rinehart, Sue Tolleson. *Gender Consciousness and Politics*. New York: Routledge, 1992.

Witt, Linda, Karen M. Paget, and Glenna Matthews. *Running as a Woman: Gender and Power in American Politics*. New York: Macmillan, 1994.

 **CHAPTER 4**

LEGISLATURES, WOMEN, AND POLICY MAKING

How have women fared in running for other elective offices? Marcia Lynn Whicker, Malcolm Jewell, and the editor find that there is an unequal representation of women in the Congress. These researchers find that, across the more than seventy years since women secured the right to participate politically with the passage of the Nineteenth Amendment, female representation in Congress has increased from a minuscule 0.2 percent of total membership in 1922 to only 5.2 percent in 1988. At that rate of increase, women will not achieve equality in representation until the year 2582. By the 104th Congress, the proportion of women increased to 10.4 percent, a sizable increase but still much below the 50 percent proportion representation by gender would entail. This study also shows that women who do obtain congressional office do so at an older age than their male counterparts, serve significantly fewer terms, and are less likely to seek reelection. Thus, the gap between democratic rhetoric and representational reality for women is great, despite a significant narrowing in the experiential backgrounds of men and women who are elected to Congress.

On the other hand, we find that women's election to state assemblies and senates has increased 100 percent from 1974 to 1984. However, Wilma Rule finds recruitment to state assemblies and senates has slipped over the past decade. Her analysis reveals that, for the 1970s, there was a building on the gains in the Republican–moralistic states most favorable to women in the 1960s. In the 1980s no political party or political culture was dominant in the states where women legislators had the most dramatic increase. Rule finds that states that led in the 1970s and 1980s continued to advance, with most of their state senates at least doubling the number of women members by the 1994 elections. In 1994 the South broke out of its mold as the "solid Democratic South" for the first time in some 100 years. The author also concludes that, at the same time, the Republican Party dominance was modified as a favorable factor for women's recruitment.

We next move from recruitment of women to state assemblies and senates to an analysis of the demographic, political, and legislative data on all women serving in the legislatures of fifteen states in 1972, 1982, and 1992. Kathleen Dolan and Lynne E. Ford also use a mail survey of the 1,373 women serving in the fifty state legislatures during the 1992 legislative session. Their findings reveal a diverse group of women in the political arena, both in experience and in interests these women bring to politics. As a group, female state legislators serving in the 1990s exhibit greater educational, occupational, political, and legislative diversity than the women who served in the past. The authors indicate that, if the launching role that state legislative experience has provided for men holds true for women, this diversity and the greater numbers of women serving in elective office at the state level should ultimately mean larger and more diverse pools of future female candidates at the national level. The question then becomes, Will the larger pool ultimately reverse some of the trends pointed out in the article by Whicker, Jewell, and Duke about the unequal representation of women in the U.S. Congress?

We turn our attention next to women and legislative bodies.

Women in Congress

Marcia Lynn Whicker
Malcolm Jewell
Lois Lovelace Duke

EXPLANATIONS OF THE PARADOX OF FEMALE VOTING STRENGTH AND REPRESENTATIONAL WEAKNESS

At one level, a paradox surrounds women in politics. While constituting about 53 percent of the population, women have held only a fraction of elected offices at all levels of government.[1] As a political group, women exhibit considerable voting strength but, simultaneously, representational weakness, especially at the national level. In 1988 women held only 28 of the 535 total seats in Congress (5.2 percent). At least partially because of the Anita Hill–Clarence Thomas controversy in late 1991, more women ran for the U.S. Congress in 1992. As a result, the 103rd Congress included seven female senators and forty-seven women in the U.S. House of Representatives (about 11 percent). The representation of women in the U.S. Congress after the 1994 GOP sweep left the numbers of women in the U.S. House at forty-seven, but included five more Republican women for a total of seventeen. After the 1994 election, women in the U.S. Senate increased to eight (five Democrats and three Republicans). These small numbers of women as a proportion of total national representation contrast with still small but nonetheless, in some instances, more than double percentages of female representation at subnational levels of government. Women held eighty-five statewide elected executive positions

Marcia Lynn Whicker is professor of public administration, Rutgers University, Newark, New Jersey. Malcolm Jewell is professor emeritus, of political science, University of Kentucky. Lois Lovelace Duke is professor of Political Science, Clemson University.

"This article originally appeared in *Free Inquiry in Creative Sociology*, Vol. 19. No. 2, 1991, Reprinted with permission."

in state government (26.2 percent) and 1,533 of the total 7,424 state legislative seats (20.6 percent) in 1995. Since 1969 the number of women serving in state legislatures has increased fivefold.[2]

Women who attempt to enter the political elite continue experiencing considerable difficulty.[3] One study of women in three midwestern state legislatures found that they polled significantly fewer votes and won significantly fewer elections than men.[4] Further, women held fewer seats in professionally developed legislatures and city councils, in part due to stiffer male opposition in states and communities where the compensation is higher, the tenure is longer, and the prestige of officeholding is greater.[5]

The weakened political position of women in elected politics has been tied to their weakened economic condition in the marketplace. Rossi anticipates that as female participation and success in the labor force increase, so will the electoral potency of women candidates.[6] Other factors offered to explain the discrepancy between female voting strength and elected legislative representation include personality differences,[7] situational factors,[8] and sex-role socialization.[9]

Situational Explanations of the Paradox

Situational factors include a lower socioeconomic status for many women, little free time, less occupational experience than men have, and lower educational status. These factors have contributed to the absence of women in state legislatures, which have frequently been "launching roles" for men elected to Congress. Yet these factors alone explain only part of the political paradox for women. According to one study using 1970s data, if women had attained the same occupational and educational status as men, they would have constituted about 25 percent of state legislatures, rather than the 5 percent of the upper houses and 8 percent of the lower houses they then constituted.[10]

Socialization Explanations of the Paradox

Socialization includes the development of stereotypical attitudes that only a restricted range of behaviors are appropriate for women, and that politics is typically a male domain.[11] "Female values" of nurturing and caretaking are viewed by both men and women as incompatible with the rough-and-tumble action and toughness that politics and effective leadership require.[12] Women have also had to deal with conflicting roles as mother and wife and political roles. Thus, women have not as readily perceived politics as a viable option for themselves.

Voter Stereotypes as Explanations of the Paradox

Women candidates have faced considerable hurdles in winning voter approval, since voters, as well as potential female candidates, have been influenced by sex-role stereotyping.[13] While men have been viewed by voters in terms of occupational roles, women have been perceived in terms of domestic roles.[14] Stereotypical bias is based on the gender of the candidate and not the voter, since men and women have shown little differences in their reported unwillingness to vote for a woman candidate.[15] In one study, women candidates were rated more intelligent and concerned about people, but men candidates were still perceived as more knowledgeable about politics and considered stronger.[16]

The disadvantage women experience in voter perceptions is stronger if they are in their childbearing years and are the mothers of small children.[17] Voter perceptions of candidate acceptability have affected the willingness of mothers of small children to become candidates. In another study, women with small children were found to be as politically active as women without small children except in running for public office. Politically active men with small children were equally as likely to be candidates as those without children.

Challenges to Voter Discrimination as the Explanation for the Political Paradox for Women

Various studies have questioned voter and contributor discrimination as an explanation of the political paradox for women, including challenges to the supposition that female candidate attractiveness can be negative, that voters and party leaders react negatively to female candidates, and that gender rather than incumbency is the primary handicap confronting women candidates.[18] Sigelman, Sigelman, and Fowler explored whether physical attractiveness contributes to voter stereotyping of female candidates.[19] They found complex and indirect effects of femininity and female candidate attractiveness on voters. While perceived attractiveness had no direct impact on voter willingness to support the female candidate, it was positively related to perceptions of dynamism and femininity, which in turn were positively related to voter willingness to vote for the woman candidate. Thus, voter stereotyping of women in domestic roles undercut their willingness to elect women, but perceptions of female candidates as dynamic and feminine enhanced their willingness to vote for women.

Other scholars have contradicted findings that women candidates are less successful than men candidates when confounding factors are controlled. In an analysis of five 1982 elections in which women ran as major-party candidates for high-level offices—governor in Vermont and Iowa, and U.S. senator in Missouri, New York, and New Jersey—Zipp and Plutzer found that the sex of the candidate had little impact on voting.[20] Another study of voters' perceptions and attitudes using data from the 1982 American National Election Survey suggests that female candidates are not at a disadvantage when controls for incumbency are considered. When incumbency was controlled, voters were more likely to have contact with female candidates; were about as likely to recognize their names; made somewhat more favorable references to female candidates; and were just as likely to vote for women.[21]

Nor are women inferior fund-raisers,[22] or forced by party leaders to run only in overwhelmingly "hopeless" races.[23] Women are more likely, however, to be challengers. The political opportunity structure for any political challenger tends to restrict the number of women elected to office, since incumbents tend to win reelection and most incumbents are men.[24]

INCREASING OPPORTUNITIES FOR WOMEN
AT THE NATIONAL LEVEL?

1984 as a Watershed Symbol Only?

If challengers to the political paradox for women are correct, opportunities for and visibility of women at the national level should be increasing, especially in the recent past. In 1984, Democrat and former House member from New York Geraldine Ferraro achieved the status of becoming the first woman vice presidential candidate for either major political party. This historic event led some observers at the time to conclude that the elections in that year may represent a watershed for women in obtaining national political visibility. In 1984, an unprecedented sixty-five women, thirty-five Republicans and thirty Democrats, also obtained a major-party nomination for U.S. House races, an 18 percent increase over the fifty-five women who received major-party nominations for House races in 1982.[25]

With offers of assistance from the Women's Campaign Fund, the Women's Trust, the National Women's Political Caucus, and the National Organization for Women, female candidate campaign organizations began to tap additional sources for assistance and to increase in professionalism.[26] Concern over a portending "gender gap," with popular reports circulating that women were beginning to disproportionately favor Democratic candidates, led the Republican party to promise to fund women senatorial candidates at levels as high as possible. Democrats responded to such pledges with their own promises of support for national female candidates.

Yet despite increased potential for advances in national political power for women, the general election outcomes in 1984 were disappointing to advocates of women as elected officials. Election results only preserved the status quo in terms of number of women in the U.S. House. While all female House incumbents who ran were victorious, two incumbents did not run, including Ferraro, who ran for vice president instead. These Democratic losses in the number of women in the House were offset by Republican gains. Thus, only twenty-two women out of 435 members were elected to the ninety-ninth Congress, constituting only 5 percent of House membership, a figure unchanged from the number and percentage of women in the ninety-fourth Congress.

A Worldwide Political Paradox for Women?

Nor is the percentage of women in Congress substantially different from the number of women in Parliament in Britain. In 1974, with women there as in the United States constituting over 50 percent of the electorate, 96 percent of all the members of the British Parliament were male. In 1976, the total number of British MPs (Members of Parliament) who were women was twenty-eight, a number roughly equivalent to the number in Congress. In the 1970s, the trend in British politics for female candidates appeared to be an increasing number of female candidates standing for election, but no significant gain in the number obtaining office.[27] Norris reports this trend continues into the late 1980s.[28]

A Decline in Stereotypical Assignments
for Women Members of Congress

Despite their small numbers within Congress, by the ninety-eighth Congress, women who did succeed in getting elected were no longer linked along sex-stereotyped lines to health, education, and children.[29] Only one of the twenty-three women in Congress at that time held a committee assignment on the Education Committee, while two or more women were on Armed Services, Appropriations, Science and Technology, Commerce, Budget, Public Works, and Transportation. The only committee associated with traditional women's issues to which a proportionately large number of women were assigned (six women) was the Special Committee on Aging.

The 104th Congress did bring about an increase in women achieving committee chairs rarely given to women. Senator Nancy Kassebaum (R-KS) became the first female chair in the Senate since 1945 when she took over the leadership of the Senate Labor and Human Resources Committee. Also, in 1995, Republican Jan Meyers of Kansas was the first woman to chair a House committee since 1977 when she became the chair of the House Small Business Committee.[30]

Some stereotypes related to women still remain, founded somewhat in reality. In a study of women who served in the House between 1915 and 1976, Gehlen found that congruent with the stereotypical niceness and nurturing often associated with female roles, women members were more reluctant than their male colleagues to oppose programs that they did not support.[31]

A Shift to Solo Campaigning with Few Gains in Numbers
until the "Year of the Woman"

By the early 1980s, the nature of congressional campaigns for female candidates had changed. With one exception, women elected in the ninety-eighth Congress entered the electoral race on their own and fought vigorous campaigns to achieve office, a shift in the prevailing pattern until recent years of women succeeding their deceased fathers and husbands.[32]

This shift from spouse succession to solo campaigning, however, has not resulted in a rise in the number of women becoming national representatives. The number of female House members and senators in the 101st Congress did not increase appreciably over previous years. With only 28 of 435 House members female, women constituted 6.2 percent of the House. With only two out of 100 senators female, women constituted a minuscule 2 percent of the U.S. Senate. Thus, of the total 535 national representatives, the 28 women serving were 5.2 percent in the 101st Congress. The 102nd Congress was made up of 6 percent women in the U.S. House and 4 percent female representation in the U.S. Senate. Even with the record gains made by women in 1992 and 1994, only forty-seven women served in the U.S. House in the 103rd and 104th Congress; seven women served in the U.S. Senate in the 103rd Congress, and eight female senators serve in the 104th Congress. The 104th Congress includes thirteen women of color: nine African-American women, three Latinas, and one Asian American/Pacific Islander woman. In addition, one

Democratic woman delegate, who is African-American, represents the District of Columbia.

DIFFERENCES BETWEEN MALE AND FEMALE MEMBERS OF CONGRESS: ARE THEIR CONGRESSIONAL CAREERS CONVERGING?

This essay examines differences between male and female members of Congress for both background characteristics and measures of congressional "success." If those who do not believe discrimination is the primary explanation for the small number of women in national office are correct, then the political career paths of men and women should become more similar across time as women enter the labor force with greater frequency and assume a variety of jobs previously held only by men. If, however, voter stereotyping and other discriminatory factors are still important, then the political career paths and measures of success for male and female members of Congress should still be different, and little convergence will occur.

Data and Methodology

The data used here are a merged set drawn from the roster of U.S. congressional officeholders and biographical characteristics of the U.S. Congress, 1789–1989, covering the 1st to the 101st Congress. The data set contains variables describing congressional service and background characteristics for each person who has served in the U.S. Congress from March 1789 through July 1989. A record exists for every Congress in which each individual has served, as well as for each chamber in which each individual has served, constituting 41,209 cases. Thus, statistics are reported here for both the total number of two-year congressional terms served by women, as well as for women as a percentage of the total number of individuals serving in Congress.

Prior to gaining the right to vote in the Nineteenth Amendment to the U.S. Constitution in 1921, women did not participate actively as a group in politics. This analysis begins after the sixty-seventh Congress, and covers the sixty-eighth through the 101st Congress. Women are compared here to men serving in Congress at the same time.

Number of Women in Congress, by Year

Table 1 shows that the number of women in Congress has always been small. In the sixty-eighth Congress, immediately after the ratification of the 1921 amendment, only one lonely woman was a national representative. Between the sixty-eighth and 101st Congresses, the percentage of women in both houses rose steadily, if slowly and not consistently, from 0.2 percent to 5.2 percent—again increasing to only 5.0 percent of the total membership of Congress in 66 years. At that average rate of increase in the number of women per 66 years, women will not achieve 50 percent of the representation in Congress until the year 2582—almost 600 years from now. By the 104th Congress, the percentage of women increased to 10.4 percent, a sizable increase but still below the 50 percent proportional representation by gender would entail.

Table 1 Number of Women in Congress, by Year

Election	Congress	President and Party	Number of Women in Congress	Percentage
1922	68	Warren G. Harding (R)	1	0.2
1924	69	Calvin Coolidge (R)	3	0.5
1926	70		5	0.9
1928	71	Herbert C. Hoover (R)	9	1.6
1930	72		8	1.5
1932	73	Franklin D. Roosevelt (D)	8	1.5
1934	74		8	1.5
1936	75	Franklin D. Roosevelt (D)	9	1.6
1938	76		9	1.6
1940	77	Franklin D. Roosevelt (D)	10	1.8
1942	78		9	1.6
1944	79	Franklin D. Roosevelt (D)	11	1.9
1946	80		8	1.4
1948	81	Harry S. Truman (D)	9	1.6
1950	82		9	1.6
1952	83	Dwight D. Eisenhower (R)	13	2.3
1954	84		16	3.0
1956	85	Dwight D. Eisenhower (R)	15	2.8
1958	86		19	3.4
1960	87	John F. Kennedy (D)	20	3.6
1962	88		14	2.5
1964	89	Lyndon B. Johnson (D)	13	2.4
1966	90		12	2.2
1968	91	Richard M. Nixon (R)	11	2.0
1970	92		15	2.7
1972	93	Richard M. Nixon (R)	16	2.9
1974	94		19	3.5
1976	95	Jimmy Carter (D)	19	3.5
1978	96		17	3.1
1980	97	Ronald Reagan (R)	24	4.4
1982	98		24	4.4
1984	99	Ronald Reagan (R)	25	4.6
1986	100		26	4.8
1988	101	George Bush (R)	28	5.2
1990	102		32	6.0
1992	103	Bill Clinton (D)	54	10.0
1994	104		55	10.4

Summary by party of president			Republican	Democrat
Number of terms			19	18
Average number of women per congress			16.3	16.3
Percentage of women per term			3.0	3.0

Table 1 also differentiates between Congresses when the White House was occupied by a Republican and those when the president was Democratic. Despite the image that Democrats are more supportive of women's rights, plus the greater frequency with which Democratic Party platforms have adopted pro-women stances in recent years, the average number of women serving in Congress under Republican presidents (16.3, or 3.0 percent) is identical to the average number of women serving under Democratic presidents (also 16.3, or 3.0 percent).

In part, this partisan equality reflects the increase in the number of women in recent years relative to the number in earlier years, and the fact that the presidency has been dominated by Republicans since 1968. Yet during the presidencies of Democrats Harry Truman, John Kennedy, and Jimmy Carter, the number and percentage of women in Congress fell, while during the presidencies of Republicans Eisenhower, Nixon, Reagan, and Bush, the number and percentage of women in Congress rose slightly. Perhaps, also, during the pro-women administrations of Democrats, pro-women voters become complacent about increasing representation, while during the less supportive administrations of Republican presidencies, pro-women voters become galvanized to work for and support women congressional candidates. Also, the number of women in Congress during the pro-family conservative years of the 1950s was slightly higher than in the activist, more liberal 1960s, a decade that saw the launching of the second major women's movement in the United States in the twentieth century.

Making Individual-Based Comparisons

Table 2 examines the differences between men and women in terms of numbers serving and background characteristics, looking at individuals as the basis for comparison. Since 1921, 3,653 individuals have served in Congress—2,993 in the House and 660 in the Senate. Woman have made up only 3.3 percent of those individuals. Throughout two centuries of U.S. history, women have had little role in national lawmaking, since only 107 women have served in the House and 14 women in the U.S. Senate. Despite the small number of women in the Senate, proportionately the number of women who have served in the House is not statistically significantly greater (probability of chi-square = .08). Nor do women differ significantly from men in the regions from which they are elected (probability = .34). While 62.0 percent of all women who have served in Congress have been Democrats, political party is also not significantly related to gender of the representative (probability = .29).

If women in Congress do not differ from their male counterparts in region, chamber to which they are elected, and political party, do they differ in background characteristics? Men and women are both equally likely to have attended public secondary school prior to entering college, but do differ in college background (significance = .03). Women are more likely to have attended private colleges (53.7 percent) than are men (44.0 percent), but men are more likely to have attended Ivy League colleges (13.7 percent) than are women (0.2 percent). A higher percentage of men (29.8 percent) attended state universities than women (25.6 percent), while

Table 2 Number of Men and Women in Congress, 68th to 101st Congress

	Men		Women		Total		Probability of Chi-Square
	Number	Per-centage	Number	Per-centage	Number	Per-centage	
Individuals serving:	3,532	96.7	121	3.3	3,653		
By chamber:							.08
House	2,886	81.7	107	88.4	2,993	81.9	
Senate	646	18.3	14	11.6	660	18.1	
By region: (1M)							.34
Northeast	928	26.3	32	26.4	960	26.3	
Midwest	1,071	30.3	29	24.0	1,100	30.1	
South	996	28.2	36	29.8	1,032	28.3	
West	536	15.2	24	19.8	560	15.3	
By party: (1M)							.29
Democrat	1,898	53.7	75	62.0	1,973	54.0	
Republican	1,612	45.6	46	38.0	1,658	45.4	
Other	21	0.6	0	0.0	21	0.6	
By relatives in Congress: (1M)							.00**
None	3,278	92.8	80	66.1	3,358	91.9	
1 or more	253	7.2	41	33.9	294	8.1	
By secondary education: (6M)							.39
Unknown	137	3.9	7	5.8	144	3.9	
Public school	2,775	78.7	89	74.2	2,864	78.6	
Private school	614	17.4	24	20.0	638	17.5	
By college: (3M)							.03*
None	442	12.5	18	14.9	460	12.6	
State university	1,051	29.8	31	25.6	1,082	29.6	
Private college	1,552	44.0	65	53.7	1,617	44.3	
Ivy League	484	13.7	7	0.2	491	13.5	
By prior service: (3M)							.00**
None	590	16.7	39	32.2	629	17.2	
Local	1,639	46.4	56	46.3	1,695	46.4	
State	1,161	32.9	23	19.0	1,184	32.4	
Federal	139	3.9	3	2.5	142	3.9	

*Significant at the .05 level. #M = number of male cases missing.

**Significant at the .01 level. #W = number of female cases missing.

Percentages are adjusted for missing cases.

a slightly higher percentage of women (14.9 percent) than men (12.5 percent) attended no college at all.

Women are now more likely to be elected to Congress on their own rather than as widows succeeding their deceased husbands. From 1916 to 1940, however, 56 percent of women elected to the House were widows of congressmen who had represented the same district. That proportion dropped to 40 percent in the 1941–1964 period and to 30 percent in the 1965–1974 period; it continued to decline to only 9 percent in the 1980 and 1982 elections.[33]

Despite the reduction in the number of women members of Congress replacing deceased fathers or husbands in recent years and the increase in the number of women engaging in solo campaigning, women differ significantly (probability of chi-square = .00) from men in having relatives in Congress. Among women, 33.9 percent had at least one relative who had served in Congress, but only 7.2 percent of men had at least one relative who had served in Congress.

Men and women also differed in prior service before entry into Congress (probability = .00). A much greater percentage of women (32.2 percent) than men (16.7 percent) had no prior government service. While similar proportions of men (46.4 percent) and women (46.3 percent) had local government experience previously, men (32.9 percent) were more likely to have gained state government experience than women (19.0 percent). Few members of either gender had previous federal experience.

Making Comparisons on the Basis of Two-Year Congressional Terms

Table 3 explores similar questions using total number of two-year terms in Congress served since 1922 (18,737) as the universe, rather than total number of individuals who served. In contrast to the proportion of women who served (3.3 percent) as a percentage of the total number of individuals in Congress during that study time span, the number of total terms served by women falls to 2.5 percent, indicating that those few women who are elected to Congress on average are serving fewer terms than their male counterparts.

When total number of terms rather than total individuals form the universe from which men and women in Congress are compared, both chamber and region are significantly related to gender at the .00 level. The number of terms women served in the House (90.9 percent) as a percentage of total terms served by women in both houses is significantly greater than the terms served by men in the House (80.7 percent) as a percentage of the total terms served by men in both houses. This contrasts with political party affiliation, where of the total terms served by men, the percentage served by men who are Democrats (57.4 percent) is virtually identical to terms served by Democratic women as a percentage of the total number of terms served by women (57.4 percent).

Women have fared considerably better in the Northeast and considerably worse in the South than have men in obtaining congressional office, relative to the performance of each gender in other regions. Women have fared marginally better

Table 3 Number of Two-Year Congressional Terms Served by Men and Women, 68th to 101st Congress

	Men		Women		Total		Probability of Chi-Square
	Number	Per-centage	Number	Per-centage	Number	Per-centage	
Terms served by men and women:	18,275	97.5	462	2.5	18,737		
By chamber:							.00**
House	14,754	80.7	420	90.9	15,174	81.0	
Senate	3,521	19.3	42	9.1	3,563	19.0	
By region: (3M)							.00**
Northeast	4,561	25.0	159	34.4	4,720	25.2	
Midwest	5,214	28.5	116	25.1	5,330	28.5	
South	5,703	31.2	98	21.2	5,801	31.0	
West	2,794	15.3	89	19.3	2,883	15.4	
By party: (1M)							.62
Democrat	10,490	57.4	265	57.4	10,755	57.4	
Republican	7,716	42.2	197	42.6	7,913	42.2	
Other	68	0.4	0	0.0	68	0.4	
By relatives in Congress: (2M)							.00**
None	16,942	92.7	321	69.5	17,263	92.1	
One or more	1,331	7.3	141	30.5	1,472	7.9	
By secondary education: (16M, 1W)							.01**
Unknown	543	3.0	25	5.4	568	3.0	
Public school	14,607	80.0	353	76.6	14,960	79.9	
Private school	3,109	17.0	83	18.0	3,192	17.1	
By college: (5M, 1W)							.00**
None	1,989	10.9	66	14.3	2,055	11.0	
State university	5,720	31.3	113	24.5	5,833	31.1	
Private college	8,105	44.4	247	53.6	8,353	44.6	
Ivy League	2,456	13.4	35	7.6	2,491	13.3	
By prior service: (9M, 1W)							.00**
None	2,799	15.3	110	23.9	2,909	15.5	
Local	8,596	47.1	237	51.4	8,833	47.2	
State	6,057	33.2	93	20.2	6,150	32.8	
Federal	814	4.5	21	4.6	835	4.5	

*Significant at the .05 level. #M = number of male cases missing.

**Significant at the .01 level. #W = number of female cases missing.

Percentages are adjusted for missing cases.

in the West and marginally worse in the Midwest than men. The percentage of terms served by women who are elected from the Northeast (34.4 percent) is significantly greater than the percentage of terms served by men elected from the Northeast (25.0 percent). The percentage of terms served by women elected from the South (21.2 percent) is significantly less than the percentage of terms men served from the South (31.2 percent). Women were somewhat more likely to be from the West (19.3 percent) than were men (15.3 percent), and somewhat less likely to be from the Midwest (25.1 percent) than were men (28.5 percent).

Using terms served as the unit of analysis, similar patterns emerge for male–female differences in relatives in Congress, college attended, and prior government service to those that appeared when individuals served was the unit of analysis. Each of these variables continues to be significantly related to gender of the member of Congress. Women are more likely to have had at least one relative in Congress and to have attended private colleges, and are less likely to have served at the state level prior to entering Congress. Additionally, secondary education is significantly related to gender, with women slightly less likely (76.4 percent) than men (80.0 percent) to have attended public schools.

Measures of Congressional Success

Table 4 examines measures of congressional success for individuals by gender. The age at which the member first entered Congress, the total years served in Congress, and the member's reason for leaving Congress are all significantly related at the .00 level to the gender of the member. In each instance, women are less successful than men. Service after leaving Congress is not related to gender.

On average, women are older (49.3 years old) than men (45.4 years of age) when they first enter Congress. Women serve an average of 6.6 years, 4.2 years less than the average years (10.8) served by men. The most common reason women leave Congress is a decision to not seek reelection (40.0 percent), while only 20.2 percent of men leave Congress because they do not seek reelection. Men (11.9 percent) are far more likely than women (2.5 percent) to have died in office. Women (6.7 percent) are slightly less likely than men (10.4 percent) to have been defeated in a general election.

Comparing Congressional Careers across Time by Decade

Table 5 examines trends in national representation by gender across time. When terms served is the unit of analysis, the proportion of women holding congressional office has increased from 0.8 percent of total congressional membership in the 1920s to 4.7 percent in the 1980s. Female representation in the House went from 1.0 percent in the 1920s to 5.3 percent in the 1980s, while Senate membership rose from 0 to 2.0 percent across the same time span.

While some aspects of qualifications had previously divided men and women—whether or not the individual had a relative who had served in Congress and the type of precongressional service held—men and women are becoming more similar. In the 1920s, 88.7 percent of all men serving in Congress did not have

Table 4   One-Way ANOVA and Contingency Table Results for Congressional Success, by Sex

Congressional Success	Male		Female		Total		Probability
	Mean		Mean		Mean		of F
ANOVA: Age first in Congress	45.4		49.3		45.5		.00**
Total years served	10.8		6.6		10.7		.00**
Frequencies, percentages:	Number	Percentage	Number	Percentage	Number	Percentage	of Chi-Square
Reason left Congress (2M. 1W)							.00**
Unknown, N.A.	992	28.1	18	15.0	1,010	27.7	
General election defeat	367	10.4	8	6.7	375	10.3	
Died in office	419	11.9	3	2.5	422	11.6	
Did not seek reelection	713	20.2	48	40.0	761	20.8	
Sought other elective office	249	7.1	12	10.0	261	7.2	
Accepted federal office	75	2.1	0	0.0	75	2.1	
Elected to other House	115	3.3	1	0.8	116	3.2	
Resigned, withdrew, expelled	92	2.6	2	1.7	94	2.6	
Still serving	508	14.4	28	23.3	536	14.7	
Number of levels after Congress (553M, 28W)							.84
None	2,207	74.1	70	75.3	2,277	74.1	
One	655	22.0	21	22.6	676	22.0	
Two	110	3.7	2	2.2	112	3.6	
Three	7	0.2	0	0.0	7	0.2	

*Significant at the .05 level.

**Significant at the .01 level.

#M = Number of male cases missing or dead.

#W = Number of female cases missing or dead.

Percentages are adjusted for missing and dead cases.

a relative who had served in the same institution, but only 22.2 percent of all women in Congress had no relative who had served there. This reflects the fact that many women were widows of members who died in office. By the 1980s, however, 95.6 percent of all men in Congress had no relative there, while 90.6 percent of all women also had no relative who had served in Congress. Plainly, women had reached almost the same percentage as men on this characteristic and were being elected in their own right, rather than on the name recognition and contacts of deceased husbands.

A similar picture emerges when the precongressional service for both genders is examined. In the 1920s, 61.1 percent of women in Congress, contrasted with only

Table 5   Men and Women, by Two-Year Term, by Decade

	Men		Women	
	Number	*Percentage*	*Number*	*Percentage*
Terms served by men and women:				
1920s	2,206	99.2	18	0.8
1930s	2,739	98.5	42	1.5
1940s	2,747	98.3	47	1.7
1950s	2,675	97.4	72	2.6
1960s	2,685	97.5	70	2.5
1970s	2,637	96.8	86	3.2
1980s	2,586	95.3	127	4.7
By chamber:				
House				
1920s	1,782	99.0	18	1.0
1930s	2,219	98.5	34	1.5
1940s	2,209	98.1	43	1.9
1950s	2,157	97.1	64	2.9
1960s	2,167	97.2	62	2.8
1970s	2,129	96.3	82	3.7
1980s	2,091	94.7	117	5.3
Senate:				
1920s	424	100.0	0	0.0
1930s	520	98.5	8	1.5
1940s	538	99.3	4	0.7
1950s	518	98.5	8	1.5
1960s	518	98.5	8	1.5
1970s	508	99.2	4	0.8
1980s	495	98.0	10	2.0
By relatives in Congress:				
None:				
1920s	1,957	88.7	4	22.2
1930s	2,464	90.0	20	47.6
1940s	2,522	91.8	23	48.9
1950s	2,498	93.4	36	50.0
1960s	2,530	94.2	44	62.9
1970s	2,499	94.8	79	91.9
1980s	2,472	95.6	115	90.6
By prior service:				
None:				
1920s	387	17.5	11	61.1
1930s	532	19.4	22	52.4
1940s	564	20.5	14	29.8
1950s	510	19.1	23	31.9
1960s	303	11.3	12	17.1
1970s	174	6.6	5	5.8
1980s	329	12.8	23	18.3
Local:				
1920s	1,067	48.4	7	38.9
1930s	1,346	49.1	17	40.5

(continued)

Table 5 (*continued*)

	Men		Women	
	Number	*Percentage*	*Number*	*Percentage*
1940s	1,340	48.8	25	53.2
1950s	1,268	47.4	40	55.6
1960s	1,196	44.6	46	65.7
1970s	1,072	40.7	40	46.5
1980s	1,305	50.6	62	49.2
State:				
1920s	677	30.7	0	0.0
1930s	750	27.4	3	7.1
1940s	742	27.0	8	17.0
1950s	792	29.6	3	4.2
1960s	1,015	37.8	7	10.0
1970s	1,214	46.0	36	41.9
1980s	867	33.6	36	28.6

17.5 percent of men there, had no prior government or political experience. By the 1980s, these two percentages had almost converged, so that only 12.8 percent of men and 18.3 percent of women in Congress had no prior government experience. In the 1980s, half of men and half of women in Congress had local experience before entering Congress. A slightly higher percentage of men (33.6 percent) than women (28.6 percent) had previous state-level experience. Despite this difference, however, the gaps between the experiential backgrounds of men and women in Congress have narrowed significantly across the sixty-six-year time span studied.

CONCLUSION

Much has been written about the inroads women have made in politics in gaining elected office in recent years, especially at the state and local levels. Greater political participation by women has been viewed as beneficial.[34] Women are said to have unique contributions to make based on their differential role socialization, their greater concern with group harmony, and their emphasis on caring for future generations. The full participation of women, as well as all disadvantaged groups, would implement democracy in its highest and purest form, producing regime legitimacy, and would expand the talent pool from which national leaders are selected.

Despite such rhetoric and a significant narrowing in the experiential backgrounds of men and women who serve in Congress, the reality is that women have played virtually no role in shaping the nation's laws. Women could not vote in most states prior to 1921, and since then have succeeded in achieving only token representation in Congress. Even though the number of women serving in the U.S. Congress roughly doubled with the 1992 election, many obstacles remain for women seeking congressional office. And, even once elected, by every measure examined here, they are less successful. The gap between democratic rhetoric and representational reality for women is great.

NOTES

1. Ronald D. Hedlund, Patricia K. Freeman, Keith E. Hamm, and Robert M. Stein, "The Electability of Women Candidates: The Effects of Sex Role Stereotypes," *Journal of Politics*, 41 (1–2) (1979), pp. 513–524; and Carol Nechemias, "Changes in the Election of Women to U.S. State Legislative Seats," *Legislative Studies Quarterly*, 12 (February 1987), pp. 125–142.

2. Center for the American Woman and Politics. Eagleton Institute of Politics (New Brunswick, NJ: 1994).

3. Irene Diamond, *Sex Roles in the State House* (New Haven, CT: Yale University Press, 1977); Susan Welch, "Recruitment of Women to Public Office," *Western Political Quarterly*, 31 (September 1978), pp. 372–380; Susan Gluck Mezey, "The Effects of Sex on Recruitment: Local Connecticut Offices," in Debra Stewart (Ed.), *Women in Local Politics* (Metuchen, NJ: Scarecrow Press, 1980); Ruth Mandel, "The Image Campaign," in James David Barber and Barbara Kellerman (Eds.), *Women Leaders in American Politics* (Englewood Cliffs, NJ: Prentice-Hall, 1986), pp. 261–271; and Robert Darcy, Susan Welch, and Janet Clark, *Women, Elections, and Representation* (New York: Longman, 1987).

4. Margery M. Ambrosius and Susan Welch, "Women and Politics at the Grassroots: Women Candidates for Office in Three States," paper presented at the annual meeting of the Western Social Science Association, April 1981.

5. Diamond, *Sex Roles*; David B. Hill, "Political Culture and Female Political Representation," *Journal of Politics*, 43 (1–2) (1981), pp. 159–168.

6. Alice S. Rossi, "Beyond the Gender Gap: Women's Bid for Political Power," *Social Science Quarterly*, 64 (1983), pp. 718–733.

7. Hedlund et al., "Electability of Women Candidates."

8. Ruth Schwartz Cowan, "The Industrial Revolution in the Home: Household Technology and Social Change in the Twentieth Century," *Technology and Culture*, 17 (1976), pp. 1–23.

9. Marcia Manning Lee, "Why Few Women Hold Public Office: Democracy and Sex Roles," *Political Science Quarterly*, 91 (1–2) (1976), pp. 297–314; and Marcia Lynn Whicker and Jennie J. Kronenfeld, *Sex Roles: Technology, Politics, and Policy* (New York: Praeger, 1986).

10. Darcy et al., *Women, Elections, and Representation*.

11. B. E. Forisha, *Sex Roles and Personal Awareness* (Morristown, NJ: General Learning Press, 1978); R. D. Hess and J. V. Torney, *The Development of Political Attitudes in Children* (Chicago: Aldine, 1967); J. Boles and H. Duriot, "Stereotyping of Males and Females in Elected Office: The Implications of an Attitudinal Study," paper presented at the annual meeting of the Midwest Political Science Association, April 1980; J. Boles and H. Duriot, "Political Woman and Superwoman: Sex Stereotyping of Females in Elected Office," paper presented at the annual meeting of the Midwest Political Science Association meeting, April 1981; R. B. Deber, "The Fault Dear Brutus: Women as Congressional Candidates in Pennsylvania," *Journal of Politics*, 44 (1982), pp. 463–479; L. Ekstrand and W. Eckert, "The Impact of Candidate's Sex on Voter Choice," *Western Political Quarterly*, 34 (1981), pp. 78–87: Hedlund et al., "Electability of Women Candidates," Virginia Sapiro, "If U.S. Senator Baker Were a Woman: An Experimental Study of Candidates' Images," *Political Psychology*, 3 (1–2) (1981–1982), pp. 61–83; Lee Sigelman and Susan Welch, "Race, Gender, and Opinion toward Black and Female Presidential Candidates," *Public Opinion Quarterly*, 48 (1984), pp. 462–475; Nancy E. McGlen and Karen O'Connor, *Women, Politics, and American Society* (Englewood Cliffs, NJ: Prentice-Hall, 1995), pp. 58–101, and Janet Clark, "Getting There: Women in Political Office," in Marianne Githens, Pippa Norris, and Joni Lovenduskit (Eds.), *Different Roles, Different Voices: Women and Politics in the United States and Europe* (New York: HarperCollins, 1994), pp. 99–110.

12. F. L. Gehlen, "Women Members of Congress: A Distinctive Role," in M. Githens and J. L. Prestage (Eds.), *A Portrait of Marginality: The Political Behavior of American Women* (New York: Longman, 1977), pp. 304–319; McGlen and O'Connor, *Women, Politics, and American Society*, pp. 80–81.

13. Elizabeth Holtzman and Shirley Williams, "Women in the Political World: Observations," *Daedalus*, 116 (1987), pp. 25–33; Leonie Huddy and Nayda Terkildsen, "Gender Stereotypes and the Perception of Male and Female Candidates," *American Journal of Political Science*, 37 (1993), pp. 119–147.

14. Marcia Lynn Whicker and Todd Areson, "The Maleness of the American Presidency," *Journal of Political Science*, 17 (Spring 1989), pp. 63–73; Mandel, "The Image Campaign"; Linda Witt, Karen M. Paget, and Glenna Matthews, *Running as a Woman: Gender Power in American Politics* (New York: Free Press 1994), pp. 1–28.

15. Susan Welch and Lee Sigelman, "Changes in Public Attitudes toward Women in Politics," *Social Science Quarterly*, 62 (June 1982), pp. 312–322.

16. Margaret Mericle, S. Lenart, and K. Heilig, "Women Candidates: Even If All Things Are Equal, Will They Get Elected?" paper presented at the annual meeting of the Midwest Political Science Association, April 1989.

17. Hedlund et al., "Electability of Women Candidates."

18. A. Karnig and B. O. Walter, "Election of Women to City Councils," *Social Science Quarterly*, 56 (1976), pp. 605–613; Ekstrand and Eckert, "The Impact of Candidate's Sex"; Robert Darcy and S. Schramm, "When Women Run against Men," *Public Opinion Quarterly*, 41 (1977), pp. 1–12; and R. Bernstein, "Why Are There So Few Women in the House?" *Western Political Quarterly*, 39 (1986), pp. 155–163; Carole Chaney and Barbara Sinclair, "Women and the 1992 House Elections," in Elizabeth Adell Cook, Sue Thomas, and Clyde Wilcox, (Eds.), *The Year of the Woman: Myths and Realities* (Boulder, CO: Westview Press, 1994), pp. 125–127.

19. Lee Sigelman, Carol K. Sigelman, and Christopher Fowler, "A Bird of a Different Feather? An Experimental Investigation of Physical Attractiveness and the Electability of Female Candidates," *Social Psychology Quarterly*, 50 (1) (1987) pp. 32–43.

20. John F. Zipp and Eric Plutzer, "Gender Differences in Voting for Female Candidates: Evidence from the 1982 Election." *Public Opinion Quarterly*, 49 (1985), pp. 179–197.

21. Darcy, Welch, and Clark, "Women, Elections, and Representation." pp. 73–81.

22. Barbara C. Burrell, "Women's and Men's Campaigns for the U.S. House of Representatives, 1972–1982: A Finance Gap?" *American Politics Quarterly*, 13 (1985), pp. 251–272; Robert M. Darcy, M. Brewer, and C. Clay, "Women in the Oklahoma Political System: State Legislative Elections," *Social Science Journal*, 21 (January 1985), pp. 67–78; Candice J. Nelson, "Women's PACs in the Year of the Woman," in Elizabeth Adell Cook, Sue Thomas, and Clyde Wilcox, (Eds.), *The Year of the Woman: Myths and Realities*, (Boulder, CO: Westview Press, 1994), pp. 181–195.

23. I. Gertzog and M. M. Simard, "Women and 'Hopeless' Congressional Candidacies: Nomination Frequencies, 1916–1978," *American Politics Quarterly*, 9 (1981), pp. 449–466; and Janet Clark, Robert Darcy, Susan Welch, and M. Ambrosius, "Women as Legislative Candidates in Six States," in J. A. Flammang (Ed.), *Political Women: Current Roles in State and Local Government* (Beverly Hills, CA: Sage, 1985).

24. Robert Darcy and James R. Choike, "A Formal Analysis of Legislative Turnover: Women Candidates and Legislative Representation," *American Journal of Political Science*, 30 (1) (1986), pp. 237–255.

25. Barbara C. Burrell, "The Political Opportunity of Women Candidates for the U.S. House of Representatives in 1984," *Women and Politics*, 8 (1988), pp. 51–68.

26. Susan Carroll, *Women as Candidates in American Politics* (Bloomington: Indiana University Press, 1985).

27. Elizabeth Vallance, *Women in the House: A Study of Women Members of Parliament* (Atlantic Highlands, NJ: Athlone Press, 1979).

28. Pippa Norris, "The Impact of the Electoral System on Election of Women to National Legislatures," in Marianne Githens, Pippa Norris and Joni Lovenduski (Eds.), *Different Roles, Different Voices: Women and Politics in the United States and Europe* (New York: HarperCollins, 1994), pp. 114–121.

29. Rossi, "Beyond the Gender Gap."

30. Curt Anderson, "Kansas Women Rise to Power in Congress," *Times-Picayune*, November 26, 1994, p. A8.

31. Gehlen, "Women Members of Congress."

32. Irwin Gertzog, "Changing Patterns of Female Recruitment to the U.S. House of Representatives," *Legislative Studies Quarterly*, 4 (1979), pp. 429–445.

33. Darcy, Welch, and Clark, *Women, Elections, and Representation.*

34. Ibid.

FURTHER READINGS

Carroll, Susan J. *Women as Candidates in American Politics*. Bloomington: Indiana University Press, 1985.

Carroll, Susan J., Debra L. Dodson, and Ruth B. Mandel. *The Impact of Women in Public Office: An Overview*. New Brunswick, NJ: Center for the American Woman and Politics, 1991.

Darcy, Robert, Susan Welch, and Janet Clark. *Women, Elections and Representation*. New York: Longman, 1987.

Fowler, Linda L., and Robert D. McClure. *Political Ambition: Who Decides to Run for Congress*. New Haven; CT: Yale University Press, 1989.

Gertzog, Irwin N. *Congressional Women: Their Recruitment, Treatment and Behavior*. New York: Praeger, 1984.

Kirkpatrick, Jeane J. *Political Woman*. New York: Basic Books, 1974.

Klein, Ethel. *Gender Politics*. Cambridge, MA: Harvard University Press, 1984.

Phillips, Anne. *Engendering Democracy*. University Park: Pennsylvania State University Press, 1991.

Fenichel Pitkin, Hanna. *The Concept of Representation*. Berkeley: University of California Press, 1967.

Witt, Linda, Karen M. Paget, and Glenna Matthews. *Running as a Woman: Gender and Power in American Politics*. New York: Free Press, 1994.

Why Are More Women State Legislators?

Wilma Rule

The 1994 elections marked the first major standstill in women's election to state legislatures in over twenty years. It was the first time that a large number of legislatures actually had declines in women members. What was going on here? Was this the end of women's advances toward equal legislative representation? Was the women's movement dead? Would this decline have negative consequences for women state leaders and members of Congress?

Hold on. There is a brighter side: Women actually increased their percentages in twenty-five of the fifty legislatures over the previous election, while in six states they held their own. In 1994 they averaged 21 percent of state legislatures, whereas ten years earlier they were 12 percent and in 1974 only 6 percent.[1] Women legislators have increased proportions by 75 percent since 1984 but have slipped from a 100 percent increase over the past decade. But the women's movement for equal political representation was more powerful than ever before.

While some trends from 1974 to 1984 remain the same, the elections of 1994 show that indeed there is much change—some for the better and some making women's recruitment to state legislatures a little worse for the next decade.

This chapter asks the following questions:

1. What were the reasons for women's steady advance from 1974 to 1984? What has changed in 1994? (see Tables 1 and 3).

Wilma Rule is adjunct professor of political science at the University of Nevada, Reno. Original article appeared in the *Western Political Quarterly*, vol. 43 (June 1990). This version, revised by the author, is reprinted with permission by the author and the University of Utah, copyright holder.

Table 1 Women in U.S. State Legislatures, 1974 and 1984

	State Senate			State House			Percentage of Women in Both Houses*	
	Number of Senators	Number of Women		Number of Members	Number of Women			
State		1974	1984		1974	1984	1974	1984
Alabama	35	0	1	105	1	5	1%	4%
Alaska	20	1	2	40	6	4	12	10
Arizona	30	3	4	60	10	12	14	18
Arkansas	35	1	0	100	2	7	2	5
California	40	1	2	80	2	12	3	12
Colorado	35	3	6	65	5	19	8	25
Connecticut	36	3	8	151	17	33	10	21
Delaware	21	1	3	41	6	7	11	16
Florida	40	1	1	120	6	18	4	16
Georgia	56	0	2	180	2	17	1	8
Hawaii	25	1	3	51	3	12	5	20
Idaho	35	1	3	70	6	12	7	14
Illinois	59	3	8	118	8	18	5	11
Indiana	50	3	4	100	6	14	6	12
Iowa	50	4	1	100	7	13	7	9
Kansas	40	1	2	125	3	21	2	13
Kentucky	38	2	2	100	3	8	4	7
Louisiana	39	1	0	105	2	5	2	3
Maine	33	1	6	151	16	35	9	22
Maryland	47	4	2	141	8	33	6	19
Massachusetts	40	2	7	160	7	19	3	9
Michigan	38	0	1	110	6	12	4	9
Minnesota	67	0	8	134	6	18	3	13
Mississippi	52	1	0	122	5	3	3	2
Missouri	34	1	1	163	10	18	6	10
Montana	50	2	2	100	7	12	6	6
Nebraska**	49	1	7	—	—	—	2	14
Nevada	21	1	2	42	4	3	8	8
New Hampshire	24	2	5	400	83	111	—	27
New Jersey	40	3	2	80	6	8	8	8
New Mexico	42	2	1	70	0	6	2	6
New York	61	3	5	150	4	15	3	10
North Carolina	50	1	6	120	8	20	5	15
North Dakota	53	3	3	106	10	12	8	10
Ohio	33	3	0	99	5	12	6	9
Oklahoma	48	0	1	101	2	10	1	7

(continued)

Table 1 (*continued*)

State	Number of Senators	Number of Women 1974	Number of Women 1984	Number of Members	Number of Women 1974	Number of Women 1984	Percentage of Women in Both Houses* 1974	Percentage of Women in Both Houses* 1984
		State Senate			*State House*			
Oregon	30	2	6	60	9	13	12	21
Pennsylvania	50	1	1	203	6	8	3	4
Rhode Island	50	1	5	100	3	13	3	12
South Carolina	46	0	2	124	5	10	3	7
South Dakota	35	1	4	70	5	10	6	13
Tennessee	33	0	1	99	4	9	3	8
Texas	31	1	0	150	5	11	3	6
Utah	29	0	1	75	6	6	6	7
Vermont	30	3	4	150	17	29	11	18
Virginia	40	0	2	100	6	11	4	9
Washington	49	1	8	98	12	19	9	18
West Virginia	34	1	2	100	9	12	7	10
Wisconsin	33	0	2	99	6	24	5	20
Wyoming	30	1	2	62	4	16	5	20
Average Percentage		3.8	8.1		7.1	13.7	5.7	12.1

*Percentages are computed on the basis of numbers of state senate and house members in 1974 and 1984. The numbers of senate and house members in this table are for 1984.

**Nebraska is unicameral.

Source: "Women State Legislators as of January, 1974" (New Brunswick, NJ: Center for the American Woman in Politics, Eagleton Institute of Politics, Rutgers, 1974) and Council of State Governments, *State Elective Officials and the Legislatures, 1983–1984* (Lexington, KY: Council of State Governments).

2. What are the factors that are more favorable in the 1980s than in the 1970s? How does 1994 compare to 1984?

EXPLAINING WOMEN'S INCREASES IN THE 1980s

In order to arrive at an explanation of women's growing power in 1984, past research is replicated and then other variables are added in an effort to understand the changes that have occurred since the 1970s. We examine whether women are still likely to be elected in states with small populations and large legislatures, as was true in the 1960s and 1970s. We also ask whether one can predict women's increases in the 1980s from the proportions in individual states in the 1970s.[2] We expect that states favorable in past decades will continue to be so, while at the same time others are now providing new opportunities for women's election to legislatures.

We also examine the relationship of Democratic or Republican Party dominance and women's recruitment to state assemblies and senates.[3] Are Republican Party–dominated states (i.e., those with 60 percent or more Republican members in the legislature) still favorable grounds for women's election, as in the 1960s and 1970s? And are Democratic Party states still unfavorable? We expect that the legislative barriers to women in the Democratic Party, particularly in the northern states, came down in the 1980s. But we also anticipate that the Republican Party states remained favorable grounds for women's election in that decade.

Competitive states—those that are not dominated by one party or another—had no relationship to women's election in the 1970s. We expect that trend to continue. This is because those states varied in the money that was spent for social welfare in the 1970s. Low-social-welfare states usually are not favorable for women's election to state legislatures, while those that spend more for this purpose are.[4]

Several scholars have observed that women are likely to be recruited in states that have a "moral" political culture, and are unlikely to be elected in "traditional" and "individualistic" states.[5] In moral states—such as those in most of New England as well as Arizona, Oregon, and Washington—politics is everybody's business. Elected officials are expected to be selfless and committed to promoting the public's interest. In the "traditional" state politics of the southern states, by contrast, government is of, by, and for a privileged few, usually white males. And in the "individualistic" states of Illinois, Massachusetts, and New York, government is viewed as if it were a business serving various competing interests for the state officeholders whose career is politics. This study anticipates that states with moral cultures will continue to be favorable and that women's recruitment in traditional and individualistic states will increase over a decade earlier.

Recently attention has turned to a new question: Does it make a difference in women's recruitment if legislators are elected under different election procedures? Yes, several scholars found, it does make a considerable difference.[6] They discovered that when voters could choose two or more representatives for the legislature instead of one from each district, many more women got elected to their state houses.

We expect that the importance of multimember districts for women's election to state legislatures will be upheld in this study. Also, we expect that the single primary (in which the candidate with the most votes wins the nomination) will be favorable to women. The double or runoff primary in some southern states requires that a candidate achieve an absolute majority vote before she or he runs in the final election.[7] A majority of votes is more difficult to achieve for a woman legislative candidate than it is for a male contestant. In consequence, the author expects that fewer women will be elected to legislatures in double-primary states.

This essay also examines whether the legislature is still a dead end for women legislators, as it was in the 1970s when few were elected to Congress. Where large proportions of women were elected to legislatures in low-population states (such as New Hampshire), few were elected to Congress; also, where a small proportion was recruited to the legislatures in high-population states (such as California), only a small number also went on to Congress.[8] We hypothesize that this situation has changed in the 1980s, with more opportunity for women legislators to move up to Congress and to statewide offices such as governor and secretary of state.

Of considerable interest is whether the women's movement has played a significant role in this period of great change in women's legislative representation. We expect that with the growth of the women's movement, there has developed a reciprocal relationship among women at various levels of government that had not been present before. Specific women's organizations, such as the National Organization for Women, are also expected to have aided women's recruitment in the 1980s.[9] In turn, an important base of women's organizations has been women in the workforce and professional women. It is expected that these changes in women's work outside the home have had a favorable impact on women's legislative recruitment in the 1980s as in the 1970s.

The factors promoting or hindering women's recruitment to state senates have been given scarce research attention, perhaps because few women were elected to them. However, the percentage of women in state senates has doubled in the last decade and in 1984 reached 8 percent. Women's recruitment to state senates may be of interest not only because it will broaden the representativeness of those chambers but also because it will provide a future pool of experienced and credible women candidates for the U.S. House of Representatives, which in 1990 was about 94 percent male.

We suggest that women's recruitment to state senates has a time-lagged, two-tiered pattern. We expect that those states where women were first elected in large numbers to state assemblies in the 1960s and 1970s, such as many in New England, will now have the largest percentages of women state senators. This is likely because women who have served some terms in the assembly and who have become well known should have greater chances for state senate election than those without a legislative background.[10]

METHODOLOGY

Our analysis required the gathering of some eighty—sometimes overlapping—political and socioeconomic contextual variables. For example, we collected data on the extent of party dominance in each house of the fifty legislatures for 1974 and 1984, as well as the strength of parties at the local and state levels. The data were collected primarily from standard sources (see Table 2).

Numerous and different statistical tests on various sets and subsets were conducted. These included Pearsonian correlations, factor analysis, and stepwise multiple regressions. The bivariate correlational analysis included separate and combined sets of the percentages of women in the assemblies and senates for the 1974 and 1984 periods in all fifty states, and in forty non-Confederate states. From this analysis, the direct relationship between women's election to state legislatures and political and socioeconomic variables was determined. The results are presented in Table 3.

Table 2 Sources for Variables

Council for State Governments. *The Book of the States*, 1972–1973, 1974–1975, 1983–1984, and 1985.

National Center for Educational Statistics. *Earned Degrees Conferred*, 1972–1973, 1973–1974, and 1979–1980.

National Organization for Women.

Official Catholic Directory. Wilmette, IL: National Register Publishing Company, 1983.

U.S. Bureau of the Census. *Characteristics of the Population, 1980; General Social and Economic Characteristics, 1980; Statistical Abstract of the United States, 1981, 1984, 1985, 1986, 1988, 1989* (Washington, DC: U.S. Government Printing Office, 1986).

Then a rotated orthogonal factor analysis using all the variables was undertaken. One objective was to verify the interpretation of the correlation analysis by employing another test using the same data; another was to provide a basis for reducing the data set. The next step involved multiple regression analyses with the reduced set of thirty-nine significant variables. Of six run only two are presented here. One regression used the decade's percentage increases in both chambers. The results are found in the section "The New Wave: States with the Most Increases 1974–1984." Another regression presented in Table 4 used the 1984 percentage of women in both chambers.

FINDINGS

Continuity and Change in All Fifty States, 1974–1984

The contextual variables related to women's political recruitment in the last decade are summarized in Table 3. They are based on simple bivariate correlations. In section I of Table 3, the continuing favorable contextual factors from the 1970s are presented. These are descriptive of Republican-dominated New England states. In section II are listed two continuing negative factors for women's recruitment— Democratic Party dominance of the assemblies and state senates and traditional culture. Although the negative correlation with Democratic Party dominance has declined in the last decade, it is still significant in the following ten former Confederate states: Alabama, Arkansas, Florida, Georgia, Louisiana, Mississippi, North Carolina, South Carolina, Texas, and Virginia.

In section III the previously unfavorable relationship of small assemblies in high-population states no longer is a negative contextual factor as, for example, in the California of 1984. Nor are states that have a low per capita income. In the following section, there are six new variables that have emerged as significant for women's recruitment during the ten-year period. These include individualistic state cultures, such as those in the Midwest, and states with multimember assembly districts.

The remaining four favorable variables relate in various ways to the growth of the women's movement. The first shows a relationship between the election of

Table 3   Continuity and Change in Women's Recruitment to State Assemblies and Senates, 1974–1984 (Based on Pearsonian Correlations)

I. Continuing favorable factors, 1974–1984
Republican Party dominance of legislatures***

Moral state political culture***

Higher AFDC payments**

No second primary**

II. Continuing unfavorable factors, 1974–1984
Democratic dominance of legislatures, especially in former Confederacy states***

Traditional southern culture***

III. Factors no longer unfavorable, 1984
Small assemblies in high-population states‡

Low-income states‡

IV. New contextual conditions aiding women's recruitment, 1984
Individualistic state culture***

Multimember assembly districts*

Women in U.S. Congress**

Women in labor force***

Professional women**

National Organization for Women***

***Significant at the .001 level.
**Significant at the .01 level.
*Significant at the .02 level.
‡Not statistically significant.

women in Congress to greater representation of women in the same state's legislatures. Women's labor force participation and the presence of a large proportion of women professionals are also significant. Finally, women's associations (as represented in our data set by ratios of chapters of the National Organization for Women to state population) are shown to be highly correlated with greater percentages of women in state legislatures.

THE 1994 ELECTION

Comparing 1994 with the earlier years, we find that Republican Party dominance has been modified somewhat as a favorable factor. This is due in part to Republican majorities in the lower houses in the Carolinas and the state senate in Florida. Fewer women were elected to the legislatures in the former, while in Florida's senate there was no change from the previous election. The traditional southern culture and Christian fundamentalism appear related to growing Southern Republicanism. Generally it differs from the Republicanism of New England on approaches to such issues as abortion, crime, education, and welfare.

In 1994 Democratic dominance of state legislatures appeared to be less of a negative factor in the former "solid South." Democratic dominance has been wan-

Table 4   Women State Legislators' Party Affiliation and Women's Legislative Representation, 1994

State	Total Number of State Legislators	Women's Party Affiliation		Women's Percentage in Both Houses	Percentage Decrease or Increase since 1992
		Democratic	Republican		
Alabama	140	6	0	4	−2
Alaska	60	6	7 (1 Ind.)	23	+1
Arizona	90	10	17	30	−3
Arkansas	135	14	3	13	+3
California	120	19	6 (1 Ind.)	22	−1
Colorado	100	16	16	32	−3
Connecticut	187	34	16	27	+2
Delaware	62	2	11	21	+7
Florida	160	23	8	19	+1
Georgia	236	29	14	18	+1
Hawaii	76	11	5	21	−3
Idaho	105	9	21	29	−1
Illinois	177	20	22	24	+1
Indiana	150	13	19	21	+2
Iowa	150	11	15	17	+2
Kansas	165	15	30	27	−2
Kentucky	138	5	6	8	+3
Louisiana	144	12	2	10	+2
Maine	186	32	18 (1 Ind.)	27	−5
Maryland	188	42	12	29	+5
Massachusetts	200	33	15	24	+1
Michigan	148	20	14	23	+3
Minnesota	201	30	20	25	−2
Mississippi	174	17	3	12	+1
Missouri	197	18	21	20	0
Montana	150	18	18	24	+4
Nebraska	49	Nonpartisan		24	+4
Nevada	63	11	11	35	+8
New Hampshire	424	49	79	30	−4
New Jersey	120	6	8	12	−0
New Mexico	112	15	8	20	+1
New York	211	29	10	18	0
North Carolina	170	11	16	16	−2
North Dakota	147	9	13	15	−1
Ohio	132	13	18	24	+3

(continued)

Table 4   (continued)

State	Total Number of State Legislators	Women's Party Affiliation		Women's Percentage in Both Houses	Percentage Decrease or Increase since 1992
		Democratic	*Republican*		
Oklahoma	149	11	5	11	+2
Oregon	90	14	10	27	0
Pennsylvania	253	15	14	12	+2
Rhode Island	150	27	8	23	−2
South Carolina	170	10	11	12	−1
South Dakota	105	8	11	18	−2
Tennessee	132	13	5	14	+2
Texas	181	21	13	19	+3
Utah	104	5	10	14	0
Vermont	180	34	19	29	−5
Virginia	140	12	4	11	0
Washington	147	34	24	40	0
West Virginia	134	13	7	15	−1
Wisconsin	132	17	15	24	−3
Wyoming	90	7	12	21	−3
Average Percentage		56%	44%	21%	+0.1%

Note: Percentages are rounded.

Source: Center for the American Woman and Politics, Fact Sheets, "Women in State Legislatures 1994," and 1995 (unofficial figures).

ing in the 1980s. Republican inroads seem to have brought more Democratic women into office as a result of party competition.

Another factor has been the Voting Rights Act. Previously gerrymandered legislative districts were redistricted in the 1980s and 1990s to give Blacks and Latinos representation previously denied them. As seats opened up, Democratic women typically have filled 10 to 15 percent of them in southern, as well as other, states.

As a whole, however, women have been disadvantaged whenever legislative election methods were changed. Thus in the 1980s and 1990s nine former multi-member legislative districts were changed to single-member ones. The result were drastic declines in some state's women's representation. Florida's, Hawaii's, and Wyoming's declined from about the fifth highest (averaging 20 percent women in 1984) to around twenty-sixth in 1994 (still with about the same average percentage of women legislators). Among the remaining multimember states, Arizona, Maryland, New Hampshire, and Washington were also leaders in 1984. They averaged 33 percent women legislators in 1994, with Washington State highest in the nation at 40 percent (see Table 4).

The decline from 100 percent to 75 percent in the growth of women's representation from 1984 to 1994 is due in part to the election system change. Switching to a semiproportional or proportional representation system for state legislatures would have brought more political equity for majority and minority women (and men).

In summary, the major changes in the last decade for women's legislative representation are a slight decline in the *favorability* of the Republican Party; a slight decline in the *unfavorability* of the Democratic Party; the unfavorable impact on women's legislative recruitment in states changing to single-member districts; and the 25 percent decline in the decade's growth rate of women's representation. The favorable factors listed in Table 2 show continuity from 1974 to 1994.

THE NEW WAVES: STATES WITH THE MOST INCREASES 1974–1994

In 1984 40 percent of the states had increases of women legislators of 100 percent or more over the previous decade. Ten years later the record was almost as good, with 36 percent growing at a high rate. Those eighteen legislatures (except for Kansas)—like the ones before them with large increases—constituted new ground for growth in women's representation (see Tables 1 and 3).

There was only one Republican-dominated state, Kansas, in the 1994 group. The remaining seventeen were politically competitive or tending in that direction, and Democrat-dominant states: Alaska, Arkansas, Georgia, Idaho, Illinois, Louisiana, Massachusetts, Michigan, Mississippi, Missouri, Montana, New Mexico, Nevada, Ohio, Pennsylvania, Texas, and Washington.

The most significant and striking growth pattern is found in five southern states. In Mississippi women's representation advanced from 2 percent to 12 percent, equaling the northern state of Pennsylvania. In addition, Mississippi, like the others, had a small contingent of Republicans among its women legislators.

The inland western states of Nevada and Montana increased 300 percent, and four other state legislatures in that region saw large increases. Five midwestern states' showed growth of 100 to 150 percent. Lastly, the two eastern states with large increases were Pennsylvania, which had growth of 200 percent, and Massachusetts, with 166 percent more women legislators than the decade before.

New wave states of 1984 with the highest growth in state assemblies continued to augment appreciably in 1994, except for Florida, Hawaii, and Wyoming, whose slowdown was explained previously. The high-growth states included California, Colorado, Kansas, Maine, Maryland, Rhode Island, and Wisconsin. They varied in political party and political culture, and all at least doubled the number of women state senators by 1994.

Viewing the 1984 and 1994 geographic and political mix of these fast-growing states, this picture emerges: From Alaska to Texas, from California to Maryland, women candidates have better chances than ever for election. A significant factor for the past decade has been the continued promotion and support of women candidates by women's organizations. Of course, there still exists a tremendous range, from 4.3 percent women legislators in Alabama to 40 percent in Washington State. And women still averaged only one-fifth of the nation's state lawmakers in 1994 although women constitute over half of America's population.

Most Powerful Predictors of Recruitment, 1984 and 1994

Our final analysis ascertains the most powerful predictors of women's assembly and senate recruitment as of 1984. In the stepwise multiple regression in Table 4, each variable may be regarded as a separate dimension. Highly intercorrelated clusters of variables have been removed through the computer routine in order to provide a parsimonious list and to avoid complicating the results with multicolinearity. The percentage that each variable explains is given in the last column of the table, and the total explained by the nine variables is 76 percent.

Table 5 contains contextual factors that relate to the two 1984 trends the data have previously shown. The first trend is the continuance of the 1974 favorable contextual pattern for assemblies and senates, as in independent variables 1 (percentage women in 1974 assemblies), 5 and 6 (higher educational and Aid to Families with Dependent Children [AFDC] expenditures), and 7 (the single primary). These four variables explain 45 percent of the variance. The second trend is that of the "new wave" states now favorable to women's election to state legislatures. These new wave variables are 2 (percentage women in congressional delegation), 3 (more professional women), 4 (percentage women statewide officials), 8 (more NOW chapters per population), and 9 (multimember state senate districts). These five variables explain 31 percent of the variance in women's 1984 legislative recruit-

Table 5   **Most Powerful Predictors of Greater Women's Recruitment to State Assemblies and Senates, 1984 (Multiple Stepwise Regression) ($N = 50$)**

Independent Variables*	Multiple Correlation Coefficient (R)	Cumulative Percentage of Variance Explained (R^2)	Percentage Variance Explained by Each Variable
1. Percentage women in 1974 state assemblies	.61	37	37
2. Percentage women in state congressional delegation, 1974–1984	.72	52	15
3. Percentage women professionals	.76	58	6
4. Percentage women statewide officials	.80	64	6
5. State educational expenditures	.82	67	3
6. State AFDC expenditures	.83	69	2
7. Single primary	.85	72	3
8. National Organization for Women	.86	75	3
9. Multimember senate districts	.87	76	1

*The F ratio when each of the variables was entered into the equation was significant at less than the .001 level.

Sources: Refer to Table 2.

ment. The two trends for 1984 set forth in Table 4 were still in place in 1995. The oldest trend is continued above-average growth in women's representation in the states that led in the 1970s, including Arizona, Connecticut, Oregon, and Vermont. These and others favorable to women twenty years ago and in 1994 generally were higher in expenditures for education and aid to dependent children.

The second trend is strengthened due to increases from 1984 to 1994 in the number of women in Congress (from 25 to 55 members) and in the number of female statewide executive officers. The single primary continues as a boon for women candidates as do the remaining states with multimember districts. Women's groups in the previous and this decade, such as the National Organization of Women, the National Women's Political Caucus and their local branches, and Emily's List providing campaign finance, are of major importance.

CONCLUSION

This analysis shows that women's recruitment to state legislatures has almost tripled in the past twenty years. For the 1970s there was a building on the gains in the Republican–moralistic states most favorable to women in the 1960s. In the 1980s no political party or political culture was dominant in the states where women legislators had the most dramatic increases. Most states that led in the 1970s and 1980s continued to advance, with state senates at least doubling women members by the 1994 elections.

In 1994 the South broke out of its mold as the "solid [Democratic] South" for the first time in some 100 years. Republicans won three legislative bodies that previously had been Democratic, but the number of women legislators decreased. Gone is the southern Democratic Party as a negative factor for women's election in five states where their proportions at least doubled. Although women legislators' numbers are growing fast, seven of the ten southern states still have the lowest proportions in the nation.

Republican Party dominance was modified as a favorable factor for women's recruitment. Contemporary southern Republicanism appears to differ from New England Republicanism in approaches to abortion, education, and welfare. Also, Democratic dominance in the South became less unfavorable for women's recruitment in 1994, in part because of Republican competition. States that are competitive generally have been good grounds for women candidates in the 1980s to 1990s.

Turning to structural arrangements, the change of election procedures for nine states from multimember districts to single ones since 1980 adversely affected women's legislative recruitment and growth in 1994. A semiproportional or proportional election system would produce a fairer result for majority and minority women and men. Some multimember assemblies remain, and in four of them women's recruitment is in the top ten nationally.

The data presented in Tables 2 and 4 further substantiate the observation by other writers, including Mandel and Carroll, that the women's movement has made considerable impact on women's election to political office.[11] In addition, the large increase in women state executives and members of Congress from 1984 to 1994 has helped women's recruitment to state legislatures, and vice versa. In turn, women's organizations have provided womanpower and campaign financing to assist women's success at the polls.

The 1994 stalling of women's advance toward equal participation in state legislatures is not the beginning of the end. The number of women legislators, it is true, declined in five times as many states than is usual. But more than half of the states increased women's representation. Although the growth for the decade declined one-fourth, women legislators' increase was still high at 75 percent. The introduction of greater competition to Democratic Party dominance in state legislatures and other favorable factors noted earlier can only foretell greater opportunity for women legislators in the years ahead. As numbers of women legislators grow, legal gains can be made not only for women and children but also for protecting and promoting the state's environment, health, and a peacetime prosperity.[12]

NOTES

1. E. Werner, "Women in the State Legislatures," *Western Political Quarterly*, 19 (1968), pp. 40–50; I. Diamond *Sex Roles in the State House* (New Haven, CT: Yale University Press, 1977); C. Nechemias, "Changes in the Election of Women to U.S. State Legislative Seats," *Legislative Studies Quarterly*, 12 (1) (February 1987), pp. 125–142.

2. Diamond, *Sex Roles*.

3. W. Rule, "Why Women Don't Run: The Critical Contextual Factors in Women's Legislative Recruitment," *Western Political Quarterly*, 34 (March 1981), pp. 60–77.

4. Ibid.

5. See Diamond, *Sex Roles*; D. Hill, "Political Culture and Female Political Representation," *Journal of Politics*, 43 (1981), pp. 159–168.

6. R. Darcy, S. Welch, and J. Clark, *Women, Elections and Representation* (Lincoln: University of Nebraska Press, 1994), pp. 160–168; W. Rule, "Multi-member Districts, Minority and Anglo Women's and Men's Recruitment Opportunity," and subsequent chapters on Maryland and Arizona in W. Rule and J. Zimmerman (Eds.), *U.S.*

Electoral Systems: Their Impact on Women and Minorities (Westport, CT: Greenwood Press, 1992).

7. A. P. Lamis, "The Runoff Primary Controversy: Implications for Southern Politics." *PS*, 7 (1984), pp. 782–787.

8. See Rule, "Why Women Don't Run."

9. T. J. Volgy, J. E. Schwartz, and H. Gottlieb: "Female Representation and the Quest for Resources: Feminist Activism and Electoral Success," *Social Science Quarterly*, 66 (1986), pp. 156–168.

10. G. Jacobson, G. Kernell, and S. Kernell, *Strategy and Choice in Congressional Elections* (New Haven, CT: Yale University Press, 1981).

11. R. Mandel, *In the Running: The New Woman Candidate* (New York: Ticknor and Fields, 1981); S. J. Carroll, *Women as Candidates in American Politics* (Bloomington: University of Indiana Press, 1985.)

12. S. Thomas, *How Women Legislate* (New York: Oxford University Press, 1994), chapters 3, 4, and 6. See also B. Burrell, *A Woman's Place Is in the House* (Ann Arbor: University of Michigan Press, 1994).

FURTHER READINGS

Burrell, B. *A Woman's Place Is in the House*. Ann Arbor: University of Michigan Press, 1994.

Darcy, R., S. Welch, and J. Clark. *Women, Elections and Representation*. Lincoln: University of Nebraska Press, 1994.

Rule, W., and J. Zimmerman (Eds.). *U.S. Electoral Systems: Their Impact on Women and Minorities*. Westport, CT: Greenwood Press, 1992.

Thomas, S. *How Women Legislate*. New York: Oxford University Press, 1994.

Contemporary Women State Legislators: A Diverse Group with Diverse Agendas

Lynne E. Ford
Kathleen Dolan

The representation of women in American political institutions has been characterized as both a "puzzle" and a "problem"[1] It is a puzzle because, although women make up over half of the U.S. population, they constitute a considerably smaller proportion of elected representatives at all levels of government. Even in 1994, women did not approach parity at any level of public office. Is this because women are somehow prevented from seeking and winning election, or is it because they have simply chosen not to enter electoral politics as candidates? Research suggests some combination of factors but does not definitively solve the puzzle. The underrepresentation of women in legislatures is a problem because it runs counter to the ideals of representative democracy. Is a representative system legitimate when the minority is consistently called upon to speak for the interests of a majority of citizens? One theme in democratic theory "concerns the distribution of power in a political community: The degree to which people are free to share in making decisions about the community, and ultimately, themselves."[2] To the extent that women are included, government is more representative of society as a whole—both substantively and symbolically.[3] Will the gains made by women in the most recent elections, particularly at the state legislative level, resolve the puzzle and the problem?

In this chapter we use two different kinds of data in order to more fully understand the nature of representation by women state legislators today and to see

Lynne E. Ford is an assistant professor of political science at the College of Charleston. Kathleen Dolan is an assistant professor of political science at the University of Wisconsin–Oshkosh.

whether the type of woman serving in the state legislature has changed over time. Using this approach, we are able to create a profile of change over time and offer a full description of contemporary women state legislators. The most striking aspect of the population of women legislators today is the diversity in their backgrounds, their reasons for seeking office, and the agendas they pursue once in office. In the aggregate, women serving today are a reflection of the constituency they serve and offer the promise that a variety of women can win a seat and serve in the state legislatures, thus enriching both the quantity of women's representation and the quality of representative democracy overall.

GAINS FOR WOMEN OVER THE LAST TWENTY YEARS: ALL THINGS ARE NOT EQUAL

State legislatures are historically important institutions for women, and it is at the state level that women have made the greatest gains in striving for some level of proportionality (see Table 1). Consider that in 1970 women held just 4 percent of all available state legislative seats, and, until 1974, no woman had been elected governor of a state in her own right. By 1984 women had tripled their participation in the state legislatures, comprising 12 percent nationwide. In 1992, called by many the "Year of the Woman," women made the largest single net gain in any one election cycle, winning 1,526, or 20.4 percent, of the 7,424 seats available.[4]

In contrast, progress at the federal level has been much slower. In 1975 women represented only 4 percent of the membership in the U.S. Congress. Ten years later, their proportion had crept to 5 percent and to merely 6 percent (thirty-two women) in 1991. Finally, the elections in 1992 increased women's presence to 10 percent of the institution—forty-seven seats in the House and seven in the Senate.[5]

At local levels, measuring progress is more difficult because of the sheer number and variation in the kinds of positions available. Between 1975 and 1988, women's representation in county elected office increased from 3 to 9 percent and from 4 to 14 percent of all municipal elected positions.[6] Most visible at the local level are female big-city mayors, and in 1994 women were mayors of eighteen of the 100 largest U.S. cities.[7]

Table 1   Women's Representation in Elective Office over Time, 1977–1993

Level of Office	1977	1981	1985	1989	1993
U.S. Congress	4%	4%	5%	5%	10%
State legislatures	9	12	13	15	21
County governing board*	4	6	8	9	NA

*There are three states without a county governing board structure: Connecticut, Rhode Island, and Vermont.

Source: "Women in Elective Office 1994," CAWP Fact Sheet (New Brunswick, NJ: Center for the American Woman and Politics).

THE IMPORTANCE OF STATE LEGISLATURES TO WOMEN'S REPRESENTATION

All in all, women enjoy the greatest electoral successes at the state legislative level, and the majority of research on women candidates and elected officials concentrates on women serving in statehouses.[8] As women won increasingly more seats during the 1970s, a robust research effort confirmed the importance of state legislatures to women's representation in politics for a number of reasons. First, evidence shows that service in the state legislature functions as a key entry point to higher office; the rate of gains for women at the state level has a direct impact on the number of women serving in the national legislature and executive positions nationwide.[9] Of the forty-eight women who held seats in the 103rd Congress, twenty-one served in their state legislatures prior to being elected to the national legislature.[10]

Additionally, state legislatures hold particular importance for women from a policy perspective; many of the issues of direct concern to women are decided at the state level. The Equal Rights Amendment, issues of pay equity, spousal retirement benefits, teen pregnancy, women's health concerns, maternity leave issues, and workplace climate concerns have all received direct attention at the state level.[11] Research finds that a higher percentage of women than men spend time promoting passage of "women's rights" bills, and that women are more likely to list "women's distinctive concerns" (defined to include policy areas like health care, welfare, and education) when asked to name their top legislative priority.[12] To many interested in the promotion of women's rights, this suggests that as the number of women serving at all levels increases, the attention devoted to policy of direct concern to women will also increase. There is some initial evidence to support this contention. Thomas, for example, found that when the proportion of women in the legislature falls below 15 percent, women, like other minority groups, are constrained in their legislative behavior. In states where the proportion of women reached or surpassed 20 percent, women legislators gave priority to bills dealing with issues of women, children, and the family and were more successful in introducing, monitoring, and passing distinctive legislation than were their male colleagues.[13]

Although, on the whole, women have increased their presence in state legislatures nationwide, the proportion of women legislators varies considerably among the fifty states (Table 2). What might account for these differences? Research in this area is still inconclusive but suggests several possibilities. One such explanation may lie in the political culture of individual states and regions of the United States.[14] Historically, the dominant national culture in America has proscribed women's active participation in politics, defining the competitive electoral arena as most appropriate for men.[15] However, the considerable variation in the proportions of female representation across the states implies that some state environments may foster women's participation at both the mass and elite levels, while others do not.[16] In the South, for example, women only held 13 percent of the seats in the region in 1994, compared with 20.4 percent nationwide.[17] Irene Diamond found that

Table 2   Women in the State Legislatures, 1993

State	Senate	House	Total	% of Total	Rank by %
Alabama	1	7	8	5.7	49
Alaska	4	9	13	21.7	21
Arizona	9	23	32	35.6	2
Arkansas	1	12	13	9.6	46
California	6	22	28	23.3	18
Colorado	8	26	34	34.0	3
Connecticut	8	39	47	25.1	13
Delaware	3	6	9	14.5	38
Florida	6	22	28	17.5	31
Georgia	6	35	41	23.2	19
Hawaii	6	12	18	23.7	16
Idaho	9	23	32	30.5	7
Illinois	11	30	41	23.2	19
Indiana	13	16	29	19.3	27
Iowa	6	16	22	14.7	37
Kansas	14	33	47	28.5	8
Kentucky	1	5	6	4.3	50
Louisiana	1	9	10	6.9	48
Maine	11	47	58	31.2	6
Maryland	10	34	44	23.4	17
Massachusetts	9	37	46	23.0	20
Michigan	3	26	29	19.6	26
Minnesota	20	35	55	27.4	9
Mississippi	4	15	19	10.9	44
Missouri	1	37	38	19.3	29
Montana	8	21	29	19.3	27
Nebraska*	10	NA	10	20.4	23
Nevada	5	12	17	27.0	11
New Hampshire	9	133	142	33.5	5
New Jersey	2	13	15	12.5	41
New Mexico	8	14	22	19.6	25
New York	7	27	34	16.1	35
North Carolina	7	24	31	18.2	30
North Dakota	8	16	24	16.3	34
Ohio	5	23	28	21.2	22
Oklahoma	6	8	14	9.4	47
Oregon	7	17	24	26.7	12
Pennsylvania	4	21	25	9.9	45
Rhode Island	11	26	37	24.7	14
South Carolina	3	19	22	12.9	40

(continued)

Table 2 (continued)

State	Senate	House	Total	% of Total	Rank by %
South Dakota	7	14	21	20.0	24
Tennessee	3	13	16	12.1	42
Texas	4	25	29	16.0	36
Utah	2	12	14	13.5	39
Vermont	11	50	61	33.9	4
Virginia	4	12	16	11.4	43
Washington	17	41	58	39.5	1
West Virginia	5	17	22	16.4	33
Wisconsin	7	29	36	27.3	10
Wyoming	5	17	22	24.4	15
United States	336	1,180	1,516	20.4	

*Nebraska has a nonpartisan, unicameral legislature.

Source: Data provided by the National Conference of State Legislatures, January 1993.

"moralistic" cultures encourage a political environment "potentially receptive to the values and style that have traditionally been associated with women—concern with public welfare rather than personal enrichment and so forth," while "traditionalistic" cultures defined politics as an exercise in maintaining the status quo, largely excluding the participation and interests of women.[18] In addition, the size of the legislative district, whether the legislature meets on a full- or part-time basis, whether it is characterized as professional or nonprofessional, and the level of pay have been found to exert some influence on the number of women elected.[19]

CHANGING PROFILES: THE "TRADITIONAL" VERSUS THE "CONTEMPORARY" WOMAN STATE LEGISLATOR

When scholars first began to study women elected to the legislatures, they compared women's characteristics, motivations for seeking the office, and legislative behaviors with those of their male legislative colleagues.[20] They found that women elected through the early 1970s were less well educated and older than their male colleagues, less likely to be married with small children at home, unlikely to have pursued a professional career outside the legislature, more likely to be motivated to seek public office by civic concerns and the desire to make life better for others, unlikely to have been tapped for the seat by their local party elites (even though they may have worked for years within the party ranks), and have little expressed desire to pursue higher office or a full-time career in politics.[21] These early women legislators were forced to follow a rather passive path to office, dependent on political ties to others and situational factors beyond their control, one characterized by a vicarious status mediated by those with more direct access to political power and leadership structures.

More recently, as career paths and socioeconomic characteristics of men and women have converged, the number of women elected to office has increased. Many of the differences between male and female candidates found previously have largely disappeared in importance for women seeking office in the 1980s and beyond.[22] Educational and occupational opportunities for women have expanded greatly, leading to ever-increasing numbers of women pursuing higher education and employment outside the home, often in areas that were previously considered "nontraditional careers."[23] Similar changes have been occurring in politics. Recent research finds that as educational, occupational, and financial doors have been opened for women in the last twenty years, their "political opportunity" has expanded as well.[24]

The recent changes in women's social and political lives raise two questions. First, are the women elected to office in the 1990s different from their predecessors of the 1970s and 1980s? Have more recently elected women been able to combine politics, work, and family in ways not possible for an earlier generation of women legislators? Are they capitalizing on educational and professional occupational networks in an effort to increase their chances of being elected to political office? Second, if women state legislators are changing, what are they like today? What new characteristics and abilities do they bring to the state legislatures, and what are the implications for the representation of women?

INDICATORS OF TRANSITION: THE EMERGENCE OF THE NEW-STYLE WOMAN LEGISLATOR OVER TIME

While others have asked a similar question—Is there a new type of woman in office?—the dominant research approach continues to focus on examining differences between men and women currently holding political office.[25] Having found that women still differ from men in a number of areas, some researchers have concluded that women legislators have not changed. In our view, this approach does not completely address the question. Simply confirming that male and female legislators do not yet resemble one another on some number of indicators does not preclude the possibility of significant changes taking place among women themselves. In order to determine whether women have changed over time in relation to those who came before them, women need to be the primary focus of the inquiry. To undertake this examination, we collected demographic, political, and legislative data on all women serving in the legislatures of fifteen states in 1972, 1982, and 1992.[26] The states were selected to capture geographic diversity, political culture, the proportion of women in the legislatures, and the level of professionalism of the legislatures.[27] There were a total of 706 women who served in these state legislatures during the time periods under analysis.[28]

In comparing the demographic and personal characteristics of women serving across the three points in time, we were interested in whether women's preparation for office, work life, and family life had changed. For comparison, we selected occupation prior to entering the legislature as well as personal factors like marital status, number of children, level of education, and age at the time of their first election. We expected that, like many women today, legislators of the 1990s would have taken advantage of expanding social and economic opportunities and therefore be more likely to have worked outside the home before serving in the legislature, have at least a college degree if not professional training, and be married.

Table 3 presents the comparative analysis results.[29] Women elected most recently are significantly more likely to be younger, married, and a member of a racial minority group than were women serving in 1972 or 1982. Further, women in 1992 were more likely to be employed in business or professional positions and less likely to be homemakers prior to entering the legislature. In looking at levels of education, the likelihood that a woman serving in the legislature has a college degree is quite consistent over the twenty-year period (33 percent in 1972 and 37 percent in 1992). The biggest change is in postgraduate education, where the number of women completing degrees beyond the bachelor's degree more than doubles, from 7 percent in 1972 to 17 percent in 1992.

In looking at women's preparation to run for political office, we focused on several political variables. In the past, women followed a path to the state legislature that required them to gain substantial political experience along the way through a series of elected or appointed offices, most often beginning with the school board. These same women often devoted substantial time to service in the political party. The traditional image of women as a part of the "lick-em and stick-em" brigade of party workers is a familiar one in American politics and proved to be one of the only ways for women to attract the attention of party elites recruiting candidates for office. Since women were less credentialed than men at the time, party service and recognition increased their viability. This is not as necessary for women in the 1990s, since their political portfolio is now more likely to include professional degrees and occupations as well as the financial backing gained through professional and occupational networks.

Table 3 compares women's previous political office experience and their service to the party, defined in this case as having held party office. There is no significant difference among women in having held elected or appointed offices prior to election to the legislature (41 percent in 1972 and 37 percent in 1992). There is, however, a significant difference in the type and level of previous office. Women in 1992 were three times more likely to enter the state legislature from a position on the town or city council (9 percent compared with 3 percent in 1972). Women in 1972 were twice as likely to have served on a state board or commission, usually in an appointed position (15 percent compared with 7 percent in 1992). Political party service reflects the same trends, but the largest differences are found between 1982 and 1992; 44 percent of women in 1982 held party office, compared with only 30 percent serving in 1992. This may mean that women no longer need the party in order to be recognized as viable candidates. It could also mean that political parties are casting a wider net in recruiting women to run for office and looking beyond the rather small pool of local party leadership. Alternatively, it may be a reflection of the general trend away from involvement with parties seen nationally among candidates, public officials, and the electorate.

**Table 3   Difference of Means Analysis for Women State Legislators
1972–1992: Demographic, Political, and Legislative Variables—
Means (percent) for Measures at Three Points in Time**

	1972	1982	1992
Total Legislators (N)	87	241	378
Occupation			
Lawyer	11	10	9
Educator	25	22	19
Homemaker	25	20	8**
Business/professional	11	16	22*
Support personnel	11	9	8
Education			
College graduate	33	35	37
Graduate school	7	13	17*
Law School	9	10	9
Age			
At first election	49	44	46**
Marital status			
Married	68	77	81*
Race			
White	96	91	86*
Previous political office			
Any office	41	32	37
Town/city council	3	5	10*
County council	3	5	6
Mayor/deputy mayor	1	2	2
State board/commission	15	9	7*
School board	13	9	9
Committee assignments			
Education	22	23	29
Health and welfare	23	24	26
Appropriations	5	8	13*
Finance	12	12	16
Industry and commerce	8	14	19*
Agriculture	6	8	13*
Committee leadership			
Any position	18	30	34*
Chair/vice chair	15	22	26*
Ranking member	—	3	7*

*$p < .05$.

**$p < .01$.

Finally, in looking at women's legislative activities inside the institution, we focused on committee service and leadership activities. Previous research found women serving on committees dealing with traditional "women's issues," defined as education, health, and welfare.[30] It is not clear whether women were relegated by assignment to "women's" committees based on sex-role stereotypes or whether women specifically chose these committees in order to concentrate their legislative impact.[31] Given that women's social and professional opportunities have expanded into nontraditional occupations over time, we might expect that women recently elected, if given the choice, would select a wider range of committee assignments, including finance, appropriations, industry and commerce, transportation, energy, agriculture, and judiciary. We expected that women serving in 1992, in order to further expand their influence within the chamber, would be more likely to gain positions of leadership both on committees and in the chamber.

Table 3 shows that women in 1992 were not moving away from "women's issue" committees. There is no significant difference in service on education or health and welfare committees between women legislators in the three time periods. There is a difference, however, in service on the nontraditional committees. Women in 1992 were more than twice as likely to serve on appropriations, industry and commerce, transportation, and agriculture committees than their 1972 predecessors. Rather than abandoning entirely issues most directly affecting women, families, and children, women legislators appear to be expanding the scope of their influence to include financial and business concerns. In the process, they may also be expanding the definition of "women's issues." In the area of leadership, we found women in 1992 more likely to hold both committee and chamber leadership positions. In 1972, 18 percent of the women held a committee position and 2 percent held a leadership office in the institution. In 1992, 34 percent led committees and 8 percent were part of the chamber leadership.

In each of the areas we examined (personal and demographic characteristics, preparation for political office, and legislative activity once elected), women in 1992 were significantly different from women serving in 1972 and 1982. The sum of the differences creates a portrait of contemporary legislators that resembles that of many modern professional women outside of politics. They are likely to be married with children, to have prepared for a career by earning a college or advanced degree, and to have entered the legislature from an occupation outside the home. These changes are important in relation to the representation of women. First, they signal political opportunities for all kinds of women—not just those who come from political dynasties or choose politics instead of a family life. Young women can decide that they want to prepare to seek political office and construct an educational and financial path that will allow them to do so. Once elected, they will share the characteristics and lifestyles of their peer group outside of politics. Symbolically this is important. Once inside the state legislature, women have moved to expand their range of interests beyond, but not instead of, the traditional issues of women, children, and the family. This will likely make them more viable candidates for higher office since they can broaden their legislative expertise in the process.

CONTEMPORARY WOMEN STATE LEGISLATORS: A DIVERSE GROUP WITH DIVERSE AGENDAS

Having seen that the characteristics and interests of women legislators have, in fact, changed over time, we turn to our second question: What are women legislators like today? In order to answer this question, we have to move beyond the information gathered through state legislative manuals. These sources do not give any information on motivations for seeking office, political aspirations, or issue priorities of the legislators; they focus almost exclusively on background characteristics and legislative assignments once in office. To get an idea of what women legislators are like in the 1990s, we needed to collect additional data from the women state legislators themselves. The data used to create a portrait of the contemporary woman state legislator come from an original mail survey of the 1,373 women serving as U.S. state legislators in all fifty states during the 1992 legislative session.[32] The survey asked women legislators for more detailed information about their political, professional, and legislative careers. Surveys were returned from all fifty states, and the number of surveys received from each state is strongly related to the number of women legislators serving in that state ($R = .95$). There were 627 surveys returned, for a response rate of 46 percent.

The women state legislators who responded to the survey closely match the entire population of women state legislators on such characteristics as political party, chamber of service, and race. For example, the political party identification distribution of all women state legislators in 1992 was 60 percent Democrat, 39 percent Republican, and 1 percent Independent. For our sample the distribution is 59 percent Democrat, 40 percent Republican, and 1 percent Independent. Seventy-eight percent of all women legislators serve in their state's lower chamber and 22 percent serve in the upper chamber. For our sample, 74 percent served in the lower house and 26 percent in the Senate. Finally, in terms of race, 88 percent of the legislators serving in 1992 were White, 9 percent were African-American, and 3 percent were other races. In our sample, 92 percent of respondents are White, 5 percent are African-American, and 3 percent are other races. Because the women who responded to the survey resemble the population from which they were selected, we feel confident about drawing an accurate portrait of the contemporary woman state legislator from our information.

In creating a more detailed portrait of women currently serving, we have focused our attention on women legislator's professional, political, and legislative attitudes and attributes. The trends suggested in the previous section are confirmed here: The current woman state legislator is decidedly different from the traditional women characterized by much of the earlier research.

PROFESSIONAL AND PERSONAL CHARACTERISTICS

In the area of demographic characteristics, we found that women serving in state legislatures in 1992 were a diverse group who have achieved a range of educational and occupational success far above that of women state legislators in the past. A survey of women state legislators done in 1977 found that 63 percent of these women had at least a college degree. Of this group, 26 percent had gone on to earn advanced degrees.[33] In 1992 fully 77 percent of the women in our sample had earned a college education, and another 18 percent had some college education. Further, 36 percent of the respondents held a master's doctoral, or law degree. Clearly, these women are taking advantage of the greater educational opportunities available to women in the United States over the last twenty years.

Women have put their education to use by pursuing professional occupations outside the home. The women legislators in our survey were involved in an impressive array of careers, including law, education, journalism, business, and the health professions. In earlier times women state legislators tended to be employed in clerical and sales positions, or not employed at all. Indeed, a 1977 survey found that 46 percent of women state legislators described themselves as housewives.[34] In our 1992 group, housewives constituted only 16 percent of the sample. This change in educational and occupational preparation for political office may prove important in determining what these women will do once they are in office.

Another important set of demographic variables to consider are those involving age and family life. In our sample the women tended to be older, married women with children. While there was significant diversity in the age ranges of our sample (the youngest respondent was twenty-six and the oldest eighty-three), the median age was fifty-four years old. That women state legislators tend to be middle-aged is likely due to the number of years they devote to educational, occupational, and family pursuits prior to their involvement in politics. In our sample, 73 percent of the respondents were married, 21 percent had been married but were presently widowed or divorced, and only 7 percent had never been married. The mast majority of these women were mothers (83 percent), and a fairly large group (20 percent) had children who were under the age of eighteen. These data seem to illustrate that contemporary women state legislators are balancing family and professional obligations, much like the vast majority of women as a whole.

POLITICAL BACKGROUND

In examining the relatively slow pace of women's integration into political office in the United States, some researchers have suggested that women lack the political ambition and experience necessary for success. Previous research has found that women traditionally entered public life through civic and volunteer activities, usually motivated by a sense of civic duty and a desire to make their community a better place. Having accomplished the specific change they sought, many of these women returned to private life without seeking additional office. Does this traditional portrait still apply to the contemporary woman state legislator? If state legislative seats are going to act as "feeder systems" for higher office, women need to develop attitudes and experiences that can propel them to progressively higher offices.

The women legislators in our sample possess significant office-holding experience prior to their election to the state legislature. In fact, only 33 percent of our respondents report having had no prior political office experience at all, and 36 percent of them have held two or more previous offices. This confirms the pattern that others have found: Women state legislators tend to come to that office after having paid their political dues in a series of other offices.[35] Further, more of them came to the legislature having previously held elected office rather than appointed office, which means they have the campaign experience necessary to successfully seek an office in the state legislature and presumably beyond.

Familiar patterns regarding women state legislators' paths to office are confirmed again when we examine the past offices our respondents have held. The three most common previously elected positions are city or town council, county council, or local school board. Additionally, 17 percent have served as appointed members of various state boards and commissions. While numerous women had held elected or appointed office at the county and state level, the majority of women in our sample (56 percent) earned their political experience in local-level politics.

Turning to an examination of the attitudes women state legislators hold about politics and their position, we see considerable diversity among our respondents. For example, when we examine their motivations for entering politics, we see that the conventional image of the civic-minded woman legislator may no longer be applicable. A vast majority of the women in our sample (75 percent) expressed motivations for seeking office that could be characterized as ambition- or opportunity-based motivations (such as being recruited to run, wanting to enter politics, or having had previous political experience), while only 32 percent expressed more traditional civic-oriented reasons (wanted to help community, liked idea of public service). Clearly, these data show that a significant portion of the sample exhibits some degree of political ambition.

On the issue of how committed our respondents are to the office of legislator and to political office more broadly, the evidence is mixed. When we asked our respondents if they considered themselves to be full-time legislators, 54 percent reported that they do. This finding is especially interesting given that only 14 percent of our respondents served in legislatures that could be considered full-time. Clearly, these women were expressing a level of commitment to their position that is largely unrelated to the constitutional responsibilities and resources of their legislatures. Yet respondents were quite evenly split on whether they consider politics and public office a career. Forty-six percent indicated that they do not think of politics as a career, 40 percent say that they do, and 14 percent are unsure at this point. If we are correct in our assumption that considering politics as a career is related to progressive ambition for higher office, this 40 percent, while not a majority, still creates a substantial pool of candidates for the future.

In response to our question about their interest in seeking an office other than the one they now hold, 38 percent indicated that they definitely or probably will run for additional office, while 42 percent said no and 20 percent were unsure. Why don't more women say that they want to seek an additional office? The most common response to our inquiry into why these women do not intend to seek other office was satisfaction with the office of state legislator. This was followed by health concerns (which is not so surprising when you consider that the average age of our respondents was fifty-four), a feeling of being burned out by politics, and a desire to have more time for self and family.

For those women who expressed ambitions for future political offices, where are they headed? Our survey asked respondents to indicate which elected office beyond the legislature they intended to seek. Since respondents were allowed to list more than one office, 235 women listed a total of 409 positions to which they aspired. The most frequently mentioned office (26 percent of all offices mentioned) was that of state senator, indicating that, for lower-chamber legislators, the upper chamber is seen as desirable and possibly a path to other offices as well. The second and third most frequently mentioned offices are U.S. representative and U.S. senator. Together these offices accounted for 20 percent of the offices mentioned. Statewide elective office was less frequently mentioned than legislative office; the governorship was mentioned 14 percent of the time, and the lieutenant governor's office 10 percent.

LEGISLATIVE ACTIVITIES

The final aspect to consider in portraying contemporary women state legislators is their legislative activity within the institution. Much of the recent research done on women state legislators suggests that women approach their legislative activities from a distinct perspective, a perspective shaped and influenced by their experiences as women.[36] For many researchers, this evidence suggests that women are concerned about issue areas having an impact on the lives of women and on areas of traditional concern to women, such as children, welfare, and education. To examine the role of these issue concerns in the legislative career of our respondents, we focused on their committee assignments, stated legislative priorities, and concerns about the problems facing women in the United States.

In looking at committee assignments, we see that our respondents were indeed focusing much of their legislative activity on these issues, but not to the exclusion of all other policy areas. Fifty-one percent of the women in our sample sat on at least one committee related to women's issues, and about 20 percent of this group sat on at least two. Further, 40 percent of respondents sat on a health and welfare committee, and 35 percent served on committees handling education policy. Yet 46 percent were members of committees such as appropriations, banking, finance, and industry and labor.

Finally, do women today list "women's issues" high on their legislative priority list? We asked our respondents to identify their top three legislative priorities during the most recent legislative session. Thirty-eight percent of the sample identified a legislative priority that we classified as being related to women's interests.

Among the most frequently offered of these priorities were issues related to child care, families, and women's health. Yet, alongside these priorities, respondents listed concerns about economic development, substance abuse, labor issues, and agricultural and environmental issues. The data on committee assignments and legislative priorities indicate that these women legislators are sensitive to the needs of women and that they pay considerable attention to the so-called women's issues. It would be misleading, however, to portray contemporary women state legislators as a group solely devoted to the needs of their descriptive constituencies to the neglect of broader issues.

CONCLUSIONS

We began this chapter with a puzzle and a problem related to women's representation in American political institutions. Why has the increase in women's representation come so slowly, and now that women are present in greater numbers, what will it mean? From the earliest debates over suffrage to women's celebrated representation on the Senate Judiciary Committee, the assumption has been that an influx of significant numbers of women into the political process would radically alter the course of public life. The precise nature of this change, however, has been a matter for speculation and study. Would women act as agents of reform, pushing for legislative action to improve the lives of women and children? In general, would they bring a distinctive "woman's" focus to their legislative work born out of their unique experiences in the private sphere? Often implied, but sometimes explicitly stated, is the underlying premise that women are women— one homogeneous body of actors sharing attitudes, agendas, and policy preferences. Very little research has been done to directly examine the diversity among women representatives and how who they are might affect what they are inclined to do as legislators.

Over the past twenty years, women in the United States have sought and won increased access to elective office at all levels of government. Nowhere has that success been more clearly documented than in the state legislatures. The 1990s, as a period of tremendous gain for women in state legislatures, present a significant opportunity to put some of these earlier assumptions about women state legislators to the test. Our examination of women state legislators, both over time and during the contemporary period, leads us to reject the earlier notions of women as a relatively homogeneous group. Indeed, our data illustrate the diversity of experience and interests these women bring to politics. As a group, women state legislators serving in the 1990s exhibit greater educational, occupational, political, and legislative diversity than the women who served in the past. Precisely how this diversity among the women themselves and in their political agendas will be reflected in the character of the legislatures in which they serve remains to be seen.

NOTES

1. R. Darcy, Susan Welch, and Janet Clark, *Women, Elections and Representation*, 2nd ed. (Lincoln: University of Nebraska Press, 1994).

2. Virginia Saprio, *Women in American Society: An Introduction to Women's Studies*, 3rd ed. (Mountain View, CA: Mayfield Publishing Company, 1994), p. 279.

3. Sue Thomas, *How Women Legislate* (New York: Oxford University Press, 1994).

4. CAWP Fact Sheet (New Brunswick, NJ: Center for the American Woman and Politics, 1993).

5. CAWP Fact Sheet, 1993.

6. Jo Freeman, *Women: A Feminist Perspective*, 5th ed. (Mountain View, CA: Mayfield Publishing Company, 1995).

7. Freeman, *Women: A Feminist Perspective*, p. 415.

8. See, for example, Jeanne Kirkpatrick, *Political Woman* (New York: Basic Books, 1974); Irene Diamond, *Sex Roles in the state House* (New Haven, CT: Yale University Press, 1977); Susan J. Carroll, *Women as Candidates in American Politics* (Bloomington: Indiana University Press, 1985); and Thomas, *How Women Legislate*.

9. Darcy, Welch, and Clark, *Women, Elections and Representation*.

10. CAWP Fact Sheet, 1993.

11. Darcy, Welch, and Clark, *Women, Elections and Representation*.

12. Ruth Mandel and Debra Dodson, "Do Women Officeholders Make a Difference?" in Sara E. Rix (Ed.), *The American Woman* (New York: Norton, 1992); Sue Thomas and Susan Welch, "The Impact of Gender on Activities and Priorities of State Legislators," *Western Political Quarterly*, 44 (1991), pp. 445–456.

13. Thomas, *How Women Legislate*; Rosabeth Kanter, "Some Effects of Proportion on Group Life: Skewed Sex Ratios and Response to Token Women," *American Journal of Sociology*, 82 (1977), pp. 965–990.

14. Daniel Elazar, *American Federalism: A View from the States*, 3rd ed. (New York: Harper and Row, 1984); Marjorie R. Hershey, "The Politics of Androgyny: Sex Roles and Attitudes toward Women in Politics," *American Politics Quarterly*, 5 (1977), pp. 261–287; David B. Hill, "Political Culture and Female Political Representation," *Journal of Politics*, 43 (1981), pp. 157–168; Diamond, *Sex Roles in the State House*.

15. Kirkpatrick, *Political Woman*; Virginia Sapiro, *The Political Integration of Women* (Urbana: University of Illinois Press, 1984).

16. Diamond, *Sex Roles in the State House*; Hill, "Political Culture and Female Political Representation"; Marjorie Spruill Wheeler, *New Women of the New South: The Leaders of the Woman Suffrage Movement in the Southern States* (New York: Oxford University Press, 1993); and Darcy, Welch, and Clark, *Women, Elections and Representation*.

17. CAWP Fact Sheet, 1993.

18. Diamond, *Sex Roles in the State House*, p. 22.

19. Sue Thomas, "Women in State Legislatures: One Step at a Time," in Elizabeth Adell Cook, Sue Thomas, and Clyde Wilcox (Eds.), *The Year of The Woman: Myths and Realities* (Boulder, CO: Westview Press, 1994), pp. 141–159; Barbara Burrell, "The Presence of Women Candidates and the Role of Gender in Campaigns for State Legislature in an Urban Setting: The Case of Massachusetts," *Women and Politics*, 10 (3) (1990), pp. 85–102.

20. Emmy E. Werner, "Women in the State Legislatures," *Western Political Quarterly*, 21 (1968), pp. 40–50.

21. See, for example, Carol Nechemias, "Changes in the Election of Women to U.S. State Legislative Seats," *Legislative Studies Quarterly*, 12 (1) (1987), pp. 125–142; Carol, Nechemias, "Geographic Mobility and Women's Access to State Legislatures," *Western Political Quarterly*, 38 (1985), pp. 119–131; Wilma Rule, "Why Women Don't Run: The Contextual Factors in Women's Legislative Recruitment," *Western Political Quarterly*, 34 (1981), pp. 60–74.

22. Joan Hulse Thompson, "Career Convergence: Election of Women and Men to the House of Representatives," *Women and Politics*, 5 (1) (1985), pp. 69–90; Darcy, Welch, and Clark, *Women, Elections and Representation*.

23. Sara Rix, *The American Woman* (New York: Norton, 1992).

24. Barbara C. Burrell, "The Political Opportunity of Women Candidates for the U.S. House of Representatives in 1984," *Women and Politics*, 8 (1) (1988), pp. 51–69.

25. A question most recently posed by Patricia Freeman and William Lyons, "Female Legislators: Is There a New Type of Woman in Office?" in Gary Moncrief and Joel Thompson (Eds.), *Changing Patterns in State Legislative Careers* (Ann Arbor: University of Michigan Press, 1992).

26. The fifteen states included in the sample are California, Georgia, Idaho, Illinois, Iowa, Nevada, New Jersey, Oklahoma, Oregon, Pennsylvania, South Carolina, South Dakota, Vermont, Virginia, and Wisconsin.

27. The fifteen states represent all three classifications of legislatures formulated by the National Council of State Legislatures. California, Illinois, New Jersey, Pennsylvania, and Wisconsin are considered full-time, professional legislatures. Iowa, Oklahoma, Oregon, South Carolina, and Virginia are classified as transitional legislatures, moving from amateur to professional status. Georgia, Idaho, Nevada, South Dakota, and Vermont are considered part-time, amateur legislatures.

28. There may be missing data on some variables (committee assignments, year of birth, race and marital sta-

tus) for some women because of variation in information reported in state legislative manuals.

29. To test the hypotheses regarding changes among women state legislators over time, we conducted difference of means tests for the several dependent variables by the time period of service (1972, 1982, 1992).

30. Diamond, *Sex Roles in the State House*; Thomas and Welch, "The Impact of Gender Activities and Priorities of State Legislators."

31. Marylin Johnson and Susan Carroll, *Profile of Women Holding Office II* (New Brunswick, NJ: Center for the American Woman and Politics, 1978); Susan Carroll and Ella Taylor, "Gender Differences in the Committee Assignment of State Legislators: Preferences or Discrimination?" paper presented at the annual meeting of the Midwest Political Science Association, Chicago, 1989.

32. The mail survey was administered during July and August of 1992. We used a two-wave mailing procedure with a reminder postcard sent between survey mailings. Each mailing occurred approximately four weeks apart.

33. Diamond, *Sex Roles in the State House*.

34. Ibid.

35. Alice Rossi, "Beyond the Gender Gap: Women's Bid for Political Power," *Social Science Quarterly*, 58 (1983), pp. 671–682.

36. Beth Reingold, "Concepts of Representation among Female and Male State Legislators," paper presented at the annual meeting of the American Political Science Association, Washington, DC, 1991; Michelle A. Saint-Germain, "Does Their Difference Make a Difference? The Impact of Women on Public Policy in the Arizona Legislature," *Social Science Quarterly*, 70 (1989), pp. 956–968; Thomas, *How Women Legislate*.

FURTHER READINGS

Carroll, Susan J. "Gender Politics and the Socializing Impact of the Women's Movement," in Roberta S. Sigel (Ed.), *Political Learning in Adulthood*. Chicago: University of Chicago Press, 1980.

Carroll, Susan J., and Wendy S. Strimling. *Women's Routes to Elective Office: A Comparison with Men's*. New Brunswick, NJ: Center for the American Woman and Politics, 1983.

Conover, Pamela. "Feminists and the Gender Gap." *Journal of Politics*, 50 (1980), pp. 985–1010.

Constantini, Edmond. "Political Women and Ambition: Closing the Gender Gap." *American Journal of Political Science*, 34 (1990), pp. 741–770.

Dodson, Debra, and Susan Carroll. *Reshaping the Agenda: Women in State Legislatures*. New Brunswick, NJ: Center for the American Woman and Politics, 1991.

Flammang, Janet A. *Political Women: Current Roles in State and Local Government*. Beverly Hills, CA: Sage, 1984.

Gurin, Patricia. "Women's Gender Consciousness." *Public Opinion Quarterly*, 49 (1985), pp. 143–163.

Hartmann, Susan M. *From Margin to Mainstream: American Women and Politics since 1960*. Philadelphia: Temple University Press, 1989.

Kelly, Rita Mae, and Jayne Burgess. "Gender and the Meaning of Power and Politics." *Women and Politics*, 9 (1) (1989), pp. 47–82.

Leeper, Mark. "The Impact of Prejudice on Female Candidates: An Experimental Look at Voter Inference." *American Politics Quarterly*, 19 (2) (1991), pp. 248–261.

Mandel, Ruth B. *In the Running: The New Woman Candidate*. New Haven, CT: Ticknor and Fields, 1981.

Rule, Wilma. "Why More Women are State Legislators: A Research Note." *Western Political Quarterly*, 42 (1989), pp. 437–448.

Ryan, Barbara. *Feminism and the Women's Movement*. New York: Routledge, 1992.

Williams, Christine B. "Women, Law and Politics: Recruitment Patterns in the Fifty States." *Women and Politics*, 10 (3) (1990), pp. 103–123.

 CHAPTER 5

THE EXECUTIVE BRANCH: WOMEN AND LEADERSHIP

A growing list of nations in this century have selected female heads. These have included Great Britain, the Philippines, Argentina, Israel, Iceland, and India. However, the United States has not yet succeeded in electing a woman as our chief executive. The U.S. presidency has remained a bastion of maleness. Marcia Lynn Whicker and Todd W. Areson have investigated the reasons for this and find four factors that account for the unlevel presidential "playing field" that women candidates face: (1) the presidential system itself, which relies more closely on direct, popular elections than does the parliamentary system, which elects its prime minister from among fellow party members; (2) the paucity of women gaining experience in the presidential "launching roles" of the vice presidency, the U.S. Senate, and governorships; (3) the difficulty women face in securing campaign funding for national and subnational races; and (4) long-standing public images of a conflict for women—and not for men—between familial and political roles. Is the lack of female presence in high elective office an issue that should be addressed by our government? If not the government, who? How can the role of women in high elective office be increased?

Sara J. Weir focuses on the growing importance of the governorship in U.S. politics and explores the implications of women as governors. Her study shows how the ten women elected to the governorship since 1974 have worked against gender stereotypes to serve in an office that demands knowledge of budgeting and fiscal policy and administrative leadership—abilities most often associated with males by voters. Although the numbers are too small to generalize, the author speculates about changing patterns in the candidacy and election of women state chief executives and the ways in which some female governors empower women and support women's issues. Positive developments include the high numbers of women serving as lieutenant governors in 1995—increasing the numbers of women in the "pool" of qualified gubernatorial candidates of the future. However, the author cautions that the number of women running for and winning in gubernatorial contests is still very small. Let us next look at the results of the Whicker and Areson study and the Weir findings.

The Maleness of the American Presidency

Marcia Lynn Whicker
Todd W. Areson

INTRODUCTION

The U.S. presidency has historically been a bastion of maleness despite comments during the early Clinton administration that First Lady Hillary Rodham Clinton would be a "copresident." Aside from being First Lady, the closest a woman has come to presidential power was the 1984 Democratic vice presidential nomination of Geraldine Ferraro. The earlier 1972 presidential candidacy of Democrat Shirley Chisholm, a Black woman from New York, was discounted by both the press and the public on sexual and racial grounds. In the 1988 primaries, Democratic U.S. Representative Pat Schroeder from Colorado briefly considered running for president but was unable to raise the necessary funds.

Yet women in more socially conservative societies, where fewer advances for women might be expected, have served as the chief executives of their countries. Throughout the decade of the 1980s, Conservative Party leader Margaret Thatcher was prime minister of Britain. In 1990 Mary Robinson became president of Ireland, which is governed through a parliamentary system. Indira Gandhi was prime minister of India from 1966 until her assassination in 1984 by religiously motivated Sikh extremists. Golda Meir, a former schoolteacher from Milwaukee, served as the prime minister of Israel during the late 1960s and early 1970s.

Marcia Lynn Whicker is a professor of public administration at Rutgers University, Newark, New Jersey. Todd W. Areson is currently manager of demonstration projects for the Virginia Division of Child Support Enforcement in Richmond, Virginia.

Isabel Perón, the second wife of Argentine leader General Juan Perón, was elected president of that country in 1974, becoming the first woman head of state in the Western Hemisphere. In 1962 Sirimavo Bandaranaike was elected prime minister of her native Sri Lanka, following the 1959 assassination of the former prime minister, her husband. And, with the fall of Ferdinand Marcos in the Philippines in 1986, Corazon Aquino was elected president there in a bitter and contentious campaign.

Why are women becoming chief executives in countries more socially traditional than the United States while still being excluded from the White House in all but secondary roles? The purpose of this essay is to explore this crucial political—and no longer merely academic—question.

THE PARLIAMENTARY SYSTEM VERSUS THE U.S. PRESIDENTIAL SYSTEM

Many of the female leaders cited here—with the exceptions of Perón and Aquino, who succeeded to leadership roles after the deaths of politically prominent husbands—achieved their power in parliamentary systems. Table 1 presents a listing of women national leaders from other countries, showing slightly more have obtained national leadership positions in parliamentary than in presidential systems. Prime ministers are not elected directly by the people but are chosen by their fellow party members, since the prime minister is the leader of the dominant party in parliament.[1] Party members and long-term colleagues likely have less traditional bias against women as political leaders than does the general electorate.[2]

In aspiring to leadership of a political party, parliamentary members start with an equally recognized legitimacy: All have been elected from their districts or

Table 1   Non-U.S. Women National Leaders

Name	Country	Years of Rule	Type of Government	Political Experience
Aquino, Maria Corazon	Philippines	1986–1992	Presidential	None
Bandaranaike, Sirimavo	Sri Lanka	1960–1965, 1970–1977	Parliamentary	None
Bhutto, Benazir	Pakistan	1988–1990	Parliamentary	Limited
Brundtland, Gro Harlem	Norway	1981, 1986–1989	Parliamentary	Extensive
Chamorro, Violetta	Nicaragua	1990–	Presidential	Limited
Charles, Mary Eugenia	Dominica	1966–1977, 1980–	Presidential	Extensive
Gandhi, Indira	India	1980–1984	Parliamentary	Extensive
Meir, Golda	Israel	1969–1974	Parliamentary	Extensive
Pascale-Trouillot, Ertha	Haiti	1990–	Presidential	Extensive
Perón, Isabel	Argentina	1974–1976	Presidential	Limited
Thatcher, Margaret	England	1979–1990	Parliamentary	Extensive

Source: Michael Genovese, "Women National Leaders: What Do We Know?" in Michael A. Genovese (Ed.), *Women as National Leaders*, (Newbury Park, CA: Sage, 1993), pp. 211–218.

in national elections, depending on whether single-member districts or proportional representation is the electoral basis. Party members seem to operate on a rough merit system, which provides rewards of power and leadership based on political and legislative performances.[3] Both male and female party members, once elected, have similar opportunities to excel in the tasks of creating national agenda, developing legislation, and shepherding proposals around or over legislative hurdles. In this arena, paying one's professional dues is important, recognized, and generally rewarded.

Only since 1980 have women come to be elected national chief executives in popular elections. In June 1980 Vigdis Finnbogadottir became the world's first popularly elected head of state in Iceland. In April 1990 Violetta Barrios de Chamorro was elected president of Nicaragua. (Michel Rocard, who became prime minister of the French Republic in June 1988, was appointed to that office by President Mitterand rather than elected.)

In the United States as well as in the various parliamentary systems, women active in party politics have become more similar to the men who are active. Table 2 shows that women national leaders were more likely to have obtained extensive political experience in parliamentary than presidential systems. Of women leaders with extensive experience, two-thirds were from parliamentary systems, and one-third were from presidential systems. Between 1964 and 1976, the differences between male and female political elites in terms of social background, political status, political careers, and perceptions of the political process—all factors affecting one's potential for leadership—were decreasing. During that period, issue orientations were predominantly a matter of party agenda rather than of gender, with the exception of issues dealing directly with gender roles.[4] A 1990 study also confirms the narrowing of the gap between men and women in "political ambition," the pursuit of public office for personal self-enhancement.[5] Across a twenty-two-year period (1964–1986), women exhibited a marked increase in political ambition not matched by similar increases for men.

The United States differs from countries with parliamentary systems in that the national political leader (the president) is elected by the people through the electoral college system. Despite concern over the biases this system causes,[6] the electoral college rarely fails to confirm the popular vote.[7] In practice, U.S. presi-

Table 2 Non-U.S. Women National Leaders by Experience and Type of Government

Type of Experience	Type of Government		
	Presidential	*Parliamentary*	*Total*
None	1 (50%)	1 (50%)	2
Limited	2 (67%)	1 (33%)	3
Extensive	2 (33%)	4 (67%)	6
Total	5	6	

dential outcomes may be based less on political and legislative merit than on effective media exposure and communications, levels of campaign funding, and the personal appeal of the candidate.[8]

Although party identification does affect outcomes in U.S. elections, the role and influence of U.S. political parties have diminished steadily in recent decades as candidates have opted to build their own campaign organizations.[9] In parliamentary systems, by contrast, party discipline has remained crucial to national political leadership: Parties control the nominating process and, through the selection of leaders, reward individuals who have provided loyal party service.

Women, while becoming leaders in political systems based more directly on merit, have fared less well in arenas where public opinion dominates.[10] In the United States, antidiscrimination legislation has been a relatively recent occurrence, dating to the 1960s. Usually changes in legislation, whether antidiscriminatory or otherwise, are influenced and supported by the pace of change in public opinion. Thus, women only achieved the right to vote in 1920, with state ratification of the Nineteenth Amendment to the Constitution.[11]

In other areas, especially in employment, where advancement for women was previously predicated on changes in public opinion, social legislation has been necessary for female gains. The Equal Pay Act of 1963, requiring equal pay for equal work by men and women, was the first federal law against sex discrimination in employment. In 1972 and again in 1974, two major expansions of that act extended coverage to executive, administrative, and professional employees and to most federal, state, and local government employees.[12]

It was the 1964 Civil Rights Act (Title VII) that safeguarded equal opportunity for women in employment in both hiring and advancement. Originally intended to protect blacks and other racial minorities, the 1964 act included equal opportunity for women as an amendment—a political miscalculation by opponents of the act. Intending to kill the act by including coverage of women, opponents were surprised when the amended act passed. Title VII also covers sexual harassment on the job.[13] The Pregnancy Disability Act of 1978, an amendment to Title VII, provides pregnancy protections for female employees.[14]

Social legislation has also been necessary to protect women from discrimination in nonemployment areas. Federal legislation has prohibited discrimination by institutions receiving federal funds. In marriage and divorce, it has taken a combination of both court suits and legislation to diverge from the English common-law assumption that husband and wife are one, with reciprocal and unequal rights.[15] Only in 1974, with the passage of the Equal Credit Opportunity Act, was sex discrimination in credit approval banned.[16]

Popular biases against women, partially overcome through social legislation, still exist in politics and can be expressed more directly in U.S. presidential electoral politics than in parliamentary selection of prime ministers. As Madison feared, majority rather than elite rule—a founding principle of the nation and one to which most citizens readily adhere—can sometimes be used as an instrument of bias and prejudice.

AN ABSENCE OF APPROPRIATE POLITICAL EXPERIENCE

A survey of the previous political experience of presidents and party nominees for president since 1960 indicates that three backgrounds emerge as the dominant training grounds for those who would be president—the offices of vice president, U.S. senator, and governor.

John F. Kennedy, the first president born and elected in this century, was a Democratic U.S. senator from Massachusetts when he ran for the presidency in 1960. Democrat Lyndon Johnson, his successor, wielded great power for years as U.S. Senate majority leader before accepting the vice presidency in 1960 after a failed presidential bid. Had he not become president as a result of Kennedy's assassination, Johnson likely would have run again for the White House.

The necessity of first being tested in these presidential proving grounds has not been limited to Democrats, of course. Republican Richard Nixon served in the U.S. Senate and as vice president prior to his unsuccessful 1960 presidential bid against Senator John Kennedy and his successful 1968 bid against Vice President Hubert Humphrey.

The pattern holds even with the one "accidental" president in recent years, Republican Gerald Ford. Ford was catapulted to the vice presidency through the resignation of Nixon's corrupt vice president, Spiro Agnew. Within a few months, Nixon's own resignation, brought about by impeachable charges of obstruction of justice in the Watergate affair, propelled Ford into the presidency in August 1974.

In recent presidential history—1976, 1980, 1984 and 1992—candidates with gubernatorial experience have captured the presidency. Democrat Jimmy Carter, elected in 1976, served as governor of Georgia before making his surprising successful bid for the White House as a Washington outsider. In both 1980 and 1984, former Republican California Governor Ronald Reagan easily defeated his Democratic opponent. In 1992, Bill Clinton, governor of Arkansas, captured the White House.

Even unsuccessful presidential nominees have acquired their political experience in the U.S. Senate, the vice presidency, and the presidency. Former Vice President Nixon, who opposed Senator Kennedy in 1960, fits this pattern. In 1964, Republican Senator Barry Goldwater ran unsuccessfully against Vice President Johnson. Former Democratic Senator from Minnesota and incumbent Vice President Hubert Humphrey was defeated by former Vice President Nixon in 1968. In 1972, President Nixon defeated South Dakota Democratic Senator George McGovern.

In 1976, former Governor Jimmy Carter defeated incumbent President Gerald Ford and, in turn, former Governor Ronald Reagan defeated incumbent President Jimmy Carter in 1980. In 1984, President Reagan's unsuccessful Democratic opponent, Walter Mondale, had been both a Democratic senator from Minnesota and Carter's vice president.

This pattern of formative political experience in the U.S. Senate, a governorship, or the vice-presidency continued to hold in 1988. All but one of the presidential and vice-presidential candidates fit the pattern, the exception being Jesse Jackson, a black Democratic candidate for president. Although Jackson ran in 1984 and again in 1988 before his candidacy was taken seriously, he did not attain his party's nomination for president or vice president.

On the Republican side, the major contenders early in the 1988 race were Vice President George Bush and U.S. Senate Majority Leader Robert Dole. Eventually, Bush gained the nomination and appointed Indiana Senator Daniel Quayle as his vice presidential running mate. All fit the pattern.

Early in the 1988 presidential primaries, the Democratic picture was more chaotic. By the date of the so-called Super Tuesday primaries in March, the three major contenders were Massachusetts Governor Michael Dukakis, the Reverend Jesse Jackson, and Tennessee Senator Albert Gore. Only Jackson, the first black to contend seriously for the White House, deviates from the norm.

Traditionally, blacks in the United States have been excluded from the highest echelons of elected office and political leadership. The sole exceptions have been former U.S. Senator Edward Brooke of Massachusetts and former Governor Douglas Wilder of Virginia. Jesse Jackson compensated for this exclusion by pursuing those avenues of political power open to him, including leadership in the black church and in the civil rights movement.

Before the close of the 1988 primaries, Governor Dukakis had secured enough votes to gain the Democratic nomination, and appointed an established political insider, Texas Senator Lloyd Bentsen, as his running mate: In 1992, Clinton defeated incumbent George Bush, continuing the pattern of extensive political training in "launching roles" for both winners and losers in presidential elections (see Table 3).

Table 3   Political Backgrounds of Recent Presidential Contenders

Year	Winner	Background	Loser	Background
1960	Kennedy	Senator	Nixon	Senator Vice president
1964	Johnson	Senator Vice president President	Goldwater	Senator
1968	Nixon	Senator Vice president	Humphrey	Senator Vice president
1972	Nixon	Senator Vice president President	McGovern	Senator
1976	Carter	Governor	Ford	Vice president President
1980	Reagan	Governor	Carter	Governor President
1984	Reagan	Governor President	Mondale	Senator Vice president
1988	Bush	Vice president	Dukakis	Governor
1992	Clinton	Governor	Bush	Vice president President

Candidates with other political backgrounds, including experience as a U.S. representative, traditionally have been unsuccessful in capturing their party's presidential nomination. Democratic Representative Morris Udall from Arizona in 1976 and Republican Representative John Anderson from Illinois in 1980 were unsuccessful presidential candidates. In 1988, the campaigns of both Democratic Representative Richard Gephardt from Missouri and Republican Representative Jack Kemp from New York faltered.

Paradoxically, five recent presidents have served in the U.S. House of Representatives—Kennedy, Johnson, Nixon, Ford, and Bush. Yet their service in the House has been coupled, *in each case*, with later experience in the Senate or the vice presidency, two of the presidential "launching roles." Although five of the last seven presidents started in the House of Representatives, House experience in itself has not been sufficient to support a successful presidential nomination. The presidential candidacies of Morris Udall (Democrat), John Anderson (Independent), Jack Kemp (Republican), and Richard Gephardt (Democrat), all of whom had held no public office higher than the House, failed.

Nor can it be stated that the three traditional political backgrounds are irrelevant to or an improper proving ground for the presidency. Each provides an opportunity to develop the qualities and skills that presidents need. The first of these characteristics is high political visibility, combined with tempered experience in the exercise of power. The second is broad legislative experience; senators, vice presidents, and governors all must sell their policies and programs to national and state legislatures as well as to the public at large.

Third, all three backgrounds require a working knowledge of national political issues and of the intricate intergovernmental balance between federal and state governments in achieving national domestic policy goals. One final advantage these backgrounds provide is rigorous practice in analyzing, staking out, communicating, and defending positions in a visible, public, and adversarial arena—not unlike what the presidential campaign trail requires.

Because few women have served in these presidential launching roles, the selection pool for female presidential candidates has been minimal. For example, in 1994 only 8 out of 100 U.S. senators and 1 out of fifty governors were women. No women have been elected vice president. Only 11 percent of the seats in the House were held by women. With such a disproportionately small pool of women presidential candidates, the odds of women achieving the presidency in the near term are statistically negligible. History shows that aspirants to the presidency usually enter politics at subnational levels through either state or local elective office. But entering politics at any level presents barriers to groups that have been excluded, including the major barrier of fund-raising.

CAMPAIGN FUNDING AND PAC POWER

Elections drive home the basic principle of politics: Money buys access to power. Political action committees (PACs), long guided by this principle, have grown in clout and number in recent years. Yet, women trying to enter politics at all levels have had difficulty raising money, especially from PACs. This is in part because they are more typically nonincumbents and in part simply because they are women.[17]

In politics as elsewhere, nothing succeeds like success. This produces a political catch-22 for would-be female candidates: PACs are more likely to support proven winners—that is, incumbents. As for nonincumbents, PACs give more freely to those perceived as more likely to win, typically white males. With lower budgets for their campaigns resulting from difficulties in fund-raising, women often cannot take full advantage of modern campaign techniques, including use of the mass media, especially television, and of political pollsters. These handicaps reduce the likelihood of female challengers being elected.

Given their difficulty in fund-raising from interest groups and especially from PACs, female candidates would benefit disproportionately from reforms in campaign financing. Public financing for presidential general elections has existed since the adoption of the Revenue Act of 1971, which provided the first-time income tax checkoff as a federal subsidy.[18] Although presidential candidates receiving public financing are limited in their total expenditures, their expenditures may be supplemented by independent spending—by PACs, for example. The Federal Election Campaign Act of 1971 established procedures for the public disclosure of contributions and expenditures of $200 or more. This law also set ceilings on the amount of contributions that presidential and vice presidential candidates and their families could contribute, as well as on the amount spent for media advertising.[19]

Because women have been considerably less successful historically in reaching the traditional presidential launching roles, they have benefited less from public financing for the presidency. Further, public financing has not been adopted for other national and subnational offices, including the U.S. Congress and major state offices, where women might compete both more readily and more successfully. Some members of Congress fear that public subsidies would encourage opponents by equalizing the resources available to incumbents and nonincumbents. Others believe, however, that the ceilings on total campaign spending that would necessarily accompany such additional public financing would further bias elections toward incumbents, who already have a proven track record and greater name recognition.

Despite such criticisms, proponents argue that the nation as a whole, not just female candidates, would benefit from the enactment of public financing legislation for Congress and other levels of government. These reforms would not only allow greater diversity in the pool of candidates for elective offices but also reduce the pressure on officials, once elected, to conform to special interests at the expense of national and constituents' interests.

THE IMAGE OF FEMALE CANDIDATES

Women have experienced additional handicaps to election to higher political office, in part because of the public image of women as candidates. Women are still viewed societally in terms of domestic roles, whereas men are viewed in terms of occupational roles. Female politicians are viewed as interlopers in the political arena who should function behind the scenes rather than out front as candidates.[20]

Female candidates, then, must convince the electorate that their home responsibilities are not too demanding to permit them to make the commitment required by political officeholding. Former Princeton, New Jersey, mayor Barbara Boggs Sigmund has referred to this as "the bind of your femininity."[21] A 1978 study of men's and women's campaigns found that women were asked more often how they would manage their family responsibilities if elected and whether their husbands and children approved of their political activity.[22] Men were not asked whether their wives and children approved of their political activity. Rather, familial approval of male political participation was assumed. In one poignant example of this double standard from the mid-1970s, U.S. Representative Martha Keys of Kansas married fellow Representative Andrew Jacobs of Indiana. They had met while serving on the House Ways and Means Committee. When each sought reelection in their districts, the political marriage became a campaign issue for Keys but not for Jacobs.[23]

Because of the political liability regarding family responsibilities that people associate with women, many female politicians are either single or widowed, or do not become active in politics until after their children are adults.[24] For example, Kathryn Whitmire, mayor of Houston, was a widow when she sought and was elected to political office. Barbara Jordan, former U.S. Representative from Texas and spokesperson for the Democratic Party, never married. Nor did Elizabeth Holtzman, a Harvard lawyer and former U.S. representative from New York, who played a highly visible role in the Watergate hearings in the early 1970s. Geraldine Ferraro, the Democratic vice presidential nominee in 1984, had older children by the time she gained national attention.

The public perception that married female candidates in their childbearing years will neglect their familial duties if they run for and hold elective office affects the likelihood of women achieving the presidency in two ways. First, it reduces the pool of available female candidates acceptable to the public. Second, it delays the entry into elective politics of those women who choose to marry and have children. Many female candidates never recoup this lost ground. During the period when women are bearing and raising children, their male counterparts who aspire to the presidency are gaining formative experience at the subnational and national levels. Men gain access to the requisite presidential launching roles on a schedule compatible with career advancement, whereas women face a substantially telescoped time frame, among other handicaps, for their advancement.

The negative image of women as candidates, especially those still in their childbearing years, continues to present a significant handicap. Election to political office requires the overt approval of over 50 percent of the electorate, in most cases. There is still a proportion of voters who will not support female candidates simply because they *are* women.[25] In highly competitive races and in races where an incumbent is being challenged—the typical races that women face—a successful candidate cannot afford to lose even a small fraction of that electorate automatically. Although the proportion of the electorate opposed to women on gender alone has been diminishing, this diminution is a slow process. Further, equality of opportunity in politics cannot be regulated or mandated given that it depends instead on shifts in public opinion. Some of the changes in political opportunities and electoral success for women, then, depend to a large extent on the pace of social change.

Birth control has played a helpful role in increasing the number of women in politics by allowing women to control the number and timing of their offspring. This control is crucial for those who contemplate a political career, especially while public perceptions continue to make it difficult for women with small children to engage in high-level elective politics.

CONCLUSION

We have discussed four factors that, traditionally, have diminished the opportunity for women to compete for the presidency:

1. The presidential system itself, which relies more closely on direct, popular election than does the parliamentary system, which elects its prime minister from among fellow party members
2. The paucity of women gaining experience in the presidential "launching roles" of the vice presidency, the U.S. Senate, and governorships—roles that men have traditionally attained before competing, successfully or unsuccessfully, for the presidency
3. The difficulty women have experienced in securing PAC and other campaign funding for national and subnational races
4. Long-standing public perceptions that the traditional childbearing and child-rearing roles of women conflict with simultaneous participation in high-level elective politics.

Equality of opportunity has not been legislated in presidential politics or, for that matter, in elective politics at any level. Reforms that encourage female participation at subnational levels, such as public financing and other campaign reforms, will certainly contribute to the available pool of female presidential candidates. Ultimately, shifts in public opinion must also occur—including a recognition that political roles no more conflict with familial roles for women than they do for men—in order to level the "playing field" of U.S. presidential politics for women.

Although legislation has not been used in the United States in the past to increase female presence in high elective office, legislation to make equal representation a major goal has a recent precedent. The actions of the European Parliament can serve as an example of how the role of women in national politics may be enhanced and sustained. In the fall of 1988, the European Parliament, which represents the twelve countries in the Common Market, passed a resolution endorsing a quota and affirmative action system calling for equal numbers of men and women in the elected bodies of its member countries. Not only did this resolution pass the European Parliament, but also at least ten of the twelve member countries

have adopted rules on quotas as well as timetables for increasing female representation in their national parliaments. Similar resolve to place women in the United States in equal numbers in presidential launching roles, as well as in appropriate subnational political roles in state legislatures and local governments, could well be legislated.

NOTES

1. Jean Blondel, *Government Ministers in the Contemporary World* (Beverly Hills, CA: Sage, 1985).

2. Marcia Lynn Whicker and Jennie Jacobs Kronenfeld, *Sex Role Changes: Technology, Politics, and Policy* (New York: Praeger, 1986).

3. Richard Rose, "Government against Sub-Governments: A European Perspective on Washington," in Richard Rose and Ezra N. Suleiman (Eds.), *Presidents and Prime Ministers* (Washington, DC: American Enterprise Institute, 1980), pp. 284–347.

4. M. Kent Jennings and Barbara G. Farah, "Social Roles and Political Resources: An Overtime Study of Men and Women in Party Elites," *American Journal of Political Science*, 25 (1981), pp. 462–482.

5. Edmond Costantini, "Political Women and Political Ambition: Closing the Gender Gap," *American Journal of Political Science*, 34 (3) (August 1990), pp. 741–770.

6. John H. Yunker and Lawrence D. Longley, "The Biases of the Electoral College: Who Is Really Advantaged?" in Donald R. Matthews (Ed.), *Perspectives on Presidential Selection* (Washington, DC: Brookings Institution, 1973), pp. 172–203. Also see Nelson W. Polsby and Aaron Wildavsky, *Presidential Elections: Strategies of American Electoral Politics*, 6th ed. (New York: Charles Scribner's Sons, 1984).

7. Max S. Power, "Logic and Legitimacy: On Understanding the Electoral College Controversy," in Donald R. Matthews (Ed.), *Perspectives on Presidential Selection* (Washington, DC: Brookings Institution, 1973), pp. 204–238.

8. Stephen Hess, *The Presidential Campaign*, 3rd ed. (Washington, DC: Brookings Institution, 1988). Also see Stephen J. Wayne, *The Road to the White House: The Politics of Presidential Elections*, 3rd ed. (New York: St. Martin's Press, 1988).

9. Frank J. Sorauf, *Party Politics in America*, 5th ed. (Boston: Little, Brown, 1984), pp. 425–429.

10. Ronna Romney and Beppie Harrison, *Momentum: Women in American Politics Now* (New York: Crown, 1988).

11. William Henry Clark, "What Votes Can Win?" in James David Barber and Barbara Kellerman (Eds.), *Women Leaders in American Politics* (Englewood Cliffs, NJ: Prentice-Hall, 1986), pp. 218–234.

12. J. E. Buckley, "Equal Pay in America," in Barrie O. Pettman (Ed.), *Equal Pay for Women: Progress and Problems in Seven Countries* (West Yorkshire, England: MCB Books, 1975).

13. U.S. Department of Labor, Bureau of Labor Statistics, *1981 Weekly Earnings of Men and Women Compared in 100 Occupations* (Washington, DC: U.S. Government Printing Office, 1982).

14. Sheila B. Kamerman, Alfred J. Kahn, and Paul Kingston, *Maternity Politics and Working Women* (New York: Columbia University Press, 1983).

15. Susan Deller Ross and Ann Barcher, *The Rights of Women: The Basic ACLU Guide to a Woman's Rights*, rev. ed. (New York: Bantam, 1983).

16. Joyce Gelb and Marian Lief Palley, *Women and Public Policies* (Princeton, NJ: Princeton University Press, 1982).

17. Whicker and Kronenfeld, *Sex Role Changes*, pp. 162–163.

18. Stephen J. Wayne, *The Road to the White House: The Politics of Presidential Elections*, 3rd ed. (New York: St. Martin's Press, 1988), pp. 36–41.

19. Ibid.

20. Ruth Mandel, "The Image Campaign," in James David Barber and Barbara Kellerman (Eds.), *Women Leaders in American Politics* (Englewood Cliffs, NJ: Prentice-Hall, 1986), pp. 261–271.

21. Lisa W. Foderaro, "Women Winning Locally, but Higher Office Is Elusive," *New York Times*, April 1, 1989, pp. 29, 32.

22. Susan Gluck Mezy, "Does Sex Make a Difference? A Case Study of Women in Politics," *Western Political Quarterly*, 31 (1978), pp. 492–501.

23. Virginia Sapiro, *Women: Political Action and Political Participation* (Washington, DC: American Political Science Association, 1983).

24. Cynthia Fuchs Epstein, "Women and Power: The Role of Women in Politics in the United States," in Cynthia Fuchs Epstein and Rose Laub Coser (Eds.), *Access to Power: Cross-National Studies of Women and Elites* (London: George Allen and Unwin, 1981).

25. Whicker and Kronenfeld, *Sex Role Changes*, p. 165.

FURTHER READINGS

Barber, James David, and Barbara Kellerman (Eds.). *Women Leaders in American Politics.* Englewood Cliffs, NJ: Prentice-Hall, 1986.

Costello, Cynthia, and Anne J. Stone. *The American Woman 1994–95: Where We Stand.* New York: Norton, 1994.

Darcy, R., Susan Welch, and Janet Clark. *Women, Elections, and Representation,* 2nd ed., revised. Lincoln: University of Nebraska Press, 1994.

Genovese, Michael A. (Ed.). *Women as National Leaders.* Newbury Park, CA: Sage, 1993.

Kelber, Mim (Ed.). *Women and Government: New Ways to Political Power.* Westport, CT: Praeger, 1994.

Witt, Linda, Karen M. Paget, and Glenna Matthews. *Running as a Woman: Gender and Power in American Politics.* New York: Free Press, 1994.

Women as Governors: State Executive Leadership with a Feminist Face?

Sara J. Weir

The growing importance of state governance in the United States' political system and of governors as both initiators and administrators of large annual budgets and major public programs make the study of state governorship increasingly important in the area of public administration and executive leadership. The governorship is also politically significant because it is so often an avenue for aspiring presidential candidates. Given the increased focus on national budgets and deficit reduction, it can be argued that governors, especially of large states, possess the necessary qualifications to serve as president. Of the five most recent U.S. presidents, three gained their political experience and national reputations by serving as governors. The case for governors as national executives is further strengthened by the experience that many governors have dealing directly with international trading partners. States such as New Jersey, Texas, and Washington depend on such trade for jobs as well as for tax revenues. While much has been written about gubernatorial races and of governors as central figures in subnational governance, an entirely new area of scholarly inquiry now explores women as governors.

Few studies of the governorship have focused on women as governors. However, from the 1925 election of Nellie Tayloe Ross (Democrat) of Wyoming to the 1993 election of Christine Todd Whitman (Republican) of New Jersey, thirteen women (eleven Democrats and two Republicans) have served as governors. While

Sara J. Weir is an assistant professor of political science at Western Washington University. The author would like to acknowledge the contributions of Kathy Luecher and Yvonne Richards for their support as research assistants and to Sue Scally of Western Washington University's Bureau for Faculty Research for her work as an editor and her assistance in the preparation of this manuscript.

these numbers are small—as compared with the proportion of women elected to statewide offices or with men elected as governors—a growing number of women are running for and winning in gubernatorial contests.

This article expands the study of gender and leadership to the case of women as governors, providing comparisons of the candidacies and administrations of several women who have served as governors. While there are not enough cases to draw generalizable conclusions, patterns do emerge. For example, what do we know about the women who have run for and served as governors? Do patterns emerge in the candidacy and election of women governors, and if so, what do recent elections tell us about future prospects for women seeking to serve as governors or to use their experience as governors to seek a place on the presidential ticket? We begin with a review of the literature and then address the questions posed.

THE STUDY OF WOMEN AS GOVERNORS

The inclusion of the study of women as state executives expands our understanding both of gender as a political variable and of the politics of executive leadership. This combination of realms of inquiry is, according to Virginia Sapiro, common in the study of women and politics.[1] When women such as Ann Richards or Christine Todd Whitman achieve top executive positions, they allow examination and force attention to socially defined gender roles.[2]

The careers of the women who have sought to be and in some cases have served as governors help us to determine if expectations about the impact of gender roles and stereotypes, and the political relevance of gender differences found in studies of women as legislators, also apply to state executives.[3] Unfortunately, the existing literature on women governors is more journalistic than scholarly— this, in part, is due to the relatively small number of cases available for study, but gender stereotypes commonly held both in the popular press and in academia have also shaped the way women candidates are portrayed and whether they are considered appropriate subjects for scholarly work.[4]

The literature includes autobiographical works (such as that of Ann Richards),[5] stories of gubernatorial races involving women (like *Prairie Politics: Kay Orr vs. Helen Boosalis, The Historic 1986 Gubernatorial Race*),[6] and comparative case studies of the campaigns of women running for governor.[7] All of these books are very readable, and each provides important insight into both the personal lives and the campaigns of several women. But to begin studying this topic more systematically, one must look beyond these studies to find existing research on women and leadership.

Leadership refers to more than simply holding office: According to Genovese and Thompson, it "is a complex phenomenon revolving around *influence*—the ability to move others in desired directions."[8] Like other chief executives, state governors are judged on their ability to exercise leadership within the confines of the political culture and institutional structure of their states. Governors also vary in the personal skills they bring to the job. The style, character, and personal attributes they possess determine how successful they will be as state executives.[9]

Like the presidency, the governorship is a highly gendered office. Executive leadership has been (and to a great extent continues to be) viewed as a traditionally masculine attribute. According to political pollster Celinda Lake, the qualities that make a good governor—toughness and executive ability—are most often associated by voters with men.[10] Do the women who seek the governorship attempt to redefine executive leadership or find ways to navigate politically by being as tough and decisive as their male counterparts?

The answer to this query is not easy or straightforward: Women candidates must work against the *soft* image put upon them by the media. For example, during the 1986 gubernatorial race in Nebraska between Kay Orr and Helen Boosalis, the candidates struggled to overcome the national media's unwillingness to view the race in conventional political terms. Although both candidates had extensive experience in state and local elective positions and although they debated the hard issues, such as taxes and the economy, it was mid-September before national newspapers were able to stop talking about the "historic race" between two women.[11] This focus on gender prompted Kay Orr to comment that the contest was "no bake-off."[12]

HISTORICAL OVERVIEW

The 1974 election of Ella Grasso (Democrat) as governor of Connecticut marked the beginning of an era for women as gubernatorial candidates. Three women served as governors prior to this time, but they all acted as replacements or surrogates for their husbands. Probably the best known of the three is Lurleen Wallace (Democrat) Alabama, who succeeded her husband, George Wallace, in 1967. In this case little effort was made to hide the fact that George Wallace continued to govern.

The era of the *independent woman governor* began with the election of Ella Grasso. In the next twenty years women were major-party candidates for governor in forty-two races, winning gubernatorial contests in ten cases. How do we examine these cases, and what patterns emerge? The review that follows focuses especially on four political variables: (1) avenues of mobility and previous political experience; (2) candidate image and image problems faced by women; (3) issue positions and candidate platform; and (4) support for women's issues and the inclusion of women in their administration.

Ella Grasso, a Democrat, was the fourth woman governor but the first to be elected or appointed independent of a husband who proceeded her in office. In 1974 Grasso defeated her Republican challenger, Robert Steele, in an open-seat contest, receiving 59 percent of the vote. She was reelected to a second four-year term in 1978, and although she again received 59 percent of the vote, it was a hotly contested primary and general election campaign. Grasso gained political experience working with John Bailey, national chairman of the Democratic Party under President John Kennedy. As a longtime party activist and elected official, Grasso avoided the *soft* image that other women governors, like Martha Layne Collins of Kentucky, struggled against.

Grasso was a fiscal conservative and a social moderate who imposed austerity programs during her first term and used her opposition to a state income tax as a major focus of both of her gubernatorial campaigns. The late Governor Grasso stepped down for health reasons in the middle of her second term.[13]

Grasso was followed by Dixie Lee Ray of Washington in 1976, Martha Layne Collins of Kentucky in 1983, and Madeleine Kunin (Democrat) of Vermont in 1984. Kunin first ran for governor in 1982. She was defeated by the incumbent Republican governor Richard Snelling, but she came back to win the gubernatorial race in 1984, defeating the Republican candidate for the open seat in a very close race. She went on to be reelected to two additional two-year terms. In 1986 she won in a race that pitted her against Peter Smith, the Republican challenger, and the former mayor of Burlington, Bernie Sanders, a Socialist, running as an Independent in the election.

The 1986 election of Kay Orr as governor of Nebraska marked two firsts in gubernatorial races involving woman. Not only was she the first Republican woman to be elected governor of any state, the 1986 Nebraska race was the first gubernatorial contest between two women candidates of major political parties. Orr served as state treasurer before running for governor. This was not a feminist contest. Orr was "opposed to legalized abortion in all instances," while Boosalis said she was personally opposed to abortion except in the case of "rape, incest or to save a mother's life."[14] Both Orr and Boosalis called for limits on tax increases, with Orr labeling herself as a "fiscal conservative." The race drew national attention because both candidates were female, but beyond this the candidates took similar positions on many issues. Orr won with 53 percent of the vote "in a state where Republicans outnumber Democrats by 75,000 registered voters."[15]

Joan Finney (Democrat) of Kansas was the first female gubernatorial candidate to defeat an incumbent governor. In 1993 Christine Todd Whitman, a Republican from New Jersey, also defeated the incumbent governor, James Florio. When she took office it brought the number of women serving as governors to four. This is the highest number of women to serve simultaneously as state chief executives.

Barbara Roberts (Democrat) of Oregon and Ann Richards (Democrat) of Texas were both elected in 1990. Roberts is the most politically liberal of all the women elected governor. She was the first woman elected governor of Oregon, but she "follows in the footsteps of Democrat Betty Roberts, who ran for governor in 1974, and Republican Norma Paulus, who ran in 1986."[16] A longtime activist in the Democratic Party, Roberts served two terms in the state house of representatives. In 1984 she ran for and was elected to the office of secretary of state. Roberts was open about her support for women's issues and her opposition to state initiatives aimed at limiting the rights and protections accorded homosexuals. For example, Roberts in 1988 opposed Measure 8, which repealed Democratic Governor Neil Goldsmith's executive order banning discrimination against homosexuals working in state government."[17] Roberts, like Joan Finney of Kansas, chose not to seek reelection in 1994.

The third woman elected to the governorship in 1990 was Ann Richards of Texas. Richards first received national attention when she addressed the Democratic National Convention in 1988. Her "poor George" comments were repeated throughout the campaign, but in Texas she was already well known. Having served eight years as state treasurer, Richards modernized the state financial system and gained a reputation as a good administrator and a smart politician. She defeated Clayton Williams in an open-seat contest in 1990. Her victory was due, at least in part, to Williams's antiwoman comments during the campaign. The gender gap in voting that favored Richards in 1990 did not materialize in 1994. Richards was defeated by George W. Bush, a more moderate Republican than Williams.

A liberal feminist, Richards made appointments that served notice that in the "New Texas" she had promised, state government would no longer be the preserve of white men. Her choices were 20 percent Hispanic, 15 percent Black, 2 percent Asian, and an eye-opening 46 percent female; there were even two openly gay appointees.[18] Campaigning as a reformer, Richards introduced measures to stabilize insurance rates and attempted to address the unresolved question of "how to equalize financing among school districts that vary widely in their ability to raise money from property taxes."[19]

Although she campaigned against a state income tax, the Democrat-controlled state legislature adopted a $2.7 billion tax increase that included a revision of the state's major tax on businesses. According to Roberto Suro, "Although the levy is not strictly an income tax, businesses that used to pay taxes only on their capital assets now pay on assets or income, whichever is greater."[20] Bush focused on these tax increases, as well as on the overall performance of the state economy, to defeat Richards in 1994.

Finally, in 1993 Christine Todd Whitman was elected governor of New Jersey. As mentioned previously, she is currently the only woman governor and one of only two women to defeat incumbents to become state chief executive. Whitman campaigned on a promise of a 30 percent tax cut. Characterized as "naive" and "aristocratic," Whitman defeated Jim Florio in a close race. The victory was tainted by allegations that Whitman's campaign "may have attempted to 'suppress' the black vote by essentially bribing black ministers not to rally their congregations for the Democrats."[21] Whitman survived the controversy and received high marks for integrity and compassion in a May 1994 poll conducted by the Asbury Park Press.

Whitman has made her reputation as a fiscal conservative and a social moderate. In January 1995 she announced a timetable for completing her promised 30 percent tax cut, yet, according to Dean Armandroff, executive director of the New Jersey Republican State Committee, she is not reflexively antigovernment. "She really believes that there are legitimate roles for government."[22] For example, even with major cuts in state spending, she continues to strongly support social service programs.

Like Ann Richards, Whitman has opened state government, especially to women. She has appointed many women to leadership positions, including the first women to serve as attorney general, chief of staff, and executive director of the New York/New Jersey Port Authority. According to the National Leadership Conference of Women Executives in State Government, "Women also represent 248 out of 700 appointments to New Jersey's Boards and Commissions."[23] She has also urged the Republican Party to take a more moderate stance on the issue of abortion. The governor commented that "abortion was a deeply personal, not political, decision and urged the GOP to remove the anti-abortion plank from its 1996 platform."[24] The promotion of women and her views on abortion may make her vulnerable to a conservative challenge within her party if she seeks a second term.

PATTERNS IN THE CANDIDACY OF WOMEN GOVERNORS

Types of Contests

As Table 1 shows, between 1974 and 1993, women ran thirty-three times as major-party candidates for governor, winning in twelve cases. (In 1994, nine women ran for governor; all were defeated.) Women candidates are most successful in *open-seat* contests, with seven of twelve victories coming in races with no incumbent (see Table 2). But what about the cases that do not fit this pattern? Table 2 shows that two women governors, Ella Grasso (Democrat) Connecticut and Madeleine Kunin (Democrat) Vermont, were first elected in open-seat contests and were reelected for a second and in Kunin's case a third term. More recently Joan Finney (Democrat) Kansas and Christine Todd Whitman defeated incumbents in their successful gubernatorial races. The other race that varied from the common pattern of election was the 1986 gubernatorial race between Kay Orr (Republican) and Helen Boosalis (Democrat). Not only was this the first race between two women candidates of major political parties, but with her victory Orr became the first Republican woman to be elected to the governorship. In 1990 Orr was defeated in her bid for a second term by her Democratic challenger, Ben Nelson.

Previous Political Experience

Most women running for governor have held other state or local elected positions. For example, Ella Grasso was elected secretary of state in Connecticut in 1958. She went on to serve two terms as a U.S. representative before her election as governor in 1974. Madelaine Kunin, who served as lieutenant governor of Vermont, was defeated by incumbent governor Richard Snelling in the 1982 gubernatorial contest. She came back to defeat Republican John Easton in an open-seat contest in 1984. Her victory in a state known as a "bastion of Republicanism" was due in part to her high name recognition and past service in state government. Both Kay Orr and Helen Boosalis were well known in Nebraska electoral politics, with Orr serving as state treasurer and Boosalis as mayor of Lincoln. Ann Richards gained political experience serving two terms as state treasurer. First elected to the position in 1982, she became the first woman to hold statewide elected office since Miriam Ferguson held office from 1925 to 1927 and again from 1933 to 1935.[25]

In sum, holding other statewide elective office gives women the experience, partisan connections, and name recognition necessary to seek the governorship.

Table 1 Women Candidates for Governor, 1974–1993: Major Party Nominees

Year	State	Women Candidates	Opponents	Seat	Results*
1993	NJ	Christine Todd Whitman—R	Jim Florio—D	Challenger	Won
1993	VA	Mary Sue Terry—D	George Allen—R	Open	Lost
1992	MT	Dorothy Bradley—D	Mark Racicot—R	Open	Lost 49%
1992	NH	Deborah Arnie Arneson—D	Steve Merril—R	Open	Lost 38%
1992	RI	Elizabeth Ann Leonard—R	Bruce Sundlun—D	Challenger	Lost 34%
1990	AK	Arliss Sturgulewski—R	Tony Knowles—D and Walter Hickel—I	Open	Lost 26%
1990	CA	Dianne Feinstein—D	Pete Wilson—R	Open	Lost 46%
1990	KS	Joan Finney—D	Mike Hayden—R	Challenger	Won 49%
1990	NE	Kay Orr—R	Ben Nelson—D	Incumbent	Lost 49%
1990	OR	Barbara Roberts—D	Dave Frohnmayer—R	Open	Won 46%
1990	PA	Barbara Hafer—R	Bob Casey—D	Challenger	Lost 32%
1990	TX	Ann Richards—D	Clayton Williams—R	Open	Won 50%
1990	WY	Mary Mead—R	Michael Sullivan—D	Challenger	Lost 35%
1988	MO	Betty Hearnes—D	John Ashcroft—R	Challenger	Lost 35%
1988	VT	Madeleine Kunin—D	Michael Bernhardt—R	Incumbent	Won 55%
1986	AK	Arliss Sturgulewski—R	Steve Coper—D and Joe Vogler—AI	Open	Lost 43%
1986	AZ	Carolyn Warner—D	Evan Mecham—R and Bill Schultz—I	Open	Lost 34%
1986	CT	Julie Belaga—R	William O'Neill—D	Challenger	Lost 41%
1986	NE	Kay Orr—R	Helen Boosalis—D	Open	Won 53%
1986	NE	Helen Boosalis—D	Kay Orr—R	Open	Lost 47%
1986	NV	Patty Cafferata—R	Richard Bryan—D	Challenger	Lost 25%
1986	OR	Norma Paulus—R	Neil Goldschmidt—D	Open	Lost 48%
1986	VT	Madeleine Kunin—D	Peter Smith—R and Bernard Sanders—I	Incumbent	Won 47%
1984	VT	Madeleine Kunin—D	John Easton—R	Open	Won 50%
1983	KY	Martha Layne Collins—D	Jim Bunning—R	Open	Won 54%
1982	IA	Roxanne Conlin—D	Terry Branstad—R	Open	Lost 47%
1982	VT	Madeleine Kunin—D	Richard Snelling—R	Challenger	Lost 44%
1978	CT	Ella Grasso—D	Ronald Sarasin—R	Incumbent	Won 59%
1976	VT	Stella Hackel—D	Richard Snelling—R	Open	Lost 40%
1976	WA	Dixy Lee Ray—D	John Spellman—R	Open	Won 53%
1974	CT	Ella Grasso—D	Robert Steele—R	Open	Won 59%
1974	MD	Louise Gore—R	Marvin Mandel—D	Challenger	Lost 37%
1974	NV	Shirley Crumpler—R	Mike O'Callaghan—D	Challenger	Lost 17%

*Percentage of the vote received by women candidates according to *The Almanac of American Politics*, except in 1990 and 1992; 1990 and 1992 figures are from secretary of state offices.

Source: Center for the American Woman and Politics (CAWP), National Information Bank on Women in Public Office, Eagleton Institute of Politics, Rutgers University.

Table 2   Type of Electoral Contest in Which Women Governors Were Elected: 1974–1994

Open Seat	Challenger	Incumbent
Grasso (D) 1974	Finney (D) 1990	Grasso (D) 1978
Ray (D) 1976	Whitman (R) 1993	Kunin (D) 1986
Collins (D) 1983		Kunin (D) 1988
Kunin (D) 1984		
Orr (R) 1986		
Richards (D) 1990		
Roberts (D) 1990		

Source: Center for the American Woman and Politics (CAWP), National Information Bank on Women in Public Office, Eagleton Institute of Politics, Rutgers University.

Current New Jersey Governor Christine Todd Whitman is an exception to this pattern, gaining the experience necessary to seek the governorship by virtue of her family background, years of political involvement, and near defeat of incumbent Senator Bill Bradley in the 1990 senatorial race.

WOMEN GOVERNORS: 1994 AND BEYOND

Nineteen ninety-four was definitely not The Year of the Woman Governor. Nine women ran for state governor in the thirty-six gubernatorial contests held—none were elected. The race in Maryland was the closest and most hotly contested. In that race the Republican candidate, Ellen Sauerbrey, continues to dispute the victory of her Democratic opponent, Paris Glendening. Losing by only 5,993 votes, out of 1.4 million votes cast, she took the matter to the Maryland State Court, "In her suit, Ms. Sauerbrey said she had been cheated through votes cast by dead people, prison inmates and unregistered" voters.[26] On January 13 a state judge ruled that Sauerbrey did not have enough evidence to overturn the election. Glendening and his running mate for lieutenant governor, Kathleen Kennedy Townsend, took office in mid-January.

In California, Kathleen Brown came into the race with the right family background, high name recognition, and previous political experience. However, like Dianne Feinstein in 1990, she was no match for Governor Pete Wilson. Christine Todd Whitman is now the focus of great attention as the only female governor, and a moderate Republican. She is being discussed as a possible candidate on the Republican national ticket in 1996.

CONCLUSION

Thirteen women have served as state governors. Today only one woman governor holds office, but nineteen women are currently lieutenant governors and many more hold offices such as secretary of state or state treasurer—offices that have given most of the women discussed in this chapter the experience and recognition necessary to be elected governor. How do we evaluate this record? What predictions can be made about the future of women as governors or the governorship as an avenue of mobility to the presidency for women? The progress made in the election of women governors is mixed.

There are several positive developments. First, more women are running for and holding statewide elected positions—putting themselves in the "experience pool." If this trend continues, we should see many qualified female candidates in gubernatorial contests in 1996 and beyond.

Second, female candidates are beginning to defeat incumbents, showing their strength as candidates and their ability to raise money as challengers. Only Finney and Whitman have defeated incumbents, but many women now holding other statewide elected positions are poised to mount challenges in the coming electoral period. Republican state officeholders have received campaign support and advice from Christine Todd Whitman—currently the model for many women seeking state elected office. Third, Whitman and former Texas governor Ann Richards are highly visible in their respective political parties, with Whitman presenting the Republican Party's response to President Clinton's 1995 State of the Union Address. Still, the picture is less than perfect.

Christine Todd Whitman is currently the only female governor, and only thirteen women have held the position in the nation's history. No more than four women have served as governor simultaneously, and all nine of the female candidates for governor in the November 1994 elections were defeated. With the growing importance of the governorship in U.S. politics, full political equality will not be achieved until more women are elected as state chief executives.

Governors, to include Whitman and Richards, suggest ways in which women can reshape state executive governance; this is to include more women in important appointed positions. They also serve as important role models for other women seeking statewide elected office.

In conclusion, this essay only begins to explore the subject of female governors. Closer examination of patterns of support for female gubernatorial candidates and analysis focusing more broadly on women holding other statewide elective offices will increase our understanding of state executive leadership. Further research on these and other related topics is clearly called for.

NOTES

1. Virginia Sapiro, *The Political Integration of Women: Roles, Socialization, and Politics* (Urbana: University of Illinois Press, 1983).

2. Margaret Conaway, Jill K. Conway, Susan C. Bourquet, and Joan W. Scott, *Learning about Women: Gender Politics and Power* (Ann Arbor: University of Michigan Press, 1987).

3. Susan Welch, "Are Women More Liberal than Men in the U.S. Congress?" *Legislative Studies Quarterly*, 10 (February 1985), pp. 125–134; Sue Thomas and Susan Welch, "The Impact of Gender on Activities and Priorities of State Legislators," *Western Political Quarterly*, 44 (June 1991), pp. 445–456; Barbara Burrell, *A Woman's Place Is in the House: Campaigning for Con-*

gress in the Feminist Era. (University of Michigan Press, 1994).

4. Kim F. Kahn, "The Distant Mirror," *Journal of Politics*, 56 (1) (February 1994), pp. 154–173.

5. Ann Richards, *Straight from the Heart* (New York: Scribner's 1989).

6. John Barrette (Ed.), *Prairie Politics: Kay Orr vs. Helen Boosalis, The Historic 1986 Gubernatorial Race* (Lincoln, Nebraska: Media Publishing and Marketing, 1987).

7. Celia Morris, *Storming the Statehouse: Running for Governor with Ann Richards and Dianne Feinstein* (New York: Simon and Schuster, 1992).

8. Genovese and Thompson, p.1 in *Women as National Leaders*, Genovese (Ed.) (Thousand Oaks, California: Sage, 1993), p.1.

9. Genovese and Thompson, p. 2 in Genovese.

10. Celinda Lake, as cited in Eleanor Clift, "Not the Year of the Woman," *Newsweek*, October 25, 1993, p. 31.

11. Barrette, *Prairie Politics*, chap. 3.

12. Interview, *New York Times Magazine*, September 22, 1986, as cited in ibid.

13. Center for the American Woman and Politics (CAWP), National Information Bank on Women in Public Office, Eagleton Institute of Politics, Rutgers University.

14. *New York Times*, as cited in Barrette, *Prairie Politics*, p. 95.

15. Barrette, *Prairie Politics*, p. 155.

16. Jeff Mapes, *The Oregonian*, December 8, 1990, p. A7.

17. Ibid., p. A12.

18. Alison Cook, "Lone Star," *New York Times Magazine*, February 7, 1993, p. 42.

19. Roberto Suro, "Texas Governor Proves Adept in Her First Year," *New York Times*, January 19, 1992, p. A16.

20. Ibid., p. 16.

21. Gloria Berger, and Matthew Cooper with Scott Minerbrook and Michael Barone, "New Jersey: An Election Controversy," *U.S. News and World Report*, November 22, 1993, p. 30.

22. Dean Armandroff, as cited in Joe Donohue, "Whitman on Cutting (Tax) Edge of Stardom," *New Jersey Star-Ledger*, March 20, 1994, p. D3.

23. National Leadership Conference of Women Executives in State Government, letter of nomination for WESG "Breaking the Glass Ceiling" Awards, 1995.

24. Governor Christine Whitman, as cited in "Whitman Condemns GOP Abortion Stance," *Philadelphia Inquirer*, July 13, 1994, p. 6.

25. Ferguson served as surrogate for her husband, who could not run for reelection.

26. *New York Times*, January 14, 1995, p. A11.

FURTHER READINGS

Barrette, John (Ed.). *Prairie Politics: Kay Orr vs. Helen Boosalis, The Historic 1986 Gubernatorial Race*. Lincoln, Nebraska: Media Publishing and Marketing, 1987.

Burrell, Barbara C. *A Woman's Place Is in the House: Campaigning for Congress in the Feminist Era*. Ann Arbor: University of Michigan Press, 1994.

Dodson, Debra (Ed.). *Gender and Policymaking: Studies of Women in Office*. New Brunswick, New Jersey: Center for the American Woman and Politics, 1991.

Genovese, Michael A. (Ed.). *Women as National Leaders*. Thousand Oaks, California: Sage, 1993.

Githens, Marianne et al. (Eds.). *Different Roles, Different Voices: Women and Politics in the United States and Europe*. New York: HarperCollins, 1994.

Morris, Celia. *Storming the Statehouse: Running for Governor with Ann Richards and Dianne Feinstein*. New York: Scribner's, 1992.

Richards, Ann, with Peter Knobler. *Straight from the Heart*. New York: Simon and Schuster, 1989.

Thomas, Sue. *How Women Legislate*. New York: Oxford University Press, 1994.

 **CHAPTER 6**

THE COURTS:
WOMEN AND DECISIONS

Does gender make a difference when it comes to the judicial branch? Karen O'Connor traces the intertwined quest for expanded rights for women and the U.S. Supreme Court's responses to those actions. She begins with an overview of the colonial period, moves to the Civil War years, addresses the suffrage movement litigation, reviews the press for state laws and for the Supreme Court to address the issue of gender, and explores the legal status of women at the workplace as well as more contemporary attempts to expand women's rights. She finds that fewer and fewer constitutional cases involving sex discrimination are coming before the Supreme Court each year—perhaps because women's rights groups are using their time and money to fend off challenges to a series of decisions adverse to abortion rights. Also, the author maintains that most of the "easy" constitutional cases have been decided, and there is fairly uniform application of the intermediate standard of review in the lower courts. Thus, most gender cases that the Supreme Court now chooses to hear involve employment discrimination and the scope of bona fide occupational qualifications permissible under Title VII of the 1964 Civil Rights Act.

If we had more female judges, could we expect to see more judicial decisions favorable to women? Elaine Martin investigates gender roles and judicial roles. The author examines three aspects of change for women within the judicial system: (1) the increase in the numbers of women judges; (2) the growing evidence in judicial research that female judges are more supportive of women's rights than are male judges; and (3) the possibility that female judges' support of women's rights is related to a feeling of obligation to represent other women. The author finds that, even though the relative numbers of female judges lag far behind the relative numbers of female state legislators, their numbers are rapidly increasing. This study used hypothetical cases to create a situation where large numbers of male and female judges would be deciding the same case. Results indicate that both gender and feminist ideology are important in predicting how judges may decide women's rights cases. The author finds that, within ideological types, women are more likely than men to vote in a pro-female manner. Based on questions answered by a sample of female judges, the author concludes that some female judges have a strong sense that part of their job is to "act for" the interests of other women. We next examine these two essays on women and the courts.

Women's Rights and Legal Wrongs: The U.S. Supreme Court and Sex Discrimination

Karen O'Connor

As early as March 31, 1776, Abigail Adams wrote to her husband, John, who was attending the Second Continental Congress:

> In the new Code of Laws . . . I desire you would Remember the Ladies, and be more generous and favourable to them than your ancestors. Do not put such unlimited power into the hands of the Husbands. Remember all men would be tyrants if they could. If particular care and attention is not paid to the Laidies [*sic*] we are determined to foment a Rebelion [*sic*], and will not hold ourselves bound by any Laws in which we have no voice, or Representation.[1]

Adams's admonitions to her husband had little impact on either the Articles of Confederation or, later, the Constitution. It was not until 1920 that the Nineteenth Amendment was added to the Constitution, offering women that most basic element of citizenship—suffrage. And, in the 1990s, despite long years of a concerted drive by women's rights groups to gain ratification of an amendment guaranteeing equal rights, the Constitution continues to afford women less protection from discrimination than men.

In this article the intertwined quest for expanded rights by women and the U.S. Supreme Court's responses to those actions are traced. Often, the Supreme Court is looked upon as ahead of its time, or at least that of public opinion, in the

Karen O'Connor is professor of government in the School of Public Affairs at The American University.

From *The Oxford Companion to the Supreme Court of the United States*, edited by Kermit L. Hall. Copyright © 1992 by Oxford University Press, Inc. Reprinted by permission.

expansion of rights to minorities. This has not been the case with the expansion or guarantee of rights to women. Instead, as a general rule, the Supreme Court—the final interpreter of the Constitution—has lagged behind societal mores and realities when it has dealt with issues of concern to women. Thus, this essay is an account of the efforts of heroic women and women's groups and the political reaction to those demands for full and equal rights under the Constitution and the Court's responses to those efforts.

THE COLONIAL PERIOD TO THE CIVIL WAR

During the colonial period, suffrage was largely determined by local custom and usage. While there are few records of women voting, it is clear some did, especially large landowners. Once individual states began to draft written constitutions, however, female suffrage evaporated. Women were also excluded by the shift from gender-neutral property-owning requirements to near-universal male suffrage. This emphasis on male suffrage also fostered the codification of many of the practices Abigail Adams denounced as contributing to the second-class citizenship of women.

Recognition and Reaction

Recognition of their own inferior legal status, however, did not come to women overnight. In 1848, in what is widely hailed as the first major step toward female equality under the Constitution, a women's rights convention was held in Seneca Falls, New York.

Eight years earlier, in 1840, two women active in the American abolitionist movement—Lucretia Mott and Elizabeth Cady Stanton—had traveled to London, for the annual meeting of the International Anti-Slavery Society. After a long and arduous journey, they were denied seating on the floor of the convention solely because they were women. Forced to take seating in the rear of the balcony, they could not help but begin to see parallels between their status and that of the slaves they were trying to free. They resolved to call a meeting to discuss women's second-class status, but their involvement in the antislavery movement and issues in their own lives kept them from calling a meeting in Seneca Falls until 1848.

At what is often called the Seneca Falls Convention and at a later meeting held in Rochester, New York, a series of resolutions and a Declaration of Sentiments were drafted, calling for expanded rights for women in all walks of life. Both documents reflected dissatisfaction with contemporary moral codes, divorce and criminal laws, and the limited opportunities for women to obtain an education, participate in the church, and to enter careers in medicine, law, and politics. While these issues continue to dominate the field of sex discrimination law today, none of the participants at the Seneca Falls Convention or subsequent conventions for women's rights saw the Constitution as a source of potential rights for women. Women's rights activists did, however, eventually see the need to amend the Constitution to achieve the right to vote.

While women continued to press for changes in state laws to ameliorate their inferior legal status, they also continued to be very active in the abolitionist movement.[2] During the Civil War (1861–1865), most women's rights activists set aside the cause of women's rights to concentrate on the war effort and abolition. Many who had been present at Seneca Falls or active in subsequent efforts for women's rights joined the American Equal Rights Association (AERA), an association dedicated to the abolition of slavery and woman suffrage. AERA members saw the issues of slavery and women's rights as inextricably intertwined, believing that woman suffrage would be granted when the franchise was extended to newly freed slaves.

The Fourteenth and Fifteenth Amendments

Even the AERA, however, soon abandoned the cause of woman suffrage with its support of the proposed Fourteenth Amendment to the Constitution. When a majority of its members agreed that "now is the Negro's hour," key women's rights activists, including Stanton and Susan B. Anthony, were outraged. They were particularly incensed by the text of the proposed amendment, which would introduce the word *male* into the Constitution for the first time. Although Article II of the Constitution does refer to the president as "he," the use of the word *male* was infuriating to many women.

Not only did Stanton and Anthony argue that women should not be left out of any attempt to secure fuller rights for freed slaves, they were also concerned that the text of the proposed amendment would necessitate the passage of an additional amendment to enfranchise women. How right they were. Soon after passage of the Fourteenth Amendment, the Fifteenth Amendment was added to the Constitution specifically to enfranchise Black males previously ineligible to vote. Feverish efforts to have the word *sex* included to the amendment's list of race, color, or previous condition of servitude as improper limits on voting were unsuccessful. Women once again were told that the rights of Blacks must come first.

Passage of the Fifteenth Amendment, and the AERA's support of it, led Anthony and Stanton to found the National Woman Suffrage Association (NWSA) in 1869. The NWSA's relatively radical demands for family and standards of dress reform, as well as its support of a well-known proponent of free love, Victoria Woodhull, led many to deride its more conservative demand for suffrage via a national constitutional amendment.

LITIGATING FOR SUFFRAGE

The NWSA's advocacy of controversial reforms led to a severe image problem for both the association and its goals. In 1869, to lend credibility to its cause as well as to short-circuit the possibility of a long battle for a universal suffrage amendment, Francis Minor, the husband of Virginia Minor, a prominent NWSA member, put forth his belief that women, as citizens, were entitled to vote under the existing provisions of the Fourteenth Amendment.[3] Minor saw the NWSA's possible resort to the courts as a means to gain favorable publicity for the organization.

Victoria Woodhull's presentation to Congress in January 1871, urging it to pass enabling legislation to give women the right to vote under the Fourteenth Amendment, provided the impetus for a concerted effort to test the logic of Minor's arguments. The day after her congressional appearance, Woodhull addressed the NWSA's annual meeting, infusing the association with a new sense of purpose and enthusiasm for the suffrage battle.

Francis Minor, along with Susan B. Anthony, quickly moved to seize upon the enthusiasm that Woodhull's suggestions created. Minor urged that test cases quickly be brought to determine if the courts would obviate the need for additional legislative action. A number of legal scholars and judges had publicly agreed with Minor's arguments; moreover, in rejecting Woodhull's request for enabling legislation, the House of Representatives had noted that if the right to vote was "vested by the Constitution . . . without regard to sex, that right can be established in the courts without further legislation."[4] And, more importantly, the newly appointed chief justice of the Supreme Court, Salmon P. Chase, had suggested that women test the parameters of the Constitution to determine whether they already were enfranchised by its provisions.

Despite Chase's encouragement, prior references to women by the Supreme Court had generally accepted only limited options for women. In *Dredd Scott v. Sandford* (1857),[5] for example, Scott's lawyer had argued that one need not have "first-class" citizenship to vote. After all, he pointed out, women were citizens yet uniformly were denied the franchise. In response, Justice Taney noted:

> Undoubtedly, a person may be a citizen, that is, a member of the community who form the sovereignty, although he exercises no share of the political power, and is incapacitated for holding particular offices. Women and minors, who form a part of the political family, cannot vote. . . . [6]

Despite this discouraging language, the NWSA initiated several test cases, hoping to have at least one case heard by the Supreme Court. Somewhat fittingly, the only one to reach the Supreme Court was *Minor v. Happersett*,[7] which involved Virginia Minor and her husband, Francis, as coplaintiffs, since married women had no legal right to sue in their own names.

Women, the Legal Profession, and the Supreme Court

Unfortunately for the NWSA, before *Minor* could be appealed to the Supreme Court, the justices heard another case involving gender discrimination under the Fourteenth Amendment. *Bradwell v. Illinois* (1873)[8] involved a challenge to the Illinois Supreme Court's refusal to admit Myra Bradwell to the practice of law solely because she was a woman. Bradwell's lawyer based her claim to practice law on the amendment's clause concerning privileges and immunities. Because Bradwell's lawyer was aware of the pending suffrage test cases, in his argument he rejected the notion that women were enfranchised under the same provisions. He carefully differentiated the practice of a chosen profession from the right to vote, putting the Court on notice that not even all women were in agreement over the scope and reach of the Fourteenth Amendment. And, despite the care he took to disassociate his client from the NWSA's tactics, the Court ruled 8 to 1 against Bradwell's petition.

The majority opinion—the first pronouncement from the Supreme Court on the issue of gender—was based on two grounds. First, because Bradwell was suing as a citizen of Illinois, the Privileges or Immunities Clause of Article IV, section 2, of the Constitution was held inapplicable to her claim and was held to apply only to matters involving U.S. citizenship. Second, since admission to the bar of any state was not one of the privileges or immunities of U.S. citizenship, the Fourteenth Amendment did not secure that right.

Far more damaging to the cause of women's rights, however, was a concurrence written by Justice Joseph P. Bradley, which is often referred to as his promulgation of the "Divine Law of the Creator." Writing for himself and two other justices, Bradley chose to base his decision on much broader grounds:

> The civil law, as well as nature herself, has always recognized a wide difference in the respective sphere and destinies of man and woman. Man is, or should be, woman's protector and defender. The natural and proper timidity and delicacy . . . (of) the female sex evidently unfits it for many of the occupations of civil life. The constitution of the family organization, which is founded in the divine ordinance, as well as in the nature of things, indicates the domestic sphere as that which properly belongs to the domain and functions of womanhood. . . . So firmly fixed was this sentiment in the founders of the common law that it became a maxim of the system of jurisprudence that a woman had no legal existence separate from her husband. . . . This very incapacity was one circumstance which the Supreme Court of Illinois deemed important in rendering a married woman incompetent fully to perform the duties and trusts that belong to the office of an attorney.
>
> . . . The paramount destiny and mission of woman are to fulfill the noble and benign offices of wife and mother. This is the law of the Creator.[9]

Other Gender-Based Claims

Two years later, in *Minor v. Happersett* (1875), the Court again ruled against a claim for expanded women's rights. After the Minors filed suit against a St. Louis voting registrar who refused to accept Virginia Minor's application to vote, the Missouri Supreme Court ruled that states had the authority to bar women from registering to vote and that the Fourteenth Amendment had no impact on that right. On appeal, in rejecting Virginia Minor's claims that the judiciary was empowered to read into the Fourteenth Amendment the right of suffrage as a natural privilege and immunity of citizenship, the newly appointed Chief Justice Morrison R. Waite, writing for a unanimous Court, argued that the states were not inhibited by the Constitution from committing "that important trust to men alone." Nevertheless, the Court stressed that women were "persons" and may even be "citizens" within the meaning of the Fourteenth Amendment.[10]

Thus, by 1875, it was clear that women could not expect constitutional protections from discrimination from the Supreme Court. And, as the NWSA lost members and vigor, it saw little reason to bring other cases to the obviously unreceptive Court.

All of the gender-based discrimination cases heard by the Supreme Court during this era involved construction of the Privileges or Immunities Clause and not the Due Process or Equal Protection Clauses of the Fourteenth Amendment. In the *Slaughterhouse Cases* (1873),[11] argued and decided shortly after *Bradwell*, the Supreme Court had meticulously examined the scope of the Fourteenth Amendment. In addition to limiting the constitutional significance of the Privileges or Immunities Clause, the Court concluded that the Equal Protection Clause "is so clearly a provision for [the Negro] that a strong case would be necessary for its application to any other."[12] Although the Fourteenth Amendment would be revived as a potential tool for women's rights soon after the beginning of the twentieth century, at the end of the nineteenth century women had yet to win a favorable decision against sex discrimination from the Supreme Court. While women were gaining greater rights within the family through passage of married women's property acts in various states and were beginning to gain entry into institutions of higher learning, the Court stuck rigidly to its interpretation that the Equal Protection Clause of the Fourteenth Amendment was intended primarily to protect African-Americans (i.e., African-American males) from discrimination, and it held fast to traditional notions concerning women's proper role in society.

LITIGATING TO PROTECT WOMEN

Although the *Slaughterhouse Cases* did not provide a useful precedent for women seeking to practice law or to vote, the Court's opinion planted the seeds for judicial adoption of a very broad state police power to enact laws to protect the public health, welfare, safety, and morals. This view was accepted in several subsequent cases. In 1887, for example, in sustaining a law prohibiting the sale of intoxicating beverages, the Court built on the *Slaughterhouse* dissents of Justices Bradley and Stephen Field, announcing that it was ready to examine the *substantive* reasonableness of such state legislation. According to the Court, when state laws involving "the public morals, the public health, or the public safety" were at issue, the Court would "look to the substance of things" so as not to be "misled by mere pretenses."[13] Ten years later, in 1897, the Court for the first time invalidated a state statute on substantive due process grounds.[14] And, in 1905, in *Lochner v. New York*, the Court similarly invalidated a law regulating the work hours of bakers.[15]

Until then, the Court had rarely looked to the substance of legislation in addressing its validity. The Court's earlier readings of the Due Process Clause of the Fourteenth Amendment (or of the Fifth Amendment when federal legislation was involved) only guaranteed that legislation be passed in a fair manner, even though it might have an arbitrary or discriminatory impact. In *Lochner*, however, state laws would fail *unless* the provisions at issue were reasonable under "common knowledge." Thus, the Court refused to accept New York's claim that a *ten-hour maximum-hour* law for bakers was reasonable to ensure the health of the bakers. Instead, the Court found that it unreasonably interfered with the employers' and employees' freedom of contract protected by the Fourteenth Amendment, and found no common knowledge to justify such actions by New York.

The importance of common knowledge cannot be understated in chronicling the Court's treatment of gender. Often, "common knowledge" has substituted for the personal views of the individual justices. As Justice Bradley's "Divine Law of the Creator" opinion made quite clear, that view could easily lead to restrictions on the rights of women.

In the early 1900s, however, concern about the public health, welfare, and morals of women led women's rights activists, particularly those closely allied with the suffrage movement, to press for state laws to upgrade the status of working women.

At the turn of the century, although large numbers of women were entering the labor force, they were doing so by necessity—if single, to support themselves; if married, to add to their families' meager wages. Most women were confined to low-paying jobs in horribly substandard conditions, a circumstance highlighted by the 1911 Triangle Shirtwaist Factory fire in New York City, in which many young female workers lost their lives. Even before that time, however, some women had begun to work to improve the working conditions of women and children. And, whether out of civic concern or moral outrage, beginning in the 1890s, resolutions were adopted annually at suffrage conventions calling for improved conditions for women workers.

The National Consumers' League and Protective Legislation

The organization most responsible for change and for the Court's again addressing issues of gender was the National Consumers' League (NCL). The NCL grew out of a meeting of retail shop girls in New York City in 1890 who wanted to publicize their long hours and deplorable working conditions. Soon they were joined in their efforts by numerous upper-class women who became the guiding forces in the organization. Although the NCL initially attempted to use moral suasion, it soon became clear that legislation would be imperative to begin to remedy some of the most outrageous conditions unearthed by its members. By 1907, through the hard work of its national staff and numerous affiliates, the NCL had secured various sorts of maximum-hour or total restriction on night work for women in eighteen states.[16] Its leaders, therefore, immediately recognized how much they had at stake when the Supreme Court decided to review *Muller v. Oregon* (1908), a case challenging the constitutionality of an Oregon statute that prohibited the employment of women for more than ten hours a day. (Muller, the owner of a small laundry, had been convicted of violating the statute.) When *Muller* was accepted for review and oral argument, the NCL went to work immediately. Its general secretary quickly asked Louis D. Brandeis, the well-known attorney brother-in-law of one of its most active members, to take the case. Brandeis did so under one condition— that he have sole control of the litigation—a condition to which Oregon gladly acceded, thus allowing the NCL to represent it in court.

Numerous state court decisions involving protective legislation for women, as well as the Supreme Court's recent decision in *Lochner*, made it clear to Brandeis that a victory could be forthcoming only by presenting information, or "common knowledge," that could persuade the Court that the dangers to women working more than ten hours a day made them more deserving of state protection than the bakers in *Lochner*, and proving that there was something different about women that justified an exception to the freedom of contract doctrine enunciated by the Court in *Lochner*. Brandeis and the NCL would not challenge the Supreme Court's right, under substantive due process, to make that judgment.

NCL researchers compiled information about the possible detrimental effects of long hours of work on women's health and morals, as well as on the health and welfare of their children, including their unborn children. Brandeis stressed women's differences and the reasonableness of the state's legislation. In fact, his brief had but three pages of strictly legal argument, as against 110 pages of sociological data culled largely from European studies of the negative affects of long hours of work on women's health and their reproductive capabilities. The information presented by Brandeis was not all that different (except in quantity) from that presented on behalf of New York in *Lochner*, yet the Court appears to have been keenly persuaded by the contents of what has come to be called the Brandeis Brief.

In holding that the Oregon law was constitutionally permissible, the Court unanimously concluded "that woman's physical structure and the performance of maternal functions place her at a disadvantage in the struggle for substince." Continued the Court:

> This is especially true when the burdens of motherhood are upon her. Even when they are not, by abundant testimony of the medical fraternity continuance for a long time on her feet at work . . . tends to injurious effects on her body, and as healthy mothers are essential to vigorous offspring, the physical well-being of woman becomes an object of public interest and care in order to preserve the strength and vigor of the race.[17]

The impact of *Muller* was immediate. State courts began to hold other forms of protective legislation for women constitutional, whether or not they involved the kind of ten-hour maximums at issue in *Muller*. Thus, eight-hour maximum-work laws in a variety of professions, outright bans on night work for women, and minimum-wage laws for women were routinely upheld under the *Muller* rationale. Much of this Court-sanctioned governmental protection, however, worked to keep women out of high-paying evening jobs or positions that they desperately needed to support their families.

The NCL's efforts to protect women from unscrupulous employers were victorious in the Supreme Court in several additional cases, but they ran into trouble in the early 1920s, ironically right around the time of the ratification of the Nineteenth Amendment. In *Stettler v. O'Hara* (1917), a lower court decision upholding Oregon's minimum-wage law for women was appealed to the Supreme Court. Forces opposed to governmental interference in contractual rights feared that a decision supporting additional protective legislation would open the floodgates of governmental regulation. Stettler's lawyers argued that a labor agreement between an employer and an employee could not be disturbed by the government. Because the Fourteenth Amendment forbade the state from denying any individual of liberty without due process of law, they argued that freedom of contract was protected by the amendment. The Court had once been amenable to this kind of argument, as attested by its decision in *Lochner*.

Building on the Court's far-ranging discussion of women and their physical, social, and legal differences from men, Brandeis, again presenting the state's case, structured his arguments similarly to those offered in *Muller*, arguing the importance of a living wage to the health, welfare, and morals of women. Before the Court could decide the case, however, a vacancy occurred on the Court and Brandeis was appointed to fill it. *Stettler* was then reargued in 1917; with Justice Brandeis not participating, the Court divided 4 to 4, thus sustaining the lower court's decision.[18]

Another NCL-sponsored case, *Bunting v. Oregon* (1917), also attracted a significant amount of attention.[19] Felix Frankfurter, Brandeis' handpicked successor as counsel for the NCL, used the same kind of arguments Brandeis had used in *Muller* and *Stettler*. In a 5-to-3 decision (with Brandeis again not participating), the Court extended *Muller* to uphold the constitutionality of the Oregon statute that established maximum hours for all factory and mill workers.

Differing Views about Protective Legislation

Although the NCL was victorious in these two cases, it had not anticipated the impact that the controversy within the suffrage movement over protective legislation would have on pending litigation. During the early twentieth century, women had come together to lobby for passage and then ratification of the Nineteenth Amendment. Once it was ratified, attempts were made to secure other rights for women. Women in the more radical branch of the suffrage movement, represented by the National Woman's Party (NWP), proposed the addition of an Equal Rights Amendment (ERA) to the Constitution. Progressives and NCL members were horrified because they perceived that an ERA would immediately invalidate the protective legislation they had lobbied so hard to enact.

When *Adkins v. Children's Hospital* (1923)[20] came to the Court, the NWP was ready. *Adkins* involved the constitutionality of a Washington, D.C., minimum-wage law for women. The NWP filed an amicus curiae brief urging the Court to rule that, in light of the Nineteenth Amendment, women should be viewed on a truly equal footing with men. The division among women concerning equal rights and protective legislation was now exposed to public view. It was a debate that was to be resurrected again and again, both in the Court and in public discourse to the present day.

In *Adkins* the Court ruled 5 to 4 that minimum-wage laws for women were unconstitutional, thus resurrecting *Lochner*, which most observers thought had been overruled *sub subsilentio* in *Bunting*. The Court was unwilling to overrule *Muller* and thus simply distinguished it because it involved maximum hours and not wages. Nevertheless, the justices clearly believed that the Nineteenth Amendment conferred more rights on women that just the right to vote. In noting the newly emancipated status of women brought on by the amendment, the Court undoubtedly was responding at last in part to the proequality arguments offered by the NWP.

Adkins, unlike *Muller*, was decided by the narrowest of majorities. But it stood as valid law and as a ringing endorsement of the doctrine of freedom of contract regarding minimum-wage laws for women until 1937 (although the Court continued to uphold state maximum-hour provisions). In *West Coast Hotel v. Parrish* (1937), the Court finally abandoned its endorsement of substantive due process, explicitly overruled *Adkins*, and upheld Washington State's minimum-wage law for women.[21] By *United States v. Darby Lumber* (1941), the Court had completely abandoned substantive due process (and an equally insidious and excessively narrow view of the power of Congress under the Commerce Clause) when it unanimously upheld the validity of the federal Fair Labor Standards Act, which prescribed maximum hours and minimum wages for all workers.[22] In hammering the last nail in the coffin of substantive due process, the Court also appeared to be escaping from the constitutional need to establish a difference between men and women.

While the Court was enunciating a view that men and women were equal as permissible objects of regulation, clearly they were not. Most states continued to bar or limit night work for women. And while a separate minimum wage for women could no longer be valid, employer practices of clustering women into certain positions at far lower wages than those paid to men continued to exist.

No new cases involving women's rights came to the Supreme Court until 1948. The NCL had obtained what it wanted, and the coalition of women's groups that had pressed for suffrage had largely disintegrated. Women were urged to support the war effort, and, after the war ended, to return home—to their traditional roles as wives and mothers. Thus, few groups were left to press for women's rights either in the legislatures or through the courts. The NWP did continue to press for equal rights and, in fact, was able to get a proposed ERA introduced into every session of Congress after 1923, but it chose to stay out of litigation until the 1970s.

NEW ATTEMPTS TO EXPAND RIGHTS

In *Goesaert v. Cleary* (1948)[23] and *Hoyt v. Florida* (1961),[24] the Court again made it clear that women were not guaranteed additional rights under the Fourteenth Amendment or elsewhere in the Constitution. Although the Fourteenth Amendment is a pledge of protection against state discrimination, over the years the Court has generally applied a two-tiered level of analysis to claims advanced under its provisions. Classifications based on race or national origin are considered suspect classifications and are entitled to be judged by the severe test of strict scrutiny. As such they are presumed invalid unless the government can show that they are "necessary to a compelling state interest" and that there are not less restrictive alternative ways to achieve those goals. In contrast, when the Court applies the less stringent level of ordinary scrutiny, which until 1976 included all other legislative classifications, a state must show only a conceivable or reasonable basis for its action.

Until 1971, the Court routinely applied this minimal rationality test to claims involving discrimination against women. In *Goesaert*, for example, it sustained a statute that prohibited women from dispensing alcoholic drinks from behind a bar unless they were the wives or daughters of male bar owners. Thus, forty years after *Muller*, the Court once again justified differential treatment of women by deferring to the state's special interest in women's social and "moral" problems. Under the reasonableness test, all that needed to be shown by the state was some rational basis for the law.

In *Hoyt* the Supreme Court accepted sex-role stereotypes as sufficient reason to uphold a Florida statute that required men to serve on juries while women could merely volunteer for jury service. When Hoyt was convicted by an all-male jury of second-degree murder for killing her husband with a baseball bat, she argued that the conviction violated her rights to equal protection of the laws and her Sixth Amendment right to be judged by a jury of her peers. The Supreme Court disagreed, holding that the Florida statute was not an arbitrary or systematic exclusion of women. Justice John M. Harlan concluded:

> Despite the enlightened emancipation of women from the restrictions and protections of bygone years, and their entry into many parts of community life formerly considered to be reserved to men, woman is still regarded as the center of home and family life.[25]

It was not until the dawn of the current women's movement that judicial perspectives on what constitutes reasonable discrimination began to change. In 1966 the National Organization for Women (NOW) was founded. Soon after, a plethora of other women's rights groups was created. Most of these groups renewed the call for passage of an ERA to the Constitution. While significant lobbying was carried out on that front, some groups, aware of the successes the National Association for the Advancement of Colored People (NAACP) had in securing additional rights for African-Americans through the courts, began to explore the feasibility of a litigation strategy designed to seek a more expansive interpretation of the Fourteenth Amendment. Although prior forays into the courts had ended unfavorably, some women believed that the times had changed enough for the justices (or some of the justices) to recognize that sex-based differential treatment of women was unconstitutional. Many believed that the status of women and the climate for change were sufficiently positive to convince even a conservative Court that some change was necessary.

The American Civil Liberties Union (ACLU), long a key player in the expansion of constitutional rights and liberties, led the planning for a comprehensive strategy to elevate sex to suspect-classification status. Its first case was *Reed v. Reed* (1971).[26] Ruth Bader Ginsburg, a member of the ACLU board, argued the case before the Supreme Court. (Ironically, like the NCL's Louis Brandeis and Felix Frankfurter before her, Ginsburg, too, was ultimately to sit on the U.S. Supreme Court.) Her enthusiasm and interest in the expansion of women's rights via constitutional interpretation led the ACLU to found the Women's Rights Project (WRP).

At issue in *Reed* was the constitutionality of an Idaho statute that required that males be preferred to otherwise equally qualified females as administrators of estates for those who died. NOW, the National Federation of Business and Professional Women, and the Women's Equity Action League all filed amicus curiae briefs urging the Court to interpret the Fourteenth Amendment as prohibiting discrimination against women on account of sex. Democratic Senator Birch Bayh of Indiana, a major sponsor of the ERA, wrote one of the briefs, in which he attempted to apprise the Court of the glaring legal inequities faced by women and to link those inequities, at least in part, to the Court's own persistent refusal to expand the reach of the Equal Protection Clause to gender discrimination. Judicial decisions such as *Goesaert* and *Hoyt*, which allowed states to discriminate against women on minimally rational grounds, had made it clear to women's rights activists that a constitutional amendment was necessary if women were ever to enjoy full citizenship under the Constitution. But *Reed* was a critical first step.

Chief Justice Warren Burger, writing for a unanimous Court in *Reed*, held that the Idaho statute that provided "different treatment . . . to the applicants on the basis of their sex . . . establishes a classification subject to scrutiny under the Equal Protection Clause."[27] With these simple words, the Supreme Court for the first time concluded that sex-based differentials were entitled to some sort of scrutiny under the Fourteenth Amendment. But what type of scrutiny? According to Burger, who quoted an earlier 1920 case, the test was whether the differential treatment was "reasonable, not arbitrary" and rested "upon some ground of difference having a fair and substantial relation to the object of the legislation, so that all persons similarly circumstanced will be treated alike." The Court then found that the state's objective of reducing the workload of probate judges was insufficient justification to warrant this kind of sex-based statute. In fact, according to the Court, this was "the very kind of arbitrary legislative choice forbidden by the Equal Protection Clause."[28]

OTHER ATTEMPTS TO EXPAND RIGHTS

This major breakthrough heartened women's rights activists. It also encouraged the WRP to launch a full-blown test case strategy like that pursued by the NAACP Legal Defense and Education Fund that had culminated successfully in *Brown v. Board of Education* (1954).[29] WRP attorneys jumped at the opportunity to assist the Southern Poverty Law Center of Alabama with the next major sex-discrimination case to come before the Supreme Court, *Frontiero v. Richardson* (1973).[30] At issue in *Frontiero* was the constitutionality of a federal statute that, for the purpose of computing allowances and fringe benefits, required female members of the armed forces to prove that they contributed more than 50 percent of their dependent husbands' support. Men were not required to make any such showing about their wives.

By an 8-to-1 vote, the Court struck down the statute, which gave male members of the armed forces potentially greater benefits than females. More importantly, though, only a plurality of four justices voted to make sex a suspect classification entitled to the strict scrutiny standard of review. While four other justices agreed that the statute violated the Equal Protection Clause, they did not agree that sex should be made a suspect classification. In fact, three of them specifically noted the pending ratification of the ERA as a reason to wait—to allow the political process to guide judicial interpretation. This was to be the high-water mark of efforts to include sex, along with race, in the category of suspect classifications.

In *Craiq v. Boren* (1976), Justice William J. Brennan Jr., author of the plurality opinion in *Frontiero*, formulated a different test, known as *intermediate* or *heightened scrutiny*, to apply to sex-discrimination cases.[31] The case involved a challenge to an Oklahoma law that prohibited the sale of 3.2 percent beer to males under the age of twenty-one and females under the age of eighteen. In determining whether this kind of gender-based differential violated the Equal Protection Clause, Brennan wrote that "classifications by gender must serve important governmental objectives and must be substantially related to achievement of those objectives."[32] He also specifically identified two governmental interests that would not justify sex discrimination: neither administrative convenience nor "fostering 'old' notions of role typing" would any longer be considered constitutionally adequate rationalizations of sex classifications.[33] Shedding many of the stereotypes that had been at the core of *Muller, Hoyt*, and *Goesaert*, the Court specifically noted that there was no more place for "increasingly outdated misconceptions concerning the role of females in the home rather than in the 'marketplace and world of ideas.' "[34] This new intermediate standard of review was subsequently used to invalidate a wide range of discriminatory practices, including some Social Security, welfare, and workers' compensation programs, alimony laws, age of majority statutes, and jury service exemptions that discriminated based on gender.

This is not to say that stereotypes do not still exert influence on the Court. In *Rostker v. Goldberg* (1981), for example, the Court considered congressional combat restrictions sufficient to rationalize the exclusion of women from the new draft registration requirements of the Military Selective Service Act.[35] A majority of the Court accepted the government's position that the statutory exclusion of women from combat positions combined with the need for combat-ready troops were sufficiently important justifications to meet the burden of the intermediate standard of review. The Court did not bother to consider the validity of the combat restrictions themselves. And, in *Michael M. v. Superior Court of Sonoma County* (1981), the Court held that California's statutory rape law, which applied only to males, did not violate the Equal Protection Clause.[36] Justice William H. Rehnquist noted that the state's concern about teenage pregnancy was a sufficiently strong state interest to justify the statute. Moreover, Rehnquist's opinion pointedly did not apply the intermediate scrutiny standard of review.

In late 1981 the Court was joined by its first female member, Sandra Day O'Connor. It was not long before she and the other justices were faced with another sex-based claim made under the Fourteenth Amendment. *Mississippi University for Women v. Hogan* (1982) involved a state policy that restricted enrollment in one state-supported nursing school to females. Writing for a five-member majority, O'Connor noted that when the purpose of a statute was to "exclude or 'protect' members of one gender because they are presumed to suffer from an inherent handicap or to be innately inferior, the objective itself is illegitimate."[37] As one commentator noted, "She out-Brennaned Justice Brennan." For example, O'Connor went even further than Brennan (long the Court's foremost liberal) by suggesting in a footnote that sex might best be treated by the Court as a suspect classification.

O'Connor's strong opinion in *Hogan* again brought to four the number of justices on the Court who apparently favored some sort of strict standard of review for sex-based classifications. But that number was quickly diminished with the elevation of William H. Rehnquist to chief justice and the appointments of Justices Antonin Scalia, Anthony Kennedy, David Souter, and Clarence Thomas to the Court by Republican presidents Ronald Reagan and George Bush. A change of but one justice in *Hogan* would have allowed Mississippi to continue its maintenance of an all-female nursing school.

Recognizing the fragile nature of even the middle tier of review and the Court's uneven application of its standards, in the 1980s some women's rights groups again sought passage of an ERA to the Constitution, seeing such an amendment as the only way to guarantee that women will ever be recognized as fully equal under the Constitution. Some saw passage of an amendment as especially important given the kinds of sex-based discrimination cases that the Court was likely to address in the near future. Although most of those involved challenges under Title VII of the Civil Rights Act of 1964 and its prohibition against discrimination in employment, Court watchers feared that without the force of an ERA to overshadow interpretation of the law, the Court's decisions could grow increasingly adverse to women's full equality. In spite of the absence of an ERA, however, even the Rehnquist Court before the addition of two Clinton appointments—Ruth Bader Ginsburg and Stephen Breyer—has revealed a reluctance to go back to pre-*Reed* days, when sex-discrimination claims never found a favorable audience with the Court. Its decisions clearly have added to a climate that frowns on blatant discrimination.

CONCLUSION

Interestingly, fewer and fewer constitutional cases involving sex discrimination are coming before the Court each year, perhaps because women's rights groups are using their time and money to fend off challenges to a series of decisions adverse to abortion rights. Moreover, most of the "easy" constitutional cases have been decided, and there is fairly uniform application of the intermediate standard of review in the lower courts. Thus, most gender cases that the Court now chooses to hear involve employment discrimination and the scope of bona fide occupational qualifications permissible under Title VII. During its 1990 term, for example, the Court heard arguments in *International Union, UAW v. Johnson Controls* (1991), which involved a company fetal-protection policy that required women in certain hazardous positions to be sterilized as a condition of their employment.[38] Many women's right activists argued that a judicial finding in support of the company policy would inevitably lead to the exclusion of women in all types of lucrative positions and to the resurrection of the paternalism of *Muller v. Oregon*. Their fears, however, proved to be unfounded. In *Johnson Controls* the Court ruled unanimously that the company's policies did not constitute bona fide occupational qualifications and thus violated Title VII. Many commentators now take this as an omen that the Court will continue to build on existing precedents and not retreat to earlier decisions more "protective" of women. Nevertheless, it is likely that the decision regarding fetal-protection policies will spur continued litigation in this area as more cases come to the Court presenting issues that involve women's reproductive capabilities and the "special treatment" some employers would like to give their female workers on account of that status. The consensus evidenced by the Court, however, and the addition of two Democratic appointees to a Court dominated by appointees by conservative Republicans leave women's rights activists far more optimistic than they were just a short time ago.

NOTES

1. Quoted in L. H. Butterfield, Marc Friedlander, and Mary-Jo Kline (Eds.), *Book of Abigail and John* (Cambridge, MA: Harvard University Press, 1975), p. 21.
2. Much of this discussion comes from Nancy E. McGlen and Karen O'Connor, *Women, Politics, and American Society* (Englewood Cliffs, NJ: Prentice-Hall, 1995), chap. 1.
3. Karen O'Connor, *Women's Organizations' Use of the Courts* (Lexington, MA: Lexington Books, 1980), chap. 3.
4. H. R. Report No. 22, 41st Congress, 3rd Sess., 1871.
5. 60 U.S. 393 (1857).
6. 60 U.S. 393 at 422.
7. 88 U.S. 162 (1875).
8. 16 Wall. (83 U.S.) 130 (1873).
9. 83 U.S. 130 at 141–142 (1873).
10. 88 U.S. 162 (1875).
11. 16 Wall. 36 (1873).
12. 16 Wall. 36 at 81.
13. *Mugler v. Kansas*, 123 U.S. 623 at 661 (1887).
14. *Allgeyer v. Louisiana*, 165 U.S. 578 (1897).
15. 198 U.S. 45 (1905).
16. Clement E. Vose, "The National Consumers' League and the Brandeis Brief," *Midwest Journal of Political Science*, 1 (November 1957), pp. 267–290.

17. *Muller v. Oregon*, 208 U.S. 412 at 421 (1908).
18. 69 Ore. 519, aff'd 243 U.S. 629 (1917).
19. 243 U.S. 426 (1917).
20. 261 U.S. 525 (1923).
21. 300 U.S. 379 (1937).
22. 312 U.S. 100 (1941).
23. 335 U.S. 466 (1948).
24. 368 U.S. 57 (1961).
25. 368 U.S. 57 at 61–62.
26. 404 U.S. 71 (1971).
27. 404 U.S. 71 at 75.
28. 404 U.S. 71 at 76.
29. Richard Kluger, *Simple Justice: The History of Brown v. Board of Education and Black America's Struggle for Equality* (N.Y.: Alfred A. Knopf, 1976).
30. 411 U.S. 677 (1973).
31. 429 U.S. 190 (1976).
32. 429 U.S. 190 at 197.
33. 429 U.S. 190 at 198.
34. 429 U.S. 190 at 198–199.
35. 453 U.S. 57 (1981).
36. 450 U.S. 464 (1981).
37. 458 U.S. 718 at 725.
38. 111 S. Ct. 2238 (1991).

FURTHER READINGS

Baer, Judith. *Chains of Protection: The Judicial Response to Women's Labor Legislation*. Westview, CT: Greenwood Press, 1978.

———. *Women in American Law*. New York: Holmes and Meier, 1991.

Boles, Janet. *The Politics of the Equal Rights Amendment: Conflict and the Decision Process*. New York: Longman, 1979.

Ginsburg, Ruth Bader. "Sexual Equality under the Fourteenth and Equal Rights Amendments." *Wash-*

ington University Law Quarterly, 161 (Winter 1979), pp. 161–201.

Goldstein, Leslie Friedman (Ed.). *Feminist Jurisprudence: The Difference Debate*. New York: Rowan and Littlefield, 1992.

———. *Constitutional Rights of Women*. Madison: University of Wisconsin Press, 1994.

Kay, Herma Hill. *Sex-Based Discrimination: Texts, Cases and Materials*. 3rd ed. St. Paul, MN: West Publishing, 1988.

Kenney, Sally K. *For Whose Protection? Reproductive Hazards and Exclusionary Policies in the United States and Great Britain*. Ann Arbor: University of Michigan Press, 1993.

McGlen, Nancy E., and Karen O'Connor. *Women, Politics, and American Society*. Englewood Cliffs, NJ: Prentice-Hall, 1995.

Mezey, Susan Gluck. *In Pursuit of Equality: Women, Public Policy, and the Federal Courts*. New York: St. Martin's Press, 1992.

O'Connor, Karen. *Women's Organizations' Use of the Courts*. Lexington, MA: Lexington Books, 1980.

Rhode, Deborah L. *Justice and Gender: Sex Discrimination and the Law*. Cambridge, MA: Harvard University Press, 1989.

Women within the Judicial System: Changing Roles

Elaine Martin

Female judges are unlike other women in politics in the way they attain public office and the way they are free to behave once they attain such office. To be eligible for judicial office, women must have graduate law degrees; thus female judges tend to be more educated than other political women. Judges are selected in a variety of ways, only one of which is by partisan election, so female judges tend to be less politically active than other women officeholders.[1] Female judges are different, too, in the institutional context they enter after taking office. In some respects, they have greater independence than their legislative or executive branch sisters, who must gain the votes of colleagues to support their agendas. In other respects, they must act within a framework of legal rules that limit that independence.

For example, trial court judges need no other judge's support to decide on criminal sentencing or civil damages. However, sentencing guidelines, legislation, and higher court rulings may sharply curtail the exercise of this judicial discretion. Appellate court judges may have greater discretion in devising policy but must garner the votes of judicial colleagues to muster a majority opinion.

This article will examine three aspects of change for women within the judicial system: (1) the increase in the numbers of female judges; (2) the growing evidence in judicial research that female judges are more supportive of women's

Elaine Martin is an associate professor of political Science at Eastern Michigan University.

The research for this article was partially funded by the Center for the American Woman and Politics, the Eagleton Institute of Politics, Rutgers University. Opinions expressed are the author's alone.

rights than are male judges; and (3) the possibility that female judges' support of women's rights is related to a feeling of obligation to represent other women.

INCREASING NUMBER OF FEMALE JUDGES

It is no news that women are underrepresented in public office in the United States, or that they are far better represented in local office than in state or federal office. Yet it may be surprising to some that women are far less well represented in state judicial office than in state legislative office. In the not so distant past, women's chances of becoming judges of any sort, state or federal, were very slim. For example, in 1977 although there were nearly 16,000 judges in the United States, twenty states had no female judges whatsoever.[2] When President Carter took office in 1976, there were only five women out of over 500 federal district and appellate court judges.

In 1985 nearly 15 percent of state legislative seats were held by women, compared with about 9 percent of state intermediate appellate court seats and 6 percent of state supreme court positions held by women. In 1987, twenty states had never had a female supreme court justice; five states had no female judge on their major trial courts; and fifteen more states had only two females.[3] By 1992, thirty-nine women sat in thirty-two states on their state's highest court, and only ten states had never had a female supreme court justice.[4] Thus, even though the relative numbers of female judges lag far behind the relative numbers of female state legislators, their numbers are rapidly increasing. It is estimated that, from 1980 to 1994, the number of female judges, state and federal, appellate and trial, has almost tripled.[5]

Two factors have improved women's chances of becoming judges: All Presidents since Carter have followed his precedent in seeking to appoint women, and more women have become lawyers. These factors illustrate two theories used to explain how women can best become judges: by changing attitudes on the part of those who are influential in selecting judges and by increasing the eligible pool of female candidates.

CHANGING ATTITUDES IN SELECTING JUDGES

The United States has not just one judicial system but a federal system and fifty different state court systems. One of the ways in which these diverse court systems vary is the manner in which they select their judges. All federal court judges, whether trial court or supreme court members, are appointed by the president and confirmed by the Senate for life. An explicit affirmative action program initiated by President Carter designed to appoint more women to the federal bench added forty new female judges.[6] Subsequent Republican presidents did not equal Carter's effort, but their appointments of female judges far outnumbered all of their predecessors except Carter. Thus, by 1992, women constituted 11 percent of the federal bench. President Clinton launched a new affirmative action initiative that promises to seat even more women on the federal bench. Clinton, in his first two years of office, raised the proportion of women from 11 percent to 14 percent.[7] Thus, changing attitudes by just four presidents have dramatically altered the gender composition of the federal courts, increasing the number of women from a total of 5 in 1976 to 120 by July 1994.

The states use several different systems to select their judges and may use different methods for higher courts than they use for lower courts. There is some evidence that states that use appointment procedures similar to the one used at the federal level are more likely to have higher percentages of female judges than those states that rely on elections.[8] This is probably because governors usually have a number of judicial slots to fill by appointment and take the opportunity to please various factions within their constituency. In the case of female appointments, a number of interest groups, organizations, and individuals have pushed for an increase in female judges. However, these groups have faced resistance from the voters in electing women. This is especially true for judicial elections because they are very low-key and fail to generate much interest or voter turnout.

THE ELIGIBLE POOL THEORY

The eligible pool theory holds that because relatively few women possess the requisite educational, political, and career credentials to be judges, they are unable to compete successfully for office. Judges are drawn exclusively from the legal profession, and historically that profession has been overwhelmingly white and male. However, since the 1980s, there have been important changes in the composition of the legal profession, and therefore in the eligible pool for judges. More women have gone to law school, and more women have become lawyers and lower court judges. In 1980 only 8 percent of lawyers were women, but by 1992 that figure had risen to 19 percent.[9] Thus, in twelve years the size of the eligible pool of female lawyers more than doubled.

There is also ample evidence that women are more likely to be successful in gaining seats on higher courts if they have had experience on lower courts.[10] For example, U.S. Supreme Court Justices Sandra Day O'Connor and Ruth Bader Ginsberg both had prior experience as lower court judges before their appointments to the Supreme Court. The number of limited-jurisdiction court judges who are women has increased from about 650 in 1987[11] to approximately 2,000 in 1993.[12]

Table 1 compares the percentage of female judges on different levels of courts in relationship with the percentage of women receiving law degrees and the percentage of lawyers who are women.

SUPPORT FOR WOMEN'S RIGHTS

In the 1980s, most studies of judicial gender necessarily began with what amounted to a disclaimer. Judicial scholars explained that because of the small number of fe-

Table 1   Percentage of Female Judges, Percentage of Women Receiving Law Degrees, and Percentage of Female Lawyers

WOMEN	1980	1987	1993
Federal judges	5.4%	7.0%	11.1%
State supreme	3.6	6.5	11.2
State trial	2.4	7.3	
Female lawyers	8.0	13.0	19.0
Law degrees	30.0	40.0	45.0

Source: Data in table derived from Epstein, 1993; Martin, 1988; Allen and Wall, 1993; and McGlen and O'Connor, 1995.

male judges, they could not conclusively determine if female judges would decide cases any differently from male judges. Today, because of the increase in the numbers of female judges, scholars are well placed to test the proposition that the presence of female judges makes a difference in the administration of justice. However, a new set of problems arises for such researchers. Just what is meant by difference, and how is it to be measured? For example, if female judges decide cases differently than men, which ones, and why?

This issue can be framed in terms of whether female judges merely "stand for" other women in the numerical sense or whether they "act for" women.[13] In these terms, all female judges would necessarily "stand for" other women merely because they are also women. Female judges would not, however, necessarily "act for" other women. That is, although they would symbolically represent women, they might or might not act in a manner to further the interests of other women. There seems to be a clear consensus that simple fairness requires numerical representation for women in political office (standing for). It is not so clear that such an increase will result in an increase in the representation of women's special interests (acting for).

The relatively new field of feminist jurisprudence argues that a significant increase of female lawyers and judges will have a profound impact on the law.[14] These scholars contend that females, because of their experience as women in this society, will bring a different perspective to the law, will employ different legal reasoning, and will seek different results from the legal process.

Although all of these contentions have not been tested by the research on female judges, it does appear from some research that women judges and justices are more likely than their male counterparts to produce pro-women decisions in cases where the issue is that of gender bias.

Research done in the 1970s and early 1980s failed to find major gender differences between male and female judges. Two studies of sentencing decisions made by male and female state judges in a large metropolitan area found the only significant difference to be the tendency of male judges to give lesser sentences to female defendants.[15] One explanation of these findings is that women who became judges during those years mostly made their success in a "man's world" and were, therefore, more likely to behave as tokens and mimic the behavior of their male colleagues.[16]

Two studies of federal judges were also done during the 1980s and failed to find major differences in the behavior of male and female judges; one of the studies, however, found female appellate court judges to be slightly more liberal than men in voting on race- and sex-discrimination cases. However, both studies focused on judges appointed by President Carter, and given that both male and female appointees were quite liberal, it was not unexpected that there would be little difference between males and females.

Research done in the late 1980s and 1990s is more supportive of the notion that women may bring a different perspective to legal issues involving sex discrimination. For example, during her first term on the U.S. Supreme Court, Justice O'Connor adopted pro-woman positions in sex-discrimination cases two-thirds of the time, although in other cases she tended to vote with the conservative bloc of the Court.[17]

In 1986, Gryski, Main, and Dixon[18] found that the presence of a female justice on a state supreme court was significantly correlated with higher rates of liberal rulings on sex discrimination. A study of voting behavior and gender on the U.S. Courts of Appeals that included judges appointed by Republican presidents after Carter concluded that the votes of women in employment-discrimination cases differed from those of their male colleagues; the study suggested that personal experience of employment discrimination may have influenced female votes.[19] Allen and Wall found that women on state supreme courts are more likely than men to be the most pro-female members of their court on women's issues.[20] McGlen and O'Connor contend that the very presence of women on the bench, particularly at the appellate level, appears to make male jurists more sensitive to problems of gender bias.[21]

All of the more recent research studied appellate courts. It is much more difficult to examine the impact of judicial gender in trial courts, because a female trial court judge is often the only member of her gender serving on her court. In order to make gender comparisons, it is necessary to have a sufficient number of both male and female judges deciding the *same or similar cases in the same jurisdiction*. One way of getting around this difficulty is to ask a large sample of judges to decide the same set of hypothetical cases.

Hypothetical Cases

In 1987, using hypothetical cases, this author conducted a large national survey of male and female state court judges to determine if male and female judges decide cases involving possible sex discrimination differently. Questionnaires were sent to all 483 female general jurisdiction trial court judges sitting in 1987 and to a random sample of 647 male judges stratified by court location. The response rate was 46 percent for the male sample and 61 percent for the women. Because it is reasonable to assume that holding feminist views influences judges' perceptions on women's rights cases, respondents were asked to indicate if they considered themselves feminists.

The five hypothetical cases raised issues of maternity leave rights, battered women's rights, abortion rights for minors, property rights for divorcing home-makers, and protection from sexual harassment on the job. Judges were asked to choose in favor of one party: the female claimants or the opposing party (private corporations, law enforcement officials, parents, or spouses). All cases were drawn from newspaper accounts of actual decisions by state court judges. A description of the cases and the judges' hypothetical votes follows. Table 2 summarizes the judges' votes, using four groups: women feminists, women nonfeminists, men feminists, and men nonfeminists.

Property Rights for Divorcing Homemakers   A fifty-five-year-old woman is sued for divorce after thirty-seven years of marriage to a successful businessman. Her four children are grown. She is willing to accept a fifty-fifty split on commu-nity property and requests no alimony, but she demands 50 percent of her spouses's substantial retirement income at age sixty-five. She did not work outside the home during her marriage but now has a job as a salesclerk. The job pays enough for her immediate needs, but the organization has no pension plan. Her husband is willing to pay her a portion of the face value of his annuities, but he re-fuses to share his income.

The female litigant in this case got her greatest amount of support from women, both feminist (94 percent) and nonfeminist (92 percent), and feminist men (91 percent). Male nonfeminists were less likely to award the woman her request for half of her spouse's retirement income (82 percent).

Maternity Leave   A state law requires companies to give women four months' maternity leave and to reinstate them in the same or similar job. No pro-vision is made for paternity leave. A woman sues because she is told no position is available when she attempts to return to work after taking her maternity leave. The company claims the law illegally discriminates against men and nonpregnant women and is too costly.

Women nonfeminist judges were the least generous of all judges in awarding this female litigant maternity leave. Ninety-three percent of female feminists, 91 percent of male feminists and 85 percent of male nonfeminists were in favor of

Table 2   Hypothetical Cases

Case	Women		Men	
	Feminists	*Nonfeminists*	*Feminists*	*Nonfeminists*
Divorce	94%	92%	91%	82%
Leave	93	77	91	85
Harassment	93	90	86	75
Abortion	92	81	85	71
Battered	67	59	48	48

the woman's claim. It may be that female nonfeminists were fearful of "protective" legislation that might make it more difficult for women of childbearing age to get jobs. Before the women's movement, such protective legislation was often used as an excuse for employment discrimination against women. It remains a controversial issue.

Protection from Sexual Harassment Two women are hired in a traditionally male-dominated occupation after a private company is ordered to end its sexually discriminatory hiring practices. Within six months, one woman resigns, refusing to discuss her reasons for doing so; the other woman files suit against the company for sexual harassment. She claims that her male coworkers created a climate of intimidation through sexually suggestive remarks, jokes, anonymous notes and cartoons, and boisterous requests for sexual favors. Despite her complaints to management, no action was taken. The company claims she is overreacting to normal male camaraderie, needs to develop a sense of humor, and is trying to cover up for her own inability to adjust to a new work environment. It would like to replace her. She wants monetary damages and wants to continue in her job with company protection from harassment.

Women, both feminists and nonfeminists, were more likely than men, both feminists and nonfeminists, to favor the female litigant in this case. The biggest difference was between women feminists (93 percent) and male nonfeminists (75 percent).

Abortion Rights for Minors A woman's boyfriend impregnates her eleven-year-old daughter. Evidence indicates he has also sexually abused her nine-year-old daughter. The two girls are removed from the home by the Department of Social Services, which requests a court-ordered abortion for the older girl. The girl says she wants the abortion, but her mother protests that abortion is against her personal beliefs.

This case engendered its strongest pro-choice support from feminists and its least support from nonfeminists. Within feminist and nonfeminist categories, however, women were clearly more supportive of abortion rights. Although 92 percent of the female feminists and 85 percent of the male feminists would have granted the abortion, only 81 percent of female nonfeminists and 71 percent of male nonfeminists would do so.

Battered Women's Rights A class action suit is filed against a metropolitan police department by a group of battered women claiming a lack of law enforcement for crimes of domestic violence. They request that the court impose new rules of intervention to replace the individual discretion of police officers and to require officer training in the new methods. The police chief objects to the possible erosion of officer discretion and the increased likelihood of suits for false arrest.

The battered women in this case got far less support in their claim than female litigants in any of the other four cases. The most dramatic drop was in the support from nonfeminist men—only 43 percent "voted" for the battered women.

Forty-eight percent of feminist men, showed considerably less support than the 59 percent of nonfeminist women. Although feminist women showed the most support (67 percent), they also dropped dramatically from their usual over-90-percent support rate in the other cases. This case is different because support of the female litigants requires active judicial intervention in the established procedures of a law enforcement agency. It is on the cutting edge of *new* law and creates *new* rights.

All Five Cases   Female feminists were the most likely to decide in favor of female litigants in each of the five hypothetical cases; male nonfeminists were the least likely to decide in favor of female litigants in four of the five cases. In two cases, maternity leave and abortion rights for minors, male feminists were more likely to decide for the females than were female nonfeminists. In the cases of property rights for divorcing homemakers, male feminists and female nonfeminists expressed comparable views. However, female nonfeminists were more likely than feminist men to side with female litigants in the sexual harassment and battered women's rights cases. They also dropped dramatically from their usual over-90-percent support rate in the other cases.

Assuming that their responses to these hypothetical cases are an accurate portrayal of how these judges might behave in real-life cases, it seems that feminist female judges are the most willing to break new ground in cutting-edge cases like the battered women's rights case. Furthermore, although in general there were no big differences between nonfeminist women and feminist men, in the particularly difficult cases of sexual harassment and battered women, nonfeminist women were more willing than feminist men to reach for new law.

REPRESENTATION OF WOMEN'S INTERESTS

The official, approved image of a judge is that of a person who is impartial and one who does not prejudge the merits of a case before hearing the evidence. What this means in a nutshell is that a good judge is supposed to put aside her or his personal feelings and values when donning the robe. The robe and all its trappings are designed to hide individual physical characteristics and, in so doing, also symbolically represent the impersonal nature of the act of judging. The formal rules of the judicial game reinforce these basic expectations. The law itself, statutes and precedents, the facts of the case, the requirements of evidence, the possibility of being overturned on appeal, even the nature of the adversarial system, all restrict the freedom of judicial discretion.

The decisions in the hypothetical cases discussed here certainly suggest that feminist judges do decide gender-bias cases somewhat differently than do nonfeminist judges. So what happens when a judge is focused not only on the process of doing justice but also on the justice of the outcome? What happens to a judge's conception of her job when she feels an obligation to represent the interests of women? What if she considers herself a feminist? Ought her personal values be left out of her job as judging?

PERCEPTIONS ABOUT THE ROLE OF WOMEN JUDGES

Picture a national conference of female judges in which panels address such topics as "Feminism: Its Impact on Judges and Judging" or "Recognizing and Dealing with Sexism" or "Gender Bias in the Courts: What Can Judges Do?" Imagine that female judges from Uganda, Kenya, Thailand, and thirty-seven other countries are invited to this conference and given funds to attend so that they can share problems and build alliances. Further, imagine that, at this conference, a female state supreme court justice publicly celebrates the special qualities of sensitivity, openness, and contextual thinking that women jurists bring to the justice system; that a panel of women law professors advises a neophyte female criminal trial court judge on how to deal with male colleagues who claim she isn't "tough enough."

This conference actually took place in November of 1989, under the sponsorship of the National Association of Women Judges. At the conference, this author asked female judges to describe specific ways in which their presence on the bench had made a "difference." The eighty-five respondents gave seven different types of answers, none of which suggested that they prejudged cases, but all of which indicated they tried to represent the interests of other women, either litigants or attorneys.

The most frequently mentioned type of behavior had to do with women's efforts to raise the consciousness of their male colleagues. About half of the female respondents made remarks such as the following: "I will not write or sign any opinion which contains gender biased language—my colleagues are learning to do the same"; or "I feel my presence as a woman on the bench has made my colleagues less macho in their conduct and perspective and has broadened their perspective as to women's rights and issues."

The next most frequently described behavior was similar but stressed the female judge's role as a kind of judicial educator. For example:

> I have been particularly open to media contact. This accessibility has resulted in much media coverage of cases in which women and children are victims. This additional information has sensitized members of the public and justice system participants to the needs of the victims. Many new programs have been developed, I believe partially as a result of the publicity.

Nearly one-third of respondents indicated efforts, both on and off the bench, to make the law more equitable for women and children. For example: "Women know they'll get a fair hearing, and their lawyers know it too. Sad though it may be, it isn't always true"; or "In the past with the push to settle cases, some judges pressed for settlements in all cases. Often, it was the woman who accommodated to settle the case. I have tried to reverse this trend to settle at all cost to the woman litigant. Settlements are desired, but not by taking advantage of one party over the other."

The fourth most frequently mentioned category of behavior involved equity in hiring, promoting, and compensating practices for courtroom personnel. "Prior to my election, the secretaries and deputy clerks were all women, and the higher-paid positions of bailiff, law clerks, and court administrators were all men."

Fifteen percent mentioned participating in their state's gender-bias task force. One respondent explained, "I am on the Select Committee for Gender Equality and participate in presenting seminars to other judges in the areas of domestic violence and misdemeanors." A similar number said they were actively involved in the recruitment and selection of other female judges. As one respondent said, "I urge women attorneys to apply for judicial positions, and inform them of the proper procedures to accomplish this."

A few respondents (7 percent) mentioned a kind of humanizing impact. According to one:

> My colleagues say our court is more collegial since I have joined them. Partly, it was because I was not embarrassed to deal with other judges on a personal level as friends—by social gestures at time of celebration or sadness. We now observe birthdays, console in time of grief, welcome new judges, fete retiring judges, etc.

Another judge said:

> My presence has made the greatest impact not of gender bias (we have had a sizable percentage of women judges in our court for several years) but rather in terms of changing stereotypical views of lesbians (and to an extent, gay men). Because I assumed my duties as an openly lesbian judge, some people, attorneys in particular, have moderated their language and conduct in my courtroom (court staff, too).

CONCLUSION

"Times are changing. The president made that clear by appointing me, and just last week, naming five other women to Article III courts." Ruth Bader Ginsberg made these remarks following her inauguration as an associate justice of the U.S. Supreme Court, on August 20, 1993. Times, indeed, are changing. Although the percentages of female judges have yet to meet those of female legislators, their numbers show a significant increase in the last decade, and the numbers of females enrolling in law schools suggest even greater increases in the eligible pool in years to come. This increase in female judges spawned new research on gender and the judiciary in the late 1980s and 1990s; these studies contradicted earlier research done in the 1970s and early 1980s when there were fewer women. Results from the early studies suggested that men's and women's similar legal training and socialization as lawyers minimized any potential gender differences in judicial behavior. More recent studies indicate that, as women's numbers move beyond the token stage, and as younger females educated after the women's movement become judges, differences based on gender emerge more clearly.

The present study used hypothetical cases to create a situation where large numbers of male and female judges would be deciding the same case. Results indicate that both gender and *feminist ideology* are important in predicting how judges may decide women's rights cases. It appears that within ideological types, women are more likely than men to vote in a pro-woman manner, and the most sizable and consistent differences in voting were between feminist female judges and nonfeminist male judges.

Possible reasons for these differences were explored by examining the responses of a sample of female judges who were attending a conference of judges that featured a number of feminist panels. Women judges were asked what they had personally done to make a "difference." Their answers made it clear that some female judges have a strong sense that part of their job is to "act for" the interests of other women. To the extent that other female judges share these sentiments, it may explain why female judges are more supportive of women's rights than their male counterparts.

Research so far suggests that the "different" perspective female judges bring to their jobs relates primarily to situations that raise issues of gender fairness. The differences in this perspective is enhanced if the woman is a feminist. Further research is needed to determine if female judges do things differently in other areas of the law or in the administrative aspects of the judicial system.

NOTES

1. Elaine Martin, "Women on the Federal Bench: A Comparative Profile," *Judicature*, 65 (6) (1982), pp. 306–313; Elliot Slotnick, "Paths to the Federal Bench," *Judicature*, 67 (6) (1984), pp. 370–376.

2. Larry Berkson, "Women on the Bench: A Brief History," *Judicature*, 65 (6) (1982), pp. 286–293.

3. David Allen and Diane Wall, "Role Orientations and Women State Supreme Court Justices," *Judicature*, 77 (3) (1993), pp. 156–165.

4. Ibid., Table 1.

5. Elaine Martin, "Women on the Bench: A Different Voice," *Judicature*, 77 (3) (1993), pp. 126–128.

6. Elaine Martin, "Gender and Judicial Selection: A Comparison of the Reagan and Carter Administrations," *Judicature*, 70 (3) (1987), pp. 136–142.

7. Sheldon Goldman and Matthew Saronson, "Clinton's Nontraditional Judges: Creating a More Representative Bench," *Judicature*, 78 (2) (1994), pp. 68–73.

8. *The Success Women and Minorities in Achieving Judicial Office* (New York: Fund for Modern Courts, 1985); Elaine Martin, "State Court Political Opportunity Structures: Implications for the Representation of Women," paper presented at the American Political Science Association meetings, Washington, DC, 1988.

9. Nancy McGlen and Karen O'Connor, *Women Politics and American Society* (Englewood Cliffs, NJ: Prentice-Hall, 1995).

10. Martin, "Women on the Federal Bench"; Martin, "State Court."

11. Martin, "State Court."

12. National Center for State Courts, Williamsburg, VA, mailing list, 1993.

13. Hannah Pitkin, *The Concept of Representation* (Berkeley: University of California Press, 1967).

14. Leslie Goldstein (Ed.), *Feminist Jurisprudence: The Difference Debate* (Savage, MD: Rowman and Littlefield, 1992).

15. John Gruhl, Cassia Spohn, and Susan Welch, "Women as Policy-makers: The Case of Trial Judges," *American Journal of Political Science*, 25 (1981), pp. 308–322; Harrold Dritzer and Thomas Uhlman, "Sisterhood in the Courtroom: Sex of Judge and Defendant in Criminal Case Disposition," *Social Science Journal*, 14 (1977), pp. 77–88.

16. Allen and Wall, "Role Orientations."

17. Karen O'Connor and Lee Segal, "The Supreme Court's Judicature Reaction to Its First Female Member," *Women and Politics*, 10 (2) (1990), pp. 95–104.

18. Gerard Gryski, Eleanor Main, and Ruth Dixon, "Models of State High Court Decision Making in Sex Discrimination Cases," *Journal of Politics*, 48 (1986), pp. 462–465.

19. Susan Davis, Susan Haire, and Donald Songer, "Voting Behavior and Gender on the U.S. Courts of Appeals," *Judicature*, 77 (3) (1993), pp. 129–134.

20. Allen and Wall, "Role Orientations."

21. Nancy McGlen and Karen O'Connor, *Women, Politics and American Society* (Englewood Cliffs, NJ: Prentice-Hall, 1995).

FURTHER READINGS

Cook, Beverly, Leslie Goldstein, Karen O'Connor, and Susan Talrico (Eds.). *Women in the Judicial Process*. Washington DC: American Political Science Association, 1988.

Crites, Laura, and Winfred Hepperle (Eds.). *Women, the Courts, and Equality*. Newbury Park, CA: Sage, 1987.

Epstein, Cynthia Fuchs. *Women in Law*. 2nd ed. Urbana: University of Illinois Press, 1993.

Goldstein, Leslie. *Feminist Jurisprudence: The Difference Debate*. Savage, MD: Rowman and Littlefield, 1992.

"Gender Bias in the Courts," special issue, *Court Review*, 26 (3) (Fall 1989).

"Women in the Judiciary," special issue, *Judicature*, 65 (6) (1982).

"Women on the Bench: A Different Voice?" special issue, *Judicature*, 77 (3) (1993).

 CHAPTER 7

WOMEN, MEDIA, AND PUBLIC OPINION

The media serve as sex-role socialization agents for young women and men. However, women are basically underrepresented in the top management positions within the mass media organizations; consequently, women have had less control in determining media content and in how women are depicted in the news. Does this influence how accurately and realistically the changing role of women in American political society is portrayed in the mass media? Do the media set an agenda that helps the general public better understand the political participation of American women within our society? The first essay in this chapter examines some of the research that has been done concerning the manner in which the mass media have reported news about American political women. Comparisons are drawn between the news about women and men in the U.S. political environment. The author concludes that clearly the role of women in all facets of American political life is changing; these changes have been and are being reported by the mass media. However, she cautions that additional studies appear warranted as the number of female candidates increases in American politics to further determine the content of this media coverage, the "reality" of political gender roles, and how the media cover these, and to compare the coverage about women who run for elective office with the coverage given male candidates.

We next examine a study that looks at gender differences in attitudes among state legislators about media coverage of state legislatures generally, and support for gavel-to-gavel continuous televised coverage of legislative affairs in particular. Using data collected from a sizable sample of female and male legislators in the fifty states, Glen Sussman and Nicholas P. Lovrich Jr. find gender differences

Female legislators tend to be less satisfied with the performance of the broadcast media than are male legislators; they are also more inclined to presume that the average citizen is interested in greater access to the work of the legislature than are their male counterparts; and the concept of broad access to unedited, live coverage of legislative debate represents an important goal of legislative work particularly for urban-based Democratic female state legislators.

Hillary Rodham Clinton has transformed the role of First Lady—she represents a new era and a new generation of the professional woman who is also smart. In our final essay in this chapter on the mass media and public opinion, Barbara Burrell and Linda J. Penaloza trace the historical perspective of public opinion polls on the popularity of the First Lady back to Pat Nixon in 1969. They then focus more specifically on public response to Hillary Rodham Clinton as captured through public opinion as measured in national surveys. The authors find a good deal of variation in people's evaluations of Hillary Rodham Clinton and her actions. Substantial numbers have felt warm toward her, and a significant minority have not. The authors conclude that, rather than the First Lady being an albatross around President Clinton's neck, she developed a positive image among the public in the early stages of the Clinton administration. Findings also show that, while 80 to 90 percent of the people polled have come to say they would support a woman as president, not all of the questions asked in the polls about the role of the First Lady show a general acceptance of a more political role for that position or a ready transition from that job to being chief executive.

Women and Sex Stereotypes: Cultural Reflections in the Mass Media

Lois Lovelace Duke

Walter Lippmann believed that people act on the basis of pictures they carry around in their heads, pictures of the way they think things are. These pictures constitute what is "real" for us, and, according to Lippmann, much of what we know about the world and our relationship to it reaches us indirectly. Lippman, who was analyzing public opinion more than seventy years ago, believed that what each person does is based not on direct observation or certain knowledge but on pictures made by the individual or given to her or him.[1] This is especially important when one considers how the mass media shape our perceptions by transmitting information.

Many images of what we interpret as real are conceived based on secondhand accounts provided by the mass media, or what Nimmo and Combs describe as "mediated" realities.[2] These mediated realities are perceptions, which are focused, filtered, and fantasized by the mass media. Because these perceived realities are shared with others, a group fantasy takes on an aura of truth that the private fantasies of individuals do not.[3]

All too often, the news about women is reported based on these "mediated" realities or on other myths driven by cultural norms and standards of what are deemed "appropriate" roles for women in American society; in some instances, it

Lois Lovelace Duke is a professor of political science at Clemson University.

A previous version of this article was presented at the 1994 Western Political Science Association Meeting, Albuquerque, New Mexico, March 10–12. I would like to thank David L. Paletz and Doris A. Graber for reading and critiquing an earlier version of this article.

is determined by institutionalized discrimination and common socialization within the news organization itself.

This article will explore some of the research that has been done concerning the manner in which the mass media have portrayed American political women in the news. Comparisons will be drawn between the news about women and men in the American political environment. For the purposes of this article, mass media will include newspapers, network television news, fiction and entertainment television programs, and political advertisements. Numerous other studies about women and the mass media have been done—far too many to cite here. For example, these studies include research into the various media cited earlier as well as analyses of movies, talk shows, music videos as shown on MTV and other stations, commercial advertisements, and magazines that explore many issues of concern to women (e.g., rape, sexual violence, aging, pornography, female health matters, sexual harassment, and the beauty myth).

INFLUENCES ON NEWS MAKING

Scholars, including Gaye Tuchman and Bernard Roshco, argue that journalists construct reality in deciding what's news rather than merely providing a "picture of reality." This portrayal of what is real is influenced by the journalists' interpretation of reality.[4] Tuchman further cites certain "strategic rituals" journalists follow in striving for "objectivity."[5] Included in these "rituals" is the process of presenting conflicting possibilities, as seen when "both sides" of a story are presented. Tuchman also explains how "topical chains of command" in the hierarchy of news organizations affect the news product and the events of day-to-day happenings that culminate as news.[6]

Other internal influences on news determination cited in previous research include recruitment, socialization, and control of the reporting staff. Lee Sigelman and Warren Breed, among others, argue that news is affected by organizational structure and relationships between reporters and editors.[7] Roshco maintains that news making is also affected by journalists' beats, sources, and organizational constraints of time and space.[8] Prior studies have also concluded that internal influences on the news from within the newspaper organization stem from the more liberal political ideology of reporters as compared with their generally more conservative editors or publishers.[9]

These internal factors have determined the construction of the news, but women, other minorities, and those less influential in our society also have not had equitable access to the news organization. Thus, in many instances, issues of concern to these groups have not been addressed in the mass media. For example, Edie N. Goldenberg researched the access of resource-poor groups to the metropolitan press in Boston.[10] Goldenberg discovered that sources rich in resources within the political system enjoy certain advantages that place them in a much stronger position to manage the news than do resource-poor interest groups. That is, the groups who maintain continuing interaction with the mass media will have much greater access than most resource-poor groups, who are unable to establish and maintain an ongoing exchange with news personnel.[11]

SPECIFIC AGENDAS PASSED THROUGH THE MEDIA

The mass media not only favor certain classes and races of news story subject matter; they also are selective in what they write about, how they play up or play down a story, the "saturation" coverage they can give, sources of their stories and how balanced these sources are, endorsement and legitimacy given to the status quo by the media, and other means of conveying information.[12]

McCombs and Shaw maintain that editors, newsroom staff, and broadcasters, in choosing and displaying news, play an important part in shaping political reality.[13] That is, readers learn not only about a given issue but also how much importance to attach to that issue from the amount of information in a news story and its position. Therefore, in reflecting what candidates are saying during a campaign, the mass media may well determine the important issues—that is, the media may set the "agenda" of the campaign.[14]

Even though women and other minorities have made recent strides into the public and governmental arena, for the most part the mass media still reflect a "cultural" lag in depicting these advances through realistic news portrayal. Lang argues the "news media are both potential agents of change and captives of their own assumptions."[15]

As but one example of the coverage given African-Americans in the news, previous research into how newspapers reported on issues of race and southern politics over a thirty-year time frame revealed that four Carolina newspapers reflected more bias in the news content about issues of intense social conflict during the civil rights movement (*Brown v. Board of Education* decision and school desegregation) than in the news coverage about those issues less socially threatening to the White community (the 1964 Civil Rights Act, the 1965 Voting Rights Act, and Senate reapportionment of the South Carolina General Assembly).[16] The bias of the dominant White influence was significantly more negative in direction when the news coverage was about a more socially and politically threatening issue. Bias appeared to be directly related to the degree of the social and political threat to the White community.

As a result, a political culture was passed along for many years. This culture was spread from the politicians of the era to the populace and the mass media. The newspapers, in turn, further fanned the racism and-stereotypes dominant in the times by catering to the White male establishment, while at the same time basically ignoring the viewpoints of the Black community.

Thus, as politicians used the issue of race and fear of integration in their campaign rhetoric as they sought state and national office, this negativity toward Blacks became an entrenched part of the culture. Newspapers picked up on this negativism, as reflected by their bias on the news pages and in their editorials against progressive change. The newspapers, in most instances, were basically a mouthpiece for the dominant social, cultural, and political views of the White southern community.[17]

MYTHS AND STEREOTYPES ABOUT WOMEN PORTRAYED IN THE MEDIA

Women also have been subjected to sex-role stereotypes, cultural standards, and myths established by societal norms and passed along through the news media. For example, Elizabeth Janeway points out that every society invents myths about itself and then proceeds to act on those myths as if they were fact.[18] The technology, format, economic costs, and journalistic presentation of the news products further lend themselves to stereotypes and myths. For example, it is much easier to package the "You've come a long way baby" new woman in a cigarette advertisement than it is to portray the so-called liberated woman in a documentary film or in-depth news story.[19]

For example, some research into how the press covered the contemporary women's movement revealed evidence of sex stereotypes. David Broader explains that when the National Organization for Women (NOW) was formed in 1966, it was not considered news in the eyes of the *Washington Post*. Even though the *New York Times* reported the event, the news was reported on the "Food, Fashion, Family and Furnishings" page. According to Broder, this news was placed "down at the bottom of the page, under the recipes for the 'traditional Thanksgiving menu' and the picture of 'the culinary star of the day, the turkey, roasted, stuffed and surrounded by other festive Thanksgiving specialties.' "[20] Alger also points out that in assessing themes depicting women in the media, women's activities have most often been portrayed as concerned with the home or with men.[21]

Broder goes on to explain that the women's movement did not make the front pages of the *Post* or the *Times* until August 1970. This happened after Betty Friedan, a key figure in the women's movement and founder of NOW, organized a strike of women workers (housewives as well as office and factory workers) and protest marches in Washington, New York, and other cities throughout the United States. The tactic worked, the movement became news, and issues of concern (discrimination in pay and employment opportunities, passage of the Equal Rights Amendment, provision of child care and abortion facilities) were finally debated.[22] Kahn and Goldenberg also examined news coverage of the women's movement; they found that the early media coverage of the women's movement did not help the movement to grow. In fact, they argue that the press coverage of the women's movement—when there was any at all—was unflattering. Their findings indicate that the movement grew despite the media.[23]

Still other scholars have identified certain patterns in the manner in which women are portrayed in the mass media. For example, Lichter, Lichter, and Rothman reviewed and identified the social background, personal traits, and activities of over 7,000 characters from a sample of television program episodes selected yearly from 1955 through 1985.[24] Themes, morals, and social commentary were also recorded and analyzed from a total of 620 episodes.

These researchers found that male roles greatly outnumbered female roles (although the gap has narrowed slightly since 1975). Two out of three men were involved in an occupation, whereas only two of five women were. From 1955 to 1985, 93 percent of all judges, 93 percent of all doctors, 86 percent of all corporate executives, 87 percent of all lawyers, and 87 percent of all college professors were played by men. More generally, nine of ten educated professionals were men. Perhaps even more significant, of those characters whose education was made known, men accounted for 85 percent of all college graduates and 89 percent of those with graduate school in the television shows.[25]

Vande Berg and Streckfuss studied 116 prime-time television program episodes that covered two weeks of programming for each of the three major U.S. commercial networks (CBS, NBC, and ABC).[26] One sample week was from the spring of 1986, and the other was from the spring of 1987. They found that male characters were found to outnumber female characters by a factor of about two to one. Females were seen far more frequently than males in household occupations and as students. The researchers also found that, proportionately, female characters were far more likely than male characters to be portrayed as enacting a humane, interpersonally focused, cooperative, concerned, information-sharing style of working and managing. Male characters, on the other hand, were far more likely to be seen fulfilling decisional, political, and operational functions in organizations. These studies concluded that relatively little has changed over forty years of prime-time television in terms of the portrayal of working women—that the overall image of women continues to be one in which they are defined primarily through stereotypical domestic roles.[27]

On the other hand, a recent study sponsored by Women, Men and Media, an organization that examines the treatment of women in the media, found more news of, and by, women. That is, news about women and reported by women is on the increase in American news media. However, men continue to receive more attention from the country's news organization. Men still dominated the news, receiving 75 percent of front-page references in February 1994, the period covered by the study, as against 25 percent for women. (Even 25 percent of news about women in 1994 was an increase, as only 11 percent of the news was about women in 1989.)[28] The group also found that photographs of women had become more prevalent. Males appeared in 67 percent of the front-page pictures, while females appeared in 39 percent. However, this was the highest representation of photographs of women since the group began its annual study in 1989.[29]

Recognizing that the role of women has changed in American society, one wonders how and why myths and stereotypes about contemporary American women continue to appear in the mass media. One explanation for this is the male control of the internal news organization. That is, the male viewpoint is still dominant in the hierarchy of the news organization and in the recruitment and socialization of media personnel.

WHITE MALE DOMINATION OF THE MEDIA

Parenti points out that the news media are largely an affluent White male domain. Women, Blacks, Latinos, Asians, and the poor are accorded brief mention on special occasions. This coverage is determined by a news organization made up predominantly of White males.[30] Still other studies have demonstrated that news making is dominated by White males; as a result, more often than not the news reflects these social and cultural biases.[31]

As recently as February 1994, men continued to write the majority of the news and opinion articles published in American newspapers. The study, sponsored by Women, Men and Media, mentioned earlier, showed that men contributed 67 percent of the front-page articles and 72 percent of the opinion articles published on newspaper op-ed pages.[32]

Alger and others point out that women still constitute a much lower percentage of newspeople than they do in the general population.[33] Therefore, newspeople have values that correspond to their middle- or upper-middle-class status. Thus, according to Alger, socioeconomic status affects their "reality judgments," and their decisions about what is news and how news should be handled.[34]

Rivers describes the differences between male reality and female reality as viewed by reporters. She explains that many events as portrayed in the mass media are depictions of what is edited, filtered, preselected—usually through the mesh of the male perspective. According to Rivers, this reflects a universe in which women are too often totally invisible—or just barely so. She uses the example of Walter Cronkite and how he used to say, at the end of the CBS newscast, "And that's the way it is." According to Rivers, he should have said, " 'And that's the way it is— as decided by a very small group of people, nearly all of whom are white, male, who make more than thirty thousand dollars a year and never take their own clothes to the cleaners."[35]

What does this mean for the element of bias one might expect in news coverage of the contemporary American woman and her changing role? Generally, women and other minorities, the poor, those outside the power order, and those with differing ideological perspectives that clash with the system will, in all probability, continue to be subject to disparities in media coverage. There is a cultural, social, political, and economic redefinition of what is news and how it should be reported. Let us next look at the studies that have been completed about news coverage of women in political elections and campaigns.

WOMEN, POLITICS, AND THE MEDIA

As women advance in all political arenas, including elective and appointive offices, how do the mass media respond? Kahn analyzed newspaper coverage in forty-seven statewide campaigns between 1982 and 1988. Findings show that the media differentiated between male and female candidates in their campaign coverage. The differences were found to be more dramatic in U.S. Senate races, but the distinctions were evident in gubernatorial contests as well. In senatorial races, women received less campaign coverage than their male counterparts; the coverage they received was more negative—emphasizing their unlikely chances of winning. In both senatorial and gubernatorial races, women received consistently less issue attention than their male counterparts. Finally, the news media seemed more responsive to the messages sent by male candidates. The media's agenda more closely resembled the agenda issued by male candidates in their televised political advertisements.[36]

Mandel has argued that "female candidates must deal with how they present themselves as women. Whatever the particular circumstances, their sex is part of women's campaign consciousness."[37] Procter, Aden, and Japp confirmed Mandel's observation in their study of the television advertising in the 1986 Nebraska gubernatorial campaign that pitted Helen Boosalis against Kay Orr, the first time in American history that two women opposed each other in such an election. The study focused on the identity-building strategies of each candidate as revealed in their television ads. They found that there continue to be gender problems for women in political campaigns. Specifically, Orr was more effective in integrating traditional women's roles and stereotypes with perceptions of leadership in order to win.[38]

On the other hand, Kaid, Myers, Pipps, and Hunter used an experimental study to test reactions to both male and female candidates in each of six advertising settings.[39] Two of these were settings traditionally associated with females, two were settings traditionally associated with males, and two were neutral settings. The researchers found that female candidates can be just as successful in television advertisements as male candidates, and that females are particularly successful when performing in male settings. In fact, the female candidate received her highest overall rating on the semantic differential scales when she appeared in a male setting, the hard hat spot. The authors suggest one possible reason is that the appearance of a female in such a role would be somewhat novel to the audience.[40]

Patty Murray (D-WA), the woman who ran for the U.S. Senate in 1992 as the "mom in tennis shoes," not only was successful in her bid for election; she also landed an assignment to the powerful Senate Appropriations Committee on her first day on the job. How did the *Seattle Times* report this committee assignment? The news was reported in the local pages instead of on the front page.[41] One has to question the placement decision by newspaper personnel, which unquestionably downplayed this news item. Would the same "news" have been subjugated to inside pages if the Washington senator had been male?

Analysis of the newspaper coverage given the nominations for attorney general of Zoe Baird and Kimba Wood revealed newspapers set an agenda that depicted typical female stereotypes. That is, the newspaper accounts tended to highlight and focus not just on the issue of lawbreaking but on the problems of female professionals and the issue of child care.[42] Of course, child care has traditionally been perceived to be a female responsibility. Our society and our government leaders have delegated the nurturing role to women, which, to many, means women are the prime caretakers of children.

To contrast perceptions of male and female roles in child care, twenty years ago it was learned that then–Deputy Attorney General William Ruckelshaus had an alien woman with an improper visa working in his home. Stories in the media attributed this arrangement to his wife, and the story quickly died.[43] Thus, even though the nominee in question had employed an alien woman, the basic issue of child care was linked to the wife's responsibility—and not that of the male nominee—and the issue was put to rest.

The nominations of Baird and Wood were withdrawn by the Clinton administration, and Janet Reno, a single woman without child care responsibility, was nominated and confirmed as the first female U.S. attorney general. Shortly thereafter, Commerce Secretary Ronald H. Brown reported that he had failed to pay Social Security taxes for a household worker. Newspaper accounts explained this double-standard in the following manner:

> What is the distinction between Mr. Brown and Judge Wood? In the screening process for Presidential nominees, Mr. Brown was not asked about his compliance with immigration and tax laws. By contrast, Judge Wood was asked several times and "she was not completely forthcoming," Mr. Stephanopoulos (Clinton spokesperson) said.
>
> Judge Wood said that she was asked if she had a 'Zoe Baird problem' and that she interpreted that to mean had she ever hired an illegal alien when it was against the law and not paid Social Security and other taxes for that worker, as Ms. Baird had. She said she had replied truthfully that she had not.[44]

Thus, we have a situation in which a woman was not confirmed although she had broken no law and a man who had not complied with the law avoided the same critical scrutiny by the press during the confirmation process. The mass media play into this double standard in other ways. The press provides not only information but the particular "spin" the public and our government officials associate with this news report or this issue.

The mass media interpret what is perceived as a "female" burden or problem and pass this along to the general populace. Public opinion coalesces around this issue, elected and other officials within government interpret this stereotypical role for women, and female professionals often are the losers.

CONCLUSION

The very nature of the news-making process dictates that reporters, journalists, editors, and/or publishers, by necessity, must make news decisions. Judgments as to what is news and what is not; decisions of how to "play" a story as far as importance; judgments regarding placement of news; the amount of coverage to be given a particular issue, event, or personality; and other internal decisions within the media organization will always be determined by institutional norms of what is and ought to be "news." These internal constraints of media organizations and personnel, by necessity, dictate the ultimate news product. As Paletz and Entman have observed, "Seeking neither to praise nor deplore, we have shown that much of the news is determined less by external 'reality' than by the internal logic of media organizations and personnel."[45]

In addition, mass media professionals bring their own culture, their own social norms, and their own political views and preferences to the news-making procedure. Despite the professionalism of the individual reporter and her or his news organization, the final news product will be influenced by any number of internal and external factors.

Thus, whether the issue is women seeking elective or appointive public office, ethnicity in the Northeast, the environment in the West, or religion or race in the Deep South, specific issues and events will be selected for coverage, while others will be ignored or downplayed. Still other issues will be addressed by giving the story a different "spin" in the newspapers' pages or in the nightly television news. And the sociological and cultural influences of the individuals making these decisions will always be a human determination.

It falls, then, to the American public to recognize media coverage for what it is and to work beyond the stereotypes that do end up in the news. The role of women in all facets of American life has changed significantly over the past four decades, and is continuing to change. Clearly, these changes have been and are being reported by the mass media. But, a number of questions remain: What is the content of this media coverage? What has been the role of the media in assessing the "reality" of some of these changes? How have these changes subsequently been reported by the mass media? Do women not deserve a great deal more coverage, even under the present constraints as outlined above, than the media give them?

Clearly, this is a preliminary article written to synthesize some of the research that has been done in the area of press coverage of women in American politics. As the number of female candidates increases and the number of women in other important positions within our government grows, further studies are indicated that will examine and analyze the media coverage given women by the press. Studies that would further explore how the news is reported about women who run for elective office and how this coverage compares with that of male candidates especially appear to be warranted. More longitudinal studies certainly appear to be warranted; as more women seek and are elected to public office, one hopes that additional research can be done in this area.

NOTES

1. Walter Lippmann, "The World Outside and the Pictures in Our Heads," in *Public Opinion* (New York: Macmillan, 1922), chap. 1.

2. Dan Nimmo and James E. Combs, *Mediated Political Realities*, 2nd ed. (New York: Longman, 1990), p. 2.

3. Ibid., pp. 1–20.

4. Gaye Tuchman, *Making News: A Study in the Construction of Reality* (New York: Free Press, 1978), p. 23; Bernard Roshco, *Newsmaking* (Chicago: University of Chicago Press, 1975), p. 4.

5. Tuchman, *Making News*, p. 667.

6. Ibid., p. 12.

7. Lee Sigelman, "Reporting the News: An Organizational Analysis," *American Journal of Sociology*, 79 (July–November 1973), pp. 132–151; Warren Breed, "Social Control in the Newsroom: A Functional Analysis," *Social Forces*, 33 (May 1955), pp. 326–335.

8. Roshco, *Newsmaking*, pp. 4–5.

9. Bob Schulman, "The Liberal Tilt of Our Newsroom," *Bulletin of the American Society of Newspaper Editors*, 654 (October 1982), pp. 3–7; Joseph Kraft, "The Imperial Media," *Commentary*, 71 (May 1981), p. 36; Robert S. Lichter and Stanley Rothman, "Media and Business Elites," *Public Opinion* 4 (5) (October/November 1981), pp. 43–44.

10. Edie N. Goldenberg, *Making the Papers* (Lexington, MA: Lexington Books, 1975), pp. 1–6.

11. Ibid., pp. 145–146, 148.

12. Among others, see Michael Parenti, *Inventing Reality: The Politics of News Media*, 2nd ed. (New York: St. Martin's Press, 1993), pp. 191–210. Also see Mark Fishman, *Manufacturing the News* (Austin: University of Texas Press, 1980); Daniel C. Hallin, "Sound Bite News," in Gary Orren (Ed.), *Blurring the Lines*. (New York: Free Press, 1990); Martin A. Lee and Norman Solomon, *Unreliable Sources* (New York: Carol Publishing Group, 1991); and Martin Linskey, *Impact: How the Press Affects Federal Policymaking* (New York: Norton, 1986).

13. Maxwell E. McCombs and Donald L. Shaw, "The Agenda-Setting Function of Mass Media," *Public Opinion Quarterly*, 36 (Summer 1972), pp. 176–187. Also see Everett M. Rogers and James W. Dearing, "Agenda-Setting Research: Where Has It Been and Where Is It Going?" in James A. Anderson (Ed.), *Communication Yearbook*, vol. 2 (Beverly Hills, CA: Sage, 1988).

14. Maxwell E. McCombs and Donald L. Shaw, "The Agenda-Setting Function of Mass Media," *Public Opinion Quarterly*, 36 (Summer 1972), p. 177.

15. Gladys Engel Lang, "The Most Admired Women: Image-Making in the News," in Gaye Tuchman, Arlene Kaplan Daniels, and James Benet, (Eds.), *Hearth and Home* (New York: Oxford University Press, 1978), p. 147.

16. Lois Lovelace Duke, "Cultural Redefinition of News: Civil Rights Issues and the Press," Ph.D. diss., University of South Carolina, 1986.

17. Among others who discuss basic distortions in the media, see Parenti, *Inventing Reality*, p. 8; Bernard Rubin, "Visualizing Stereotypes: Updating Walter Lippmann," in Bernard Rubin (Ed.), *When Information Counts: Grading the Media* (Lexington, MA: D. C. Heath, 1985) pp. 29–58; and Kathleen Hall Jamieson and Karlyn Kohrs Campbell, *The Interplay of Influence* (Belmont, CA: Wadsworth, 1992); especially pp. 98–124.

18. Elizabeth Janeway, *Man's World, Woman's Place* (New York: Dell, 1971); and Caryl Rivers, "Women, Myth, and the Media," in Rubin (Ed.), *When Information Counts*, p. 4.

19. Rubin, "Visualizing Stereotypes: Updating Walter Lippman," in Rubin (Ed.), *When Information Counts*, p. 34.

20. David S. Broder, *Behind the Front Page* (New York: Simon and Schuster, 1987), p. 126.

21. Dean E. Alger, *The Media and Politics* (Englewood Cliffs, NJ: Prentice-Hall, 1989), p. 26.

22. Broder, *Behind the Front Page*, pp. 125–127.

23. Kim Fridkin Kahn and Edie N. Goldenberg, "The Media: Obstacle or Ally of Feminists?" *Annals of the American Academy of Political and Social Science*, 515 (1991), pp. 104–113.

24. S. Robert Lichter, Linda S. Lichter, and Stanley Rothman, "From Lucy to Lacy: TV's Dream Girls, *Public Opinion*, 9 (3) (September/October 1986), pp. 16–19; and Alger, *The Media and Politics*, p. 26.

25. Ibid.

26. Leah R. Vande Berg and Diane Streckfuss, "Prime-Time Television's Portrayal of Women and the World of Work: A Demographic Profile," *Journal of Broadcasting and Electronic Media*, 36 (Spring 1992), pp. 195–208.

27. Ibid.

28. William Glaberson, "Study Finds More News of, and by, Women," *New York Times*, April 13, 1994, p. A10.

29. Ibid.

30. Parenti, *Inventing Reality*, p. 8.

31. Among others, see J. P. Henningham, "Ethnic Minorities in Australian Media," in Y. Atal (Ed.), *Mass Media and the Minorities* (Bangkok: UNESCO Regional Office, 1986); Lee Becker, Gerald Kosicki, and Felecia Jones "Racial Differences in Evaluations of the Mass Media," *Journalism Quarterly*, 69 (1) (1992), pp. 124–134; and Diana Owen and Jack Dennis, "Sex Differences in Politicization: The Influence of Mass Media," *Women and Politics*, 12 (4) (1992), pp. 19–41.

32. Glaberson, "Study Finds More News of, and by, Women," p. A10.

33. Alger, *The Media and Politics*, pp. 104–105; Clint C. Wilson II and Felix Gutierrez, *Minorities and Media Diversity and the End of Mass Communication* (Newbury Park, CA: Sage, 1985), pp. 159–163.

34. Alger, *The Media and Politics*, pp. 104–105; Herbert Gans, *Deciding What's News* (New York: Vintage Books, 1980), pp. 208–209.

35. Rivers, "Women, Myth, and the Media," p. 4.

36. Kim Fridkin Kahn, "The Distorted Mirror: Press Coverage of Women Candidates for Statewide Office," *Journal of Politics*, 56 (1) (February 1994), pp. 154–173; also see Kahn and Goldenberg, "Women Candidates in the News: An Examination of Gender Differences in U.S. Senate Campaign Coverage," *Public Opinion Quarterly* 55 (Summer 1991), pp. 180–199; Kahn, "Does Being Male Help? An Investigation of the Effect of Candidate Gender and Campaign Coverage on Evaluations of U.S. Senate Candidates," Ph.D. diss., University of Michigan, 1989.

37. Ruth B. Mandel, *In the Running: The New Woman Candidate* (New York: Ticknor and Fields, 1981), pp. 33–62.

38. David E. Procter, Roger C. Aden, and Phyllis Japp, "Gender/Issue Interaction in Political Identity Making: Nebraska's Woman vs. Woman Gubernatorial Campaign," *Central State Speech Journal*, 39 (Fall/Winter 1988), pp. 190–203.

39. Lynda Lee Kaid, Sandra L. Myers, Val Pipps, and Jan Hunter, "Sex Role Perceptions and Televised Political Advertising: Comparing Male and Female Candidates," *Women and Politics*, 4 (Winter 1984), pp. 41–53.

40. Ibid.

41. Junior Bridge, "The Media Mirror: Reading between the (News) Lines," *Quill*, January/February 1994, pp. 18–19.

42. See numerous accounts in major newspapers during the period January–February 1993. In particular, see Anna Quindlen, "The Sins of Zoe Baird," *New York Times*, January 20, 1993, p. A23.

43. "It's Gender Stupid," *New York Times*, February 8, 1993, p. A17.

44. "Nominees Are Screened for Illegal Hiring," *New York Times*, February 9, 1993, p. A1.

45. David L. Paletz and Robert M. Entman, *Media Power Politics* (New York: Free Press, 1981), p. 24.

FURTHER READINGS

Bagdikian, Ben H. *The Media Monopoly*. 4th ed. Boston: Beacon Press, 1992.

Broder, David S. *Behind the Front Page: A Candid Look at How the News is Made*. Simon and Schuster, 1987.

Bennett, W. Lance. *The Politics of Illusion*. White Plains, NY: Longman, 1988.

Epstein, Edward J. *News from Nowhere*. New York: Random House, 1973.

Gans, Herbert. *Deciding What's News*. New York: Pantheon Books, 1979.

Gitlin, Todd. *The Whole World Is Watching*. Berkeley and Los Angeles: University of California Press, 1980.

Graber, Doris A. *Mass Media and American Politics*. 4th ed. Washington, DC: Congressional Quarterly Press, 1993.

Iyengar, Shanto. *Is Anyone Responsible? How Television Frames Political Issues*. Chicago: University of Chicago Press, 1991.

Iyengar, Shanto, and Donald R. Kinder. *News That Matters*. Chicago: University of Chicago Press, 1987.

Nesbit, Dorothy D. *Videostyle in Senate Campaigns*. Knoxville: University of Tennessee Press, 1988.

Neuman, W. Russell. *The Paradox of Mass Politics: Knowledge and Opinion in the American Electorate*. Cambridge, MA: Harvard University Press, 1986.

Paletz, David L., and Robert M. Entman. *Media Power Politics*. New York: Free Press, 1981.

Ranney, Austin. *Channels of Power*. New York: Basic Books, 1983.

Tuchman, Gaye. *Making News: A Study in the Construction of Reality*. New York: Free Press, 1978.

Tuchman, Gaye, Arlene Kaplan Daniels, and James Benet (Eds.). *Hearth and Home Images of Women in the Mass Media*. New York: Oxford University Press, 1978.

Gender Differences in State Legislators' Perceptions of Media Coverage of Public Affairs

Glen Sussman

Nicholas P. Lovrich Jr.

This article examines gender differences in attitudes among state legislators about media coverage of state legislatures generally, and support for gavel-to-gavel continuous televised coverage of legislative affairs in particular. Consideration is also given to several explanatory variables and their relative impact on gender differences among state legislators. The study is based on data collected from a sizable sample of female and male legislators in the fifty states.

A considerable body of research has explored the reasons for women's difficulties in recruitment to public office.[1] However, after women have secured positions within a political institution, their effective use of television as a political tool or as a means to reach out to constituents during routine legislative activities has received little scholarly consideration outside of electoral politics. As Kaid, Myers, Pipps, and Hunter have stated, "In order for women to be successful participants in the political system, they must use effectively the tools of the system."[2] The similarities and differences in male and female legislators' attitudes about the media generally, and gavel-to-gavel television programming in particular, represent an important area of gender difference research requiring further investigation.

Although women have been conspicuous in their absence from legislative assemblies in the United States historically,[3] women's limited numbers in political institutions have been increasing incrementally in recent years.[4] Women now hold approximately 20 percent of all seats in state legislative bodies.[5] As the presence of

Glen Sussman is an assistant professor of political science at Old Dominion University. Nicholas P. Lovrich Jr. is professor of political science at Washington State University.

women has increased in political institutions, research has also intensified regarding women in public office; this has included studies exploring gender differences among elected officials in attitudes about a variety of public policies and institutional practices.

Over the last twenty years or so, several studies of gender differences among state legislators found that women differed demographically from male legislators, that women had a minimum of prior political experience, that women were limited in the types of political resources they employed within the legislative institution, that women tended to be drawn to "domestic" or "women's" issues, and that women paid more attention to constituent service activities than did their male colleagues.[6] However, by the late 1980s, some research indicated that women have become increasingly similar to male legislators in their level and frequency of political activities within the legislative chamber, and in the achievement of their legislative goals.[7] In addition to the more common "gender-linked policy differences" research, gender differences in voting patterns among state legislators,[8] male and female legislators' attitudes toward the role of women in the legislative body,[9] as well as the impact of increasing numbers of women in state legislative assemblies[10] are topics that have been explored in more recent research on women in politics. While these numerous studies of the role of women in state legislatures have addressed a broad range of subjects regarding gender-related differences in political behavior and public policy priorities, gender-based orientations about the role of the media in covering state legislatures has received scant attention. Consequently, the study reported here can be viewed as being exploratory in nature and one that breaks new research ground in the substantive area of gender-based attitudes.

It is important to note that the role of the media as it relates to women in society generally has received considerable research attention. Research has focused on how women have been treated by the media,[11] on how the media are used by women in various positions of power in American society,[12] or on gender-based differences in female and male viewing habits.[13] The type of media used by women and the frequency of use of the media by women have been explored and compared with that of men. For example, women in the general population are inclined to gain information from watching television, while men tend to use both television and newspapers as primary sources of public affairs information.[14] The effective use of the media by women and men in political campaigns has been given consideration in some studies. For instance, in recent elections women's ability to successfully employ television advertising in political campaigns was found to be comparable to that of male candidates.[15]

Traditionally women have been prominent "outsiders" in the American political process. As the proportion of women continues to grow in state legislative bodies across the country, it is likely that they will bring distinctive skills, experiences, and viewpoints that challenge some aspects of the status quo.[16] In so doing, we expect that among these challenges to the status quo is greater *support for opening up the political process* to citizens. One can argue that direct and continuous televised coverage of state legislative affairs represents an important means of democratizing the legislative process. Public affairs televised coverage of legislative proceedings has been in effect for some time in several states. At the subnational level, televised coverage of state legislative proceedings was first implemented about two decades ago, although the precise formats for broadcast media coverage have differed in the several states.[17] During this time, very few states have implemented unedited, continuous televised programming of legislative affairs. Assuming that women will be inclined to support "open government" initiatives, we expect that women legislators will be more supportive of gavel-to-gavel televised programming of legislative proceedings than their male counterparts in their respective legislative chambers.

Early research about media coverage of political institutions and public affairs has indicated that ample coverage of issues considered important by legislators was provided by the media.[18] On the other hand, increasing interest in gavel-to-gavel televised programming in recent years has generated a new debate about the quality and character of contemporary media coverage of public affairs in the fifty states. The study reported here joins this discussion by investigating gender differences in attitudes about media coverage of state politics; we assess the extent to which male and female legislators support the gavel-to-gavel public affairs communication format in the legislative chambers in the states. In this endeavor, it is important to assess the impact of gender and compare sex differences to the effects of several commonly observed intervening variables known to be related to expectations about and attitudes toward the broadcast media.

INFLUENCES ON LEGISLATORS' ATTITUDES TOWARD THE MEDIA

On the one hand, our purpose is to investigate legislative attitudes about media coverage of the legislative chambers in the fifty states. On the other hand, we also seek to determine the relationship between several sociopolitical variables and attitudes about the media and state legislatures. Any linkages among these variables, and attitudes will add to our understanding of their influence on gender-based variation in attitudes about the role of the media in state politics generally, and media policy within political institutions in particular.

Age and level of formal education are two conventional demographic variables employed in the study. These two personal characteristics are considered to be fundamental factors in much social science research as they have been found, in many circumstances of social choice, to constitute a major influence on political attitudes and behavior among citizens and political elites alike. An overview of state legislatures shows that, in the past, women in state legislatures have tended to be somewhat older and somewhat less well educated than their male counterparts. In recent years, a broader and more diverse cohort of women has been recruited to legislative assemblies in many American states, although younger female legislators continue to remain relatively few in number.[19]

Political party affiliation, political ideology, and value orientation have also been selected as plausible predictors of legislators' attitudes toward the broadcast media. Whether a legislator is a Democrat or a Republican, a liberal or a conservative, political orientation is generally considered an important potential indicator of her or his orientation toward public policy issues. As far as contemporary state legislatures are concerned, women in legislative chambers tend to be more liberal than men, although the gap has been declining.[20] Also, women candidates for state legislative offices tend to hold a Democratic affiliation more often than they hold a Republican party identification.[21] An individual's value orientation might also be associated with specific public policy preferences. We employ Inglehart's widely used four-item value scale to distinguish legislators on the basis of three categories of value type—namely, postmaterialist, materialist, and mixed value orientation.[22] For the purpose of this study, we are concerned with the influence of postmateralism, which is associated with Maslowian *higher-order needs*—with greater citizen involvement in the public policy process being one such higher-order felt need. Support for unrestricted televised coverage of legislative proceedings plausibly can be considered a reflection of the call for expanding democratic participation in state politics.

The type of district represented, years of service, and personal relations (adversarial versus friendly) with broadcast journalists serve as structural variables in this study. In addition, the urban, suburban, or rural character of one's district might be expected to have a noteworthy impact on legislators' attitudes about unedited, public affairs televised coverage of legislative business. The degree of "professionalism" of the legislative body—that is, whether it is an organization that is full-time, with large staff, and well compensated or one that meets for short periods, has few staff, and offers little compensation—is also a likely key factor. It is easier for legislators to accommodate media coverage where experienced staff are available to structure and make provisions for media coverage. A ranking of the legislator's state on a legislative professionalism continuum is included among the predictors of support for gavel-to-gavel coverage. Younger, more recently elected, and urban-based state legislators are expected to be more supportive of expanded broadcast coverage and the use of a gavel-to-gavel format for public affairs programming.

One of the key considerations in the examination of women and politics is *access*—access to positions in political institutions and access to the decision-making process.[23] In recent years, women have gained increasing access to public office at the state level. Studies of contemporary state legislatures indicate, for example, that women tend to run and hold office in more urbanized districts.[24] However, it is much more likely for male legislators, who tend to enjoy the political resources and benefits of public office, to be incumbents than women. Still, women incumbents are generally as successful in winning reelection as are men.[25] Thus, incumbency (i.e., length of service) is an important consideration that might affect women's attitudes about matters concerning how their state legislatures should be accorded broadcast coverage.

The relationship between legislators and journalists is also an important consideration in assessing the political orientations of legislators. While some studies have indicated that female and male legislators tend to receive comparable media coverage,[26] other studies have shown that female candidates receive differential treatment by the media compared with male candidates.[27] As Kahn and Goldenberg argue, "Eliminating gender differences in coverage could even the political field, thereby improving women's access to the electoral arena."[28] It will be interesting to see, on the basis of our national cross-section of state legislators, how contemporary women legislators assess the extent and quality of broadcast media coverage of their own legislative assemblies as compared with their male counterparts.

Finally, the perception of professional integrity of the news media covering legislative business is plausibly an important consideration in assessing legislators' attitudes about the media and politics. The attitudes of state lawmakers toward the broadcast media are likely affected by legislators' perceptions of the degree of bias and level of accuracy reflected in broadcast news reporting. One might expect that legislators who believe the news media are likely to exhibit professional integrity in reporting the news would be more likely to support unedited, gavel-to-gavel programming than those who think less highly of the journalism community.

RESEARCH QUESTIONS

The following research questions will be addressed in the forthcoming analyses:

1. To what extent do female and male state legislators differ in their level of satisfaction with the quality of media coverage of state politics?
2. Are gender differences evident in the level of support for gavel-to-gavel televised coverage of legislative affairs?
3. What is the independent impact of several predictor variables (e.g., party, ideology) on the attitudes of male and female state legislators across the United States toward gavel-to-gavel televised programming?

We will use multiple regression (ordinary least squares) analysis.

METHODS

This study examines attitudes held among a nationwide sample ($N = 259$) of equal proportions of female and male state legislators about media coverage of the state legislative process. The survey was conducted in 1994 by the Division of Governmental Studies and Services at Washington State University. Gender differences are investigated with regard to perceptions of the amount and quality of media coverage of state politics generally, as well as support for continuous, unedited coverage of legislative affairs in particular. Determinants of support for public affairs coverage of legislators' activities in the legislative assembly—namely, accuracy in news reporting, age, bias in news reporting, education, ideology, length of service, party affiliation, postmaterialist value orientation, status of relations with journalists, type of district represented, and degree of professionalization of the respondent's legislature—will be examined to assess the likelihood of differential effects of these background characteristics on male and female legislators' attitudes toward the broadcast media in their political environment.

The data employed in this study were obtained using a mail survey of female and male legislators in all fifty states. Questionnaires were distributed to legislators in both chambers of each state legislature using Dillman's "total design method," which employs multiple waves of questionnaires to be sent to survey respondents.[29] The sample of legislators consisted of 250 women and 250 men in the fifty states. Survey responses were received from each of the fifty states; the overall response rate achieved was 52 percent with three waves of mailings, with a minimum of 40 percent returns from some states to a maximum of 70 percent returns from others.

In order to tap the political orientations of female and male legislators about the media and the state legislature generally, the following two survey questions were employed: (1) Attitudes about the amount of media coverage were determined by asking legislators to respond to the following: "Generally speaking, compared with the amount of media coverage of national and local governments, how would you rate the amount of broadcast media coverage devoted to state government?" A seven-point scale was employed, anchored at one end by "too little coverage" and at the other end by "too much coverage." The scale midpoint was labeled "about right." (2) Legislators were asked: "How satisfied are you with the quality of broadcast coverage of state politics?" Respondents were provided a seven-point scale, with "very dissatisfied" at one end and "very satisfied" at the other end. The satisfaction scale midpoint was labeled "uncertain." In addition to these evaluative sentiments, legislators were also asked to indicate what expectations they held concerning the "likely effects" of greater broadcast coverage of legislative affairs. The effects in question relate to whether greater coverage would improve or worsen the legislative process, and whether enhanced broadcast coverage would increase or decrease public confidence in the political process.

The major dependent variable in the study is an item measuring support for gavel-to-gavel televised coverage. The item in question read "Some states have gavel-to-gavel televised coverage of the state legislature. To what extent would you support this type of broadcast media coverage of the state legislature?" Legislators were presented with a seven-point scale, anchored at one end by "should be established" and at the other end by "should be prevented." The scale midpoint was labeled "undecided."

In order to address the research questions concerned with the relative impact of the several intervening variables on the attitudes of members of the state legislative chambers on gavel-to-gavel broadcast coverage, we employed a standard form of multiple regression analysis. The eleven independent variables employed in the study are described in brief in the following:

1. ACCURACY OF MEDIA—a five-point scale was used with a question lead stating that broadcast news was "accurate," anchored at one end by "strongly disagree" and at the other end by "strongly agree."
2. AGE—each legislator was asked to indicate the year of her or his birth; age was calculated from that year.
3. BIAS IN MEDIA—a five-point scale was employed with a question lead stating that broadcast news was "unbiased," anchored at one end by "strongly agree" and at the other end by "strongly disagree."

4. EDUCATION—each legislator was provided a listing of levels of educational attainment, ranging from "completed high school" to "advanced degree."

5. IDEOLOGY—each legislator was asked to place him- or herself on a five-point scale ranging from "very conservative" to "very liberal." The scale midpoint was labeled "middle of the road."

6. LENGTH OF SERVICE—years of membership in the state legislature.

7. PARTY AFFILIATION—each legislator was asked to place him- or herself on a five-point scale ranging from "strong Democrat" to "strong Republican." The midpoint was labeled "Independent."

8. POSTMATERIALISM—Inglehart's four-alternative scale was employed. Each member of the sample of lawmakers was asked to choose what he or she considers to be the two most important goals among the following four choices: (1) maintaining order in the nation, (2) giving people more say in important decisions, (3) fighting rising prices, or (4) protecting freedom of speech. Legislators who selected goals 2 and 4 were classified as "postmaterialists."

9. RELATIONS WITH JOURNALISTS—a seven-point scale was used, ranging from "adversarial relationship" at one end to "friendly relationship" at the other. The midpoint was labeled "somewhat friendly."

10. TYPE OF DISTRICT—self-placement on a three-item scale using rural, urban, and suburban as categories.

11. PROFESSIONALISM OF STATE LEGISLATURE—rank of state on "professionalism" scale developed by P. Squire (vol. 17) based on member pay, staff members per legislator, and total days in session.[30]

The following section reports the results of the several bivariate and multivariate analyses performed with the national survey of legislators.

FINDINGS

The first research question of interest pertains to the extent to which female and male state legislators differ or agree in their level of satisfaction with the extent and quality of broadcast media coverage of state politics. The question of difference and similarity in the expectations held by male and female state legislators for outcomes resulting from enhanced broadcast coverage—outcomes for the legislative process and for public confidence in the political process—is also assessed. The findings in this area are reported in Table 1.

Female state legislators are inclined to be somewhat less positive in their assessment of the extent and quality of broadcast coverage of state affairs than are their male counterparts. They are more likely than male solons to express the view that there is either too little (64 percent) or too much (12 percent) coverage, and fewer than one in four believes that broadcast coverage is "about right;" the comparable figure for "about right" assessments for male legislators is one in three solons. As to the matter of the quality of broadcast coverage being given, the female legislators are more inclined than their male colleagues to express dissatisfaction. While somewhat more than six in ten male legislators indicate dissatisfaction with the quality of media coverage, over seven in ten female legislators express this view.

Table 1 Comparison of Views of Male and Female State Legislators Regarding Quality of Broadcast Media Coverage of State Affairs

	Women Solons (N = 122)	Men Solons (N = 135)
Amount of Broadcast Coverage		
Too little coverage	77 (64%)	79 (59%)
About right amount	29 (24%)	44 (33%)
Too much coverage	14 (12%)	11 (8%)
Satisfaction with Quality of Coverage		
Satisfied with coverage	23 (19%)	32 (24%)
Uncertain	12 (10%)	19 (14%)
Dissatisfied with coverage	86 (71%)	83 (62%)
Expected Effect of More Coverage on Legislative Process		
Positive effect	79 (68%)	90 (67%)
No effect	18 (16%)	18 (13%)
Negative effect	19 (16%)	27 (20%)
Expected Effect of More Coverage on Public Confidence in Political Process		
Less confidence	32 (26%)	31 (24%)
No effect	14 (12%)	29 (22%)
More confidence	75 (62%)	71 (54%)

While gender differences seem to be present in assessments of the extent and quality of broadcast media coverage of state affairs, there is little evidence that such differences are based in differing expectations about what would happen if enhanced broadcast coverage were to occur. Fully two-thirds of both male and female state legislators believe that enhanced broadcast coverage of legislative business would *improve* the legislative process. Similarly, only one in four male and female state legislators is of the view that increased coverage would produce detrimental effects on public confidence in the political process.

What can be said of gender effects in the question of support for expanded broadcast media coverage of state affairs? Findings from the survey pertinent to this question are set forth in Table 2. First, what belief do male and female legislators hold with respect to citizen preferences for expanded broadcast coverage? Are male legislators more likely than their female counterparts to sense that citizens are disinterested in state legislative affairs? This question can be answered in the affirmative—female legislators are more likely to assume that citizens want expanded coverage than are male state legislators, and less likely to assume that citizens are either neutral or negative on the issue.

With regard to our central concern, support for the format of gavel-to-gavel coverage, there is no appreciable difference between male and female state legislators. Equal percentages (59 percent) of both male and female state solons favor the establishment of gavel-to-gavel coverage for their own legislative bodies, and one

Table 2   Comparison of Views of Male and Female State Legislators Regarding Expanded Broadcast Media Coverage in General and Gavel-to-Gavel Coverage in Particular

	Women Solons (N = 122)	Men Solons (N = 135)
Perception of Citizen Preferences on Expanded Broadcast Coverage of State Affairs		
Support	85 (71%)	77 (60%)
Neutral	33 (28%)	46 (36%)
Oppose	1 (1%)	6 (5%)
Support for Gavel-to-Gavel Coverage		
Favor establishment	68 (59%)	79 (59%)
Undecided	20 (17%)	20 (15%)
Prevent the practice	28 (24%)	25 (26%)

in four male and female legislators say they would like to prevent the practice from arising. While gender is not directly connected to preferences on gavel-to-gavel adoption, the following discussion of multivariate analyses will illustrate that gender does indeed play an important role in the politics of gavel-to-gavel coverage.

One fruitful way to probe the depths of support for gavel-to-gavel broadcast coverage is to employ a method of multivariate analysis, incorporating into a single statistical model a variety of hypothesized correlates. Such models provide for the testing of relative effects of each predictor variable, simultaneously controlling for the effects of all other model measures. In the case of uncorrelated predictors (independent variables not correlated above a .70 threshold), the regression coefficients generated by a multiple regression analysis provide a standardized measure of relative effect upon a dependent variable. In the case in point, the eleven predictor variables used here to account for variation in support for gavel-to-gavel coverage are not interrcorrelated to any significant degree; none of the eleven predictor variables is correlated above .48, and most covary only slightly, if at all.

Of particular interest, in this regard, would be the results of such an analysis run separately for female state legislators and for their male colleagues. Do the same characteristics and conditions produce the same effects for male and female state legislative leaders with respect to support for gavel-to-gavel coverage? Or, is it the case that support for "live coverage" of the legislative process has different roots for male and female legislators? If the latter were the case, then the gender dimension is surely one deserving both scholarly and practical political attention. The results of this type of analysis are reported in Table 3.

The findings reported in Table 3 indicate that the several hypothesized correlates of support for gavel-to-gavel coverage, taken in combination, can account for a significant proportion of variance in support for live television coverage of the state legislative process among legislators from across the country. For both male and female legislators, better than 16 percent of the variance in support for gavel-to-gavel coverage can be accounted for by this set of eleven variables. What is of particular interest, however, is the fact that different factors stand out as important

Table 3   Comparison of Effects of Selected Hypothesized Influences on Male and Female State Legislators' Support for Gavel-to-Gavel Coverage: Results of a Multiple Regression Analysis

Men Solons (N = 127)

Factor	Standardized Regression Coefficient	Statistical Significance
Years legislative service	.000	.993
Postmaterialist values	**−.162**	**.075**
Liberal–conservative ideology	.052	.572
Broadcast media is unbiased	−.061	.583
Professionalism of legislature	**−.176**	**.051**
Democrat–GOP party identification	.064	.483
Urban–suburban–rural district	.131	.145
Level of education	.029	.746
Friendliness with media	**−.174**	**.058**
Age	.140	.166
Broadcast media are accurate	−.020	.860

Summary statistics: R square = .166; f = 2.08; significance of F = .0275

Women Solons (N = 108)

Factor	Standardized Regression Coefficient	Statistical Significance
Years legislative service	.133	.221
Postmaterialist values	**−.177**	**.061**
Liberal–conservative ideology	.008	.933
Broadcast media is unbiased	.038	.756
Professionalism of legislature	−.139	.141
Democrat–GOP party identification	**.194**	**.055**
Urban–suburban–rural district	**.226**	**.024**
Level of education	−.021	.831
Friendliness with media	.049	.611
Age	−.023	.829
Broadcast media are accurate	−.026	.837

Summary statistics: R square = .189; f = 2.03; significance of F = .033

predictors for women and for men state legislators. Both male and female legislators have three specific predictors that produce multiple regression coefficients with a statistical significance (of t) of less than .10, but two of those three predictors are not shared across genders.

For male solons the *level of professionalism* of the state legislature in which they serve produces the most powerful effect. For the male state legislators the presence of staff support and the tradition of more full-time service is connected to the view that the television cameras ought to be set up to capture the proceedings of law-making. For female legislators there is a slight effect in evidence but not of such magnitude as to achieve even a permissive .10 standard of statistical significance commonly employed in exploratory analyses such as this particular study. The second most important predictor for male legislators is a more personal factor—namely, the extent to which the solon enjoys a friendly as opposed to an adversarial relationship with media representatives. The picture that emerges from these findings for male state legislators is that they are making *pragmatic assessments* of the ability of their legislative body to manage the presence of televised coverage and the trustworthiness of the media to use greater access to the legislative process with proper professional discretion.

For female legislators the most salient correlates of support for gavel-to-gavel coverage are quite different. First, the strongest predictor of support is found in the type of legislative district: It is the *urban* (rather than suburban or rural) area representatives among the female legislators surveyed who are most supportive of the broadened coverage offered by continuous telecasting of proceedings. Television media markets are organized on the basis of population centers, of course, and among female legislators it seems clear that there is particular interest in the television medium as a primary connection between legislator and constituent. The second most important predictor of support for gavel-to-gavel coverage for the female legislators is *partisanship*: The more inclined female legislators are to indicate that they are either a "strong Democrat" or a "Democrat" as opposed to a Republican Party partisan, the more likely they are to support the establishment of gavel-to-gavel coverage of their respective legislature. The picture that emerges here is that among the female legislators it is the urban Democrats—who tend to be young, highly educated, and often of a minority background or representing minority districts—who are the strongest supporters of "bringing the legislative process to the people." They would seem to be motivated most by the sense of this being an effective way of connecting to their own constituents, perhaps even as an effective means of providing "role models" for other Democrat-affiliated young women. Rather than being concerned as much with the practical questions of the legislature's and the broadcast media's capacity to pull off the task of coverage, the female legislators who support the idea appear to be concerned primarily with reaching a particular audience with whom they would like to establish a connection.

The one factor that is of common salience to male and female legislators is the measure of postmaterialist values developed by Ronald Inglehart in *The Silent Revolution* and most commonly used in comparative political analysis. The measure is used in the study of "value change" associated with the advent of the postindustrial society in Western democracies, and has been utilized in numerous studies of American politics. The fundamental argument underlying the measure is that the period of prolonged peace and prosperity experienced by the advanced democracies of North America, Western Europe, and Japan have led to the development of "higher-order needs"—particularly among more well-placed elites—such that in the area of politics a direct concern with economic benefits in legislation is being displaced by concern for more "quality-of-life" concerns such as environmental protection, public involvement, gender equity, and achieving a broader range in lifestyle choices (e.g., gay rights, cultural diversity, accommodation of disabilities). The postmaterialist values index is designed to measure the degree to which people ascribe to this "higher-order need" conception of contemporary political choices. From the findings reported here it is clear that both male and female state legislators who are inclined to express support for postmaterialist values are also inclined to favor gavel-to-gavel coverage of the legislative process. Ascription to these values evidently carries with it a strong sense of the need for greater public access to information bearing on democratic self-governance, and among legislators sharing these values, gavel-to-gavel coverage is seen as an appropriate means for providing that access.

CONCLUSION

Several noteworthy findings deserve particular attention in way of summary and conclusions. Female state legislators continue to differ from their male counterparts in a number of important ways. While some studies may indicate that the differences between male and female legislators are narrowing in some respects, it is clear that in the area of media perceptions and legislative process reform to provide for greater access for broadcast journalists there continues to be a gender difference. Female legislators tend to be less satisfied with the performance of the broadcast media than are men legislators, and they are more inclined to presume that the average citizen is interested in greater access to the work of the legislature than are their male counterparts. Particularly for urban-based Democratic female state legislators, perhaps the most pro-feminist state-level political elite, the concept of broad access to unedited, live coverage of legislative debate and formal decisional processes represents an important goal of legislative work.

As important as these observations might be for understanding the political dynamics of gavel-to-gavel coverage, what is even more important to note is that the same factors often have different effects for male and female legislators. How female state legislators sized up the issue of increased broadcast media access was apparently quite different from the way in which male legislators are inclined to do so. For the male solons, the pragmatic issues of managerial and professional competence reign supreme, while for the women legislators a definite geopolitical social agenda construction of the issue seems to have been a common inclination. This finding speaks volumes for the continuing need to assess gender-based differences in how political issues are being approached and how policy preferences are being derived, and of the particular utility of investigating these issues among political elites such as state legislators. Judging from the findings reported here, there continues to be a gender gap in policy preferences in many areas, as well as noteworthy differences in the ways in which public policy issues are conceptualized by men and women engaged in the work of American politics.

NOTES

1. Barbara Burrell, "The Political Opportunity of Women Candidates for the U.S. House of Representatives in 1984," *Women and Politics*, 8 (1988), pp. 51–69; Patrick Pierce, "Gender Role and Political Culture: The Electoral Connection," *Women and Politics*, 9 (1989), pp. 21–46.

2. Lynda Lee Kaid, Sandra Myers, Val Pipps, and Jan Hunter, "Sex Role Perceptions and Televised Political Advertising: Comparing Male and Female Candidates," *Women and Politics*, 4 (Winter 1984), pp. 41–52.

3. Donald Matthews, "Legislative Recruitment and Legislative Careers," in Gerhard Loewenberg, Samuel Patterson, and Malcolm Jewell (Eds.), *Handbook of Legislative Research* (Cambridge, MA: Harvard University Press, 1985), pp. 21–22.

4. Janet Clark, "Getting There: Women in Political Office," in Marianne Githens, Pippa Norris, and Joni Lovenduski (Eds.), *Different Roles, Different Voices* (New York: HarperCollins, 1994), pp. 99–110; Sue Thomas, "Women in State Legislatures: One Step at a Time," in Elizabeth Adell Cook, Sue Thomas, and Clyde Wilcox (Eds.), *The Year of the Woman* (Boulder, CO: Westview Press, 1994), pp. 141–159; Wilma Rule, "Why More Women Are State Legislators," *Western Political Quarterly*, 43 (June 1990), pp. 437–448.

5. Kathleen Dolan and Lynn E. Ford, "Women State Legislators and Change over Time: 1972–1992," paper presented at the annual meeting of the American Political Science Association, New York, 1994.

6. Irene Diamond, *Sex Roles in the House* (New Haven, CT: Yale University Press, 1977); Jeane Kirkpatrick, *Political Woman* (New York: Basic Books, 1974); Emmy Werner, "Women in Legislatures," *Western Political Quarterly*, 21 (March 1968), pp. 40–50.

7. Sue Thomas, *How Women Legislate* (London: Oxford University Press, 1994).

8. Sue Thomas, "Voting Patterns in the California Assembly: The Role of Gender," *Women and Politics*, 9 (1989), pp. 43–53; Shelah Gilbert Leader, "The Policy Impact of Elected Women Officials," in Louis Maisel and Joseph Cooper (Eds.), *The Impact of the Electoral Process* (Beverly Hills, CA: Sage, 1977), pp. 265–284.

9. Patricia Freeman and William Lyons, "Legislators' Perceptions of Women in State Legislatures," *Women and Politics*, 10 (1990), pp. 121–132.

10. Thomas, "Women in State Legislatures."

11. Kim Fridkin Kahn and Edie N. Goldenberg, "The Media: Obstacle or Ally of Feminists?" *The Annals of the American Academy of Political and Social Science*, 515 (May 1991), pp. 104–113; Laurily Keir Epstein (Ed.), *Women and the News* (New York: Hasting House, 1978).

12. Carolyn Johnson and Lynne Gross, "Mass Media Use by Women in Decision-Making Positions," *Journalism Quarterly*, 62 (Winter 1985), pp. 850–854, 950.

13. Doris Graber, "Agenda Setting: Are There Women's Perspectives?" in Laurily Keir Epstein (Ed.), *Women and the News* (New York: Hasting House, 1978), pp. 15–37.

14. Joanne Rajoppi, *Women in Office* (Westport, CT: Bergin and Garvey, 1993).

15. Kaid, Myers, Pipps, and Hunter, "Sex Role Perceptions."

16. Thomas, *How Women Legislate*; Thomas, "Women in State Legislatures."

17. Arthur Stevens, "Televising Floor Proceedings in State Legislatures: A Summary of Survey Findings," *State Communications with the People*, 94th Congress, 2nd session, Washington, DC: U.S. Government Printing Office.

18. Kendall Baker and B. Oliver Walter, "The Press as a Source of Information about Activities of a State Legislature," *Journalism Quarterly*, 52 (Winter 1975), pp. 735–740, 761.

19. Thomas, *How Women Legislate*, p. 47; Rita Mae Kelly, Michelle Saint-Germaine, and Jody Horn, "Female Public Officials: A Different Voice?" *The Annals of the American Academy of Political and Social Science*, 515 (May 1991), pp. 77–87.

20. Kelly, Saint-Germaine, and Horn, "Female Public Officials."

21. Malcolm Jewell and Marcia Lynn Whicker, *Leadership in the American States* (Ann Arbor: University of Michigan Press, 1994), pp. 159–160.

22. Ronald Inglehart, *The Silent Revolution: Changing Values and Political Styles among Western Publics* (Princeton, NJ: Princeton University Press, 1977).

23. Ellen Boneparth, "Resources and Constraints on Women in the Policymaking Process: State and Local Arenas," in Janet Flammang (Ed.), *Political Women* (Beverly Hills, CA: Sage, 1984), pp. 280–281.

24. Jewell and Whicker, *Legislative Leadership*, p. 168.

25. Clark, "Getting There," p. 107.

26. Diane Silver, "A Comparison of Newspaper Coverage of Male and Female Officials in Michigan," *Journalism Quarterly*, 63 (Spring 1986) pp. 144–150.

27. Kahn and Goldenberg, "The Media."

28. Ibid., p. 113.

29. Don Dillman, *Mail and Telephone Surveys: The Total Design Method* (New York: Wiley, 1978).

30. P. Squire, "Legislative Professionalization and Membership Diversity in State Legislatures," *Legislative Studies Quarterly*, 17 (February 1992), pp. 69–79.

FURTHER READINGS

Cook, Elizabeth Adell, Sue Thomas, and Clyde Wilcox. *The Year of the Woman*. Boulder, CO: Westview Press, 1994.

Crain, W. Mark, and Brian L. Goff. *Televised Legislatures*. Boston: Kluwer Academic Publishers, 1988.

Fisher, Karen. "Legislatures in the Living Room." *State Legislatures*, 17 (August 1991), pp. 14–17.

O'Donnell, Robert. "What's Wrong with the Media's Coverage of the Legislature?" *State Legislatures*, 11 (1985), pp. 29–30.

Renstrom, Mary. "Legislative Television Programming in the States." *State Legislative Report*, 17 (1992), pp. 1–3.

Rinehart, Sue Tolleson. *Gender Consciousness and Politics*. New York: Routledge, 1992.

Saint-Germaine, Michelle. "Does Their Differences Make a Difference? The Impact of Women in Public Policy in the Arizona Legislature." *Social Science Quarterly*, 70 (December 1989), pp. 956–968.

Sapiro, Virginia. *The Political Integration of Women*. Urbana, University of Illinois Press, 1983.

Strate, John, Coit Cook Ford, and Thomas Jankowski. "Women's Use of the Print Media to Follow Politics." *Social Science Quarterly*, 75 (March 1994), pp. 166–186.

Sussman, Glen, Byron W. Daynes, Jonathan P. West, and Nicholas P. Lovrich. "Support for Television Coverage of the Legislative Process among State Legislatures: A Comparison of Iowa, Utah, and Florida." *Political Communication* (forthcoming).

Public Opinion of Hillary Rodham Clinton as First Lady

Barbara C. Burrell
Linda J. Penaloza

A central issue for feminists has been the division of the world into private and public domains and the implications of this dichotomy for equality for women. The symbol of the First Lady in American politics joins in a unique way these two domains, and it has the potential of dramatically altering the idea of what is private and what is public in the political realm. The woman who serves as First Lady is there because of her relationship to a man. The idea of "lady" in this context emphasizes the expressive, supportive, traditional role of women as wives, mothers, and homemakers. The idea of "first" suggests that she is to be a role model for others. But she functions in a very public arena. What the nature of that "public" should be has been left rather unstructured, although subject to great cultural constraints.

Hillary Clinton has transformed the role of the First Lady. She represents a new era, a new generation, the age of the professional woman, the smart woman. She has not and will not exercise influence only behind the scenes, while onstage merely gazing adoringly at her husband. As the *Wall Street Journal* characterized her potential in December 1992, she "promises to be something unique: both a major political power center in her own right, and the first modern working mother in the White House." According to the *Economist*, "There has never before been a woman in the White House who had both a successful career and an independent powerbase before she arrived there. . . . She is a genuine trail-blazer."[1] She has also

Barbara C. Burrell is a researcher and Head of Survey Design of the University of Wisconsin–Extension Survey Research Laboratory. Linda J. Penaloza is associate director and Head of Field Operations at the University of Wisconsin–Extension Survey Research Laboratory.

been the lightning rod for all of the ambivalent feelings Americans have had about the changing roles of women. This article examines public reaction to this phenomenon and considers its implications for women in political leadership.

Public response to Hillary Rodham Clinton as First Lady is captured here through public opinion as measured in national surveys. Not only has Hillary Rodham Clinton been the subject of much media attention, she has been the focus of polls from the early days of the campaign season. Never before has the public been asked so consistently what they think about a First Lady. As the *Public Perspective* has put it, "This first lady's standing has been measured more often by more pollsters than that of any other presidential spouse."[2] Both people's general responses to her as First Lady, and what they think of her in a great variety of domains have been investigated. Here we trace the poll coverage of Hillary Rodham Clinton's odyssey to the White House and her performance as First Lady in the first year and a half she and Bill Clinton occupied the executive mansion. We address both the quantity and the quality of the polls, describe the range of subject matter that has been covered in these polls, and analyze their findings. Finally, we theorize about the First Lady's relationship with the people and the impact of her assuming a public policy role for women in politics.

HISTORICAL PERSPECTIVE

Records of public opinion polls on the popularity of the First Lady are archived back to Pat Nixon's entrance into the White House in 1969. After she had been in the White House for six months, 54 percent of the people said they approved of the job she was doing as First Lady, only 6 percent disapproved, and 40 percent said they had no opinion. Betty Ford was viewed positively by 71 percent of the people, while 24 percent had a negative opinion in the one national poll that is available.[3]

No early readings are available on the public's impression of Rosalynn Carter.[4] But in 1979 she obtained a 55 percent favorable and 33 percent unfavorable response from the public,[5] and during the 1980 campaign she received a 46 percent favorable and a 9 percent unfavorable rating, while 37 percent said they did not know enough to respond.[6]

Nancy Reagan began her sojourn in the White House with a 28 percent favorable rating, while 10 percent said they had an unfavorable opinion and 57 percent said they did not know enough about her to have an opinion, according to a CBS/*New York Times* poll. She became quite popular during her time in the White House, especially after the first year, when she began to respond to the negative press she had received for her gifts, table settings, and so on. Through most of the Reagan administration, she was viewed favorably by over 60 percent of the people, and occasionally the polls reached 70 percent. At the end of Reagan's presidency, however, a bare majority was expressing approval of the First Lady, and about three in ten said they disapproved.

Bush strategists in the 1988 campaign feared that Barbara Bush would be a detriment primarily because "her white hair and wrinkles tended to remind voters of her husband's age."[7] In an NBC October 1988 poll, 48 percent of likely voters said they had a favorable impression of her, 11 percent had an unfavorable impression, and 41 percent said they were unsure.[8] When she entered the White House in January 1989, 34 percent of the public had a favorable opinion, only 3 percent were unfavorable, and the remainder were undecided or had not heard enough to give an opinion.[9] After being in the White House for six months, she received an excellent or pretty good job rating from 66 percent of the public, while 28 percent rated her as doing an only fair or poor job.[10] By the 1992 campaign, Barbara Bush was considered a great asset, obtaining an 85 percent favorable rating in an August 1992 poll.[11] Seldom did as many as 20 percent of the people view her unfavorably during the Bush administration.

Prior to Hillary Rodham Clinton's becoming First Lady, the polls of the public's views of the First Lady were rather sporadic. In addition, different question wordings make it difficult to make comparisons.

FAVORABLE AND UNFAVORABLE RATINGS OF HILLARY RODHAM CLINTON

Pollsters have most frequently inquired about the public's general opinion of Hillary Clinton. More than any other question, the public has been asked if they have a favorable or unfavorable opinion of her. Four polls have most consistently explored public opinion of Ms. Clinton: Yankelovich/*Time*/CNN, NBC/WSJ, Gallup/*USA Today*/CNN, and CBS/*NYT*. As with the president, they have conducted polls on how she is doing on almost a monthly basis. This regular polling represents concern with the "copresidency" nature of the Clinton administration.

As early as February 1992, national pollsters were ascertaining Hillary's favorability ratings with the public. Yankelovich/*Time*/CNN and NBC/WSJ found that about one-quarter of the public had a favorable opinion, while 9 percent in the former poll and 18 percent in the latter poll expressed an unfavorable opinion.

Between February 1992 and June 1994, these four national polls explored Hillary Clinton's favorability with the public sixty-four times. In only two of these polls did unfavorable opinions surpass favorable ones. NBC/WSJ reported a rating of 29 percent unfavorable to 24 percent favorable in April 1992, and a 30 percent to 22 percent negative advantage in July 1992. But at the same time that NBC/WSJ was reporting higher unfavorable than favorable ratings of the future First Lady, Yankelovich/*Time*/CNN was reporting a 43 percent to 23 percent favorable advantage, and CBS/*NYT* had her favorable rating at 29 percent and her unfavorable rating at 14 percent.[12]

Evaluating the Polls

These differences in the polls illustrate one of the basic issues in polling: the effect of question wording. Whereas Yankelovich, Gallup, and CBS ask about favorable and unfavorable opinions, NBC asks respondents to rate their feelings toward a person as either very positive, somewhat positive, neutral, somewhat negative, or very negative (see Box entitled "National Polls Favorability Question Wording"). When given only one positive and one negative option as in the two former polls, people are more likely to go with the positive option; however, a rating scale allows respondents to spread themselves out in the middle ranges and into less positive ratings without being totally negative.[13] In evaluations of Hillary Rodham Clinton, the larger number of options often but not consistently produced higher unfavorables (Figures 1 and 2).

A second methodological issue also becomes evident as one looks across these opinion ratings. Since January 1993, CBS/*NYT* has consistently had the smallest portion of respondents making a judgment. This national poll differs from Yankelovich and Gallup by inviting survey participants to say they are undecided. It is not just a volunteered response. "Experimental research shows that many more people will say 'don't know' when that alternative is explicitly offered than when it is not."[14] That research is borne out in these polls. Yankelovich gives people the option of saying they are not familiar enough to give an opinion, and NBC allows people to give a neutral response.

Hillary Clinton received her highest favorability rating to date in a January 1993 Gallup Poll. Here 67 percent of the public had a favorable opinion. Her favorability ratings remained high in the first months of the administration as she took on the high-profile job of heading the president's Health Care Task Force. They dipped a little at the hundred-day mark in May and then climbed

---

National Polls Favorability Question Wording

Yankelovich/*Time*/CNN:
  Please tell me whether you have generally favorable or generally unfavorable impressions of that person, or whether you are not familiar enough with that person to say one way or the other.
NBC/WSJ:
  I'm going to read you the names of several people and institutions who are active in public affairs. I'd like you to rate your feelings toward each one as either very positive, somewhat positive, neutral, somewhat negative, or very negative. If you don't know the name, please just say so.
Gallup/*USA Today*/CNN:
  I'd like your overall opinion of some people in the news. In general, do you have a favorable or unfavorable opinion of . . . ?
CBS/*NYT*:
  Is your opinion of Hillary Clinton favorable, not favorable, undecided, or haven't you heard enough about Hillary Clinton yet to have an opinion?

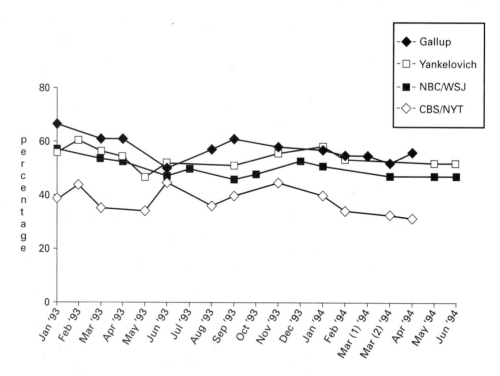

Figure 1 Trend in Favorability Ratings for Hillary Clinton

Source: Prepared by the Wisconsin Survey Research Laboratory

somewhat through the summer and fall of 1993. (At the same time, during the first year, between two and three out of ten people viewed Hillary Clinton unfavorably [Figure 3]). By the end of the first year, she was being referred to as "the very popular" First Lady.

The First Lady's ratings have compared favorably with the president's, surpassing him during the first year but falling behind as Whitewater[15] took center stage in media reports (Figure 4). The close parallel between the ratings of the two indicates the degree to which Hillary Rodham Clinton is viewed in partisan terms rather than as a traditional First Lady above the political fray.

In contrast to the favorable attention she received in the first year, the first half of the second year of the Clinton administration proved a trying time for Hillary Rodham Clinton as the Whitewater affair attracted much media attention and the president's health care plan ran into trouble on Capitol Hill. Her favorability ratings started to dip below 50 percent and fell considerably lower in the CBS/*New York Times* polls, which, probably because of methodological reasons cited earlier, have consistently been lower. Her unfavorable ratings also started to climb, with four out of ten expressing a negative opinion in some polls. The First Lady's popularity was suffering right along with the president's (see Figures 5–16).

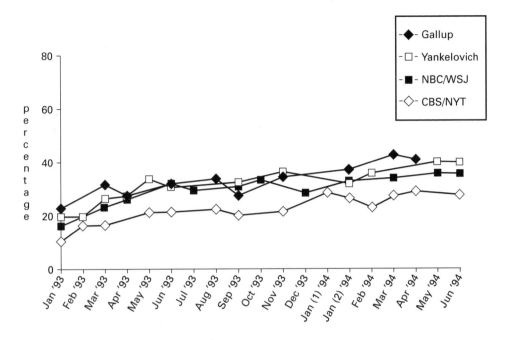

Figure 2   Trend in Unfavorability Ratings for Hillary Clinton

Source: Prepared by the Wisconsin Survey Research Laboratory

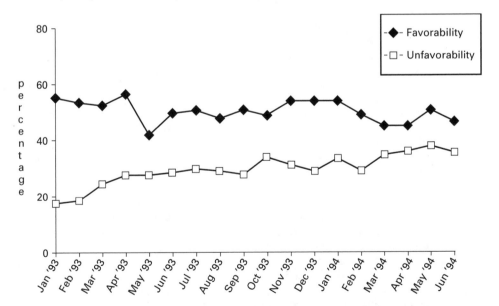

Figure 3   Average Favorability and Unfavorability Ratings for Hillary Clinton

Source: Prepared by the Wisconsin Survey Research Laboratory

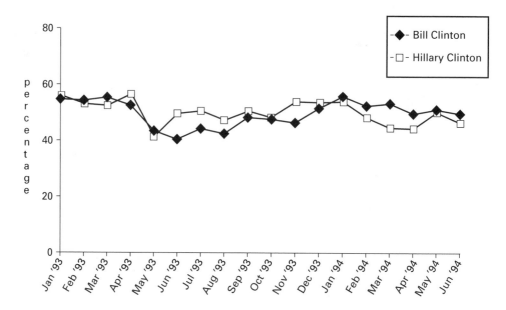

Figure 4   Average Favorability Ratings for Hillary and Bill Clinton

Source: Prepared by the Wisconsin Survey Research Laboratory

ADVISER TO THE PRESIDENT

Not only have national polls explored overall impressions, they have also examined Hillary Rodham Clinton's role as First Lady, perceptions about her involvement in public policy, and how much influence she has had on the president.

During the campaign and prior to the inauguration, the public did not favor a cabinet post for the First Lady but did support the idea of her being involved in policy making. To summarize the poll results, two-thirds were not worried about Hillary Clinton having too large a role in the Clinton administration. The public seemed not to have a problem with the future First Lady being a major adviser to the president (see box entitled "Hillary Clinton as Policy Adviser Preadministration" on page 273). One might wonder what all the fuss was about during the campaign.[16]

Based on the results of its December 1992 poll, the *Wall Street Journal* concluded that the prospect of Hillary Clinton's being an influential White House adviser was "fine by most Americans." The poll revealed that "By 63 percent to 24 percent, Americans believe Mrs. Clinton has the knowledge and personal characteristics that qualify her to be an adviser to her husband." But a strong majority opposed her being named to any official position in her husband's administration (59 percent opposed, 32 percent favored).

The message from the people became more mixed once the Clintons entered the White House with the public quite divided about the First Lady's policy-mak-

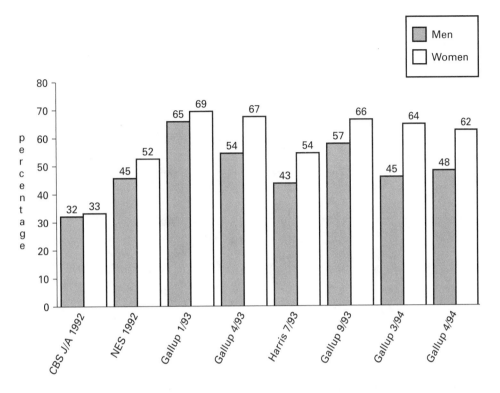

Figure 5 Hillary Clinton Favorability Ratings by Sex

Source: Prepared by the Wisconsin Survey Research Laboratory

ing role, influence, and power (see box entitled "Hillary Clinton as Policy Adviser, Administration" on page 274). In January 1993, as the new administration got under way, *US News & World Report* found the people fairly evenly split as to whether Hillary Clinton's playing a major role in advising her husband about appointments and politics would help or hurt his presidency—47 percent said she would help; 40 percent said she would hurt. (This question was not addressed in personal terms; some respondents could have been responding to general impressions of how others would view her role.) Only 37 percent favored her sitting in on cabinet meetings, and 34 percent believed she should be a major adviser on appointments and policy.

Involvement in Policy Making

Gallup Polls found that after Hillary Clinton's first nine months in the White House, including leadership on the Health Care Task Force, a position in which she primarily had received praise, and having obtained an overall positive image, absolutely no change had occurred in the percentage who felt she should be actively involved in policy making—a large segment of the populace disapproved of her

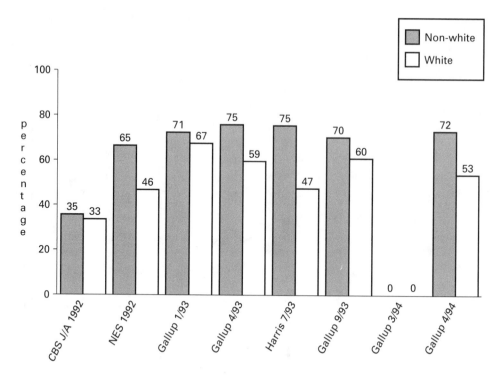

Figure 6   Hillary Clinton Favorability Ratings by Race

Source: Prepared by the Wisconsin Survey Research Laboratory

participating in policy making. Both in January and at the end of September, 49 percent of the people said she should not be involved in policy making. But by December 1993, a substantial majority (59 percent) approved of the way Hillary Rodham Clinton was handling her duties as an adviser to the president (while 28 percent disapproved), and 62 percent approved of the way she was handling her duties as first lady (24 percent disapproved).

Influence

In January 1993, at the beginning of the administration, 37 percent felt Hillary Clinton had too much influence in the Clinton administration. In September, 41 percent felt that way. In November 1993 an ABC News/*Washington Post* poll reported that a majority of the public (52 percent) believed she had too much influence over the president, while one-third thought she had the right amount and 10 percent felt she did not have enough influence. We once more must note the effect of question wording, however. In this poll one had to volunteer the response that she had the right amount of influence. In Gallup's version, the "right amount" option was given to respondents by the interviewer: 48 percent gave that response in their September 1993 poll and 49 percent in their January 1994 poll. Our conclusions

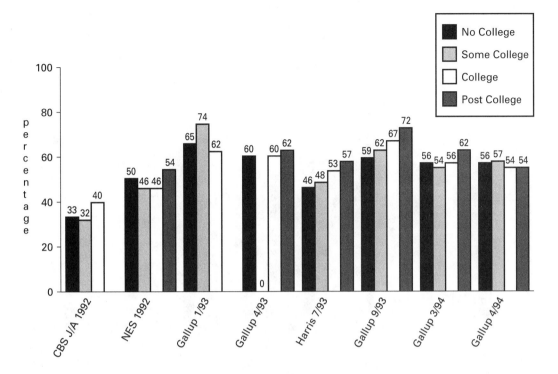

Figure 7   Hillary Clinton Favorability Ratings by Education

Source: Prepared by the Wisconsin Survey Research Laboratory

about the public's opinion of her influence are conditioned by the way in which the question is framed. It is important to examine different polls to assess public feelings.

At the beginning of the second year of the Clinton administration, a majority of the people (55 percent) disagreed with the statement "President Clinton depends too much on his wife Hillary when it comes to policy decisions;" 32 percent disagreed strongly, and 23 percent disagreed somewhat. At the same time, 36 percent either agreed strongly (22 percent) or agreed somewhat (14 percent). Asked about her power, 42 percent stated she had too much, while 47 percent felt she had about the right amount and 4 percent believed she had too little in a January 1994 national poll.

However, in the midst of the Whitewater affair, 53 percent said she had too much influence as opposed to only 39 percent who felt she had the right amount.[17] Negative opinions about her influence receded slightly by mid-April, when 49 percent responded that she had too much influence and 42 percent said she had the right amount. At the same time, only 35 percent of the public believed Hillary Rodham Clinton was "knowledgeable and experienced and should be actively involved in policy-making," while 62 percent believed she "was not elected by the

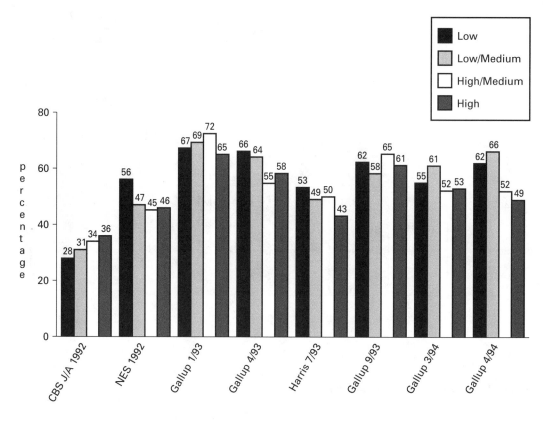

Figure 8   Hillary Clinton Favorability Ratings by Income

Source: Prepared by the Wisconsin Survey Research Laboratory

American people and, therefore, should not be actively involved in policy-making," a rather devastating critique. Clearly, the Whitewater affair had taken its toll.

TASK FORCE ON HEALTH CARE REFORM

In the first weeks of his presidency, Bill Clinton appointed Hillary Rodham Clinton head of his Task Force on Health Care Reform. Other First Ladies, most notably Rosalynn Carter, had their own public policy projects. But never before had a First Lady been put in charge of a major administrative initiative. Public reaction would be crucial to her success and for the institutionalization of this role for presidential spouses.

Pollsters quickly moved to gauge the opinion of the public to this decision of President Clinton (see box entitled "Hillary Clinton and The Health Care Task Force" on page 275). What they found was high support for the First Lady's assuming this job but somewhat less confidence among the public that it would make

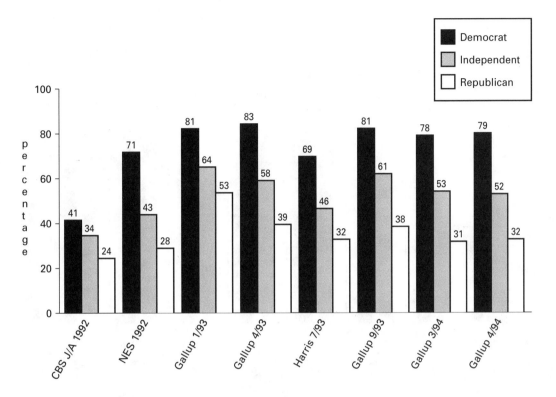

Figure 9   Hillary Clinton Favorability Ratings by Party

Source: Prepared by the Wisconsin Survey Research Laboratory

a difference, and a decline in that confidence over time. In the early stages of the debate (or perhaps before the debate really started), the public approved the job she was doing. By the time the First Lady appeared to testify before House and Senate committees at the end of September, 60 percent approved of her handling of health care policy, while 29 percent disapproved (Gallup Poll); 74 percent said she was doing an excellent or pretty good job (Harris Poll). A month later, Harris found that the percentage of the public saying she was doing an excellent or good job had declined slightly to 68 percent. By early April 1994, however, approval had plummeted to 47 percent and disapproval had climbed to 47 percent;[18] the percentage rating the job she was doing developing and presenting the president's health care plan as either excellent or good had dropped to 53 percent (Harris) after the plan had undergone enormous attacks and White House attention had been diverted by the Whitewater affair and foreign policy problems.

As the health care debate continued to be played out in the 103rd Congress (and ultimately ended in defeat for the Clintons), a majority still felt Hillary Clinton was helping rather than hurting efforts to improve the nation's health care system (55 percent), while 36 percent believed she was hurting efforts. The public was

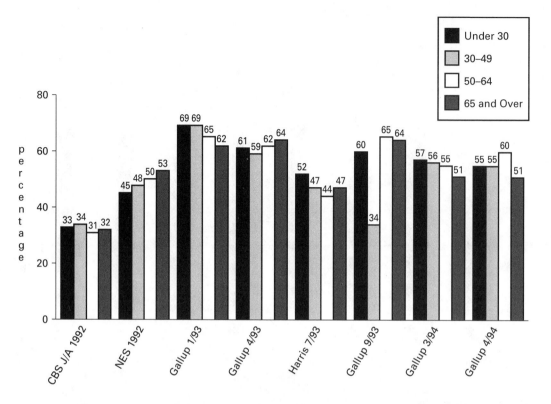

Figure 10   Hillary Clinton Favorability Ratings by Age

Source: Prepared by the Wisconsin Survey Research Laboratory

also divided on whether putting Hillary Clinton in charge of it had made health care reform more likely, made it less likely, or hadn't made any difference—24 percent said she had made health care reform more likely, 35 percent said less likely, and 38 percent said no difference. In July 1994, 52 percent still rated the job she was doing in developing and presenting the president's health plan as excellent or pretty good (while 42 percent rated her efforts as only fair or poor), a slight reversal of the April findings.

In November 1994 the White House announced that Hillary Rodham Clinton would no longer head the Health Care Task Force. The president's wife and her task force had created an enormously complex scheme to revamp the health care system in the United States. They had developed much of it in secret, although the First Lady had traveled extensively around the country, listening to and talking with American citizens as she led the Task Force. The secrecy and the complexity had worked against the ability of the Clintons to sell the plan.

The president had gambled when he put the First Lady in charge of one of the most important and difficult initiatives of his administration. The gamble was not in her ability to perform the task, but in the effect on the administration if she failed,

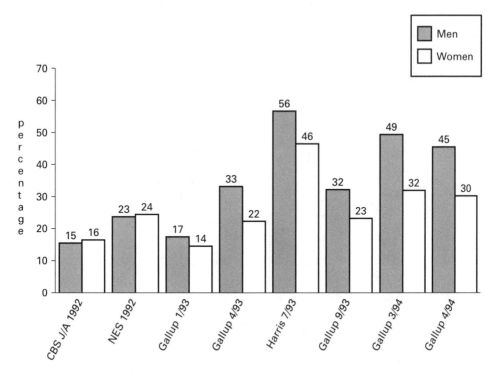

Figure 11   Hillary Clinton Unfavorability Ratings by Sex

Source: Prepared by the Wisconsin Survey Research Laboratory

and in the impact on the office of the First Lady. Would it be more difficult to achieve other goals if the First Lady were not successful, and who would be held accountable? What would it imply about Bill Clinton's leadership abilities? It would certainly affect gender politics. The immediate fallout from the defeat of the Clinton plan for health care reform appeared to be disillusionment with his administration in general rather than condemnation of the First Lady. She was criticized for what she wrought but not so much that she was the one who wrought it—probably because the whole administration seemed to be in disarray. This failure, however, suggests that the First Lady will have to find other, perhaps less public, ways of exerting influence. That occurrence would be a setback for legitimizing the public nature of the job of First Lady and institutionalizing her role as a policy maker.

PERSONAL QUALITIES

In addition to her actions, Hillary Rodham Clinton's personal character and qualities have been the subject of polls. She has been "dissected" as has no other First Lady. We might have expected First Ladies' personalities to have been the subject

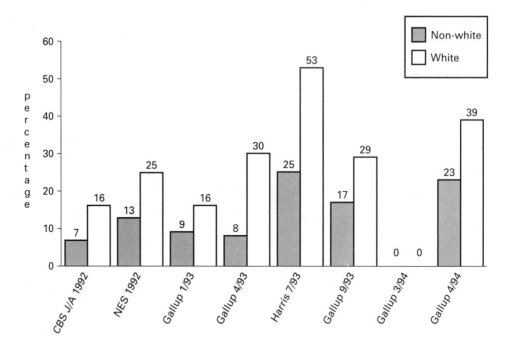

Figure 12   Hillary Clinton Unfavorability Ratings by Race

Source: Prepared by the Wisconsin Survey Research Laboratory

of polls, given a traditional concern with their characters, but prior to Hillary Rod-ham Clinton that seemed not to be the case. The broad range of aspects of her per-sonality addressed in the various polls reflects the intersection between the per-sonal and public domains of the First Lady role.

In *Vanity Fair*, Gail Sheehy reported the results of an early national poll (March 27–29, 1992) of the people's perceptions of the Democratic candidate's wife:

> 55 percent think she is an asset to her husband's campaign: 24 percent think she's a li-ability. . . . Those surveyed use the following descriptions of Hillary: intelligent (75 percent); tough-minded (65 percent); a good role model for women (48 percent); a fem-inist in the best possible sense (44 percent). The negatives: power-hungry (44 percent); too intense (36 percent); a wife who dominates her husband (28 percent).[19]

Hillary Rodham Clinton was already etching a strong picture in the minds of the voters. During the campaign and in the first year of the administration the pub-lic primarily attributed positive traits to her, as well as strong political ones. She was viewed as intelligent (40 percent thought she was smarter than her husband), ambitious, and tough, but also warm and likable or friendly. A majority also thought she cared about people like themselves, shared their values, and was a

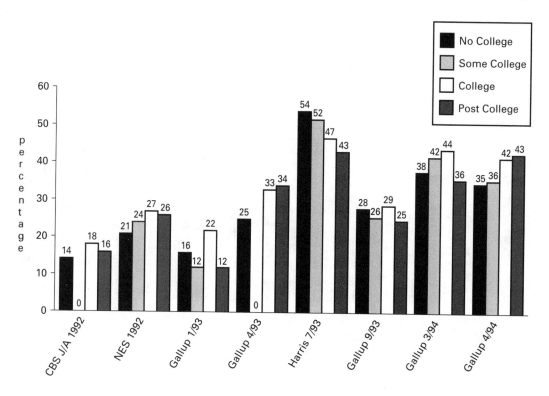

Figure 13   Hillary Clinton Unfavorability Ratings by Education

Source: Prepared by the Wisconsin Survey Research Laboratory

good role model for girls and women in general. She has also been viewed as being power-hungry and manipulative, but in a June 1992 *Time*/CNN poll 56 percent of respondents stated that they did not think she was too ambitious to make a good First Lady, while 21 percent felt she was too ambitious. And in a March 1993 poll, Gallup reported that 60 percent of respondents felt she inspired confidence and 67 percent viewed her as an effective manager. Overall, she scored high on the more expressive characteristics. She has also scored fairly high on the more masculine characteristics, not always in a negative sense, although a reservoir of negativity is present.

The Whitewater affair took a toll on positive ratings of these qualities. The difficulties arising from previous financial involvements pushed favorable ratings on those characteristics downward, especially the qualities of honesty and trust-worthiness, which declined from 82 percent when she first entered the White House to 52 percent, a bare majority in April 1994. In June 1992 NBC News/*Wall Street Journal* reported 42 percent believing she was either very or mostly honest, while 55 percent thought she was either just somewhat honest or not very honest.

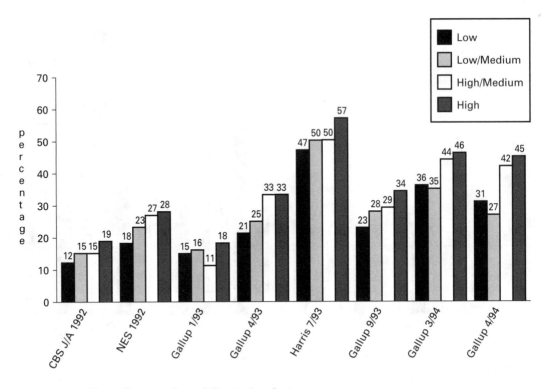

Figure 14   Hillary Clinton Unfavorability Ratings by Income

Source: Prepared by the Wisconsin Survey Research Laboratory

Whitewater and Perceptions of the First Lady's Character

The Clinton administration was dogged by many problems in its first eighteen months. One major concern was the reemergence in 1994 of questions about the president and the First Lady's investments in the Whitewater real estate venture and attempts by Hillary Rodham Clinton to help a partner in that deal with legal problems his savings and loan firm was having in the mid-1980s while she was a law partner in the Rose law firm and Bill Clinton was governor of Arkansas. New questions also emerged about Hillary Rodham Clinton's trading in commodities markets in the late 1970s. These allegations hurt the Clintons' credibility and resulted in the appointment of a special prosecutor to investigate them. The press (and Republicans), of course, have made a major issue of these events, and pollsters have undertaken innumerable testings of the public's response to them in the first half of 1994 and beyond. The polls have asked about people's knowledge and interest in the affair, their views of media coverage of it, the importance of the issue, and opinions of the First Lady's and the president's ethical and legal behavior in the matter. Here we concentrate on the latter set of issues regarding Hillary Rodham Clinton.

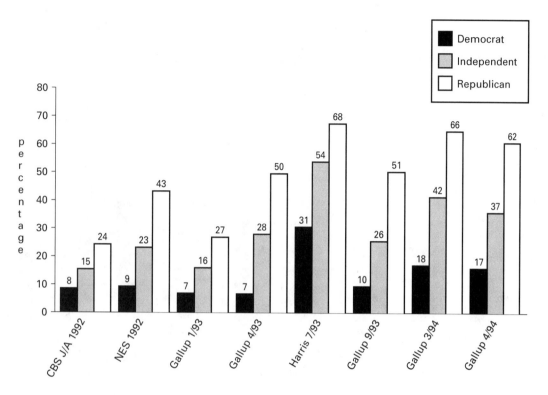

Figure 15   Hillary Clinton Unfavorability Ratings by Party

Source: Prepared by the Wisconsin Survey Research Laboratory

Between January and May 1994, approximately one-third of the public felt she had done something illegal in the Whitewater matter. Twenty-two percent felt this way in January; that proportion increased to 37 percent at the end of March and declined slightly to 35 percent early in May. At the same time, approximately four out of ten thought she had not done something illegal. That percentage increased to a majority (51 percent) at the end of March when opinions were most polarized (with only 12 percent volunteering that they either had no opinion or were unsure). Belief in her innocence declined to 42 percent in May, while uncertainty increased to 22 percent.

Between April and September 1994, CBS/*New York Times* inquired whether the public thought Bill and Hillary Clinton did or did not do something wrong in connection with the real estate development Whitewater, or didn't know enough about it yet to say. With the offered option of "don't know enough," percentages believing something had or had not been done wrong declined. Mainly the public felt that they did not know enough to give an opinion (see box entitled "Evaluations of Actions in the Whitewater Development" on page 276). Very few immediately

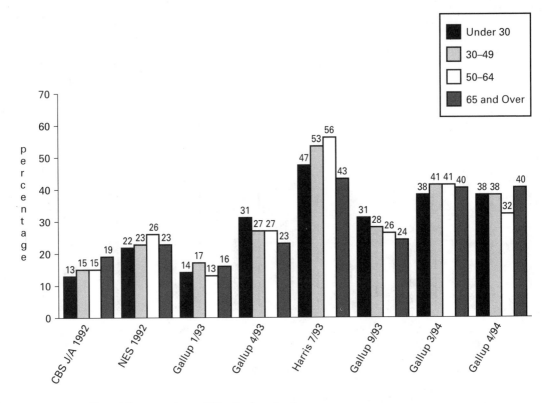

Figure 16   Hillary Clinton Unfavorability Ratings by Age

Source: Prepared by the Wisconsin Survey Research Laboratory

believed the Clintons had done something wrong as the story began to take center stage. The percentages increased some over time, but never to more than three out of ten persons.

Allegations of wrongdoing in the Whitewater real estate development and commodities trading clearly affected the ability of the Clinton administration to concentrate on promoting its public policy program in its second year. The First Lady even had to hold a press conference to answer questions about her involvement. While the administration did have significant legislative successes in its first two years, they were not translated into political success at the polls. The 1994 midterm elections were a debacle for Democrats. With the Republicans in control of the Congress in 1995 and the special prosecutor continuing his investigation, events around Whitewater will continue to plague the Clinton administration and affect Hillary Rodham Clinton's ability to play a major policy-making role as First Lady.

Hillary Clinton as Policy Adviser, Preadministration

Gallup, 7/92: Do you favor or oppose having a First Lady who is involved in the President's policy decisions and the day-to-day operations of the White House staff?

Approve 58%   Oppose 35%   Not sure 7%

Gallup, 11/10/92: Which worries you more—that Hillary Clinton won't have a large enough role in the Clinton administration or that she will have too large a role, or does neither worry you very much?

Role not large enough	4%
Too large a role	26%
Neither	67%
No opinion	3%

Newsweek, 11/20/92: Do you think Hillary Clinton is playing too great a role in the transition process?

Not too great 62%   Too great 25%

U.S. *News & World Report*, 1/25/93: Do you favor or oppose these roles for Hillary Clinton?

	Favor	Oppose
Sitting in on cabinet meetings	37%	58%
Being a traditional First Lady	70	21
Being an advocate for policies and programs to benefit children	90	7
Being a major adviser on appointments and policy	34	59
Testifying before Congress on issues that concern her	71	22

GROUP SUPPORT AND OPPOSITION TO THE FIRST LADY

Given the dramatic change Hillary Rodham Clinton has made in how we think about the role of First Lady, one would expect diversity of opinion among the people's evaluations of her and what she stands for regarding women in political leadership. We have found a good deal of variation in people's evaluations of her and her actions. Substantial numbers have felt warm toward her, and a significant minority have not. In this section we examine levels of support among groups of Americans.

Some First Ladies have been viewed as being above politics, with partisanship having had little effect on their support. People in general felt warm toward them. The public had no reason to substantially oppose such a First Lady unless they were to project their opinions of her husband onto her. However, we should expect differences between Democrats and Republicans in their views of Hillary Rodham Clinton, given her partisan nature and her involvement in public policy. We would also hypothesize that women would express more positive feelings than

Hillary Clinton as Policy Adviser, Administration

In your opinion, does Hillary Clinton have too much, too little, or the right amount of influence in the Clinton administration?

Gallup	1/29/93	9/29/93	1/15/94	3/8/94	4/22/94
Too much	37%	41%	44%	53%	49%
Too little	4	4	5	4	5
Right amount	48	48	49	39	42
No opinion	11	7	3	4	4

Which one of the following statements comes closer to your view: Hillary Clinton is knowledgeable and experienced and should be actively involved in policy making—or—Hillary Clinton was not elected by the American people and should, therefore, not be actively involved in policy making?

Gallup	1/29/93	9/29/93	4/22/94
Should be involved	46%	47%	35%
Should not	49	49	62
No opinion	5	3	3

Times Mirror, 12/2/93: Do you approve or disapprove of the way Hillary Clinton is handling her duties as an adviser to the president?

Approve 59%	Disapprove 28%	Don't know/refused 13%

ABC News/*Washington Post*, 11/11/93: Just your best guess, would you say that Hillary Clinton has too much influence over (President) Bill Clinton, not enough influence, or what?

Too much	52%
Not enough	10
About the right amount (vol)	33
No opinion	5

Tarrance Group & Mellman, Lazarus & Lake, 1/17/94: As First Lady, do you think Hillary Rodham Clinton has too much power, about the right amount of power or too little power?

Too much	42%	About right	47%
Too little	4	Unsure	8

men, especially younger women, and that baby boomers would give her the highest ratings. They would identify with her.

That Hillary Rodham Clinton would not be viewed as a nonpartisan First Lady admired by the vast majority of Americans was apparent early on as the Clintons made their run for the White House. It was quickly noted that she would be admired more by some groups than by others. According to a *USA Today* headline

Hillary Clinton and the Health Care Task Force

Gallup, 1/29/93: As you may know, President Clinton has appointed Hillary to head his task force on health care reform. In your opinion, is this an appropriate position for a First Lady, or not?

Yes 59%   No 37%   DK 4%

Yankelovich variation, 4/28/93
Appropriate 58%   Inappropriate 38%   DK 4%

Do you think Hillary Clinton will do a good job coming up with a health care plan, or not?

Yes 62%   No 21%

Newsweek, 9/9/93: Do you approve or disapprove of (President) Bill Clinton naming his wife, Hillary, to lead administration efforts to reform the country's health care system?

Approve 56%   Disapprove 38%   No opinion 6%

Time, 5/10/93: How much confidence do you have in Hillary Clinton's ability to handle her role in health care policy and other domestic issues?

A lot 33%   Some 49%   None 16%

CBS: Do you think with Hillary Clinton chairing the commission, health care reform is more likely, less likely, or won't that make much difference?

	Feb '93	Mar '93	Aug 2 '93	Sept '94
More likely	45%	46%	34%	24%
Less likely	6	7	11	35
Won't make much difference	40	39	50	38
DK/NA	9	8	5	3

CNN/*USA TODAY*: How do you think Hillary Clinton is handling health care policy?

	Sept 12	Sept 28	Apr 22 '94
Approve	50%	60%	47%
Disapprove	33	29	47
Other	17	11	

Harris: How would you rate the job Hillary Rodham Clinton has done in developing and presenting the president's health plan—excellent, pretty good, only fair or poor?

10/10/93: Excellent 36%   Pretty good 38%   Only fair 17%   Poor 7%
11/11/93: Excellent 24%   Pretty good 44%   Only fair 21%   Poor 9%
 4/4/94: Excellent 17%   Pretty good 36%   Only fair 25%   Poor 18%

Evaluation of Actions in the Whitewater Development

CBS: Do you think (President) Bill and Hillary Clinton did or did not do something wrong in connection with the real estate development Whitewater, or don't you know enough about it yet to say?

	1/15/94	2/15/94	4/21/94	7/26/94	9/8/94
Did something wrong	17%	15%	30%	20%	28%
Did not do something wrong	12	12	21	13	18
Don't know enough yet	68	69	45	61	51
Don't know/no answer	3	4	4	6	3

ABC/*Washington Post*: Again, your best guess, do you think Hillary Rodham Clinton did anything illegal in the Whitewater matter or not?

	1/23/94	3/7/94	3/27/94	5/4/94
Yes	22%	36%	37%	35%
No	43	42	51	42
No opinion, not sure	35	22	12	22

in March 1992, she rated highest among women and the young. By November 1992, however, that same newspaper noted, "Women and older people have the most favorable opinion of Hillary Clinton." Among women most likely to identify with the First Lady designate were easterners, college graduates, and urbanites, according to *USA Today*. Those least likely to identify with her were midwesterners, suburbanites, high school dropouts, and baby boomers. Nearly a year later, however, the First Lady was back to being most popular among the young, *USA Today* reported.

Figures 5 and 6 on pages 261–262 show favorable and unfavorable ratings of Hillary Rodham Clinton among a variety of groups during the campaign and the first sixteen months of the Clinton administration as found in a number of polls. Women have quite consistently felt more favorable toward Hillary Rodham Clinton than have men. At the time of the inauguration, at the height of her popularity, both men and women were very favorable. Support among men then began to decline, while support among women has been maintained at a fairly high level. Support has been higher among minorities than among whites. Support has varied little by education and income levels, nor has age been a major factor in distinguishing between supporters and detractors. Party affiliation has been the major factor in accounting for support for Hillary Rodham Clinton. Except at the time of the inauguration, when even a majority of Republicans felt favorable toward the new First Lady, Republicans have disliked Hillary Rodham Clinton about as much as Democrats have liked her. Independents have consistently been in between the two parties in their ratings.

In June 1993 only 23 percent of Republican men and 39 percent of Republican women had a favorable opinion of the First Lady, compared with 60 percent of Democratic men and 75 percent of Democratic women. A large gap existed between the support of independent men and independent women. Only 35 percent of the former, but 60 percent of the latter, had a favorable opinion. Early in the administration, the First Lady seemed to be advantaged by the support she received from independent women and disproportionate support from Republican women (relative to Republican men).

THE FUTURE

The first year of the Clinton administration was a positive one for an activist First Lady publicly involved in policy making. Hillary Rodham Clinton seemed to be successfully moving the role of First Lady into new directions compatible with contemporary visions of new social and political roles for women. Although we have not examined the extent to which Hillary Rodham Clinton combined her policy-making role with traditional First Lady duties of hostess and homemaker, the White House did make a concerted effort to be attuned to public desires that that aspect of the role of First Lady not be diminished. Newspaper headlines and cover stories with appropriate accompanying pictures throughout the year attested to the merging of the two roles.[20]

The second year was not a good one for the administration in general, and the First Lady was a prominent actor in the problems it confronted regarding Whitewater and health care reform. Her role had to be reviewed after the midterm elections, along with a reassessment of the whole program of the president. Of course, the president himself had not projected an image of leadership on many occasions, and the concerns of the White House entailed much more than what role Hillary Rodham Clinton should play. Conservative Republicans, however, were continuing to talk negatively about the administration in terms of the *Clintons*, trying to connect the public's ambivalence to the changing roles of women to the First Lady in the White House and her policy entrepreneurship.

The public have been quizzed by pollsters not only about Hillary Clinton as First Lady but also about her political abilities apart from that role. The results show a continuing hesitancy on the part of the public about seeing an integration of this position with political leadership for women, although we have to be careful about generalizing to political leadership more broadly from individual responses to Hillary Clinton in this role.

When asked in a Gallup Poll at the end of September 1993 whether they would, "personally, like to see Hillary Clinton run for president someday, or not," 56 percent said no, 36 percent said yes, and less than a majority thought she was qualified to be president of the United States someday (47 percent qualified, 45 percent not qualified) (see box entitled "Hillary Rodham and the Future").

While the public was hesitant about her ability to be president, they were more supportive of the idea of her serving in a White House position. Asked whether they agreed with the statement "She would be qualified to serve in a high White House position, even if her husband were not president," 41 percent strongly

---

Hillary Rodham and the Future

Gallup, 9/29/93: Would you, personally, like to see Hillary Clinton run for president someday, or not?

Yes 36%   No 56%

Gallup: Do you think Hillary Clinton is qualified to be president of the United States someday, or not?

	9/29/93	1/15/94
Yes, qualified	47%	45%
No, not qualified	45	50

Gallup, 9/29/93: Please tell me whether you strongly agree, moderately agree, moderately disagree, or strongly disagree with the following statement about Hillary Clinton. She would be qualified to serve in a high White House position, even if her husband were not president.

Strongly agree	41%
Moderately agree	30
Moderately disagree	11
Strongly disagree	16
Don't know/refused	3

---

agreed, 30 percent moderately agreed, 11 percent moderately disagreed, and 16 percent strongly disagreed. Support declined, however, in March 1994 to 59 percent agreeing and 39 percent disagreeing.

One can conclude from these many and varied polls that rather than Hillary Rodham Clinton being viewed an albatross around Bill Clinton's neck, as she was described in early days of the campaign, she had developed a positive image among the public in the early stages of the Clinton administration. The people seemed to like her, and taking on a visible policy-making role, as she was naturally inclined to do, did not cause problems in the first year of the administration. She seemed to successfully traverse the course from a traditional nonpartisan image of First Lady into a more independent political role at least in *personal terms*.

One could assume that the positive response of the first year would have been sustained, and perhaps people would have been more comfortable with a greater policy-making role for the position of First Lady, had the Clintons not become embroiled in concerns over their investments in Arkansas, had the administration (and the First Lady) done a better job of developing and presenting a health care reform package, and had the president seemed more focused. Whether the personal problems of this First Lady will be overcome, and how much they will be translated into public uneasiness over a public policy-making role for the president's spouse obviously remains to be seen. Being a first means that personal foibles influence the institutional development of a position. And clearly her success is linked to the success of the president.

While 80 to 90 percent of the people have come to say they would support a woman as president, not all of the questions that have been asked about the role of the First Lady in these polls show a general acceptance of a more political role for that position or a ready transition from that job to being chief executive. That 45 percent of the public in September 1993 said Hillary Clinton was not qualified to be president is a telling statistic. The mixed messages of these polls highlight the complexity for women of achieving acceptance in executive leadership positions and how traditional private functions can interact with public ones. What positions for women can be successfully used as launching pads for winning the highest office in the land? Is it possible to take a largely ascriptive position, but one that maintains high visibility and access to the power centers of the nation, and turn it into an achievement-oriented one? Why can others be advisers to the president but not his spouse? Questions of the gendered nature of American politics emerge in broad scope as we explore the public's response to Hillary Rodham Clinton in the White House.

NOTES

1. "Hillary Clinton, Trail-blazer." *The Economist*, December, 1992. p. 30.

2. "Hillary Rodham Clinton." *Public Perspective*, July-August, 1993. p. 97.

3. Poll taken by Harris and Associates, July 1976. However, the people were queried on a number of occasions about Betty Ford's active support for women's rights.

4. However, Carl Anthony has reported that after Rosalynn Carter was sent by the president to visit heads of state in South America, a national poll "gave her a 74 percent approval rating as ambassador"; see Carl Sterrazza Anthony, *First Ladies: The Sage of the Presidents' Wives and Their Power, 1961–1990*, vol. 2 (New York: William Morrow, 1991), p. 274

5. Yankelovich, October 1979.

6. CBS/*New York Times*, October 1980.

7. Campbell, Karlyn Hohrs. *Shadowing with Stereotypes: The Press, the Public, and the Candidates' Wives*. Research Paper R-9. (Cambridge, MA: John F. Kennedy School of Government, Harvard University, 1993).

8. At the same time, 42 percent said they had a favorable opinion of Kitty Dukakis, 11 percent were unfavorable, and 47 percent were unsure.

9. CBS/*New York Times*, 1989.

10. Harris Poll, July 1989.

11. Gallup Poll, August 1992.

12. In addition, the *Los Angeles Times*, ABC/*Washington Post*, *Newsweek*, and *U.S. News & World Report* have sampled national opinion but not as consistently as these four polls.

13. This has been found in some of the presidential ratings between questions asking the public whether they approve or disapprove of the job the president is doing, and those asking the public to rate the job the president is doing as either excellent, good, fair, or poor. The latter set of response options tends to elicit lower ratings for the president.

14. Converse, Jean and Stanley Presser. *Survey Questions; Handcrafting the Standardized Questionnaire*. (Newbury Park, CA: Sage, 1984).

15. Whitewater was a real estate venture in which Bill and Hillary Clinton had a partnership to buy and develop the land. A partner in the deal, James McDongal, also owned a savings and loan institution that ran into financial problems in the mid-1980s. As an attorney at the Rose law firm in Little Rock, Arkansas, Hillary Rodham Clinton helped the savings and loan company with dealings with the state government. At issue are conflicts of interest.

16. A major part of the fuss was Republican concern with her public policy agenda. As Suzanne Garment put it, this type of criticism was actually progress for women and for First Ladies because Hillary Clinton was not being attacked for her character or her finances as other First Ladies had been, but for her views and positions; see Garment, "Attacking Hillary's Views Is Progress," *Los Angeles Times*, August 23, 1992.

17. Gallup Poll, March, 1994.

18. Ibid.

19. Sheehy, Gail. "What Hillary Wants." *Vanity Fair*, May, 1992. pp. 142–147; 212–217.

20. Gibbs, Nancy. "The Trials of Hillary." *Time*, March 21, 1994. pp. 28–37.

NOTES TO FIGURES 5 THROUGH 16

a. NES refers to the American National Election Study. For the first time in its series of election studies, the 1992 American National Election Study included the potential First Ladies in their "feeling thermometer" questions about a number of political leaders and other people in the news. (Interviewees are told that "ratings between 50 degrees and 100 degrees mean that you feel favorable and warm toward the person. Ratings between 0 degrees and 50 degrees mean that you don't feel favorable toward the person and that you don't care too much for that person. You would rate the person at the 50 degree mark if you don't feel particularly warm or cold toward the person. If we come to a person whose name you don't recognize, you don't need to rate that person.") Nine percent of survey respondents said they could not rate Hillary Clinton on the feeling thermometer scale, not knowing enough about her or not recognizing her name. Twenty-six percent rated her at 50 degrees, feeling neither warm not cold, while 43 percent felt warm toward her (rating their feelings above 50 degrees on the scale) and 23 percent felt cold (rating her below 50 degrees).

b. The Gallup Poll for January 1993 asked about approval or disapproval of the job she was doing as First Lady.

c. The Harris Poll asked, "How would you rate the job Hillary Rodham Clinton is doing as First Lady—excellent, pretty good, only fair, poor?

d. The CBS, NES, and Harris Polls include only Blacks in the non-White category.

e. The April 1994 Gallup Poll age categories were 18–29, 30–44, 45–59, and 60+.

f. Each poll used different groupings in its income scale.

FURTHER READINGS

Anthony, Carl Sferazza. *First Ladies: The Saga of the Presidents' Wives and their Power 1789–1961*, vol. 1. New York: William Morrow, 1990.

———. *First Ladies: The Saga of the Presidents' Wives and their Power 1961–1990*, vol. 2. New York: William Morrow, 1991.

Cantor, Dorothy, and Toni Bernay. *Women in Power*. Boston: Houghton Mifflin, 1992.

Caroli, Betty. *First Ladies*. New York: Oxford University Press, 1987.

Genovese, Michael A. *Women as National Leaders*. Newbury Park, CA: Sage, 1993.

Grimes, Ann. *Running Mates*. New York: William Morrow, 1990.

Witt, Linda, Karen Paget, and Glenna Matthews. *Running as a Woman: Gender and Power in American Politics*. New York: Free Press, 1994.

 **CHAPTER 8**

PUBLIC POLICY:
THE FEMINIST PERSPECTIVE

Public policy in this country significantly influences the lives of American women. Diane D. Blair's article deals with the politics of reproduction and the implications for women as policy makers determine what is personal and what is political for women. Blair compares Margaret Atwood's novel *The Handmaid's Tale* (1986) and Ben Wattenberg's book *The Birth Dearth* (1987). Both works deal with the politics of reproduction, but from completely different perspectives. Atwood, writing from a feminist perspective, describes an imaginary future of total misery and wretchedness for women, one in which women have been reduced to the function of breeders. On the other hand, Wattenberg, writing from what Blair describes as a "nationalistic perspective," deplores the current American "birth dearth," blaming it primarily on "working women" and proposing a variety of pro-natalist remedies. Both books use a simple style to convey a complex message. Blair argues that among the significant implications of these two books, especially when they are read in tandem, are the following:

1. That pro-natalism, justified by the United States' relatively low fertility rate, has climbed high on many conservative agendas
2. That this movement seriously jeopardizes many of the gains achieved by feminists in recent years
3. That the contemporary pro-natalist drive has long and powerful historical precedents.

Joan Hulse Thompson traces the history and origin of the Family and Medical Leave Act (FMLA). This legislation was passed in 1990 and again in 1992, but

President Bush vetoed the bill both times and the Congress was unable to override either veto. Both chambers passed the bill again in 1993, and President Clinton signed it, making it effective on August 5, 1993. The author describes the influence of the Congressional Caucus for Women's Issues (CCWI) in developing this legislation, building a bipartisan coalition across committee jurisdictions, and coordinating the efforts of outside advocacy groups. She concludes the CCWI symbolizes what has been called the "second stage" of the women's movement because it is a partnership of congresswomen and congressmen. Thompson's case study of this act provides insight into legislation before Congress—the benefits and challenges that come from forging coalitions and compromises.

We next move from birth control as an issue of politics and the intricacies of the FMLA to the role of the Supreme Court in shaping public policy. Despite the numerous laws prohibiting sex discrimination in a variety of public policy areas, Ruth Bamberger finds the insurance industry has retained the practice of discriminating by gender in determining coverage and premium rates. The industry argues its position on cost-efficiency and actuarial grounds. Civil rights and feminist groups have criticized such discrimination on grounds of fairness and prevailing social policy. Although these groups have pursued their cause through multiple channels of government, the Supreme Court is perceived to be a primary agent of policy change. The Court has signaled that sex may be at risk as an insurance classification, but its role as shaper of public policy in this issue has been incremental at best.

Finally, in this chapter, we examine affirmative action and the program designed to correct past inequities in treatment of women and other minorities. Roberta Ann Johnson offers a generic definition of affirmative action and then does three things. First, she traces the development of the federal affirmative action policy from the issuing of Executive Orders by Presidents Roosevelt, Kennedy, and Johnson to its full implementation in the Department of Labor. Second, she summarizes and evaluates all the affirmative action cases decided by the Supreme Court, starting with the *Bakke* decision. Finally, using Census Bureau and Department of Labor statistics and secondary sources, she considers the ways affirmative action increases opportunities for women. Throughout her essay, the author recognizes affirmative action for its redistributive thrust.

The Handmaid's Tale *and* The Birth Dearth: *Prophecy, Prescription, and Public Policy*

Diane D. Blair

Six children [are] the minimum number for people of "normal" stock; those of better stock should have more.

THEODORE ROOSEVELT, 1907

As that great author and scientist, Mr. Brisbane, has pointed out, what every woman ought to do is have six children.

SINCLAIR LEWIS, 1935

There is nothing to compare to the joy of having six children. If every American family did that, we'd certainly have the greatest nation in the world.

PHYLLIS SCHLAFLY, 1987[1]

This article looks at two recent works on the politics of reproduction: *The Handmaid's Tale*, by Margaret Atwood, and *The Birth Dearth*, by Ben Wattenberg.[2] Since the former is an imaginative work by a popular novelist and the latter is a research report by a senior fellow at the American Enterprise Institute, one might assume that they would have little in common. In fact, however, these two books provide some direct, and often disturbing, points of comparison.

Both, for example, open with a selection from the Book of Genesis. Wattenberg's choice is from Book 1, Chapter 28: "Be fruitful and multiply, and replenish the earth. . . ." Wattenberg does not dwell upon this specific scriptural imperative, but human reproduction, and the need for much more of it in the contemporary United States, is the theme of his book. *The Birth Dearth* consists of three major parts, all laden with demographic and other data. In the first part, Wattenberg documents (and deplores) what he calls the United States' "fertility free-fall," a recent sharp decline in the total fertility rate (TFR) to below the population replacement rate of 2.1 children per woman. In the second part, Wattenberg offers his explana-

Diane D. Blair is a professor of political science at the University of Arkansas.

tions for this "birth dearth" and outlines what he considers to be its most alarming economic, geopolitical, and personal consequences. Finally, Wattenberg suggests a long list of possible pro-natalist remedies for this present-day problem and impending crisis.

Atwood's scriptural epigram is both longer and more specifically woven into her novel. Indeed, the following biblical episode becomes both raison d'être and central ritual in the twenty-first-century political system she posits:

> And when Rachel saw that she bare Jacob no children, Rachel envied her sister; and said unto Jacob, Give me children or else I die. And Jacob's anger was kindled against Rachel; and he said, Am I in God's stead, who hath withheld from thee the fruit of the womb? And she said, Behold my maid Bilhah, go in unto her; and she shall bear upon my knees, that I may also have children by her (Genesis 30:1–3).

As the novel opens, fundamentalists, justifying their coup primarily on the grounds of an acute birth dearth, have seized power and established the Republic (actually the monotheocracy) of Gilead. The governing patriarchy, known as Commanders, has forced all women into rigidly stratified, socially useful functions. There are Wives, physically sterile but socially prominent women, who serve their Commander husbands as hostesses and household managers; Marthas, who do the cooking and cleaning; and Aunts, who run the Rachel and Leah Reeducation Centers in which women who have viable ovaries (that is, those who have given birth previously) and are "available" (divorced women, those married to divorced men, widows, and those deliberately widowed by the state) are trained to become proper Handmaids.

Handmaids, like the novel's narrator Offred (literally "of Fred," the name of the Commander to whom she is assigned) have only one function: to reproduce. As Offred wryly notes, she and her sister Handmaids are women of "reduced circumstances" (p. 8)—reduced, that is, to being nothing more than "two-legged wombs" (p. 136). Because their fecundity is so vital to natural survival, the Handmaids are well fed, relieved of all arduous work, and protected from physical danger. They are also, however, "protected" from many other ordinary activities which Offred, too late, realizes had been central to her previous happiness: reading, paid work, discussions of current events, privacy (as opposed to solitude), friendship (as opposed to a sterile "sisterhood"), and love (as opposed to enforced breeding).

During a Handmaid's period of maximum fertility, she is "serviced" by her Commander while lying between the spread legs of the Commander's Wife, a peculiar but strangely nonsexual arrangement. If sperm meets seed, there is an elaborate birthing ceremony nine months later in which the Handmaid delivers upon the Wife's welcoming knees. If repeated attempts at conception are unsuccessful, or if the resulting children are repeatedly born dead or deformed, the Handmaid is eventually exiled to a Third World colony to clean up toxic waste. In Gilead, a literal interpretation has been given to Rachel's "Give me children, or else I die."

THE SIMILARITY OF THE TWO WORKS

Other than their genesis in Genesis, their central premise of a population shortfall, and their popularity (*The Handmaid's Tale* ran thirty-six weeks on the *New York Times* best-seller list, and a shortened and serialized version of *The Birth Dearth* was syndicated in many U.S. newspapers), what do these two works have in common? First, both books are didactic; that is, they were designed to be instructive. Wattenberg acknowledges at the outset that his book is both "a speculation and a provocation" (p. 1). It is his genuine fear about the consequences of the birth dearth that has propelled him, a self-described optimist, into writing this "alarmist tract" (p. 10). According to Wattenberg, the very survival of Western civilization is at stake, and he chastises both liberals and conservatives for their failure to come right out and say what Wattenberg thinks urgently needs to be said: American women should be having more babies.

Atwood is somewhat more reticent in acknowledging the instrumentality of her intentions. "This book won't tell you who to vote for," she has said. "I do not have a political agenda of that kind."[3] Atwood, however, has long used her fiction for social criticism, and with specific reference to *The Handmaid's Tale* has observed: "Speculative fiction is a logical extension of where we are now. I think this particular genre is a walking along of a potential road, and the reader as well as the writer can then decide if that is the road they wish to go on. Whether we go that way or not is going to be up to us."[4]

This leads to the second point of clear comparability between the two works. Both are projectionist: They are grounded in present events and trends that are at least suggestive of a possible future. Wattenberg's projections are based on data and interpretations of data gathered from an impressive array of sources. Wherever he looks he finds evidence that in the "modern, industrial, free" nations (the United States, Canada, the nations of Western Europe, Japan, Australia, and Israel), the TFR is well below replacement rates. In contrast, the population of the "Soviet bloc" (the Soviet Union and Eastern Europe) will be increasing. Most alarming to Wattenberg, despite a "heartening" decline in Third World fertility, is that we are now

> awash in the fruit of those TFR's in the six-plus range from a generation ago. Today there are 1.1 billion women of child-bearing age in the less-developed world! Even if those women reduce their fertility as the U.N. projects, there will be a flood of Third World babies, a real flood. Third World population, which is now 3.7 *billion* persons, is slated to rise to over 8 *billion* people in the middle of the next century! (p. 44)

What concerns Wattenberg most deeply is that, if present reproductive trends continue, by 2025 the Westernized nations will constitute only 9 percent of the world's population, down from 22 percent in 1950 and 15 percent in the 1990s; and that 9 percent will not be enough to spread democratic values, technological advances, and economic benefits. Wattenberg ruefully notes, " 'Manifest destiny' was not the cry of a no-growth continent of old people" (p. 71).

Atwood's novel contains no charts and graphs. It is obvious, however, that she, like Wattenberg, is a very close follower of current events, from which she has gleaned a number of happenings and ideas, which she has woven into a grim dystopia. In the contemporary United States, for example, abortion clinics have frequently been bombed and burned. In Romania, doctors performing abortions until recently were subject to twenty-five years' imprisonment or even death.[5] In Atwood's imagined Gilead, abortionists are executed and their bodies hung from hooks on "The Wall," as a deterrent, or else they are dismembered in gruesome "particicution" ceremonies. In the United States, homosexuals are often subject to legal and social penalties; in Gilead, "gender treachery," being nonproductive, is a capital offense. In the last few years, courts in at least eleven U.S. states have ordered women, against their wishes, to submit to cesarean section surgery when doctors decided that conventional childbirth could harm the fetus, and there have been increasing instances of litigation by the state in behalf of "fetus patients" against the bearing mothers; in Gilead, Handmaids are nothing but fetus-bearing vessels and must sacrifice all personal choice and pleasure in the fetus's behalf.[6] As in Gilead, so in the United States today, many major companies bar women under forty-five from certain jobs that might diminish their fertility or damage a fetus; toxic wastes are increasingly being shipped to Third World nations; "pro-life" forces have frequently held symbolic "funerals" for fetuses; and at least one state legislature has now required "dignified" burial or disposal of fetal remains.[7]

As Atwood has emphasized, although her novel is futuristic, it is not utterly fantastic. "There are no spaceships, no Martians, nothing like that," she has pointed out. In fact, when asked if Gilead could possibly happen here, she responds that some of it "is happening now," and that, "There is nothing in *The Handmaid's Tale*, with the exception of one scene, that has not happened at some point in history."[8]

Obviously, both Wattenberg and Atwood have looked closely at certain contemporary events and circumstances, have extrapolated these events into a highly undesirable future, and have written their books to alert readers to the dangers the authors see ahead. Since in some ways the "solutions" Wattenberg advocates are related to the dangers Atwood warns against, it is somewhat surprising to find as much agreement as there is between the two regarding the major factors that have depressed present birth rates.

FACTORS PRODUCING THE BIRTH DEARTH

Both Wattenberg, with long lists and charts, and Atwood, by indirection throughout the novel and in a "scholarly" appendix at the novel's end, suggest that among the factors producing the "baby bust" have been better contraceptive techniques, more education and higher income for females, delayed marriage, more frequent divorce, more abortions due to legalization, increased infertility and more open homosexuality. Most interesting, however, is that both writers—Wattenberg centrally, Atwood peripherally—implicate the women's liberation movement as possibly pushing us into undesirable futures.

For Wattenberg, the cause-and-effect relationship is very clear and entirely adverse. According to his analysis, "One clear root thought of the original [women's liberation] movement was this: Marriage, raising a family, or a large family, was no longer necessarily considered to be the single most important thing in a woman's life" (p. 127). As he has written elsewhere,

> About twenty years ago, corresponding almost exactly with the Birth Dearth—many women began to forge a new economic contract for themselves. They exchanged what anthropologists tell us was the original female contract—trading childbearing capabilities for economic sustenance in the home—for a version of the male practice—trading physical and mental labor for economic sustenance in the market.[9]

Hence, women's liberation led to women's presence in the workforce; and "working women," according to Wattenberg, are "probably the single most important factor" causing the birth dearth.[10]

Such generalizations may disturb at least some of Wattenberg's readers, and certainly his feminist ones. Especially when the policy implications of Wattenberg's philosophy are being considered, however, it is good that he has made his central premises so plain. Wattenberg insists, for example, that he wants pro-natalist policies that will expand rather than limit women's choices, and he suggests scores of possibilities. If "working women" are the "single greatest cause" of the birth dearth, however, it seems obvious that all solutions will be partial until women leave the workforce and resume their "original contracts."

For Atwood, the line between contemporary women's liberation and future Gileadean oppression is much more circuitous. In the "old times" (which, of course, are our times), Offred was sufficiently "liberated" to have had a college degree, a job, and a lover who eventually became her husband. Although she chose to have a child, many of her friends—working women who did not want the economic and other burdens of children, or who feared the fragility of the environment or the inevitability of nuclear catastrophe—did not. Others, because of the fertility-depressing and abortifacient effects of environmental pollutants, nuclear radiation, and toxic wastes, could not conceive or bear a healthy child. Furthermore, the sexual freedom and excesses of the "old times" produced not only fertility-impeding sexually transmitted diseases but also an escalating atmosphere of contempt for and violence against women. Hence, among the chief demands of women's liberationists were increased respect for women and improved physical protection. Offred's own mother, she recalls, marched in demonstrations to "take back the night," enthusiastically participated in pornographic-book burnings, and often mouthed antimale slogans such as "A man is just a woman's strategy for making other women."

Society was "dying of too much choice," Offred recalls (p. 25):

> Women were not protected then. . . . Now we walk along the same street, in red pairs, and no man shouts obscenities at us, speaks to us, desires us. . . . There is more than one kind of freedom, said Aunt Lydia. Freedom to and freedom from. In the days of anarchy it was freedom to. Now you are being given freedom from. Don't underrate it (p. 24).

Following an emotional birthing ceremony from which all males, all doctors, and all anesthetics have been excluded, Offred utters one of the book's most poignant lines: "Mother, I think: Wherever you may be. Can you hear me? You wanted a woman's culture. Well, now there is one. It isn't what you meant, but it exists" (p. 127).

Atwood is a feminist, and the oppressions she describes can be much more clearly traced to the religious right than to the feminist left. Atwood's warning signals, however, are flashed at radical feminism as well as religious fundamentalism. Please remember, she seems to be saying, that the "protection" of women has always been the major justification for their oppression, and sometimes, however unfortunately, one must choose between freedom *from* and freedom *to*. Or, as Offred's Commander reminds her, "Better never means better for everyone. It always means worse for some" (p. 211).

As should be obvious by now, these two authors have written "message" books in order to convey diametrically different messages. Before further discussing those differences, however, one final similarity should be noted: Both authors employ a very simple style to clothe a highly complex message.

For many readers and book reviewers, it is the prosaic, unemotional tone with which Offred relates the most degrading and horrifying arrangements that makes the book so deeply disturbing. Leaving a particicution ceremony, where the Handmaids have been emotionally stampeded into tearing an accused rapist apart with their bare hands, they wish each other the conventional "You have a nice day" (p. 281). Thoughts can quickly turn from death to dinner, from bodies hanging on The Wall to sundresses and ice cream cones.

Oddly, while the novelist is presenting her grim forecast with restrained but imaginative force, it is the research fellow who hammers the reader with tones of breathless, desperate urgency. As the material already quoted indicates, Wattenberg's voice is shrill, overwrought, semihysterical. His favorite punctuation mark is the exclamation point. And in his determination to persuade the widest possible audience, his words and sentences often go beyond the simple to the simplistic. In outlining possible economic incentives to produce additional offspring, for example, Wattenberg holds out the promise of "a nice green check" (p. 154), "a green federal check" (p. 157), "a green Social Security check" (p. 157), and "real green cash money" (p. 158). "In a nonfree country," he lectures his apparently unsophisticated readers, "the ruler, or rulers, can sit down around a big table and make policy" (p. 143). One of his pieces of pictorial persuasion is a python (the United States) swallowing a pig (the post–World War II baby boom). Should the pictures not be sufficiently clear, Wattenberg supplies the sound effects: "Gobble, gobble, suck, suck" (p. 34).

DIFFERENCES BETWEEN THE TWO WORKS

The following short excerpts, the first from Atwood, the second from Wattenberg, illustrate not only the unadorned style employed by each author but also the profoundly different assumptions and values they bring to their work. In *The Hand-maid's Tale*, Offred has been taken by her Commander to an illegal nightclub where the women are dressed in everything from chorus girls' shifts to old cheerleading costumes. Offred is dumbfounded, amused, and wildly curious, but any display of emotions could be fatal. Hence, she warns herself, "All you have to do, I tell my-self, is keep your mouth shut and look stupid. It shouldn't be that hard" (p. 236). In the penultimate paragraph of *The Birth Dearth*, Wattenberg summarizes his solution to the impending crisis as follows: "After all, it's not such a big deal. All it involves is having another baby" (p. 169).

The reader quickly realizes that Atwood's "all" reverberates with the irony of centuries. In two simple lines, the author has captured the conventional wisdom passed down to women, and keeping them down, through the ages: Feign igno-rance; don't ask questions; accept your lot; suffer in silence; what you don't know can't hurt you. In contrast, Wattenberg seems oblivious to the irony, and revolu-tionary implications, of his "all." Because women not only bear children but gener-ally have had the major responsibility for nurturing and raising them to adulthood, the ability to control one's reproductive choices is the sine qua non of woman's ability to live in relative freedom. Almost all the advances of recent decades have recognized the centrality of reproductive freedom to any other meaningful kind of economic, political, or personal freedom for women. Yet Wattenberg, with off-hand ease, is apparently ready to jettison these hard-won achievements, and to do so with no apparent recognition of the magnitude of what he is advocating.

To be fair, Wattenberg rejects any overtly coercive solutions to the birth dearth. He opposes outlawing either contraception or abortion, and suggests that enthusiastically pro-natalist public education (using three-children-each Jeane Kirkpatrick and Sandra Day O'Connor as prominent role models, for example) could be effective when coupled with some lucrative economic incentives. Among the many possibilities he suggests are much more extensive and less expensive day care, very profitable tax incentives, forgiveness of college loans to child-producing couples, and reorganizing Social Security in recognition of the fact that people who have no children or even one child are "cheating": They are "free riders" who "end up drawing full pensions paid for by children who were raised and reared—at a large expense—by children of other people" (p. 154). Wattenberg suggests every-thing from personal ads in the *New York Times* (to destigmatize these possible paths to marriage and children) to kibbutz-style collectives in the suburbs, without ever advocating anything even approaching the Gileadean model of society.

His perspective, however, is a nationalistic one. His goal, he says, is to pre-serve and promote precious political and economic freedoms that can only survive if the "free world" remains stronger than the Communist world and than the less developed nations, which are only beginning to absorb the values and benefits of the Western model. If some individuals must sacrifice a little bit of liberty to secure the future of freedom, so be it.

Atwood is also centrally concerned with freedom; how easily it is underval-ued (Offred wistfully remembers going to a laundromat with her own dirty gar-ments and her own money in her own jeans pocket, or checking into a hotel room);

how quickly it can be taken away (shortly after the coup, all Compucounts [credit cards] coded female are canceled, rendering all women economically dependent in a noncash economy); and above all, how important it is to watch, as Offred regrets she has not, as Atwood hopes her readers will, for signs of its endangerment.

Here especially *The Handmaid's Tale* brilliantly demonstrates the relevance of good social science fiction to politics. By taking a few parts of contemporary reality, exaggerating them, and extrapolating them into a possible future, Atwood makes her readers see the present more clearly, and recognize the possible dangers in what may otherwise appear beneficent, or at least benign.

IMPLICATIONS OF THE TWO WORKS

Read by itself, *The Handmaid's Tale* provides a fresh and interesting, sometimes alarming and sometimes amusing perspective on contemporary events and policies. When it is read in tandem with *The Birth Dearth*, three implications seem especially noteworthy.

First, the mere fact that the "birth dearth" has climbed high on at least some conservative agendas is important for all political observers and policy makers to recognize. Pat Robertson's attempt in the October 1987 televised Republican presidential debate to propose a prohibition on abortion as the best way to "ensure the fiscal stability of the Social Security system" was widely dismissed as an isolated bit of idiocy; but references, following Wattenberg, to child-free families as "freeloaders" on Social Security are becoming increasingly common. As further examples of the rising popularity of strategic demography, Jack Kemp has been warning that "no nation can long remain a world power when its most precious resource (i.e. its population) is a shrinking resource"; Gary Bauer, when serving as President Reagan's domestic policy adviser, noted "a lot of very worrying evidence on the population decline"; Allan Carlson of the Rockford Institute has taken up the cause of pro-natalism; and Phyllis Schlafly, as quoted at the outset, is proselytizing the need for and joys of much larger families.[11]

Thus far, these seem to be only sentiments, but could the increased popularity of strategic demography help to explain the explosive sudden popularity of day care?[12] Does it not seem surprising that federal child care legislation, vetoed so vehemently by President Nixon in 1971 for its family-weakening implications, denounced so thoroughly over the decades by the political right for its communal overtones, had emerged by 1988 as Senator Orrin Hatch's "number one policy issue"?[13] In *The Birth Dearth*, published in 1987, Wattenberg pointed out the strategic value of an issue like day care with the potential for uniting feminists and pronatalists. Even earlier, in a 1986 interview on the meanings in *The Handmaid's Tale*, Atwood pointed out that:

> Any power structure will co-opt the views of its opponents, to sugarcoat the pill. The regime gives women some of the things the women's movement says they want—control over birth, no pornography—but there is a price. . . . Anyone who wants power

will try to manipulate you by appealing to your desires and fears, and sometimes your best instincts. Women have to be a little cautious about that kind of appeal to them. What are we being asked to give up?[14]

Presumably, nothing must be "given up" to get good day care legislation. If it is easier for women to work and to have children, women can work more comfortably, possibly at better jobs, and also have more children. Still, does it make a difference that at least some recent converts to day care advocacy may be less concerned with the welfare of working women than with the number of their progeny? Should a beneficial public policy be rejected simply because the motives of at least some of its advocates may be distasteful? Probably not—but certainly one should be aware of these purposes and be alert to attempts to advance them.

Especially after reading *The Handmaid's Tale*, reading Wattenberg can seem a bit like being parachuted behind enemy lines—an infuriating experience, but also highly instructive. Senator Orrin Hatch's proposed day care bill, much like Wattenberg's suggested scheme, has no income test and emphasizes the free enterprise and corporate sector. It does not authorize even greater federal funding for women who stay home and have three or four or more children as Wattenberg suggests would be even more expeditious (since even working women with day care will probably stop at one or two children). Others on the right, however, are beginning to suggest that this would be not only the most equitable but also the most progeny-producing policy.[15] How will feminists respond to those who say that *they* are pro-woman and only want to provide equal treatment for those who choose the "traditional" female functions? If feminists want greater economic opportunities for women, can economic opportunities be denied to those who want to be Wives, or even Handmaids?

The debate over surrogate motherhood has just begun, and has already sharply divided feminists.[16] At least some, however, would argue for the legality of an arrangement under which a woman who desperately wanted her husband's child could freely contract with a willing surrogate, who might find surrogacy much more pleasant and profitable than her other employment options. However, what if surrogacy, and in vitro fertilization, gained legal status primarily as part of a national pro-natal policy? If it is acceptable to countenance using a woman's womb to produce children for potential parents who want them, is it more or less acceptable to use modern technology to increase a nation's population count?

Wattenberg frets that fewer children will mean fewer housing starts, fewer consumers, fewer soldiers, and a weaker national defense: "At an estimated cost of approximately $300 billion, it [he is referring to the Strategic Defense Initiative] could be put together only by amortizing it over a large population."[17] Are housing starts and aircraft carriers less or more valid reasons for surrogate motherhood than personal satisfaction? And if women want their unique reproductive function recognized and subsidized by a grateful nation, does the public good have more or fewer claims on private reproductive choices? With the Wattenberg thesis fresh in mind, it is somewhat alarming to note economist Sylvia Hewlett approvingly quoting Charles de Gaulle to the effect that "having a child for a woman is a little like doing military service for a man. Both are essential for the welfare of the nation, and we should support both activities with public monies."[18]

This leads to a second important implication of these two works: The line between what is personal and what is political is a very fragile one, which must be constantly patrolled. With the contemporary Supreme Court edging ever closer to what had come to be considered clear constitutional zones of privacy, this is surely a timely reminder, and one that feminists in particular may wish to ponder.

One of the earliest and most formidable obstacles that contemporary feminism encountered was a definition of politics so narrow as to exclude many of the issues and concerns of most importance to many women. There was a political sphere, which involved such matters as the gross national product and international spheres of influence and partisan realignment, and there was a personal sphere, which included such items as childbirth and child care. Policy makers, the media, even political scientists, did not "do" the politics of the family, or of rape, or of pornography, or of reproduction. Feminists have worked hard, and successfully, to get certain subjects into the public domain. It is largely because of their efforts that presidential candidates must now seriously address a whole range of "family" issues, that members of the U.S. Congress now regularly debate everything from teenage pregnancy to premenstrual syndrome, and that political scientists now schedule panels and sections on gender politics. What these two books suggest, however, is that once "women's" issues are in the public domain, they can become fair game for those who are not sympathetic to feminist aspirations. Feminists may see as obvious the legitimacy of demands for state entry into family affairs to prohibit and punish spouse abuse versus the nonlegitimacy of state regulation of maternal treatment of the fetus. Nonfeminists, however, may not recognize such a distinction.

Finally, these two predictive works, while focusing on the future, strongly suggest the advisability of remembering the past. There is absolutely nothing new about the concept of pro-natalism. Most of the world's cultures are now, and have always been, pro-natalist, and this specifically includes the United States. As the epigrams at the outset were selected to suggest, American women have periodically attempted to reduce and limit the size of their families only to be rebuked for their shameful lack of maternal and patriotic sentiments. The shame-sayers in the past were also nativist, jingoist, and ethnocentric. And, as in the past, white middle-class women are the favored scapegoats.

In the late nineteenth and early twentieth centuries, the political establishment, which of course was white and male, alarmed over the large families of recent immigrants as compared with the smaller families of earlier settlers, warned of "race suicide." Socialists countercharged that the call for large families was merely cloaking the capitalists' desire to fill their factories and armies.[19] Charlotte Perkins Gilman stormed at male hypocrisy:

> All this for and against babies is by men. One would think the men bore the babies, nursed the babies, reared the babies. . . . The women bear and rear the children. The men kill them. Then they say: We are running short of children—make some more. . . . [20]

Despite these and other protests, however, proponents of large families succeeded, temporarily at least, in idealizing them—and they could succeed again. As often as women have watched the hard-earned gains of periodic feminism swept back in succeeding waves of familialism, it is still easy to become time-bound, easy to assume that the contemporary women's movement is some kind of irreversible culmination of long centuries of progress. But the pro-natalist observations of strategic demographers have become a regular feature of the influential *Atlantic Monthly*.[21] And there is no small irony in the fact that one of the last issues of *Ms.* magazine styled itself a "Special Mother's Issue"; featured on the front a classic, cover-girl mother and serene child; and, in an article on "Careers and Kids," highlighted three-child Justice Sandra Day O'Connor and five-child Judge Patricia Wald, both of whom temporarily dropped out of the labor force when their children were small. The pro-natal message is everywhere.[22]

Wattenberg himself seems genuinely insistent that coercive solutions to the birth dearth are unacceptable. Never, however, does he explicitly acknowledge what he tacitly assumes: the coercive potential of public opinion. Nor, of course, can he guarantee that those whom he persuades of the birth dearth's dire nature will be as observant of privacy and choice as he would prefer them to be.

It is often assumed that the biggest barrier to smaller families in years past, and still around the world today, has been the lack of efficient contraceptive methods. In fact, however, "Birth control has always been primarily an issue of politics, not of technology."[23] As demographers have documented at length, contraceptive methods are, and always have been, less significant than attitudes in shaping women's reproductive choices.[24] It is these attitudes that Wattenberg very much hopes to change, and that Atwood warns may be very, very malleable.

NOTES

1. Theodore Roosevelt, quoted in Linda Gordon, *Women's Body, Women's Right* (New York: Grossman, 1976), p. 141. Sinclair Lewis quote from *It Can't Happen Here* (New American Library, 1970), p. 19. Phyllis Schlafly's remarks from address to the Arkansas Governor's School for the Gifted and Talented, quoted in *Arkansas Democrat*, June 24, 1987.

2. Margaret Atwood, *The Handmaid's Tale* (Boston: Houghton Mifflin, 1986); Ben J. Wattenberg, *The Birth Dearth* (New York: Pharos Books, 1987).

3. Quoted in Caryn James, "The Lady Was Not for Hanging," *New York Times Book Review*, February 9, 1986, p. 35.

4. Cathy N. Davidson, "A Feminist 1984," *Ms.*, February 1986, pp. 24–26, esp. p. 26.

5. For an analysis of thirty reported abortion clinic bombings between May 1982 and January 1985, see David C. Nice, "Abortion Clinic Bombings as Political Violence," *American Journal of Political Science*, 32 (February 1988), pp. 178–195. Romanian pro-natal policies are described in Dirk J. van de Kaa, "Europe's Second Demographic Transition," *Population Bulletin*, 42 (1987), pp. 3–57, esp. p. 30.

6. See Janet Gallagher, "Fetal Personhood and Women's Policy," in Virginia Sapiro (Ed.), *Women, Biology and Public Policy* (Beverly Hills, CA: Sage, 1985), pp. 91–116; Lisa M. Krieger, "Fetus Definitions Create Medical, Legal Inconsistencies," *Arkansas Democrat*, January 27, 1988, p. 7A; and Eve W. Paul, "Amicus Brief in Forced Caesarean Case," *Insider*, February 1988, p. 2.

7. On workplace restrictions, see Cynthia Ganney, "The Fine Line between Fetal Protection and Female Discrimination," *Washington Post National Weekly Edition*, August 24, 1987, p. 11. On toxic wastes, see "Toxic Shipments to Third World Likely to Increase," *Springdale (Arkansas) News*, April 26, 1987. On Minnesota act requiring burial of fetal remains, see "Judge Blocks Forced Fetal Burial," *Arkansas Democrat*, August 22, 1987.

8. Quoted in Davidson, "A Feminist 1984," p. 24.

9. Ben J. Wattenberg and Karl Zinsmeister, "The Birth Dearth: The Geopolitical Consequences," *Public Opinion*, 8 (December–January 1986), pp. 7–13, esp. p. 13.

10. Wattenberg, *The Birth Dearth*, p. 120.

11. Pat Robertson's formula is as follows: "By the year 2000 we will have aborted 40 million children in this country. Their work product by the year 2020 will amount to $1.4 trillion, the taxes from them would amount to $330 billion and they could ensure the fiscal stability of the Social Security System." Quoted and criticized by Charles Krauthammer, "Win, Place, Show Ridiculous in Politics," *Arkansas Democrat*, February 21, 1988. "The child-free families of today are the free-loaders on social security tomorrow," according to George Gilder, "Children and Politics," *Public Opinion*, 10 (March–April 1988), pp. 10–11, esp. p. 11. Jack Kemp and Gary Bauer, quoted in Allan L. Otten, "Birth Dearth," *Wall Street Journal*, June 18, 1987. Allan Carlson's views in "High-Tech Societies Don't Have High Enough Birthrates," *Washington Post National Weekly Edition*, April 28, 1986, pp. 23–24, and "What to Do, Part I," *Public Opinion*, 10 (March–April 1988), pp. 4–6. On Schlafly, see n. 1.

12. On the recent popularity of day care, see Barbara Kantrowitz with Pat Wingert. "The Clamor to Save the Family," *Newsweek*, February 29, 1988, pp. 60–61; and Cindy Skrzycki and Frank Swoboda, "Congress Has Discovered a New Problem: Child Care," *Washington Post National Weekly Edition*, February 29–March 6, 1988, p. 33.

13. On President Nixon's veto and past conservative opposition to day care legislation, see Jill Norgren, "In Search of a National Child-Care Policy: Background and Prospects," in Ellen Boneparth (Ed.), *Women, Power and Policy* (Elmsford, NY: Pergamon Press, 1982), pp. 124–139. Senator Orrin Hatch statement made on *The McNeil-Lehrer News Hour*, January 7, 1988.

14. Quoted in James, "The Lady Was Not for Hanging," p. 35.

15. Carlson, "What to Do, Part I," p. 5. Mrs. Pat Robertson quoted to this effect in *Arkansas Democrat*, March 2, 1988.

16. See Robyn Rowland, "Technology and Motherhood: Reproductive Choice Reconsidered," *Signs*, 12 (Spring 1987), pp. 512–528.

17. Wattenberg and Zinsmeister, "The Birth Dearth," pp. 9–10.

18. Sylvia Hewlett, "What to Do, Part II," *Public Opinion*, 10 (March–April 1988), p. 7.

19. Gordon, *Women's Body, Women's Right*, pp. 140–145.

20. Quoted in ibid., p. 145.

21. See R. J. Hernstein, "IQ and Falling Birth Rates," *Atlantic Monthly*, May 1989, pp. 73–79, and Jonathan Rauch, "Kids as Capital," *Atlantic Monthly*, August 1989, pp. 56–61.

22. See Edith Fierst, "Careers and Kids," *Ms.*, May 1988, pp. 62–64.

23. Gordon, *Women's Body, Women's Right*, p. xii.

24. Richard L. Clinton, "Population, Politics and Political Science," in Richard L. Clinton (Ed.), *Population and Politics* (Lexington, MA: Lexington Books, 1973), pp. 51–71, esp. pp. 54–55.

FURTHER READINGS

Chesler, Ellen. "Stop Coercing Women." *New York Times Magazine*, February 6, 1994, pp. 31, 33.

Daniels, Cynthia R. *At Women's Expense: State Power and the Politics of Fetal Rights*. Cambridge, MA: Harvard University Press, 1993.

DeGama, Katherine. "A Brave New World? Rights Discourse and the Politics of Reproductive Anatomy." *Journal of Law and Society*, 21 (Spring 1993), pp. 114–130.

Dixon-Mueller, Ruth. *Population Policy and Women's Rights*. Westport, CT: Praeger, 1993.

Elshtain, Jean Bethke. "If You're An Addict, It's Now A Crime to Give Birth." *The Progressive* 54 (December 1990), pp. 26–28.

Gallagher, Janet. "Prenatal Invasions and Interventions: What's Wrong with Fetal Rights." *Harvard Women's Law Journal*, 10 (1987), pp. 9–58.

Hartmann, Betsey. *Reproductive Rights and Wrongs*. New York: Harper and Row, 1987.

Kent, Bonnie. "Protecting Children, Born and Unborn." *Report from the Institute for Philosophy and Public Policy*, 11 (Winter 1991), pp. 13–15.

"The Politics of Pregnancy: Policy Dilemmas in the Maternal-Fetal Relationship." *Women and Politics*, 13 (3 and 4) (1993), entire issue.

Roberts, Dorothy E. "The Future of Reproductive Choice for Poor Women and Women of Color." *Women's Rights Law Reporter*, 14 (Spring/Fall 1992), pp. 305–314.

The Family and Medical Leave Act: A Policy for Families

Joan Hulse Thompson

> My name is Liberia Johnson. In 1978, I was employed by a retail store in Charleston, South Carolina. . . . I became pregnant. . . . I tried to work because the income was so important to my family. My doctor told me that I was hypertensive and I had a thyroid problem. . . . If I did not stop working I would have a miscarriage. . . . The store manager . . . told me my job would be there after my baby was born. . . . I left at three months pregnant. I had a difficult pregnancy. I was in the hospital three times because I almost lost my baby. When I had my baby, I went and got my six weeks checkup and the same day I went back to the store and asked for my job. . . . There was a new manager and he told me "I don't have a job."[1]

On October 17, 1985, Ms. Johnson, married and the mother of five children, told her story to a joint oversight hearing on Disability and Parental Leave chaired by Congresswoman Patricia Schroeder (D-CO). Congresswoman Mary Rose Oakar (D-OH) and nine congressmen, six Democrats and three Republicans, attended part of the three-hour hearing, which featured medical and academic experts, corporate and union representatives, and a local government official as well as another public witness, a single mother with an adopted daughter.

    An oversight hearing is designed to attract attention from members of Congress, the press, and the public to an issue in hopes of gathering support for government action. Public witnesses like Liberia Johnson can play a brief but significant role. According to a veteran committee staff member, anecdotes are "the only thing that move people. A good public witness draws the rapt attention of the

Joan Hulse Thompson is an associate professor of political science at Beaver College in Glenside, Pennsylvania.

members."[2] They convince members of Congress in a very personal way that legislation is needed to remedy an injustice. The more heart-wrenching their stories, the better.

How did a Black woman, who formerly worked a cash register and became a baker at a small hospital, get to tell her story to Congress? Public witnesses are usually found by interest groups or by subcommittee staff, but in this case the Congressional Caucus for Women's Issues was responsible. Several caucus members, the caucus staff, and a few interested attorneys had been working on parental leave since early 1984. This issue illustrates the role of congresswomen and their caucus in developing and promoting a policy proposal to respond to the economic needs of women.

The House and Senate passed the Family and Medical Leave Act (FMLA) in 1990 and again in 1992, but President Bush vetoed the bill both times and the Congress was unable to override either veto. Both chambers passed the bill again on February 4, 1993, and President Clinton signed it the next day, making it effective on August 5 of that year (see Table 1). The 1992 election, hailed as the "Year of the Woman," made the difference for the FMLA. The number of women in the House increased from twenty-nine to forty-eight and in the Senate from two to six.[3]

WOMEN IN CONGRESS AND THEIR CAUCUS

Since the first woman entered the House of Representatives in 1917, congresswomen have been outsiders. None ever belonged to either party's powerful yet informal social and political groups, such as Speaker Rayburn's Board of Education or the Republican Chowder and Marching Society founded by Richard Nixon and Gerald Ford, among others.[4] As female politicians, they were isolated from the social network of male politicians and also from that of more traditional women outside of politics.

The congresswomen needed a support group. Congressmen have them, usually centered on the gymnasium or the golf course. One congresswoman explained the significance of such social groups as follows:

> Members who don't or can't participate in them are like the kid in college who has no one to study with; no one to exchange ideas with to get a broader idea of what's going on in the class; no one to work with to get the right kind of "vibes" about the course and the teacher. It takes longer for that kid to understand what is going on and often that student is never as good as he or she could be.[5]

The Congresswomen's Caucus, founded in 1977 by Elizabeth Holtzman (D-NY), Margaret Heckler (R-MA), and Shirley Chisholm (D-NY), had both social and policy goals. All the members were committed to the Equal Rights Amendment (ERA) and to increasing the number of women in public office. Frequent meetings provided an opportunity for "conviviality, affection, and good feelings."[6] Bipartisanship strengthened the organization's claim to speak for women nationally.

Table 1   Provisions of the Family and Medical Leave Act (PL 103-3) Signed by President Clinton on February 5, 1993

1. Family leave—Employees may take up to 12 weeks of unpaid leave per year for the care of a new-born, newly adopted, or newly placed foster child, or for the care of a seriously ill child, parent, or spouse.

2. Medical leave—Employees may take up to 12 weeks of unpaid leave per year for their own serious medical condition. When medically necessary, employers must permit intermittent leave for treatment, but workers may be required to temporarily transfer to another equivalent position.

3. Exemption—Employers with fewer than 50 employees within 75 miles of a work site are exempt. Approximately 5 percent of all employers are covered and about 45 percent of all employees.

4. Coverage—Employees must have worked at least 12 months and at least 1,250 hours (an average of 25 hours per week) during the previous year to be eligible for leave. Highly paid workers (top 10 percent) in a firm may be denied reinstatement, if they received timely notice and the employer can demonstrate substantial and grievous economic injury would occur. Other eligible workers are entitled to the same or equivalent positions upon their return to work.

5. Conditions—Health insurance, if it is provided by the employer, must be continued on the same basis during the period of the leave. Employees are not entitled to more than 12 weeks leave in one year regardless of circumstances. Employees are required to give 30 days' notice when the need for leave is foreseeable. Employers may require that a health care provider certify the serious health condition of the employee or their family member in order to qualify for leave and reinstatement.

6. Paid leave—Workers may choose to substitute accrued paid vacation, personal or family leave for unpaid family leave mandated by the FMLA. Employers are not required to permit workers to take paid sick leave for the care of a new or ill family member. However, employers may require workers to substitute any paid leave they have accrued for all or part of their unpaid FMLA leave.

7. Enforcement—Administrative and civil procedures are available for enforcement under the supervision of the Wage and Hours Division of the Department of Labor. Violators are liable for lost wages, benefits and other compensation, or actual monetary losses sustained by the employee up to the equivalent of 12 weeks pay. If employers can demonstrate a good-faith effort to comply with the law, they will not be assessed an additional monetary penalty as punishment for the violation.

8. Federal employees—Federal government workers are also entitled to 12 weeks of family or medical leave after 12 months of employment. The Office of Personnel Management is responsible for enforcement.

9. Congressional employees—Employees of the House of Representatives and the Senate are eligible for 12 weeks of family or medical leave, the same as private employees. Previous employee rights bills have usually exempted congressional employees.

The Congresswomen's Caucus was not the first such organization, although its focus on member, rather than constituency, characteristics was unusual. Responding to the narrow circles of power in the prereform Congress and paralleling the growth of special-interest groups in the larger society, caucuses have flourished in the House. The Democratic Study Group was first in 1959. There were ten caucuses in 1974 and ninety by 1987.[7] Officially known as *legislative service organizations,* caucuses are voluntary associations of House members formed to help fulfill goals of representation, personal power, policy promotion, and reelection. Members from constituencies dependent upon the maritime industry have formed the

Port Caucus, those with steel mills have joined the Steel Caucus, and so forth. Caucuses gather and distribute information, seek to influence congressional agendas, and attempt to build policy coalitions.

Whether or not congresswomen initially felt that they should represent women nationally, most soon realized that if they did not speak for women, no one else would.[8] However, not all congresswomen believed that the problems of women could best be addressed at the national level. Because they favored state, local, or private initiatives, most Republican congresswomen and some Democrats were out of step with the underlying liberal perspective of the Congresswomen's Caucus. Steps taken to convince all the women to join inhibited the caucus from taking positions on issues important to its most active members. But requiring greater policy agreement threatened to make the caucus a tiny, exclusively Democratic group with little hope of fulfilling its policy goals, especially in the conservative atmosphere of the early 1980s.

A COED CAUCUS EXPANDS ITS INFLUENCE

Recurrent financial problems, a House rules change, the conservative national tide, and a desire to be more effective on women's issues combined to lead the members of the Congresswomen's Caucus to invite congressmen to join their organization late in 1981. The following year the organization took on a new name, the Congressional Caucus for Women's Issues, and established an executive committee of congresswomen to set policy. The group has grown from a membership of 10 to 150 by 1994, with 42 congresswomen and 108 congressmen. Although some congresswomen do not belong,[9] caucus leaders were in a far better position with their expanded membership to command the attention of the media and the public, and to pursue policy change in an institution where men hold the power positions.

Congresswomen do sit on the most powerful committees, but no woman chaired a committee in 1994,[10] and the five subcommittees they chaired were not among the most powerful. Women have been part of the leadership structure in both parties, but not yet as high as the party leader or the party whip.[11] The concerns of other caucuses, such as the Congressional Black Caucus, have won greater recognition as their members gained positions within the formal power structure. But due to electoral defeats, retirements, and attempts for higher office, that path has not worked very well for women.

Expanding the women's caucus to include supportive congressmen proved to be a shortcut. By 1985, the male members of the caucus included the Speaker, majority whip, nine committee chairs, including Rules, and three select committee chairmen. Although only about a dozen Republicans belonged, they included ranking members of four committees. In 1993–1994, male members of the caucus chaired fourteen House committees and forty-four subcommittees, with ranking positions on three committees and two subcommittees. Having men in the caucus in the 103rd Congress had the effect of increasing its representation on the five committees that form an oligarchy of power in Congress from fifteen seats to sixty-six seats.[12] When the FMLA passed the House, the caucus male membership included the Speaker, majority leader, majority whip, Democratic Caucus chairman and the chairman of the Rules Committee. Although neither party leaders nor committee chairs can assure congressional passage, it does help women's issues to have publicly committed supporters in high places.

POLICY DEVELOPMENT BY THE CAUCUS

Attempts by the Congresswomen's Caucus to build coalitions or "to fashion and implement legislative strategies were . . . infrequent and superficial."[13] The expanded caucus could do more. The same year the caucus invited men to join, it also became the House coordinator for the Economic Equity Act, a package of bills initiated by Senator David Durenberger (R-MN) in response to the fate of the ERA. The Ninety-eighth Congress (1983–1984) was a very productive one for the caucus, largely because of the much-publicized gender gap. Public opinion polls showed President Reagan to be much less popular with women than with men. Republican congressmen feared the women's vote, and Democrats in Congress were anxious to exploit their potential advantage. Child support enforcement and pension reform legislation, both included in the Economic Equity Act, were enacted before the 1984 election.[14]

After President Reagan's landslide victory over Walter Mondale and caucus leader Geraldine Ferraro (D-NY), a caucus staff member reflected that "feminists are just poison"[15] now on the Hill. In a caucus-sponsored report, then–Caucus Director Anne Radigan explained:

> On Capitol Hill, legislators reacted negatively to the failure of the Democratic presidential ticket and its feminist adherents. Where only a few weeks earlier politicians had beaten a path to their doors, now feminist women's groups found themselves and their agenda held at a cool and measured distance.[16]

In order to advance women's economic issues in the Ninety-ninth Congress, the caucus adopted a new strategy of describing legislative proposals as "profamily" rather than for women. The plan was to seize that politically popular label from conservatives and the religious right. The FMLA even bridged the politically devisive abortion issue by making it more economically feasible for women to choose to have children. By the 1988 presidential election, both candidates were talking about family policy proposals, including both parental leave and child care.

During the Bush administration, the FMLA was joined on the House agenda by new women's equity legislation developed through the caucus. The Women's Health Equity Act, first introduced in July 1990 and enacted under Clinton in June 1993, will increase research efforts on breast and ovarian cancer, menopause, osteoporosis, contraception, and infertility. The Economic Equity Act package was redesigned with thirty bills divided into sections on workplace fairness, economic opportunity, work and family, and economic self-sufficiency for women. The Violence against Women Act, first introduced in 1990 and enacted with the crime bill in 1994, expands rape shield laws, creates federal offenses for interstate spousal abuse, and provides funds for rape crisis shelters, additional police, prosecutors, and victim advocates.

Although abortion has been the driving issue for most feminist groups in the last few years, the caucus had primarily an informational, rather than advocacy, role on abortion rights until January 1993. The 1992 elections added twenty-two new pro-choice women to the executive committee while two pro-life caucus congresswomen did not return to Congress. The new executive committee voted overwhelmingly to support the Freedom of Choice Bill to codify the *Roe v. Wade* Supreme Court decision. In the 103rd Congress, the caucus was committed to removing restrictions on abortion funding and including abortion services in health care reform. The FMLA has been a priority for the caucus since 1985, but certainly not its only concern.

PROS AND CONS OF GENDER NEUTRALITY

According to Anne Radigan, the caucus has long been committed to supporting gender-neutral legislation. Therefore, a bill for parental, not maternity, leave was introduced. Protective laws, such as weight-lifting restrictions, have been used to keep women out of higher-paying, nontraditional jobs. Mandatory maternity leave, by treating pregnancy as a special condition, could well lead to further workplace discrimination against women, such as a reluctance to hire or promote a woman who might become pregnant.

The Pregnancy Discrimination Act (PDA), an amendment to Title VII of the Civil Rights Act of 1964, was enacted in 1978 in response to a U.S. Supreme Court decision. The decision, *Gilbert v. General Electric*, interpreted the previous law as permitting employers to treat pregnancy differently from other medical conditions with respect to health insurance and leave policies. Under the PDA, women unable to work due to pregnancy or childbirth would have to be treated the same as other employees unable to work for other medical reasons. The law was gender-neutral, but it left millions of women unprotected because their employers provided no health insurance or disability benefits. It also ignored the bonding needs of newborn infants and their families.

Also in 1978, the California legislature enacted a mandatory maternity leave program covering all employers in the state. However, the law was challenged in 1983 by a private employer who claimed that the state law was reverse discrimination against males and violated the federal mandate for gender neutrality. In 1984 this argument was successful in the federal trial court, although an appellate court later reversed the decision.

Representative Howard Berman (D-CA), who had sponsored the state law while in the legislature, and other California representatives decided to sponsor a bill at the national level that would mandate maternity and some paternity leave. They had the support of many California feminists who believed that "since women alone bear children they are at an indisputable disadvantage compared to working men and require an edge to help them remain competitive in the workplace."[17] The aftermath of giving birth includes more than just physical recovery.

Also in 1984, a small drafting group of lawyers who had fought for the PDA and a caucus staff attorney began to look for a way to respond to the federal court decision—a manner in which to fill the coverage gap and recognize the needs of women and their families, without abandoning the principle of gender neutrality. Their solution was to frame a broad policy mandating parental leave for both parents and medical disability leave for all workers.

A more narrowly drawn bill for pregnant women with a small paternity leave, to encourage a greater role for fathers in the care of newborns, would have had an easier time gaining support. Making parental leave optional for either parent enabled opponents to score points with such remarks as "This is ludicrous in the extreme. I don't need 18 weeks off if my wife has a baby."[18] Including all those temporarily medically disabled increased the cost of the bill to employers and, therefore, their resolve to oppose it. Republican Senator Durenberger, usually a dependable ally on women's issues, expressed concern in 1990 that the costs of temporary medical leaves and leaves for the care of sick family members were "virtually untested in the private sector"[19] and therefore very difficult to predict.

CHARGES OF ELITISM AND DAMAGING REGULATION

Choosing to make the mandated leave unpaid kept the cost down and made the policy self-policing, but at the price of raising difficult issues of social class. Women's groups, like most interest groups, are composed primarily of members from the middle class and above. They are potentially vulnerable to charges of insensitivity to the real problems of working-class women when their organizations engage in conflicts over abstract principles of equality. That was why both the public witnesses at the October 1985 oversight hearing were African-American. One of Pat Schroeder's concluding remarks expressed her pleasure that, while "The bill looks like it is for 'Yuppies,' " the hearing had demonstrated that "It's for everyone." Demonstrating universality was clearly one of the goals of the congresswomen, the caucus staff, and the women's groups when they planned the initial hearing.

Nevertheless, opponents described the women's groups as "powerful special-interest groups" seeking to dictate policy against the best interests of both employers and the very employees whose interests they claimed to represent. Testimony from the U.S. Chamber of Commerce at subsequent legislative hearings included references to the fact that "all employees . . . will be subject to a uniform parental leave law, . . . whether they can afford to take advantage of it or not."[20] Furthermore, the business community argued, "Any mandated benefit is likely to replace other, sometimes more preferable, employee benefits . . . (such as) flextime, child-care, dental or liberalized leave benefits."[21] In 1989 a Texas Republican expressed the view that only the upper classes would be able to take the leaves while all workers would share the costs. He described the bill as " 'Yuppie' welfare—a perverse redistribution of income."[22]

The mandatory nature of the legislation was critical for both sides and could not be compromised. Supporters proclaimed that the proposal "breaks new ground in labor law"[23] and, of course, business groups opposed it for exactly that reason. Proponents could and did compromise the number of weeks of leave and the number of employees a company must have to be covered; however, eliminating the mandatory nature of the regulation would leave nothing of substance. For business interests and their supporters in Congress, "Such legislation results in a loss of freedom of choice—the hallmark of our economic system."[24]

Government already regulates wages and working conditions. Further intrusions must be fought, according to the U.S. Chamber of Commerce, for the sake of maintaining the nation's international competitiveness and high rate of economic growth. Figures for employee benefit costs as a percentage of the payroll for Korea, Japan, and Taiwan were cited and shown to put U.S. industry at a disadvantage. European nations that grant paid family leaves were praised by supporters but criticized by the Chamber of Commerce for rates of job creation below that of the United States. The chamber argued that the costs of mandated family leave would devastate small businesses. It might lead to discrimination in hiring, making it difficult for women of childbearing age to even find employment.

To opponents, family leave was another well-intentioned but misguided intervention in the employer–employee relationship. They argued that it would not serve the interests of the nation or even those of working women. To proponents, family leave was the next step toward a more humane society, just as child labor and minimum-wage laws were fifty years ago. In response to complaints about cost, prime sponsor Senator Christopher Dodd (D-CT), declared, "It's mortifying that we can't offer a benefit like this that is a minimum standard of human decency."[25] Normal family life adjusts to adult employment schedules on a daily basis. Family and medical leave is for times of transition and crisis, when accommodating the business needs of employers would cause great harm to the family.

BUILDING SUPPORT FOR THE FMLA

According to then caucus director, Anne Radigan, the legislative strategy for the FMLA assumed compromise would be necessary for success. She described the plan in 1985 as follows: "At first, try to be as all encompassing as possible, then go for as much as you can (realistically hope for), and finally get what you can."[26] Members of Congress tend to be pragmatic because they want accomplishments to claim credit for back home.

Because public support is essential to win congressional support, the initial hearing and every subsequent hearing were planned with the media in mind. The first hearing had a star witness, Dr. T. Berry Brazelton, who has the charisma of a cable television star and the authority of a noted pediatrician and author. His testimony gave the bill the advantage of backing in the medical community. As hoped, he drew a feature story in the *Washington Post*. Subsequent hearings heard from a retail manager who recovered from cancer but was unemployed for two years, and a daughter who lost her job when she was absent caring for her father during the last weeks of his life.

After the first hearing the caucus staff monitored the media coverage and was both encouraged and discouraged. Both the Associated Press and the United Press International wire services carried the story, but both talked about maternity leave. "What did we do wrong?" lamented Anne Radigan. "How was that connection, the language . . . misunderstood? We are talking so very clearly about parents, mothers *and fathers*." On the other hand, there was good coverage and an opportunity to build support before opposition surfaced. Reflecting on the media strategy three years later, Anne Radigan recalled that "most reporters covering the issue gave the bill a favorable spin."[27]

By 1989, the *Congressional Quarterly* was referring to the FMLA as "a key item on the agenda . . . of organized labor."[28] At the first hearing in 1985, this point was made by a coal miner who prefaced his remarks with the question, "What's an official of a macho male coal miners union doing in a place like this?" He then described the parental leave proposal that the coal companies refused to accept in national contract talks in 1984, the growing number of women in coal mining, the changing family patterns in mining communities, and the special hardships facing rural families when their children are seriously ill. Medical treatment for cancer, for instance, is available only in major cities, requiring time off from work for travel to hospitals as far as 200 miles away.

Although his stories were emotionally compelling, the United Mine Workers spokesman made it clear that he was coming to Congress because the union had been unable to get parental leave through in contract negotiations. In a sense, he was asking Congress to circumvent the collective bargaining process. Unions want mandatory benefits so that their bargaining can focus on other issues.

Representative William Clay (D-MO), a Black congressman and union ally, called the FMLA "preventive medicine, (because it) . . . goes to the heart of what is causing families to struggle."[29] As a cosponsor, Clay, the chairman of the Labor Management Subcommittee of the House Education and Labor Committee, proved valuable. However, his advocacy may also have strengthened the resolve of the business community. Clay is known for angry rhetoric but not for legislative effectiveness beyond his own committee.

Furthermore, Education and Labor is perceived as a partisan, ideological committee where liberals can win bills that will not pass in the more moderate House chamber or in the Senate. Opponents are more interested in compromise, when they fear that without it they may suffer total defeat, than when they can realistically anticipate eventual victory. Union support, while necessary for committee approval, was less important for enactment than the media coverage that would build support within the general public and therefore in the full chamber.

EXPANDING THE FMLA COALITION

Early in 1985, Schroeder's original bill provided for disability leaves, defining disability as "a total inability to perform a job, a notion of disability that the disabled rights advocates had been struggling for years to overcome."[30] Substituting "medical leave" resolved the objections of the disabled and gained the support of five organizations, including the Disability Rights Education and Defense Fund.

At the suggestion of Congresswoman Roukema (R-NJ), ranking minority member of Clay's subcommittee, the proposal was expanded in 1987 from parental to family leave by including leave to care for seriously ill, elderly parents. This inclusion brought the politically powerful American Association of Retired Persons and another group into the coalition.

Public testimony made it clear that women with difficult pregnancies and those who could not afford to risk losing their jobs might choose to have an abortion for financial reasons. Congresswomen Mary Rose Oakar, a Roman Catholic and pro-life member, said at the initial hearing that "nothing is more sacred than children in their formative weeks," making parental leave "a real, positive, minimum response." She also pledged, in her role as chair of the subcommittee responsible for federal employee benefits, that the federal government would be a model employer. Dale Kildee (D-MI), also a devout Roman Catholic, added that the bill promised to be "a real vehicle for making this government pro-family." Other pro-life members, including Republican Henry Hyde of Illinois, and the U.S. Catholic Conference supported the bill. However, antiabortion forces could not develop a maximum lobbying effort for anything other than a prohibition of abortion.

In March 1989 the House Education and Labor Committee approved amendments to add a title including congressional employees among covered workers and a section outlining special rules for instructural personnel at public and private schools. The rules for educators were negotiated by the National School Board Association, professional unions representing teachers, and other education organizations to provide employee coverage even at small schools and to prevent undue disruption in classroom instruction from intermittent leaves or teachers returning at the very end of the term.

Businesses would be paying the cost of the FMLA, so members of Congress would want to see evidence of at least some business support. After questioning ten major companies about their leave provisions, a caucus staff member invited General Foods Corporation to testify at the first hearing in 1985. The company has a policy of *paid* disability and child care leaves as part of its plan to "meet contemporary and future needs of employees," explained its representative. Male employees had been reluctant to ask for leave, she continued, but recently a "very highly placed executive" had taken parental leave to be with his new baby and "he's being looked at as the domino."

Such a company had an incentive to support the FMLA. The governmental mandate would require its competitors to pay the cost of a minimal benefit, while its benefit package would remain attractive to prospective employees. At a subsequent hearing, Southern New England Telephone testified that parental leave enabled the company to retain trained employees.

While the U.S. Chamber of Commerce, the National Federation of Independent Business, and the American Society for Personnel Administration testified against the bill, congressional staff found other small-business representatives to argue for the bill. These included the National Federation of Business and Professional Women's Clubs and the National Association of Women Business Owners. Congresswoman Pat Schroeder said that from small business owners in her district she heard that "parental leave policies save employers the cost of hiring and training new employees. Most of all these policies help attract the best and the brightest, and retain a valued and trusted work force."[31]

The cosponsorship of the four subcommittee chairs with jurisdiction was sufficient for success at that stage in the legislative process. The primary focus during full committee consideration was the cost for business, especially small business, to continue health insurance coverage of workers on leave and to hire replacements. The original bill applied to employers with five or more workers, repeated concessions raised that number to fifty, provided a legal means to deny some highly paid employees reinstatement, shortened the number of weeks of leave, restricted workers to either family or medical leave during a twelve-month period, and raised the number of weeks worked to be eligible. The bill still covered some part-time as well as full-time workers, allowed intermittent as well as continuous leave, mandated continued health benefits if offered, and provided job guarantees for family and medical leaves. Since 95 percent of all private employers have fewer than fifty workers, only about 5 percent of companies and 45 percent of the workforce is covered by the FMLA mandate.

CREATING AN FMLA STUDY COMMISSION

Released in early 1987, the original annual cost estimate from the Chamber of Commerce for family leave alone was $16 billion; but this figure was based on the faulty assumptions that all workers would be replaced and that replacements would be paid more than regular workers. Under pressure, the chamber reduced the estimated cost to $2.6 billion. After initial compromises, the nonpartisan Government Accounting Office estimated that the bill would cost $188 million annually.[32] Based on these figures, supporters estimate that the FMLA would cost employers only $6.50 per year per eligible worker. A report, produced by the caucus research arm and the Women's Legal Defense Fund, found that unemployment resulting from the absence of parental leave costs American families at least $607 million a year and costs taxpayers about $108 million a year for government assistance programs.[33]

While the caucus saw the FMLA as a first step in a new and desirable direction, opposition groups feared more costly encroachments if the bill succeeded in any form. Marian Wright Edelman of the Children's Defense Fund published a book in 1987 urging a comprehensive family policy. Her program, just as business anticipated, goes beyond the FMLA, with calls for private and public funding for about six months of paid maternity and paternity leave. She also urged a reduction in the number of hours in a normal workweek, an increase in the minimum wage, and more flexible scheduling of work time.[34]

Academic specialists, comparing the United States with other Western democracies in Europe and with Canada, have pointed out that in those countries payments are available to compensate for lost wages after childbirth. Realizing that such a proposal was too costly to win passage, successive versions of the FMLA provided for a study commission. This group would recommend means to provide salary replacement for employees taking parental and medical leaves. Those who wanted paid leaves were thus partially satisfied since a study commission could improve prospects for a future program of leaves paid for by employers, Social Security, or some other means.

The final version of the FMLA Commission mandate focused on examining the administrative and implementation costs business groups feared from the law as enacted. Issues of productivity, alternative benefits, job creation, federal enforcement, and economic growth by sector had been added to the commission mandate in response to business criticism, and as a result the examination of paid leave provisions greatly reduced in importance. Consideration of the needs of employees who had been covered by the original proposal, but are not eligible for mandatory leaves under the new law, were also added to the commission's charge. The commission report is due in late 1995 and will surely reflect its bipartisan membership, including advocates and opponents of the FMLA.

A PRECEDENT FOR HEALTH CARE REFORM

More ominous to the business community than the FMLA itself was the prospect that once one benefit became mandatory others would follow. Employers could be required to offer not only paid parental and medical leaves but also health insurance to all employees and their families. Early in 1990 a congressional commission recommended such a mandatory benefits program for employers of over 100 persons to cover hospital and surgical services, prenatal care, and also mental health care.[35] In an era of tight federal budgets, the tendency is to shift social welfare costs, borne by the national government in many countries, to private business in order to avoid calling for higher tax revenues.

The implications of enacting family and medical leave then went beyond the narrow domain of women's issues. Opting for a gender-neutral policy meant that passage, if accomplished, would be a major precedent both for governmental regulation of business and for passing costs of social welfare programs on to private industry. Although this made passage more difficult, it also helped supporters attract a broader coalition than they could have for a narrowly drawn maternity leave bill.

President Clinton's health care reform proposal, introduced in November 1993, did include an employer mandate to cover 80 percent of the cost of health insurance for employees and their families, with government subsidies for small employers. Employer mandates were defended as the only practical means to guarantee universal coverage, the primary goal of the Clinton administration. The mandate was criticized by the U.S. Chamber of Commerce and other business representatives with the familiar argument that more governmental regulation would cost jobs in the private sector. The FMLA had been "yet another Democratic effort to regulate industry, increase the bureaucracy and set the stage for costly litigation."[36] To these concerns, Republican opponents of Clinton's health reform added the prediction that it would create massive new governmental bureaucracies to administer cost controls and force an increase in taxes to pay for those presently uninsured.

At first, it seemed that no one wanted to be against universal health insurance coverage any more than they had wanted to position themselves against family leave, but Clinton's health reform lost public support after insurance industry advertisements raised fears that those currently insured would have to pay more for less coverage. Congresswomen Nancy Johnson of Connecticut, a moderate Republican member of the caucus, "rose to prominence when Republicans recognized that they had a health care expert in their midst."[37] Congressional Democrats, however, were unable to either unite around one proposal in a partisan coalition or work with Republicans, such as Johnson, to develop a bipartisan proposal that could pass. "From the Republican point of view, Democrats had turned a deaf ear to their longstanding warnings that a big bill could never gain broad support because there would always be more risks associated with passing it than clear gains."[38] Eventually Republicans, led by Senator Gramm of Texas, discovered that outright opposition to major health reform did play well with voters.

The 103rd Congress began with the easy passage of the FMLA, which, unlike health reform, had bipartisan support, limited implications, and an incremental approach, putting off paid leave and universal coverage to the future. While health reform dominated the agenda of the entire 103rd Congress, compromise efforts by the Democrats came too little and too late, and the bill failed to pass in any form. The public appeal of major health reform proposals has declined, but opponents will remain prepared for a revival of interest in some form of federal governmental regulation of the health insurance industry.

THE POLITICS OF CONGRESSIONAL PASSAGE

With its strong public appeal, the FMLA was viewed as a potentially powerful political issue throughout its consideration. Although not at the top of the congressional agenda until 1993, it attracted and sustained public support from 1985 until its enactment. The story of its approval by Congress in 1990, 1992, and 1993 demonstrates that party politics and media strategies were decisive on the FMLA.

The bill did not reach the floor of the House until 1990, but it was debated on the Senate floor in 1988. Just before the presidential and congressional elections, Democratic senators brought minimum-wage increases, parental leave, and child care to the floor "in an openly partisan fashion," according to the *Congressional Quarterly Almanac*. "While the Senate waited for conference reports on fiscal 1989 appropriations bills, Democrats used their power as the majority party to put on the floor all the labor and social legislation they wanted to highlight in the closing weeks before the November 8 elections."[39] No vote was taken on the bills due to a Republican filibuster.

In 1989 Schroeder said, "The worst rumor we hear up here is that the (Republican) administration will ask us to schedule the bill (for floor action) around Mother's Day and then take men out of the bill."[40] Instead, the Democratic Speaker arranged for the FMLA to pass the House, with its gender neutrality and governmental mandate intact, just in time for Mother's Day 1990. As the supporters of the FMLA celebrated its first-ever passage in the House, opponents declared it dead.

A lobbyist for the National Association of Wholesaler–Distributors, Mary Tavenner, reported, "I had John Sununu (White House chief of staff) look me straight in the eye and say that the president would veto it."[41] After refusing to meet with Republican supporters of the bill, President Bush vetoed it on the last Friday afternoon before the July 4th holiday, a time when the media and the public would be least attentive.

The vetoed bill was a substitute proposal, negotiated just prior to House floor consideration. It eliminated the possibility that the same worker would be eligible for both family and medical leave, totaling twenty-five weeks, in one year. The cap would be twelve weeks for either or both, and the small-employer exemption was modified as well. Such changes made the law less burdensome for business and therefore picked up support. This revised 1990 version, which for the first time included care of a seriously ill spouse, was supported by 198 Democrats and 39 Republicans, while 54 Democrats and 133 Republicans opposed it. Three planned amendments were actually withdrawn by Republicans at the request of the White House because their passage might have made the bill more attractive and made a veto more difficult to sustain.

One-third of the senators faced reelection in 1990. Those who opposed the FMLA were not anxious to participate in another filibuster or take a recorded vote on the bill. Senate Majority Leader George Mitchell, a Democrat, worked out a deal with Senator Robert Dole, the Republican leader, to permit the FMLA to pass on a voice vote on the condition that Mitchell would schedule a vote on a constitutional amendment to make flag desecration a crime. Thus each party was able to advance an issue it hoped would work to its advantage in the coming congressional elections.

While the 1990 Bush veto killed the bill for that session, the issue remained for the fall congressional campaign, the next Congress, and the 1992 election. In a national public opinion survey taken in June 1990, 74 percent favored a law guaranteeing up to twelve weeks of unpaid parental leave.[42] One columnist predicted that the 1990 veto of the FMLA, veto number 13 for Bush, would turn out to be unlucky for the president.[43] Although hardly decisive, the issue did contribute to the defeat of President Bush in 1992.

In 1991 Senator Christopher Dodd, the prime Senate sponsor, negotiated an additional compromise with Republican Senators Bond of Missouri and Coates of Indiana, who wanted to be responsive to business and also support pro-family legislation. This version added a provision allowing employers to deny reinstatement to their highest-paid employees, if necessary to avoid "substantial and grievous economic injury to the operations of the employer" (Public Law 103-3). The bill passed both the House and the Senate in the fall of 1991, but no conference committee met until August 1992.

During the summer and fall of 1992, Al Gore, then senator and vice presidential candidate, spoke movingly "of how fortunate he had been to take time off from work when his young son lay critically ill in the hospital after he was hit by a car."[44] The Senate passed the conference committee bill by unanimous consent on August 11, and the House followed suit by a vote of 241 to 161 on September 10, 1992. Advocating a new proposal to grant a tax credit to small and mid-sized companies who voluntarily granted family leave, President Bush sided with opponents who would not accept any form of mandatory leave. His veto was overridden in the Senate 68 to 31, but the House failed to attain the necessary two-thirds vote, voting 258 to 169.

The new Congress in 1993 moved quickly through the reconsideration of the FMLA with hearings in January highlighting administration support and House and Senate passage early in February. On the final vote, the FMLA was supported by 224 Democrats and 40 Republicans, with 29 Democrats and 134 Republicans opposed. Although an amendment, negotiated with the Clinton administration, was added in the Senate calling for a full review of policy on homosexuals in the military, the FMLA became President Clinton's first legislative victory. At the signing ceremony, he declared that "America's families . . . have beaten the gridlock in Washington to pass family leave."

CONCLUSION

Despite President Bush's vetoes, the concept of family leave entered the agenda of the state governments during the years it was debated in Washington. Eighteen states, Puerto Rico, and the District of Columbia have some form of job protection for at least some workers who need family leave. A few of these measures are more generous than the FMLA; the others are the same or less comprehensive. Laws in ten states provide only maternity leave, but the newer statutes tend to be gender-neutral.[45]

Experience with family and medical leave laws at the state level provided information on actual costs and benefits that was used to argue for the national approach. When finally enacted, the FMLA did not supersede any provision of state law or local ordinances that provided more generous family or medical leave rights. If a state law provides for sixteen weeks of leave every two years, an eligible worker could, if family circumstances dictated, take sixteen weeks of leave one

year under state law and twelve weeks the next year under the FMLA. Corporations with work sites in more than one state would have preferred one federal
requirement, but after the long delay in enactment, Congress refused to override
benefits granted in the meantime by state legislatures. Some employers are therefore faced with both state and national standards to reconcile with guidance from
the rules and regulations issued by the Department of Labor.

In the first year of implementation, the Labor Department received more than
125,000 requests for information about the FMLA from employers and employees.
Of the 965 complaints it received, over 90 percent were resolved quickly, often with
just a phone call. In about 60 percent of the cases the employer was violating the
act, and in about 30 percent the employer was not violating the act. About ninety
cases were pending at the end of the first year, and the department filed two lawsuits against employers in September 1994.

Advocates for women, such as the Women's Legal Defense Fund, have urged
that the Labor Department take steps to publicize the FMLA more widely and that
Congress expand its reach to more workers and seek a means of partial wage
replacement.[46] The United States Chamber of Commerce continues to oppose employer mandates. It argues that "the FMLA does not expand the range of benefits
available to employees; it simply locks one benefit into the package, thereby reducing the ability of employees to negotiate for other benefits they need more."[47]

Whether or not one hails the FMLA as a first step toward creating a new
United States business culture friendly to families, its passage illustrates the role of
the Caucus for Women's Issues in developing legislation, building a bipartisan
coalition across committee jurisdictions, and coordinating the efforts of outside advocacy groups. Having leaned heavily on caucus staff in the early stages, committee and personal staffs gradually took over staff responsibilities once the bill was
launched. The caucus presence was continued through its information services
and represented by its members, especially the congresswomen and their legislative assistants for women's issues. The current director, Lesley Primmer, once a
legislative assistant to Olympia Snowe, observes "moving legislation is done
by personal and committee staff primarily, with the caucus serving in an intermediate role."[48]

The caucus symbolizes what has been called the "second stage" of the
women's movement because it is a partnership of congresswomen and congressmen.[49] Anne Radigan once explained its goal as follows:

> To get across to the public at large, that women's issues are everybody's issues.
> Women don't live in a vacuum, they don't exist alone, and they certainly don't exist
> in a "we against them" adversary relationship. Women are wives who are dependent,
> women are wives who are working, women are daughters who are going to school,
> women are elderly parents who are vulnerable. . . . This is a family sort of preroga-
> tive. . . . Women's issues affect everyone.[50]

Women's issues such as the FMLA were a priority after the 1992 election, but
after the 1994 election the very survival of the caucus was in doubt. On December
6, 1994, the Republican Conference voted to eliminate provisions in the House rules

that permit representatives to use office staff funds to support legislative service organizations. If the vote is confirmed by the full House, the caucus will be forced to move off the Hill and seek private financing under the new cochairs elected in March 1995. The conservative tide and the defeat of nine Democratic caucus women will have a major impact on the organization regardless. The decision to take a pro-choice stance after sixteen years of remaining neutral on abortion was a response to the influx of Democratic women in 1992, but it may make it more difficult for returning caucus women to recruit new members from the incoming class of eight Republican and three Democratic congresswomen.

NOTES

1. Liberia Johnson, Joint Hearing on Disability and Parental Leave, 2261 Rayburn House Office Building, October 17, 1985, tape-recorded by the author. Subsequent quotations from testimony at the same hearing will not be footnoted.

2. Anonymous staff interview with the author for a case study of pension reform legislation, Washington, DC, July 19, 1984.

3. The number rose to seven in June 1993, when Kay Bailey Hutchison (R-TX) won a special election for the Senate. Although nine Democratic women lost in the Republican sweep of 1994, eight new Republican and three new Democratic women were elected to the House. The 104th Congress has forty-six women in the House and eight in the Senate. Olympia Snowe of Maine left the House and won a seat in the Senate.

4. Irwin N. Gertzog, *Congressional Women: Their Recruitment, Treatment, and Behavior* (Westport, CT; Praeger, 1984), pp. 80–87.

5. Ibid., p. 89.

6. Ibid., p. 197.

7. Susan Webb Hammond, "Congressional Caucuses in the Policy Process," in Lawrence C. Dodd and Bruce I. Oppenheimer (Eds.), *Congress Reconsidered*, 4th ed. (Washington, DC: C.Q. Press, 1989), p. 355; and Roger H. Davidson and Walter Oleszek, *Congress and Its Members*, 4th ed. (Washington, DC: C.Q. Press, 1994), p. 307.

8. Joan Hulse Thompson, "Role Perceptions of Women in the Ninety-fourth Congress," *Political Science Quarterly*, 95 (Spring 1980), p. 73.

9. Marge Roukema (R-NJ), a supporter of the FMLA since 1987, joined the caucus in mid-1993. There were fifty-five women in the 103rd Congress—forty-eight in the House and seven in the Senate. In the House, forty-two women belonged to the Caucus Executive Committee and three women senators were among the ten senators who subscribed to the caucus newsletter. There were thirty-five Democrats and seven Republicans on the Executive Committee in 1994.

10. Pat Schroeder was expected to become chair of the Education and Labor Committee in the 104th Congress. Since the Republicans won control of the House, she is ranking minority member rather than chair. Instead, caucus member Jan Meyers (R-KS) of the Small Business Committee will be the first woman to chair a House committee in twenty years. In the Senate, Republican Nancy Kassebaum, also of Kansas, will take over as chair of the Labor and Human Resources Committee as a result of her party's victory. Both Meyers and Kassebaum voted no on final passage of the FMLA.

11. After the 1994 elections, the diminished number of House Democrats reelected Barbara Kennelly (CT) over fellow caucus member Louise Slaughter (NY) to the party post of Democratic Caucus vice chair by a vote of 93 to 90. The minority leader, minority whip, and caucus chair are the three higher-ranking party leadership positions.

12. The most powerful committees are Appropriations, Budget, Ways and Means, Rules, and Energy and Commerce. See Lawrence C. Dodd and Bruce I. Oppenheimer, "Consolidating Power in the House: The Rise of a New Oligarchy," in *Congress Reconsidered*, pp. 48–50.

13. Gertzog, *Congressional Women*, p. 202.

14. Joan Hulse Thompson, "The Women's Rights Lobby in the Gender Gap Congress, 1983–84," *Commonwealth*, 2 (1988), pp. 19–35. The other side of the gender gap, higher support among men for Republican candidates, played a major role in Democratic defeats in 1994. Richard L. Berke, "Defections among Men to G.O.P. Helped Insure Rout of Democrats," *New York Times*, November 11, 1994, p. A1.

15. Anonymous staff interview with author, October 1985.

16. Anne L. Radigan, *Concept and Compromise: The Evolution of Family Leave Legislation in the U.S. Congress* (Washington, DC: Women's Research and Educational Institute, 1988), p. 12.

17. Ibid., p. 8.

18. Macon Morehouse, "Parental, Medical Leave Bill Gets Markup in Senate," *Congressional Quarterly Weekly Report*, 47 (April 22, 1989), p. 892.

19. Ibid.

20. Christine A. Russell, director of the Small Business Center, U.S. Chamber of Commerce, "America's Small Businesses Cannot Afford Mandated Leave," public information release, no date, pp. 1–2 (obtained from its author, January 1990).

21. Ibid.

22. Brian Nutting, "Parental-Leave Bill Passed by Panel," *Congressional Quarterly*, 47 (March 11, 1989), p. 519.

23. Radigan, *Concept and Compromise*, p. 2.

24. Russell, "America's Small Businesses," p. 2. One precedent does exist. The Veterans' Reemployment Rights Act (1940) mandates up to four years of leave with job security for workers called to active military duty.

25. Morehouse, "Markup in Senate," p. 892.

26. Anne Radigan, executive director, Congressional Caucus for Women's Issues, personal interview with author, Washington, DC, October 18, 1985.

27. Radigan, *Concept and Compromise*, p. 15. Indeed, Ms. Radigan notes that some of the reporters had a special interest in the story because they were dissatisfied with the parental leave policies of their own employers.

28. Nutting, "Parental-Leave Bill Passed by Panel," p. 519.

29. "Family and Medical Leave Act of 1987 Introduced," *Update*, February 27, 1987, p. 13.

30. Radigan, *Concept and Compromise*, p. 16.

31. "Family and Medical Leave Hearings in D.C. and on West Coast," *Update*, August 7, 1987, np.

32. "Capitol Boxscore," *Congressional Quarterly*, 47 (February 4, 1989), p. 243.

33. Roberta Spalter, Heidi Hartmann, and Sheila Gibbs, *Unnecessary Losses: Costs to Workers in the States of the Lack of Family and Medical Leave* (Washington, DC: Institute for Women's Policy Research, 1989), p. 3.

34. Marian Wright Edelman, *Families in Peril: An Agenda for Social Change* (Cambridge, MA: Harvard University Press, 1987).

35. *Philadelphia Inquirer*, March 3, 1990, p. A5.

36. "Family Leave Waits for Clinton," *Congressional Quarterly Almanac*, 48 (1992), p. 355.

37. Alissa Rubin, "Demise of Health Care Overhaul Produced Big Winners and Losers," *Congressional Quarterly*, 52 (October 1, 1994), p. 2799.

38. Alissa Rubin, "Overhaul Issue Unlikely to Rest in Peace," *Congressional Quarterly*, 52 (October 1, 1994), p. 2800.

39. "Democrats Stymied on Parental-Leave Bill," *Congressional Quarterly Almanac*, 44 (1988), p. 263.

40. "Parental-Leave Bill Moves Forward," *Congressional Quarterly*, 47 (April 15, 1989), p. 815.

41. Alyson Pytte, "House Passes Parental Leave: White House Promises Veto," *Congressional Quarterly*, 48 (May 12, 1990), 1471.

42. A Louis Harris Associates poll of 1,254 with a margin of error of plus or minus 3 percent. The other results were opposed to such a law (24 percent) and unsure (2 percent); cited in the *New York Times*, July 26, 1990.

43. Ellen Goodman, "Ambushing Bush on Family Leave," *Philadelphia Inquirer*, August 1, 1990, p. A9.

44. "Clinton Signs Family Leave Act," *Congressional Quarterly Almanac*, 49 (1993), p. 389.

45. Donna Lenhoff and Sharon Stoneback, "Review of State Legislation Guaranteeing Jobs for Family or Medical Leaves," Women's Legal Defense Fund, August 1989, pp. 5–6; *New York Times*, July 27, 1990, p. A8; and "Family and Medical Leave Legislation in the States," Women's Legal Defense Fund, June 1991.

46. "News from WLDA," press release from the Women's Legal Defense Fund, August 2, 1994, and the telephone interview with Donna Lentoff, WLDF general counsel, August 16, 1994.

47. "Comments of the United States Chamber of Commerce Regarding the Interim Regulations Implementing the Family and Medical Leave Act of 1993," provided by Nancy Reed Fulco, human resources attorney, U.S. Chamber of Commerce.

48. Primmer interview, July 28, 1989.

49. Betty Friedan, *The Second Stage* (New York: Summit, 1981), pp. 250–255.

50. Radigan interview, October 18, 1985.

FURTHER READINGS

Burrell, Barbara C. *A Woman's Place Is in the House: Campaigning for Congress in the Feminist Era*. Ann Arbor: University of Michigan Press, 1994.

Carroll, Susan J. *Women as Candidates in American Politics*. 2nd ed. Bloomington: Indiana University Press, 1994.

Conway, M. Margaret, David W. Ahern, and Gertrude A. Steuernagel. *Women and Public Policy: A Revolution in Progress*. Washington, DC: Congressional Quarterly, 1995.

Costain, Anne N. *Inviting Women's Rebellion: A Political Process Interpretation of the Women's Movement*. Baltimore: Johns Hopkins University Press, 1992.

Gelb, Joyce, and Marian Lief Palley. *Women and Public Policies*. 2nd ed. Princeton, NJ: Princeton University Press, 1987.

Gertzog, Irwin N. *Congressional Women: Their Recruitment, Treatment and Behavior.* 2nd ed. Westport, CT: Praeger, 1995.

Haas, Linda. *Equal Parenthood and Social Policy: A Study of Parental Leave in Sweden.* Albany: New York State University Press, 1992.

Klein, Ethel. *Gender Politics: From Consciousness to Mass Politics.* Cambridge, MA: Harvard University Press, 1984.

Mezey, Susan Gluck. *In Pursuit of Equality: Women, Public Policy, and the Federal Courts.* New York: St. Martin's Press, 1992.

Margolies-Mezvinsky, Marjorie. *A Woman's Place: The Freshmen Women Who Changed the Face of Congress.* Southbridge, MA: Crown, 1994.

Stetson, Dorothy McBride. *Women's Rights in the U.S.A.: Policy Debates and Gender Roles.* Pacific Grove, CA: Brooks/Cole, 1991.

Thomas, Sue. *How Women Legislate.* New York: Oxford University Press, 1994.

Women's Research and Education Institute. *The American Woman: A Status Report.* New York: Norton, 1986, 1988, 1990, 1992, 1994.

Sex at Risk in Insurance Classifications? The Supreme Court as Shaper of Public Policy

Ruth Bamberger

Since the onset of the women's movement in the late 1960s, the private insurance industry has been confronted by civil rights groups, particularly feminist organizations, and government agencies over the treatment of insurance consumers whose risk potential is determined in part by gender classification. Numerous studies by congressional committees, state insurance commissions, and feminist ad hoc groups revealed practices whereby women in the same occupation, age, and health categories as men were subjected to demeaning underwriting criteria, denied equal access to coverage and benefits, particularly in health and disability insurance, and charged higher premium rates. Men, too, were found to be victimized by gender classification, especially in life and in auto insurance, where companies charge young males more than women of the same age.

As a result of political pressures on the insurance industry, almost half of the fifty states have adopted insurance regulations prohibiting differential treatment in coverage and benefits of males and females.[1] But gender is still widely used as a classification in setting premium rates for individual health, life, disability, auto, and retirement insurance. Only one state, Montana, prohibits by law the use of the gender classification for any purpose, including rate setting.[2] Five other states ban the gender classification only in auto insurance, where it is seen to disadvantage men.[3] Selective prohibition of gender discrimination and inattention to the disparate economic impact of sex-divided pricing on women by the insurance indus-

Ruth Bamberger is a professor of Political Science at Drury College.

try are presently legally defensible in the absence of a constitutional presumption that sex classification violates women's right to equal protection of the law.

The insurance industry's reluctance to forego the gender classification is a direct consequence of insurance marketing methods that use classification to exclude some customers and price-compete for others. Actuarial tables demonstrate that women and men have different morbidity and mortality experience, though some studies conclude otherwise.[4] The gender classification, selectively used, promotes the impression that classifications are impelled by costs, not selling strategies. Most companies charge women higher prices for health, disability, and retirement plans, while men pay higher prices for life insurance, and young men pay more for auto insurance. These price differences originated as sales discounts and continue to serve that function. In auto insurance, for example, women's discounts cease around age twenty-five, although men at every age average more accidents than women.

CRITIQUE OF INSURER'S USE OF THE GENDER CLASSIFICATION

Criticisms of the insurance industry's use of the gender classification are numerous. The most basic is its acceptance of gender as an a priori differential. Simply stated, gender is used to justify using gender. What actuarial data tell us, then, is something about the average woman or man, but application of these averages to individuals grossly distorts reality, with unequal treatment as the result.[5] Stated another way, overreliance on the gender classification allows other meaningful risk factors to be overlooked.

Critics also argue that continued use of the gender classification perpetuates traditional stereotypes of men and women. For example, underwriting manuals well into the 1970s labeled women as "malingerers, marginal employees working mainly for convenience, and delicately balanced machines eagerly awaiting a breakdown. . . . If a woman has disability coverage, the temptation exists to replace her earnings with an insurance income once work loses its attractiveness."[6]

Finally, insurers should not use a classification scheme over which the insured have no control. Sex, like race, is an immutable characteristic and therefore should not be used as a basis for determining costs and coverage of insurance policies. Critics document insurance practices prior to the civil rights movement whereby race was casually employed as a classification. This practice was eliminated because it was not constitutionally acceptable, even though Blacks and Whites had different morbidity and mortality rates. Although sex discrimination is not unconstitutional, the same social policy should apply to the sex classification.[7]

FEDERAL COURTS AND SEX DISCRIMINATION IN INSURANCE

Even though the campaign to eliminate sex discrimination in insurance has been waged largely at the state level, where the insurance industry is regulated, a major vehicle for challenging industry practice has been the federal courts via Title VII of the Civil Rights Act of 1964. The law states that it is an unlawful employment practice for an employer "to fail or refuse to hire or to discharge any individual, or otherwise to discriminate against any individual with respect to compensation, terms, conditions, or privileges of employment, because of such individual's race, color, religion, sex, or national origin. . . ."[8] The Equal Employment Opportunity Act of 1972 broadened Title VII to include in the definition of *employer* government agencies at the state and local levels.

Because many companies and government agencies provide compensation by way of insurance benefits to their employees (over 80 percent of all Americans are enrolled in employer-sponsored health, disability, and pension plans), sex-based insurance plans became a viable target for calling into question the common practice of classification by sex. Civil rights and feminist groups surmised that if the federal courts would strike down sex-based employer plans that affected large numbers of people, this would have a spillover effect on the insurance industry. A careful examination of Supreme Court opinions in key cases provides clues about the direction of public policy in the controversy over the sex classification in insurance.

WOMEN AND THE SEX CLASSIFICATION IN DISABILITY AND RETIREMENT INSURANCE

Beginning with the 1970s, the Supreme Court decided several cases that have played a major role in defining the parameters of sex classification schemes in disability and retirement insurance. The disability cases, *Geduldig v. Aiello* (1974) and *General Electric v. Gilbert* (1976), raised the question of whether employer-sponsored disability plans that excluded pregnancy constituted unlawful sex discrimination.[9] In both cases, the majority of the Court upheld the plans, arguing that the pregnancy exclusion was not a sex-based classification but a classification of "pregnant . . . and non-pregnant persons."[10]

Geduldig and *Gilbert* demonstrated the unwillingness of the Court to undo established insurance practice. The insurance industry has never considered normal pregnancy a disability; moreover, it argued in *Gilbert* that if pregnancy were included in an employee group plan, it would significantly drive up employers' costs.[11] Public reaction after the *Gilbert* decision was so great that in 1978 Congress passed the Pregnancy Discrimination Act as an amendment to Title VII, requiring employers with disability plans to include pregnancy benefits.[12]

In 1978 the Supreme Court considered the validity of a sex differential in an employee retirement plan in *Los Angeles Department of Water and Power v. Manhart*.[13] The case involved a pension program of the Los Angeles department whereby females made larger contributions from their salaries to the pension fund than males, on the basis that women as a class live longer than men. The department had calculated, from a study of mortality tables and its own employee experience, that women should contribute 14.84 percent more per monthly paycheck than men because they would draw more monthly payments from the fund over their average life span. The Court struck down the plan on a 6–2 vote. The central argument of the majority opinion, written by Justice Stevens, was that Title VII specifically prohibits discrimination against any *individual* on the basis of sex, and therefore it is illegal to treat one gender group differently from the other.

Although it appears that Stevens was attacking the common insurance practice of classifying by gender, he tempered the majority opinion by stating that Title VII was not intended to revolutionize the insurance industry: All that is at issue today is a requirement that men and women make unequal contributions to an employer-sponsored pension fund. Nothing in our holding implies that it would be unlawful for an employer to set aside equal retirement contributions for each employee and let each retiree purchase the largest benefit that his or her accumulated contributions could command in the open market. Nor does it call into question the insurance industry practice of considering the composition of an employer's workforce in determining the probable cost of a retirement or death benefit plan.[14]

In 1983 the Supreme Court reaffirmed. *Manhart* in *Arizona Governing Committee v. Norris*, though by a narrower margin, 5–4.[15] The State of Arizona's retirement plan differed from the Los Angeles plan in that employee contributions were not determined by sex; upon retirement, however, women's monthly payments were lower because of their longer life expectancy. The plan provided employees three options at retirement—a lump sum benefit, a fixed monthly payment over a fixed number of years, or a lifetime annuity. Women's benefits under the first two options were the same as men's, but the lifetime annuity option gave women a smaller monthly payment than men. The litigant in the case, Natalie Norris, in opting for the lifetime annuity, would be paid $320 per month at age sixty-five, whereas a man in an identical situation would collect $354 a month.

Justice Marshall, who wrote the majority opinion, reaffirmed the Court's position in *Manhart*: "We have no hesitation in holding . . . that the classification of employees on the basis of sex is no more permissible at the payout stage of a retirement plan than at the pay-in stage."[16]

In defending the retirement plan, the state of Arizona contended that Title VII was not applicable in their case, since retirement options were being offered through a third party (an insurance company) whose policies were comparable to what was available in the open market. The Court rebutted this argument by noting that when the state entered into such an agreement, it was the responsible agent for employee pension plans, and hence subject to Title VII requirements.

It should be noted that Justice Powell, who voted with the majority in *Manhart*, was on the minority side in *Norris*, precisely because the Arizona plan was provided by a third-party insurer. He believed that striking down such a plan, where the insurer used actuarially sound sex-based mortality tables, amounted to revolutionizing the insurance and pension industries, which *Manhart* went out of its way to avoid.[17]

MEN AND THE SEX CLASSIFICATION IN RETIREMENT INSURANCE

The Supreme Court decisions in *Manhart* and *Norris* ended discriminatory treatment for women in a prospective manner, but women did not get retroactive relief of any kind, and the Court grandfathered into the future unequal payments to women already retired. Two years before the *Manhart* decision, however, the Supreme Court was more generous with men in the settlement of a dispute over a retirement plan for state employees of Connecticut. The case, *Fitzpatrick v. Bitzer* (1976), was brought by current and retired male employees of the state on the allegation that the statutory retirement plan discriminated against them on the basis of their sex.[18] The Connecticut plan allowed female employees with over twenty-five years of service to the state to retire at age fifty with full retirement benefits, while men were not eligible until age fifty-five. Reduced retirement benefits were also available to employees who left state employment before they were eligible to retire. The plan adversely affected men, who, if they left at age fifty-five, would receive less than a woman of similar age, who could already be drawing full benefits after age fifty. The Court not only struck down the retirement plan on Title VII grounds but concluded that all retirees and their survivors were entitled, under protection of the Fourteenth Amendment, to retroactive payments dating back to the adoption of the pension program in 1939.

Surprisingly, the Supreme Court did not cite the *Fitzpatrick* decision in either *Manhart* or *Norris*. All three cases involved violations of Title VII of the Civil Rights Act of 1964, as amended in 1972. The awarding of back pay to male employees in the *Fitzpatrick* decision was rendered on Fourteenth Amendment grounds, namely, that Congress could require states to correct sex discrimination practices, even if the costs were significant.[19]

FITZPATRICK, MANHART, NORRIS, *AND THEIR AFTERMATH*

The Supreme Court's decisions on gender discrimination in group retirement plans have had a wide impact on employer-sponsored pension plans. The TIAA-CREF retirement plan for college teachers is a case in point. The system of unequal payments to male and female retirees had been in the federal court pipeline for several years prior to *Norris* in 1983. On the same day that the Supreme Court handed down its decision in *Norris*, it remanded to the appellate courts two cases challenging the TIAA-CREF plan.[20] As a result, all TIAA-CREF participants now receive unisex benefits on annuity income payments made after May 1, 1980.[21]

On the question of retroactive payments to employees, the Supreme Court, on a 9–0 vote, granted relief to all male retirees and their survivors in *Fitzpatrick* but was less kindly disposed to women retirees in *Manhart* and *Norris*. In *Manhart*, seven justices argued against retroactive pay. Justice Stevens, speaking for the majority, alluded to a precedent in *Albemarle Paper Co. v. Moody*, where the Court established generous guidelines for awarding back pay for violations of Title VII, but it was not to be given automatically in every case.[22] Granting retroactivity in a case like *Manhart* would not be practical, according to Stevens, as pension plans could be jeopardized by drastic changes in the rules.[23] It was enough of a blow to employers to adapt to the Court's decision requiring equal contributions from men and women.

In *Norris* the number of justices arguing against retroactive payments was reduced to five, while four supported some kind of retroactive relief. Justice O'Connor, whose vote was crucial in the 5–4 vote striking down the Arizona plan, did not go along with the four justices who thought that relief should apply to all benefit payments made after the federal district court's judgment in *Norris*. O'Connor maintained, as did Stevens in *Manhart*, that the magnitude of a decision awarding retroactive relief would have the effect of disrupting current pension plans.[24] In contrast, retroactive relief for male employees in *Fitzpatrick* was awarded. The Supreme Court granted men equal protection of the law in *Fitzpatrick* but denied this protection to women in *Manhart* and *Norris*.

PROSPECTS FOR ELIMINATION OF THE SEX CLASSIFICATION IN INSURANCE

One immediate consequence of the *Manhart* and *Norris* decisions was the introduction of bills in Congress in the late 1970s and early 1980s to prohibit insurance companies nationwide from using gender classification in determining coverage, benefits, and prices. Known as the Non-Discrimination in Insurance Act in the House and the Fair Insurance Practices Act in the Senate,[25] the bills were introduced under Congress's prerogative in the McCarran–Ferguson Act[26] and its authority to regulate interstate commerce and to legislate in matters of civil rights. While the legislation received wide support from women's groups and organizations such as the American Association of University Professors, the American Association of Retired Persons, and the Leadership Conference on Civil Rights, the insurance industry waged an expensive lobbying campaign to kill the legislation, and was successful.[27]

Thus far, most state equal rights amendments and equal protection provisions have failed to protect women against sex discrimination in insurance. The insurance industry continues to use sex as a rate classification, despite the numerous efforts of women's organizations to reverse public policy.[28]

THE SUPREME COURT AND PROSPECTS FOR ELIMINATING THE SEX CLASSIFICATION IN INSURANCE

It would be an overstatement to say that the Supreme Court has been the primary mover and shaker in shaping public policy on sex discrimination in the insurance industry. But one could cogently argue that in the American constellation of political decision makers, it has been a strategic actor. The Court's decisions in *Fitzpatrick, Manhart,* and *Norris* serve notice to the insurance industry that gender discrimination in insurance merits heightened scrutiny. But the Court has also made it clear that it will not definitively reject gender discrimination.

Women's rights and civil rights organizations must look beyond the judiciary to eliminate the practice of insurance sex discrimination. One possible avenue is a

reintroduced federal Equal Rights Amendment (ERA) that incorporates a legislative history clearly articulating that the scope of equal rights for women and men
extends to insurance practices. Sex, just like race, would be excluded as a rate classification in insurance, because it would be unconstitutional. Only when gendered
human beings have constitutional protection under an ERA will the Supreme
Court, as guardian of the Constitution, speak out clearly against sex discrimination
in insurance.

NOTES

1. Primary regulation of the insurance industry rests
with the fifty states. This arrangement dates back to the
middle of the nineteenth century, when individual
states legislated regulatory agencies to oversee the
growing business of insurance. The McCarran–
Ferguson Act, passed by Congress in 1945, reaffirmed
state regulation, though not exclusively. Congress reserved for itself the authority to enact insurance legislation under the following clause in McCarran: "No Act
of Congress shall be construed to invalidate, impair, or
supersede any law enacted by any State for the purpose
of regulating the business of insurance . . . unless such
Act specifically relates to the business of insurance."
15 U.S.C. 1012(b) (1982).

2. Montana Code Ann. 49–2–309 (1983).

3. Hawaii, Massachusetts, Michigan, North Carolina,
and Pennsylvania. For pathbreaking work on automo-
bile insurance sex discrimination, see Patrick Butler,
Twiss Butler, and Laurie Williams, "Sex-Divided
Mileage, Accident, and Insurance Cost Data Show That
Auto Insurers Overcharge Most Women," parts 1 and 2
Journal of Insurance Regulation, 6 (1988), pp. 243–284,
373–420.

4. See U.S. Congress, Joint Economic Committee, *Hearings, Economic Problems of Women*, 93rd Cong., 1st sess.,
1973, pp. 151–220; "The Weaker Sex." *Life Notes*,
National Association of Life Underwriters, April
1974; California Commission on the Status of Women,
Women and Insurance, 1975.

5. An excellent example is the sex differential used in
dental and vision care insurance. No medical explanations are available to verify differences in men and
women. Yet the insurance industry uses the sex classification anyway, and indeed has established such a differential, with the result that women pay higher rates.
Robert Randall, "Risk Classification and Actuarial
Tables as They Affect Insurance Pricing for Women
and Minorities," in *Discrimination against Minorities and
Women in Pensions and Health, Life, and Disability Insurance*. Vol. 1. U.S. Commission on Civil Rights (Ed.),
(Washington, DC: Government Printing Office, 1978),
pp. 568, 576.

To further illustrate, studies of mortality differences
by sex show a considerable overlap between men and

women with respect to the age at which death occurs.
For over 80 percent of males, one can find a matching
female who died at approximately the same time. Sex
is not a reliable predictor of mortality, so that it would
be misleading even to talk about an average man or
average woman. For references to the debate over overlapping death rates of men and women, see Spencer
Kimball, "Reverse Sex Discrimination: *Manhart*," *American Bar Foundation Research Journal* 83 (1979), pp.
120–123; and Lea Brilmayer et al., "Sex Discrimination
in Employer-Sponsored Insurance Plans: A Legal and
Demographic Analysis," *University of Chicago Law
Revue*, 47 (1980), pp. 530–531.

6. Quoted in Suzanne Stoiber, "Insured: Except in Case
of War, Suicide, and Organs Peculiar to Females," *Ms.*
(June 1973), p. 114.

7. Anne C. Cicero, "Strategies for the Elimination of Sex
Discrimination in Insurance," *Harvard Civil Rights-Civil
Liberties Law Review* 20 (1985), p. 211; Brilmayer et al.,
"Sex Discrimination," pp. 526–529.

8. 42 U.S.C. 2000e-2(a) (1).

9. *Geduldig v. Aiello*, 417 U.S. 484 (1974). This case, challenging a California state disability plan, was argued on
Fourteenth Amendment equal protection grounds. With
the exception of *Fitzpatrick v. Bitzer*, 427 U.S. 445 (1976),
infra 17, which was argued on both Title VII and Fourteenth Amendment grounds, other federal court cases
referred to in this study were argued on Title VII grounds
only; *General Electric v. Gilbert*, 429 U.S. 125 (1976).

10. 417 U.S. at 496–497 n. 20.

11. 429 U.S. at 131.

12. Pregnancy Discrimination Act as codified at 42
U.S.C. 2000e (k) (1982).

13. *Los Angeles Department of Water and Power v. Manhart*, 435 U.S. 702 (1978).

14. Ibid., at 717–718.

15. *Arizona Governing Committee v. Norris*, 463 U.S. 1073
(1983).

16. Ibid., at 1081.

17. Ibid., at 1099.

18. *Fitzpatrick v. Bitzer*, 427 U.S. 445 (1976). The significance of the 1976 *Fitzpatrick* decision was first described

by Ruth Weyand, who was a senior attorney with the federal Equal Employment Opportunity Commission. See the *14th National Conference on Women and the Law Sourcebook* pp. 303–304 for Weyand's list of Title VII pension cases that ended early retirement pay discrimination against men with back pay before the retirement pay discrimination against women was ended without back pay.

19. A U.S. District Court's opinion on attorney's fees stated that the *Fitzpatrick* settlement would eventually cost Connecticut almost $400 million over forty years. 445 F. Supp. 1338, 1343 (D. Conn., 1978).

20. *Teachers Insurance and Annuity Association v. Spirt* and *Long Island University v. Spirt*, 691 F.2d 1054, 463 U.S. 1223 (1983); *Peters v. Wayne State University*, 691 F.2d 235, 463 U.S. 1223 (1983).

21. For a complete summary of TIAA-CREF action after *Norris*, see *News from TIAA-CREF*, October 9, 1984.

22. *Albermarle Paper Co. v. Moody*, 422 U.S. 405 (1975).

23. 435 U.S. at 718–723.

24. 463 U.S. at 1109–1111. Five years after *Norris*, the Supreme Court ruled that the State of Florida did not have to pay $43.6 million in retroactive payments to male state employees whose spouses shared in their pension plans prior to *Norris*. At dispute in this case was a plan where male employees with spouses were paid less than female employees with spouses, on the basis that female spouses lived longer than the male

spouses of female employees. *Florida v. Hughlan Long*, *U.S. Law Week*, 56 (1988), pp. 4718–4725.

25. For the House version of this legislation, see *Non-Discrimination in Insurance Act of 1983: Hearings on H.R.100 before the Subcommittee on Commerce, Transportation, and Tourism of the Committee on Energy and Commerce*, 98th Cong., 1st sess. 1–15 (1983). H.R. 100 was significantly weakened through the adoption of an amendment that would exempt sex discrimination in individual private insurance contracts. For the Senate version of this legislation, see *Fair Insurance Practices Act: Hearings on S. 372 before the Committee on Commerce, Science, and Transportation*, 98th Cong., 1st sess., 2–16 (1983).

26. *Supra*, 1.

27. The campaign cost the industry almost $2 million. A group called the Committee for Fair Insurance Rates was financed by thirty-three companies for the express purpose of "educating" the public about the adverse consequences of H.R. 100 and S. 372. Common Cause *NEWS*, September 21, 1983; *National Underwriter* (Life and Health Edition), October 1, 1983, p. 2.

28. The National Organization for Women maintains an office in Washington, D.C., committed to eliminating insurance sex discrimination. I am indebted to Dr. Patrick Butler, director of the NOW Insurance Project, for current information about action at the federal and state levels on sex discrimination in insurance.

FURTHER READINGS

Abraham, Kenneth S. *Distributing Risk: Insurance, Legal Theory, and Public Policy*. New Haven, CT: Yale University Press, 1986.

Benston, George J. "The Economics of Gender Discrimination in Employee Fringe Benefits: *Manhart* Revisited." *University of Chicago Law Review* 49 (1982), pp. 489–542.

———. "Discrimination and Economic Efficiency in Employee Fringe Benefits: A Clarification of Issues and a Response to Professors Brilmayer, Laycock, and Sullivan"; Brilmayer, Lea, Douglas Laycock, and Teresa Sullivan. "The Efficient Use of Group Averages as Nondiscrimination: A Rejoinder to Professor Benston." *University of Chicago Law Review* 50 (1983), pp. 222–279.

Brilmayer, Lea, Richard Hekeler, Douglas Laycock, and Teresa Sullivan. "Sex Discrimination in Employer-Sponsored Insurance Plans: A Legal and Demographic Analysis." *University of Chicago Law Review* 47 (1980), pp. 505–560.

Butler, Patrick, Twiss Butler, and Laurie Williams. "Sex-Divided Mileage, Accident, and Insurance Cost

Data Show That Auto Insurers Overcharge Most Women." *Journal of Insurance Regulation* 6 (1988), pp. 243–284, 373–420.

Cicero, Anne C. "Strategies for the Elimination of Sex Discrimination in Insurance." *Harvard Civil Rights–Civil Liberties Review* 20 (1985), pp. 211–267.

Commission on Civil Rights. *Discrimination against Women and Minorities in Pensions and Health, Life, and Disability Insurance*. Washington, DC: U.S. Government Printing Office. Vol. 1 (1978).

Comptroller General of the United States. *Economic Implications of the Fair Insurance Practices Act*. Report to Sen. Orrin G. Hatch et al., GAO/OCE-84-1, April 6, 1984.

Jerry, Robert H. II. "Gender and Insurance." In M. Margaret Conway, David W. Ahern, Gertrude A. Steuernagel. (Eds.). *Women and Public Policy*. Washington, DC: Congressional Quarterly Press, 1994, pp. 102–123.

Kimball, Spencer L. "Reverse Sex Discrimination: *Manhart*." *American Bar Foundation Research Journal* (Winter 1979), pp. 83–139.

Affirmative Action as a Woman's Issue

Roberta Ann Johnson

Debate about affirmative action is often heated and emotionally charged. It generates discussions about "merit";[1] it buries academics in Department of Labor statistics;[2] it absorbs lawyers and historians in interpretation of congressional intent;[3] and it bogs down the public policy experts with narrow implementation matters.[4] All this often misses the essential point about affirmative action, which is that its goal is redistribution.[5]

In what ways does a policy of affirmative action assist women to become fully integrated into schools, training programs, and jobs? This article will (1) define affirmative action, (2) detail the development of federal affirmative action guidelines, (3) describe Supreme Court decisions relating to affirmative action and Congress's reaction, and (4) consider the ways in which affirmative action is a woman's issue.

AFFIRMATIVE ACTION DEFINED

Affirmative action is a generic term for programs that take some kind of initiative, either voluntarily or under the compulsion of law, to increase, maintain, or re-

Roberta Ann Johnson is a professor of politics at the University of San Francisco.

"This is a revised version of an article that appeared in the *Journal of Political Science*, vol. 17, Nos. 1 and 2 (Spring 1989). Reprinted with permission."

The author would like to acknowledge Megan Andesha, a student at the University of San Francisco, who assisted in the research of the most recent Supreme Court cases.

arrange the number or status of certain group members, usually defined by race or gender, within a larger group. When these programs are characterized by race or gender preference, "especially when coupled with rigorously pursued 'goals,' [they] are highly controversial because race and gender are generally thought to be 'irrelevant' to employment and admissions decisions" and are "immutable characteristics over which individuals lack control."[6]

AFFIRMATIVE ACTION AND FEDERAL GUIDELINES

Significant moves to prohibit discrimination in the public sector began in the late 1930s and early 1940s, according to David Rosenbloom, who describes a series of executive orders, starting with the Roosevelt administration, that called for a policy of nondiscrimination in employment.[7] However, it is President John F. Kennedy's executive order, issued March 16, 1961, that is usually seen as representing the real roots of present-day affirmative action policy.[8] Executive Order 10,925 required government contractors to take affirmative action and established specific sanctions for noncompliance.[9] Nevertheless, even the order's principal draftsperson admitted that the enforcement process led to a great deal of complainant frustration.[10]

Before another executive order would be issued, civil rights exploded onto the public agenda. A march on Washington held on August 28, 1963, brought 200,000 Black and White supporters of civil rights to the Capitol. In response to this and other demonstrations, and as a result of shifting public sentiment, President Kennedy sent a civil rights bill to Congress; it was passed in 1964, after his assassination. The Civil Rights Act of 1964 included in its provisions Title VI, which prohibited discrimination on the basis of race, color, or national origin by all recipients of federal funds, including schools, and Title VII, which made it unlawful for any employer or labor union to discriminate in employment on the basis of race, color, religion, sex, or national origin. Title VII also created the Equal Employment Opportunity Commission (EEOC) for enforcement in the private sector.

The following year, 1965, President Lyndon B. Johnson issued Executive Order 11,246 barring discrimination on the basis of race, color, religion, or national origin by federal contractors and subcontractors.[11] On October 13, 1967, it was amended by Executive Order 11,375 to expand its coverage to women. One major innovation of the order was to shift enforcement to the secretary of labor by creating an Office of Federal Contract Compliance (OFCC). Starting in 1968, the government established the enforceability of the executive order with legal action[12] and, for the first time, issued notices of proposed debarment (contract cancellation) using its administrative process.[13]

Prodded to be more specific about its standards, the OFCC began to spell out exactly what affirmative action meant in the context of the construction industry, and that became a model for all affirmative action programs.[14] During this period, President Richard Nixon played the role of champion of affirmative action, saving LBJ's executive order.

In 1968 the OFCC focused on Blacks in the construction industry. The result was the Philadelphia Plan, which was developed in three stages. First, the OFCC required preaward affirmative action plans from low bidders in some labor market areas, like Philadelphia. But because there were no guidelines for acceptability, the industry pressured Congress, which stimulated an opinion from the comptroller general, who recommended that the OFCC provide minimum requirements and standards by which programs would be judged. The second or revised Philadelphia Plan was then developed. It required that contractors submit a statement of "goals" of minority employment together with their bids, which took into account the minority participation and availability in the trade, as well as the need for training programs. On September 23, 1969, the Labor Department issued its third and final set of guidelines for the Philadelphia Plan after having determined the degree to which there was discrimination in construction crafts. This final plan established ranges within which the contractor's goals had to fall and recommended filling vacancies and new jobs approximately on the basis of one minority craftsman for each nonminority craftsman.

The comptroller general found the revised plan illegal on the ground that it set up quotas. But the attorney general issued an opinion declaring the plan to be legal and advised the secretary of labor to ignore the comptroller general's opinion. The comptroller general then urged the Senate Subcommittee on Deficiencies and Supplementals to attach a rider onto its appropriations bill prohibiting the use of funds to pay for efforts to achieve specific minority employment goals. The Nixon administration lobbied hard in the House and succeeded in eliminating the rider. On reconsideration, the Senate also defeated the rider, and the Philadelphia Plan was saved.

In 1971 the Department of Labor issued general guidelines that had the same features as the Philadelphia Plan, making it clear that "goals and timetables" were meant to "increase materially the utilization of minorities and women," with underutilization being spelled out as "having fewer minorities or women in a particular job classification than would reasonably be expected by their availability. . . ."[15] The 1971 Department of Labor guidelines, called Revised Order 4, were to govern employment practices by government contractors and subcontractors in industry and higher education.

Hole and Levine, in *Rebirth of Feminism*, document the initial exclusion of women from the guidelines. In 1970 Secretary of Labor Hodgson even publicly remarked that he had "no intention of applying literally exactly the same approach for women" as was applied to eliminate discrimination against minorities.[16] However, because of publicity and pressure by women's groups, by April 1973 women were finally included as full beneficiaries in the Revised Order 4.

What is important about the Philadelphia Plan and the Department of Labor guidelines is that they established not only the principle but also the guidelines for the practice of affirmative action that other civil rights enforcement agencies and even the courts would follow.

During the 1970s, administrative changes strengthened affirmative action. The Office of Management and Budget enlarged and refined the definition of *mi-*

nority group and, under President Carter, affirmative action efforts were consolidated. By executive order on October 5, 1978, the OFCC went from overview responsibility, whereby each department had responsibility for the compliance of its own contractors (with uneven results), to consolidated contract compliance, whereby the OFCC was given enforcement responsibility over all contractors;[17] overnight, 1,600 people who had been working for other departments were now working for Labor. The expanded program now was called the Office of Federal Contract Compliance Programs (OFCCP).

During the 1980s, there were attempts to weaken affirmative action. The Reagan administration publicly and continually criticized goals and timetables, calling them quotas.[18] By 1982 the OFCCP's budget and number of workers were significantly reduced. By 1983, while President Reagan used attitudes toward affirmative action as a litmus test to successfully reorganize the U.S. Commission on Civil Rights, his attempt to rescind or revise Executive Order 11,246 by specifically prohibiting numerical hiring goals was successfully stopped by opposition from within his own administration.[19] Nevertheless, during these years, the administration whittled away at the policy. In 1983 it instituted changes within the OFCCP that affected the agency's case determinations and remedies, although by January 1987 some of these changes were rescinded. On January 21, 1987, Joseph N. Cooper, director of the OFCCP, quit his job in protest. In an interview, he spoke candidly about the "number of officials in the Labor Department and elsewhere in the Administration who were intent on destroying the contract compliance program."[20]

While President George Bush, during his four-year term, was no friend to affirmative action, he seemed to oppose it for tactical political reasons rather than because of strident political ideology. Even Democratic President Bill Clinton seemed gun-shy when it came to affirmative action. Clinton abandoned Lani Guinier, his choice for director of the Civil Rights Division of the Justice Department, when she was portrayed by the media as the "quota queen." Although this characterization was untrue, Clinton quickly disassociated himself from Guinier and withdrew his nomination in the interest of maintaining his own centrist image.

THE BAKKE DECISION AND OTHER COURT DECISIONS

Affirmative action policy for student admissions has a very different history. Its source is Title VI of the Civil Rights Act of 1964 and Title IX of the Educational Amendments of 1972, not Executive Order 11,246. Title VI *requires* affirmative action steps to be taken in admissions *only as a remedy* for past discrimination. However, most minority affirmative action admission programs were self-imposed.[21] Title IX (subpart B, section 106.17) of the Educational Amendments of 1972, which prohibits *sex* discrimination, also calls for affirmative steps to be taken to remedy "past exclusion." A case having to do with minority affirmative action in admissions became the most well known and celebrated test of the principle of affirmative action.

Justice Lewis Powell announced the *Bakke v. University of California* Supreme Court decision to a hushed courtroom on the morning of June 28, 1978. He said, "We speak today with notable lack of unanimity." In fact, the 154 pages of judicial text presented *six* separate opinions and *two* separate majorities.[22]

Allan Bakke wanted to be a medical doctor. In 1973, at age thirty-three, while employed as a full-time engineer, he applied to a dozen medical schools, one of which was the University of California–Davis, and was turned down by all of them. The next year, after a second rejection from the twelve medical schools, Bakke sued the University of California in the California Court system, claiming that Davis's use of racial quotas was what had excluded him from medical school.

The *Bakke* case was not a strong one for those who supported affirmative action. On trial was an admissions program that reserved 16 of its 100 places for minority students (Blacks, Hispanics, and Asians), which looked like an admissions "quota" system. Furthermore, the Davis Medical School was founded in 1968, so the school could not claim that affirmative action was a remedy for past years of discrimination.

In this case, fifty-eight amicus curiae briefs were filed, and "The Court seemed less a judicial sanctum than a tug of war among contesting lobbyists."[23] When the dust cleared, the Court found a way both to admit Allan Bakke, now age thirty-eight, to the Davis Medical School and to defend the practice of affirmative action. By a 5–4 margin, the Court rejected the Davis program with a fixed number of seats for minorities; but also, by a different 5–4 margin, the Court accepted race-conscious admissions as being consistent with the Constitution and with Title VI.[24]

OTHER COURT DECISIONS AFTER BAKKE

Two cases that followed *Bakke*, *Weber* in 1979 and *Fullilove* in 1980, helped clarify the legal picture on affirmative action. In a 5–2 decision in *Weber* (two Supreme Court members did not participate), it was ruled permissible under Title VII for the private sector voluntarily to apply a compensatory racial preference for employment.

Brian Weber was an unskilled laboratory employee at the Gramercy, Louisiana, plant of the Kaiser Aluminum and Chemical Corporation. In 1974, while Blacks made up 39 percent of Gramercy's general labor force, at the Kaiser plant, only 2 percent of the 273 skilled craft workers were Black. Kaiser instituted a training program for its unskilled workers, earmarking half the trainee openings for Blacks until the percentage of Black craftspeople corresponded to their proportion in the labor force. Weber had more seniority than some of the Blacks chosen for the program. The Court, however, argued that Kaiser's affirmative action program was a reasonable response to the need to break down old patterns of segregation.

The following year, in *Fullilove*, the Supreme Court decided, 6–3, that a congressional affirmative action program, a 10 percent set-aside of federal funds for minority business people, provided in the Public Works Employment Act of 1977, was also permissible under the Constitution.

Fullilove v. Klutznick was decided during the summer of 1980.[25] Chief Justice Burger wrote the majority opinion, which found the "limited use of racial and ethnic criteria" constitutionally permissible when its purpose was to remedy the present effects of past racial discrimination. With this case, Father Mooney suggests that, with certain qualifications, the Supreme Court legitimized affirmative action as a policy for U.S. society.[26] But not so when it came to layoffs.

In 1984, when layoffs were concerned, the Court shifted from its permissive view on classwide "race conscious remedies." On June 12, 1984, the Supreme Court issued its decision in *Firefighters Local Union No. 1784 v. Stotts*, which focused on the extent to which seniority systems may be overridden as part of court-ordered relief to remedy discrimination in employment. It was a 6–3 decision.

Carl Stotts was a Black firefighter in the Memphis, Tennessee, Fire Department. He brought a class action lawsuit into federal district court in 1977, alleging discriminatory hiring and promotion practices in the department. This resulted in a consent decree in 1980 requiring that the percentage of Black employees in each job classification be increased to the proportion of Blacks in the local labor force.

The next year, because of budget problems, the city began to make plans to lay off firefighters on a seniority basis (last hired, first fired). "Black firefighters asked the court to prohibit the layoff of Black employees. The court ordered the city not to apply its seniority policy in a manner that would reduce the percentage of blacks in the department. The case was appealed to the Supreme Court."[27]

The Supreme Court said that the seniority system could not be disregarded in laying people off and that although there was protection for actual victims of discrimination, "mere membership in the disadvantaged class was an insufficient basis for judicial relief."[28] In other words, a seniority system could be used to lay people off even though many Blacks would be the first to go. The same was true in *Wygant v. Jackson Board of Education*, which was decided May 19, 1986.

In *Wygant*, nonminority teachers in Jackson, Michigan, challenged their terminations under a collective bargaining agreement requiring layoffs in reverse order of seniority unless it resulted in more minority layoffs than the current percentage employed. This layoff provision was adopted by the Jackson Board of Education in 1972 because of racial tension in the community that extended to its schools. In a 5–4 decision, the court said that this system of layoffs violated the rights of the nonminority teachers even though (unlike the case of *Stotts*) it was a part of their collective bargaining agreement. Powell, writing for the Court, argued that he could not find enough to justify the use of racial classifications.[29] Affirmative action was not as important as seniority when it came to layoffs.

Nevertheless, the "principle" of affirmative action actually survived in the majority's opinion in *Wygant*. The Court again affirmed that under certain circumstances policies using race-based classifications were justified. It was just that, for the majority, these were not the right circumstances. Marshall's words written in his dissenting opinion ring true: "Despite the Court's inability to agree on a route, we have reached a common destination in sustaining affirmative action against constitutional attack."[30] His assessment was to be proved correct in the February

25, 1987, case *US v. Paradise*, and in the March 25, 1987, case *Johnson v. Transportation Agency, Santa Clara County*.

In a 5–4 decision, in the *Paradise* case, the Court upheld a federal district court judge's order requiring Alabama to promote one Black state police trooper for each White trooper from a pool of qualified candidates. Justice Brennan wrote the plurality opinion justifying the affirmative action program because of the "egregious" nature of previous bias against Blacks. Justice Powell, in a concurring opinion, emphasized that the "quota" did not disrupt seriously the lives of innocent individuals; Justice Stevens's concurring opinion emphasized that the Court-imposed plans fell within the bounds of reasonableness, whereas the dissenters emphasized the undue burden the plan placed on the White troopers.

In the *Johnson* case, six of the nine Supreme Court Justices approved of Santa Clara county's affirmative action program. In 1978 Santa Clara's transit district's board of supervisors adopted a goal of a workforce whose proportion of women, minorities, and the disabled equaled the percentage of the county's labor force at all job levels. Women constituted 36.4 percent of the relevant labor market, and although women made up 22.4 percent of the district workers, they were mostly in clerical positions, with none in the 238 skilled jobs. In 1979 Diane Joyce and Paul Johnson competed, along with five others who were all deemed "well qualified," for the job of dispatcher, a skilled position. They had all scored over 70, the passing grade, in an oral examination conducted by a two-person panel. Johnson tied for second with a score of 75, and Joyce ranked third with 73. After a second interview, first Johnson was chosen, but then, because of affirmative action considerations, Joyce got the job. Johnson sued, contending that he was better qualified. In 1982 a judge ruled that Johnson had been a "victim of discrimination." The Reagan administration joined attorneys for Johnson and appealed to the Supreme Court.[31]

Justice William Brennan, in writing for the Court, put its stamp of approval on voluntary employer action designed to break down old patterns of race and sex segregation. " 'Given the obvious imbalance in the skilled craft category' in favor of men against women, Brennan said, 'it was plainly not unreasonable . . . to consider the sex of Ms. Joyce in making the promotion decision.' " Brennan called the affirmative action plan "a moderate, flexible case by case approach to effecting a gradual improvement in the representation of minorities and women in the agency's work force."[32] Justice Antonin Scalia responded with a scathing dissent, emphasizing the burden that falls on the "Johnsons of the country," whom he called "the only losers in the process."[33]

THE COURT AND THE PUBLIC ARE DIVIDED ON AFFIRMATIVE ACTION

The Supreme Court remained divided on affirmative action, and by a bare majority the Court supported affirmative action for purposes of hiring and promotion, but not to determine layoff lists. A Gallup Poll conducted in June 1987 following the *Johnson* decision showed that the public also continued to be divided on the issue of affirmative action and that the majority of those polled continued to be opposed (see Table 1).

Eight years in the White House allowed President Reagan to accomplish, with judicial appointments, what he was not able to do with judicial arguments. When Supreme Court justices retired, he used his power of appointment to add conservatives Sandra Day O'Connor and Antonin Scalia to the bench—and he appointed conservative William H. Rehnquist to be chief justice. Even so, as we have seen, affirmative action programs continued to win majority Court approval through 1987. Then, however, when Justice Powell, the "swing" vote, retired, and Reagan replaced him with conservative Anthony M. Kennedy, the Court was packed for the next affirmative action case.

On January 24, 1989, the Supreme Court announced its decision on the *Richmond v. Croson* case. The Court ruled, 6–3, that a 1983 Richmond, Virginia, ordinance that channeled 30 percent of public works funds to minority-owned construction companies violated the Constitution. Justice O'Connor, who wrote the majority opinion, argued that "laws favoring blacks over whites must be judged by the same constitutional test that applies to laws favoring whites over blacks"— namely, that classifications based on race are suspect and have to be scrutinized very carefully.

In scrutinizing this case, O'Connor did not see the necessary evidence of past discrimination that would justify using race-based measures. Black people made up 50 percent of the Richmond population, she noted, and although there was a "gross statistical disparity" between "the number of prime contracts awarded to minority firms and the minority population of the city of Richmond," still, she argued, this case does not "constitute a prima facie proof of a pattern of practice of discrimination." The appropriate pool for comparison is not the general population but the "number of minorities qualified to undertake the task," and O'Connor pointed out that the city did not know exactly how many minority business enterprises (MBEs) there were in the relevant market that were qualified to undertake prime or subcontracting work in public construction projects. Even if there were a

Table 1   Affirmative Action Ruling

	Approved	Disapproved	No Opinion
National	29%	63%	8%
Democrats	37	54	9
Republicans	22	74	4
Independents	27	64	9
Men	26	66	8
Women	32	59	9
Whites	25	67	8
Blacks	56	34	10
Hispanics	46	47	7

Source: George Gallup Jr., "Little Support for High Court Ruling on Hiring," *San Francisco Chronicle*, June 15, 1987.

low number of MBEs, she argued, maybe it was not because of discrimination but because of "black career and entrepreneurial choices." "Blacks may be dispropor-tionately attracted to industries other than construction."[34]

Justice Thurgood Marshall, in his dissent, found it "deeply ironic" that the majority did not find sufficient evidence of past discrimination in Richmond, Vir-ginia, the former capital of the Confederacy. "Richmond knows what racial dis-crimination is; a century of decisions by this and other Federal courts has richly documented the city's disgraceful history . . . ," he wrote, and Marshall defended, again, the use of race-conscious measures to redress the effects of prior discrimi-nation.[35]

The *Richmond* case did not end the debate, but perpetuated the uncertainty surrounding affirmative action plans. Now such plans could stand only if they could survive strict judicial scrutiny—for example, if they were adopted to elimi-nate "patently obvious, egregious discrimination that can be linked to the deliber-ate acts of identifiable parties." Mere numerical disparities would not be enough. Experts predicted that the lower courts would be flooded with challenges to affirmative action by White plaintiffs.[36]

OTHER CASES THAT INFLUENCED AFFIRMATIVE ACTION

On June 5, 1989, the court again decided a case that would affect affirmative action policy. In *Wards Cove Packing v. Atonia*, the court ruled, 5–4, that plaintiffs who are not employers have the burden of proving whether a job requirement that is shown statistically to screen out minorities or women is a "business necessity." The case redrew the ground rules unanimously established by the Court in 1971, which pro-hibited not only employment practices *intended* to discriminate but also practices that had discriminatory *impact*.

The plaintiffs in this case were non-Whites—Filipino and Alaskan native can-nery workers who were channeled into lower-paid unskilled jobs. Noncannery jobs were filled by the company with predominantly White workers who were hired in Washington and Oregon. With these statistics showing disparate impact, and con-sistent with precedent, the lower court asked the salmon canneries to justify, on grounds of "business necessity," the business practice of flying in Whites for man-agerial jobs and hiring local non-Whites to work in the cannery. Justice Byron White, writing for the majority, overturned eighteen years of precedent. He said that the cannery business did not have to prove anything. It was up to the non-White can-nery workers to disprove the company's claim that there was no discrimination.

Justice John Paul Stevens, in his dissent, called the decision "the latest sojourn into judicial activism," accusing the majority of "[t]urning a blind eye to the mean-ing and purpose of Title VII. . . ."[37]

One week after the *Wards Cove* decision, the court dealt an even more lethal blow to affirmative action. In *Martin v. Wilks*, five members of the court ruled that Whites may bring reverse discrimination claims against judge-approved affirma-tive action plans. This meant that consent decrees, which settle many discrimination suits and had been thought to be immune from subsequent legal attack, were now fair game.

The *Martin v. Wilks* case had its roots in the early 1970s, when a local chapter of the National Association for the Advancement of Colored People (NAACP), supported by the federal government, sued the city of Birmingham, Alabama, on the grounds that Blacks were being discriminated against in hiring and promotion in the city's fire department. Several years later a settlement was reached, although the union representing the "almost all white work force" objected to the settlement at the hearing.[38] The Federal District Court "approved the settlement and entered a consent decree under which blacks and whites would be hired and promoted in equal number until the number of black firefighters approximated the proportion of blacks in the civilian labor force." A few months later, fifty white firefighters sued the city, claiming discrimination. The Federal District Court dismissed the suit. In 1987 the Eleventh Circuit Court overturned that dismissal, a decision inconsistent with those of every other circuit court, and reinstated the white firefighters in the city of Birmingham; a group of black firefighters appealed to the Supreme Court.

Chief Justice William Rehnquist wrote the majority opinion, in which he agreed with the Eleventh Circuit Court, arguing that a decree could be binding only on parties who had been part of the original lawsuit. "Outside groups" could not be required to join such a suit, and if they were not bound by the decree, they could sue. Justice Stevens's dissent pointed out that the Court's decision "would subject large employers who seek to comply with the law by remedying past discrimination to a never-ending stream of litigation and potential liability. He called the results 'unfathomable' and 'counterproductive.' "[39]

RESPONSES TO THE COURT DECISIONS

These decisions of the Court stimulated two important responses. First, across the country, lawsuits were filed by White male workers who now had standing in the Court to allege that they had suffered reverse discrimination because of affirmative action programs, even programs that were court-imposed or that resulted from full trials. The effects were felt from San Francisco[40] to Birmingham.[41] The second important response to the Court's decisions came from Congress.

For six months, civil rights organizations and their congressional allies worked together to prepare legislation that would basically reverse three of the Supreme Court decisions, two that related to affirmative action, the *Wards Cove* case, "in which the Court ruled that . . . the plaintiff has the burden of proving that an employer had no business reason for a practice with discriminatory effects," and the *Martin v. Wilks* case, "in which the Court held that Court-approved affirmative action plans can be challenged as reverse discrimination. . . ."[42] The proposed legislation would also reverse another civil rights (but non–affirmative action) case, *Paterson v. McClean Credit Union*, "in which the Court ruled that an 1866 law prohibiting racial discrimination in contracts applies only to hiring agreements, not to on-the-job discrimination."[43]

The civil rights bill's sponsors, Senator Edward Kennedy (D-MA) and Representative Augustus Hawkins (D-CA), were confident about getting the majority necessary to pass the law. The challenge, which kept them negotiating behind closed doors, was to line up the sixty Senate cloture votes needed to shut off debate and to get the sixty-seven votes to guarantee override of a possible presidential veto. This civil rights bill, because it dealt with more subtle issues like "burden of proof" and "right to sue," was not as "sexy" as, for example, the Voting Rights Act, and the fear was that the supporting public might be less attentive to its fate.[44] Nevertheless, the White House watched closely.

At the end of May 1990, reporters were describing the "tough test" faced by the Bush administration. Although the president originally had warned he would veto the civil rights bill, by spring he was backing off from his threat. There seemed to be two reasons for his change of heart. First, it appeared that many Republicans in the Senate were ready to break with the White House to support the bill. The president's veto might not be sustained. The second reason for the president to look for compromise was his concern about his reelection. President Bush was eager to court the African-American vote in 1992; in mid-1990, he had a 56 percent Black approval rating and was the most popular Republican president among Blacks since Dwight Eisenhower.[45] A compromise on the civil rights bill seemed likely. Thus, in 1990 it appeared that a committed pro–civil rights core in Congress and a pragmatic White House would help important elements of affirmative action to survive. But in the fall of 1990 President Bush vetoed the civil rights bill, and Congress was unable to override his veto. That December, Robert Allen, chairman of AT&T, arranged a private dinner between top business and civil rights leaders. A coalition of 200 top CEOs, the so-called Business Roundtable, voted to continue these talks, and both sides agreed to have lawyers meet to try to "hammer out their differences." Saving affirmative action and the civil rights bill now seemed probable.

The Bush administration, however, was unhappy with the prospect of such a compromise. Preparing for the presidential campaign of 1992, GOP strategists believed that a Republican anti–affirmative action position would be very effective and that a compromise bill would dilute the Republican political advantage on the quota issue. Therefore, the White House proceeded to destroy the business civil rights negotiations. Roundtable members were warned that their talks undermined business support for the president's version of a civil rights bill, and Chief of Staff John Sununu personally drummed up opposition among smaller companies. The White House campaign was blunt and vicious. Even Robert Allen came under personal attack from conservative columnist Paul Gigot in the *Wall Street Journal* because of his involvement. The participants who had seemed so hopeful buckled under the political pressure.[46] Then, a turn of events which no one could have predicted, made the passage of the congressional act virtually inevitable.

In Louisiana, an avowed racist and self-described Klan member, David Duke, became the Republican candidate for Senate. This represented a serious problem for the Republican party, which wanted desperately to disassociate themselves from him. Continuing with an anti–civil rights position, therefore, became problematic for Bush because such a position would seem too similar to Duke's position. Bush reversed himself on the civil rights bill; by the end of 1991, President Bush was on record supporting the civil rights legislation, and he signed it into law.

AFFIRMATIVE ACTION: A WOMAN'S ISSUE

The aim of affirmative action is the redistribution of benefits and opportunities. Has the program benefited women?

According to the Department of Labor guidelines, starting in April 1982, women were to be included in the special class or "protected class" benefiting from compensatory policies. Note, however, that in all the Supreme Court landmark cases except the *Johnson* case, women were not the protected class directly benefiting from the affirmative action programs in question. Thus, even with the Department of Labor guidelines, there is no guarantee that women, as a protected class, will be included in affirmative action pools, which are up to each employer to define.

Industrywide figures consistently have painted a mixed picture for employed women under affirmative action. For example, Goldstein and Smith analyzed minority and female employment changes in over 74,000 separate companies between 1970 and 1972. They compared contractor and noncontractor companies with a presumption that federal contractors are more likely to conform to affirmative action goals. What they found surprised them.

Although, as expected, Black males did economically better in employment in contractor companies between 1970 and 1972, so did *White males*. The big losers during these years were White women. Between 1970 and 1972, before the OFCC revised guidelines included women, White women not only showed no employment gains, they showed significant employment losses. In fact, White women's losses were equal in magnitude to the significant gains made by White males.[47]

Under the revised guidelines, it appears that the effect of including women in the federal affirmative action program, as a protected class, is mixed. From 1967 to 1980, for White women, "Rough stability prevailed over this period in their wages relative to White men," according to Smith and Welch. Sociologist Paul Burstein suggests an interesting explanation, rarely considered by economists, to account for why White women have not experienced a large wage advance under the 1972 guidelines. As a group, their "seeming decline" in income is probably due to the steady influx of relatively inexperienced female workers into the labor force. Women as a group are better off, but their average income drops.[48] The story on wages for Black women is different. Between 1967 and 1980 the largest wage advances were achieved by Black women, who went from earning 74 percent of the wage of similarly employed White women in 1967 to almost complete racial parity in 1980.[49] It has been suggested that "part of the reason for nonwhite women's gains . . . may be their having been so badly off initially that their jobs and incomes could improve considerably without posing any real threat to the normal workings of the economy."[50]

In a National Bureau of Economic Research paper, Jonathan Leonard studied the effectiveness of affirmative action for the employment of minorities and women.[51] Focusing on the period between 1974 and 1980, he also compared *contractor and noncontractor* establishments. Leonard compared the mean employment share of targeted groups and controlled for establishment size, growth, region, industry, occupation, and corporate structure. He found that members of protected groups grew faster in contractor than in noncontractor establishments, 3.8 percent faster for Black males, 7.9 percent faster for other minority males, 2.8 percent for White females, and 12.3 percent for Black females.[52] This suggests that affirmative action programs benefit Black women and tend to help White women, though not as much as they benefit minorities.

When Leonard focused on the effect of compliance reviews—that is, the role they played over and above that of contractor status—he found that they advanced Black males by 7.9 percent, other minority males by 15.2 percent, and Black females by 6.1 percent. It *retarded* the employment growth of Whites (including White women). Thus, he concluded, *"with the exception of white females*, compliance reviews have had an additional positive impact on protected group employment beyond the contractor effect."[53] His data also show that White women were not benefiting from affirmative action when it comes to promotions.[54]

Leonard suggests an explanation for why White women's position in contractor companies has not improved significantly compared with noncontractor companies. It is that these women have so flooded the employment market that they have been hired in *both* contractor and noncontractor companies. As he says, "female [employment] share" has "increase[d] at all establishments because of the supply shift. . . ." Thus, his comparison of contractor and noncontractor hiring does not show the general large increase in White women hired. His explanation seems plausible considering the clear increase in the number of women employed, which is reflected by Bureau of the Census data for the period between 1970 and 1980.[55]

Although it appears that not all women have benefited directly from affirmative action, there are many specific cases where women (including White women) have directly benefited from an affirmative action approach. Affirmative action, with its emphasis on numbers and parity, can indirectly benefit women (including White women) because it inevitably shifts our focus from rhetoric to results. Thus, in some areas, such as academic admissions (which falls under Title IX protection), public scrutiny was all that was necessary to make possible a large redistribution of places to all women. Quoting McGeorge Bundy, Wilkinson wrote, "Since 1968 the number of women entering medical schools has risen from 8 percent to 25 percent of the total. A parallel increase has occurred in law schools. No constitutional issue is raised by this dramatic change, . . . the women admitted have had generally competitive records on the conventional measures."[56]

Even though they score competitively, I am arguing that affirmative action has helped these women get admitted to professional schools by focusing public attention on admissions criteria and admission results. In this context let us remember a Charlotte Perkins Gilman line in a poem that focuses on Socialist change. "A lifted world lifts women up," she wrote.

Thus, there is a mixed answer to the question "Does affirmative action benefit women?" Non-white women seem to have most clearly benefited directly from the program, but all women may be benefiting indirectly. Might affirmative action be a women's issue for reasons other than women's benefits?

Perhaps affirmative action could be seen as a woman's issue, in the tradition of social feminism, because it calls for a fairer distribution of social benefits. Of course, I am not suggesting that women be insensitive to the catalog of arguments, some of them practical, that have been made against affirmative action.[57] What I would suggest is that women (and men) be wary of falling into the trap of characterizing affirmative action as the "opposite" of a merit system. It is not. After all, proportionality is used even to select justices on the Supreme Court, where there may be a Jewish seat, a southern seat, a Black seat, and now a woman's seat.[58]

The major issue raised by affirmative action is not merit but redistribution. Allan Bakke's arguments were made against a special program benefiting minorities. Over and over he raised the flag of "fair competition," but Davis Medical School had another special program, which Bakke did not complain about—the dean's special admissions program "under which white children of politically well-connected university supporters or substantial financial contributors have been admitted in spite of being less qualified than other applicants, including Bakke."[59] Thus, the Bakke issue is not, and never was, special programs. The issue is who will be benefiting from these special programs—and that is a matter not of merit but of politics.

NOTES

1. See Allan P. Sindler, *Equal Opportunity: On the Policy and Politics of Compensatory Minority Preferences* (Washington, DC: American Enterprise Institute for Public Policy Research, 1983).

2. See Jonathan S. Leonard, "The Effectiveness of Equal Employment Law and the Affirmative Action Regulation," Working Paper No. 1745, NBER Working Paper Series, National Bureau of Economic Research, November 1985 (unpublished).

3. See Thomas Sowell, *Civil Rights: Rhetoric or Reality?* (New York: William Morrow, 1984); and James E. Jones Jr., "The Bugaboo of Employment Quotas," *Wisconsin Law Review*, 5 (1970) p. 341.

4. Daniel C. Maguire provides the most complete compendium of practical "problems" in *A New American Justice* (New York: Doubleday, 1980).

5. This, to the credit of its author, is the focus of Daniel C. Maguire's book cited in note 4.

6. Arval A. Morris, "Affirmative Action and 'Quota' Systems," Commentary, 26 Ed. *Law Report*, 1985.

7. David H. Rosenbloom, *Federal Equal Employment Opportunity Politics and Public Personnel Administration* (New York: Praeger, 1977), p. 60; see also James E. Jones, "Twenty-one Years of Affirmative Action: The

Maturation of the Administrative Enforcement Process under the Executive Order 11,246 as Amended," *Chicago Kent Law Review*, 59 (Winter 1982); pp. 66–122; Paul Burstein, *Discrimination, Jobs, and Politics* (Chicago: University of Chicago Press, 1985), pp. 8, 13.

8. U.S., Federal Register, March 6, 1961, 26, pt. 2: 1977

9. Rosenbloom, *Federal Equal Employment Opportunity Politics*, pp. 67–69.

10. Jones, "Twenty-one Years," p.f. 72.

11. *U.S. Federal Register*, 30, pt. 10: 12319

12. In *U.S. v. Local 189*, United Papermakers and Paperworkers, 290F2d 368, and Crown Zellerbach Corp., 282F Supp. 39 (E. D. La. 1968) "the government sought an injunction against the union's interference with the company's contractual obligations under Executive Order 11,246. . . ." Ibid., p. 83.

13. There are many who criticize the way affirmative action has been implemented. For an overview, see Leonard, Working Paper No. 1745, and Leonard, "Affirmative Action as Earnings Redistribution: The Targeting of Compliance Reviews," *Journal of Labor Economics*, 3 (3) (July 1985), pp. 380–384; see also James P. Smith and Finis Welch, "Affirmative Action and Labor Markets," *Journal of Labor Economics*, 2 (April 1984), pp. 285–286, 298.

14. Leonard, Working Paper No. 1745, p. 4.

15. Sowell, *Civil Rights* p. 41.

16. Judith Hole and Ellen Levine, *Rebirth of Feminism* (New York: New York Times Book Company, 1971), p. 46; see also Morris Goldstein and Robert Smith, "The Estimated Impact of the Antidiscrimination Program Aimed at Federal Contractors," *Industrial and Labor Relations Review*, 29 (4) (July 1976). pp. 523–543.

17. Interview with Joseph Hodges, assistant regional director, Office of Federal Contract Compliance, U.S. Department of Labor, Region IX, February 6, 1987.

18. See, for example, Joann S. Lublin and Andy Pasztor, "Tentative Affirmative Action Accord Is Reached by Top Reagan Officials," *Wall Street Journal*, December 11, 1985, p. 4; and Robert Pear, "Rights Chief Assails Hiring Goals as Failure," *New York Times*, November 1, 1985, p. 19.

19. Lublin and Pasztor, "Tentative Affirmative Action Accord."

20. Kenneth B. Noble, "Labor Dept. Aide Quits in Protest Over 'Lip Service' to Jobs Rights," *New York Times*, January 21, 1987; see also "Job-Bias Official Quits Labor Post," *Washington Post*, January 21, 1987.

21. Interview with Paul Grossman, head of the Attorney's Division, Office for Civil Rights, U.S. Department of Education, Region IX, February 6, 1987.

22. Christopher F. Mooney, S.J., *Inequality and the American Conscience* (New York: Paulist Press, 1982), p. 5.

23. J. Harvey Wilkinson III, *From Brown to Bakke: The Supreme Court and School Integration* (New York: Oxford University Press, 1979), p. 255.

24. Ibid., p. 301. Since Justice Powell was the "swing" vote, "An irony of Bakke, wrote Washington attorney and civil rights activist Joseph Rauh, was that 'Affirmative action was saved by a conservative Southern justice.' "

25. Mooney, *Inequality*, p. 101.

26. Ibid., p. 103.

27. United States Commission on Civil Rights, *Toward an Understanding of Stotts,* Clearinghouse Publication 85, January 1985, p. 2.

28. Ibid.

29. Wygant v. Jackson Board of Education in *United States Law Week*, 54 (45) (May 20, 1986), pp. 4480f.

30. Ibid., p. 4489.

31. David G. Savage, "Landmark Ruling Upholds Job Preferences for Women," *Los Angeles Times*, March 2, 1987, pp. 10, 22.

32. Ibid., p. 22. See also "Caveats Reversed in Workplace Equality," Insight, *Washington Times*, April 27, 1987, pp. 8–12.

33. Ibid., "Caveats Reversed."

34. Linda Greenhouse, "Court Bars Plan Set Up to Provide Jobs to Minorities," *New York Times*, January 24, 1989, pp. 1, A12; Sandra Day O'Connor, "Excerpts from Court Opinions in Voiding of Richmond's Contracting Plan," *New York Times*, January 24, 1989, p. A12.

35. Thurgood Marshall, "Excerpts," ibid., p. A12.

36. Linda Greenhouse, "Signal on Job Rights," *New York Times*, January 25, 1989, pp. 1, A9.

37. Linda Greenhouse, "Court, Ruling 5 to 4, Eases Burden on Employers in Some Bias Suits," *New York Times*, June 6, 1989, pp. 1, A24; "Excerpts from Court Opinions about Job Rights," *New York Times*, June 6, 1989, p. A24.

38. Linda Greenhouse, "Court 5–4, Affirms a Right to Reopen Bias Settlements," *New York Times*, June 13, 1989, p. A7.

39. Ibid.

40. Martin Halstuk, "White Cops' Suit Alleges Bias in S.F. Promotions," *San Francisco Chronicle*, September 26, 1989, p. 1.

41. Ronald Smothers, "Ruling on Firefighters Is Debated in Alabama," *New York Times*, June 14, 1989, p. A18.

42. Susan Rasky, "Rights Groups Work on Measure to Reverse Court's Bias Rulings," *New York Times*, December 30, 1989, p. A11.

43. Ibid.

44. Ibid.

45. Larry Martz, Ann McDaniel, and Bill Turque, "Bush's Pledge: 'I Want to Do the Right Thing,' " *Newsweek*, May 28, 1990, pp. 20, 21.

46. Bob Cohn and Thomas M. DeFrank, "A White House Torpedo," *Newsweek*, April 29, 1991, p. 35.

47. Goldstein and Smith, "Estimated Impact."

48. Burstein, *Discrimination*, p. 148.

49. James P. Smith and Finis Welch, "Affirmative Action and Labor Markets," *Journal of Labor Economics*, 2 (2) (April 1984).

50. Burstein, *Discrimination*, p. 150.

51. Leonard, Working Paper No. 1745.

52. Ibid., p. 10.

53. Ibid., p. 11.

54. Ibid., p. 17.

55. See, for example, a study by Cynthia M. Taeuber and Victor Valdisera, *Women in the American Economy*, Current Population Reports, Special Studies Series P-23, No. 146, U.S. Department of Commerce, Bureau of the Census, p. 23, which focuses on occupations with major employment gains for women and shows that in many of the male-dominated fields, the percentage of women employed rose sharply.

56. Wilkinson, *From Brown to Bakke*, pp. 262–263.

57. The best list of arguments against affirmative action is in Maguire, *A New American Justice*, pp. 31–39.

58. Wilkinson, *From Brown to Bakke*, p. 269.

59. Charles Lawrence III, "The Bakke Case: Are Racial Quotas Defensible?" *Saturday Review*, October 15, 1977, p. 14.

FURTHER READINGS

Cahn, Steven M. *Affirmative Action and the University: A Philosophical Inquiry*. Philadelphia: Temple University Press, 1993.

Greene, Kathanne W. *Affirmative Action and Principles of Justice*. New York: Greenwood Press, 1989.

Jones, James E., Jr. "The Bugaboo of Employment Quotas," *Wisconsin Law Review*, 5 (1970), p. 341.

Maguire, Daniel C. *A New American Justice*. New York: Doubleday, 1980.

Mooney, Christopher F., S.J. *Inequality and the American Conscience*. New York: Paulist Press, 1982.

Orlans, Harold, and June O'Neill. "Affirmative Action Revisited," *Annals of the American Academy of Political and Social Science*, 523 (September 1992), pp. 144–158.

Rosenfeld, Michel. *Affirmative Action and Justice: A Philosophical and Constitutional Inquiry*. New Haven, CT: Yale University Press, 1991.

Sindler, Allan P. *Equal Opportunity: On the Policy and Politics of Compensatory Minority Preferences*. Washington, DC: American Enterprise Institute for Public Policy Research, 1983.

Sowell, Thomas. *Civil Rights: Rhetoric or Reality?* New York: William Morrow, 1984.

United States Commission on Civil Rights. *Toward an Understanding of Stotts*. Clearinghouse Publication 85, January 1985, p. 2.

Wilkinson, Harvey J. III. *From Brown to Bakke: The Supreme Court and School Integration*. New York: Oxford University Press, 1979.

 **CHAPTER 9**

WOMEN ACTIVISTS: ATTITUDES, TACTICS

We have thus explored the issue of women in politics. We began with a theoretical component; moved to political attitudes, voting, and elections; looked at women and government; and continued with an analysis of women and national policy. We began with theory and conclude this volume with practice. In our concluding chapter, we look at two essays that deal with a feminist framework for organizations and the relationship between coffee, coffeehouse cultures, political discourse, and gender.

In her essay Kathleen P. Iannello identifies a modified consensual structure in which routine decisions are made by a few and critical decisions are made by the entire group membership. Other important characteristics of these model organizations include the following: (1) recognition of ability or expertise rather than rank or position, (2) the notion of power as the ability to accomplish or achieve goals (as opposed to the idea of power as domination), and (3) clarity of goals, which are arrived at through a consensual process. The author uses a case study of the governing body of one women's studies program at a small liberal arts college to illustrate the challenges and benefits of organizing consensually. The implications for women in this structure include experiences in an environment of trust and support as opposed to the more traditional hierarchical organizations in which only those at the top (all too often male figures) make critical policy with varying degrees of input from lower levels.

Our final article examines the often complex relationships between coffee, coffeehouse cultures, and gender, along with how these relationships have shifted historically. Elizabeth A. Kelly concludes with a look at the countercultural institutions which have emerged in the last two decades that draw on the traditions of free speech and cultural and political criticisms that were integral to the coffeehouse cultures of centuries past. The author describes the feminist community organizing and the cultural work since the late 1960s that has often centered around coffeehouses, sometimes in tandem with feminist bookstores and other forms of cultural expression. She describes two feminist coffeehouses and the political struggles attached to building alternative social and cultural institutions that prioritize women and their concerns or needs. Let us further examine female activism and how female attitudes and tactics can bring about change.

Anarchist Feminism and Student Power: Is This Any Way to Run a Women's Studies Program?

Kathleen P. Iannello

Since 1970, when the first women's studies program was established at San Diego State University, women's studies programs have flourished at colleges and universities in America as well as throughout the world. Recent data show there are now 621 women's studies programs in the United States alone.[1] As these programs have evolved, women on college campuses, like their sisters in the larger social and political arena, have striven to organize "differently." This difference has meant attempts at building consensual organization and decision making rather than hierarchical organization based on parliamentary process according to that well-worn "road map" of procedure: *Robert's Rules*. While nearly everyone has had experience with centralized, hierarchical decision-making structures, signified by the typical "executive board" that makes decisions for the rest of the group, few have experienced the consensual approach. Within consensual organization, power is shared and the concept of an executive or management level of the structure is completely nonexistent.

This means that in order to build consensual structures, people often have to *learn* to *participate* in organizations in different ways than they have in the past. This "new process" is often a challenge for those who encounter it for the first time. For students involved in the governing organizations of women's studies programs, the challenge is even greater when they discover that consensual decision making means they have as much power over their own course of study as do faculty, staff,

Kathleen P. Iannello is an associate professor of political science at Gettysburg College.

and administrators. However, shared power also means shared responsibility, which can seem quite overwhelming to those who are unaccustomed to it.

Faculty, administrators and students *are* sharing power. Is this any way to run a women's studies program? A case study of the governing body of one women's studies program, called the Women's Studies Program Advisory Council (WSPAC), sheds some light on the specific challenges as well as benefits of organizing consensually in an academic environment. The study also raises important questions regarding student participation. But first, in order to consider what might be unique to the academic setting in developing consensual organization, an overview of the history and evolution of feminist consensual structure in the nonacademic setting is useful for those who are unfamiliar with it.

ANARCHIST FEMINISTS AND CONSENSUAL STRUCTURE

By now students of feminist theory recognize that feminism is not a monolith. Variations of liberal, Marxist, socialist, radical, multicultural, and postmodern feminism abound (to name a few!). What these differing theories have most in common is their goal of reducing or eliminating male domination or patriarchy from society. Of these feminist frameworks, anarchist feminism, sometimes viewed as a part of radical feminism, focuses most specifically on the relationship between patriarchy and hierarchy. Anarchist feminists examine forms of organization that provide unequal access to economic, political, and social resources.[2] They argue that power, defined as domination, "originates in, and is transmitted through" these organizational structures, which they define as centralized, hierarchical forms.[3]

The way to begin the task of eliminating this power, they argue, is to build "alternative forms of organization alongside the institutions of the larger society."[4] By alternative forms of organization, they mean groups in which leadership positions are rotated and responsibility is shared among group members. In doing so, they attempt to "eradicate all the structural factors that create and maintain leaders and followers."[5] This is something that must be practiced on a daily basis, they argue, and not put off while waiting for larger social change. "For social anarchists . . . the revolution is a process, not a point in time; and how one lives one's daily life is very important. People don't learn that they can live without leadership elites by accepting socialist ones; they do not end power relationships by creating new ones."[6] Instead, there must be a redefinition of power—a qualitative change. This means a change from *power as domination* to *power as the ability to accomplish or achieve goals:* empowerment.

The women's consciousness-raising groups of the 1960s and early 1970s represent an attempt to build alternative organizations. According to Jo Freeman's account of their experiences, they succeeded in raising consciousness but not in operating in nonhierarchical ways. As Freeman indicates, there was a kind of "tyranny of structurelessness," in that lack of structure gave way to the development of informal leaders—individuals who gained power due to media attention or personal characteristics.[7] Such leaders were not chosen by the group and thus could not be removed by the group. Lack of a leadership "process" created a kind of tyranny—unaccountable leadership.

Since then, many women's groups have come to learn that nonhierarchy does not mean nonstructure. Combining the concept of nonhierarchical *structure* with theories of empowerment, anarchist feminists have developed what some call a modified consensual model of organization. What does this modified consensual *structure* look like? What follows are two examples. Both organizations exist in the same small New England city and are similar in size but differ in services performed and explicit goals. They are referred to here by fictitious names: the feminist peace group and the women's health collective.[8]

Feminist Peace Group

This organization describes itself as a group of feminist activists working for disarmament and social justice in its immediate community and the world. It is part of a larger women's peace organization that has branches in nations around the world. The local branch formed in the spring of 1983. The members describe themselves as

> feminist activists who were seeking a diverse, effective and explicitly feminist women's peace group. . . . (We) embrace feminism as the most effective and comprehensive analysis of our political, economic, social, and military institutions. We see the rule of men over women as the model for other forms of dominance and oppression. And we strive for a radically different society which values cooperation, non-violence, nurturance and spiritual integrity.[9]

The organization, which has a mailing list of over 100, relies on three categories of members: (1) active members who participate in project groups and retreats, (2) supporting members who attend events and participate in telephone trees, and (3) sponsoring members who provide financial support for projects and actions. The approximately fifteen active members meet once a month; they also divide into a number of project groups, which they say "allow us to divide responsibility and to work easily with new people."[10] The project groups offer a way for the organization to involve and assimilate new members. They view the project groups as a way of dealing with a growing membership—the groups allow them to maintain a system of shared decision-making and leadership roles. All group decisions are made through consensus, which means that all members present at meetings must agree on, or at least not object to, decisions being made. Meetings are "facilitated" by members, on a rotating basis. Both the meeting agenda and the decision about who will "facilitate" are determined in the first few minutes of every full meeting.

The three groups of members mentioned earlier provide a network of communication and support that hinges on each member's ability to contribute to the organization—whether that contribution is simply monetary, communicative, or time invested. Within the "active" group, ability and interest are recognized through the various project groups. An example is a media project called "redirection." This group designed a series of radio ads against the development and sale of war toys. They also developed a follow-up telephone survey to attempt to measure the influence of the ads on the local community. Some of the project groups have been in existence since the beginning of the organization, while new ones have been created and old ones dissolved. The membership of the project groups changes with the shifting interests and abilities of the overall group membership. The organization has also recruited new members simply by sparking interest in the community through specific projects such as the media project described previously.

One difficulty for this organization has been related to what it called the "housekeeping" chores, which include the collection of member dues, distribution of other monies raised through grants, keeping of membership lists and organization files, and preparation of two yearly social and informational public events. In the past these tasks simply fell to those interested and willing to do them. However, those falling into this category have numbered fewer as member interests and energies have been more focused toward the project groups.

It was decided by the active membership that a project group would be formed to deal with these housekeeping tasks. Members who placed themselves within this group were those who did not want to make a larger time commitment to other project groups. In other words, the development of this group provided active members yet another option of participation that best reflected their abilities at the time. That housekeeping became a problem for this group underscores the fact that every organization has a number of tasks that must be tended to in order to keep the organization functioning. This is important in that some aspect of the organization's operating procedures must speak to this issue. This may be a reason why some collectivist groups fail: they lack the *structure* to deal with basic operating problems or needs.

The Women's Health Collective

This organization describes itself as a "modified collective," numbering approximately fifteen member–workers. The organization's focus is on women's reproductive health. It was formed in 1972 by community members, as a nonprofit organization, "in response to the need for safe, legal abortion services for . . . women." Its mission statement indicates the goals of the organization as follows:

> To provide high quality, cost-accessible, health care for and by women that includes but is not limited to gynecological and abortion services.
> To empower women by informing them medically and politically and by training women healthworkers.
> To be a woman-operated business striving for consensual power-sharing and equality of worker input in major policy decisions.
> To have our business structure be seen as a working model for other interested groups.[11]

In more than two decades, the health collective has gone through two major organizational and structural changes. At the time of its inception, the organization was established with a staff that made decisions about the day-to-day operation of the clinic. There was a separate (outside) board composed of community members, which met with the staff every two weeks to make major policy decisions. As the staff members explain, "This was helpful in the beginning, as a broad range of experience and opinions were needed."[12] However, by the end of the first two years, the board had become what the staff described as a "technical legality," and was dissolved.

At this point the full staff became the board as well, and all staff members participated in all decision making, according to consensus. The staff/board met weekly at that time and made all routine as well as critical policy decisions, including the hiring of staff and determination of salaries. At this point in their development, the staff decided that all salaries would be the same for all members. In terms of jobs and tasks, as they explain, "The philosophy of the collectivity involves the idea that each staff member should ideally be trained to do any given task. Most staff members rotate positions of counselor, coordinator and phone counselor. Training programs are arranged for staff to learn more specialized tasks such as lab work, administrative skills and physician assistant skills."

After nearly ten years of operating in this fashion, the health collective once again changed or modified its structure. Members indicate that there were two major reasons for a change: (1) a need to make the "business" of the organization more efficient and (2) a need to recognize, through position and salary, the expertise of certain members. The structure that recently developed out of these needs is one in which there are currently three coordinators who have responsibility for areas such as personnel, medical, and business matters. These tasks have been delegated to them by the full staff. The women in the organization describe how the coordinator positions evolved from the expertise certain women brought with them when they joined the clinic. For instance, one member, who had worked in another medical organization, brought with her knowledge of medical protocol. She eventually became the medical coordinator.

It is also important to note that when expertise is lost, through the departure of a member, the position the member held is dissolved. For example, a woman who brought "political and communication" skills to the organization became outreach coordinator. When she left the organization, the outreach coordinator's position was dissolved. While coordinator positions do not rotate, coordinators do make an effort to share knowledge and information with the rest of the group. While this new structure brought with it some differentiation as to position and salary, the full staff still makes policy decisions in these areas. The full staff now meets once a month to consider critical policy questions, with routine decisions delegated to coordinators.

Within the women's health collective, individual members said they joined because they were looking for a female-managed business where they expected to find a supportive work environment, more flexible working hours, and coworkers who really understood the individual's needs both inside and outside the workplace. In short, these individuals expressed a commitment to a distinctly feminist ethic of care.[13] None of these women were opposed to the kind of structure the health collective utilizes. However, some of them were surprised, upon being hired, to find that they would need to learn about consensus decision making in order to work within this group.

Like the feminist peace group, one of the most significant aspects of the women's health collective is the recognition of ability or expertise within the membership without the creation of hierarchy. Coordinators are *delegated* responsibility from the entire staff. Yet they also have a responsibility to educate the remaining staff in a specific area of routine work such as medical protocol.

This is a model of nonhierarchy that demonstrates the concept of empowerment, in that organization members become enriched or gain personal power through the expertise of others. The development of expertise in the health collective may be more important than in the peace group because of the external constraints: The health collective is a business that must deal with external hierarchies of the marketplace, of the medical as well as political worlds. For this group, the development and sharing of expertise may be much more a matter of survival than it is for the peace group, which is a volunteer organization with fewer time-constrained goals.

Modified Consensual Structure

The most significant aspect of these organizations is their structure (see Figure 1). This is evident in the way the women of the peace group and health collective make decisions. First, they are keenly aware of the distinction between critical and routine decisions. Decisions that are "critical" have the potential for changing the direction of the organization. Those that are "routine" are important to the operation of the organization on a daily basis—but are not likely to raise significant questions about changes in overall policy.[14]

In both the peace group and the health collective, critical decisions are reserved for the entire membership of the organization, while routine decisions are delegated horizontally. For example, in the peace group the project groups make routine decisions. In the health collective, it is the coordinators and their respective committees who make decisions about problems they are close to and have information about. It is recognized that routine decisions have the potential for becoming critical. In the event that they do, they are reconsidered by the entire group.

What is unique about the structure of these anarchist feminist groups is that everyone is involved in making critical policy. In hierarchical organizations, only those at the top, with varying degrees of input from lower levels, make critical policy. Additionally, in the anarchist groups, routine decisions are delegated horizontally to those who have an interest in making them. While such delegation can involve additional responsibility, authority, and expertise, it does not result in a superordinate–subordinate relationship.

In the peace group, some rotation of members according to tasks helps to ensure that hierarchy does not develop. Because it is a volunteer organization, the peace group can afford the organizational costs involved in retraining members in new areas. The health collective decided that it could not afford those costs and

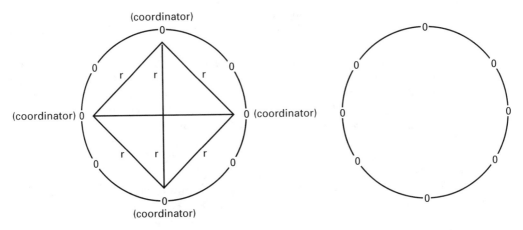

Modified Consensual Organization
Routine decisions are made inside
the circle, critical decisions are
made on the circle.

Consensual Organization
All decisions, critical and
routine, are made on the circle.

Key: 0 = organization members
r = routine decisions
Lines on the circles and within the circle
represent paths of communication
within the organization.

Figure 1   Consensual and Modified Consensual Organization.

therefore relied more on the "process" of the organization, including trust among members, to avoid the development of hierarchy.

Thus, while the most important defining element of these structures is the reserving of critical decisions for the entire membership, and the outward delegation of routine decisions to the few, other aspects of the internal environment are important to the maintenance of nonhierarchial structure. These aspects are best described by the term *process*. This includes the concepts of consensus, empowerment, and emerging leadership. Without the trust among members that is fostered through consensus decision making and the conscious effort to avoid domination, hierarchy would be difficult to avoid. In this way, the political ideals of the members and the ideological commitment to nonhierarchy are vitally important.

From the study of these two anarchist feminist groups, a modified consensual structure has been identified. Again, the most important defining element is the *outward*, not downward, delegation of routine decisions to the few and the reserving of critical decisions for the entire membership. Other important elements of the model include (1) recognition of ability or expertise rather than rank or position, (2) the notion of empowerment as a basis of consensual "process" and (3) clarity of goals that are arrived at *through* this consensual process.

IS THIS ANY WAY TO RUN A WOMEN'S STUDIES PROGRAM?

Keeping in mind what has been learned about modified consensual structure through the examples of the peace group and health collective, we can return to the question: Is this any way to run a women's studies program? A case study of one program at a small liberal arts college serves as a starting point for this discussion.

In 1987 the Women's Studies Program Advisory Council (WSPAC) was established as the governing body for the women's studies program at Gettysburg College. While first consisting of seven faculty members, the organization soon expanded to include anyone on campus who wished to be a member. Today the council is composed of thirty-one members, with fourteen faculty members, thirteen students, one support staff person, and three administrators. The WSPAC sets policy for the women's studies program, which supports both a major and a minor and also plans cocurricular, campuswide events.[15]

There is a women's studies coordinator who serves a five-year term and is considered the equivalent of a department chairperson. She oversees the daily administration of the program with the assistance of an administrative assistant and one or more student assistants. The coordinator is a tenured faculty member in an academic department receiving one course release each semester for her administrative responsibilities.

Despite the existence of a coordinator, the WSPAC makes decisions consensually. In fact, in this case, the coordinator's commitment to shared decision making has fostered an atmosphere in which consensual process is more likely to thrive. The group meets every other week during the academic year and is structured very similarly to the peace group and health collective discussed earlier.

Each meeting is facilitated by members, on a rotating basis. The agenda is reviewed by the entire membership and is efficiently discussed, with a specific amount of time allotted for each item. This time designation is important for moving discussion along. Meetings last an hour and a half, rarely exceeding the designated time.

Everyone is asked to "check in" at the beginning of the meeting; each member says something about herself or the business at hand. This has the effect of fostering an "ethic of care" and the importance of participation within the organization. Likewise at the end of each meeting, everyone is asked to "check out" by evaluating the meeting "process," and again making any more personal comments they wish to make. Students, in particular, seem to feel comfortable with this part of the process. They describe the meetings as "relaxing." "It doesn't feel like work," one student remarked. Another student said: "No one has ever asked me to do this before, it makes me feel important to the organization."

The WSPAC does recognize the difference between critical and routine decisions and delegates routine decisions outward to various smaller committees that bring major policy issues back to the entire group. It is clearly structured as a modified consensual model. However, there are factors unique to the WSPAC, but common to campus organizations, that pose additional challenges with regard to maintaining consensual process.

One is its changing membership. From year to year, and sometimes from semester to semester, WSPAC membership changes. There is a basic core of faculty and the women's studies coordinator and administrative assistant, most of whom were among the founders of the group, who are ongoing members. Some of the administrators are continual members, and some are not. As expected, the student members are the most changeable due to the fact that they are only on campus for four years and during that time may or may not be participants.

Like new members of the peace group and health collective, new WSPAC members are often unfamiliar with consensual process and have *to learn* how to participate. One WSPAC faculty member explained, "You don't simply 'attend' a WSPAC meeting, you 'participate' and that places a lot more responsibility on you as a member. When I go to other committee meetings on campus I know the chairperson will do most of the work. That's not the case in a consensual organization." Frequent membership changes make the WSPAC's time invested in teaching "process" even greater. Since the turnover in students is most significant, the WSPAC assigns mentors, who are experienced members, to help students learn the nature of consensus versus voting, that there are no "motions" moved to the floor, and that everyone is a guardian of the process.

Along with the issue of changing membership come questions of differing knowledge. For example, students tend to be less familiar with the tenure and promotion process that affects faculty in women's studies. They may also be less aware of the role of particular administrators on campus. Likewise, faculty and administrators may be totally unaware of students' experiences in particular courses or their needs on campus. Because of this, the organization's "process" must allow for each member's vantage point. This is difficult under the pressures to get things done, such as major curriculum decisions for the next year. While this is sometimes a problem for the other organizations described in this article, it is not as much of a concern because their memberships are more constant and homogeneous. Furthermore, their deadlines are not tied to the time frame of academic semesters.

For the WSPAC this also raises the question of membership balance. The health collective and peace group might think of balance in terms of race, age, or ethnicity. While these are questions for women's studies committees as well, a central question for these organizations is the faculty–student ratio. This year the WSPAC's faculty–student ratio is almost even. In past years there have been many more faculty members than students. When this was the case, the faculty members of the group were constantly worried that student voices were not being heard. This year members of the WSPAC were struck by the novelty of one member asking with regard to an issue: "Has the *faculty* perspective been heard?"

What would happen if there were many more students than faculty? Could the organization adjust to the shift in the base of knowledge? Does a shift in the base of knowledge mean a shift in the base of power? Would women's studies at Gettysburg College or on any campus, become a "student-run" program? These are just a few of the questions raised due to increased student participation.

If the organization is truly consensual, it would be impossible to say that it was "run" by students or faculty. This means that no matter what the exact membership is, the "process" of the organization maintains a balanced perspective. One of the greatest difficulties in developing a consensual women's studies organization is the immediate environment. Colleges and universities are hierarchies. WSPAC members automatically bring to the organization their "position" on campus whether it be student, faculty member, administrator, or support staff member. These are not identities that can be checked at the door like a coat or umbrella. This reality puts additional pressure on the "process" of the organization to place all members on common ground with equal decision-making capability. This is particularly difficult when faculty and students are obviously not "equal" in the classroom. It is hard to say whether working toward equality in the WSPAC requires more effort on the part of the faculty or the students.

There is excitement among WSPAC members about the increased level of student involvement in the organization. As one nonstudent member explained it, "The larger student presence on WSPAC makes us even more committed to a process that creates equality." Likewise, the students are energized. "It's great to spend time with the other 'resident feminists' on campus," one student remarked. "Our participation will bring more positive attention to women's studies here." Similarly, another student said, "This is a new way for us to be taken seriously on campus."

Along with this new sense of importance, students also expressed uncertainties about their increased role. "I'm sometimes intimidated by the decisions we are making," one student said with regard to discussion about the hiring of part-time faculty. "We are affecting people's careers." Note here that students are intimidated by the nature of the *decision*, not by the other members of the organization. However, in these discussions students indicated the tendency to look to the coordinator or other faculty or administrators for direction when they thought the issue at hand was "too overwhelming." "They're the experts," one student commented. "When you've been in that professor's class, you tend to look to her for 'the answer.' " Yet the same students thought that their expertise as students was a factor, too. "We were able to give faculty information about our experiences in courses that they wouldn't have gotten otherwise," one student noted. "There was a real exchange."

As with the health collective, the sharing of knowledge and expertise in WSPAC contributes to a sense of equality. The recognition and analysis of differences in perspectives within the group is an open, ongoing process. One nonstudent member of the group said, "The legitimacy to air these issues makes the inequalities easier to deal with. If we are not willing to discuss and disagree then the process is not working. When it is working we are able to accomplish so much in a rational, responsive and respectful way. That's how it feels this year."

Beyond the mechanics of the modified consensual structure, the element of mutual respect and trust are central to the effective operation of this primarily faculty–student organization. Faculty members, students, and other WSPAC members have a mutual commitment to the goal of administering a high-quality women's studies program. It is to the benefit of all involved to reach that goal.

Is this any way to run a women's studies program? The National Women's Studies Association's report to the profession suggests that places of "liberal learning" provide a context, or moments in which theory and experience work together to transform students' sense of self and their relation to the world. "Women's studies' central responsibility is to facilitate such moments of recognition and to follow them with moments of empowerment."[16] In light of this statement, it seems entirely appropriate that women's studies students experience empowerment through participation in consensual organizations designed to administer women's studies programs.

NOTES

1. *Liberal Learning and the Women's Studies Major* (College Park: National Women's Studies Association, 1991), p. 7.

2. Lydia Sargent, *Women and Revolution* (Boston: South End Press, 1981), p. 116.

3. Ibid., p. 115.

4. Ibid., p. 114.

5. Ibid., p. 116.

6. Ibid.

7. See Jo Freeman, *The Politics of Women's Liberation* (White Plains, NY: Longman, 1975).

8. Methods used to study these organizations were qualitative. Information was gathered through two years of personal observation of organization meetings, including special committee meetings and special projects/events, interviews with a cross section of women from both organizations, and the reading and

researching of documents related to the history and operation of the organizations. Similar methods were used to gather data on the WSPAC.

9. Organization mission statement, feminist peace group, pp. 1–2.

10. Ibid.

11. Organization mission statement, women's health collective, p. 1.

12. From a history of the women's health collective.

13. See Carol Gilligan, *In a Different Voice* (Cambridge, MA: Harvard University Press, 1982).

14. For a discussion of critical and routine decisions in organizations, see Philip Selznick, *Leadership in Administration* (Evanston, IL: Harper and Row, 1957), p. 56.

15. From a history of the WSPAC included in the *Policies and Procedures* manual.

16. National Women's Studies Association report, p. 1.

FURTHER READINGS

Building United Judgment. Madison, WI: Center for Conflict Resolution, 1981.

Eisenstein, Hester. *Gender Schock*. Boston: Beacon Press, 1991.

Ferguson, Kathy E. *The Feminist Case against Bureaucracy*. Philadelphia: Temple University Press, 1984.

Gilligan, Carol. *In a Different Voice*. Cambridge, MA: Harvard University Press, 1982.

Gilligan, Carol, Nona P. Lyons, and Trudy J. Hanmer. *Making Connections*. Cambridge, MA: Harvard University Press, 1990.

Hartsock, Nancy. "Foucault on Power: A Theory for Women?" in Linda Nicholson (Ed.), *Feminism/Postmodernism* (New York: Routledge, 1990).

Hirschmann, Nancy J. *Rethinking Obligation*. Ithaca; NY: Cornell University Press, 1992.

Iannello, Kathleen P. *Decisions without Hierarchy*. New York: Routledge, 1992.

Leidner, Robin. "Stretching the Boundaries of Liberalism: Democratic Innovation in a Feminist Organization," *Signs* 16 (2) (1991), pp. 263–289.

Liberal Learning and the Women's Studies Major. College Park: National Women's Studies Association, University of Maryland, 1991.

Love, Nancy. *Dogmas and Dreams*. Chatham, NJ: Chatham House, 1991.

Martin, Patricia Yancey. "Rethinking Feminist Organizations," *Gender and Society*, (June 1990), pp. 182–206.

Sargent, Lydia. *Women and Revolution*. Boston: South End Press, 1981.

Swerdlow, Amy. "Motherhood and the Subversion of the Military State: Women's Strike for Peace Confronts the House Committee on Un-American Activities," in Elshtain, Jean Bethke and Sheila Tobias (Eds.), *Women, Militarism and War*, (Savage, MD: Rowman and Littlefield, 1990).

Tong, Rosemarie. *Feminist Thought*. Boulder, CO: Westview Press, 1989.

Grounds for Criticism: Coffee, Passion, and the Politics of Feminist Discourse

Elizabeth A. Kelly

More than one-third of the world's people drink coffee today, but coffee has never been merely a beverage. Three centuries or so have gone by since it became an overnight rage among the fashionable and witty in cities across Europe. Jürgen Habermas, among others, has drawn attention to the role played by coffeehouses in the formation of a bourgeois public sphere in the late eighteenth century. Indeed, the role of the coffeehouse as a bastion of free speech had far-reaching implications: Coffee and the establishments serving it played an integral role in the founding of the United States and continue to provide arenas where discourses of resistance and alternatives to established "politics as usual" may take place. The GI coffeehouse movement, for example, promoted resistance to U.S. involvement in the Vietnam Conflict; places like Chicago's Mountain Moving Coffeehouse, established over twenty years ago and still operating today, have been focal points for the development of a feminist "women's culture" and served as safe spaces for the articulation of feminist and lesbian–feminist political thought.

This paper will explore the relationship between coffee and political discourse, paying particular attention to the role of coffeehouses as alternative public spheres. It will also examine the often complex relationships between coffee, coffeehouse cultures, and gender, along with how these relationships have shifted historically. Considered by turns as cure-all or the "devil's brew," the common peo-

Elizabeth A. Kelly is an assistant professor of political science and women's studies at De Paul University. I am grateful to Uma Narayan, Jacqueline Taylor, and Linda Hillman for their careful readings, encouragement, and insights. Michael Forman, Carl Larsen, and John Martin also deserve thanks for reading and commenting on an earlier version of this paper and for providing the moment of its "conception."

ple's drink or the liquor of the elite, object of disdain or cause for celebration, coffee has seldom failed to elicit one emotion that perhaps best explains its powerful political impact: passion. I will argue that such emotions, often overlooked by political theory, indeed stand at the center of a critical theory of coffee drinking.

ORIGINS OF COFFEE

The origins of coffee drinking are shrouded in mystery; legends abound, but there is little factual evidence to show precisely when people began to drink this seductive brew, let alone who first concocted it. Remarkably similar accounts from Arab chronicles credit either King Solomon or the Prophet Muhammad with first "discovering" coffee. As the story goes, the great man interrupts a journey to visit a town whose inhabitants suffer from a strange, unnamed illness. On command from the Angel Gabriel, he roasts coffee beans and prepares a beverage whose curative powers are truly miraculous; the townsfolk recover completely after taking only a few sips.[1] Another tale has the dreaming Prophet visited by an angel, who commands Muhammad to fetch a bowl of water to a nearby field. When the water stops moving, a sign from Allah will appear. The next morning, Muhammad carries out these instructions: When the water in the bowl is still, he kneels in prayer. A shrub appears before him, and a voice commands him to taste its fruit. Obeying, he experiences a great surge of energy and leaves the field refreshed. The fruit, of course, is the coffee bean.[2]

A variation on the "discovery" theme centers on the dervish Omar, who is awakened one midnight by a huge apparition, the spirit of his long-dead mentor, which guides him to a coffee tree. Omar and his disciples at first attempt to eat the berries; they then try to soften them in water. When this fails, they drink the liquid in which the berries have been boiled. Shortly thereafter, victims of an epidemic of itching rampant in Mocha come to consult with Omar and are cured after drinking the brew. Their gratitude allows Omar to enter Mocha with honors; he becomes the patron saint of coffee growers, owners of coffeehouses, and coffee drinkers alike.[3]

Perhaps the most commonly told story of coffee's origins is that of the "dancing goats." Here Kaldi, a young Ethiopian goatherd, is depressed. Weary of searching for greener pastures and faced with a flock of tired, hungry goats, he rests, unable to move on. The herd begins to nibble sweet red berries off nearby bushes; suddenly all the goats begin behaving very strangely. The oldest billy goat kicks up his heels, cavorting ecstatically; the others quickly join him in a manic dance. Startled, Kaldi, decides to try the berries himself. He, too, begins leaping giddily about the hillside, his troubles forgotten. A passing monk is astonished to see shepherd and flock dancing about the meadow; he samples the berries, and invites other monks to join in. That night during prayers, the monks all feel remarkably alert. They spread news of the amazing discovery throughout the religious community; the fame of the coffee berries—and the beverage brewed from them— spreads throughout the land.[4]

It seems safe to say that whoever the first coffee drinkers may have been, they experienced sensations ranging from exhilaration to religious ecstasy. None of the serious histories of coffee I looked at in the course of preparing this essay contains any mention—whether couched in terms of legend or fact—of the possibility that a *woman* may very well have been the first to hit on the concept of roasting, grinding, and brewing coffee beans into a beverage. This is peculiar, because women have historically been responsible for roasting, brewing, stewing, and fermenting all sorts of substances in the course of preparing food and drink. Given the highly gender-specific ways in which coffee has been both utilized and symbolized—from the days of dervishes and dancing goats down through the present—it is perhaps not surprising.

EARLY HISTORY OF COFFEE AND COFFEE DRINKING

Once legends of origin are dispensed with, coffee's history becomes much more prosaic. The practice of roasting coffee beans probably began around the thirteenth century, when the drink appears to have become popular in connection with Sufi Muslim religious practices. It was first widely used in the Yemen, but soon spread to Mecca and Medina. References to the beverage are found in scientific literature, philosophical tracts, folklore, and religious texts. The eleventh-century physician and philosopher Avicenna wrote that coffee "fortifies the members, cleans the skin, dries up the humidities that are under it, and gives an excellent smell to the body." Another Islamic physician claimed that "it is by experience found to conduce the drying of colds, persistent coughs and catarrh, and to unblock constipation and provoke urination; it allays high blood pressure, and is good against smallpox and measles." He added a cautionary note that adding milk to the brew might "bring one in danger of leprosy." By the end of the fifteenth century, Muslim pilgrims had extolled coffee's restorative powers throughout the Islamic world. While the beverage remained one of the props of the nocturnal devotional services of the Sufi religious order, those who were less spiritually inclined found it a pleasant stimulus to talk and sociability. Here, the coffeehouse was born.[5]

COFFEEHOUSE CULTURE IN SIXTEENTH-CENTURY ISLAM

The story of how coffee drinking fueled a democratic fad for coffeehouse culture across Europe during the seventeenth and eighteenth centuries, especially in England, is familiar. It has often been told in relation to demands for freedom of speech and freedom of the press, which were central to the politics of an emergent bourgeois public sphere. However, the historical and political antecedents of European coffeehouses in sixteenth-century Islam are far less well known. The actual preparation of the beverage differed depending on the cultural context, but in fifteenth-century Mecca and Cairo coffee's popularity—along with its tendency to encourage people to speak freely as they gathered in public places—was not just noteworthy but highly politically charged and acutely gender-specific.

In the Arab world, coffeehouses were essentially Muslim establishments, whose clientele was therefore exclusively male. They served as practical alternatives to the proscribed taverns where wines and other alcoholic beverages were served. With wine and other fermented drinks forbidden under Islamic law, local water often scarce and brackish, and goat's milk barely palatable, coffee was a perfect thirst quencher. It was served and drunk hot, but generally savored slowly; this all but demanded stationary, relatively protected places of consumption, where patrons could take their time, and which in turn served as the perfect setting for talk and socializing with others. Gaming, dancing, music, and singing—activities frowned upon by the strictest followers of Islam—went on in the coffeehouses, along with freewheeling social, political, and religious discussions. All of this was viewed by the authorities with suspicion, and many Islamic officials saw coffee as subversive. It gathered people together; it sharpened their wits and loosened their tongues; it stimulated political arguments and, at least potentially, fomented revolts.

In 1511 an official in Mecca, whose office apparently combined aspects of consumer advocacy and protection with the enforcement procedures of a vice squad, put coffee on trial. He convened a meeting of religious scholars who heard evidence from physicians regarding the putatively detrimental effects of coffee drinking and from religious leaders and government officials regarding the immoral and impious behavior of coffeehouse denizens. For a brief time the sale and consumption of coffee were banned in the city. However, the sultan turned out to be a coffee aficionado; within a year the official who had instigated the ban had been removed from his post, and coffeehouses once again flourished. However, in 1525–1526 a more serious incident surrounding coffee took place in Mecca, where a distinguished jurist, Muhammad ibn al-'Arraq, succeeded in closing down the coffeehouses for nearly two years.[6]

A similar pattern of opposition to coffeehouses and coffee drinking emerged in Cairo, where attempts were made to ban all coffee in 1532–1533 and where rioting broke out in the streets on several occasions during 1534–1535 when authorities attempted to shut down the coffeehouses. Here, again, secular and religious leaders were suspicious of the potential threats to their authority symbolized by nocturnal gatherings where people spoke freely and critically on any and all issues. These fears were real and sometimes took substantive form. In Istanbul, in 1633, Sultan Marat IV ordered all coffeehouses torn down on the pretext of fire prevention; they remained closed, "desolate as the heart of the ignorant," until the last quarter of the century. Perhaps the most remarkable, and definitely the most savage, example of the sporadic attempts to prohibit coffee drinking was seen in Turkey, where the grand vizier banned coffee outright in 1656. For a first violation of the ban, the punishment was the cudgel; for a second, the offender would be sewn into a leather bag and thrown into the Bosphorus, where the straits claimed many souls.[7]

Attempts to curtail coffee drinking or coffeehouse culture proved futile, however, over the long run. Throughout the Arab world, social life had been permanently and irrevocably altered by the ever-growing use of coffee, for in cities, towns, and villages, a previously unknown *public* institution—the coffeehouse—had grown up around the production and sale of this commodity. Talk, whether in the form of casual banter or passionate literary disputes and political arguments, was central to the new institution, as was a certain egalitarian spirit. The traveler Pedro Teixeira reported that in Baghdad coffee was "prepared and sold in public houses built to that end; wherein all men who desire it meet to drink it, be they great or mean."[8] In place of newspapers or other public forums, coffeehouses had quickly become places where information of all kinds, from place gossip to the latest trades in the market, could be exchanged simply by word of mouth. At least one Islamic critic bemoaned the way in which coffeehouse patrons "really extend themselves in slander, defamation, and throwing doubt on the reputations of virtuous women. What they come up with are generally the most frightful fabrications, things without a grain of truth in them."[9] This complaint retains its resonance today, although the sports bar or health club locker room might come more readily to mind as places where tall tales of male sexual prowess or conquest may be routinely overheard.

INTRODUCTION OF COFFEE IN EUROPE

The introduction of coffee to Europe, most likely through Venice and other Italian port cities, recapitulated many of the patterns that had been set in Arab lands a century or so earlier. In Europe, as in Islam, coffee drinking initially had religious connotations; in both cases the practice quickly gave rise to the public institution of the coffeehouse, which was often viewed with suspicion by authorities, if not deemed downright subversive of the state. A relatively egalitarian ethic, free speech, and the exchange of news and information also prevailed as the fad for coffee caught on in areas where both the beverage and the institutions it encouraged had previously been unknown. At first European Christians were skeptical about what was seen as a "pagan brew." Italian priests attacked the beverage virulently and successfully petitioned Pope Clement VIII in the hope that he would place coffee under papal interdiction throughout Christendom. The priests argued that coffee was the drink of the devil. Satan, they reasoned, had forbidden the Muslim infidels the use of wine (central to the Christian sacrament of Holy Communion), supplying them instead with his "hellish black brew." The pope, however, found the pungent aroma of the cup of coffee brought before him as evidence of this diabolical intrigue to be utterly irresistible. After tasting the drink, he pronounced it delicious and declared that it would be dreadful to let the infidels have exclusive use of the beverage. Pope Clement turned the tables on Satan by baptizing coffee on the spot. Thus sanctified, coffee no longer required an apothecary's prescription; ordinary people flocked to try the drink, which was sold on street corners throughout Italy.[10]

With this incident, we see a striking connection to the legends surrounding coffee's origin; clearly, the perceptions of the beverage's magical or medicinal properties have something to do with how its advent, whether in the Arab world or some chamber deep within the Vatican, is culturally remembered. In both contexts, religion, spirituality, and much medical healing were clearly and emphatically defined as exclusively male preserves—even, in many cases, at the expense of longstanding traditions of female dominance in these realms.[11] Thus it is particularly interesting that when coffee makes its appearance in Europe, it does so only after receiving papal approbation—in essence, recapitulating the earlier Islamic legends. In both cases, spiritually enlightened males get the credit for discovering, sanctioning, or sanctifying coffee drinking.

In 1650 the first European coffee house opened in Oxford, England, "at the Angel in the parish of St.-Peter-in-the-East."[12] It took another ten years before coffeehouses became truly popular in the university town, but complaints about them grew as their popularity increased. Neither the university nor the coffeehouses springing up in its environs welcomed women, either as scholars or as customers. By 1661 Anthony Wood opined that scholarship was in decline, since "nothing but news, and the affaires of Christendom is discoursed off and that also generally at coffee houses."[13] Roger North held that "the Scholars are so Greedy after News (which is none of their business) that they neglect all for it . . . a vast loss of Time grown out of a pure Novelty; for who can apply close to a subject with his Head full of the din of a Coffee House?"[14] By 1677 the vice chancellor of the University was ordering coffee sellers not to open after evening prayers on Sundays, but he opined that "at five of the clock they flocked all the more" to their favorite haunts. Three years later, a Puritan mayor attempted to close the coffeehouses down entirely on Sundays, but it seems highly unlikely that this edict was ever enforced, let alone obeyed.[15]

POPULARITY OF COFFEEHOUSES IN LONDON

Nowhere were coffeehouses so popular as in London, where the first one had opened in 1652. By 1700 there were about 3,000 coffeehouses in the city, which at the time had a population of around 600,000; this works out to an almost unbelievable ratio of one coffeehouse for every 200 people. Coffeehouses represented a spectrum of interests, ranging from commerce to politics and literature. They generally opened off the street and were rather crudely furnished, with tables and chairs scattered about a sanded floor. Eventually booths were added and the walls covered with broadsides and newspapers of all kinds, playbills, handbills, and posters. Macaulay described the company at the famous literary establishment, Wills,' as consisting of "earls in stars and garters, clergymen in cassocks, pert templars, sheepish lads from the Universities, translators and index-makers in ragged coats."[16] Here, classes mixed more freely than they might elsewhere; no one who could put a penny on the bar was excluded. All were welcome in these centers of male networking; all, that is, except women.

Coffeehouses arrived on the London scene along with Puritan rule; they were especially suited to the social climate of the day, offering an antidote to taverns and alcoholism. One approving entry into the pamphlet wars that raged shortly after the advent of coffeehouse culture praised "this coffee drink" for having "caused a greater sobriety among the Nations," and added, by way of explanation: "Whereas formerly Apprentices and clerks with others used to take the morning's draught in Ale, Beer, or Wine, which, by the dizziness they Cause in the Brain, made many unfit for business, they use now to play the Good-fellows in this wakeful and civil drink."[17] While tea and chocolate were also available in the coffeehouses, alcoholic drinks were not; sobriety and moderation were the order of the day, and rules governing the behavior of coffeehouse patrons were prominently displayed on the walls of these establishments. Manners mattered in these places, although it is doubtful that all of the posted regulations were followed to the letter.[18]

Even allowing for a gap between theory and practice when it came to rules and regulations, the democratic character of the English coffeehouse and the sobriety encouraged there were significant at a time when the bourgeoisie was newly organizing as a class. Progressive ideas were in the air, and the coffeehouse as a public space where such thoughts could be aired was as novel a concept as coffee was a beverage. Here, as Habermas and others have noted, *men*, not only could meet to talk over the issues of the day but also begin to articulate a critique of the theory and practice of absolutist domination. Eventually these expressions of "public opinion" legitimated by rational consensus among relatively equal citizens would take on a political dimension of their own, as the bourgeoisie deployed this new, critical public sphere as a revolutionary instrument of class emancipation. The public sphere, insofar as it served to build public opinion in support of values like free speech, democracy, or the rule of law, also served to protect individuals from arbitrary actions of the state, and to mediate between the state and civil society. New technologies allowed newspapers, journals, and books to be produced cheaply and quickly; these media became more widely available than ever before, facilitating lively political debate and opposition—much of which, of course, took place in coffeehouses. The bourgeois public sphere may thus be seen as an arena where democratic discourse was not only available—at least to a limited extent— but, especially as exemplified by English coffeehouse culture, could flourish.[19]

GENDER POLITICS OF COFFEEHOUSE CULTURE

Joan Landes's contention that Habermas's notion of the "bourgeois public sphere" was essentially, and not just contingently, masculinist, bears mention here. Landes takes Habermas to task for not paying adequate attention to the way in which the eighteenth-century public sphere, described in outline here, was shaped by gendered categories and overtly sexist strategies, such as Rousseau's ideology of republican motherhood. The equation of "men" and "citizens" is thus not generic, for the public sphere was just as exclusive of women as the coffeehouse—whether located in fifteenth-century Cairo or eighteenth-century London.[20]

Clear evidence of this was seen in 1674, when unhappy wives published *The Women's Petition against Coffee*. The authors of this pamphlet declared that it was unhealthy for men to be spending so much time away from their homes. Men who became addicted to coffee, they argued, were becoming "as unfruitful as the deserts, from where that unhappy berry is said to be brought." The women complained that they were being neglected by their husbands, whose enjoyment of coffeehouse society placed "the whole race . . . in danger of extinction."[21] Especially interesting here is the way in which women's resentment of coffeehouses would appear to stem less from their exclusion from these male preserves than from the way in which the coffeehouse drew husbands and fathers away from the home (and the marriage bed). Coffeehouses, like taverns, were comfortable retreats from the responsibilities of family life, where men could both reduce the time and attention spent on domestic affairs and fritter away scarce financial resources, leaving less available for family needs. Not only did these public spaces exclude women; they also competed with women and domestic life for the time and money of men. Thus an interest in politics and public life could often provide a convenient excuse for men to hang out in such places, shirking their family responsibilities.

The gender politics of coffeehouse culture allow us to ask whether the political "fraternity" encouraged within the bourgeois public sphere of the eighteenth century resulted from something more than the mere exclusion of women. In spending long hours at the coffeehouse discussing the affairs of the day, men were withdrawing from the demands of family life at a time when the family constituted the basic economic unit of society. Thus women's responsibilities for domestic affairs and the household economy were only increased in the absence of men. Perhaps the democratic discourse of the new public spaces was built not just on the exclusion of women and the creation of specifically gendered categories like "republican motherhood," but also at the cost of increased anxiety and family labor on the part of wives, mothers, and daughters.[22]

COFFEEHOUSES, POLITICAL DISCOURSE, AND REVOLUTION

The coffeehouse played an integral role in revolutionary politics on the North American continent as well as in Europe. European settlers brought coffee with them to the colonies throughout the seventeenth and early eighteenth centuries. Four years after the British took control of Dutch New Amsterdam in 1664, coffee had eclipsed beer as the preferred breakfast drink of New Yorkers. In Boston the Green Dragon Coffee House, founded in 1697, would in later years be named the "headquarters of the Revolution" by no less than Daniel Webster. At the Green Dragon John Adams, Paul Revere, and others reportedly planned the Boston Tea Party, which made coffee drinking a patriotic act. Another Boston coffeehouse, the Bunch of Grapes, provided the stage for the first public reading of the Declaration of Independence. New York's Merchants Coffee House, located at the southeast corner of Wall and Water Streets, served as another focal point for revolutionary politics. The Sons of Liberty met there on April 18, 1774, to repel a shipment of tea arriving on a British ship; a month later citizens gathered there to draft a letter calling for a "virtuous and spirited Union" of the colonies against Great Britain, along with a congress of deputies—which would become the First Continental Congress. After the Revolution, the coffeehouse continued to play a political role, most notably hosting a huge reception on April 23, 1789, in honor of President–elect George Washington. Coffee was thus bound up, in the early days of the Republic, with a revolutionary politics of liberty and critical public opinion.[23]

Women were, for the most part, excluded from this political community, despite the fact that prewar boycotts and the need to quarter and provision the revolutionary army had politicized household economies before and after independence was declared.[24] Indeed, women had mounted public actions to police local merchants who hoarded scarce commodities in Poughkeepsie, Philadelphia, and elsewhere. On at least one occasion, coffee played a central role in such activity. In July, 1778, Abigail Adams reported to her husband, John, that "a Number of Females, some say a hundred, some say more assembled with a cart and trucks, marched down to the Ware House" of an "eminent, wealthy, stingy Merchant" who was believed to be hoarding coffee in Boston. When the merchant refused to deliver the keys, "one of them seazd him by his Neck and tossed him into the cart. . . . he delivered the keys. . . . they . . . opened the Warehouse. Hoisted out the Coffee themselves, put it into trucks and drove off. . . . A large concourse of Men stood amazed silent Spectators."[25] By the end of the war, however, such patriotic activity on the part of women would be deflected into benevolence, with service and reform societies directing women's energies back into the private world of home and family.

Much the same state of affairs prevailed in Europe, although in the case of the French Revolution, comparable women's riots were more desperate, frequent, and violent; the issue was bread, not the luxury of coffee or tea.[26] The historian Michelet described coffee as "the great event which created new customs, and even modified human temperaments," ascribing to the beverage the intangible and spontaneous flow of wit characteristic of the age of the philosophes—but this was entirely gender-specific. Coffeehouse culture flourished in France after the famous Café Procope opened its doors in 1689. Located across from the Comédie Francaise, this establishment attracted authors, actors, dramatists, and musicians, along with philosophers and politicians. Voltaire, who is rumored to have consumed over seventy cups of coffee a day, was a frequent patron. So were Rousseau, Diderot, Beaumarchais, and—during the days of the Revolution—Marat, Robespierre, and Danton. As in England, French coffeehouse culture emphasized temperance, luring customers away from the taverns and wine sellers.[27]

The café society central to the revolutionary public sphere remained relatively intact throughout the nineteenth and early twentieth centuries in France, but by the end of the eighteenth century coffeehouse culture in England had all but vanished. For the wealthier classes, select "gentlemen's clubs" became the preferred place to assemble in the company of one's social peers; the poorer and less exclusive establishments reverted to their earlier roles as taverns or chop houses, and a new fad for drinking tea eclipsed the coffee-drinking habit. As the public life of coffee declined in England, it found new favor on the domestic scene in Germany, as a breakfast and afternoon drink in middle-class homes.

Coffee was not unknown in Germany. Its use, however, had ambivalent connotations, notably the notion that coffee drinking made men and women sterile, which spared a movement aimed at preventing women from drinking the brew. In 1732 Johann Sebastian Bach composed a "Coffee Cantata," inspired by his love of the brew, which includes the aria "Ah! How sweet coffee tastes! Lovelier than a thousand kisses, sweeter far than muscatel wine! I must have my coffee." The fact that Bach had two wives and fathered twenty children also tended to give the lie to claims regarding coffee's putative links to sterility. We are left wondering, however, just what the mothers of these children might have felt about any of this.[28]

In 1777 Frederick the Great of Prussia attempted to ban coffee consumption by ordinary citizens. Annoyed with the large sums of cash that were flowing to foreign coffee merchants, he declared:

> It is disgusting to note the increase in the quantity of coffee used by my subjects and the amount of money that goes out of the country in consequence. Everybody is using coffee. If possible, this must be prevented. My people must drink beer. His Majesty was brought up on beer, and so were his officers. Many battles have been fought and won by soldiers nourished on beer; and the King does not believe that coffee-drinking soldiers can be depended upon to endure hardships or to beat his enemies in case of the occurrence of another war.[29]

Retired soldiers were recruited as "coffee smellers" to go about arresting anyone caught secretly roasting or brewing the beverage, while physicians were encouraged to tell their patients that drinking coffee would make them sterile. This move of Frederick's generated numerous expressions of passive and active resistance. The public's desire for coffee, however, won out in the end. Yet in Germany, coffee drinking became a private, domestic activity; coffee replaced flour soup or beer at breakfast and took on a new, gender-specific dimension as the focus of socializing among women in the afternoons. Breakfast coffee retained vestiges of the public functions of the coffeehouse, marking the start of the working day. After a cup or two in the morning, people were alert and ready to face the business day. In the nineteenth century the newspaper, another émigré from the coffeehouse, was added to this ritual. But the real impetus for the spread of coffee's popularity in Germany came from women of the new burgher class.

WOMEN AND "COFFEE CIRCLES" CULTURE

Recently arrived from the countryside, freed from work in the fields, townswomen gathered to drink coffee in the afternoons at one another's homes. The *Kaffeekränzchen*, or "coffee party," (literally "coffee circle") was entirely a women's affair; it demanded the relative freedom and leisure attached to the bourgeois cult of domesticity. Amaranthes's *Frauenzimmerlexikon*, the "Woman's Lexicon," defined it as "a daily or weekly gathering of several closely acquainted women, each taking her turn as hostess, and in which the members divert and amuse themselves with drinking coffee and playing *Ombre* [a popular card game of the day]." One way to "read" the significance of these gatherings is to suggest that women approached them with a passion that must be seen as compensation for their exclusion from other, more public, domains. In many respects, afternoon coffee parties served as a sort of exclusively female parallel to the exclusively male socializing of coffee-houses and taverns, often becoming the objects of ridicule. Indeed, to this day the word *Kaffeeklatsch* ("ladies gossip circle") retains extremely pejorative—and heavily gendered—connotations.[30] An alternative interpretation, however, might focus on the fact that women might simply have found the company of other women more interesting and stimulating than mixed company.[31]

Without romanticizing the women's coffee parties, it is important to protest the prevailing portrait of them as venues for trivial (i.e., domestic) gossip, especially as contrasted to images of coffeehouses as places where important (i.e., public) speech and activity would prevail. This serves to obscure the reality of how much time spent in taverns or coffeehouses—male preserves of "publicity"—was likely devoted to forms of "male" gossip, or conversations about sports, sexual conquest, tall tales, and the like, instead of (or, more charitably, in addition to) the serious political discourse that is often spoken of by theorists of the bourgeois public sphere. Perhaps there is something threatening to men in the image of women getting together and talking among themselves. The language is, indeed, replete with pejorative synonyms for "girl talk": *gab, gossip, chat, chitchat, chatter, babble, prattle,* and *hen party* are only a few of the terms used to devalue women in their verbal interactions. But perhaps this is not so much a matter of male fear as it is a question of women's internalization of second-class status. As Deborah Cameron notes, "Men trivialize the talk of women not because they are afraid of such talk, but in order to make women themselves down-grade it. If women feel that all interaction with other women is a poor substitute for mixed interaction and trivial compared with the profundities of men's talk, their conversations will indeed be harmless."[32]

Even more is at stake here than the use of language—powerful though language may be as a cultural significator of power and power-structured relationships. Ambivalence and anxiety about women's leisure time seem to have accompanied the rise of the bourgeois family; derogative responses to women's coffee parties may have been one manifestation of bourgeois male concerns in this regard. On the one hand, a wife's leisure may be taken as a positive reflection of her husband's status and affluence. On the other, however, this newfound leisure might give rise to a whole new set of worries about what "mischief" women might get up to if they have too much free time on their hands. Such concerns would eventually be borne out when Betty Friedan's germinal analysis of a "feminine mystique" emerging among middle-class women was published in the United States—a century after women's coffee parties were all the rage among the German bourgeoisie.[33]

COFFEE'S CHANGING ROLE IN TWENTIETH CENTURY

The movement of coffee out of the public sphere and into the private realm of the bourgeois family and its imitators in nineteenth-century Germany was paralleled in the United States, where, by the start of the twentieth century, the beverage had been thoroughly domesticated. Indeed, its gendered connotations underwent a further transformation when coffee drinking was promoted by the Women's Christian Temperance Union (WCTU) as an alternative to the alcoholic beverages that were readily available in saloons across the nation. The American Public Health

Association supported the WCTU, claiming that there was "a physiological antag-
onism between coffee and alcohol, as well as between coffee and opium," and des-
ignating coffee a healthy stimulant, "much favored by brain workers," as well as
an antimalarial agent.[34] Female reformers of the Progressive Era often suggested
founding coffeehouses in the slums as a means of displacing saloons. They looked
favorably on the popularity of coffeehouses among Jewish and Italian immigrants,
whose sobriety was noteworthy compared with that of many other immigrant
groups. In the early 1900s, Jane Addams praised these working-class cafés as the
"Salons of the Ghetto" and cited them for "performing a function somewhat
between the eighteenth century coffee house and the Parisian cafe."[35]

The public sphere of the coffeehouses—whether in medieval Islam or eighteenth-century London and New York—had been an exclusively male domain.
Throughout the twentieth century in the United States the domestic use of coffee
would become something of a feminized cultural icon, central to the spread of commodity goods and consumer capitalist culture. George Lipsetz analyzed coffee's
changing role as a cultural icon in a case study of the women's roles in the CBS network television show *I Remember Mama*, which consistently ranked among the top
ten programs during its eight-year run in the 1950s. Both this production and a
1948 feature film of the same name were inspired by a collection of short stories by
Kathryn Forbes entitled *Mama's Bank Account*, as were a Broadway play and radio
performance. The stories, and their various media interpretations, dealt with Nor-
wegian immigrant life in the years before the Great Depression. Lipsetz contrasted
the role of coffee drinking in the movie and the television series, which was (not
incidentally) sponsored by Maxwell House Coffee.[36]

In the motion picture one of "Mama's" teenage daughters was permitted to join
her parents in a cup of coffee after she proved herself as an adult by rejecting a showy
dresser set and accepting a piece of family jewelry for her high school graduation
gift. The young woman's rejection of consumer goods in favor of traditional values
was seen by moviegoers as praiseworthy. However, this was turned upside down in
the television series, where tradition served only to legitimate the purchase of more
and more consumer goods, and the family story became a lure to bring the audience
commercial messages from the program's sponsor. As Lipsetz put it, "The product
becomes a member of the Hansen family, while tradition and emotional support become commodities to be secured through the purchase of Maxwell House coffee."[37]

Coffee was cast in the dramatic narratives of the show in a variety of ways.
Mama and Papa drank it together in the kitchen; it served as a means of calming
down rambunctious children, as a spark for women's conversations, or as an excuse for having company; it facilitated clear thinking and problem solving. Perhaps
more importantly, its magical attributes served to draw viewers toward other commodities seen in an equally respectful, if not quite so consistently magical, light.[38]
A fundamental connection was established between the warmth of these nostalgic
scenes of idyllic family life and the impetus of a consumer capitalist economy toward ever-expanding commodity purchases. In the context of the television series,
the domestication of coffee drinking stands in sharp relief as an example of the sub-
sumption by the "culture industry" of the critical public sphere of political dis-

course formerly found in coffeehouse culture. This iconography demonstrates the extent to which the industry's attendant forms of "publicity" and "entertainment" have come to serve as stand-ins for free speech and cultural critique.

Indeed, contemporary coffee advertisements would seem to demonstrate that coffee today has moved almost totally out of the public sphere and into the realm of privacy and intimacy. Television commercials for Folger's Coffee, for instance, evoke "traditional" family values far more insistently (and effectively) than any of the speakers at the 1992 Republican National Convention. In a typical spot we see the young African-American soldier returning home, duffle bag over his shoulder, to share a cup of coffee with Mom in the family kitchen along with an affectionate hug—and "masculine" toss of a football—with a kid brother. In another, a young White woman returns home after college, and, by taking over the chore of making morning coffee, demonstrates that for all her education she still aspires to be "just like mom." Every December the handsome young son returns, we know not from just where—perhaps an Ivy League college?—his arms filled with brightly wrapped packages. The presents get put under the Christmas tree before he awakens his delighted family with the aroma of a pot of freshly brewed Folger's. Images are, indeed, often more powerful than words!

In this context it is also important to think of the unfolding heterosexual romance portrayed in a recent, ongoing series of commercials for Taster's Choice instant coffee or the call to "celebrate the moments of our lives" by drinking General Foods International Coffees. The latter ads often display various forms of female bonding, with sisters or former college roommates drinking coffee while engaging in nostalgic conversation. These relationships between women are depicted as either emphatically asexual or prophetically heterosexual, as when college pals reminisce about the handsome waiter at a European café. They are indicative of the confinement of female discourse, and especially the "symbolic speech" of female sexuality, to domesticity within an overarching framework of compulsory heterosexuality.[39] Indeed, coffee drinking is often equated with women making time for themselves in the midst of competing demands: an instant cappuccino, one ad implies, can make the conflicting demands of children, housework, a profession, and caring for elderly relatives melt away to nothing—and in just "an instant." Only rarely do we see coffee advertised in more "public" settings, notably the Folger's commercials that show diners in fancy restaurants drinking instant coffee that's been "switched" for a freshly brewed beverage. And even then the domestic message is clear: "I'll serve this at home" is, explicitly or implicitly, the tag line spoken by these putatively surprised patrons.

It might seem, in the United States at least, as if the pendulum had swung entirely from one side to the other, from a heavily male (public) sphere of coffeehouses and coffee drinking to a specifically female (private) realm of idyllic domesticity where coffee is just one of many commodities to be purchased and consumed. Indeed, it would not be difficult to develop a wholly negative, one-sided critique in the style of Horkheimer and Adorno, where the golden (masculine) age of the coffeehouse is valorized at the expense of a debased (feminine) mode of domestic coffee drinking. But such a critique would ignore the ways in which vestiges of the older traditions not only remain in contemporary society but on occasion have been manipulated consciously by members of progressive social movements in ways that subvert both the established "culture industry" and the gendered distinctions of the "public" and "private" spheres.

COFFEE AND ALTERNATIVE SOCIAL AND CULTURAL INSTITUTIONS

Countercultural institutions have emerged in the last two decades that draw on the traditions of free speech and cultural and political criticism that were integral to the coffeehouse cultures of centuries past. Indeed, these institutions may be situated in a context of political discourse that includes the café societies of Bohemian Paris at the turn of the twentieth century and Weimar Germany after the First World War.[40] The GI coffeehouse movement was a focal point, on and around a number of military installations, for organizing against the Vietnam Conflict. By the early 1970s, some peace protestors had shifted their efforts away from college campuses to military bases around the country. At Mountain Home Air Force Base in Idaho, for example, peace workers "opened a coffeehouse for GIs in an abandoned theater downtown; they called it the Helping Hand. They had meetings that advised enlisted personnel how to assist the antiwar movement. They published an antiwar newspaper for the base, began counseling GIs on how to file for conscientious-objector status, and opened a small library of radical books."[41] Comparable efforts were made across the country, with coffeehouses springing up in the vicinity of almost every major military base. Over a hundred underground newspapers would be published, often in conjunction with coffeehouse activities. For a while there was even talk of unionizing the military. In at least some cases, these initiatives involved discussions of class relationships (between middle-class and working-class peace organizers and between civilians and GIs) and confrontations with feminist issues that sparked difficult and lively debates.[42]

Since the late 1960s, in cities and towns across the United States, feminist community organizing and cultural work has often centered around coffeehouses, sometimes in tandem with feminist bookstores and other forms of cultural expression. While some of these businesses have been relatively short-lived experiments in collectivity and other alternatives to capitalist organizations, others have survived and continue to do so despite an often hostile economic climate. In Chicago, for example, the Mountain Moving Coffeehouse celebrated its twentieth anniversary in 1993. Its very name connotes the political struggles attached to building alternative social and cultural institutions—it is no easy task to "move the mountains" of entrenched sexism and homophobia that militate against feminist organizational agendas prioritizing women and their concerns or needs.

Technically speaking, Mountain Moving is set somewhat apart from the "tradition" of coffeehouse culture, not just in that it provides a space for feminist/lesbian cultural expression but also because this space is not permanently devoted to the consumption of coffee or any other comestibles. Rather, Mountain Moving Coffeehouse has met on Saturday nights in space made available by at least two

Chicago churches. Coffee, tea, soda, and sweets are served at intermissions or before and after programs, and are somewhat incidental to the featured events. At large-drawing concerts, the bulk of the audience never leaves the sanctuary space of the church to visit the third floor of the building where the library and refreshments are available. Smaller events, such as a popular crafts fair held during the December holiday season, take place entirely on the third floor, and in these instances coffee is more integrated. In addition to sponsoring a variety of ongoing reading, discussion, and support groups for women and children, with an emphasis on lesbian political issues, Mountain Moving Coffeehouse has brought a wide range of cultural programming to Chicago's feminist community (at affordable prices). A typical month includes events ranging from comedy to folksingers to a jazz duo, along with showings of artwork by differently abled women.

Despite its departures from more conventional forms, the heart of traditional coffeehouse culture has been retained insofar as Mountain Moving's clientele sustains a lively alternative to more mainstream forms of information sharing, community support, and entertainment. The importance of countercultural institutions such as this should not be underestimated. In addition to providing safe spaces for critical discourse and cultural events, they are places where symbolic speech, represented by styles of dress, bodily presentation, and other nonverbal forms of behavior, may find free expression. For some women this freedom to "speak" symbolically is a luxury unavailable in other venues of everyday life.

A young woman who is a recent graduate of the college where the author teaches poignantly expresses the importance of such symbolic speech and the need for places where it may be freely and safely articulated. She describes herself as "a walking stereotype of a young 'Generation X' lesbian" who is a "regular" at Mountain Moving events, saying, "I look like a twelve year old boy—short hair, no makeup, no dresses, no skirts, definitely no high heels; when people aren't sure, they assume I'm male." She is frequently the object of homophobic verbal assaults on the streets of Chicago, but at coffeehouse events she looks "like everyone else." At Mountain Moving there are no "gender police" to call her to account for transgressing standards of "feminine" appearance or behavior, so she can feel comfortable just being herself. Coffeehouse events serve to remind her that she is not "alone in the world"; she feels empowered "to know that there's a group of people trying to move the mountain together, and not just me." When she was first coming out as a lesbian in Chicago, "it was really affirming to be surrounded by other lesbians, given that there's so much homophobia in the 'real' world." She still sees the coffeehouse as a place where she is guaranteed community and conviviality: "It's as if I'm a battery that runs down in the real world, but I can go to Mountain Moving and get recharged."[43]

Lynette J. Eastland spent several months studying Twenty Rue Jacob, a feminist coffeehouse and bookstore in Salt Lake City, Utah. She described her experiences as a participant–observer in this ethnographic study, citing the importance of everyday relationships to the coffeehouse community:

> The days I liked the best were those heavily loaded with people. . . . Sometimes they purchased something, but most often these days were primarily socially oriented. We

would sell a lot of cups of coffee, some lunches and maybe a record or two. The women would great each other warmly with hugs and smiles and catch up on the news of each others' lives. Some would come in to check the bulletin board and posters for local activities . . . or to see who was there, but mostly they came to pass time with one another, to find a friendly face.[44]

Here, it would seem, the exclusively male atmosphere of the eighteenth-century coffeehouse has been irrevocably altered by the social and political needs of women "customers"; while the gender specificity may have been inverted, traditions of free speech, public information, and sociability have been retained.

Indeed, in some instances, the explicitly political connections have been positively exploited. Eastland recounts how a typical day at Twenty Rue Jacob might include a scene such as the following, which involved

two young women who came in early afternoon and ordered two cups of coffee. They were obviously upset and isolated themselves from the few people gathered around the counter. . . . they asked to speak to [the manager, who] pulled up a chair and sat down. The two women held hands across the table as they talked. Both appeared very young, very attractive and were wearing dresses and high heels. . . . They needed the name of a lawyer, they said, who would be sensitive to their problem. They were being threatened by the ex-husband of one of the women, who said he would take [her] child away if they continued to see each other. They were confused and afraid and needed help.

The manager of the coffeehouse supplied the women with the name and phone number of an attorney; while we do not know "the rest of the story," it is clear that Twenty Rue Jacob played an integral role in making available to patrons information that might otherwise be unavailable or difficult to obtain from "mainstream" sources. Once again, echoes of past traditions linger, though with a twist.[45]

Oppositional and progressive coffeehouse cultures such as the two described here represent viable alternatives to the commodity culture of the mass media and serve as reminders of how it may still be possible to create public spheres where critical political discourse may be sustained in troubled times. Perhaps more importantly, as the vitality of feminist coffeehouses today would tend to indicate, such publicly discursive moments can be recreated in ways that inform a new generation of citizens. Here the links between the passions stimulated by coffee drinking and free speech undertaken in public association not only reach back through time to medieval Islam or the Enlightenment but also stretch forward to an as yet unimagined future. For those who prize a good cup of coffee along with democracy and passionate critical discourse, there may yet be hope.

NOTES

1. Aytoun Ellis, *The Penny Universities: A History of the Coffee-Houses* (London: Secker and Warburg, 1956), p. 3; Ralph S. Hattox, *Coffee and Coffeehouses: The Origins of a Social Beverage in the Medieval Near East* (Seattle: University of Washington Press, 1985), p. 12.

2. Ellis, *The Penny Universities*, p. 17.

3. Claudia Roden, *Coffee* (New York: Penguin, 1977), p. 20; David Joel, and Karl Schapira, *The Book of Coffee and Tea* (New York: St. Martin's Press, 1982), pp. 5–6.

4. Sara Perry, *The Complete Coffee Book* (San Francisco: Chronicle Books, 1991), p. 7; Roden, *Coffee*, p. 20; Schapira, *The Book of Coffee and Tea*, p. 6.

5. Norman Kolpas, *A Cup of Coffee* (New York: Grove Press, 1993), p. 14; Hattox, *Coffee and Coffeehouses*, pp. 22–28; Perry, *The Complete Coffee Book*, p. 7; Roden, *Coffee*, p. 20.

6. Hattox, *Coffee and Coffeehouses*, p. 37.

7. Ibid., pp. 32–39; Roden, *Coffee*, p. 21.

8. Hattox, *Coffee and Coffeehouses*, p. 93.

9. Ibid., p. 101.

10. Perry, *The Complete Coffee Book*, p. 8; Roden, *Coffee*, p. 21; Schapira, *The Book of Coffee and Tea*, p. 9.

11. David F. Noble, *A World without Women: The Christian Clerical Culture of Western Science* (New York: Knopf, 1992), esp. pp. 3–39.

12. Ellis, *The Penny Universities*, p. 19.

13. Ibid., p. 24.

14. Ibid., p. 27.

15. Ibid., p. 24.

16. Quoted in Roden, *Coffee*, p. 28.

17. Quoted in Edward Robinson, *The Early English Coffee House, with an Account of the First Use of Coffee* (1893) (Christchurch, Hants.: Dolphin Press, 1972), p. 117.

18. Ibid., pp. 109–110.

19. Jürgen Habermas, *The Structural Transformation of the Public Sphere: An Inquiry into a Category of Bourgeois Society*, trans. Thomas Burger with the assistance of Frederick Lawrence (Cambridge, MA: MIT Press, 1989).

20. See Joan B. Landes, *Women and the Public Sphere in the Age of the French Revolution* (Ithaca, NY: Cornell University Press, 1988), pp. 7, 129.

21. The Women's Petition Against Coffee, representing to publick consideration the grand inconveniences accruing to their sex from the excessive use of that drying, enfeebling liquor. Presented to the right honorable the keepers of the library of Venus by a wellwiller. London, 1674.

22. Thanks to Uma Narayan for this insight. On the family as an economic unit, see Laurel Thatcher Ulrich, *Good Wives: Image and Reality in Northern New England, 1650–1750* (New York: Oxford University Press, 1982).

23. Kolpas, *A Cup of Coffee*, p. 22.

24. Linda K. Kerber, *Women of the Republic: Intellect and Ideology in Revolutionary America* (New York: Norton, 1986), p. 35.

25. L. H. Butterfield (Ed.) Abigail Adams to John Adams, July 31, 1778, *Adams Family Correspondence* (Cambridge, MA: Belknap Press, 1963), II, p. 295, quoted in Kerber, *Women of the Republic*, p. 44.

26. Ibid., p. 44.

27. Roden, *Coffee*, p. 25.

28. Perry, *The Complete Coffee Book*, p. 17; Josh Glenn, "Coffee Time," *Utne Reader*, November/December 1994, p. 62.

29. Roden, *Coffee*, p. 22.

30. Wolfgang Schivelbusch, *Tastes of Paradise: A Social History of Spices, Stimulants, and Intoxicants*, translated from the German by David Jacobson (New York: Vintage Books, 1993), p. 69.

31. See, for example, Carroll Smith-Rosenberg, "The Female World of Love and Ritual Relations between Women in Nineteenth-Century America," *Signs*, 1 (1) (1975), pp. 1–29.

32. Deborah Cameron, *Feminism and Linguistic Theory*, cited in Jane Mills, *Womanwords: A Dictionary of Words about Women* (New York: Free Press, 1989), p. 44. See also Dale Spender, *Man Made Language*, 2nd ed. (New York: Pandora, 1991), p. 106–108.

33. Betty Friedan, *The Feminine Mystique* (New York: Norton, 1963).

34. "The Abuse of Alcohol from a Sanitary Standpoint," *American Kitchen Magazine*, 5 (1) (April 1896), p. 33, quoted in Harvey A. Levenstein, *Revolution at the Table: The Transformation of the American Diet* (New York: Oxford University Press, 1988), p. 99.

35. Jane Addams, "Immigration: A Field Neglected by the Scholar," *The Commons*, January 1905, p. 16.

36. George Lipsetz, "Why Remember Mama? The Changing Face of a Women's Narrative," in *Time Passages: Collective Memory and American Popular Culture* (Minneapolis: University of Minnesota Press, 1990), pp. 77–96.

37. Ibid., p. 89.

38. Ibid., p. 90.

39. Adrienne Rich, "Compulsory Heterosexuality and Lesbian Existence," *Signs*, 5 (4) (1980), pp. 631–660.

40. See, for example, Georges Bernier, *Paris Cafes: Their Role in the Birth of Modern Art* (New York: Wildenstein, 1985); and Henry Pachter, "Expressionism and Café Culture," in *Weimar Etudes* (New York: Columbia University Press, 1982).

41. Randy Shilts, *Conduct Unbecoming: Gays and Lesbians in the U.S. Military* (New York: St. Martin's Press, 1993), p. 152.

42. See Ellen Willis, "Radical Feminism and Feminist Radicalism" in Sonya Sayres, et. al (Eds.), *The 60s without Apology* (Minneapolis: University of Minnesota Press, in cooperation with Social Text, 1984), pp. 111–112.

43. Suzy Stanton, personal communication, October 20, 1994. Suzy is a 1994 graduate of De Paul University. At De Paul, she was instrumental in founding an organization for lesbian, gay, and bisexual students and for developing and administering a survey of homophobic attitudes on campus—no mean feats at a Catholic institution of higher education.

44. Lynette J. Eastland, *Communication, Organization and Change within a Feminist Context: A Participant Observation of a Feminist Collective* (Lewiston, NY: E. Mellen Press, 1991), p. 176.

45. Ibid., pp. 184–185.

FURTHER READINGS

Eastland, Lynette J. *Communication, Organization and Change within a Feminist Context: A Participant Observation of a Feminist Collective.* Lewiston, NY: E. Mellen Press, 1991.

Kerber, Linda K. *Women of the Republic: Intellect and Ideology in Revolutionary America.* New York: Norton, 1986.

Landes, Joan B. *Women and the Public Sphere in the Age of the French Revolution.* Ithaca, NY: Cornell University Press, 1988.

Rich, Adrienne. "Compulsory Heterosexuality and Lesbian Existence." *Signs,* 5 (4) (1980), pp. 631–660.

Smith-Rosenberg, Carroll. "The Female World of Love and Ritual: Relations between Women in Nineteenth-Century America," *Signs,* 1 (1) (1975), pp. 1–29.

CONTRIBUTORS

Todd W. Areson is currently manager of demonstration projects for the Virginia Division of Child Support Enforcement. He is managing a federal demonstration to develop a methodology for staffing standards for individual child support offices. Previously, he was a local government consultant in Richmond, Virginia, dealing with issues of policy management, organizational effectiveness, and intergovernmental linkages confronting elected and appointed officials. He has extensive experience directing university–government consortia at all three levels of the intergovernmental system. Areson holds a Ph.D. in education and organizational change from the University of Michigan (1974). He has published in the areas of policy analysis, program evaluation, and organizational innovation.

Ruth Bamberger is professor of political science and chair of the Department of History and Political Science at Drury College, Springfield, Missouri. She has researched extensively in the area of sex discrimination in insurance since it became a major public policy issue in the mid-1970s. She has written papers on the topic, which have been presented at the Midwest Political Science Association, the Southern Political Science Association, and the Southwestern Social Science Association. In the spring of 1981, Bamberger was granted an honorary research fellowship at the University of Durham, England, where she researched sex discrimination in insurance in the British system.

Irene Barnett is a doctoral student in Kent State University's Department of Political Science. Her interests are in comparative politics and women in politics.

Linda L. M. Bennett is an associate professor and chair, Department of Political Science, Wittenberg University, Springfield, Ohio. Her research interests include American national government and politics. She is the author of *Symbolic State Politics: Education Funding in Ohio* (1984) and coauthor of *Living with Leviathan: Americans Coming to Terms with Big Government* (1990). She has also authored or co-authored articles on American government and politics. She is working on studies of public knowledge of and attitudes about Congress and of challengers in congressional elections.

Stephen E. Bennett is a professor of political science, senior research associate in the Institute for Policy Research, and director of the Center for the Study of Democratic Citizenship, at the University of Cincinnati. His research interests focus on American political behavior. He is the author of *Apathy in America, 1960–1984* (1986) and coauthor of *Living with Leviathan: Americans Coming to Terms with Big Government* (1990). He has also authored or coauthored articles on mass belief systems, political participation, and political information. He is working on studies of Americans' knowledge of and attitudes about Congress, and of the impact of political indifference and ignorance on American political life.

Diane D. Blair, a professor of political science at the University of Arkansas, has published two books and numerous articles dealing with women and politics, state and local government, and Arkansas politics. She chaired the Arkansas Governor's Commission on the Status of Women (1971–1973) and now serves, by presidential appointment, on the Board of the Corporation for Public Broadcasting.

Lewis Bowman is a retired professor of political science who taught most recently in the Department of Government and International Affairs at the University of South Florida (USF), in Tampa, Florida, and in the Department of Political Science at the University of North Texas. He has taught and done research in American politics, political parties and interest groups, and electoral behavior.

Charles S. Bullock III is the Richard R. Russell Professor of Political Science at the University of Georgia. He received his Ph.D. from Washington University, St. Louis, and has done research on Congress, civil rights, and policy implementation. He is the coauthor of *Law and Social Change* (1974); *Racial Equality in America* (1975); *Coercion to Compliance* (1976); *Public Policy and Politics in America*, 2nd ed. (1984); *Public Policy in the Eighties* (1983); *Implementation of Civil Rights Policy* (1984); *Government in America* (1984); and *Runoff Elections in the United States* (1992), which received the Southern Political Science Association's V.O. Key Book Award. He is on the editorial boards of the *Journal of Politics* and *Social Science Quarterly*. In 1991 he received the William A. Owens Creative Research Award.

Barbara Burrell, Ph.D., is a researcher and head of survey design at the University of Wisconsin–Extension Survey Research Laboratory. She is the author of *A Woman's Place Is in the House: Campaigning for Congress in the Feminist Era* (1994) and is currently completing a book on Hillary Rodham Clinton and public opinion.

Nancie Caraway is a political theorist and feminist scholar. Her research interests include multicultural feminist theory, women's global human rights, and media and cultural studies. Currently she is at work on a screenplay about the German Green activist and feminist Petra Kelly and a play about racial politics in Hawaii. Caraway lives, writes, and teaches in Hawaii and Washington, D.C.

Cal Clark is professor and head of the Department of Political Science at Auburn University. He received his Ph.D. from the University of Illinois and previously taught at New Mexico State University, the University of Wyoming, and Chung Yuan Christian University in Taiwan. His primary teaching and research interests include international political economy, East Asain development, comparative public policy, and U.S. competitiveness. He is the author of *Taiwan's Development*; coauthor of *Women in Taiwan Politics* and *Flexibility, Foresight, and Fortuna in Taiwan's Devel-*

opment; and coeditor of *Studies in Dependency Reversal, State and Development*, and *The Evolving Pacific Basin*. His work has appeared in such journals as the *American Political Science Review, Business and the Contemporary World, Comparative Political Studies, Harvard International Review, International Studies Quarterly, Jerusalem Journal of International Relations, Journal of Conflict Resolution, Policy Studies Journal, Political Methodology*, and *Western Political Quarterly*.

Janet Clark is professor and chair of political science at West Georgia College. She received her Ph.D. in political science from the University of Illinois and previously taught at New Mexico State University, the University of Wyoming, and Chung Yuan Christian University in Taiwan. Her primary teaching and research interests include women in politics, American government, and state and local politics. She is the coauthor of *Women, Elections, and Representation, Government and Politics in Wyoming*, and *Women in Taiwan Politics*. Her work has appeared in such journals as the *American Politics Quarterly, International Journal of Public Administration, Journal of Political Science, Policy Studies Journal, Social Science Quarterly, Western Political Quarterly*, and *Women and Politics*. She has served as president of the Western Social Science Association and of the Women's Caucus for Political Science. She is the current editor of *Women and Politics* and served a term as book review editor of the *Social Science Journal*.

Elizabeth Adell Cook is a visiting assistant professor of government at The American University. She is the co-author of *Between Two Absolutes: Public Opinion and the Politics of Abortion* (1992) and coeditor of *The Year of the Woman: Myths and Realities* (1994). She has also published many scholarly articles on feminist consciousness and abortion politics.

Iva Ellen Deutchman is associate professor of political science at Hobart and William Smith Colleges. She has published in numerous journals, primarily in the area of gender and politics in the U.S. and Australia. She has been a visiting scholar and visiting lecturer at the University of Melbourne.

Kathleen Dolan is an assistant professor of political science at the University of Wisconsin–Oshkosh. She has written several articles on women state legislators and attitudes toward women candidates. Her research interests include electoral behavior, women and politics, and legislative behavior.

Lois Lovelace Duke is professor of political science at Clemson University and author of many pieces on women and politics and on U.S. national government, including a coedited volume with James MacGregor Burns, William Crotty, and Lawrence Longley, *The Democrats Must Lead: The Case for a Progressive Democratic Party*. Her research interests also include mass media and politics, and state and local government. Currently, she is working on a manuscript featuring civil rights activists and their contributions to the civil rights movement in the Deep South. She is a past president of the Women's Caucus for Political Science: South; is the current president of the South Carolina Political Science Association; and is the current president of the Clemson Area League of Women Voters. She is the recipient of the Clemson University Chapter of the American Association of University Professors (AAUP) Award of Merit for distinctive contributions to the academic profession (May 1992).

Lynne E. Ford, assistant professor of political science, College of Charleston, teaches courses on U.S. politics, political parties and interest groups, political psychology, and women and politics. Her research interests include women and politics, citizenship through service learning, and the development of political attitudes in adolescents. With Kathleen Dolan, she has written on women state legislators based on an original survey of sitting women legislators in all fifty states.

Joanne V. Hawks, director of Sarah Isom Center for Women's Studies, University of Mississippi, teaches courses on the history of southern and American women and the role of women in society. With Carolyn Ellis Staton she has researched and written articles on women in southern legislatures from the 1920s to the present.

William E. Hulbary is an associate professor of political science in the Department of Government and International Affairs at the University of South Florida (USF), in Tampa, Florida. He teaches courses and does research in political behavior, political parties, American politics, and research methods and statistics.

Kathleen P. Ianello is an associate professor of political science at Gettysburg College in Gettysburg, Pennsylvania. She teaches courses in American politics, public policy, and feminist theory. She is the author of *Decisions without Hierarchy*.

Malcolm Jewell, professor emeritus of political science at the University of Kentucky in Lexington, has taught in the areas of legislatures and political parties. He has written extensively about legislative elections, primary elections, and state politics. His coauthored book, *Legislative Leadership in the American States*, includes a chapter on women in legislative leadership.

Roberta Ann Johnson is a professor of politics at the University of San Francisco. She has a B.A. degree (magna cum laude, Phi Beta Kappa) from Brooklyn College, and M.A. and Ph.D. degrees from Harvard University. From 1980 to 1985 she was a technical assistance specialist in the Office for Civil Rights, U.S. Department of Education. In 1992 she had a Fulbright Grant to teach American politics and women's studies at the University of Indonesia, Jakarta. In 1993–1994 she was the National Endowment for the Humanities Chair at the University of San Francisco. In 1994 she received federal funding through the Campus Compact program to develop a service-learning course on the homeless. She has published numerous articles on minorities, women, the disabled, and civil rights–related topics in journals such as the *Western Political Quarterly, Policy, Revista/Review InterAmericana*, and *Policy and Politics*. She has also published a book, *Puerto Rico: Commonwealth or Colony?* (1980).

Anne E. Kelley is an emeritus associate professor of political science in the Department of Government and International Affairs at the University of South Florida (USF), in Tampa, Florida. She has taught and done research in political parties and interest groups, Florida politics, women and politics, and American political theory.

Elizabeth A. Kelly is an assistant professor of political science and women's studies at De Paul University in Chicago. She is the author of *Education, Public Knowledge, and Democracy* (1995) and is currently working on a book about Jane Addams's social and political thought. She enjoys a good cup of coffee.

Nicholas P. Lovrich Jr. is professor of political science and has served as director, Division of Governmental Studies and Services, at Washington State University for the past fifteen years. The division provides applied research services to agencies of federal, state, and local government; manages grant and contract activities in the Department of Political Science; assists faculty and graduate student research; maintains a year-round internship program (twelve-month T.A.); and publishes reports and a series of occasional papers. He holds a B.A. from Stanford University and M.A. and Ph.D. degrees in political science (public Administration subfield) from UCLA. His research has been published in such journals as *Policy Studies Journal, Policy Studies Quarterly, Social Science Quarterly, State and Local Government Review, Public Administration Quarterly, International Journal of Public Administration, Public Productivity and Management Review, Urban Affairs Quarterly,* and *Journal of Urban Affairs*. He is currently the principle investigator for grants from the Washington Traffic Safety Commission, Washington State Patrol, Whitman County Enhanced 911 project and the Washington State Association of Counties. Dr. Lovrich has been either the principle investigator or coprinciple investigator on grants from agencies such as the U.S. Fish and Wildlife Service, the Canadian National Government, the W. K. Kellogg Foundation, and the U.S. Federal District Court for Eastern Washington.

Susan A. MacManus is professor of public administration and political science in the Department of Government and International Affairs at the University of South Florida (USF), Tampa, Florida. Her research interests include urban and minority politics, public policy analysis, and public budgeting and finance. Her articles on women and politics have appeared in the *Journal of Politics, Western Political Quarterly, Social Science Quarterly, Women and Politics, National Civic Review, Journal of Political Science, The Municipal Year Book,* and in numerous edited books. She is past president of the Southern Political Science Association and frequently serves as a political commentator. In 1991 she received USF's Theodore and Venette Askounes-Ashford Distinguished Scholar Award.

Elaine Martin, associate professor of political science, Eastern Michigan University, Ypsilanti, Michigan, teaches courses in judicial politics, women in politics, and public administration. She has published extensively on the subject of gender and the judiciary, and is now at work on a book: *Distinguished Women: Voices from the Bench.*

Karen O'Connor is a professor of government in the School of Public Affairs at The American University. A past president of the Women's Caucus for Political Science, she has written extensively on interest groups, women and politics, and the law. Her most recent books include *Women, Politics, and American Society* (1995), with Nancy E. McGlen, and *American Government: Roots and Reform,* 2nd ed. (1995), with Larry J. Sabato.

Linda J. Penaloza is associate director and head of Field Operations at the University of Wisconsin–Extension Survey Research Laboratory. She has a B.A. in sociology from Trinity University, San Antonio, Texas; an M.A. in sociology from the University of Minnesota, Minneapolis; and is working toward a Ph.D. in journalism and mass communications from the University of Wisconsin–Madison.

Wilma Rule is an adjunct professor of political science at the University of Nevada at Reno and coeditor with Joseph F. Zimmerman of *U.S. Electoral Systems: Their Impact on Women and Minorities* (1992) and *Electoral Systems in Comparative Perspective: Their Impact on Women and Minorities* (1994). She is the author of numerous articles on women's recruitment to state and national legislatures.

Carolyn Ellis Staton is acting vice chancellor for Academic Affairs and professor of Law at the University of Mississippi Law School. She received her undergraduate degree from Tulane University, her master's degree from Columbia University, and her juris doctorate from Yale Law School. Formerly, she was in private practice in New York and was an assistant United States attorney in the District of New Jersey. She was also a Fulbright Fellow in Germany. Currently Ms. Staton serves as reporter on evidence for the Mississippi Supreme Court Advisory Committee on Rules. She is the author of books and articles on evidence, criminal procedure, and sex discrimination. She teaches courses on evidence, sex discrimination, criminal procedure, and school law.

Gertrude A. Steuernagel is professor of political science at Kent State University. Her most recent book is a work coauthored with M. Margaret Conway and David W. Ahern, *Women and Public Policy: A Revolution in Progress* (1995). She is currently working with Conway and Ahern on a book involving women and political participation. Her teaching and research interests are in women and politics and political theory.

Glen Sussman is an assistant professor of political science at Old Dominion University in Norfolk, Virginia. He teaches courses on American politics, electoral politics, media and politics, political behavior, and the presidency. His publications include articles on gender politics, the media and politics, political behavior and presidential–congressional relations.

Joan Hulse Thompson, associate professor of political science, Beaver College, Glenside, Pennsylvania, served as an American Association of University Women Education Foundation Fellow at the Congressional Caucus for Women's Issues in 1983–1984. She was an American Political Science Association Congressional Fellow in 1985–1986.

Sara J. Weir is an assistant professor of the political science at Western Washington University in Bellingham, Washington. She teaches courses in domestic policy analysis and women and politics. Her current research is in the area of women and leadership.

Marcia Lynn Whicker is a professor of public administration in the Graduate School at Rutgers, Newark. Prior to moving to Rutgers, she held faculty positions at Virginia Commonwealth University in Richmond, the University of South Carolina in Columbia, Temple University in Philadelphia, and Wayne State University in Detroit. She holds a Ph.D. (1976) and M.A. (1974) in political science and an M.S. (1974) in economics from the University of Kentucky in Lexington, an M.P.A. (1971) in public administration from the University of Tennessee in Knoxville, a B.A. (1970) in political science and economics from the University of North Carolina at Chapel Hill, and an associate degree in electronic engineering technology (1986) from Midlands Technical College in Columbia, South Carolina. Whicker has worked for various government agencies, including the U.S. Senate Budget Committee and a U.S. House member as an APSA Congressional Fellow; the Department of Health, Education, and Welfare; the Tennessee Valley Authority; and the U.S. Comptroller as a national bank examiner. She has published thirteen books and numerous scholarly and journalistic articles in the areas of public policy, public administration, American national politics, and leadership. She has contributed to the application of computer simulation models to test the effectiveness and representativeness of governmental structures and systems.

Thomas Yantek is an associate professor of political science at Kent State University. His research has been published in such journals as the *American Journal of Political Science, Western Political Quarterly, Policy*, and *Policy Studies Journal*.